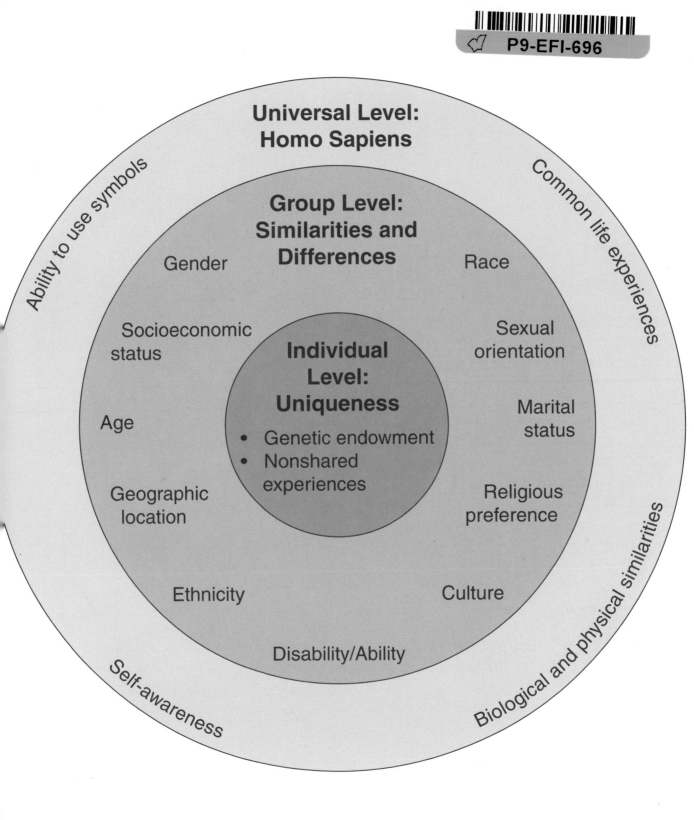

Counseling the
Culturally Diverse

Counseling the
Culturally Diverse

Theory and Practice

Fourth Edition

Derald Wing Sue
David Sue

JOHN WILEY & SONS, INC.

Copyright © 2003 by John Wiley & Sons. All rights reserved.

Published simultaneously in Canada.

Library of Congress Cataloging-in-Publication Data

Sue, Derald Wing.
  Counseling the culturally diverse : theory and practice / by Derald Wing Sue, David Sue — 4th ed.
    p. cm.
  Rev. ed. of: Counseling the culturally different.
  Includes bibliographical references and indexes.
  ISBN 0-471-41980-X (alk. paper)
    1. Cross-cultural counseling. I. Sue, David. II. Sue, Derald Wing. Counseling the culturally different. III. Title.
  BF637.C6 S85 2002
  158'.3—dc21

                                                                        2002071444

Printed in the United States of America.

10 9 8 7 6

Chapter 7 _____

Part IV

Chapter 8 _____

Chapter 9

Chapter 10

Chapter 13 _____
Counseling Asian Americans   327

Chapter 14 _____
Counseling Hispanic/Latino Americans   343

Since publication of the first three editions of *Counseling the Culturally Different: Theory and Practice,* the text has maintained its stature as a classic in the field of multicultural counseling and therapy, has become the most frequently cited text in the field of ethnic minority psychology, and is now the standard reference for nearly all courses in minority mental health and treatment. We believe that the fourth edition continues the legacy of scholarly excellence without sacrificing its provocative, hard-hitting, intense, and practice-oriented approach to the field. Knowing that many users of this text are practitioners, we have made a special effort to address implications for clinical practice by constantly relating theory and research to practice and by providing an end section in every chapter on "Implications for Clinical Practice" or "Guidelines for Clinical Practice." Preliminary reviews show an almost universal positive response to these new and enhanced features.

Longtime users of the text will immediately notice the slight change in the title: *culturally diverse* instead of *culturally different.* The change reflects two important philosophical trends in our own thinking. First, the phrase "culturally different" begs the question: "Different from what?" In almost all cases the comparison standard is related to White Euro-American norms and has the unintended consequence of creating a hierarchy among different groups (race, culture, ethnicity, etc.) in our society. Second, our definition of diversity includes group markers such as race, gender, culture, sexual orientation, and disability as well.

We have maintained the balance between the need for mental health professionals to understand not only cultural differences reflected in worldviews but also the sociopolitical nature of clinical applications has been maintained. The major thesis of this edition is that counseling and psychotherapy are rooted in and reflect the dominant values of the larger society. As a result, forms of treatment may represent cultural oppression and may reflect primarily a Eurocentric worldview that may damage and do great harm to culturally different clients. In order to be culturally competent, mental health professionals must be able to free themselves from the cultural conditioning of their personal and professional training, to understand and accept the legitimacy of alternative worldviews, to begin the process of developing culturally appropriate intervention strategies in working with a diverse clientele, and to become aware of systemic forces affecting both their clients and themselves.

We continue to use generous clinical and real-life examples to illustrate the concepts of multicultural counseling and therapy. Because the field has evolved with new developments in research, theory, and practice, the new edition operates from a broadened but more precise definition of multiculturalism, cultural competence, and multicultural counseling and therapy.

The opening chapter provides a strong conceptual and philosophical framework for understanding the meaning of multiculturalism, multicultural counseling and therapy, and cultural competence. It seeks to tackle hot-button issues related to race, gender, sexual orientation, and other group markers. Chapter 1 introduces a tripartite framework for understanding individual uniqueness; group differences related to race, gender, sexual orientation, disability, and so on; and universal similarities. Unlike other texts on multicultural psychology, this volume presents working definitions of cultural competence and multicultural counseling and therapy. The main thesis of Chapter 1 is our stance that multicultural counseling and therapy are superordinate to counseling/clinical competence.

As in the previous editions, Chapter 2 makes it clear that counseling and psychotherapy are sociopolitical acts as well. The mental health profession is taken to task by documenting its ethnocentric, monocultural features; by revealing how counseling and therapy have historically portrayed racial/ethnic minorities as pathological; by discussing how mental health practices have oppressed minorities; by showing how the mental health profession reflects the larger biases, assumptions, practices and prejudices of the larger society; and by pointing out the cultural biases in the American Psychological Association and the American Counseling Association's Code of Ethics and Standards of Practice. A "Call to Conscience" for drastic changes in mental health practice is necessary if we are to provide culturally relevant services to a diverse population.

While Chapter 2 deals with the politics of counseling and psychotherapy from a much more societal and historical perspective, Chapter 3 emphasizes how the discrimination, prejudice, and stereotyping experienced by various racial/ethnic minority groups have affected their perceptions of the counseling/therapy process. Greater emphasis is given to how the issue of trust and mistrust of mental health professionals is played out in the therapeutic process. Numerous case examples illustrate issues and principles.

Chapter 4 has been updated considerably. Since it was published in 1980, it is gratifying to see how the other major competitors consider it to be a cornerstone of the field. The concepts in this chapter have become part of the knowledge base in the field. We continue to use case examples to illustrate our concepts.

Chapter 5 challenges the universal models of helping and suggests that mental health professionals must begin the process of developing appropriate and effective intervention strategies in working with culturally different clients. This means that traditional clinical practice must accept the notion of culture-specific strategies in the helping process. Traditional taboos of Eurocentric counseling and therapy are questioned. We have added new material stressing prevention and remediation approaches, the use of psychoeducational methods, and systems intervention, as well as traditional one-to-one relationships. We stress the importance of mental health practitioners for making use of indigenous helping/healing approaches that already exist in the minority community. The rationale, importance, description, and use of alternative helping roles in multicultural counseling/therapy are major features of this chapter.

Much work on family ethnicity and mental health practice has accumulated over the past years. In Chapter 6, our basic premise is that the family counselor/therapist must be aware of how racial/ethnic minority groups view the family. Not only do groups differ in defining the family (vs. the nuclear family), but also roles and processes differ from Euro-American structures and processes. Specific suggestions and guidelines are given to the multicultural family therapist.

All helping originates from a particular cultural context. Within the United States, counseling and psychotherapy are the dominant psychological healing methods; in other cultures, however, indigenous healing approaches continue to be used widely. Chapter 7 begins with a description of the historic and continuing "shamanic" practice of healers often called *witches, witch doctors, wizards, medicine men* or *women, sorcerers, or magic men* or *women*. These individuals are believed to possess the power to enter an altered state of consciousness and in their healing rituals journey to other planes of existence beyond the physical world. We describe the three major therapeutic approaches that Western science might find helpful.

Much research has now clarified the parameters of the competing theories of racial identity development. While we discuss the various theories and their pros and cons, the major emphasis in Chapter 8 is an integrative attempt to describe the various "stages" or "ego states" (a controversy in the field) and their implications for assessment and therapeutic intervention.

White identity development, "White privilege," and how the Euro-American worldview affects perception of race-related issues have become important aspects of the dialogue in mental health practice. The thesis of Chapter 9 is that multiculturally competent White mental health professionals (a) must realize that they are victims of their cultural conditioning; (b) have inherited the racial biases, prejudices, and stereotypes of their forebears; (c) must take responsibility for the role they play in the oppression of minority groups; and (d) must move toward actively redefining their Whiteness in a nondefensive and nonracist manner. Discussion of the interplay between varying levels of White awareness and working with culturally different clients is a major part of this chapter.

Chapter 10 remains generally unchanged. How race, culture, ethnicity, gender, and sexual orientation influence worldviews has now become increasingly recognized as an important dimension to study and understand. In the field of mental health practice, being able to understand the worldview of your culturally different clients is considered one of the cornerstones of cultural competence. Again, it is now an accepted knowledge base of the profession, and it must be an integral part of our text. Though unchanged in content and focus, the chapter has been updated to reflect contemporary work in the multicultural field.

Chapters 11 through 14 maintain the integration of the most recent research and clinical findings on specific racial/ethnic minority populations, balanced with practical suggestions and therapeutic implications. Feedback from users of our text has also resulted in a major chapter on counseling multiracial individuals as well (Chapter 15).

Chapters 16 through 18 are new and expanded chapters that represent our first step to extend the definition and practice of multicultural counseling/therapy to other multicultural populations. While the focus has primarily been on racial/ethnic minorities, the topics of prejudice, racism, oppression, and discrimination apply also to other culturally different groups. We illustrate this by a discussion of gays and lesbians, women, the physically challenged, and the elderly in our society. Major focuses include similarities and differences between these groups with respect to the sociopolitical dynamics of being different and how counseling/therapy can benefit from the principles of multiculturalism. We make a case that all counseling, in some respects, is multicultural in nature.

Increasingly, we have begun to realize that both clients and counselors function under the umbrella of many institutions: mental health agencies, schools, businesses, industries, and municipalities. We are products of our school systems; we are employed by organizations; we seek health care from the medical establishment; and we function under governmentally developed social policies. What happens when the very organizations that educate us, employ us, and police us are monocultural and harm or oppress rather than heal or liberate? What happens if it is the policies, practices, and structures of organizations that are the causes of human suffering and misery? What if our clients' problems are not internal but external (i.e., they reside in the social system)? What if mental health providers are culturally competent, but the organizations that employ them prevent them from manifesting those competencies? Chapter 20 views organizations as clients and discusses how mental health professionals can become agents of system change as well.

There is an African American proverb that states, "We stand on the head and shoulders of many who have gone on before us." Certainly, this book would not have been possible without their wisdom, commitment, and sacrifice. We thank them for their inspiration, courage, and dedication and hope that they will look down on us and be pleased with our work. We would also like to acknowledge the dedicated multicultural pioneers in the field who have journeyed with us along the path of multiculturalism before it became fashionable. While there are too many to name, our professional and personal lives have been especially enriched by these individuals: Patricia Arredondo, Donald Atkinson, Carolyn Attneave, Price Cobbs, William Cross, Ursula Delworth, A. J. Franklin, Leo Goldman, Thomas Gunnings, Robert Guthrie, Janet Helms, Asa Hilliard, Allen Ivey, James Jones, Barbara Kirk, Teresa LaFromboise, Amado Padilla, Thomas Parham, Paul Pedersen, Rene A. Ruiz, Stanley Sue, Ronald Samuda, Dalmas Taylor, Charles Thomas, Joseph Trimble, Melba Vasquez, Clement Vontress, Joe White, and Robert Williams.

Working on this fourth edition has proven to be a labor of love. It would not have been possible, however, without the love and support of our families, who provided the patience and nourishment that sustained us throughout our work on the text. Derald Wing Sue wishes to express his love for his wife, Paulina, his son, Derald Paul, and his daughter, Marissa Catherine. David Sue wishes to express his love to his wife, Diane, and his daughters, Jenni and Cristi.

We hope that *Counseling the Culturally Diverse: Theory and Practice,* fourth edition, will stand on "the truth" and continue to be the standard bearer of multicultural counseling and therapy texts in the field.

DERALD WING SUE
DAVID SUE

THE CONCEPTUAL DIMENSIONS OF MULTICULTURAL COUNSELING/THERAPY

The Superordinate Nature of Multicultural Counseling/Therapy

1
Chapter

What is multicultural counseling/therapy? Isn't "good counseling," good counseling? How applicable are our standards of clinical practice for racial/ethnic minority populations? Is there any difference between counseling a White client and counseling a Black client? What do we mean by multiculturalism and diversity? Do other special populations such as women, gays and lesbians, the elderly, and those with disabilities constitute a distinct cultural group? What do we mean by the phrase *cultural competence*?

Professor Jonathon Murphy felt annoyed at one of his Latina social work graduate students. Partway through a lecture on family systems theory, the student had interrupted him with a question. Dr. Murphy had just finished an analysis of a case study on a Latino family in which the 32-year-old daughter was still living at home and could not obtain her father's approval for her upcoming marriage. The caseworker's report suggested excessive dependency as well as "pathological enmeshment" on the part of the daughter. As more and more minority students entered the program and took Dr. Murphy's classes on social work and family therapy, this sort of question began to be asked more frequently, and usually in a challenging manner.

STUDENT: *Aren't these theories culture-bound? It seems to me that counseling strategies aimed at helping family members to individuate or become autonomous units would not be received favorably by many Latino families. I've been told that Asian Americans would also find great discomfort in the value orientation of the White social worker.*

PROFESSOR: *Of course we need to consider the race and cultural background of our clients and their families. But it's clear that healthy development of family members must move toward the goal of maturity, and that means being able to make decisions on their own without being dependent or enmeshed in the family network.*

STUDENT: *But isn't that a value judgment based on seeing a group's value system as pathological? I'm just wondering whether the social worker might be culturally insensitive to the Latino family. She doesn't appear culturally competent. To describe a Latino family member as "excessively dependent" fails to note the value placed on the importance of the family. The social worker seems to have hidden racial biases, as well as difficulty relating to cultural differences.*

PROFESSOR: *I think you need to be careful about calling someone incompetent and "racist." You don't need to be a member of a racial minority group to understand the experience of discrimination. All counseling and therapy is to some extent multicultural. What we need to realize is that race and ethnicity are only one set of differences. For example, class, gender, and sexual orientation are all legitimate group markers.*

STUDENT: *I wasn't calling the social worker a racist. I was reading a study that indicated the need for social workers to become culturally competent and move toward the development of culture-specific strategies in working with racial minorities. Being a White person, she seems out of touch with the family's experience of discrimination and prejudice. I was only trying to point out that racial issues appear more salient and problematic in our society and that. . . .*

PROFESSOR [INTERRUPTING AND RAISING HIS VOICE]: *I want all of you [class members] to understand what I'm about to say. First, our standards of practice and codes of ethics have been developed over time to apply equally to all groups. Race is important, but our similarities far exceed differences. After all, there is only one race, the human race! Second, just because a group might value one way of doing things does not make it healthy or right. Culture does not always justify a practice! Third, I don't care whether the family is red, black, brown, yellow, or even white: Good counseling is good counseling! Further, it's important for us not to become myopic in our understanding of cultural differences. To deny the importance of other human dimensions such as sexual orientation, gender, disability, religious orientation, and so forth is not to see the whole person. Finally, everyone has experienced bias, discrimination, and stereotyping. You don't have to be a racial minority to understand the detrimental consequences of oppression. As an Irish descendant, I've heard many demeaning Irish jokes, and my ancestors certainly encountered severe discrimination when they first immigrated to this country. Part of our task, as therapists, is to help all our clients deal with their experiences of being different.*

In one form or another, difficult dialogues such as the previous one are occurring throughout our training institutions, halls of ivy, governmental agencies, corporate boardrooms, and community meeting places. Participants in such dialogues come with different perspectives and strong convictions and often operate from culturally conditioned assumptions outside their levels of awareness. These assumptions, however, are important to clarify because they define different realities and determine our actions. In the helping professions, insensitive counseling and therapy can result in cultural oppression rather than liberation. Let us explore more thoroughly the dialogue between professor and student to understand the important multicultural themes being raised.

Theme One: Cultural Universality versus Cultural Relativism

One of the primary issues raised by the student and professor relates to the *etic* (culturally universal) versus *emic* (culturally specific) perspectives. The professor operates from the etic position. He believes, for example, that good counseling is good counseling; that disorders such as depression, schizophrenia, and sociopathic behaviors appear in all cultures and societies; that minimal modification in their diagnosis and treatment is required; and that Western concepts of normality and abnormality can be considered universal and equally applicable across cultures (Draguns, 1985; Howard, 1992).

The student, however, operates from an emic position and challenges these assumptions. She tries to make the point that lifestyles, cultural values, and worldviews affect the expression and determination of deviant behavior. She argues that all theories of human development arise from a cultural context and that using the Euro-American value of "independence" as healthy development—especially on collectivistic cultures such as Latinos or Asian Americans—may constitute bias (C. Hall, 1997; Paniagua, 2001; D. Sue, Sue, & Sue, 2000).

This is one of the most important issues currently confronting the helping professions. There is little doubt that to a large degree the code of ethics and standards of practice in counseling, psychotherapy, social work, and other mental health specialties assume universality. Thus, if the assumption that the origin, process, and manifestation of disorders are similar across cultures were correct, then guidelines and strategies for treatment would appear to be appropriate in application to all groups.

In the other camp, however, are mental health professionals who give great weight to how culture and life experiences affect the expression of deviant behavior and who propose the use of culture-specific strategies in counseling and therapy (Atkinson, Morten, & Sue, 1998; Herring, 1999; Parham, White, & Ajamu, 1999; D. W. Sue, 2001). Such professionals point out that current guidelines and standards of clinical practice are culture-bound and often inappropriate for racial/ethnic minority groups.

Which view is correct? Should treatment be based on cultural universality or cultural relativism? Few mental health professionals today embrace the extremes of either position, although most gravitate toward one or the other. Proponents of cultural universality focus on disorders and their consequent treatments and minimize cultural factors, whereas proponents of cultural relativism focus on the culture and on how the disorder is manifested and treated within it. Both views have validity. It is naive to believe that no disorders cut across different cultures/societies or share universal characteristics. In addition, one could make the case that even though hallucinating may be viewed as normal in some cultures (cultural relativism), proponents of cultural universality argue that it still represents a breakdown in "normal" biological-cognitive processes. Likewise, it is equally naive to believe that the relative frequencies and manners of symptom formation for various disorders do not reflect the dominant cultural values and lifestyles of a society. Nor would it be beyond our scope to entertain the notion that various diverse groups may respond better to culture-specific therapeutic strategies. A more fruitful approach to these opposing views might be to address the following two questions: "What is universal in human behavior that is also relevant to counseling and therapy?" and "What is the relationship between cultural norms, values, and attitudes, on the one hand, and the manifestation of behavior disorders and their treatments, on the other?"

Theme Two: The Emotional Consequences of "Race"

A tug-of-war appears to be occurring between the professor and the student concerning the importance of "race" in the therapeutic process. Disagreements of this type are usually related not only to differences in definitions, but also to hot buttons being pushed in the participants. We address the former shortly but concentrate on the latter because the interaction between the professor and the student appears to be related more to the emotive qualities of the topic. What motivates the professor, for example, to make the unwarranted assumption that the Latina was accusing the social worker of being a racist? What leads the professor, whether consciously or unconsciously, to minimize or avoid considering race as a powerful variable in the therapeutic process? He seemingly does this by two means: (a) diluting the importance of race by using an abstract and universal statement ("There is only one race, the human race") and (b) shifting the dialogue to discussions of other group differences (gender, sexual orientation, disability, and class) and equating race as only one of these many variables.

We are negating neither the importance of other group differences in affecting human behavior nor the fact that we share many commonalities regardless of our race or gender. These are certainly legitimate points. We submit, however, that the professor is uncomfortable with open discussions of race because of the embedded or nested emotions that he has been culturally conditioned to hold. For example, discussions of race often evoke strong passions associated with racism, discrimination, prejudice, personal blame, political correctness, anti-White attitudes, quotas, and many other emotion-arousing concepts. At times, the deep reactions that many people have about discussions on race interfere with their ability to communicate freely and honestly and to listen to others (D'Andrea & Daniels, 2001; Reynolds, 2001). Feelings of guilt, blame, anger, and defensiveness (as in the case of the professor) are unpleasant. No wonder it is easier to avoid dealing with such a hot potato. Yet it is precisely these emotionally laden feelings that must be expressed and explored before productive change will occur. In Chapter 9 we devote considerable space to this issue. Until mental health providers work through these intense feelings, which are often associated with their own biases and preconceived notions, they will continue to be ineffective in working with a culturally diverse population.

Theme Three: The Inclusive or Exclusive Nature of Multiculturalism

While the professor may be avoiding the topic of race by using other group differences to shift the dialogue, he raises a very legitimate content issue about the inclusiveness or exclusiveness of multicultural dialogues. Are definitions of multiculturalism based only on race, or does multiculturalism encompass gender, sexual orientation, disability, and other significant reference groups? Isn't the professor correct in observing that almost all counseling is multicultural? We believe that resistance to including other groups in the multicultural dialogue is related to three factors: (a) Many racial minorities believe that including other groups (as in the previous example) in the multicultural dialogue will enable people who are uncomfortable with confronting their own biases to avoid dealing with the hard issues related to race and racism; (b) taken to the extreme, saying that all counseling is multicultural makes the concept meaningless because the ultimate extension equates all differences with individual differences; and (c) there are philosophical disagreements among professionals over whether gender and sexual orientation, for example, constitute distinct overall cultures.

We believe that each of us is born into a cultural context of existing beliefs, values, rules, and practices. Individuals who share the same cultural matrix with us exhibit similar values and belief systems. The process of socialization is generally the function of the family and occurs through participation in many cultural groups. Reference groups related to race, ethnicity, sexual orientation, gender, age, and socioeconomic status exert a powerful influence over us and influence our worldviews.

Whether you are a man or a woman, Black or White, gay or straight, disabled or able-bodied, married or single, and whether you live in Appalachia or New York all result in sharing similar experiences and characteristics. While this text is focused more on racial/ethnic minorities, we also believe in the inclusive definition of multiculturalism.

Theme Four: The Sociopolitical Nature of Counseling/Therapy

The dialogue between professor and student illustrates nicely the symbolic meanings of power imbalance and power oppression. Undeniably, the relationship between the professor and student is not an equal one. The professor occupies a higher-status role and is clearly in a position of authority and control. He determines the content of the course, the textbooks to read, and right or wrong answers on an exam, and he evaluates the learning progress of students. Not only is he in a position to define reality (standards of helping can be universally applied; normality is equated with individualism; and one form of discrimination is similar to another), but he can enforce it through grading students as well. As we usually accept the fact that educators have knowledge, wisdom, and experience beyond that of their students, this differential power relationship does not evoke surprise or great concern, especially if we hold values and beliefs similar to those of our teachers. However, what if the upbringing, beliefs, and assumptions of minority students render the curriculum less relevant to their experiential reality? More important, what if the students' worldviews are a more accurate reflection of reality than are those of the professors?

Many racial/ethnic minorities, gays and lesbians, and women have accused those who hold power and influence of imposing their views of reality upon them. The professor, for example, equates maturity with autonomy and independence. The Latina student points out that among Hispanics collectivism and group identity may be more desirable than individualism. Unfortunately, Dr. Murphy fails to consider this legitimate point and dismisses the observation by simply stating, "Culture does not always justify a practice." In the mental health fields, the standards used to judge normality and abnormality come from a predominantly Euro-American perspective. As such, they are culture-bound and may be inappropriate in application to culturally diverse groups. When mental health practitioners unwittingly impose these standards without regard for differences in race, culture, gender, and sexual orientation, they may be engaging in cultural oppression (Neville, Worthington, & Spanierman, 2001). As a result, counseling and psychotherapy become a sociopolitical act. Indeed, a major thesis of this book is that counseling and psychotherapy have done great harm to culturally diverse groups by invalidating their life experiences, by defining their cultural values or differences as deviant and pathological, by denying them culturally appropriate care, and by imposing the values of a dominant culture upon them.

Theme Five: The Nature of Multicultural Counseling Competence

The Latina student seems to question the social worker's clinical or cultural competence in treating a family of color. In light of the professor's response to his student, one might question his cultural competence as a teacher as well. If counseling, psychotherapy, and education can be viewed as socio-political acts, and if we accept the fact that our theories of counseling are culture-bound, then is it possible that mental health providers trained in traditional Euro-American programs may be guilty of cultural oppression in working with clients of color? The question our profession must ask is this: Is counseling/clinical competence the same as multicultural counseling competence? Dr. Murphy seems to believe that "good counseling" subsumes cultural competence, or that it is a subset of good clinical skills. Our contention, however, is that cultural competence is superordinate to counseling competence. Let us briefly explore the rationale for our position.

While there are disagreements over the definition of cultural competence, many of us know clinical incompetence when we see it; we recognize it by its horrendous outcomes, or by the human toll it takes on our minority clients. For example, for some time the profession and mental health professionals themselves have been described in very unflattering terms by multicultural specialists: (a) they are insensitive to the needs of their culturally diverse clients, do not accept, respect, and understand cultural differences, are arrogant and contemptuous, and have little understanding of their prejudices (Thomas & Sillen, 1972); (b) clients of color, women, and gays and lesbians frequently complain that they feel abused, intimidated, and harassed by non-minority personnel (Atkinson et al., 1998; President's Commission on Mental Health, 1978); (c) discriminatory practices in mental health delivery systems are deeply embedded in the ways in which the services are organized and in how they are delivered to minority populations, and are reflected in biased diagnosis and treatment, in indicators of "dangerousness," and in the type of personnel occupying decision-making roles (T. L. Cross, Bazron, Dennis, & Isaacs, 1989); and (d) mental health professionals continue to be trained in programs in which the issues of ethnicity, gender, and sexual orientation are ignored, regarded as deficiencies, portrayed in stereotypic ways, or included as an afterthought (Laird & Green, 1996; Meyers, Echemedia, & Trimble, 1991).

From our perspective, mental health professionals have seldom functioned in a culturally competent manner. Rather, they have functioned in a monoculturally competent manner with only a limited segment of the population (White Euro-Americans), but even that is debatable. We submit that much of the current therapeutic practice taught in graduate programs derives mainly from clinical experience and research with middle- to upper-class

White folks. Even though our profession has advocated moving into the realm of empirically supported treatments (EST), little evidence exists that they are applicable to racial/ethnic minorities (Atkinson, Bui, & Mori, 2001; D. W. Sue, Bingham, Porche-Burke, & Vasquez, 1999). A review of studies on EST reveals few, if any, on racial minority populations, which renders assumptions of external validity questionable when applied to people of color (Atkinson et al., 2001; Hall, 2001; S. Sue, 1999). If we are honest with ourselves, we can only conclude that many of our standards of professional competence (Eurocentric) are derived primarily from the values, belief systems, cultural assumptions, and traditions of the larger society.

Thus, values of individualism and psychological mindedness and using "rational approaches" to problem solve have much to do with how competence is defined. Yet many of our colleagues continue to hold firmly to the belief that good counseling is good counseling, thereby dismissing the centrality of culture in their definitions. The problem with traditional definitions of counseling, therapy, and mental health practice is that they arose from monocultural and ethnocentric norms that excluded other cultural groups. Mental health professionals must realize that good counseling uses White Euro-American norms that exclude three quarters of the world's population. Thus, it is clear to us that the more superordinate and inclusive concept is that of multicultural counseling competence, not clinical/counseling competence. Standards of helping derived from such a philosophy and framework are inclusive and offer the broadest and most accurate view of cultural competence.

A Tripartite Framework for Understanding the Multiple Dimensions of Identity

All too often, counseling and psychotherapy seem to ignore the group dimension of human existence. For example, a White counselor who works with an African American client might intentionally or unintentionally avoid acknowledging the racial or cultural background of the person by stating, "We are all the same under the skin" or "Apart from your racial background, we are all unique." We have already indicated possible reasons why this happens, but such an avoidance tends to negate an intimate aspect of the client's group identity. As a result, the African American client might feel misunderstood and resentful toward the helping professional, hindering the effectiveness of multicultural counseling. Besides unresolved personal issues arising from the counselor, the assumptions embedded in Western forms of therapy exaggerate the chasm between therapist and minority client.

First, the concepts of counseling and psychotherapy are uniquely Euro-American in origin, as they are based on certain philosophical assumptions and values that are strongly endorsed by Western civilizations. On the one side are beliefs that people are unique and that the psychosocial unit of operation is the individual; on the other side are beliefs that clients are the same and that the goals and techniques of counseling and therapy are equally applicable across all groups. Taken to its extreme, this latter approach nearly assumes that persons of color, for example, are White and that race and culture are insignificant variables in counseling and psychotherapy. Statements like "There is only one race, the human race" and "Apart from your racial/cultural background, you are no different from me" are indicative of the tendency to avoid acknowledging how race, culture, and other group dimensions may influence identity, values, beliefs, behaviors, and the perception of reality (Carter, 1995; Helms, 1990; D. W. Sue, 2001).

Related to the negation of race, we have indicated that a most problematic issue deals with the inclusive or exclusive nature of multiculturalism. A number of psychologists have indicated that an inclusive definition of multiculturalism (gender, ability/disability, sexual orientation, etc.) can obscure the understanding and study of race as a powerful dimension of human existence (Carter, 1995; Carter & Qureshi, 1995; Helms, 1995; Helms & Richardson, 1997). This stance is not intended to minimize the importance of the many cultural dimensions of human identity but rather emphasizes the greater discomfort that many psychologists experience in dealing with issues of race rather than with other sociodemographic differences (Carter, 1995). As a result, race becomes less salient and allows us to avoid addressing problems of racial prejudice, racial discrimination, and systemic racial oppression. This concern appears to have great legitimacy. We have noted, for example, that when issues of race are discussed in the classroom, a mental health agency, or some other public forum, it is not uncommon for participants to refocus the dialogue on differences related to gender, socioeconomic status, or religious orientation (à la Dr. Murphy).

On the other hand, many groups often rightly feel excluded from the multicultural debate and find themselves in opposition to one another. Thus, enhancing multicultural understanding and sensitivity means balancing our understanding of the sociopolitical forces that dilute the importance of race, on the one hand, and our need to acknowledge the existence of other group identities related to social class, gender, ability/disability, age, religious affiliation, and sexual orientation, on the other (D. W. Sue et al., 1999).

There is an old Asian saying that goes something like this: "All individuals, in many respects, are (a) like no other individuals, (b) like some individuals, and (c) like all other individuals." While this statement might sound confusing and contradictory, Asians believe these words to have great wisdom and to be entirely true with respect to human development and identity. We have found the tripartite framework shown in Figure 1.1 (D. W. Sue, 2001) to be useful in exploring and understanding the formation of personal

Figure 1.1

**Tripartite Development of
Personal Identity**

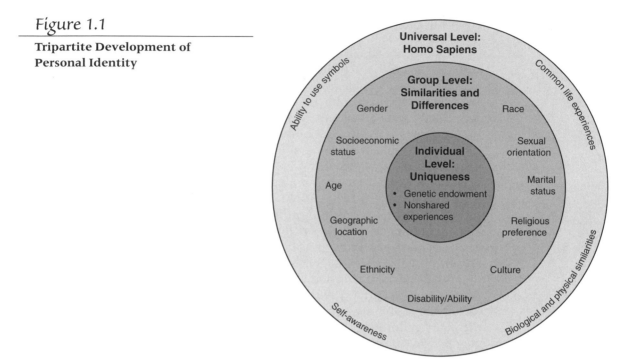

identity. The three concentric circles illustrated in Figure 1.1 denote individual, group, and universal levels of personal identity.

Individual level: "All individuals are, in some respects, like no other individuals." There is much truth in the saying that no two individuals are identical. We are all unique biologically, and recent breakthroughs in mapping the human genome have provided some startling findings. Biologists, anthropologists, and evolutionary psychologists had looked to the Human Genome Project as potentially providing answers to comparative and evolutionary biology, to find the secrets to life. Although the project has provided valuable answers to many questions, scientists have discovered even more complex questions. For example, they had expected to find 100,000 genes in the human genome, but approximately 30,000 were found—only two or three times more are found in a fruit fly or a nematode worm. Of those 30,000 genes, only 300 unique genes distinguish us from the mouse. In other words, human and mouse genomes are about 85% identical! While it may be a blow to human dignity, the more important question is how so relatively few genes can account for our humanness.

Likewise, if so few genes can determine such great differences between species, what about within the species? Human inheritance almost guarantees differences because no two individuals ever share the same genetic endowment. Further, no two of us share the exact same experiences in our society. Even identical twins who theoretically share the same gene pool and are raised in the same family are exposed to both shared and nonshared experiences. Different experiences in school and with peers, as well as qualitative differences in how parents treat them, will contribute to individual uniqueness. Research indicates that psychological characteristics and behavior are more affected by experiences specific to a child than are shared experiences (Plomin, 1989; Rutter, 1991).

Group level: "All individuals are, in some respects, like some other individuals." As mentioned earlier, each of us is born into a cultural matrix of beliefs, values, rules, and social practices (D. W. Sue, Ivey, & Pedersen, 1996). By virtue of social, cultural, and political distinctions made in our society, perceived group membership exerts a powerful influence over how society views sociodemographic groups and over how its members view themselves and others (Atkinson et al., 1998). Group markers such as race and gender are relatively stable and less subject to change. Some markers, such as education, socioeconomic status, marital status, and geographic location, are more fluid and changeable. While ethnicity is fairly stable, some argue that it can also be fluid. Likewise, debate and controversy surround the discussions about whether sexual orientation is determined at birth and whether we should be speaking of sexuality or sexualities. Nevertheless, membership in these groups may result in shared experiences and characteristics. They may serve as powerful reference groups in the formation of worldviews. On the group level of identity, Figure 1.1 reveals that people may belong to more than one cultural group (i.e., an Asian American female with a disability), that some group identities may be more salient than others (race over religious orientation), and that the salience of cultural group identity may shift from one to the other depending on the situation. For example, a gay man with a disability may find that his disability identity is more salient among the able-bodied but that his sexual orientation is more salient among those with disabilities.

Universal level: "All individuals are, in some respects, like all other individuals." Because we are members of the human race and belong to the species *Homo sapiens,* we share many similarities. Universal to our commonalties are (a) biological and physical similarities, (b) common life experiences (birth, death, love, sadness, etc.), (c) self-awareness, and (d) the ability to use symbols such as language. In Shakespeare's *Merchant of Venice,* Shylock attempts to acknowledge the universal nature of the human condition by asking, "When you prick us, do we not bleed?" Again, while the Human Genome Project indicates that a few genes may cause major differences between and within species, it is startling how similar the genetic material within our chromosomes is and how much we share in common.

Individual and Universal Biases in Psychology and Mental Health

Unfortunately, psychology and mental health professionals in particular have generally focused on either the individual or universal levels of identity, placing less importance on the group level. There are several reasons for this orientation. First, our society arose from the concept of rugged individualism, and we have traditionally valued autonomy, independence, and uniqueness. Our culture assumes that individuals are the basic building blocks of our society. Sayings such as "be your own person," "stand on your own two feet," and "don't depend on anyone but yourself" reflect this value. Psychology and education represent the carriers of this value, and the study of individual differences is most exemplified in the individual intelligence testing movement that pays homage to individual uniqueness (Samuda, 1998).

Second, the universal level is consistent with the tradition and history of psychology, which has historically sought universal facts, principles, and laws in explaining human behavior. Although an important quest, the nature of scientific inquiry has often meant studying phenomena independently of the context in which human behavior originates. Thus, therapeutic interventions from which research findings are derived may lack external validity (S. Sue, 1999).

Third, we have historically neglected the study of identity at the group level for sociopolitical and normative reasons. As we have seen, issues of race, gender, sexual orientation, and disability seem to touch hot buttons in all of us because they bring to light issues of oppression and the unpleasantness of personal biases (Carter, 1995; Helms & Richardson, 1997; D. W. Sue et al., 1998). In addition, racial/ethnic differences have frequently been interpreted from a deficit perspective and have been equated with being abnormal or pathological (Guthrie, 1997; Lee, 1993; White & Parham, 1990). We have more to say about this in the next chapter.

Nevertheless, disciplines that hope to understand the human condition cannot neglect any level of our identity. For example, psychological explanations that acknowledge the importance of group influences such as gender, race, culture, sexual orientation, socioeconomic class, and religious affiliation lead to more accurate understanding of human psychology. Failure to acknowledge these influences may skew research findings and lead to biased conclusions about human behavior that are culture-bound, class-bound, and gender-bound.

Thus, it is possible to conclude that all people possess individual, group, and universal levels of identity. A holistic approach to understanding personal identity demands that we recognize all three levels: individual (uniqueness), group (shared cultural values and beliefs), and universal (common features of being human). Because of the historical scientific neglect of the group level of identity, this text focuses primarily on this category.

Before closing this portion of our discussion, however, we would like to add a caution. While the concentric circles in Figure 1.1 might unintentionally suggest a clear boundary, each level of identity must be viewed as permeable and ever-changing in salience. In counseling and psychotherapy, for example, a client might view his or her uniqueness as important at one point in the session and stress commonalties of the human condition at another. Even within the group level of identity, multiple forces may be operative. As mentioned earlier, the group level of identity reveals many reference groups, both fixed and nonfixed, that might impact our lives. Being an elderly, gay, Latino male, for example, represents four potential reference groups operating on the person. The culturally competent helping professional must be willing and able to touch all dimensions of human existence without negating any of the others.

The Impact of Group Identities on Counseling and Psychotherapy

Accepting the premise that race, ethnicity, and culture are powerful variables in influencing how people think, make decisions, behave, and define events, it is not far-fetched to conclude that such forces may also affect how different groups define a "helping relationship" (Dumas, Rollock, Prinz, Hops, & Blechman, 1999; Fraga, Atkinson, & Wampold, 2002; D. W. Sue, 2001). Multicultural psychologists have noted, for example, that theories of counseling and psychotherapy represent different worldviews, each with its own values, biases, and assumptions about human behavior (Ivey, Ivey, & Simek-Morgan, 1997; Katz, 1985). Given that schools of counseling and psychotherapy arise from Western-European contexts, the worldview that they espouse as reality may not be that shared by racial/ethnic minority groups in the United States, nor by those who reside in different countries (Parham et al., 1999). Each cultural/racial group may have its own distinct interpretation of reality and offer a different perspective on the nature of people, the origin of disorders, standards for judging normality and abnormality, and therapeutic approaches.

Among many Asian Americans, for example, a "self orientation" is considered undesirable while a "group orientation" is highly valued. The Japanese have a saying that goes like this: "The nail that stands up should be pounded back down." The meaning seems clear: Healthy development is considering the needs of the entire group, while unhealthy development is thinking only of oneself. Likewise, relative to their Euro-American counterparts, many African Americans value the emotive and affective quality of interpersonal interactions as qualities of sincerity and authenticity (Parham,

1997; Parham et al., 1999). Euro-Americans often view the passionate expression of affect as irrational, lacking objectivity, impulsive, and immature on the part of the communicator. Thus, the autonomy-oriented goal of counseling and psychotherapy and the objective focus of the therapeutic process might prove antagonistic to the worldviews of Asian Americans and African Americans, respectively.

It is therefore highly probable that different racial/ethnic minority groups perceive the competence of the helping professional differently than do mainstream client groups. Further, if race/ethnicity affects perception, what about other group differences, such as gender and sexual orientation? If that is the case, minority clients may see a clinician who exhibits therapeutic skills that are associated primarily with mainstream therapies as having lower credibility. The important question to ask is, "Do groups such as racial/ethnic minorities define cultural competence differently than do their Euro-American counterparts?" Anecdotal observations, clinical case studies, conceptual analytical writings, and some empirical studies seem to suggest an affirmative response to the question (Fraga et al., 2002; McGoldrick & Giordano, 1996; Nwachuku & Ivey, 1991; D. W. Sue & Sue, 1999; Wehrly, 1995).

What Is Multicultural Counseling/Therapy?

In light of the previous analysis, let us define *multicultural counseling/therapy (MCT)* as it relates to the therapy process and the roles of the mental health practitioner:

> *Multicultural counseling and therapy can be defined as both a helping role and process that uses modalities and defines goals consistent with the life experiences and cultural values of clients, recognizes client identities to include individual, group, and universal dimensions, advocates the use of universal and culture-specific strategies and roles in the healing process, and balances the importance of individualism and collectivism in the assessment, diagnosis, and treatment of client and client systems. (D. W. Sue, in press)*

This definition often contrasts markedly with traditional definitions of counseling and psychotherapy. A more thorough analysis of these characteristics is described in Chapter 4. For now, let us extract implications for counseling practice from the definition just given.

1. *Helping role and process.* MCT involves broadening the roles that counselors play and expands the repertoire of therapy skills considered helpful and appropriate in counseling. The more passive and objective stance taken by therapists in clinical work is seen as only one method of

helping. Likewise, teaching, consulting, and advocacy can supplement the conventional counselor or therapist role.

2. *Consistent with life experiences and cultural values.* Effective MCT means using modalities and defining goals for culturally diverse clients that are consistent with their racial, cultural, ethnic, gender, and sexual orientation backgrounds. Advice and suggestions, for example, may be effectively used for some client populations.

3. *Individual, group, and universal dimensions of existence.* As we have already seen, MCT acknowledges that our existence and identity are composed of individual (uniqueness), group, and universal dimensions. Any form of helping that fails to recognize the totality of these dimensions negates important aspects of a person's identity.

4. *Universal and culture-specific strategies.* Related to the second point, MCT believes that different racial/ethnic minority groups might respond best to culture-specific strategies of helping. For example, research seems to support the belief that Asian Americans are more responsive to directive/active approaches and that African Americans appreciate helpers who are authentic in their self-disclosures. Likewise, it is clear that common features in helping relationships cut across cultures and societies as well.

5. *Individualism and collectivism.* MCT broadens the perspective of the helping relationship by balancing the individualistic approach with a collectivistic reality that acknowledges our embeddedness in families, significant others, communities, and cultures. A client is perceived not just as an individual, but as an individual who is a product of his or her social and cultural context.

6. *Client and client systems.* MCT assumes a dual role in helping clients. In many cases, for example, it is important to focus on the individual clients and encourage them to achieve insights and learn new behaviors. However, when problems of clients of color reside in prejudice, discrimination, and racism of employers, educators, and neighbors, or in organizational policies or practices in schools, mental health agencies, government, business, and society, the traditional therapeutic role appears ineffective and inappropriate. The focus for change must shift to altering client systems rather than individual clients.

What Is Cultural Competence?

Consistent with this definition of MCT, it becomes clear that a culturally competent healer is working toward several primary goals (D. W. Sue et al., 1982; D. W. Sue, Arredondo, & McDavis, 1992; D. W. Sue et al., 1998). First, a culturally competent helping professional is one who is actively in the process of becoming aware of his or her own assumptions about human behavior, values, biases, preconceived notions, personal limitations, and so forth. Second, a culturally competent helping professional is one who actively attempts to understand the worldview of his or her culturally different client. In other words, what are the client's values and assumptions about human behavior, biases, and so on? Third, a culturally competent helping professional is one who is in the process of actively developing and practicing appropriate, relevant, and sensitive intervention strategies and skills in working with his or her culturally different client. These three goals make it clear that cultural competence is an active, developmental, and ongoing process and that it is aspirational rather than achieved. Let us more carefully explore these attributes of cultural competence.

Competency One: Therapist Awareness of One's Own Assumptions, Values, and Biases

In almost all human service programs, counselors, therapists, and social workers are familiar with the phrase, "Counselor, know thyself." Programs stress the importance of not allowing our own biases, values, or hang-ups to interfere with our ability to work with clients. In most cases, such a warning stays primarily on an intellectual level, and very little training is directed at having trainees get in touch with their own values and biases about human behavior. In other words, it appears to be easier to deal with trainees' cognitive understanding about their own cultural heritage, the values they hold about human behavior, their standards for judging normality and abnormality, and the culture-bound goals toward which they strive.

What makes examination of the self difficult is the emotional impact of attitudes, beliefs, and feelings associated with cultural differences such as racism, sexism, heterosexism, able-body-ism, and ageism. For example, as a member of a White Euro-American group, what responsibility do you hold for the racist, oppressive, and discriminating manner by which you personally and professionally deal with persons of color? This is a threatening question for many White people. However, to be effective in MCT means that one has adequately dealt with this question and worked through the biases, feelings, fears, and guilt associated with it. It would appear, then, that a culturally competent therapist would have developed beliefs and attitudes consistent with the characteristics outlined in Table 1.1.

Competency Two: Understanding the Worldview of Culturally Diverse Clients

It is crucial that counselors and therapists understand and can share the worldview of their culturally diverse clients. This statement does not mean

Table 1.1 Cultural Competence: Awareness

1. **The culturally competent mental health professional is one who has moved from being culturally unaware to being aware and sensitive to his or her own cultural heritage and to valuing and respecting differences.**

The therapist has begun the process of exploring his/her values, standards, and assumptions about human behavior. Rather than being ethnocentric and believing in the superiority of his or her group's cultural heritage (arts, crafts, traditions, language), there is acceptance and respect for cultural differences. Other cultures and sociodemographic groups are seen as equally valuable and legitimate. It is clear that a counselor or therapist who is culturally unaware is most likely to impose his or her values and standards on a minority client. As a result, an unenlightened therapist may be engaging in an act of cultural oppression.

2. **The culturally competent mental health professional is aware of his or her own values and biases and of how they may affect minority clients.**

The therapist actively and constantly attempts to avoid prejudices, unwarranted labeling, and stereotyping. Beliefs that African Americans and Hispanic Americans are intellectually inferior and will not do well in school, that Asian Americans make good technical workers but poor managers, that women belong in the home, or that the elderly are no longer useful in society are examples of widespread stereotyping that may hinder equal access and opportunity. Culturally competent providers try not to hold preconceived limitations and notions about their culturally diverse clients. As a check on this process, they actively challenge their assumptions; they monitor their functioning via consultations, supervision, or continuing education.

3. **Culturally competent mental health professionals are comfortable with differences that exist between themselves and their clients in terms of race, gender, sexual orientation, and other sociodemographic variables. Differences are not seen as being deviant.**

The culturally competent counselor/therapist does not profess color blindness or negate the existence of differences in attitudes and beliefs among different groups. The basic concept underlying color blindness, for example, is the humanity of all people. Regardless of color or other sociodemographic differences, each individual is equally human. While its original intent was to eliminate bias from treatment, it has served to deny the existence of differences in clients' perceptions of society arising from membership in different groups. The message tends to be, "I will like you only if you are the same," instead of, "I like you because of and in spite of your differences."

4. **The culturally competent mental health practitioner is sensitive to circumstances (personal biases; stage of racial, gender, and sexual orientation identity; sociopolitical influences; etc.) that may dictate referral of the client to a member of his or her own sociodemographic group or to another therapist in general.**

A culturally competent helper is aware of his or her limitations in MCT and is not threatened by the prospect of referring a client to someone else. This principle, however, should not be used as a cop-out for therapists who do not want to work with culturally diverse clients, or who do not want to work through their own personal hang-ups.

5. **The culturally competent mental health professional acknowledges and is aware of his or her own racist, sexist, heterosexist, or other detrimental attitudes, beliefs, and feelings.**

A culturally competent helper does not deny the fact that he or she has directly or indirectly benefited from individual, institutional, and cultural biases and that he or she has been socialized into such a society. As a result, the culturally competent provider inherits elements in the socialization process that may be detrimental to culturally diverse clients. Culturally competent counselors accept responsibility for their own racism, sexism, and so forth and attempt to deal with them in a nondefensive, guilt-free manner. They have begun the process of defining a new nonoppressive and nonexploitative attitude. In terms of racism, for example, addressing one's Whiteness is crucial for effective MCT.

that providers must hold these worldviews as their own, but rather that they can see and accept other worldviews in a nonjudgmental manner. Some have referred to the process as cultural role taking: The therapist acknowledges that he or she has not lived a lifetime as an Asian American, African American, American Indian, or Hispanic American person. It is almost impossible for the therapist to think, feel, and react as a racial minority individual. Nonetheless, cognitive empathy, as distinct from affective empathy, may be possible. In cultural role taking the therapist acquires practical knowledge concerning the scope and nature of the client's cultural background, daily living experience, hopes, fears, and aspirations. Inherent in cognitive empathy is the understanding of how therapy relates to the wider sociopolitical system with which minorities contend every day of their lives. Table 1.2 explicates some of these qualities.

Competency Three: Developing Appropriate Intervention Strategies and Techniques

Effectiveness is most likely enhanced when the therapist uses therapeutic modalities and defines goals that are consistent with the life experiences and cultural values of the client. This basic premise will be emphasized throughout future chapters. Studies have consistently revealed that (a) economically and educationally marginalized clients may not be oriented toward "talk therapy"; (b) self-disclosure may be incompatible with the cultural values of Asian Americans, Hispanic Americans, and American Indians; (c) the sociopolitical atmosphere may dictate against self-disclosure from racial minorities and gays and lesbians; (d) the ambiguous nature of counseling may be antagonistic to life values of certain diverse groups; and (e) many minority clients prefer an active/directive approach to an inactive/nondirective one in treatment. Therapy has too long assumed that clients share a similar background and cultural heritage and that the same approaches are equally effective with all clients. This erroneous assumption needs to be buried.

Because groups and individuals differ from one another, the blind application of techniques to all situations and all populations seems ludicrous. The interpersonal transactions between the counselor and client require differential approaches that are consistent with the person's life experiences (Sue et al., 1996). In this particular case, and as mentioned earlier, it is ironic that equal treatment in therapy may be discriminatory treatment! Therapists need to understand this. As a means to prove discriminatory mental health practices, racial/ethnic minority groups have in the past pointed to studies revealing that minority clients are given less preferential forms of treatment (medication, electroconvulsive therapy, etc.). Somewhere, confusion has occurred, and it was believed that to be treated differently is akin to discrimination. The confusion centered on the distinction between equal access and

Table 1.2 Cultural Competence: Knowledge

1. **The culturally competent mental health professional must possess specific knowledge and information about the particular group with which he or she is working.**

The professional must be aware of the history, experiences, cultural values, and lifestyles of various sociodemographic groups in our society. The greater the depth of knowledge of one cultural group and the more knowledge the professional has of many groups, the more likely it is that the therapist can be an effective helper. Thus, the culturally competent counselor is one who continues to explore and learn about issues related to various minority groups throughout his or her professional career.

2. **The culturally competent mental health professional will have a good understanding of the sociopolitical system's operation in the United States with respect to its treatment of marginalized groups in our society.**

The culturally competent professional understands the impact and operation of oppression (racism, sexism, etc.), the politics of counseling, and the racist, sexist, and homophobic concepts that have permeated the mental health helping professions. Especially valuable for the therapist is an understanding of the role that ethnocentric monoculturalism plays in the development of identity and worldviews among minority groups.

3. **The culturally competent mental health professional must have a clear and explicit knowledge and understanding of the generic characteristics of counseling and therapy.**

These encompass language factors, culture-bound values, and class-bound values. The therapist should understand the value assumptions (normality and abnormality) inherent in the major schools of therapy and how they may interact with values of the culturally different. In some cases, the theories or models may limit the potential of persons from different cultures. Likewise, being able to determine those that may be useful to culturally diverse clients is important.

4. **The culturally competent mental health professional is aware of institutional barriers that prevent some diverse clients from using mental health services.**

Important factors include the location of a mental health agency, the formality or informality of the decor, the languages used to advertise the services, the availability of minorities among the different levels, the organizational climate, the hours and days of operation, and the offering of the services needed by the community.

---

opportunities versus equal treatment. Racial/ethnic minority groups may not be asking for equal treatment so much as they are asking for equal access and opportunities. This dictates a differential approach that is truly nondiscriminatory. Table 1.3 outlines specific cultural skills needed to function effectively.

Thus, to be an effective multicultural helper requires cultural competence. In light of the previous analysis, we define it in the following manner:

Cultural competence is the ability to engage in actions or create conditions that maximize the optimal development of client and client systems. Multicultural counseling competence is defined as the counselor's acquisition of awareness, knowledge, and skills needed to function effectively in a pluralistic democratic society (ability to communicate, interact, negotiate, and intervene on behalf of clients from diverse backgrounds), and on a organizational/societal level, advo-

Table 1.3 **Cultural Competence: Skills**

1. **At the skills level, the culturally competent mental health professional must be able to generate a wide variety of verbal and nonverbal responses.**

Mounting evidence indicates that different groups may not only define problems differently from their majority counterparts, but also respond differently to counseling therapy styles. It appears that the wider the repertoire of responses the therapist possesses, the better helper he or she is likely to be. We can no longer rely on a very narrow and limited number of skills in counseling and therapy. We need to practice and be comfortable with a multitude of response modalities.

2. **The culturally competent mental health professional must be able to send and receive both verbal and nonverbal messages accurately and appropriately.**

The key words "send," "receive," "verbal," "nonverbal," "accurately," and "appropriately" are important. These words recognize several things about MCT. First, communication is a two-way process. The culturally skilled counselor must be able not only to communicate (send) his or her thoughts and feelings to the client, but also to read (receive) messages from the client. Second, MCT effectiveness may be highly correlated with the counselor's ability to recognize and respond to both verbal and nonverbal messages. Third, sending and receiving a message accurately means the ability to consider cultural cues operative in the setting. Fourth, accuracy of communication must be tempered by its appropriateness. This concept, which deals essentially with communication styles, is difficult for many to grasp. In many cultures, subtlety and indirectness of communication are a highly prized art. Likewise, others prize directness and confrontation.

3. **The culturally competent mental health professional is able to exercise institutional intervention skills on behalf of his or her client when appropriate.**

This implies that giving help may involve out-of-office strategies (outreach, consultant, change agent, ombudsman roles, and facilitators of indigenous support systems) that discard the intrapsychic counseling model and view the problems or barriers as residing outside the minority client.

4. **The culturally competent mental health professional is aware of his or her helping style, recognizes the limitations that he or she possesses, and can anticipate the impact on the culturally different client.**

All helpers have limitations in their ability to relate to culturally different clients. It is impossible to be all things to everyone; that is, no matter how skilled we are, our personal helping style may be limited. This is nothing to be ashamed of, especially if a therapist has tried and continues to try to develop new skills. When therapy-style adjustments appear too difficult, the next best thing to do may be to (a) acknowledge the limitations, and (b) anticipate your impact on the client. These things may communicate several things to the culturally different client: first, that you are open and honest about your style of communication and the limitations or barriers they may potentially cause; second, that you understand enough about the client's worldview to anticipate how this may adversely affect your client; third, that as a counselor, it is important for you to communicate your desire to help despite your limitations. Surprisingly, for many culturally different clients, this may be enough to allow rapport building and greater freedom on the part of counselors to use techniques different from those of the client.

Table 1.3 continued

5. **The culturally competent mental health professional is able to play helping roles characterized by an active systemic focus, which leads to environmental interventions. Such a mental health professional is not trapped into the conventional counselor/therapist mode of operation.**

In the *consultant role*, for example, helping professionals attempt to serve as resource persons to other professionals or minority populations in developing programs that would improve their life conditions through prevention and remediation. The *outreach role* requires that counselors and therapists move out of their offices and into their clients' communities (Atkinson, Thompson, & Grant, 1993). For example, since many African Americans are deeply involved in their church and respect their Black ministers, outreach and preventive programs could be delivered through the support of interdenominational Black ministerial alliances or personnel in the churches (Thomas & Dansby, 1985). Home visits are another outreach tactic that has been used traditionally by social workers. This approach enables therapists to meet the needs of minority clients (financial difficulties with transportation), to see the family in their natural environment (perhaps allowing the therapist to observe directly the environmental factors that are contributing to the families problems), to make a positive statement about their own personal commitment and involvement with the family, and to avoid the intimidating atmosphere of large, formal, and unfamiliar institutions. The *ombudsman role,* which originated in Europe, functions to protect citizens against bureaucratic mazes and procedures. In this situation, the therapist would attempt to identify institutional policies and practices that may discriminate or oppress a minority constituency. As a facilitator of indigenous support systems, the counselor would structure their activities to supplement, not supplant, the already existing system of mental health. Collaborative work with folk healers, medicine persons, or community leaders would be very much a part of the therapist's role.

cating effectively to develop new theories, practices, policies, and organizational structures that are more responsive to all groups. (Sue, in press)

This definition of cultural competence in the helping professions makes it clear that the conventional one-to-one, in-the-office, objective form of treatment aimed at remediation of existing problems may be at odds with the sociopolitical and cultural experiences of their clients. Like the complementary definition of MCT, it addresses not only clients (individuals, families, and groups) but also client systems (institutions, policies, and practices that may be unhealthy or problematic for healthy development). This is especially true if problems reside outside rather than inside the client. For example, prejudice and discrimination such as racism, sexism, and homophobia may impede healthy functioning of individuals and groups in our society.

Second, cultural competence can be seen as residing in three major domains: (a) attitudes/beliefs component—an understanding of one's own cultural conditioning that affects the personal beliefs, values, and attitudes of a culturally diverse population; (b) knowledge component—understanding and knowledge of the worldviews of culturally diverse individuals and groups; and (c) skills component—an ability to determine and use culturally appropriate intervention strategies when working with different groups in our society.

Third, in a broad sense, this definition is directed toward two levels of cultural competence: the person/individual and the organizational/system levels. The work on cultural competence has generally focused on the micro level, the individual. In the education and training of psychologists, for example, the goals have been to increase the level of self-awareness of trainees (potential biases, values, and assumptions about human behavior); to acquire knowledge of the history, culture, and life experiences of various minority groups; and to aid in developing culturally appropriate and adaptive interpersonal skills (clinical work, management, conflict resolution, etc.). Less emphasis is placed on the macro level: the profession of psychology, organizations, and the society in general (Barr & Strong, 1987; T. L. Cross et al., 1989; J. M. Jones, 1997; Lewis, Lewis, Daniels, & D'Andrea, 1998; D. W. Sue, 1991a). We suggest that it does little good to train culturally competent helping professionals when the very organizations that employ them are monocultural and discourage or even punish psychologists for using their culturally competent knowledge and skills. If our profession is interested in the development of cultural competence, then it must become involved in impacting systemic and societal levels as well.

Last, our definition of cultural competence speaks strongly to the development of alternative helping roles. Much of this comes from recasting healing as involving more than one-to-one therapy. If part of cultural competence involves systemic intervention, then roles such as a consultant, change agent, teacher, and advocate supplement the conventional role of therapy. In contrast to this role, alternatives are characterized by the following:

1. Having a more active helping style
2. Working outside the office (home, institution, or community)
3. Being focused on changing environmental conditions as opposed to changing the client
4. Viewing the client as encountering problems rather than having a problem
5. Being oriented toward prevention rather than remediation
6. Shouldering increased responsibility for determining the course and outcome of the helping process

It is clear that these alternative roles and their underlying assumptions and practices have not been perceived as activities consistent with counseling and psychotherapy.

The Superordinate Nature of Multicultural Counseling/Therapy   **25**

Multidimensional Model of Cultural Competence in Counseling

Elsewhere, one of the authors (D. W. Sue, 2001) has proposed a *multidimensional model of cultural competence (MDCC)* in counseling/therapy. This was an attempt to integrate three important features associated with effective multicultural counseling: (a) the need to consider specific cultural group worldviews associated with race, gender, sexual orientation, and so on; (b) components of cultural competence (awareness, knowledge, and skills); and (c) foci of cultural competence. These dimensions are illustrated in Figure 1.2. This model is used throughout the text to guide our discussion because it allows for the systematic identification of where interventions should potentially be directed.

Dimension I: Group-Specific Worldviews

In keeping with our all-encompassing definition of multiculturalism, we include the human differences associated with race, gender, sexual orientation, physical ability, age, and other significant reference groups. Figure 1.2 originally identified only five major groups organized around racial/ethnic categories. This dimension can be broadened to include multiracial groups and other culturally diverse groups such as sexual minorities, the elderly, women, and those with disabilities. In turn, these group identities can be further broken down into specific categories along the lines of race/ethnicity (African Americans, American Indians, Asian Americans, and Euro-Americans), sex-

Figure 1.2

A Multidimensional Model for Developing Cultural Competence

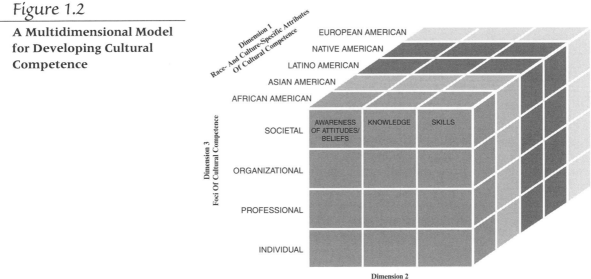

ual orientation (straights, gays, lesbians, and bisexuals), gender (men and women), and so forth. We are aware that a strong case can be made for including socioeconomic status, religious preference, and other group differences as well. Unfortunately, space limitations force us to make hard choices about which groups to cover.

Dimension II: Components of Cultural Competence

As we have already stated, most multicultural specialists have used the divisions of awareness, knowledge, and skills to define cultural competence. To be effective multicultural therapists, specialists must be aware of their own biases and assumptions about human behavior, must acquire and have knowledge of the particular groups they are working with, and must be able to use culturally appropriate intervention strategies in working with different groups.

Dimension III: Foci of Therapeutic Interventions

A basic premise of MCT is that culturally competent helping professionals must not confine their perspectives to just individual treatment, but must be able to intervene effectively at the professional, organizational, and societal levels as well. Figure 1.3 reveals the four foci of intervention and development.

Focus 1: Individual. To provide culturally effective and sensitive mental health services, helping professionals must deal with their own biases, prejudices, and misinformation/lack of information regarding culturally diverse groups in our society. In this case, positive changes must occur in their attitudes, beliefs, emotions, and behaviors regarding multicultural populations.

Focus 2: Professional. It is clear that our profession has developed from a Western European perspective. As a result, how we define psychology (the study of mind and behavior) may be biased and at odds with different cultural groups. Further, if the professional standards and codes of ethics in mental health practice are culture bound, then they must be changed to reflect a multicultural worldview.

Focus 3: Organizational. Since we all work for or are influenced by organizations, it is important to realize that institutional practices, policies, programs, and structures may be oppressive to certain groups, especially if they are monocultural. If organizational policies and practices deny equal access and opportunity for different groups or oppress them (redlining in home mortgages, laws against domestic partners, inequitable mental health care, etc.), then they should become the targets for change.

Focus 4: Societal. If social policies (racial profiling, misinformation in educational materials, inequities in health care, etc.) are detrimental to the mental

Figure 1.3

The Foci of Cultural Competence: Individual, Professional, Organizational, and Societal

and physical health of minority groups, for example, does not the mental health professional have a responsibility to advocate for change? Our answer, of course, is affirmative.

Often, psychologists treat individuals who are the victims of failed systemic processes. Intervention at the individual level is primarily remedial when a strong need exists for preventive measures. Because psychology concentrates primarily on the individual, it has been deficient in developing more systemic and large-scale change strategies.

Implications for Clinical Practice

Using our tripartite levels of identity model (Figure 1.1), the multidimensional model of cultural competence (Figure 1.2), and the foci of cultural competence (Figure 1.3), we can discern several guiding principles for effective MCT.

1. Understand the terms "sociodemographic" and "diverse backgrounds" in the MCT definition to be inclusive and encompass race, culture, gender, religious affiliation, sexual orientation, elderly, women, disability, and so on.

2. Realize that you are a product of cultural conditioning and that you are not immune from inheriting hot buttons and biases associated with culturally diverse groups in our society. As such, you must be vigilant of emotional reactions that may lead to a negation of other group values and lifestyles.

3. When working with different cultural groups, attempt to identify culture-specific and culture-universal domains of helping. Do not neglect the ways in which American Indians, Latinos/Hispanics, and African Americans, for example, may define normality-abnormality, the nature of helping, and what constitutes a helping relationship.

4. Be aware that persons of color, gays/lesbians, women, and other groups may perceive mental illness/health and the healing process differently than do Euro-Americans. To disregard differences and impose the conventional helping role and process on culturally diverse groups may constitute cultural oppression.

5. Be aware that Euro-American healing standards originate from a cultural context and represent only one form of helping that exists on an equal plane with others. As a helping professional, you must begin the task of recognizing the invisible veil of Euro-American cultural standards that influence your definitions of a helping relationship. As long as counselors and therapists continue to view Euro-American standards as normative, they will unwittingly set up a hierarchy among the groups.

6. Realize that the concept of cultural competence is more inclusive and superordinate than is clinical competence. Do not fall into the trap of "good counseling is good counseling." Know that cultural competence must replace clinical competence. The latter is culture-bound, ethnocentric, and exclusive. It does not acknowledge racial, cultural, and gender differences sufficiently to be helpful. To assume universality of application to all groups is to make an unwarranted inferential leap.

7. If you are planning to work with the diversity of clients in our world, you must play roles other than that of the conventional counselor. Simply concentrating on the traditional clinical role ignores the importance of interventions at other levels. New helping roles such as consultant, advisor, change agent, facilitator of indigenous healing systems, and so on have been suggested as equally valuable.

8. Realize that organizational/societal policies, practices, and structures may represent oppressive obstacles that prevent equal access and opportunity. If that is the case, systems intervention is most appropriate.

9. Use modalities that are consistent with the lifestyles and cultural systems of clients. In many cases, psychoeducational approaches, working outside of the office, and engaging in practices that violate traditional

Euro-American standards (advice giving and self-disclosure) may be dictated.

10. Finally, but most important, realize that MCT (and cultural competence) is inclusive because it includes all groups (including Whites, males, and heterosexuals). Conventional counseling and therapy are exclusive and narrow and are based on Euro-American norms. As such, cultural competence is superordinate to clinical competence.

THE POLITICAL DIMENSIONS OF MENTAL HEALTH PRACTICE

The Politics of Counseling and Psychotherapy

2

Chapter

The White Supremacist

In 1998 John William King and two accomplices killed African American James Byrd in Jasper, Texas. In courtroom testimony, the description of the attack and torture of Byrd was both stunning and sickening. The three men picked up 49-year-old Byrd, chained him to a truck, and dragged him for miles through the town. His cries of pain did little to prevent the three from continuing their inhumane torture, and Byrd's body was shredded and his head decapitated. In the aftermath of the event and during his trial, King expressed little remorse but rather bragged about his deed and expressed his hate defiantly. On his way to death row a reporter asked if he had anything to say to Byrd's family. His reply: "Yeah, they can suck my dick!" In his prison cell he wrote a friend and bragged, "Regardless of the outcome of this, we made history." It was signed "with much Aryan love."

The Athlete

In 2000 Atlanta Braves pitcher John Rocker triggered outrage in New York and in his native Georgia with printed remarks in Sports Illus-trated. *Saying that he would rather retire than play for New York, he explained, "Imagine having to take the [No.] 7 train to [Shea Stadium] looking like you're in Beirut next to some kid with purple hair, next to some queer with AIDS, right next to some dude who got out of jail for the fourth time, right next to some 20-year-old mom with four kids. The biggest thing I don't like about New York are the foreigners. You can walk an entire block in Times Square and not hear anybody speaking English. Asians and Koreans and Vietnamese and Indians and Russians and Spanish people and everything up there. How the hell did they get in this country?"*

The Teacher

A White female elementary school teacher in Oklahoma had planned an ethnic minority appreciation day for her sixth-grade class. As there were a

33

large number of American Indian students in her class, part of the day was devoted to a unit on Native American heritage. One of the American Indian students had designed a bonnet and dress of her tribe. While her fellow students expressed appreciation and admiration for her costume and tribal dance demonstration, the teacher was reported to have remained silent. Several days later the female student received a low grade for her participation in the activities. According to the student, the teacher had praised her dance technique and beautiful costume but had stated that (a) the costume was not typical of her tribe, (b) her dance was not traditional, and (c) the assignment was graded on "authenticity, not fantasy." When the parents heard about the remarks, they demanded a meeting with the teacher and principal. During the meeting, the father expressed anger at "White folks always telling Indians who we are." The teacher's only response was to show the parents an anthropology book with what she claimed to be the typical headgear and costume of the family's tribe.

The Corporation

American Airlines was caught red-faced over major racial gaffes when it became known in 1998 that their pilots' manual contained derogatory and stereotypic references to their Latin American customers. The manual suggested that Latin Americans "like to get drunk and call in false bomb threats when running late for a plane." American Airlines was forced to make a public apology and stated that future revisions of the manual would remove any such racially charged assertions.

The Politician

During the presidential primaries, candidate John McCain used the highly offensive term "gooks" to describe his North Vietnamese captors. While it is understandable that he harbored deep resentment toward his captors, the term is a dehumanizing one that assaults everyone of Asian descent, on par with epithets against Blacks, Latinos, and gays. McCain refused to apologize or retract his derogatory statements.

The Scientist

Nobel laureate James Watson, whose codiscovery of DNA earned him the highest scientific recognition, made extremely controversial remarks during a guest lecture at the University of California, Berkeley, in 2000. Many in the audience branded his statements and beliefs as both sexist and racist. He equated darker skins with greater sexual urges and activity ("Latin lovers"), made demeaning remarks about obese people, and made repeated sexist references to women.

These and countless other examples indicate that racism, sexism, and homophobia are alive, well, and thriving in the United States. Indeed, the 1990s saw a historic rise in the incidents of overt bigotry throughout the country. The incidents have ranged from murder and mayhem to physical attacks, threats, and all forms of psychological harassment: A study by Klanwatch and the Militia Task Force (Serrano, 1998) recorded a record number of hate groups in 1997, a 20% increase over the previous year; reports of the burning of Black churches in the mid-1990s seemed commonplace; a report by the National Asian Pacific American Legal Consortium (1997) showed a 17% increase of hate crimes directed toward Asian Americans; and one study revealed an 8% increase of anti-gay violence in the United States (National Coalition of Anti-Violence Programs, 2001).

These reports are even more disturbing in light of the apparent erosion of the nation's oldest civil rights law. For example, over the past 12 years the U.S. Supreme Court, with a conservative majority, has ruled that (a) cities may not set aside a fixed percentage of public contracts for minorities, (b) civil rights plaintiffs may not use statistics on job segregation to prove illegal discrimination, (c) White males may file reverse discrimination challenges against court-approved affirmative action programs, and (d) minorities or women may not challenge an unfair seniority policy after it has been in force for 300 days. In addition, in a stunning 2000 decision the U.S. Supreme Court ruled that the Boy Scouts of America could not be compelled by a New Jersey antidiscrimination law to allow an openly gay scoutmaster to serve in the organization.

California, a state often considered to be forward thinking in the areas of diversity and multiculturalism, passed (a) Proposition 187, the divisive and mean-spirited legislation that sought to expel from public schools children who were in the U.S. illegally and deny them health care and other social services; (b) Proposition 209, an antiaffirmative action initiative that effectively eliminates any such programs in the state; and (c) Proposition 227, an initiative that sharply reduces bilingual education in California schools. The assault on affirmative action programs has spread to many other states as well, where the courts have struck down policies of the University of Texas and University of Michigan Law Schools. In 2001 a federal appeals court ruled unanimously that the affirmative action program used by the University of Georgia was unconstitutional. Similar movements are taking place in the business, educational, and governmental sectors.

In addition to these legal attacks, university and college campuses—supposed bastions of enlightenment and democracy—have experienced an alarming rise of prejudice and discrimination. Ugly racial incidents have been well documented, such as the burning of a cross in a Black student's dormitory room, the taunting of a Black female as "dark meat" by Dartmouth football players, the spray painting of racial slurs on the walls of a minority cultural center at Smith

College, the victimizing of Hispanic students with racial epithets and attacks by a fraternity group in Berkeley, and racial incidents at Duke and Stanford.

More recently, the destruction of the World Trade Center in New York City, the attack on the Pentagon in Washington, D.C., the downing of an airplane in Pennsylvania, and the loss of thousands of innocent lives have left a nation stunned and shocked. Naturally, many have reacted with horror over the tragic events, sadness for those who perished, empathy for loved ones left behind, fear about their personal safety, feelings of helplessness, and grief over a lost way of life (whether real or imagined). Despite our collective pain and anger toward our tormentors, it is very important to resist the primitive impulse of revenge in favor of a rational long-term strategy that remains true to our democratic ideals.

We have been concerned, for example, about increased hate crimes directed at Arabs, Middle Easterners, Afghans, and Sikhs. Reports of beatings, hate mail, verbal harassment, and airline profiling have been directed not only at Muslims but also at non-Muslim minorities (Asian Americans and Hispanics) who are mistakenly associated with terrorists. It is important to remember the lessons of World War II, when the United States incarcerated 120,000 loyal Japanese Americans (two-thirds U.S. citizens by virtue of birth) and deprived them of their civil liberties. While we strongly condemn the actions of the terrorists, and believe that those responsible should be hunted down and brought to justice, it is important to remember two things. First, Islam does not condone the actions or beliefs of the terrorists; there is a difference between Muslims and the terrorists. Second, we must be careful to walk the fine line between deprivation of civil liberties, scapegoating, and the inconvenience of citizens for safety reasons.

It may seem surprising and unusual for us to open a chapter on *Counseling the Culturally Diverse* with these examples. Aren't these incidents only tangentially related to the topic of multicultural counseling/therapy? Why should we give them such broad prominence? After all, as mental health practitioners, we are here to help people, not oppress them. While these last statements may be correct in philosophy, they fail to recognize several important facets of counseling and psychotherapy with minority clients.

First, the worldview of persons of color and other marginalized groups is ultimately linked to the historical and current experiences of oppression in the United States. A racial minority client, for example, is likely to approach counseling and therapy with a great deal of healthy suspicion regarding the therapist's conscious and unconscious motives in a multicultural context. That a therapist is "supposed to help" or that definitions of therapy encompass certain philosophical assumptions such as (a) a concern and respect for the uniqueness of clients; (b) an emphasis on the inherent worth and dignity of all people regardless of race, creed, color, or sex; (c) a high priority placed on helping others attain their own self-determined goals; (d) valuing freedom and the opportunity to explore one's own characteristics and potentials; and

(e) a future-oriented promise of a better life is not enough to foster trust in light of the current sociopolitical climate (Atkinson et al., 1998; Katz, 1985; D. W. Sue et al., 1996). Many of these goals had their roots in the educational guidance movement of the early twentieth century and reflected democratic ideals such as "equal access and opportunity," "pursuit of happiness," "liberty and justice for all," and "fulfillment of personal destiny." While these lofty ideals may seem highly commendable and appropriate for the mental health profession, they have often been translated in such a manner as to justify support for the status quo (D'Andrea & Daniels, 1995; Katz, 1985; M. L. Jackson, 1995; D. W. Sue et al., 1998).

That mental health practice has failed to fulfill its promises to culturally diverse populations has been a frequent theme voiced by minority group authors since the mid-1960s and continues to this very day (Fernando, 1988; M. L. Jackson, 1995; Meyers et al., 1991; Pine, 1972; President's Commission on Mental Health, 1978; Surgeon General's Report, 2000).

Discouragingly, minority group perceptions of the discriminatory nature of the helping profession continue to have great legitimacy and indicate a gap between the ideals of the mental health profession and its actual operation with respect to marginalized groups in our society. While mental health practice enshrines the concepts of freedom, rational thought, tolerance of new ideas, and equality and justice for all, those in power can use it as an oppressive instrument to maintain or to protect the status quo. In this respect, mental health practice becomes a form of oppression in which there is an unjust and cruel exercise of power to subjugate or mistreat large groups of people. When used to restrict rather than enhance the well-being and development of racial minorities, it may entail overt and covert forms of prejudice and discrimination. Thus, the worldview of persons of color who come for therapy boils down to one important question: "What makes you, a counselor/therapist, any different from all the others out there who have oppressed me and discriminated against me?"

This question brings us back to a more personal observation. Just as the White supremacist, famous sports figure, teacher, corporation, politician, and scientist could be racist in thought, beliefs, and deeds, so also can counselors and therapists be subject to inheriting and acting out the biases of the society. Racism runs deep and dies hard! Scratch the surface and you will find beliefs that are evidence of the sociopolitical climate in which we are raised—beliefs, for example, that Muslims and Asian Americans are aliens and potential terrorists or spies, that Blacks lack the intellectual qualities to advance in our society, that immigrants are to be blamed for draining our economic resources, that there is nothing worse than the intermingling of races, that Hispanic people are lower than animals and should be destroyed, that American Indians must fit preconceived White definitions, and that persons of color are aliens in their own land.

To say that we have somehow escaped our racist, sexist, and homophobic upbringing, that we are not perpetrators of bias and discrimination, or that the racial climate is good is to deny social reality. As mental health professionals, we have a personal and professional responsibility to (a) confront, become aware of, and take actions in dealing with our biases, stereotypes, values, and assumptions about human behavior; (b) become aware of the worldviews, values, biases, and assumptions of clients who differ from us, (c) develop appropriate help-giving practices, intervention strategies, and structures that take into account the historical, cultural, and environmental experiences and influences of our clients; and (d) change the policies, practices, programs, and structures of the institutions that oppress groups in our society.

This book is about providing appropriate mental health care to a culturally diverse population. Its main thesis is that counseling and psychotherapy do not take place in a vacuum isolated from the larger sociopolitical influences of our society. Multicultural counseling often mirrors the state of interracial relationships in the wider society as well as the dominant-subordinate relationships of other marginalized groups (gays/lesbians, women, and the physically challenged). It serves as a microcosm reflecting Black-White, Asian-White, Hispanic-White, American Indian–White, interethnic, and minority-majority relations.

This chapter attempts to explore the many ways in which counseling and psychotherapy have failed to provide culturally appropriate mental health services to disempowered groups in our society. It does this by using racial minorities as an example of the damaging majority-minority relationships that historically characterize many other marginalized groups. Only by honestly confronting these unpleasant social realities and accepting responsibility for changing them will our profession be able to advance and grow (B. R. Strickland, 2000). For racial/ethnic minorities, these failures can be seen in three primary areas: (a) the education and training of mental health professionals, (b) biased and inaccurate therapeutic and mental health literature, and (c) the inappropriate process and practice of counseling and psychotherapy. We deal with only the first two areas in this chapter. Therapeutic process and practice is discussed in Chapters 4 and 5. Prior to our journey, however, it is important to present some important demographic data regarding the diversification of the United States and its implications for our society and the mental health profession.

The Diversification of the United States

People of color have reached a critical mass in the United States, and their numbers are expected to continue increasing. The rapid increase in racial/ethnic minorities in the United States has been referred to as the "Diversification of the United States" or, literally, the "Changing Complexion of Society." From 1990 to 2000, the U.S. population increased 13% to over 281 million (U.S. Bureau of the Census, 2001). Most of the population increase consisted of visible racial/ethnic minority groups (VREG): The Asian American/Pacific Islander population increased by almost 50%, the Latino/Hispanic population by over 58%, African Americans by 16%, and American Indians/Alaska Natives by 15.5%, in marked contrast to the 7.3% increase of Whites. Currently, people of color constitute over 30% of the U.S. population, approximately 45% of whom are in the public schools (D. W. Sue et al., 1998; U.S. Bureau of the Census, 2000). Projections indicate that persons of color will constitute a numerical majority sometime between 2030 and 2050 (D. W. Sue et al., 1998).

The rapid demographic shift stems from two major trends: immigration rates and differential birthrates. The current immigration rates (documented immigrants, undocumented immigrants, and refugees) are the largest in U.S. history. Unlike the earlier immigrants who were primarily White Europeans oriented toward assimilation, the current wave consists primarily of Asian (34%), Latin American (34%), and other VREGs who may not be readily assimilated (Atkinson et al., 1998). In addition, the birthrates of White Americans have continued to decline (Euro-American = 1.7 per mother) in comparison to other racial/ethnic minorities (e.g., African American = 2.4, Mexican American = 2.9, Vietnamese = 3.4, Laotians = 4.6, Cambodians = 7.4, and Hmong = 11.9).

Societal Implications

Societal implications of the diversification of the United States are many:

1. Approximately 75% of those now entering the labor force are visible racial/ethnic minorities and women. The changing complexion and feminization of the workforce have become a reality.

2. By the time the so-called baby boomers (those born between 1946 and 1961) retire, the majority of people contributing to the social security and pension plans will be racial/ethnic minorities. In other words, those planning to retire (primarily White workers) must depend on their coworkers of color. If racial/ethnic minorities continue to encounter the glass ceiling and to be the most undereducated, underemployed, underpaid, and unemployed, the economic security of retiring White workers looks grim.

3. Businesses are aware that their workforces must be drawn increasingly from a diverse labor pool and that the current U.S. minority marketplace equals the entire gross domestic product of Canada; projections are that it will become immense as the shift in demographics continues. The economic viability of businesses will depend on their ability to manage a diverse workforce effectively, allow for equal access and opportunity, and appeal to consumers of color.

4. Students of color now constitute 45% of the population in our public schools. Some school systems such as that in California reached 50%

students of color as early as the late 1980s. Thus, it appears that our educational institutions must wrestle with issues of multicultural education and the development of bilingual programs.

5. The diversity index of the United States stands at 49, indicating that there is a nearly one in two chance that two people selected at random are racially or ethnically different.

6. The changing demographics are uneven and have differential effects on different parts of the country. We have mentioned California trends several times not because it is more important than other states but because it represents one of the most diverse regions in the country, thus representing a harbinger of things to come as our nation becomes increasingly diverse. Some parts of the country undergoing rapid transformation are the following:

- Over half the population of California is composed of racial/ethnic minorities.
- Thirty percent of New York City residents were born outside of this country.
- Seventy percent of the District of Columbia is African American.
- Two thirds of Miami is Hispanic.
- Approximately 37% of the population of San Francisco is Asian/ Asian American.
- Nearly two thirds of Detroit is African American.
- Over 10,000 Laotian Hmongs have immigrated to Minneapolis/St. Paul, Minnesota.

Following are the regions/states that will have the greatest percentages of minority representation by the year 2020:

State/Region	% Minority
D.C.	72.6
New Mexico	67.8
Hawaii	64.6
California	62.3
Texas	53.9
Maryland	44.9
Arizona	44.0
New York	43.5
Nevada	42.5
New Jersey	42.0

In recognition of the changing composition of the nation, business and industry have moved toward diversity training, multicultural concepts have been infused into school curricula, and there have been many attempts to fight bigotry, bias, and discrimination in our social, economic, and political systems. Nonetheless, the changing demographics have also caused alarm in many of our White citizens and have often resulted in conflict and major clashes. Perhaps this is to be expected as different worldviews, lifestyles, and value systems challenge the myth of the melting pot concept as we move from a monocultural to a multicultural society.

Mental Health Implications

As with our society in general, the implications for the mental health professions are many:

1. First, the clash of worldviews, values, and lifestyles is inescapable not only in the therapist's personal life but in his or her professional practice as well. It will be impossible for any of us to avoid client groups who differ from us in terms of race, culture, and ethnicity. Increasingly, therapists will come into contact with clients who may not share their worldview of what constitutes normality-abnormality, who define helping in a manner that contrasts sharply with our codes of ethics and standards of practice, who require culture-specific strategies and approaches in counseling and psychotherapy, and who may perceive the profession as a sociopolitical tool.

2. If counselors and therapists are to provide meaningful help to a culturally diverse population, we must reach out and not only acquire new understandings but also develop new culturally effective helping approaches. To prepare counselors with multicultural expertise means (a) revamping our training programs to include accurate and realistic multicultural content and experiences, (b) developing multicultural competencies as core standards for our profession, and (c) providing continuing education for our current service providers (D. W. Sue et al., 1999).

3. Because therapeutic and ethical practice may be culture-bound, therapists who work with culturally different clients may be engaging in cultural oppression using unethical and harmful practices for that particular population. Our professional organizations need to adopt ethical guidelines, codes of ethics, standards of practice, and by-laws that are multicultural in scope (D. W. Sue, 2001). Omission of such standards and failed translation into actual practice are inexcusable and represents

a powerful statement of the low priority and lack of commitment to cultural diversity. If we are indeed committed to multiculturalism, then each and every one of us must become advocates in demanding that our professional associations seriously undertake a major revision of standards used to ascertain counseling competence. Furthermore, these multicultural criteria must be infused into licensing and credentialing standards as well.

4. The education and training of psychologists have, at times, created the impression that the theories and practices of psychology are apolitical and value-free. Yet we are often impressed by the fact that the actual practice of therapy can result in cultural oppression; that what happens in the therapist's office may represent a microcosm of race relations in the larger society; that the so-called psychological problems of minority groups may reside not within, but outside of our clients; and that no matter how well intentioned helping professionals may be, they are not immune from inheriting the racial biases of their forebears.

5. Because none of us is immune from inheriting the images/stereotypes of the larger society, we can assume that most therapists are prisoners of their own cultural conditioning. As a result, they possess stereotypes and preconceived notions that may be unwittingly imposed on their culturally different clients. These may affect how they define problems, the goals that they develop, and the standards that they use to judge normal and abnormal behavior. If their biases and prejudices influence their work with culturally diverse clients, they may potentially oppress and harm them. Thus it is imperative that all therapists explore their own stereotypes and images of various minority groups. Since many of our stereotypes are unconscious, we must work tirelessly to uncover them with as little defensiveness as possible. One of the greatest obstacles is our fear that others will see our racism, sexism, heterosexism, and biases. Thus we try to deny their existence or to hide them from public view. This works against our ability to uncover them.

The Education and Training of Mental Health Professionals

While national interest in the mental health needs of ethnic minorities has increased in the past decade, the human service professions have historically failed to meet the particular mental health needs of this population (Samuda, 1998; Surgeon General's Report on Minority Mental Health, 2000). Evidence reveals that in addition to the common stresses experienced by everyone else, the minority population is more likely to encounter problems such as immigrant status, poverty, cultural racism, prejudice, and discrimination. Yet studies continue to reveal that American Indians, Asian Americans, African

Americans, and Latino/Hispanic Americans tend to underutilize traditional outpatient mental health services (Cheung & Snowden, 1990; F. T. L. Leong, 1994). Further, some years back, S. Sue and colleagues found that clients tended to terminate counseling/therapy at a rate of more than 50% after only one contact with the therapist. This was in marked contrast to the termination rate of less than 30% among White clients (S. Sue, Allen, & Conaway, 1975; S. Sue, Fujino, Hu, Takeuchi, & Zane, 1991; S. Sue & McKinney, 1974; S. Sue, McKinney, Allen, & Hall, 1974). While utilization data for minority groups are changing, these early findings led many to search for enlightened explanations.

For example, some researchers hypothesized that minority-group individuals underutilize and prematurely terminate counseling/therapy because of the biased nature of the services themselves (D. W. Sue & Sue, 1977; S. Sue et al., 1974). The services offered are frequently antagonistic or inappropriate to the life experiences of the culturally different client: They lack sensitivity and understanding, and they are oppressive and discriminating toward minority clients. Many believed that the presence of ill-prepared mental health professionals was the direct result of a culture-bound and biased training system (Korman, 1973; Meyers et al., 1991; Mio & Morris, 1990). While directors of training programs report that multicultural coursework has increased significantly (Bernal & Castro, 1994; Hills & Strozier, 1992) in mental health education, it is interesting to note that graduate students in mental health programs have a different view. They report few courses offered in multicultural psychology and inadequate coverage of work with diverse populations within required core courses (Allison, Crawford, Echemendia, Robinson, & Knepp, 1994; Mintz, Bartels, & Rideout, 1995). For example, courses in family therapy, theories of psychotherapy, assessment and testing, and research seldom include or infuse multicultural content into the overall curriculum. Further, the training of mental health professionals has often resulted in therapists' inheriting the racial and cultural biases of their forebears because stereotyped perceptions of minorities are reinforced by the biased content of the programs (Guthrie, 1997; Katz, 1985; Wrenn, 1985).

It is our contention that reports of increased multicultural coverage (while gaining a degree of prominence) are inflated or superficially developed. Most graduate programs continue to give inadequate treatment to the mental health issues of ethnic minorities. Cultural influences affecting personality formation, career choice, educational development, and the manifestation of behavior disorders are infrequently part of mental health training or are treated in a tangential manner (Bernal & Castro, 1994; Parham, White, & Ajamu, 1999). When minority group experiences are discussed, they are generally seen and analyzed from the White Euro-American, middle-class perspective. In programs where minority experiences have been discussed, the focus tends to be on their pathological lifestyles or on the maintenance of false stereotypes. The result is twofold: (a) Professionals who deal with mental health problems of ethnic minorities lack understanding and knowledge about ethnic values and their consequent interaction with a racist society, and (2) mental health practitioners are graduated from our programs believing that minorities are inherently pathological and that therapy involves a simple modification of traditional White models.

This ethnocentric bias has been highly destructive to the natural help-giving networks of minority communities. Often, mental health professionals operate under the assumption that racial and ethnic minorities never had such things as counseling and psychotherapy until they were invented and institutionalized in Western cultures. For the benefit of "those" people, the mental health movement has delegitimized natural help-giving networks that have operated for thousands of years by labeling them as unscientific, supernatural, mystical, and inconsistent with professional standards of practice. Then mental health professionals are surprised to find that there is a high incidence of psychological distress in the minority community, that their treatment techniques do not work, and that the culturally different do not utilize their services.

Contrary to this ethnocentric orientation, we need to expand our perception of what constitutes mental health practices. Equally legitimate methods of treatment include the informal or natural support systems so powerful in many minority groups (family, friends, community self-help programs, and occupational networks), folk-healing methods, and formal indigenous systems of therapy (C. C. Lee, 1996; Pedersen, 1994; D. W. Sue, Ivey, & Pedersen, 1996; D. W. Sue et al., 1998). Instead of attempting to destroy them, we should actively try to find out why they may work better than Western forms of counseling and therapy.

Definitions of Mental Health

A number of individuals have pointed out how counseling and psychotherapy often tend to assume universal (etic) applications of their concepts and goals to the exclusion of culture-specific (emic) views (Pedersen, 2000; Trimble, 1990). Likewise, graduate programs have often been accused of fostering *cultural encapsulation,* a term first coined by Wrenn (1962). The term refers specifically to (a) the substitution of modal stereotypes for the real world, (b) the disregarding of cultural variations in a dogmatic adherence to some universal notion of truth, and (c) the use of a technique-oriented definition of the counseling process. The results are that counselor roles are rigidly defined, implanting an implicit belief in universal concepts of "healthy" and "normal."

If we look at criteria used by the mental health profession to judge normality and abnormality, this deficiency becomes glaring. Several fundamental approaches that have particular relevance to our discussion have been identified (D. Sue et al., 2000): (a) normality as a statistical concept, (b) normality as ideal mental health, and (c) abnormality as the presence of certain behaviors (research criteria).

First, statistical criteria equate normality with those behaviors that occur most frequently in the population. Then, abnormality is defined in terms of those behaviors that occur least frequently. For example, data collected on IQs may be accumulated and an average calculated. IQ scores near the average are considered normal, and relatively large deviations from the norm (in either direction) are considered abnormal. In spite of the word *statistical,* however, these criteria need not be quantitative in nature: Individuals who talk to themselves, disrobe in public, or laugh uncontrollably for no apparent reason are considered abnormal according to these criteria simply because most people do not behave in that way. Statistical criteria undergird our notion of a normal probability curve so often used in IQ tests, achievement tests, and personality inventories.

Statistical criteria may seem adequate in specific instances, but they are fraught with hazards and problems. For one thing, they fail to take into account differences in time, community standards, and cultural values. If deviations from the majority are considered abnormal, then many ethnic and racial minorities that exhibit strong cultural differences from the majority must be so classified. When we resort to a statistical definition, the dominant or most powerful group generally determines what constitutes normality and abnormality. For example, what would it mean if a group of African Americans were to be administered a personality test and it was found that they were more suspicious than their White counterparts?

Some psychologists and educators have used such findings to label African Americans as paranoid. Statements by Blacks that "the Man" is out to get them may be perceived as supporting a paranoid delusion. This interpretation, however, has been challenged by many Black psychologists as being inaccurate (Grier & Cobbs, 1968; Guthrie, 1997; A. C. Jones, 1985; Parham, White, & Ajamu, 1999). In response to their slave heritage and a history of White discrimination against them, African Americans have adopted various behaviors (in particular, behaviors toward Whites) that have proven to be important for survival in a racist society. "Playing it cool" has been identified as one means by which Blacks, as well as members of other minority groups, may conceal their true thoughts and feelings. A Black person who is experiencing conflict, anger, or even rage may be skillful at appearing serene and composed. This tactic is a survival mechanism aimed at reducing one's vulnerability to harm and exploitation in a hostile environment (J. L. White & Parham, 1990).

The personality test that reveals Blacks as being suspicious, mistrustful, and paranoid needs to be understood from a larger sociopolitical perspective.

Minority groups who have consistently been victims of discrimination and oppression in a culture that is full of racism have good reason to be suspicious and mistrustful of White society. In their classic book *Black Rage,* Grier and Cobbs (1968) point out how Blacks, in order to survive in a White racist society, have developed a highly functional survival mechanism to protect them against possible physical and psychological harm. The authors perceive this "cultural paranoia" as adaptive and healthy rather than dysfunctional and pathological. Indeed, some psychologists of color have indicated that the absence of a *paranorm* among minorities may be more indicative of pathology than is its presence. The absence of a paranorm may indicate either poor reality testing (denial of oppression-racism in our society) or naïveté in understanding the operation of racism.

Second, humanistic psychologists have proposed the concept of ideal mental health as one of the criteria of normality. Such criteria stress the importance of attaining some positive goal. For example, consciousness-balance of psychic forces (Freud, 1960; C. G. Jung, 1960); self-actualization/creativity (Maslow, 1968; C. R. Rogers, 1961); competence, autonomy, and resistance to stress (Allport, 1961; R. W. White, 1963); and self-disclosure (Jourard, 1964) have all been historically proposed. The discriminatory nature of such approaches is grounded in the belief of a universal application (all populations in all situations) and reveals a failure to recognize the value base from which the criteria are derived. The particular goal or ideal used is intimately linked with the theoretical frame of reference and values held by the practitioner. For example, the psychoanalytic emphasis on insight as a determinant of mental health is a value in itself (London, 1989). It is important for the mental health professional to be aware, however, that certain socioeconomic groups and ethnic minorities do not particularly value insight. Furthermore, the use of self-disclosure as a measure of mental health tends to neglect the concept of the paranorm. One characteristic often linked to the healthy personality is the ability to talk about the deepest and most intimate aspects of one's life—to self-disclose. This orientation is very characteristic of our counseling and therapy process, in which clients are expected to talk about their lives in a very personal manner. The fact that many minorities are initially reluctant to self-disclose can place them in a situation in which they are judged to be mentally unhealthy and, in this case, paranoid.

Definitions of mental health such as competence, autonomy, and resistance to stress are related to White middle-class notions of individual maturity (Ahuvia, 2001; Triandis, 2000). The mental health professions originated from the ideological milieu of individualism (Ivey, Ivey, & Simek-Morgan, 1997). Individuals make their lot in life. Those who succeed in society do so on the basis of their *own* efforts and abilities. Successful people are seen as mature, independent, and possessing great ego strength. Apart from the potential bias in defining what constitutes competence, autonomy, and resistance to stress, the use of such a person-focused definition of maturity places the blame on the individual. When a person fails in life, it is because of his or her own lack of ability, interest, maturity, or some inherent weakness of the ego. If we see minorities as being subjected to higher stress factors in society and placed in a one-down position by virtue of racism, then it becomes quite clear that the definition will tend to portray the lifestyle of minorities as inferior, underdeveloped, and deficient. W. Ryan (1971) was the first to coin the phrase "blaming the victim" to refer to this process. Yet a broader system analysis would show that the economic, social, and psychological conditions of minorities are related to their oppressed status in America.

Thus, the use of ideal mental health as the sole criterion tends to present multiple problems. Which goal or ideal should be used? The answer depends largely on the particular theoretical frame of reference or values embraced by those posing the criteria. Their unbridled imposition without regard to sociocultural influences would lead us to conclude that almost all minorities in the United States are unhealthy.

An alternative to the previous two definitions of abnormality is research-oriented. For example, in determining rates of mental illness in different ethnic groups, psychiatric diagnosis, presence in mental hospitals, and scores on objective psychological inventories are frequently used (Samuda, 1998). Diagnosis and hospitalization present a circular problem: The definition of normality-abnormality depends on what mental health practitioners say it is! In this case, the race or ethnicity of mental health professionals is likely to differ from that of minority clients. Bias on the part of the practitioner with respect to diagnosis and treatment is likely to occur (Cheung & Snowden, 1990; Snowden & Cheung, 1990). The inescapable conclusion is that minority clients tend to be diagnosed differently and to receive less preferred modes of treatment (Paniagua, 2001).

Furthermore, the political and societal implications of psychiatric diagnosis and hospitalization were forcefully pointed out over 30 years ago by Laing (1967, 1969) and Szasz (1970, 1971). While it appears that minorities underutilize outpatient services, they seem to face greater levels of involuntary hospital commitments (Snowden & Cheung, 1990). Laing believes that individual madness is but a reflection of the madness of society. He describes schizophrenic breakdowns as desperate strategies by people to liberate themselves from a false self used to maintain behavioral normality in our society. Attempts to adjust the person back to the original normality (sick society) are unethical.

Szasz states this opinion even more strongly:

In my opinion, mental illness is a myth. People we label "mentally ill" are not sick, and involuntary mental hospitalization is not treatment. It is punishment. . . . The fact that mental illness designates a deviation from an ethical rule of conduct, and that such rules vary widely, explains why upper-middle-class psychiatrists can so easily find evidence of "mental illness" in lower-class individuals; and why so many prominent persons in the past fifty years or so have been diagnosed by their enemies as suffering from some types of insanity. Barry Goldwater was called a paranoid schizophrenic . . . Woodrow Wilson, a neurotic. . . . Jesus Christ, according to two psychiatrists . . . was a born degenerate with a fixed delusion system. (Szasz, 1970, pp. 167–168)

Szasz (1987, 1999) sees the mental health professional as an inquisitor, an agent of society exerting social control on those individuals who deviate in thought and behavior from the accepted norms of society. Psychiatric hospitalization is believed to be a form of social control for persons who annoy or disturb us. The label *mental illness* may be seen as a political ploy used to control those who are different, and therapy as a way to control, brainwash, or reorient the identified victims to fit into society. It is exactly this concept that many minorities find frightening. For example, many Asian Americans, American Indians, African Americans, and Hispanic/Latino Americans are increasingly challenging the concepts of normality and abnormality. They believe that their values and lifestyles are often seen by society as pathological and thus that they are unfairly discriminated against by the mental health professions (Paniagua, 2001).

In addition, using "objective" psychological inventories as indicators of maladjustment may also place minorities at a disadvantage. One example concerns the paranorm mentioned earlier. Most minorities are aware that the test instruments used on them have been constructed and standardized according to White middle-class norms. The lack of culturally unbiased instruments makes many feel that the results obtained are invalid. Indeed, in a landmark decision in the State of California (*Larry P. v. California,* 1986), Judge Peckham ruled in favor of the Association of Black Psychologists' claim that individual intelligence tests such as the Wechsler Intelligence Scale for Children–Revised (WISC-R), Wechsler Adult Intelligence Scale–Revised (WAIS-R), and Stanford-Binet Intelligence Scale could not be used in the public schools on Black students. The improper use of such instruments can lead to the exclusion of minorities in jobs and promotion, to discriminatory educational decisions, and to biased determination of what constitutes pathology and cure in counseling/therapy (Halleck, 1971; London, 1988; Samuda, 1998).

D. Sue et al. (2000) have noted some primary objections to testing and the consequent classification that often results. When a diagnosis becomes a label, it can have serious consequences. First, a label can cause people to interpret all activities of the affected individual as pathological. No matter what Black people may do or say that breaks a stereotype, their behavior will seem to reflect the fact that they are less intelligent than others around them. Second, the label may cause others to treat individuals differently even when they are perfectly normal. Third, a label may cause those who are labeled to believe that they do indeed possess such characteristics.

A study by Rosenthal and Jacobson (1968) showed how a label can cause differential treatment. The authors randomly assigned school children to either of two groups. Teachers were told that tests of one group indicated that they were intellectual "bloomers" (gaining in competence and maturity); the other group was not given this label. After a one-year interval, children from both groups were retested (they had also been tested the year before). The experimenters found that the group identified as "bloomers" showed dramatic gains in IQs. Understanding how this occurs has significant implications for racial/ethnic minorities, women, and other groups subjected to widespread stereotyping.

Differential Treatment and the Self-Fulfilling Prophecy

Many have speculated that the label led teachers to have higher intellectual expectations for the "bloomers" and thus to treat them differently. Even though there was no significant difference in IQ between the two groups to begin with, differences were present by the end of the year. It is not difficult to speculate that stereotypes of various racial and ethnic minorities will result in differential treatment based on preconceived notions. In addition, the Rosenthal and Jacobson (1968) study suggests not only that teachers behave differently, but also that labels may affect the children. It is possible that when people are constantly told by others that they are stupid or smart, they may come to believe such labels (self-fulfilling prophecy). If people ascribe certain stereotypical traits to a racial minority or an ethnic group, then it is reasonable to believe that they will behave differently toward the group and cause cognitive and behavioral changes among members of the group. These factors lend support to the belief that therapy is an ethnocentric part of the establishment that interprets behavior exclusively from its reference point and attempts to fit minorities into the White experience.

Stereotype Threat
Nowhere are stereotypes more powerful and damaging for African Americans, Latinos, and women than in the academic performance arena. The belief that Blacks and Latinos are intellectually inferior and that women are weaker in math than men is widespread. Steele and colleagues (Spencer, Quinn, & Steele, 2001; Steele, 1997; Steele & Aronson, 1995) have proposed a theory of stereotype threat that accounts for the differential performance between minorities and their White counterparts. His ingenious studies reveal that when evaluated in a situation likely to arouse a threat of fulfilling stereotypes about them, equally prepared and bright African Americans stu-

dents often underperform in comparison with White students. Several components appear to be operating here: (a) apprehension that one will confirm a group stereotype about oneself, (b) feelings of threat that are sufficiently intense to disrupt the task at hand, and (c) protective disidentification in which the person rejects or disidentifies with the task at hand.

For example, an African American male student in a testing situation who believes that his performance may confirm a stereotype may become sufficiently anxious that it interferes with his ability to perform maximally on the task. Further, to deal with the threat or fear, the student may disengage psychologically from the situation by minimizing its importance. Unlike the self-fulfilling prophecy, the person experiencing stereotype threat need not have internalized the stereotype or believe that he or she is incapable of performing well on the task! Interestingly, Steele and Aronson (1995) also found that women performed worse in math under a stereotype threat condition and that even White students performed poorer than Asian students when stereotype threat (i.e., that Asian Americans are better in math than Whites) was invoked for them.

Curriculum and Training Deficiencies

It appears that many of the universal definitions of mental health that have pervaded the profession have been due primarily to severe deficiencies in training programs. Various specialists (Arredondo et al., 1996; Z. Chen, 2001; Mio & Morris, 1990) have asserted that the major reason for ineffectiveness in working with culturally different populations is the lack of culturally sensitive material taught in the curricula. The field has ethnocentrically assumed that the material taught in traditional mental health programs is equally applicable to all groups. Even now, when there is high recognition of the need for multicultural curricula, infusing such concepts into course content remains a battle. As a result, course offerings continue to lack a non-White perspective, to treat cultural issues as an adjunct or add-on, to continue portraying cultural groups in stereotypic ways, and to create an academic environment that does not support minority concerns, needs, and issues (Grieger & Toliver, 2001).

This very issue of cultural encapsulation and its detrimental effects on minorities has generated training recommendations from many sources (Casas, Pavelski, Furlong, & Zanglis, 2001; D'Andrea, Daniels, Arredondo, et al., 2001; Korman, 1974). Multicultural specialists have noted the serious lack and inadequacy of psychology training programs in dealing with religions, racial, ethnic, sexual, and economic groups. Selected recommendations include advocating (a) that professional psychology training programs at all levels provide information on the political nature of the practice of psychology, (b) that professionals need to "own" their value positions, (c) that client populations ought to be involved in helping determine what is "done to them", (d) that evaluation of training programs should include not only the content but also an evaluation of the graduates, and (e) that continuing professional development should occur beyond the receipt of any advanced degree.

Perhaps the most important recommendation to arise from multicultural psychologists and educators was the importance of identifying and assessing competencies of psychologists as they relate to the culturally different (D. W. Sue et al., 1982; D. W. Sue, Arredondo, & McDavis, 1992; American Psychological Association [APA], 1993; Arredondo et al., 1996; D. W. Sue et al., 1998). In addition, the importance of providing educational experiences that generate sensitivity and appreciation of the history, current needs, strengths, and resources of minority communities was stressed. Students and professionals should be helped to understand the development and behavior of the group being studied, thus enabling them to (a) use their knowledge to develop skills in working with minority groups and (b) develop strategies to modify the effects of political, social, and economic forces on minority groups. The curriculum must focus on immediate social problems and needs. It must stimulate an awareness of minority issues caused by economic, social, and educational deprivation. The curriculum must also be designed to stimulate this awareness not solely at a cognitive level. It must enable students to understand feelings of helplessness and powerlessness, low self-esteem, and poor self-concept, as well as how they contribute to low motivation, frustration, hate, ambivalence, and apathy. Each course should contain (a) a consciousness-raising component, (b) an affective/experiential component, (c) a knowledge component, and (d) a skills component.

Counseling and Mental Health Literature

Many writers have noted how the social science literature, and specifically research, has failed to create a realistic understanding of various ethnic groups in America (Guthrie, 1997; J. M. Jones, 1997; Samuda, 1998; D. W. Sue & S. Sue, 1972; A. Thomas & Sillen, 1972). In fact, certain practices are felt to have done great harm to minorities by ignoring them, maintaining false stereotypes, or distorting their lifestyles. As mentioned earlier, mental health practice may be viewed as encompassing the use of social power and functioning as a handmaiden of the status quo (Halleck, 1971; Highlen, 1996; Katz, 1985). It is clear that organized social science is part of a culture-bound social system from which its researchers are usually drawn; moreover, organized social science often depends on it for financial support. Ethnic minorities frequently see the mental health profession in a similar way: as a discipline concerned with maintaining the status of those in power (Highlen,

1996). As a result, the person collecting and reporting data is often perceived as possessing the social bias of his or her society.

Social sciences, for example, have historically ignored the study of Asians in America (Hong & Domokos-Cheng Ham, 2001; Leong, 1986; Root, 1998). This deficit has contributed to the perpetuation of false stereotypes that has angered many younger Asians concerned with raising consciousness and group esteem. When studies have been conducted on minorities, research has been appallingly unbalanced. Many social scientists (Billingsley, 1970; J. M. Jones, 1997; Wilson & Stith, 1991) have pointed out how "White social science" has tended to reinforce a negative view of African Americans among the public by concentrating on unstable Black families rather than on the many stable ones. Such unfair treatment has also been the case in studies on Latinos that have focused on the psychopathological problems encountered by Mexican Americans (Falicov, 1996). Other ethnic groups such as Native Americans (Atkinson, Morten, & Sue, 1998; LaFromboise, 1998) and Puerto Ricans (Garcia-Preto, 1996) have fared no better. Even more disturbing is the assumption that the problems encountered by minorities are due to intrinsic factors (racial inferiority, incompatible value systems, etc.) rather than to the failure of society (Katz, 1985; Samuda, 1998).

In a classic study of stereotype evolution, S. Sue and Kitano (1973) analyzed the literature portrayal of the Chinese and Japanese in the United States and concluded that there is a strong correlation between stereotypes and the conditions of society. When economic conditions were poor, Asians were portrayed as nonassimilable, sexually aggressive, and treacherous. However, when economic conditions dictated a cheap labor supply, stereotypes became more favorable. While there are many aspects of how minorities are portrayed in the social science literature, two of them seem crucial for us to explore: minorities and pathology and the role of scientific racism in research.

Minorities and Pathology

When we seriously study the "scientific" literature of the past, we are immediately impressed with how an implicit equation of minorities and pathology is a common theme. The historical use of science in the investigation of racial differences seems to be linked with White supremacist notions (Guthrie, 1997; J. M. Jones, 1997; Samuda, 1998). The classic work of A. Thomas and Sillen (1972) refers to this as *scientific racism* and cites several historical examples to support the authors' contention: (a) 1840 census figures (fabricated) were used to support the notion that Blacks living under unnatural conditions of freedom were prone to anxiety; (b) mental health for Blacks consisted of contentment with subservience; (c) psychologically normal Blacks were faithful and happy-go-lucky; (d) influential medical journals presented (falsely) facts supporting the belief that the anatomical, neurological, or endocrinological aspects of Blacks were always inferior to those of Whites; (e) the Black person's brain is smaller and less developed; (f) Blacks were less prone to mental illness because their minds were so simple; and (g) the dreams of Blacks are juvenile in character and not as complex as Whites. More frightening, perhaps, is a survey that found that many of these stereotypes continue to be accepted by White Americans: 20% publicly expressed a belief that African Americans are innately inferior in thinking ability; 19% believe that Blacks have thicker craniums; and 23.5% believe that they have longer arms than Whites (Plous & Williams, 1995). One wonders how many White Americans hold similar beliefs but do not publicly voice them because of social pressures.

Furthermore, the belief that various human groups exist at different stages of biological evolution was accepted by G. Stanley Hall in 1904. He stated explicitly that Africans, Indians, and Chinese were members of adolescent races and in a stage of incomplete development. In most cases, the evidence used to support these conclusions was fabricated, extremely flimsy, or distorted to fit the belief in non-White inferiority (A. Thomas & Sillen, 1972). For example, Gossett (1963) reported that when one particular study in 1895 revealed that the sensory perception of Native Americans was superior to that of Blacks and that of Blacks to Whites, the results were used to support a belief in the mental superiority of Whites, whose "reactions were slower because they belonged to a more deliberate and reflective race than did the members of the other two groups" (p. 364). The belief that Blacks were "born athletes" as opposed to scientists or statesmen derives from this tradition. The 1987 statement by then–Dodger executive Al Campanis that Blacks are not mentally capable of being front-office executives or managers indicates that such stereotypes still operate. Even respected professional golfer Jack Nicklaus is reported to have stated that African American golfers are born with the wrong muscles to play at the highest level in golf (Hatfield, 1996). The success of Tiger Woods has done little to dispel this belief. The fact that Hall was a well-respected psychologist, is often referred to as the father of child study, and was the first president of the American Psychological Association did not prevent him from inheriting the racial biases of the times.

The Genetically Deficient Model

The portrayal of persons of color in literature has generally taken the form of stereotyping them as deficient in certain desirable attributes. For example, de Gobineau's (1915) *Essay on the Inequality of the Human Races* and Darwin's (1859) *The Origin of Species by Means of Natural Selection* were used to support the genetic intellectual superiority of Whites and the genetic inferiority of the "lower races." Galton (1869) wrote explicitly that African "Negroes" were "half-witted men" who made "childish, stupid and simpleton-like mistakes," while

Jews were inferior physically and mentally and were designed only for a parasitical existence on other nations of people. Using the Binet scales to test Black, Mexican American, and Spanish Indian families, Terman (1916) concluded that they were uneducable.

The genetic deficient model is present in the writing of educational psychologists and academicians (Hernstein, 1971; A. Jensen, 1969; Shockley, 1972; Shuey, 1966). At the American Association for the Advancement of Science convention in 1989, Phillip Rushton of the University of Western Ontario presented a much-criticized study. He claimed that human intelligence and behavior were largely determined by race, that Whites have bigger brains than Blacks, and that Blacks are more aggressive. These "scientists" have adopted the position that genes play a predominant role in the determination of intelligence. Shockley (1972) has expressed fears that the accumulation of weak- or low-intelligence genes in the Black population will seriously affect overall intelligence. Thus, he advocates that people with low IQs should not be allowed to bear children; they should be sterilized. Andy Rooney, a well-known commentator on *60 Minutes,* may have expressed this same train of thought when he said, "Blacks have watered down their genes because the less intelligent ones are the ones that have the most children. They drop out of schools early, do drugs, and get pregnant." In all fairness to Rooney, we must note that he denies making such comments, although CBS did take disciplinary action.

Allegations of scientific racism can be seen also in the work of the eminent British psychologist Cyril Burt, who fabricated data to support his contention that intelligence is inherited and that Blacks have inherited inferior brains. Such an accusation is immensely important when one considers that Burt is a major influence in American and British psychology, is considered by many to be the father of educational psychology, was the first psychologist to be knighted, and was awarded the American Psychological Association's Thorndike Prize; furthermore, his research findings form the foundation for the belief that intelligence is inherited. The charges leveled by several people (Dorfman, 1978; Gillie, 1977; Kamin, 1974) can be categorized into four assertions: (a) that Burt guessed at the intelligence of parents he interviewed and later treated his guesses as scientific facts, (b) that two of Burt's collaborators never existed and that Burt wrote the articles himself while using their names, (c) that Burt produced identical figures to three decimal points from different sets of data (a statistical impossibility), and (d) that Burt fabricated data to fit his theories. In a thorough review of one of Burt's most influential publications, Dorfman (1978) concludes:

> *Cyril Burt presented data in his classic paper "Intelligence and Social Class" that were in perfect agreement with a genetic theory of IQ and social class. A detailed analysis of these data reveals, beyond reasonable doubt, that they were fabricated*

from a theoretical normal curve, from a genetic regressions equation, and from figures published more than 30 years before Burt completed his surveys. (p. 1177)

More recently, the publication of *The Bell Curve: Intelligence and Class Structure in American Life* (Hernstein & Murray, 1994) has reignited the controversy in both the public and academic domains. Again, the assertions by the two authors echo a familiar refrain: intelligence is inherited to a large degree; race is correlated with intellect; and programs such as Head Start and Affirmative Action should be banished because they do no good. Instead, resources and funding should be reallocated to those who can profit from it. Samuda (1998) concludes about the authors, "Simply stated, they essentially recommend that those of lower intelligence should serve those of higher intelligence. . . . *The Bell Curve* remains astonishingly antiquated and immune to evidence from the physiological and neurobiological sciences, quantitative genetics, and statistical theory, and it overlooks the significance of environmental factors that research has uncovered" (p. 175–176). The problem with *The Bell Curve* is that it presents a good deal of genuine science sprinkled with science fiction and a political ideology aimed at creating an elite class in America (Gould, 1996; A. Ryan, 1995; Willie, 1995).

The question of whether there are differences in intelligence between races is both complex and emotional. The difficulty in clarifying this question is compounded by many factors. Besides the difficulty in defining "race," there exist questionable assumptions regarding whether research on the intelligence of Whites can be generalized to other groups, whether middle-class and lower-class ethnic minorities grow up in environments that are similar to those of middle- and lower-class Whites, and whether test instruments are valid for both minority and White subjects. More important, we should recognize that the average values of different populations tell us nothing about any one individual. Heritability is a function of the population, *not* a trait. Ethnic groups all have individuals in the full range of intelligence, and to think of any racial group in terms of a single stereotype goes against all we know about the mechanics of heredity. Yet much of the social science literature continues to portray ethnic minorities as being genetically deficient in one sense or another. Those interested both in the issues and consequences related to the testing of American minorities and in the technical and sociopolitical analyses of *The Bell Curve* are directed to the excellent rebuttal by Samuda (1998).

The Culturally Deficient Model
Well-meaning social scientists who challenged the genetic deficit model by placing heavy reliance on environmental factors nevertheless tended to perpetuate a view that saw minorities as culturally "disadvantaged," "deficient,"

or "deprived." Instead of a biological condition that caused differences, the blame now shifted to the lifestyles or values of various ethnic groups (Dana, 1993; Samuda, 1998). The term cultural deprivation was first popularized by Riessman's widely read book, *The Culturally Deprived Child* (1962). The term was used to indicate that many groups perform poorly on tests or exhibit deviant characteristics because they lack many of the advantages of middle-class culture (education, books, toys, formal language, etc.). In essence, these groups were culturally impoverished! Samuda (1975, 1998) summarized studies about how a numerous factors place many minority persons in such a position as to hinder their success in school and society at large: (a) nutritional factors—malnutrition contributing to physical and mental impairment; (b) environmental factors—crowded and broken homes, dilapidated and unaesthetic areas (lack of books, toys, pictures, etc.); (c) psychological factors—lower self-concepts, poor motivation, absence of successful male models, lack of parental encouragement and interest in education, fear of competing with Whites; (d) sociocultural factors—exposure to a culture with slum and ghetto values; and (e) linguistic factors.

While Riessman meant such a concept to add balance to working with minorities and ultimately to improve their condition in America, some educators of the time (K. B. Clark, 1963; K. B. Clark & Plotkin, 1972; Mackler & Giddings, 1965) strenuously objected to the term. First, the term *cultural deprivation* means lacking a cultural background (e.g., slaves arrived in America culturally naked), which is contradictory because everyone inherits a culture. Second, such terms cause conceptual and theoretical confusions that may adversely affect social planning, educational policy, and research. For example, the oft-quoted Moynihan Report (Moynihan, 1965) asserts that "at the heart of deterioration of the Negro society is the deterioration of the Black family. It is the fundamental source of the weakness in the Negro community" (p. 5). Action thus was directed toward infusing "White" concepts of the family into the Black concepts. Third, cultural deprivation is used synonymously with the deviation from and superiority of White middle-class values. Fourth, these deviations in values become equated with pathology, and the group's cultural values, families, or lifestyles are thought to transmit the pathology. Thus, the concept provides a convenient rationalization and alibi for the perpetuation of racism and the inequities of the socioeconomic system.

The Culturally Diverse Model
Many researchers now maintain that the culturally deficient model serves only to perpetuate the myth of minority inferiority. The focus tends to be a person-blame one, an emphasis on minority pathology, and a use of White middle-class definitions of desirable and undesirable behavior. Social science's use of a common standard assumption implies that to be different is to be deviant, pathological, or sick. Mercer (1971) claims that intelligence and

personality scores for minority group children actually measure how Angli-cized a person has become. Minorities should no longer be viewed as defi-cient, but rather as "culturally diverse." The goal of society should be to recognize the legitimacy of alternative lifestyles, the advantages of being bicultural (i.e., capable of functioning in two different cultural environ-ments), and the value of differences.

Since publication of the first three editions of this text, there has been increasing use of the term *cultural diversity*. The title of the first three editions included the phrase "culturally different." We dropped the former phrase be-cause it begs the question "different from what?" Inevitably, the answer was "White Euro-American" norms and society, creating a hierarchy and lesser status to other groups. Our switch to "culturally diverse" implies that all racial/ethnic groups operate on a level playing field and that comparisons and descriptions are not made against only one standard (Whites).

Relevance of Research

So far, our discussion of minority portrayal in the professional literature has been a general one. We have made minimal reference to research as it relates to minorities in particular. Research findings are supposed to form the basis of any profession that purports to be a science. The data generated from research should be objective and free of bias. As we saw in the last section, what a re-searcher proposes to study and how he or she interprets such findings are inti-mately linked to a personal, professional, and societal value system. Cheek (1987) goes so far as to assert that social science is a vehicle of White supremacy.

It is an inescapable conclusion that personal and societal values often af-fect the interpretation of data related to minorities (Atkinson et al., 2001). A very similar analogy can be drawn with respect to the mental health pro-fession. For example, the profession's preoccupation with pathology tends to encourage the study of personality deficits and weaknesses rather than strengths or assets. Racist attitudes may intensify this narrow view, as mi-norities may be portrayed in professional journals as neurotics, psychotics, psychopaths, parolees, and so on, instead of as well-rounded persons.

It is not surprising that minority groups are often suspicious of the re-searcher's motives. The researcher of ethnic matters may find his or her atti-tudes and values toward minority groups being challenged. No longer can the researcher claim that research is solely in the interest of science and morally neutral. The late Carl Rogers, a well-known humanistic psychologist, has stated, "If behavioral scientists are concerned solely with advancing their sci-ence, it seems most probable that they will serve the purpose of whatever group has the power" (quoted in Brecher & Brecher, 1961, p. 20). C. W. Thomas (1970) has voiced this thought in stronger form:

White psychologists have raped Black communities all over the country. Yes raped. They have used Black people as the human equivalent of rats run through Ph.D. experiments and as helpless clients for programs that serve middle-class White administrators better than they do the poor. They have used research on Black people as green stamps to trade for research grants. They have been vultures. (p. 52)

R. L. Williams (1974) discusses two scientific research projects that illustrate this statement: the Tuskegee experiment and the Colville Indian Reservation Study.

The Tuskegee experiment was carried out from 1932 to 1972 by the U.S. Public Health Service. Over 600 Black men from Alabama were used as guinea pigs in the study of what damage would occur to the body if syphilis were left untreated. Approximately 399 were allowed to go untreated even when medication was available. Records indicated that seven died as a result of syphilis, and an additional 154 died of heart disease that may have been caused by the untreated syphilis. In a moving ceremony in 1997, President Clinton officially expressed regret to the few survivors and apologized to Black America. Experiments of this type are ghastly and give rise to suspicions that minorities are being used in other experiments of this sort.

That exploitation occurs in other ethnic communities is exemplified in the Colville Indian reservation disposition (R. L. Williams, 1974). After gaining the trust and confidence of the Colville Indians in Washington, an anthropologist conducted a study of factionalism among the tribe. A subsequent study by another group of White researchers recommended that the best course of action for the Colville reservation was to liquidate its assets, including its land, rather than consider economic development. Part of the justification for liquidation stemmed from the results obtained from the first study, and termination of the reservation was recommended. Several primary issues about the actions merit attention. First, the reservation was composed of 1.4 million acres of land that was rich in timber and minerals. There was strong pressure on the part of Whites to obtain the land. Second, the problems of factionalism were actually created by a society that attempted to "civilize" the Indians via Christianity and by White businesses that offered promises of riches. Third, many of the Indians confided in the White researcher and were led to believe that the information obtained would not be released.

It is this type of study, as well as the continual portrayal of ethnic communities and groups as deviants, that makes minorities extremely distrustful of the motives of the White researcher. Whereas social scientists in the past have been able to enter ethnic communities and conduct their studies with only minimal justification to those studied, researchers are now being received with suspicion and overt hostility. Minorities are actively raising questions and issues regarding the values system of researchers and the outcome of their research.

Concern with the ethics of research has led most educational institutions and government agencies to establish review boards whose purposes are to survey all research being conducted or proposed by investigators. The American Psychological Association adopted a set of guidelines titled *Ethical Principles in the Conduct of Research with Human Participants,* part of which is intended to endorse and promote ethical principles in psychological research. The APA has also established a committee on scientific and professional ethics and conduct that has the power to levy sanctions on members for violations of varying seriousness. The document published by the APA raises questions such as the following: Under what conditions is it ethically acceptable to study residents of a ghetto, minority group members, the poor, prisoners, intellectually handicapped individuals, or college students? What are the researcher's motives? Is research conducted for some definable good, or is it opportunistic, exploitative, and potentially damaging to the target populations?

Furthermore, many members of ethnic minorities find it difficult to see the relevance or applicability of much research conducted on them (Atkinson et al., 2001; S. Sue, 1999). This is especially true when they view the researcher as a laboratory specialist dealing with abstract, theoretical ideas rather than with the real human condition. Much hostility is directed toward the researcher who is perceived in this way. There is a growing feeling among ethnic minorities that research should go beyond the mere explanation of human behavior. Research should contribute to the concerns and betterment of the groups being studied. This concern is voiced not only by minorities, but also by many students, scholars, and the public. Ethnic minorities often view the researcher as a laboratory specialist interested in abstract theoretical ideas rather than as a person interested in the applicability of his or her findings. Psychological researchers are often guilty of perpetuating this belief by failing to make clear and explicit the goals of their pursuits. Indeed, many find this task distasteful. Much hostility, therefore, is directed at researchers of ethnic matters whom many minorities feel conduct narrow, irrelevant studies that will not improve the human condition. There seems to be much justification for these charges.

First, graduate programs in the social sciences have traditionally been much more concerned with the training of academicians than of practitioners. In their analysis of graduate education, several psychologists (Highlen, 1996; Katz, 1985; Mio & Iwamasa, 1993) point out that most programs present the experimental research scientist as the paradigm for the psychological researcher. This model has frequently hindered research dealing with social and psychological problems facing humankind. Since much exploratory work is needed in investigating complex social problems, the strong emphasis on rigorous methodology discourages much meaningful research dealing with problems of complex social issues (Hoshmand, 1989; Ponterotto & Casas, 1991). This discouragement is often seen in the status hierarchy of graduate programs. Experimental research is at the top of the ladder, and exploratory work at the bottom. Furthermore, many professional journals only reluctantly accept manuscripts that may have meaningful implications in social contexts but that may not lend themselves to rigorous experimentation. Ethnic minorities who seek solutions to pressing social problems become alienated from such programs, which they feel are irrelevant and encapsulated from real social settings.

Second, many social researchers feel that their responsibility is discharged with the publication of their results. Research data reported in the professional journals may be understandable to fellow professionals, but certainly not to many students and laypeople. All too often the publication of articles is intended to impress colleagues and insure promotion and tenure. The individuals and communities in such studies are often forgotten. Feedback in a form that is intelligible and usable by the particular communities is seriously lacking, and this contributes to feelings of exploitation. Researchers are increasingly being asked, "How will this study help us? Tell us in concrete terms, without your professional rationalizations and jargon, and we will decide whether you can have access to us or not."

Implications for Clinical Practice

If the mental health profession and its practitioners are to receive acceptance from racial/ethnic minority groups, they must demonstrate, in no uncertain terms, their good faith and ability to contribute to the betterment of a group's quality of life. This demonstration can take several directions.

1. The mental health profession must take initiative in confronting the potential political nature of mental health practice. For too long we have deceived ourselves into believing that the practice of counseling/therapy and the database that underlie the profession are morally, ethically, and politically neutral. The results have been (a) the subjugation of minority groups, (b) the perpetuation of the view that they are inherently pathological, (c) the perpetuation of racist practices in treatment, and (d) the provision of an excuse to the profession for not taking social action to rectify inequities in the system.

2. Mental health professionals must move quickly to challenge certain assumptions that permeate our training programs. We must critically reexamine our concepts of what constitutes normality and abnormality, begin mandatory training programs that deal with these issues, critically examine and reinterpret past and continuing literature dealing with the culturally different, and use research in such a manner as to improve the life conditions of the researched populations.

3. We must make sure that educational programs can no longer present a predominantly White Euro-American orientation. The study of minority group cultures must receive equal treatment and fair portrayal on all levels of education. Courses dealing with minority group experiences and internship practices must become a required part of training. Training programs also need to reorganize the professional reward structure so that the practitioner receives equal status with the academician, and action or applied research should be encouraged even though it may not involve the epitome of rigorous experimental controls.

4. Research can be a powerful means of combating stereotypes and of correcting biased studies. The fact that previous studies have been used to perpetuate stereotypes does not preclude the usefulness of research. If social scientists believe that research has been poorly conducted or misinterpreted to the detriment of minority groups, they should feel some moral commitment to investigate their beliefs. Unfortunately, this self-correcting process of ethnic research remains underdeveloped because of the shortage of minority social scientists contributing a minority-group point of view. Researchers cannot escape the moral and ethical implications of their research and must take responsibility for the outcome of their study. They should guard against misinterpretations and take into account cultural factors and the limitations of their instruments.

5. There is a strong need for counseling to attract more ethnic minorities to the profession, complex as this issue is. Although many White professionals have great understanding and empathy for minorities, they can never fully appreciate the dilemmas faced by a minority member. Ethnic minorities can offer a dimension and a viewpoint that act as counterbalances to the forces of misinterpretation. Furthermore, the cry for more minority professionals demonstrates the presence of a credibility gap between counseling/therapy and minority members. With the addition of more minority psychologists, trust among ethnic minorities may be enhanced.

6. Social scientists must realize that many so-called pathological socio-emotional characteristics of ethnic minorities can be attributed directly to unfair practices in society. There must be a shift in research, from focusing on the poor and culturally diverse to focusing on the groups and institutions that have perpetuated racism and obstructed needed changes.

7. We need to balance our study by focusing also on the positive attributes and characteristics of ethnic minorities. Social scientists have had a tendency to look for pathology and problems among minorities. Too much research has concentrated on mental health problems and culture con-

flict of minorities, while little has been done to determine the advantages of being bicultural. Hopefully, such an orientation will do much to present a more balanced picture of different minority groups.

8. Last, making research with minorities a community endeavor can do much to lower hostility and develop trust between researcher and subject. For example, a social scientist investigating minority groups in the community is often more effective if he or she discusses ideas with community leaders and obtains their cooperation. The inclusion of community members in different phases of research (interviewers, coordinators, etc.) can facilitate trust. This would require social scientists to articulate clearly their goals and methods to the community. Many research subjects and communities seldom know the implications or outcomes of the research conducted on them. Involving minorities at all stages of research can benefit its subjects in the following ways: (a) answering their questions and concerns, (b) helping others acquire an understanding of them, and (c) teaching them research skills. In this way, research will be educational for those being studied as well.

Sociopolitical Considerations of Trust and Mistrust

3

Chapter

I have worked with very few African American clients during my internship at the clinic, but one particular incident left me with very negative feelings. A Black client named Malachi was given an appointment with me. Even though I'm White, I tried not to let his being Black get in the way of our sessions. I treated him like everyone else, a human being who needed help.

At the onset, Malachi was obviously guarded, mistrustful, and frustrated when talking about his reasons for coming. While his intake form listed depression as the problem, he seemed more concerned about nonclinical matters. He spoke about his inability to find a job, about the need to obtain help with job-hunting skills, and about advice in how best to write his résumé. He was quite demanding in asking for advice and information. It was almost as if Malachi wanted everything handed to him on a silver platter without putting any work into our sessions. Not only did he appear reluctant to take responsibility to change his own life, but also I felt he needed to go elsewhere for help. After all, this was a mental health clinic and not an employment agency. Confronting him about his avoidance of responsibility would probably prove counterproductive, so I chose to focus on his feelings. Using a humanistic-existential approach, I reflected his feelings, paraphrased his thoughts, and summarized his dilemmas. This did not seem to help immediately, as I sensed an increase in the tension level, and he seemed antagonistic toward me.

After several attempts by Malachi to obtain direct advice from me, I stated, "You're getting frustrated at me because I'm not giving you the answers you want." It was clear that this angered Malachi. Getting up in a very menacing manner, he stood over me and angrily shouted, "Forget it, man! I don't have time to play your silly games." For one brief moment, I felt in danger of being physically assaulted before he stormed out of the office.

This incident occurred several years ago, and I must admit that I was left with a very unfavorable impression of Blacks. I see myself as basically a good person who truly wants to help others less fortunate than myself. I know it sounds racist, but Malachi's behavior only reinforces my belief that they have trouble controlling their anger, like to take the easy way out, and find it difficult to be open and trusting of others. If I am wrong in this belief, I hope this workshop [multicultural counseling/therapy] will help me better understand the Black personality.

A variation of the above incident was supplied at an in-service training workshop by a White male therapist and is used here to illustrate some of the major issues addressed in this chapter. In Chapter 2 we asserted that mental health practice is strongly influenced by historical and current sociopolitical forces that impinge on issues of race, culture, and ethnicity. Specifically, we made a point that (a) the therapeutic session is often a microcosm of race-relations in our larger society, (b) the therapist often inherits the biases of his or her forebears, and (c) therapy represents a primarily Euro-American activity that may clash with the worldviews of culturally different clients. In this case, we question neither the sincerity of the White therapist nor his desire to help the African American client. However, it is obvious to us that the therapist is part of the problem and not the solution. The male therapist's preconceived notions and stereotypes about African Americans appear to have affected his definition of the problem, assessment of the situation, and therapeutic intervention. Let us analyze this case in greater detail to illustrate our contention.

First, statements about Malachi's wanting things handed to him on a "silver platter," his "avoidance of responsibility," and his "wanting to take the easy way out" are symbolic of social stereotypes that Blacks are lazy and unmotivated. The therapist's statements that African Americans have difficulty "controlling their anger," that Malachi was "menacing," and that the therapist was in fear of being assaulted seem to paint the picture of the hostile, angry, and violent Black male—again an image of African Americans to which many in this society consciously and unconsciously subscribe. While it is always possible that the client was unmotivated and prone to violence, studies suggest that White Americans continue to cling to the image of the dangerous, violence-prone, and antisocial image of Black men (J. M. Jones, 1997). Is it possible, however, that Malachi has a legitimate reason for being angry? Is it possible that the therapist and the therapeutic process are contributing to Malachi's frustration and anger? Is it possible that the therapist was never in physical danger, but that his own affectively based stereotype of the dangerous Black male caused his unreasonable fear? Might not this potential misinterpretation be a clash of different communications styles that triggers unrealistic racial fears and apprehensions? We strongly encourage you to explore these questions with colleagues and students.

Second, mental health practice has been characterized as primarily a White middle-class activity that values rugged individualism, individual responsibility, and autonomy (Atkinson et al., 1998; Highlen, 1994, 1996). Because people are seen as being responsible for their own actions and predicaments, clients are expected to "make decisions on their own" and to "be primarily responsible for their fate in life." The traditional therapist's role should be to encourage self-exploration so that the client can act on his or her own behalf. The individual-centered approach tends to view the problem as residing within the person. If something goes wrong, it is the client's fault. In the last chapter we pointed out how many problems encountered by minority clients reside externally to them (bias, discrimination, prejudice, etc.) and that they should not be faulted for the obstacles they encounter. To do so is to engage in victim blaming (Lewis, Lewis, Daniels, & D'Andrea, 1998; Ridley, 1995; W. Ryan, 1971).

Third, therapists are expected to avoid giving advice or suggestions and disclosing their thoughts and feelings not only because they may unduly influence their clients and arrest their individual development, but also because they may become emotionally involved, lose their objectivity, and blur the boundaries of the helping relationship (Herlihy & Corey, 1997). Parham (1997) states, however, that a fundamental African principle is that human beings realize themselves only in moral relations to others (collectivity, not individuality): "Consequently, application of an African-centered worldview will cause one to question the need for objectivity absent emotions, the need for distance rather than connectedness, and the need for dichotomous relationships rather than multiple roles" (p.110).

In other words, from an African American perspective, the helper and helpee are not separated from one another but are bound together both emotionally and spiritually. The Euro-American style of objectivity encourages separation that may be interpreted by Malachi as uninvolved, uncaring, insincere, and dishonest—that is, "playing silly games" (Paniagua, 1998).

Fourth, the more active and involved role demanded by Malachi goes against what the helping profession considers "therapy." Studies seem to indicate that clients of color prefer a therapeutic relationship in which the helper is more active, self-disclosing, and not adverse to giving advice and suggestions when appropriate (D. W. Sue, Ivey, & Pedersen, 1996). The therapist in this scenario fails to entertain the possibility that requests for advice, information, and suggestions may be legitimate and not indicative of pathological responding. The therapist has been trained to believe that his role as a therapist is to be primarily nondirective; therapists do "therapy," not provide job-hunting information. This has always been the conventional counseling and psychotherapy role, one whose emphasis is a one-to-one, in-the-office, and remedial relationship aimed at self-exploration and the achievement of insight (Atkinson, Thompson, & Grant, 1993). We will have more to say about how these generic characteristics of counseling and psychotherapy may act as barriers to effective multicultural counseling/therapy in the next chapter.

Many of the previous conflicts lead us to our fifth point. If the male therapist is truly operating from unconscious biases, stereotypes, and preconceived notions with his culturally different client, then much of the problem seems to reside within him and not with Malachi. In almost every introductory text on counseling and psychotherapy, lip service is paid to the axiom, "Counselor, know thyself." In other words, therapeutic wisdom endorses the notion that we become better therapists the more we understand our own motives, biases, values, and assumptions about human behavior (Wehrly, 1995). Unfortunately, most training programs are weak in having their students explore their values, biases, and preconceived notions in the area of racist/sexist/homophobic attitudes, beliefs, and behaviors. We are taught to look at our clients, to analyze them, and to note their weaknesses, limitations, and pathological trends; less often do we either look for positive healthy characteristics in our clients or question our conclusions. Questioning our own values and assumptions, the standards that we use to judge normality and abnormality, and our therapeutic approach is infrequently done. As mental health professionals, we may find it difficult and unpleasant to explore our racism, sexism, and homophobia, and our training often allows us the means to avoid it.

When the therapist ends his story by stating that he hopes the workshop will "help me better understand the Black personality," his worldview is clearly evident. There is an assumption that multicultural counseling/therapy simply requires the acquisition of knowledge, and that "good intentions" are all that is needed. This statement represents one of the major obstacles to self-awareness and dealing with one's own biases and prejudices. While we tend to view prejudice, discrimination, racism, and sexism as overt and intentional acts of unfairness and violence, unintentional and covert forms of bias may be the greater enemy because they are unseen and more pervasive. Like this therapist, well-intentioned individuals experience themselves as moral, just, fair-minded, and decent. Thus, it is difficult for many mental health professionals to realize that what they do or say may cause harm to their minority clients:

> *Unintentional behavior is perhaps the most insidious form of racism. Unintentional racists are unaware of the harmful consequences of their behavior. They may be well-intentioned, and on the surface, their behavior may appear to be responsible. Because individuals, groups, or institutions that engage in unintentional racism do not wish to do harm, it is difficult to get them to see themselves as racists. They are more likely to deny their racism. . . . The major challenge facing counselors is to overcome unintentional racism and provide more equitable service delivery. (Ridley, 1995, p. 38)*

Sixth, the therapist states that he tried to not let Malachi's "being Black get in the way" of the session and that he treated him like any other "human being." This is a very typical statement made by Whites who unconsciously subscribe to the belief that being Black, Asian American, Latino American, or a person of color is the problem. In reality, color is not the problem. It is society's perception of color that is the problem! In other words, the locus of the problem (racism, sexism, and homophobia) resides not in marginalized groups, but in the society at large. Often this view of race is manifested in the myth of color blindness: If color is the problem, let's pretend not to see it. Our contention, however, is that it is nearly impossible to overlook the fact that a client is Black, Asian American, Hispanic, and so forth. When operating in this manner, color-blind therapists may actually be obscuring their understandings of who their clients really are. To overlook one's racial group membership is to deny an intimate and important aspect of one's identity. Those who advocate a color-blind approach seem to operate under the assumption that Black is bad and that to be different is to be deviant.

Last, and central to the thesis of this chapter, is the statement by the counselor that Malachi appears guarded and mistrustful and has difficulty being open (self-disclosing). We have mentioned several times that a counselor's inability to establish rapport and a relationship of trust with culturally diverse clients is a major therapeutic barrier. When the emotional climate is negative, and when little trust or understanding exists between the therapist and the client, therapy can be both ineffective and destructive. Yet if the emotional climate is realistically positive and if trust and understanding exist between the parties, the two-way communication of thoughts and feelings can proceed with optimism. This latter condition is often referred to as *rapport* and sets the stage in which other essential conditions can become effective. One of these, self-disclosure, is particularly crucial to the process and goals of counseling because it is the most direct means by which an individual makes him- or herself known to another (Carter, 1995; Parham et al., 1999).

This chapter attempts to discuss the issue of trust as it relates to minority clients. Our discussion does not deal with cultural variables among certain groups (Asian Americans, American Indians, etc.) that dictate against self-disclosure to strangers. This topic is presented in Chapter 4. We first present a brief discussion of the sociopolitical situation as it affects the trust-mistrust dimension of certain culturally different populations. Second, we look at factors that enhance or negate the therapist's cultural effectiveness as it relates to the theory of social influence. Third, we systematically examine how therapist credibility and similarity affect a client's willingness to work with a therapist from another race/culture.

Effects of Historical and Current Oppression

Mental health practitioners must realize that racial/ethnic minorities and other marginalized groups (women, gays/lesbians, and the disabled) in our society live under an umbrella of individual, institutional, and cultural forces that often demean them, disadvantage them, and deny them equal access and opportunity (Atkinson & Hackett, 1998; J. M. Jones, 1972, 1997; Laird & Green, 1996; B. R. Strickland, 2000). Experiences of prejudice and discrimination are a social reality for the culturally different and affect their worldview of the helping professional who attempts to work in the multicultural arena. Thus, mental health practitioners must become aware of the sociopolitical dynamics that form not only their clients' worldviews, but their own as well. As in the clinical case presented earlier, racial/cultural dynamics may intrude into the helping process and cause misdiagnosis, confusion, pain, and a reinforcement of the biases and stereotypes that both groups have of one another. It is important for the therapist to realize that the history of race relations in the United States has influenced us to the point that we are extremely cautious about revealing to strangers our feelings and attitudes about race. In an interracial encounter with a stranger (i.e., in therapy), each party will attempt to discern gross or subtle racial attitudes of the other while minimizing vulnerability. For minorities in the United States, this lesson has been learned well. While White Americans may also exhibit caution similar to that of their minority counterparts, the structure of society places more power to injure and damage in the hands of the majority culture. In most self-disclosing situations, White Americans are less vulnerable than their minority counterparts.

As the individual chapters on American Indians, Asian Americans, Blacks, Hispanics, and other culturally different groups (gays/lesbians, women, persons with disabilities, and the elderly) will reveal, the histories and experiences of the culturally different have been fraught with oppression, discrimination, and racism. Institutional racism has created psychological barriers among minorities and White Americans that are likely to interfere with the therapy process. Understanding how the invisibility of ethnocentric monoculturalism has affected race, gender, and sexual orientation relationships is vital to successful multicultural competence.

Ethnocentric Monoculturalism

It is becoming increasingly clear that the values, assumptions, beliefs, and practices of our society are structured in such a manner as to serve only one narrow segment of the population (D. W. Sue, 2001). Most mental health professionals, for example, have not been trained to work with anything other than mainstream individuals or groups. This is understandable in light of the historical origins of education, counseling/guidance, and our mental health systems, which have their roots in Euro-American or Western cultures (Highlen, 1994; Wehrly, 1995). As a result, American (U.S.) psychology has been severely criticized as being ethnocentric, monocultural, and inherently biased against racial/ethnic minorities, women, gays/lesbians, and other culturally diverse groups (Carter, l995; Laird & Green, l996; Ridley, l995). As voiced by many multicultural specialists, our educational system and counseling/psychotherapy have often done great harm to our minority citizens. Rather than educate or heal, rather than offer enlightenment and freedom, and rather than allow for equal access and opportunities, historical and current practices have restricted, stereotyped, damaged, and oppressed the culturally different in our society.

In light of the increasing diversity of our society, mental health professionals will inevitably encounter client populations that differ from themselves in terms of race, culture, and ethnicity. Such changes, however, are believed to pose no problems as long as psychologists adhere to the notion of an unyielding universal psychology that is applicable across all populations. While few mental health professionals would voice such a belief, in reality the very policies and practices of mental health delivery systems do reflect such an ethnocentric orientation. The theories of counseling and psychotherapy, the standards used to judge normality-abnormality, and the actual process of mental health practice are culture-bound and reflect a monocultural perspective of the helping professions (Highlen, l994; Katz, l985; D. Sue, 1990). As such, they are often culturally inappropriate and antagonistic to the lifestyles and values of minority groups in our society. Indeed, some mental health professionals assert that counseling and psychotherapy may be handmaidens of the status quo, instruments of oppression, and transmitters of society's values (Halleck, l971; D. W. Sue & Sue, l990; A. Thomas & Sillen, l972).

We believe that ethnocentric monoculturalism is dysfunctional in a pluralistic society such as the United States. It is a powerful force, however, in forming, influencing, and determining the goals and processes of mental health delivery systems. As such, it is very important for mental health professionals to unmask or deconstruct the values, biases, and assumptions that reside in it. Ethnocentric monoculturalism combines what Wrenn (1962, 1985) calls *cultural encapsulation* and what J. M. Jones (1972, 1997) refers to as *cultural racism*. In a publication by a combined multicultural task group from the American Psychological Association's Division of Counseling Psychology and the Society for the Psychological Study of Ethnic Minority Issues (D. W. Sue et al., 1998), five components of ethnocentric monoculturalism were identified.

Belief in Superiority

First, there is a strong belief in the superiority of one group's cultural heritage (history, values, language, traditions, arts/crafts, etc.). The group norms and values are seen positively, and descriptors may include such phrases as "more advanced" and "more civilized." Members of the society may possess conscious and unconscious feelings of superiority and feel that their way of doing things is the best way. In our society, White Euro-American cultures are seen as not only desirable, but normative as well. Physical characteristics such as light complexion, blond hair, and blue eyes; cultural characteristics such as a belief in Christianity (or monotheism), individualism, Protestant work ethic, and capitalism; and linguistic characteristics such as standard English, control of emotions, and the written tradition are highly valued components of Euro-American culture (Katz, 1985). People possessing these traits are perceived more favorably and often are allowed easier access to the privileges and rewards of the larger society. McIntosh (1989), a White woman, refers to this condition as *White privilege:* an invisible knapsack of unearned assets that can be used to cash in each day for advantages not given to those who do not fit this mold. Among some of the advantages that she enumerates are the following (paraphrased):

- I can if I wish arrange to be in the company of people of my race most of the time.
- I can turn on the television or open to the front page of the paper and see people of my race widely represented.
- When I am told about our national heritage or about "civilization," I am shown that people of my color made it what it is.
- I can be sure that my children will be given curricular materials that testify to the existence of their race.

Belief in the Inferiority of Others

Second, there is a belief in the inferiority of the entire group's cultural heritage, which extends to their customs, values, traditions, and language. Other societies or groups may be perceived as less developed, uncivilized, primitive, or even pathological. The group's lifestyles or ways of doing things are considered inferior. Physical characteristics such as dark complexion, black hair, and brown eyes; cultural characteristics such as belief in non-Christian religions (Islam, Confucianism, polytheism, etc.), collectivism, present time orientation, and the importance of shared wealth; and linguistic characteristics such as bilingualism, non-standard English, speaking with an accent, use of nonverbal and contextual communication, and reliance on the oral tradition are usually seen as less desirable by the society. Studies consistently reveal that individuals who are physically different, who speak with an accent, and who adhere to different cultural beliefs and practices are more likely to be evaluated more negatively in our schools and workplaces. Culturally different individuals may be seen as less intelligent, less qualified, and more unpopular, and as possessing more undesirable traits.

Power to Impose Standards

Third, the dominant group possesses the power to impose their standards and beliefs on the less powerful group. This third component of ethnocentric monoculturalism is very important. All groups are to some extent ethnocentric; that is, they feel positively about their cultural heritage and way of life. Minorities can be biased, can hold stereotypes, and can strongly believe that their way is the best way. Yet if they do not possess the power to impose their values on others, then hypothetically they cannot oppress. It is power or the unequal status relationship between groups that defines ethnocentric monoculturalism. The issue here is not to place blame but to speak realistically about how our society operates. Ethnocentric monoculturalism is the individual, institutional, and cultural expression of the superiority of one group's cultural heritage over another combined with the possession of power to impose those standards broadly on the less powerful group. Since minorities generally do not possess a share of economic, social, and political power equal to that of Whites in our society, they are generally unable to discriminate on a large-scale basis. The damage and harm of oppression is likely to be one-sided, from majority to minority group.

Manifestation in Institutions

Fourth, the ethnocentric values and beliefs are manifested in the programs, policies, practices, structures, and institutions of the society. For example, chain-of-command systems, training and educational systems, communications systems, management systems, and performance appraisal systems often dictate and control our lives. Ethnocentric values attain "untouchable and godfather-like" status in an organization. Because most systems are monocultural in nature and demand compliance, racial/ethnic minorities and women may be oppressed. J. M. Jones (1972, 1997) labels institutional racism as a set of policies, priorities, and accepted normative patterns designed to subjugate, oppress, and force dependence of individuals and groups on a larger society. It does this by sanctioning unequal goals, unequal status, and unequal access to goods and services. Institutional racism has fostered the enactment of discriminatory statutes, the selective enforcement of laws, the blocking of economic opportunities and outcomes, and the imposition of forced assimilation/acculturation on the culturally different. The sociopolitical system thus attempts to define the prescribed role occupied by minorities. Feelings of powerlessness, inferiority, subordination, deprivation, anger and rage, and overt/covert resistance to factors in interracial relationships are likely to result.

The Invisible Veil

Fifth, since people are all products of cultural conditioning, their values and beliefs (worldviews) represent an *invisible veil* that operates outside the level of conscious awareness. As a result, people assume universality: that regardless of race, culture, ethnicity, or gender, everyone shares the nature of reality and truth. This assumption is erroneous but is seldom questioned because it is firmly ingrained in our worldview. Racism, sexism, and homophobia may be both conscious (intentional) and unconscious (unintentional). Neo-Nazis, skinheads, and the Ku Klux Klan would definitely fall into the first category. While conscious and intentional racism as exemplified by these individuals, for example, may cause great harm to culturally different groups, it is the latter form that may ultimately be the most insidious and dangerous. As mentioned earlier, it is well-intentioned individuals who consider themselves moral, decent, and fair-minded that may have the greatest difficulty in understanding how their belief systems and actions may be biased and prejudiced. It is clear that no one is born wanting to be racist, sexist, or homophobic. Misinformation related to culturally diverse groups is not acquired by our free choice, but rather is imposed through a painful process of social conditioning; all of us were taught to hate and fear others who are different in some way (D. W. Sue et al., 1998). Likewise, because all of us live, play, and work within organizations, those policies, practices, and structures that may be less than fair to minority groups are invisible in controlling our lives. Perhaps the greatest obstacle to a meaningful movement toward a multicultural society is our failure to understand our unconscious and unintentional complicity in perpetuating bias and discrimination via our personal values/beliefs and our institutions. The power of racism, sexism, and homophobia is related to the invisibility of the powerful forces that control and dictate our lives. In a strange sort of way, we are all victims. Minority groups are victims of oppression. Majority group members are victims who are unwittingly socialized into the role of oppressor.

Historical Manifestations of Ethnocentric Monoculturalism

The European-American worldview can be described as possessing the following values and beliefs: rugged individualism, competition, mastery and control over nature, a unitary and static conception of time, religion based on Christianity, separation of science and religion, and competition (Katz, 1985). It is important to note that worldviews are neither right or wrong, nor good or bad. They become problematic, however, when they are expressed through the process of ethnocentric monoculturalism. In the United States, the historical manifestations of this process are quite clear. First, the European colonization efforts toward the Americas operated from the assumption that the enculturation of indigenous peoples was justified because European culture was superior. Forcing the colonized to adopt European beliefs and customs was seen as civilizing them. In the United States, this practice was clearly evident in the treatment of Native Americans, whose lifestyles, customs, and practices were seen as backward and uncivilized, and attempts were made to make over the "heathens." Such a belief is also reflected in Euro-American culture and has been manifested also in attitudes toward other racial/ethnic minority groups in the United States. A common belief is that racial/ethnic minorities would not encounter problems if they assimilate and acculturate.

Monocultural ethnocentric bias has a long history in the United States and is even reflected as early as the uneven application of the "Bill of Rights," which favored White immigrants/descendants over "minority" populations (Barongan et al., 1997). Over some 200 years ago, Britain's King George III accepted a "Declaration of Independence" from former subjects who moved to this country. This proclamation was destined to shape and reshape the geopolitical and sociocultural landscape of the world many times over. The lofty language penned by its principal architect, Thomas Jefferson, and signed by those present was indeed inspiring: "We hold these truths to be self-evident, that all men are created equal."

Yet as we now view the historic actions of that time, we cannot help but be struck by the paradox inherent in those events. First, all 56 of the signatories were White males of European descent, hardly a representation of the current racial and gender composition of the population. Second, the language of the declaration suggests that only men were created equal; what about women? Third, many of the founding fathers were slave owners who seemed not to recognize the hypocritical personal standards that they used because they considered Blacks to be subhuman. Fourth, the history of this land did not start with the Declaration of Independence or the formation of the United States of America. Nevertheless, our textbooks continue to teach us an ethnocentric perspective ("Western Civilization") that ignores over two thirds of the world's population. Last, it is important to note that those early Europeans who came to this country were immigrants attempting to escape persecution (oppression) who in the process did not recognize their own role in the oppression of indigenous peoples (American Indians) who already resided in this country for centuries. As Barongan et al. (1997, p. 654) described,

> *the natural and inalienable rights of individuals valued by European and European American societies generally appear to have been intended for European Americans only. How else can European colonization and exploitation of Third World countries be explained? How else can the forced removal of Native Americans from their lands, centuries of enslavement and segregation of African Americans, immigration restrictions on persons of color through history, incarceration*

of Japanese Americans during World War II, and current English-only language requirements in the United States be explained? These acts have not been perpetrated by a few racist individuals, but by no less than the governments of the North Atlantic cultures. . . . If Euro-American ideals include a philosophical or moral opposition to racism, this has often not been reflected in policies and behaviors.

We do not take issue with the good intentions of the early founders. Nor do we infer in them evil and conscious motivations to oppress and dominate others. Yet the history of the United States has been the history of oppression and discrimination against racial/ethnic minorities and women. The Western European cultures that formed the fabric of the United States of America are relatively homogeneous compared not only to the rest of the world, but also to the increasing diversity in this country. This Euro-American worldview continues to form the foundations of our educational, social, economic, cultural, and political systems.

As more and more White immigrants came to the North American continent, the guiding principle of blending the many cultures became codified into such concepts as the "melting pot" and "assimilation/acculturation." The most desirable outcome of this process was a uniform and homogeneous consolidation of cultures—in essence, to become monocultural. Many psychologists of color, however, have referred to this process as *cultural genocide,* an outcome of colonial thought (Guthrie, 1976, 1997; Parham et al., 1999; Samuda, 1998; A. Thomas & Sillen, 1972). Wehrly (1995, p. 24) states, "Cultural assimilation, as practiced in the United States, is the expectation by the people in power that all immigrants and people outside the dominant group will give up their ethnic and cultural values and will adopt the values and norms of the dominant society—the White, male Euro-Americans."

While ethnocentric monoculturalism is much broader than the concept of race, it is race and color that have been used to determine the social order (Carter, 1995). The "White race" has been seen as being superior and White culture as normative. Thus, a study of U.S. history must include a study of racism and racist practices directed at people of color. The oppression of the indigenous people of this country (Native Americans), enslavement of African Americans, widespread segregation of Hispanic Americans, passage of exclusionary laws against the Chinese, and the forced internment of Japanese Americans are social realities. Thus it should be of no surprise that our racial/ethnic minority citizens may view Euro-Americans and our very institutions with considerable mistrust and suspicions. In health care delivery systems and especially in counseling and psychotherapy, which demand a certain degree of trust among therapist and client groups, an interracial encounter may be fraught with historical and current psychological baggage related to issues of discrimination, prejudice, and oppression. Carter (1995, p. 27) draws the following conclusion related to mental health delivery systems: "Because any institution in a society is shaped by social and cultural forces, it is reasonable to assume that racist notions have been incorporated into the mental health systems."

Therapeutic Impact of Ethnocentric Monoculturalism

Many multicultural specialists (Herring, 1997; Kochman, 1981; Locke, 1997; Parham et al., 1999; Ponterotto & Casas, 1991; Stanback & Pearce, 1985) have pointed out how African Americans, in responding to their forced enslavement, history of discrimination, and America's reaction to their skin color, have adopted toward Whites behavior patterns that are important for survival in a racist society. These behavior patterns may include indirect expressions of hostility, aggression, and fear. During slavery, to rear children who would fit into a segregated system and who could physically survive, African American mothers were forced to teach them (a) to express aggression indirectly, (b) to read the thoughts of others while hiding their own, and (c) to engage in ritualized accommodating-subordinating behaviors designed to create as few waves as possible (Willie, Kramer, & Brown, 1973). This process involves a "mild dissociation" whereby African Americans may separate their true selves from their roles as "Negroes" (C. A. Pinderhughes, 1973). In this dual identity the true self is revealed to fellow Blacks, while the dissociated self is revealed to meet the expectations of prejudiced Whites. From the analysis of African American history, the dissociative process may be manifested in two major ways.

First, "playing it cool" has been identified as one means by which African Americans or other minorities may conceal their true feelings (Greene, 1985; Grier & Cobbs, 1971; A. C. Jones, 1985). This behavior is intended to prevent Whites from knowing what the minority person is thinking or feeling and to express feelings and behaviors in such a way as to prevent offending or threatening Whites (Parham et al., 1999; Ridley, 1995). Thus, a person of color who is experiencing conflict, explosive anger, and suppressed feelings may appear serene and composed on the surface. This is a defense mechanism aimed at protecting minorities from harm and exploitation.

Second, the *Uncle Tom syndrome* may be used by minorities to appear docile, nonassertive, and happy-go-lucky. Especially during slavery, Blacks learned that passivity is a necessary survival technique. To retain the most menial jobs, to minimize retaliation, and to maximize survival of the self and loved ones, many minorities have learned to deny their aggressive feelings toward their oppressors.

We are reminded of the skit performed by Richard Pryor, the Black comedian, in which the issue of Black awareness of personal vulnerability was sarcastically portrayed. Pryor mimiced how he recently purchased a brand-new Cadillac and was proudly driving about when he was pulled over by a

White police officer. Aware that many White officers have preconceived notions about "dangerous Black males" and not wanting to be "blown away," Pryor humorously enacted how he immediately raised his arms loudly, claiming, "Look, no hidden weapons!" When asked for his driver's license, Pryor stated, "I will now take my right hand and use only two fingers to get my wallet located in the left breast pocket of the jacket." Pryor tipped his body slightly to the left so that his jacket flopped open and said, "No hidden weapons there, either." Ever so slowly, he advanced his right hand toward the wallet to retrieve it. The skit continued in this very sarcastic but realistic statement about the nature of Black-White relations in our society.

The overall result of the experiences of minorities in the United States has been to increase their vigilance and sensitivity to the thoughts and behaviors of Whites in society. We mentioned earlier that African Americans have been forced to read the thoughts of others accurately in order to survive. This has resulted in some studies (Kochman, 1981; E. J. Smith, 1981; D. W. Sue, 1990) revealing that certain minority groups such as African Americans are better readers of nonverbal communication. This will be discussed in greater detail in Chapter 5. Many African Americans have often stated that Whites say one thing but mean another. This better understanding and sensitivity to nonverbal communication has enhanced Black people's survival in a highly dangerous society. As we see later, it is important for the minority individual to read nonverbal messages accurately—not only for physical survival, but for psychological reasons as well.

In summary, it becomes all too clear that past and present discrimination against certain culturally diverse groups is a tangible basis for minority distrust of the majority society (Ridley, 1984, 1995). White people are perceived as potential enemies unless proved otherwise. Under such a sociopolitical atmosphere, minorities may use several adaptive devices to prevent Whites from knowing their true feelings. Because multicultural counseling may mirror the sentiments of the larger society, these modes of behavior and their detrimental effects may be reenacted in the sessions.

The fact that many minority clients are suspicious, mistrustful, and guarded in their interactions with White therapists is certainly understandable in light of the foregoing analysis. Despite their conscious desires to help, White therapists are not immune from inheriting racist attitudes, beliefs, myths, and stereotypes about Asian American, African American, Latino/Hispanic American, and American Indian clients. For example, White counselors often believe that Blacks are nonverbal, paranoid, and angry and that they are most likely to have character disorders (Carter, 1995; A. C. Jones, 1985) or to be schizophrenic (Pavkov, Lewis, & Lyons, 1989). As a result, they view African Americans as unsuitable for counseling and psychotherapy. Mental health practitioners and social scientists who hold to this belief fail to understand the following facts:

1. As a group, African Americans tend to communicate nonverbally more than their White counterparts and to assume that nonverbal communication is a more accurate barometer of one's true feelings and beliefs (E. T. Hall, 1976; Kochman, 1981; Stanback & Pearce, 1985; Weber, 1985). E. T. Hall (1976) observed that African Americans are better able to read nonverbal messages (high context) than are their White counterparts and that they rely less on verbalizations than on nonverbal communication to make a point. Whites, on the other hand, tune in more to verbal messages than to nonverbal messages (low context). Because they rely less on nonverbal cues, Whites need greater verbal elaborations to get a point across (D. W. Sue et al., 1996). Being unaware of and insensitive to these differences, White therapists are prone to feel that African Americans are unable to communicate in "complex" ways. This judgment is based on the high value that therapy places on intellectual/verbal activity.

2. Rightfully or not, White therapists are often perceived as symbols of the Establishment who have inherited the racial biases of their forebears. Thus, the culturally diverse client is likely to impute all the negative experiences of oppression to them (Katz, 1985; Vontress, 1971). This may prevent the minority client from responding to the helping professional as an individual. While the therapist may be possessed of the most admirable motives, the client may reject the helping professional simply because he or she is White. Thus, communication may be directly or indirectly shut off.

3. Some culturally diverse clients may lack confidence in the counseling and therapy process because the White counselor often proposes White solutions to their concerns (Atkinson, Morten, & Sue, 1989; Atkinson, Morten, et al., 1998). Many pressures are placed on minority clients to accept an alien value system and reject their own. We have already indicated how counseling and psychotherapy may be perceived as instruments of oppressions whose function is to force assimilation and acculturation. As some racial/ethnic minority clients have asked, "Why do I have to become White in order to be considered healthy?"

4. The "playing it cool" and "Uncle Tom" responses of many minorities are present also in the therapy sessions. As pointed out earlier, these mechanisms are attempts to conceal true feelings, to hinder self-disclosure, and to prevent the therapist from getting to know the client. These adaptive survival mechanisms have been acquired through generations of experience with a hostile and invalidating society. The therapeutic dilemma encountered by the helping professional in working with a client of color is how to gain trust and break through this maze. What the therapist ultimately does in the sessions will determine his or her trustworthiness.

To summarize, culturally diverse clients entering counseling or therapy are likely to experience considerable anxiety about ethnic/racial/cultural differences. Suspicion, apprehension, verbal constriction, unnatural reactions, open resentment and hostility, and passive or cool behavior may all be expressed. Self-disclosure and the possible establishment of a working relationship can be seriously delayed or prevented from occurring. In all cases, the therapist's trustworthiness may be put to severe tests. A culturally effective therapist is one who (a) can view these behaviors in a nonjudgmental manner (i.e., they are not necessarily indicative of pathology but a manifestation of adaptive survival mechanisms), (b) can avoid personalizing any potential hostility expressed toward him or her, and (c) can adequately resolve challenges to his or her credibility. Thus, it becomes important for us to understand those dimensions that may enhance or diminish the culturally different client's receptivity to self-disclosure.

Credibility and Attractiveness in Multicultural Counseling

In the last section, we presented a case to explain how the political atmosphere of the larger society affects the minority client's perception of a multicultural therapy situation. Racial/ethnic minorities in the United States have solid reasons for distrusting White Americans. Lack of trust often leads to guardedness, inability to establish rapport, and lack of self-disclosure on the part of culturally different clients. What therapists say and do in the sessions can either enhance or diminish their credibility and attractiveness. A therapist who is perceived by clients as highly credible and attractive is more likely to elicit trust, motivation to work or change, and self-disclosure. These appear to be important conditions for effective therapy to occur (S. Sue & Zane, 1987).

Theories of counseling and psychotherapy attempt to outline an approach designed to make them effective. It is our contention that multicultural helping cannot be approached through any one theory of counseling (Rogler, Malgady, Constantino, & Blumenthal, 1987; D. W. Sue et al., 1996). There are several reasons for such a statement. First, theories of counseling are composed of philosophical assumptions regarding the nature of "man" and a theory of personality. As pointed out earlier, these characteristics are highly culture-bound (Katz, 1985; D. W. Sue, 1995a). The "true" nature of people is a philosophical question. What constitutes the healthy and unhealthy personality is also debatable and varies from culture to culture and from class to class.

Second, theories of counseling and psychotherapy are composed also of a body of therapeutic techniques and strategies. These techniques are applied to clients with the hope of effecting change in behaviors, perceptions, or attitudes. A theory dictates what techniques are to be used and, implicitly, in what proportions (D. W. Sue et al., 1996; Corey, 2001). For example, it is clear that humanistic-existential therapists behave differently than do rational-emotive ones. The fact that one school of counseling/therapy can be distinguished from another has implications: It suggests a certain degree of rigidity in working with culturally different clients who might find such techniques offensive or inappropriate. The implicit assumption is that these techniques are imposed according to the theory and not based on client needs and values.

It is very important that the therapist be aware of the implications regarding minority reading of nonverbal behavior. "Playing it cool" and the Uncle Tom syndrome, as well as other challenges, are frequently employed to assess the counselor's nonverbal message rather than the verbal one. When topics related to racism are brought up in the session, what the therapist says may often be negated by his or her nonverbal communication. If this is the case, the minority client will quickly pick up the inconsistency and conclude that the therapist is incapable of dealing with cultural/racial diversity.

Third, theories of counseling and psychotherapy have often failed to agree among themselves about what constitutes desirable outcomes. This makes it extremely difficult to determine the effectiveness of counseling and therapy (Herring, 1997; Kleinke, 1994). For example, the psychoanalytically oriented therapist uses "insight"; the behaviorist uses "behavior change"; the client-centered person uses "self-actualization"; and the rational-emotive person uses "rational cognitive content/processes." The potential for disagreement over appropriate outcome variables is increased even further when the therapist and client come from different cultures. While the counseling outcome is extremely important, we attempt to concentrate our discussion on "process" elements. We are more concerned here with *how* change occurs (the process) during therapy rather than with *what* change (the outcomes) results from therapy.

Counseling as Interpersonal Influence

When people engage in interactions with one another, they inevitably attempt to exert influence. These social-influence attempts may be overt/covert or conscious/unconscious. Whether the intent is to create a favorable impression when meeting people, to toilet train a young child, to convince people that cigarette smoking is harmful, to gain acceptance from a desired group, or to sell goods, these social-influence attempts are all aimed at changing attitudes, perceptions, or behaviors.

Likewise, therapy may be conceptualized as an interpersonal-influence process in which the counselor uses social power to influence the client's attitudes and behaviors. Strong (1969) is probably the person most credited with providing a conceptual framework for understanding parallels between the role of the therapist, the process of therapy, and the outcome of therapy with those of the persuasive communicator, the influencing process, and opinion/behavior change, respectively. Specifically, communication attributes that had been established as important determinants of attitude change in the field of social psychology seemed similar to those that make an effective therapist (Heesacker & Carroll, 1997). Counselors who are perceived by their clients as credible (expert and trustworthy) and attractive are able to exert greater influence than are those perceived as lacking in credibility and attractiveness. A sufficient number of counseling reviews and studies support this contention (Corrigan, Dell, Lewis, & Schmidt, 1980; Heesacker, Conner, & Pritchard, 1995; Heppner & Claiborn, 1989; Heppner & Frazier, 1992; Lent & Maddux, 1997; Schmidt & Strong, 1971; Stoltenberg, McNeill & Elliot, 1995; Strong & Schmidt, 1970). Using social-influence theory as a means to analyze counseling not only has empirical validity and concentrates on process variables, but also seems to be equally applicable to all approaches. Regardless of the counseling orientation (person-centered, psychoanalytic, behavioral, transactional analysis, etc.), the therapist's effectiveness tends to depend on the client's perception of his or her expertness, trustworthiness, and attractiveness.

Most of the studies mentioned have dealt exclusively with a White population (Heesacker et al., 1995). Thus, findings that certain attributes contribute to a counselor's credibility and attractiveness may not be so perceived by culturally different clients. It is entirely possible that credibility, as defined by credentials indicating specialized training (e.g., MFCC, MSW, PsyD, PhD, or MD), might only indicate to a Latino client that the White therapist has no knowledge or expertise in working with Latinos. This assumption is based on the fact that most training programs are geared for White middle-class clients and are culturally exclusive.

Our focus in this section is twofold: (a) We outline the various ways clients perceive their therapist's attempts to influence them, and (b) we discuss the dimensions of therapist expertness, trustworthiness, and similarity as they relate to culturally different clients. We are then able to lay the foundation for a theory of multicultural counseling, which is presented and discussed later.

Psychological Sets of Clients

The therapist's credibility and attractiveness depend very much on the psychological set or frame of reference for the culturally different client. We all know individuals who tend to value rational approaches to solving problems and others who value a more affective (attractiveness) approach. It would seem reasonable that a client who values rationality might be more receptive to a counseling approach that emphasizes the counselor's credibility. Thus, understanding a client's psychological set may facilitate the therapist's ability to exert social influence in counseling. In a very useful model, Collins (1970) proposed a set of conceptual categories that can be used to understand people's receptivity to pressures for change. We apply those categories here with respect to the therapy situation. These five hypothetical sets or frames of mind are elicited in clients for several different reasons. Race, ethnicity, and the experience of discrimination often affect the type of set that will be operative in a minority client.

1. The problem-solving set: Information orientation. In the problem-solving set, the client is concerned about obtaining correct information (solutions, outlooks, and skills) that has adaptive value in the real world. The client accepts or rejects information from the therapist on the basis of its perceived truth or falsity: Is it an accurate representation of reality? The processes that are used tend to be rational and logical in analyzing and attacking the problem. First, the client may apply a consistency test and compare the new facts with earlier information. For example, a White male therapist might try to reassure an African American client that he is not against interracial marriage, but hesitate in speech and tense up whenever the topic is broached. In this case, the verbal or content message is inconsistent with nonverbal cues, and the credibility and social influence of the therapist are likely to decline. Second, the Black client may apply a corroboration test by actively seeking information from others for comparison purposes. If he or she hears from a friend that the therapist has racial hang-ups, then again the therapist's effectiveness is likely to be severely diminished. The former test makes use of information that the individual already has (understanding of nonverbal meanings), while the latter requires him or her to seek out new information (asking a trusted African American friend).

Through socialization and personal experiences, we have learned that some people are more likely to provide accurate/helpful information (i.e., being credible) than others are. Sources that have been dependable in the past and that have high status, possess great reputations, occupy certain roles, and are motivated to make accurate representations are more likely to influence us. Minorities, on the other hand, may have learned that many Whites have little expertise when it comes to their lifestyles and that the information or suggestions that they give are White solutions or labels.

It is highly possible that racial/ethnic groups may vary in their information orientation. For example, D. W. Sue (1981) has indicated that many Puerto Ricans who come for counseling and therapy expect information, advice, and direct suggestions. Likewise, it has been found that many Asian Americans not only tend to prefer a structured, direct, and practical orientation, but also often seek advice, consolation, and suggestions from therapists.

Therapists who do not value the problem-solving set and who may be affectively oriented may actually have great difficulties in relating to the client.

2. The consistency set. People are operating under the consistency set whenever they change an opinion, belief, or behavior in such a way as to make it consistent with other opinions, beliefs, or behaviors. This principle is best illustrated in Festinger's classic book *A Theory of Cognitive Dissonance* (1957). Stated simply, the theory says that when a person's attitudes, opinions, or beliefs are met with disagreement (inconsistencies), cognitive imbalance or dissonance will be created. The dissonance is psychologically uncomfortable and produces tension with drive characteristics. The result is an attempt to reduce the dissonance. In reality, the consistency set may really be a by-product of the problem-solving set. This is so because we assume that the real world is consistent. For example, since therapists are supposed to help, we naturally believe that they would not do something to hurt us. If they do, then it creates dissonance. To reduce this inconsistency, we may discredit or derogate the therapist (e.g., he or she is not a good person after all!) or in some way excuse the act (e.g., he or she did it unintentionally). The rules of the consistency set specify that "good people do good things" and "bad people do bad things." It is important to note that the consistency set states that people are not necessarily *rational* beings but *rationalizing* ones. A therapist who is not in touch with personal prejudices or biases may send out conflicting messages to a minority client. The counselor may verbally state, "I am here to help you," but at the same time indicate racist attitudes and feelings nonverbally. This can destroy the counselor's credibility very quickly, for example, in the case of a minority client who accurately applies a consistency set such as, "White people say one thing, but do another. You can't believe what they tell you."

Generally, minority clients who enter therapy with a White therapist will tend to apply a consistency test to what the therapist says or does. That is because the client is trying to test the therapist to determine whether he or she has the knowledge, understanding, and expertise to work with a minority individual. A culturally different client will actively seek out disclosures on the part of the therapist to compare them with the information he or she has about the world. Should the therapist pass the test, new information may be more readily accepted and assimilated. As we mentioned, persons of color apparently are better readers of nonverbal cues. As a result, the therapist who sends out conflicting verbal and nonverbal messages may easily be dismissed as being unable to help the client.

3. The identity set. In the identity set, the individual generally desires to be like or similar to a person or group held in high esteem. Much of our identity is formed from those reference groups to which we aspire. We attempt to take on the reference group's characteristics, beliefs, values, and behaviors because they are viewed as favorable. An individual who strongly identifies with a particular group is likely to accept the group's beliefs and conform to behaviors dictated by the group. If race or ethnicity constitutes a strong reference group for a client, then a counselor of the same race/ethnicity is likely to be more influential than is one who is not.

A number of studies (see reviews by Atkinson, 1983, 1985; Atkinson & Schein, 1986) indicate that certain similarities between the counselor and client may actually enhance therapeutic longevity and therapist preference. For example, racial similarity between therapist and client may actually increase willingness to return for therapy and facilitate effectiveness. The studies on this are quite mixed, as there is considerable evidence that membership group similarity may not be as effective as belief or attitude similarity. Furthermore, a number of studies (Parham, 1989; Parham & Helms, 1981, 1985) suggest that the stage of cultural or racial identity affects which dimensions of similarities will be preferred by the racial/ethnic minority client. We have much more to say about cultural identity development later.

4. The economic set. In the economic set, the person is influenced because of the perceived rewards and punishments that the source is able to deliver. In this set, a person performs a behavior or states a belief in order to gain rewards and avoid punishments. In the counseling setting, this means that the therapist controls important resources that may affect the client. For example, a therapist may decide to recommend the expulsion of a student from the school or deny a positive parole recommendation to a client who is in prison. In less subtle ways, the therapist may ridicule or praise a client during a group-counseling session. In these cases, the client may decide to alter his or her behavior because the therapist holds greater power. The major problem with the use of rewards and punishments to induce change is that while it may assure *behavioral compliance,* it does not guarantee *private acceptance.* As noted, racial/ethnic minorities are well versed in recognizing power differentials and behaving accordingly (i.e., playing it cool or using the Uncle Tom approach). Furthermore, for rewards and coercive power to be effective, the therapist must maintain constant surveillance. Once the surveillance is removed, the client is likely to revert back to previous modes of behavior. For culturally diverse clients, therapy that operates primarily on the economic set is more likely to prevent the development of trust, rapport, and self-disclosure.

The economic set is probably the strongest indicator of cultural oppression in therapy (D. W. Sue, 1981). We in the mental health professions like to believe that counseling and psychotherapy are aimed at helping people, freeing them, and allowing them greater autonomy and choice in life situations. Unfortunately, in working with culturally diverse clients whose lifestyles and values may differ from our own, we often engage in cultural oppression. That is, we attempt to make them conform to our standards and ways of behavior. In doing this, we can exercise the economic set strongly by making our clients feel inadequate for being different. As mental health professionals, we need to realize that counseling and therapy can be very oppressive at an unintentional level.

5. The authority set. Under this set, some individuals are thought to have a particular position that gives them a legitimate right to prescribe attitudes or behaviors. In our society, we have been conditioned to believe that certain authorities (police officers, chairpersons, designated leaders, etc.) have the right to demand compliance. This occurs via training in role behavior and group norms. Mental health professionals, like counselors, are thought to have a legitimate right to recommend and provide psychological treatment to disturbed or troubled clients. It is this psychological set that legitimizes the counselor's role as a helping professional. Yet for many minorities, it is exactly these roles in society that are perceived as instruments of institutional oppression and racism. The 1996 O. J. Simpson trial and verdict brought out major differences in how African Americans and White Americans perceived the police. African Americans were more likely, as a group, to entertain the notion that police officers deliberately tampered with evidence because Simpson was a Black man; White Americans, however, were much less inclined to believe the police could act in such a manner. Even when audiotapes of detective Mark Fuhrman revealed an admission of evidence tampering and racist beliefs, White Americans continued to cling to the belief that it was an isolated incident or that Fuhrman was "an exception to the rule."

None of the five sets or frames is mutually exclusive. These sets frequently interact, and any number can operate at the same time. For example, it is possible that you are influenced by a therapist you find highly credible. It is also possible that you like the therapist or find him or her very attractive. Are you accepting his or her influence because the therapist is credible (problem-solving set), attractive (identification set), or both?

It should be clear at this point that characteristics of the influencing source (therapist) are of the utmost importance in eliciting types of changes. In addition, the type of mental or psychological set placed in operation often dictates the permanency and degree of attitude/belief change. For example, the primary component in getting compliance in the economic and authority set is the power that the person holds over you (i.e., the ability to reward or punish); in identification (the identity set), it is the attractiveness or liking of the therapist; and in internalization (the problem-solving and consistency set), credibility or truthfulness is important.

While these sets operate similarly for both majority and minority clients, their manifestations may be quite different. Obviously, a minority client may have great difficulty identifying (identification set) with a counselor from another race or culture. Also, what constitutes credibility to minority clients may be far different from what constitutes credibility to a majority client. We now focus on how counselor characteristics affect these sets as they apply to the culturally different.

Therapist Credibility

Credibility (which elicits the problem-solving, consistency, and identification sets) may be defined as the constellation of characteristics that makes certain individuals appear worthy of belief, capable, entitled to confidence, reliable, and trustworthy. Expertness is an "ability" variable, while trustworthiness is a "motivation" variable. Expertness depends on how well-informed, capable, or intelligent others perceive the communicator (counselor). Trustworthiness is dependent on the degree to which people perceive the communicator (therapist) as motivated to make invalid assertions. In counseling and therapy, these two components have been the subject of much research and speculation (Barak & Dell, 1977; Barak & La Crosse, 1975; Dell, 1973; Heesacker et al., 1995; La Crosse & Barak, 1976; LaFromborse & Dixon, 1981; Lent & Maddux, 1997; S. B. Spiegel, 1976; Sprafkin, 1970; Strong, 1969; Strong & Schmidt, 1970). The weight of evidence supports our commonsense beliefs that the helping professional who is perceived as expert and trustworthy can influence clients more than can one who is perceived to be lower on these traits.

Expertness. Clients often go to a therapist not only because they are in distress and in need of relief, but also because they believe the counselor is an expert, that is, that he or she has the necessary knowledge, skills, experience, training, and tools to help (problem-solving set). Perceived expertness is typically a function of (a) reputation, (b) evidence of specialized training, and (c) behavioral evidence of proficiency/competency. For culturally different clients, the issue of therapist expertness seems to be raised more often than when clients go to a therapist of their own culture and race. As mentioned previously, the fact that therapists have degrees and certificates from prestigious institutions (authority set) may not enhance perceived expertness. This is especially true of clients who are culturally different and aware that institutional bias exists in training programs. Indeed, it may have the opposite effect by reducing credibility! Additionally, reputation-expertness (authority set) is unlikely to impress a minority client unless the favorable testimony comes from someone of his or her own group.

Thus behavior-expertness, or demonstrating the ability to help a client, becomes the critical form of expertness in effective multicultural counseling (problem-solving set). It appears that using counseling skills and strategies appropriate to the life values of the culturally diverse client is crucial. We have already mentioned evidence that certain minority groups prefer a much more active approach to counseling. A counselor playing a relatively inactive role may be perceived as being incompetent and unhelpful. The following example shows how the therapist's approach lowers perceived expertness.

> *ASIAN AMERICAN MALE CLIENT: It's hard for me to talk about these issues. My parents and friends . . . they wouldn't understand . . . if they ever found out I was coming here for help. . . .*
>
> *WHITE MALE THERAPIST: I sense it's difficult to talk about personal things. How are you feeling right now?*
>
> *ASIAN AMERICAN CLIENT: Oh, all right.*
>
> *WHITE THERAPIST: That's not a feeling. Sit back and get in touch with your feelings. [pause] Now tell me, how are you feeling right now?*
>
> *ASIAN AMERICAN CLIENT: Somewhat nervous.*
>
> *WHITE THERAPIST: When you talked about your parents' and friends' not understanding and the way you said it made me think you felt ashamed and disgraced at having to come. Was that what you felt?*

While this exchange appears to indicate that the therapist could (a) see the client's discomfort and (b) interpret his feelings correctly, it also points out the therapist's lack of understanding and knowledge of Asian cultural values. While we do not want to be guilty of stereotyping Asian Americans, many do have difficulty, at times, openly expressing feelings publicly to a stranger. The therapist's persistent attempts to focus on feelings and his direct and blunt interpretation of them may indicate to the Asian American client that the therapist lacks the more subtle skills of dealing with a sensitive topic or that the therapist is shaming the client (see Chapter 13).

Furthermore, it is possible that the Asian American client in this case is much more used to discussing feelings in an indirect or subtle manner. A direct response from the therapist addressed to a feeling may not be as effective as one that deals with it indirectly. In many traditional Asian groups, subtlety is a highly prized art, and the traditional Asian client may feel much more comfortable when dealing with feelings in an indirect manner.

In many ways, behavioral manifestations of therapist expertness override other considerations. For example, many educators claim that specific therapy skills are not as important as the attitude one brings into the therapeutic situation. Behind this statement is the belief that universal attributes of genuineness, love, unconditional acceptance, and positive regard are the only things needed. Yet the question remains: How does a therapist communicate these things to culturally diverse clients? While a therapists might have the best of intentions, it is possible that his/her intentions might be misunderstood. Let us use another example with the same Asian American client.

ASIAN AMERICAN CLIENT: *I'm even nervous about others seeing me come in here. It's so difficult for me to talk about this.*
WHITE THERAPIST: *We all find some things difficult to talk about. It's important that you do.*
ASIAN AMERICAN CLIENT: *It's easy to say that. But do you really understand how awful I feel, talking about my parents?*
WHITE THERAPIST: *I've worked with many Asian Americans and many have similar problems.*

In this sample dialogue we find a distinction between the therapist's intentions and the effects of his comments. The therapist's intentions were to reassure the client that he understood his feelings, to imply that he had worked with similar cases, and to make the client feel less isolated (i.e., that others have the same problems). The effects, however, were to dilute and dismiss the client's feelings and concerns and to take the uniqueness out of the situation.

Likewise, a therapist who adheres rigidly to a particular school of counseling, or who relies primarily on a few therapy responses is seriously limited in his or her ability to help a wide range of clients. Advocates of a single school of thought do not realize that when they make statements about their therapeutic orientation (such as "I am Rogerian," "I am behavioral," "I am rational-emotive in orientation," etc.), they conceptualize people in the same way and respond toward them in a therapeutic mode that is similar regardless of race, color, creed, religion, and gender. Counselors and therapists who respond in such a manner fail to take into account that people differ in a number of ways along these dimensions. While counseling and psychotherapy theories are important, psychology training programs have an equally strong responsibility to teach helping skills that cut across schools of therapy. Only in this way will future therapists be better able to engage in a wide variety of therapy behaviors when working with culturally diverse groups.

Trustworthiness. Perceived trustworthiness encompasses such factors as sincerity, openness, honesty, or perceived lack of motivation for personal gain. A therapist who is perceived as trustworthy is likely to exert more influence over a client than is one who is not. In our society, many people assume that certain roles such as ministers, doctors, psychiatrists, and counselors exist to help people. With respect to minorities, self-disclosure is very much dependent on this attribute of perceived trustworthiness. Because mental health professionals are often perceived by minorities to be "agents of the Establishment," trust is something that does not come with the role (authority set). Indeed, many minorities may perceive that therapists cannot be trusted unless otherwise demonstrated. Again, the role and reputation you have as being trustworthy must be evidenced in behavioral terms. More than anything, challenges to the therapist's trustworthiness will be a frequent theme blocking further exploration and movement until it is resolved to the satisfaction of the client. These verbatim transcripts illustrate the trust issue.

> WHITE MALE THERAPIST: *I sense some major hesitations. . . . It's difficult for you to discuss your concerns with me.*
>
> BLACK MALE CLIENT: *You're damn right! If I really told you how I felt about my [White] coach, what's to prevent you from telling him? You Whities are all of the same mind.*
>
> WHITE THERAPIST [ANGRY]: *Look, it would be a lie for me to say I don't know your coach. He's an acquaintance, but not a personal friend. Don't put me in the same bag with all Whites! Anyway, even if he were a close friend, I hold our discussion in strictest confidence. Let me ask you this question: What would I need to do that would make it easier for you to trust me?*
>
> BLACK CLIENT: *You're on your way, man!*

This verbal exchange illustrates several issues related to trustworthiness. First, the minority client is likely to test the therapist constantly regarding issues of confidentiality. Second, the onus of responsibility for proving trustworthiness falls on the therapist. Third, to prove that one is trustworthy requires, at times, self-disclosure on the part of the mental health professional. That the therapist did not hide the fact that he knew the coach (openness), became angry about being lumped with all Whites (sincerity), assured the client that he would not tell the coach or anyone about their sessions (confidentiality), and asked the client how he would work to prove he was trustworthy (genuineness) were all elements that enhanced his trustworthiness.

Handling the "prove to me that you can be trusted" ploy is very difficult for many therapists. It is difficult because it demands self-disclosure on the part of the helping professional, something that graduate training programs have taught us to avoid. It places the focus on the therapist rather than on the client and makes many uncomfortable. In addition, it is likely to evoke defensiveness on the part of many mental health practitioners. Here is another verbatim exchange in which defensiveness is evoked, destroying the helping professional's trustworthiness:

> BLACK FEMALE CLIENT: *Students in my drama class expect me to laugh when they do "steppin' fetchin'" routines and tell Black jokes. . . . I'm wondering whether you've ever laughed at any of those jokes.*
>
> WHITE MALE THERAPIST: [long pause] *Yes, I'm sure I have. Have you ever laughed at any White jokes?*
>
> BLACK CLIENT: *What's a White joke?*
>
> WHITE THERAPIST: *I don't know* [nervous laughter]; *I suppose one making fun of Whites. Look, I'm Irish. Have you ever laughed at Irish jokes?*

> BLACK CLIENT: *People tell me many jokes, but I don't laugh at racial jokes. I feel we're all minorities and should respect each other.*

Again, the client tested the therapist indirectly by asking him if he ever laughed at racial jokes. Since most of us probably have, to say "no" would be a blatant lie. The client's motivation for asking this question was to find out (a) how sincere and open the therapist was and (b) whether the therapist could recognize his racist attitudes without letting it interfere with therapy. While the therapist admitted to having laughed at such jokes, he proceeded to destroy his trustworthiness by becoming defensive. Rather than simply stopping with his statement of "Yes, I'm sure I have," or making some other similar one, he defends himself by trying to get the client to admit to similar actions. Thus the therapist's trustworthiness is seriously impaired. He is perceived as motivated to defend himself rather than help the client.

The therapist's obvious defensiveness in this case has prevented him from understanding the intent and motive of the question. Is the African American female client really asking the therapist whether he has actually laughed at Black Jokes before? Or is the client asking the therapist if he is a racist? Both of these speculations have a certain amount of validity, but it is our belief that the Black female client is actually asking the following important question of the therapist: "How open and honest are you about your own racism, and will it interfere with our session here?" Again, the test is one of trustworthiness, a motivational variable that the White male therapist has obviously failed.

To summarize, expertness and trustworthiness are important components of any therapeutic relationship. In multicultural counseling/therapy, however, the counselor or therapist may not be presumed to possess either. The therapist working with a minority client is likely to experience severe tests of his or her expertness and trustworthiness before serious therapy can proceed. The responsibility for proving to the client that you are a credible therapist is likely to be greater when working with a minority client than with a majority client. How you meet the challenge is important in determining your effectiveness as a multicultural helping professional.

We have come quite a long way in terms of examining how credibility and trustworthiness on the part of the therapist are affected by racial-cultural factors. We have also briefly discussed similarity and the evocation of the identification set. Do minority clients actually prefer a member of their own race in therapy? This is a very important question, but the findings seem to be mixed or varying.

It is quite obvious that we know minority individuals who prefer seeing people of their own race and cultural background as well as some who apparently do not care. We may also know some minority individuals who would prefer to see therapists not of their own race. What are the determining factors that affect this selection process? How important are membership group similarity and attitude similarity in a culturally different client's preference for members of his or her own race? It appears that certain types of similarities and dissimilarities may affect the credibility of the helping professional differentially. Relevant similarities seem more powerful than irrelevant ones. Also, the minority individual's stage of cultural identity may cause him or her to interact quite differently with this question. Later we discuss cultural identity development and how it may affect a minority client's preference for a therapist of his or her own race.

Implications for Clinical Practice

It is clear that counseling and psychotherapy, in both process and goals, contain a powerful sociopolitical dimension. How minority clients relate to therapists different from themselves often mirrors the state of interracial relationships in the wider society. Several guidelines suggested from this chapter can aid us in our journey toward cultural competence.

1. In working with minority clients, it is important to distinguish between behaviors indicative of a true mental disorder and those that result from oppression and survival. A client of color may not readily self-disclose to you and may engage in behaviors for self-protection. These represent functional survival skills rather than pathology.

2. Do not personalize the suspicions a client may have of your motives. If you become defensive, insulted, or angry with the client, your effectiveness will be seriously diminished.

3. Monitor your own reactions and question your beliefs. All of us are victims of our social conditioning and have unintentionally inherited the racial biases of our forebears. A culturally competent mental health professional is willing to question his or her own worldview and standards used to judge normality and abnormality, and is willing to understand and overcome his or her own stereotypes, biases, and assumptions about other cultural groups.

4. Be aware that that clients of color or other marginalized groups may consider your professional credentials as insufficient. Know that your credibility and trustworthiness will be tested. Evidence of specialized training is less impressive than factors such as authenticity, sincerity, and openness. Tests of credibility may occur frequently in the therapy session, and the onus of responsibility for proving expertness and trustworthiness lies with the therapist.

5. In multicultural counseling/therapy you may be unable to use the

client's identification set (membership group similarity) to induce change. At times, racial dissimilarity may prove to be so much of a hindrance as to render therapy ineffective. In this situation, referring out should not be viewed negatively or as a defeat. One could argue that a counselor or therapist who is aware of limitations and is nondefensive enough to refer out is evidencing cultural competence.

6. Some have argued that attitudinal similarity may be more important than racial similarity in counseling. Research in this area is inconclusive. It seems to depend on several factors: (a) the type of presenting problems, (b) the degree and stage of racial/ethnic identity, and (c) certain characteristics of the therapist that may override race differences.

7. Be aware that difficulties in multicultural counseling may not stem from race factors per se, but from the implications of being a minority in the United States and thus having secondary status. In any case, a broad statement on this matter is overly simplistic. By virtue of its definition, multicultural therapy implies major differences between the client and the helper. How these differences can be bridged and under what conditions a therapist is able to work effectively with culturally diverse clients are key questions.

THE PRACTICE DIMENSIONS OF MULTICULTURAL COUNSELING/THERAPY

Barriers to Effective Multicultural Counseling/Therapy

4

Chapter

One of the most difficult cases I have ever treated was that of a Mexican American family in Southern California. Fernando M. was a 56-year-old recent immigrant to the United States. He had been married some 35 years to Refugio, his wife, and had fathered 10 children. Only four of his children, three sons and one daughter, resided with him.

Fernando was born in a small village in Mexico and resided there until three years ago, when he moved to California. He was not unfamiliar with California, having worked as a bracero *for most of his adult life. He would make frequent visits to the United States during annual harvest seasons.*

The M. family resided in a small, old, unpainted, rented house that sat on the back of a dirt lot and was sparsely furnished with their belongings. The family did not own a car, and public transportation was not available in their neighborhood. While their standard of living was far below poverty levels, the family appeared quite pleased at their relative affluence when compared with their life in Mexico.

The presenting complaints concerned Fernando. He heard threatening voices, was often disoriented, and stated that someone was planning to kill him and that something evil was about to happen. He became afraid to leave his home, was in poor physical health, and possessed a decrepit appearance, which made him essentially unemployable.

When the M. family entered the clinic, I was asked to see them because the bilingual therapist scheduled that day had called in sick. I was hoping that either Fernando or Refugio would speak enough English to understand the situation. As luck would have it, neither could understand me, nor I them. It became apparent, however, that the two older children could understand English. Since the younger one seemed more fluent, I called upon him to act as a translator during our first session. I noticed that the parents seemed reluctant to participate with the younger son, and for some time the discussion between the family members was quite animated. Sensing something wrong and desiring to get the session underway, I interrupted the family and asked the son who spoke English best what was wrong. He hesitated for a second, but assured me that everything was fine.

During the course of our first session, it became obvious to me that Fernando was seriously disturbed. He appeared frightened, tense, and, if the interpretations from his son were correct, hallucinating. I suggested to Refugio that she consider hospitalizing her husband, but she was adamant against this course. I could sense her nervousness and fear that I would initiate action in having her husband committed. I reassured her that no action would be taken without a follow-up evaluation and suggested that she return later in the week with Fernando. Refugio said that it would be difficult since Fernando was afraid to leave his home. She had to coerce him into coming this time and did not feel she could do it again. I looked at Fernando directly and stated, "Fernando, I know how hard it is for you to come here, but we really want to help you. Do you think you could possibly come one more time? Dr. Escobedo [the bilingual therapist] will be here with me, and he can communicate with you directly." The youngest son interpreted.

The M. family never returned for another session, and their failure to show up has greatly bothered me. Since that time I have talked with several Latino psychologists who have pointed out multicultural issues that I was not aware of then. Now I realize how uninformed and naive I was in working with Latinos and only hope the M. family have found the needed help elsewhere.

W hile the last chapter dealt with the sociopolitical dynamics affecting multicultural counseling/therapy, this chapter discusses the cultural barriers that may render the helping professional ineffective, thereby denying help to culturally diverse clients. The above example illustrates important multicultural issues that are presented in this series of questions:

1. Was it a serious blunder for the therapist to see the M. family or to continue to see them in the session when he could not speak Spanish? Should he have waited until Dr. Escobedo returned?

2. While it may seem like a good idea to have one of the children interpret for the therapist and the family, what possible cultural implications might this have in the Mexican American family? Can one obtain an accurate translation through family interpreters? What are some of the pitfalls?

3. The therapist tried to be informal with the family in order to put them at ease. Yet some of his colleagues have stated that how he addresses clients (last names or first names) may be important. When the therapist used the first names of both husband and wife, what possible cultural interpretation from the family may have resulted?

4. The therapist saw Mr. M.'s symptoms as indications of serious pathology. What other explanations might he entertain? Should he have so blatantly suggested hospitalization? How do Latinos perceive mental health issues?

Barriers to Effective Multicultural Counseling/Therapy

5. Knowing that Mr. M. had difficulty leaving home, should the therapist have considered some other treatment avenues? If so, what may they have been?

The clash of cultural and therapeutic barriers exemplified in the questions above is both complex and difficult to resolve. They challenge mental health professionals to (a) reach out and understand the worldviews, cultural values, and life circumstances of their culturally diverse clients; (b) free themselves from the cultural conditioning of what they believe are correct therapeutic practice; (c) develop new but culturally sensitive methods of working with clients; and (d) play new roles outside of conventional psychotherapy in the helping process (Atkinson, Thompson, & Grant, 1995; D. W. Sue et al., 1998). Three major potential barriers to effective MCT are illustrated in this case: class-bound values, language bias/misunderstanding, and culture-bound values.

First, Fernando's "paranoid reactions and suspicions" and his hallucinations may have many causes. An enlightened mental health professional must consider whether there are sociopolitical, cultural, or biological reasons for his symptoms. Can his fears, for example, symbolize realistic concerns (fear of deportation, creditors, police, etc.)? How do Latino cultures view hallucinations? Some studies indicate that cultural factors make it more acceptable for some Spanish speaking populations to admit to hearing voices or seeing visions. Indeed, Appendix I of the American Psychiatric Association's *Diagnostic and Statistical Manual of Mental Disorders* (2000) now recognizes a large group of *culture-bound syndromes,* disorders that seem to appear only in specific cultures and societies. Another consideration is the life circumstance of Fernando's work. Could his agricultural work and years of exposure to pesticides and other dangerous agricultural chemicals be contributing to his mental state? Counseling and psychotherapy often focus so much on internal dynamics of clients that there is a failure to consider external sources as causes. It is important for the therapist to consider these explanations.

In addition, mental health practice has been described as a White middle-class activity that often fails to recognize the economic implications in the delivery of mental health services. Class-bound factors related to socioeconomic status may place those suffering from poverty at a disadvantage and deny them the necessary help that they need. For example, Fernando's family is obviously poor; they do not own an automobile; and public transportation is not available in the rural area in which they reside. Poor clients have difficulties traveling to mental health facilities for treatment. Not only is attending sessions a great inconvenience, but it can also be costly to arrange private transportation for the family. It might seem that meeting the needs of the M. family might entail home visits or some other form of outreach. If the M. family is unable to travel to the therapist's office for treatment, what blocked the therapist from considering a home visit or a meeting point between the destinations? Many therapists feel disinclined, fearful, or uncomfortable in doing the former. Their training dictates that they practice in their offices and that clients come to them. When mental health services are located away from the communities that they purport to serve, when outreach programs are not available, and when economic considerations are not addressed by mental health services, institutional bias is clearly evident.

Second, linguistic or language barriers often place culturally diverse clients at a disadvantage. The primary medium by which mental health professionals do their work is through verbalizations ("talk therapies"). Ever since Freud developed the *talking cure,* psychotherapy has meant that clients must be able to verbalize their thoughts and feelings to a practitioner in order to receive the necessary help required. In addition, because of linguistic bias and monolingualism, the form of talk is via standard English. Clients who do not speak standard English, who possess a pronounced accent, or who have limited command of English (like the M. family) may be victimized.

The need to understand the meaning of linguistic differences and language barriers in counseling and psychotherapy has never been greater. As we mentioned previously, the result of changing demographics is that many of our clients are born outside of the United States and speak English as their second language. While the use of interpreters might seem like a solution, such a practice may suffer from certain limitations. For example, can interpreters really give an accurate translation? Cultural differences in mental health concepts are not equivalent in various cultures. In addition, many concepts in English and Spanish do not have equivalent meanings. Likewise, the good intentions of the therapist to communicate with the M. family via the son, who seemed to speak English fluently, might result in a cultural family violation. It may undermine the authority of the father by disturbing the patriarchic role relationships considered sacred in traditional Latino families. There is no doubt that the need for bilingual therapists is great. Yet the lack of bilingual mental health professionals does not bode well for linguistic minorities.

Third, a number of culture-bound issues seemed to be played out in the delivery of services to the M. family. The therapist's attempt to be informal and to put the family at ease resulted in greeting Mr. M. by using his first name (Fernando) as opposed to a more formal one (Mr. M.). In traditional Latino and Asian cultures, such informality or familiarity may be considered a lack of respect for the man's role as head of the household. Another cultural barrier might be operative in asking the son whether something was wrong. It is highly probable that the animated family discussion was based on objections to the son's interpreting by placing the father and mother in a dependency position. Yet as you recall, the son denied that anything was wrong. Many traditional Latinos do not feel comfortable airing family issues in public and might consider it impolite to turn down the therapist's suggestion (to have the younger son interpret).

Let us use another case to help illustrate other barriers to effective multicultural counseling/therapy.

Several years ago I was asked by a student services committee at a large public university to help identify factors that would make their services more relevant to the needs of minority students. Apparently, the office of student services, especially the counseling center, was under considerable pressures from minority groups to make changes amid charges of racism. The director of the counseling center and several staff members reported that they had tried to encourage minority students to come for counseling, but their efforts had met with no success. A recent study by the university had revealed that while the student population was comprised of 16% Asian Americans, 17% African Americans, 3% Latino/Hispanic Americans, and less than 1% American Indians, very few minorities used the center's services. The counseling center had a nationally known reputation as a fertile training program for interns doing work in socioemotional problems.

My own investigation revealed that not only were the services heavily clinical (personal/emotional counseling) in nature, but they subscribed to the traditional one-to-one model as well. When counselors were asked about the types of cases they preferred to work with, 85% of the counseling staff listed clinical, while only 15% chose educational/vocational cases. Indeed, I quickly sensed a status hierarchy among the staff. At the top of the pecking order were those who primarily did clinical work, and at the bottom were the educational/vocational counselors. In addition, the staff of 28 in the center had only three minority members.

This case identifies another set of possible barriers or impediments that may work against culturally diverse clients. For example, is the institution discouraging certain culturally diverse clients from making use of its services? If so, what are these characteristics, and why? Is the traditional counselor-client model effective in counseling minorities (nontraditional clients)?

The underrepresentation of minority clients in mental health services is not unusual. As summarized in Chapter 3, American Indians, Asian Americans, African Americans, and Latinos/Hispanics underutilize traditional mental health services and are more likely to terminate sessions earlier than are their White counterparts. In this case example, several primary reasons of why the counseling center has such low utilization rates can be identified.

First, it became obvious by a casual inspection that the counseling center staff was predominantly White. Of the minority group members present, one was an African American counselor, but the others were an African American clerical staff member and an Asian American vocational librarian. The lack of minority professionals in the counseling center was a loud and clear message to certain culturally diverse students concerning the commitment of the institution and and the center. The perception of many minority students was that the counseling center did not care about culturally diverse students, that it lacked understanding about their lifestyles and experiences, and that its efforts toward encouraging participation were not genuine and sincere. Right or wrong, many students assumed that the staff would not be able to relate to the minority-group experience of the students and, indeed, that the low minority representation resulted from racist policies and practices that discriminated against hiring minority staff. Based on these perceptions, many of the students were actively discouraged from utilizing the services.

Second, how the services were offered to the university community was also crucial in its ability to relate to a culturally diverse student body. This case makes it clear that the traditional services were one-to-one in nature: The counselor received clients in his or her office. This type of approach, as Atkinson, Kim, and Caldwell (1998) pointed out, may actually be less appropriate than meeting the client in a different contextual environment. Like the case of the M. family, rather than demanding that the client adapt to the counselor's culture, it may be better for the counselor to adjust to and work within the client's culture. In other words, alternative roles involve the counselor more actively in the client's life experiences than what we have traditionally been trained to do. Outreach roles, consultant roles, change-agent roles, and the use of the client's indigenous support systems may be more appropriate. Many minority group individuals find the one-to-one/in-office type of counseling very formal, removed, and alien. When counselors move out of their offices into the environments of their clients, it again indicates commitment and interest in the individual. According to this nontraditional view, counseling is not simply sitting down and talking with a client, but may involve shooting basketball with the client in his or her home environment, playing billiards with the client, and working in situations where the minority individual is found (dormitories, the student union, etc.). Unfortunately, most training in counseling and clinical psychology does not give adequate experiences with these types of change-agent outreach programs. Indeed, counselors are often discouraged from meeting clients on their home turf because it is "unprofessional" and not a part of the counselor's role.

Third, the counseling center in this example is defined as one that is very well known in terms of socio-emotional counseling and emphasis. This again is not unusual in most counselor education training programs. Often, counselor trainees are more intrigued with personal-emotional (psychiatric) issues than with educational or vocational concerns. Yet it appears that many minority individuals are much more concerned with their vocational, educational, and career goals. For example, as we will see in Chapter 13, Asian Americans tend to be much more concerned with educational-vocational counseling and will come for these services at a high rate when offered. Much of this is due to cultural factors operating in the lives of Asian Americans. When counselors tend to perceive educational-vocational counseling as less prestigious, then it is entirely possible that this is communicated to the student population. Additionally, many minority individuals may not trust talking about personal issues with White counselors and may be more amenable to dealing directly with vocational-educational career issues. This subject is discussed further in later chapters.

In Chapter 2 we mentioned how the mental health profession had failed to contribute to the betterment of culturally diverse groups in America. Psychology training programs and the portrayal of minorities in both the popular and scientific literature have often instilled within counselor trainees (a) monocultural assumptions of mental health, (b) negative stereotypes of pathology for minority lifestyles, and (c) ineffective, inappropriate, and antagonistic counseling approaches to the values held by minorities. As in the counseling center illustration, this damage is clearly seen in the actual practice of counseling and therapy.

Characteristics of Counseling/Therapy

Counseling and psychotherapy may be viewed legitimately as a process of interpersonal interaction, communication, and social influence. For effective therapy to occur, the therapist and client must be able to *send and receive both verbal and nonverbal messages appropriately and accurately.* While breakdowns in communication often happen between members who share the same culture, the problem becomes exacerbated between people of different racial or ethnic backgrounds. Many mental health professionals have noted that racial or ethnic factors may act as impediments to therapy by lowering social influence (Locke, 1998; Paniagua, 1998; D. W. Sue, 2001; Vontress, 1981). Misunderstandings that arise from cultural variations in communication may lead to alienation or an inability to develop trust and rapport. Culture clashes can often occur between the values of counseling/psychotherapy and the values of culturally different groups.

At this point, we turn our attention to a much more formal analysis of how these values may distort communication or affect the therapeutic relationship. We discuss implications for therapy and present a conceptual scheme that can be used to compare and contrast how language, culture, and class variables can be used to determine appropriate interventions. Such a comparative analysis is helpful in providing a means for examining the appropriateness of counseling approaches—not only for culturally different clients but for other special populations as well (women, gay/lesbians, the physically handicapped, and the elderly).

Generic Characteristics of Counseling/Therapy

We have repeatedly emphasized that counseling and psychotherapy are influenced by the sociocultural framework from which it arises. In the United States, White Euro-American culture holds certain values that are reflected in this therapeutic process. All theories of counseling and psychotherapy are influenced by assumptions that theorists make regarding the goals for therapy, the methodology used to invoke change, and the definition of mental health and mental illness. Counseling and psychotherapy have traditionally been conceptualized in Western individualistic terms (Atkinson, Morten, et al., 1998; Ivey, Ivey, Simek-Morgan, 1997). Whether the particular theory is psychodynamic, existential-humanistic, or cognitive-behavioral in orientation, a number of multicultural specialists (Corey, 2001; Ivey et al., 1997) indicate that they share certain common components of White culture in their values and beliefs. Katz (1985) has described these components of White culture. These values and beliefs have influenced the actual practice of counseling and psychotherapy, as can be seen clearly in Tables 4.1 and 4.2.

In the United States and in many other countries as well, psychotherapy and counseling are used mainly with middle- and upper-class segments of the population. As a result, culturally diverse clients do not share many of the values and characteristics seen in both the goals and the processes of therapy. Schofield (1964) has noted that therapists tend to prefer clients who exhibit the *YAVIS* syndrome: young, attractive, verbal, intelligent, and successful. This preference tends to discriminate against people from different minority groups or those from lower socioeconomic classes. This has led Sundberg (1981) to sarcastically point out that therapy is not for *QUOID* people (quiet, ugly, old, indigent, and dissimilar culturally). Three major characteristics of counseling and psychotherapy, which may act as a source of conflict for culturally diverse groups, were identified in the early 1970s (D. W. Sue & D. Sue, 1972).

First, therapists often expect their clients to exhibit some degree of openness, psychological-mindedness, or sophistication. Most theories of helping place a high premium on verbal, emotional, and behavioral expressiveness and the obtaining of insight. These are either the end goals of therapy or the medium by which "cures" are effected. Second, therapy is traditionally a one-to-one activity that encourages clients to talk about or discuss the most intimate aspects of their lives. Individuals who fail in or resist self-disclosure may be seen as resistant, defensive, or superficial. Third, the counseling or therapy situation is often an ambiguous one. The client is encouraged to discuss problems while the counselor listens and responds. Relatively speaking, the therapy situation is unstructured and forces the client to be the primary active participant. Patterns of communication are generally from client to therapist.

Four other factors identified as general characteristics of therapy are its (a) monolingual orientation, (b) emphasis on long-range goals, (c) distinc-

Table 4.1 **Generic Characteristics of Counseling**

Culture	Middle Class	Language
Standard English	Standard English	Standard English
Verbal communication	Verbal communication	Verbal communication
Individual centered		
	Adherence to time schedules (50-minute sessions)	
Verbal/emotional/ behavioral expressiveness		
Client-counselor communication	Long-range goals	
	Ambiguity	
Openness and intimacy		
Cause-effect orientation		
Clear distinction between physical and mental well-being		
Nuclear family		

tion between physical and mental well-being, and (d) emphasis on cause-effect relationships. Furthermore, since therapy is generally isolated from the client's environment and contacts are brief (50 minutes, once a week), it is by nature aimed at seeking long-range goals and solutions.

Another important and often overlooked factor in therapy is the implicit assumption that a clear distinction can be made between mental and physical illness and health. Contrary to this Western view, many cultures may not distinguish clearly between the two. Such a separation may be confusing to some culturally diverse clients and cause problems in therapy.

Ornstein's early work (1972), in which he identifies the dual hemispheric functioning of the brain, has intriguing implications for therapy as well. While the left hemisphere of the brain is involved with linear, rational, and cognitive processes, the right half tends to be intuitive, feeling, and experientially oriented. When both hemispheres are operating in a mutually interdependent fashion, they facilitate our functioning as human beings. Ornstein points out that the linear/logical/analytic/verbal mode of the left brain dominates Western thinking. The intuitive/holistic/creative/nonverbal functioning of the right brain has been neglected in Western culture and seen as a less legitimate mode of expression.

An analysis of the various American schools of therapy leads to the inevitable conclusion that Western mental health practice is left-brain oriented (Highlen, 1994, 1996). Such an approach or worldview may definitely clash with Eastern and American Indian philosophy. Thus, a left-brain orientation means a linear emphasis on cause-effect approaches and a linear concept of time. We deal with these concepts in greater detail later.

Table 4.2   **Racial/Ethnic Minority Group Variables**

Culture	Lower Class	Language
Asian Americans		
Asian language	Nonstandard English	Bilingual background
Family centered	Action oriented	
Restraint of feelings	Different time perspective	
One-way communication from authority figure to person	Immediate, short-range goals	
Silence is respect		
Advice seeking		
Well-defined patterns of interaction (concrete structured)		
Private versus public display (shame/disgrace/pride)		
Physical and mental well-being defined differently		
Extended family		
African Americans		
Black language	Nonstandard English	Black language
Sense of "people-hood"	Action oriented	
Action oriented	Different time perspective	
Paranorm due to oppression	Immediate, short-range goals	
Importance placed on nonverbal behavior	Concrete, tangible, structured approach	
Extended family		
Latino/Hispanic Americans		
Spanish-speaking	Extended family	Bilingual background
Group centered	Nonstandard English	
Temporal difference	Action oriented	
Family orientation	Different time perspective	
Different pattern of communication	Immediate short-range goals	
Religious distinction between mind/body	Concrete, tangible, structured approach	

Table 4.2 **continued**

Culture	Lower Class	Language
American Indians		
Tribal dialects	Nonstandard English	Bilingual background
Cooperative, not competitive individualism	Action oriented	
	Different time perspective	
Present-time orientation	Immediate, short-range goals	
Creative/experimental/intuitive/nonverbal	Concrete, tangible, structured approach	
Satisfy present needs		
Use of folk or supernatural explanations		
Extended family		

In summary, the generic characteristics of counseling/therapy can be seen to fall into three major categories:

1. Culture-bound values: individual centered, verbal/emotional/behavioral expressiveness, communication patterns from client to counselor, openness and intimacy, analytic/linear/verbal (cause-effect) approach, and clear distinctions between mental and physical well-being

2. Class-bound values: strict adherence to time schedules (50-minute, once- or twice-a-week meetings), ambiguous or unstructured approach to problems, and seeking long-range goals or solutions

3. Language variables: use of standard English and emphasis on verbal communication

Tables 4.1 and 4.2 summarize these generic characteristics and compare their compatibility to those of four racial/ethnic minority groups. As mentioned earlier, such a comparison can also be done for other groups that vary in gender, age, sexual orientation, ability/disability, and so on.

Sources of Conflict and Misinterpretation in Therapy

While an attempt has been made to delineate clearly three major variables that influence effective therapy, these variables are often inseparable from one another. For example, use of standard English in counseling and therapy definitely places those individuals who do not speak it fluently at a disadvantage. However, cultural and class values that govern conventions of conversation can also operate via language to cause serious misunderstandings. Furthermore, the fact that many African Americans, Latino/Hispanic Americans, and American Indians come from a predominantly lower-class background often compounds class and culture variables. Thus it is often difficult to tell which are the sole impediments in therapy. Nevertheless, this distinction is valuable in conceptualizing barriers to effective multicultural counseling/therapy.

Culture-Bound Values

In simple terms, *culture* consists of all those things that people have learned in their history to do, believe, value, and enjoy. It is the totality of ideals, beliefs, skills, tools, customs, and institutions into which each member of society is born. While D. W. Sue and D. Sue (1972) have stressed the need for social scientists to focus on the positive aspects of being bicultural, such dual membership may cause problems for many minorities. The term *marginal person* was first coined by Stonequist (1937) and refers to a person's inability to form dual ethnic identification because of bicultural membership. Racial/ethnic minorities are placed under strong pressures to adopt the ways of the dominant culture. The cultural deficit models tend to view culturally different individuals as possessing dysfunctional values/belief systems that are often handicaps to be overcome, to be ashamed of, and to be avoided. In essence, racial/ethnic minorities may be taught that to be different is to be deviant, pathological, or sick.

Many social scientists (Carter, 1995; Guthrie, 1997; Halleck, 1971; Katz, 1985; Parham et al., 1999; D. W. Sue et al., 1982) believe that psychology and therapy may be viewed as encompassing the use of social power and that therapy is a handmaiden of the status quo. The therapist may be seen as a societal agent transmitting and functioning under Western values. An early outspoken critic, Szasz (1970) believes that psychiatrists are like slave masters using therapy as a powerful political ploy against people whose ideas, beliefs, and behaviors differ from the dominant society. Several culture-bound characteristics of therapy may be responsible for these negative beliefs.

Focus on the Individual
Most forms of counseling and psychotherapy tend to be individual centered (i.e., they emphasize the "I-thou" relationship). Pedersen (2000) notes that U.S. culture and society is based on the concept of individualism and that competition between individuals for status, recognition, achievement, and so forth, forms the basis for Western tradition. Individualism, autonomy, and the ability to become your own person are perceived as healthy and desirable goals. If we look at most Euro-American theories of human development

(Piaget, Erickson, etc.), we are struck by how they emphasize "individuation" as normal and healthy development. Pedersen notes that not all cultures view individualism as a positive orientation; rather, it may be perceived in some cultures as a handicap to attaining enlightenment, one that may divert us from important spiritual goals. In many non-Western cultures, identity is not seen apart from the group orientation (collectivism). The Japanese language does not seem to have a distinct personal pronoun *I*. The notion of *atman* in India defines itself as participating in unity with all things and not being limited by the temporal world.

Many societies do not define the psychosocial unit of operation as the individual. In many cultures and subgroups, the psychosocial unit of operation tends to be the family, group, or collective society. In traditional Asian American culture, one's identity is defined within the family constellation. The greatest punitive measure to be taken out on an individual by the family is to be disowned. What this means in essence is that the person no longer has an identity. While being disowned by a family in Western European culture is equally negative and punitive, it does not have the same connotations as in traditional Asian society. Although they may be disowned by a family, Westerners are always informed and told that they have an individual identity as well. Likewise, many Hispanic individuals tend to see the unit of operation as residing within the family. African American psychologists (Mays, 1985; Parham, 1997; Parham et al., 1999) also point out how the African view of the world encompasses the concept of "groupness."

Our contention is that racial/ethnic minorities often use a different psychosocial unit of operation in that collectivism is valued over individualism. This worldview is reflected in all aspects of behavior. For example, many traditional Asian American and Hispanic elders tend to greet one another with the question, "How is your family today?" Contrast this with how most U.S. Americans tend to greet each other: "How are you today?" One emphasizes the family (group) perspective, while the other emphasizes the individual perspective.

Affective expressions in therapy can be strongly influenced also by the particular orientation one takes. When individuals engage in wrongful behaviors in the United States, they are most likely to experience feelings of *guilt*. In societies that emphasize collectivism, however, the most dominant affective element to follow a wrongful behavior is *shame*, not guilt. Guilt is an individual affect, while shame appears to be a group one (it reflects on the family or group).

Counselors and therapists who fail to recognize the importance of defining this difference between individualism and collectivism will create difficulties in therapy. Often we are impressed by the number of our colleagues who describe traditional Asian clients as being "dependent," "unable to make decisions on their own," and "lacking in maturity." Many of these judgments are based on the fact that many Asian clients do not see a decision-making process as an individual one. When an Asian client states to a counselor or therapist, "I can't make that decision on my own; I need to consult with my parents or family," he or she is seen as being quite immature. After all, therapy is aimed at helping individuals make decisions on their own in a "mature" and "responsible" manner.

Verbal/Emotional/Behavioral Expressiveness
Many counselors and therapists tend to emphasize the fact that verbal/emotional/behavioral expressiveness is important in individuals. For example, we like our clients to be verbal, articulate, and able to express their thoughts and feelings clearly. Indeed, therapy is often referred to as talk therapy, indicating the importance placed on standard English as the medium of expression. Emotional expressiveness is also valued, as we like individuals to be in touch with their feelings and to be able to verbalize their emotional reactions. In some forms of counseling and psychotherapy, it is often stated that if a feeling is not verbalized and expressed by the client, it may not exist. We tend to value and believe that behavioral expressiveness is important as well. We like individuals to be assertive, to stand up for their own rights, and to engage in activities that indicate that they are not passive beings.

All these characteristics of therapy can place culturally diverse clients at a disadvantage. For example, many cultural minorities tend not to value verbalizations in the same way that U.S. Americans do. In traditional Japanese culture, children have been taught not to speak until spoken to. Patterns of communication tend to be vertical, flowing from those of higher prestige and status to those of lower prestige and status. In a therapy situation, many Japanese clients, to show respect for a therapist who is older, "wiser," and who occupies a position of higher status, may respond with silence. Unfortunately, an unenlightened counselor or therapist may perceive this client as being inarticulate and less intelligent.

Emotional expressiveness in counseling and psychotherapy is frequently a highly desired goal. Yet many cultural groups value restraint of strong feelings. For example, traditional Hispanic and Asian cultures emphasize that maturity and wisdom are associated with one's ability to control emotions and feelings. This applies not only to public expressions of anger and frustration, but also to public expressions of love and affection. Unfortunately, therapists unfamiliar with these cultural ramifications may perceive their clients in a very negative psychiatric light. Indeed, these clients are often described as inhibited, lacking in spontaneity, or repressed.

One author of this text (D. W. Sue) once did a research study at a well-known university in Southern California. The study involved identifying symptomology among Japanese American students using counseling and psychiatric services. He was quite shocked and surprised when many of the psychiatric staff indicated that they were very pleased to see research being done on Japanese American clients because, as they put it, "Did you know they are one of the most repressed groups we have ever encountered?" We submit that this statement tends to overlook the fact that cultural forces may be operative in the Japanese American clients' overall behavior in the psychiatric session. While the clients may be repressed, the failure to consider cultural factors that dictate against public disclosures and feelings may prove a serious consequence.

In therapy it has become increasingly popular to emphasize expressiveness in a behavioral sense. For example, one need only note the proliferation of cognitive-behavioral assertiveness training programs throughout the United States and the number of self-help books that are being published in the popular mental health literature. Many of these, such as *Pulling Your Own Strings* and *Stand Up for Your Own Rights,* attest to the importance placed on assertiveness and individual rights. This orientation fails to realize that there are cultural groups in which subtlety is a highly prized art. Yet doing things indirectly can be perceived by the mental health professional as evidence of passivity and the need for an individual to learn assertiveness skills.

Therapists who value verbal, emotional, and behavioral expressiveness as goals in therapy may be unaware that they are transmitting their own cultural values. These generic characteristics of counseling are antagonistic not only to lower-class values, but to different cultural ones as well. In their excellent review of assertiveness training, Wood and Mallinckrodt (1990) warn that therapists need to make certain that gaining such skills is a value shared by the minority client, and not imposed by therapists. For example, statements by some mental health professionals that Asian Americans are the most repressed of all clients indicate that they expect their clients to exhibit openness, psychological-mindedness, and assertiveness. Such a statement may indicate the therapist's failure to understand the background and cultural upbringing of many Asian American clients. Traditional Chinese and Japanese cultures may value restraint of strong feelings and subtleness in approaching problems.

Insight

Another generic characteristic of counseling is the use of insight in both counseling and psychotherapy. This approach assumes that it is mentally beneficial for individuals to obtain insight or understanding into their underlying dynamics and causes. Brought up in the tradition of psychoanalytic theory, many theorists tend to believe that clients who obtain insight into themselves will be better adjusted. While many behavioral schools of thought may not subscribe to this, most therapists in their individual practice use insight either as a process of therapy or as an end product or goal.

We need to realize that insight is not highly valued by many culturally diverse clients. There are major class differences as well. People from lower socioeconomic classes frequently do not perceive insight as appropriate to their life situations and circumstances. Their concern may revolve around questions such as "Where do I find a job?" "How do I feed my family?" and "How can I afford to take my sick daughter to a doctor?" When survival on a day-to-day basis is important, it seems inappropriate for the therapist to use insightful processes. After all, insight assumes that one has time to sit back, reflect, and contemplate motivations and behavior. For the individual who is concerned about making it through each day, this orientation proves counterproductive.

Likewise, many cultural groups do not value insight. In traditional Chinese society, psychology has little relevance. It must be noted, however, that a client who does not seem to work well in an insight approach may not be lacking in insight or lacking in psychological-mindedness. A person who does not value insight is not necessarily one who is incapable of insight. Thus, several major factors tend to affect insight.

First, many cultural groups do not value this method of self-exploration. It is interesting to note that many Asian elders believe that thinking too much about something can cause problems. In a study of the Chinese in San Francisco's Chinatown, Lum (1982) found that many believe the road to mental health was to "avoid morbid thoughts." Advice from Asian elders to their children when they encountered feelings of frustration, anger, depression, or anxiety was simply, "Don't think about it." Indeed, it is often believed that the reason why one experiences anger or depression is precisely that one is thinking about it *too much!* The traditional Asian way of handling these affective elements is to "keep busy and don't think about it." Granted, it is more complex than this, because in traditional Asian families the reason why self-exploration is discouraged is precisely because it is an individual approach. "Think about the family and not about yourself" is advice given to many Asians as a way of dealing with negative affective elements. This is totally contradictory to Western notions of mental health, namely, that it is best to get things out in the open in order to deal with them.

Second, many racial/ethnic minority psychologists have felt that insight is a value in itself. For example, it was generally thought that insight led to behavior change. This was the old psychoanalytic assumption that when people understood their conflicts and underlying dynamics, the symptoms or behavior would change or disappear. The behavioral schools of thought have since disproved this one-to-one connection. While insight does lead to behavior change in some situations, it does not always seem to do so. Indeed, behavioral therapies have shown that changing the behavior first may lead to insight (cognitive restructuring and understanding) instead of vice-versa. As an example, one of the authors once had considerable difficulties and apprehensions about asking members of the opposite sex out on social occasions.

He would find it highly anxiety-provoking to call a female friend on the phone and ask her out for a date. This bothered him so much that he sought counseling and was able to understand the basis of his anxieties. Briefly, it boiled down to the fact that he feared rejection and that the rejection, if it came, was always in some sense correlated with his own concept of masculinity. This insight made the author feel much better but did not ever help him pick up the phone to ask a female friend out on a date! Of course, one can claim that the author did not achieve "true insight." We would then ask the question, "When does a person have insight?" We submit that the only answer, which is a highly value-based one, is that a client has insight when the therapist says that person has insight. This varies from therapist to therapist and from theory to theory.

Self-Disclosure (Openness and Intimacy)
Most forms of counseling and psychotherapy tend to value one's ability to self-disclose and to talk about the most intimate aspects of one's life. Indeed, self-disclosure has often been discussed as a primary characteristic of the healthy personality. The converse of this is that people who do not self-disclose readily in counseling and psychotherapy are seen as possessing negative traits such as being guarded, mistrustful, or paranoid. There are two difficulties in this orientation toward self-disclosure. One of these is cultural, and the other is sociopolitical.

First, intimate revelations of personal or social problems may not be acceptable because such difficulties reflect not only on the individual but also on the whole family. Thus, the family may exert strong pressures on the Asian American client not to reveal personal matters to strangers or outsiders. Similar conflicts have been reported for Hispanics (Leong, Wagner, & Tata, 1995; Paniagua, 1998) and for American Indian clients (Herring, 1999; LaFromboise, 1998). A therapist who works with a client from a minority background may erroneously conclude that the person is repressed, inhibited, shy, or passive. Note that all these terms are seen as undesirable by Western standards.

Related to this example is many health practitioners' belief in the desirability of self-disclosure. Self-disclosure refers to the client's willingness to tell the therapist what he or she feels, believes, or thinks. Jourard (1964) suggests that mental health is related to one's openness in disclosing. While this may be true, the parameters need clarification. Chapter 2 used as an example the paranorm of Grier and Cobbs (1968). People of African descent are especially reluctant to disclose to Caucasian counselors because of hardships that they have experienced via racism (Parham et al., 1999; Ridley, 1995). African Americans initially perceive a White therapist more often as an agent of society who may use information against them than as a person of goodwill. From the African American perspective, uncritical self-disclosure to others is not healthy.

The actual structure of the therapy situation may also work against intimate revelations. Among many American Indians and Hispanics, intimate aspects of life are shared only with close friends. Relative to White middle-class standards, deep friendships are developed only after prolonged contacts. Once friendships are formed, they tend to be lifelong in nature. In contrast, White Americans form relationships quickly, but the relationships do not necessarily persist over long periods of time. Counseling and therapy seem also to reflect these values. Clients talk about the most intimate aspects of their lives with a relative stranger once a week for a 50-minute session. To many culturally different groups who stress friendship as a precondition to self-disclosure, the counseling process seems utterly inappropriate and absurd. After all, how is it possible to develop a friendship with brief contacts once a week?

Scientific Empiricism

Counseling and psychotherapy in Western culture and society have been described as being highly linear, analytic, and verbal in their attempt to mimic the physical sciences. As indicated by Table 4.1, Western society tends to emphasize the so-called scientific method, which involves objective, rational, linear thinking. Likewise, we often see descriptions of the therapist as being objective, neutral, rational, and logical in thinking (Highlen, 1994; Katz, 1985; Pedersen, 1988). The therapist relies heavily on the use of linear problem solving as well as on quantitative evaluation that includes psychodiagnostic tests, intelligence tests, personality inventories, and so forth. This cause-effect orientation emphasizes left-brain functioning. That is, theories of counseling and therapy are distinctly analytical, rational, and verbal, and they strongly stress the discovery of cause-effect relationships.

The emphasis on symbolic logic contrasts markedly with the philosophies of many cultures that value a more nonlinear, holistic, and harmonious approach to the world (D. W. Sue & Constantine, in press). For example, American Indian worldviews emphasize the harmonious aspects of the world, intuitive functioning, and a holistic approach—a world view characterized by right-brain activities (Ornstein, 1972), minimizing analytical and reductionistic inquiries. Thus, when American Indians undergo therapy, the analytic approach may violate their basic philosophy of life.

It appears that the most dominant way of asking and answering questions about the human condition in U.S. society tends to be the scientific method. The epitome of this approach is the so-called experiment. In graduate schools we are often told that only in the experiment can we impute a cause-effect relationship. By identifying the independent and dependent variables and controlling for extraneous variables, we are able to test a cause-effect hypothesis. While correlation studies, historical research, and and other approaches may be of benefit, we are told that the experiment represents the epitome of "our science" (Seligman & Csikszentmihalyi, 2001). As indicated, other cultures may value different ways of asking and answering questions about the human condition.

Distinctions between Mental and Physical Functioning

Many American Indians, Asian Americans, Blacks, and Hispanics hold different concepts of what constitutes mental health, mental illness, and adjustment. Among the Chinese, the concept of mental health or psychological well-being is not understood in the same way as it is in the Western context. Latino/Hispanic Americans do not make the same Western distinction between mental and physical health as do their White counterparts (Rivera, 1988). Thus, nonphysical health problems are most likely to be referred to a physician, priest, or minister. Culturally diverse clients operating under this orientation may enter therapy expecting therapists to treat them in the same manner that doctors or priests do. Immediate solutions and concrete tangible forms of treatment (advice, confession, consolation, and medication) are expected. For example, both authors (currently psychologists) remember the period in their lives when they entered the field of psychology. Their parents asked one question that drove home the differences in worldview that various cultural groups have concerning this concept of psychology, psychological well-being, psychological adjustment, and mental health and mental illness: "How can you be called a doctor when you're not really a doctor?" This question indicates that our parents considered medical doctors (MDs), but not doctors of philosophy (PhDs), to be doctors. When our work with clients was explained as "sitting down and talking with individuals and helping them explore their thoughts and feelings," our father's response was, "Humph, they pay you for that?" Again, it was obvious that this was not a legitimate form of work to them. After all, avoidance of morbid thoughts is the way to deal with psychological problems, not sitting down and talking about them.

Ambiguity

The ambiguous and unstructured aspect of the therapy situation may create discomfort in clients of color. The culturally different may not be familiar with therapy and may perceive it as an unknown and mystifying process. Some groups, such as Hispanics, may have been reared in an environment that actively structures social relationships and patterns of interaction. Anxiety and confusion may be the outcome in an unstructured counseling setting. The following example of a Hispanic undergoing vocational counseling illustrates this confusion:

> *Maria W. was quite uncomfortable and anxious during the first interview dealing with vocational counseling. This anxiety seemed to be related more to the*

ambiguity of the situation than to anything else. Maria appeared confused about the direction of the counselor's comments and questions. At this point, the counselor felt an explanation of vocational counseling might facilitate the process.

COUNSELOR: *Let me take some time to explain what we do in vocational counseling. Vocational counseling is an attempt to understand the whole person. Therefore, we are interested in your likes and dislikes, what you do well, your skills, and what they mean with respect to jobs and vocations. The first interview is usually an attempt to get to know you—especially your past experiences and reactions to different courses you've taken, jobs you've worked at, and so forth. Especially important are your goals and plans. If testing seems indicated, as in your case, you'll be asked to complete some tests. After testing we'll sit down and talk about what they mean. When we arrive at possible vocations, we'll use the vocational library and find out what these jobs require in terms of background, training, and so forth.*

CLIENT: *Oh! I see. . . .*

COUNSELOR: *That's why we've been talking about your high school experiences. Sometimes the hopes and dreams can tell us much about your interests.*

After this explanation, Maria participated much more in the interviews.

Patterns of Communication

The cultural upbringing of many minorities dictates different patterns of communication that may place them at a disadvantage in therapy. Counseling, for example, initially demands that communication move from client to counselor. The client is expected to take the major responsibility for initiating conversation in the session, while the counselor plays a less active role.

However, American Indians, Asian Americans, and Hispanics function under different cultural imperatives, which may make this difficult. These three groups may have been reared to respect elders and authority figures and not to speak until spoken to. Clearly defined roles of dominance and deference are established in the traditional family. Evidence indicates that Asians associate mental health with exercising will power, avoiding unpleasant thoughts, and occupying one's mind with positive thoughts. Therapy is seen as an authoritative process in which a good therapist is more direct and active while portraying a father figure (Henkin, 1985; Mau & Jepson, 1988). A racial/ethnic minority client who is asked to initiate conversation may become uncomfortable and respond with only short phrases or statements. The therapist may be prone to interpret the behavior negatively, when in actuality it may be a sign of respect. We have much more to say about these communication style differences in the next chapter.

Class-Bound Values

As mentioned earlier, class values are important to consider in therapy because many racial/ethnic minority groups are disproportionately represented in the lower socioeconomic classes (Lewis et al., 1998). Mental health practices that emphasize assisting the client in self-direction through the presentation of the results of assessment instruments and self-exploration via verbal interactions between client and therapist are seen as meaningful and productive. However, the values underlying these activities are permeated by middle-class values that do not suffice for those living in poverty. We have already seen how this operates with respect to language. As early as the 1960s, Bernstein (1964) investigated the suitability of English for the lower-class poor in psychotherapy and has concluded that it works to the detriment of those individuals.

For the therapist who generally comes from a middle- to upper-class background, it is often difficult to relate to the circumstances and hardships affecting the client who lives in poverty. The phenomenon of poverty and its effects on individuals and institutions can be devastating. The individual's life is characterized by low wages, unemployment, underemployment, little property ownership, no savings, and lack of food reserves. Meeting even the most basic needs of hunger and shelter is in constant jeopardy. Pawning personal possessions and borrowing money at exorbitant interest rates only leads to greater debt. Feelings of helplessness, dependence, and inferiority develop easily under these circumstances. Therapists may unwittingly attribute attitudes that result from physical and environmental adversity to the cultural or individual traits of the person.

For example, note the clinical description of a 12-year-old child written by a school counselor:

> *Jimmy Jones is a 12-year-old Black male student who was referred by Mrs. Peterson because of apathy, indifference, and inattentiveness to classroom activities. Other teachers have also reported that Jimmy does not pay attention, daydreams often, and frequently falls asleep during class. There is a strong possibility that Jimmy is harboring repressed rage that needs to be ventilated and dealt with. His inability to directly express his anger had led him to adopt passive aggressive means of expressing hostility (i.e., inattentiveness, daydreaming, falling asleep). It is recommended that Jimmy be seen for intensive counseling to discover the basis of the anger.*

After six months of counseling, the counselor finally realized the basis of Jimmy's problems. He came from a home life of extreme poverty, where hunger, lack of sleep, and overcrowding served to diminish severely his energy level and motivation. The fatigue, passivity, and fatalism evidenced by Jimmy were more a result of poverty than of some innate trait.

Likewise, poverty may bring many parents to encourage children to seek employment at an early age. Delivering groceries, shining shoes, and hustling other sources of income may sap the energy of the schoolchild, leading to truancy and poor performance. Teachers and counselors may view such students as unmotivated and potential juvenile delinquents.

Research concerning the inferior and biased quality of treatment to lower-class clients is historically legend (Atkinson, Morten, et al., 1998; Pavkov et al., 1989; Rouse, Carter, & Rodriguez-Andrew, 1995). In the area of diagnosis, it has been found that the attribution of mental illness was more likely to occur when the person's history suggested a lower rather than higher socioeconomic class origin. Many studies seem to demonstrate that clinicians given identical test protocols tend to make more negative prognostic statements and judgments of greater maladjustment when the individual was said to come from a lower- rather than a middle-class background.

In the area of treatment, Garfield, Weiss, and Pollock (1973) gave counselors identical descriptions (except for social class) of a 9-year-old boy who engaged in maladaptive classroom behavior. When the boy was assigned upper-class status, more counselors expressed a willingness to become ego-involved with the student than when lower-class status was assigned. Likewise, Habemann and Thiry (1970) found that doctoral-degree candidates in counseling and guidance programmed students from low socioeconomic backgrounds into a noncollege-bound track more frequently than into a college-preparation one.

In an extensive historic research of services delivered to minorities and low socioeconomic clients, Lorion (1973) found that psychiatrists refer to therapy those persons who are most like themselves: White rather than non-White and from upper socioeconomic status. Lorion (1974) pointed out that the expectations of lower-class clients are often different from those of psychotherapists. For example, lower-class clients who are concerned with survival or making it through on a day-to-day basis expect advice and suggestions from the counselor. Appointments made weeks in advance with short, weekly, 50-minute contacts are not consistent with the need to seek immediate solutions. Additionally, many lower-class people, through multiple experiences with public agencies, operate under what is called "minority standard time" (Schindler-Rainman, 1967). This is the tendency of poor people to have a low regard for punctuality. Poor people have learned that endless waits are associated with medical clinics, police stations, and governmental agencies. One usually waits hours for a 10- to 15-minute appointment. Arriving promptly does little good and can be a waste of valuable time. Therapists, however, rarely understand this aspect of life and are prone to see this as a sign of indifference or hostility.

People from a lower socioeconomic status may also view insight and attempts to discover underlying intraphysic problems as inappropriate. Many lower-class clients expect to receive advice or some form of concrete tangible treatment. When the therapist attempts to explore personality dynamics or to take a historical approach to the problem, the client often becomes confused, alienated, and frustrated. Abad, Ramos, and Boyce (1974) used the case of Puerto Ricans to illustrate this point. The authors felt that the passive psychiatric approach that requires the client to talk about problems introspectively and to take initiative and responsibility for decision making is not what is expected by the Puerto Rican client. Several writers (Menacker, 1971; Schindler-Rainman, 1967) have taken the position that poor people are best motivated by rewards that are immediate and concrete. A harsh environment, where the future is uncertain and immediate needs must be met, makes long-range planning of little value. Many clients of lower socioeconomic status are unable to relate to the future orientation of therapy. To be able to sit and talk about things is perceived as a luxury of the middle and upper classes.

Because of the lower-class client's environment and past inexperience with therapy, the expectations of the minority individual may be quite different, or even negative. The client's unfamiliarity with the therapy process may hinder its success and cause the therapist to blame the client for the failure. Thus, the minority client may be perceived as hostile and resistant. The results of this interaction may be a premature termination of therapy. Considerable evidence exists that clients from upper socioeconomic backgrounds have significantly more exploratory interviews with their therapists, and that middle-class patients tend to remain in treatment longer than lower-class patients (Gottesfeld, 1995; Leong, Wagner, & Kim, 1995; Neighbors, Caldwell, Thompson, & Jackson, 1994). Furthermore, the now-classic study of Hollingstead and Redlich (1968) found that lower-class patients tend to have fewer ego-involving relationships and less intensive therapeutic relationships than do members of higher socioeconomic classes.

Poverty undoubtedly contributes to the mental health problems among racial/ethnic minority groups, and social class determines the type of treatment a minority client is likely to receive. In addition, as Atkinson, Morten, et al. (1998, p. 64) conclude,

> *ethnic minorities are less likely to earn incomes sufficient to pay for mental health treatment, less likely to have insurance, and more likely to qualify for public assistance than European Americans. Thus, ethnic minorities often have to rely on public (government-sponsored) or nonprofit mental health services to obtain help with their psychological problems.*

Language Barriers

Western society is definitely monolingual. Use of standard English to communicate may unfairly discriminate against those from a bilingual or lower-class background. This is seen not only in our educational system, but in the therapy relationship as well. The bilingual background of many Asian Americans, Latino/Hispanic Americans, and American Indians may lead to much misunderstanding. This is true even if a minority group member cannot speak his or her own native tongue. Early language studies (M. E. Smith, 1957; M. E. Smith & Kasdon, 1961) indicate that simply coming from a background where one or both of parents have spoken their native tongue can impair proper acquisition of English.

Even African Americans who come from a different cultural environment may use words and phrases (Black Language, or Ebonics) not entirely understandable to the therapist. While considerable criticism was directed toward the Oakland Unified School District with their short-lived attempt to recognize Ebonics in 1996, the reality is that such a form of communication does exist in many African American communities. In therapy, however, African American clients are expected to communicate their feelings and thoughts to therapists in standard English. For some African Americans, this is a difficult task, since the use of nonstandard English is their norm. Black language code involves a great deal of implicitness in communication, such as shorter sentences and less grammatical elaboration (but greater reliance on nonverbal cues). On the other hand, the language code of the middle and upper classes is much more elaborate, relies less on nonverbal cues, and entails greater knowledge of grammar and syntax.

Romero (1985) indicated that counseling psychologists are finding that they must interact with consumers who may have English as a second language, or who may not speak English at all. The lack of bilingual therapists and the requirement that the culturally different client communicate in English may limit the person's ability to progress in counseling and therapy. If bilingual individuals do not use their native tongue in therapy, many aspects of their emotional experience may not be available for treatment. For example, because English may not be their primary language, they may have difficulty using the wide complexity of language to describe their particular thoughts, feelings, and unique situations. Clients who are limited in English tend to feel like they are speaking as a child and choosing simple words to explain complex thoughts and feelings. If they were able to use their native tongue, they would easily explain themselves without the huge loss of emotional complexity and experience.

Understanding Black communication styles and patterns is indispensable for therapists working in the African American community. Failure to understand imagery, analogies, and nuances of cultural sayings may render the therapist ineffective in establishing relationships and building credibility.

In therapy, heavy reliance is placed on verbal interaction to build rapport. The presupposition is that participants in a therapeutic dialogue are capable of understanding each other. Therapists often fail to understand an African American client's language and its nuances for rapport building. Furthermore, those who have not been given the same educational or economic opportunities may lack the prerequisite verbal skills to benefit from talk therapy.

A minority client's brief, different, or "poor" verbal responses may lead many therapists to impute inaccurate characteristics or motives. A minority client may be seen as uncooperative, sullen, negative, nonverbal, or repressed on the basis of language expression alone.

Since Euro-American society places such a high premium on one's use of English, it is a short step to conclude that minorities are inferior, lack awareness, or lack conceptual thinking powers. Such misinterpretation can also be seen in the use and interpretation of psychological tests. So-called IQ and achievement tests are especially notorious for their language bias.

Generalizations and Stereotypes: Some Cautions

White cultural values are reflected in the generic characteristics of counseling (Table 4.1; see also Table 9.1). These characteristics are summarized and can be compared with the values of four racial/ethnic minority groups: American Indians, Asian Americans, Blacks, and Hispanics (see Table 4.2). Although it is critical for therapists to have a basic understanding of the generic characteristics of counseling and psychotherapy and the culture-specific life values of different groups, overgeneralizing and stereotyping are ever-present dangers. For example, the listing of racial/ethnic minority group variables does not indicate that all persons coming from the same minority group will share all or even some of these traits. Furthermore, emerging trends such as short-term and crisis intervention approaches and other less verbally oriented techniques differ from the generic traits listed. Yet it is highly improbable that any of us can enter a situation or encounter people without forming impressions consistent with our own experiences and values. Whether a client is dressed neatly in a suit or wears blue jeans, is a man or a woman, or is of a different race will likely affect our assumptions.

First impressions will be formed that fit our own interpretations and generalizations of human behavior. Generalizations are necessary for us; without them, we would become inefficient creatures. However, they are guidelines for our behaviors, to be tentatively applied in new situations, and they should be open to change and challenge. It is exactly at this stage that generalizations remain generalizations or become stereotypes. *Stereotypes* may be defined as rigid preconceptions we hold about *all* people who are members of a particular group, whether it be defined along racial, religious, sexual, or other lines. The belief in a perceived characteristic of the group is applied to all members without regard for individual variations. The danger of stereotypes is that they are impervious to logic or experience. All incoming information is distorted to fit our preconceived notions. For example, people who are strongly anti-Semitic will accuse Jews of being stingy and miserly and then, in the same breath, accuse them of flaunting their wealth by conspicuous spending.

The information in Tables 4.1, 4.2, and 9.1 should act as guidelines rather than absolutes. These generalizations should serve as the background from which the "figure" emerges. For example, belonging to a particular group may mean sharing common values and experiences. Individuals within a group, however, also differ. The background offers a contrast for us to see individual differences more clearly. It should not submerge but rather increase the visibility of the figure. This is the figure-ground relationship that should aid us in recognizing the uniqueness of people more readily.

Implications for Clinical Practice

In general, it appears that Western forms of healing involve processes that may prove inappropriate and antagonistic to many culturally diverse groups. The mental health professional must be cognizant of the culture-bound, class-bound, and linguistic barriers that might place minority clients at a disadvantage. Some suggestions to the clinician involve the following:

1. Become cognizant of the generic characteristics of counseling and psychotherapy. It is clear that mental health services arise from a particular cultural context and are imbued with assumptions and values that may not be applicable to all groups.

2. Know that we are increasingly becoming a multilingual nation and that the linguistic demands of clinical work may place minority populations at a disadvantage. Be sensitive and ready to provide or advocate for multilingual services.

3. Consider the need to provide community counseling services that reach out to the minority population. The traditional one-to-one, in-the-office delivery of services must be supplemented by those that are more action oriented. In other words, effective multicultural counseling must involve roles and activities in the natural environment of the clients

(schools, churches, neighborhoods, playgrounds, etc.) rather than just in mental health clinics.

4. Realize that the problems and concerns of many minority groups are related to systemic and external forces rather than internal psychological problems. Poverty, discrimination, prejudice, immigration stress, and so forth indicate that counselors might be most effective in aiding clients to deal with these forces rather than self-exploration and insight approaches.

5. While most theories of counseling and psychotherapy prescribe the types of actions and roles played by a therapist, these may prove minimally helpful to minority clients. The more passive approach must be expanded to include roles and behaviors that are more action oriented and educational in nature. As a helping professional, you may need to expand your repertoire of helping responses.

6. Be careful not to overgeneralize or stereotype. Knowing general group characteristics and guidelines is different from rigidly holding on to preconceived notions. In other words, knowing that certain groups such as African Americans and Asian Americans may share common values and worldviews does not mean that all Asian Americans, for example, are the same. Nor does our discussion imply that Euro-American approaches to therapy are completely inapplicable to minority groups.

7. Try not to buy into the idea that clinical work is somehow superior to other forms of helping. We are aware that many of you are attracted to the conventional psychotherapist role, that your professors may unintentionally give you the impression that it is the epitome of the therapeutic relationship, or that it represents a higher and more sophisticated form of helping. Such an attitude of arrogance not only may be detrimental to those being served but also limits your ability to work with a culturally diverse population.

Culturally Appropriate Intervention Strategies

5

Dr. Paul S., a Black professor in the doctoral program, was addressing the entire graduate faculty about the need for a multicultural perspective in the department and the need to hire a Latina psychologist. Several of his White colleagues raised objections to the inclusion of more minority curricula in the program because it would either (a) raise the number of units students would have to take to graduate or (b) require the dropping of a course to keep units manageable. At one point, Dr. S. rose from his seat, leaned forward, made eye contact with the most vocal objector, and, raising his voice, asked, "What would be wrong in doing that?" The question brought about the following exchange:

WHITE MALE PROFESSOR: The question is not whether it's right or wrong. We need to look at your request from a broader perspective. For example, how will it affect our curriculum? Is your request educationally sound? What external constraints do we have in our ability to hire new faculty? Even if university funds are available, would it be fair to limit it to a Hispanic female? Shouldn't we be hiring the most qualified applicant rather than limiting it to a particular race or sex?

DR. S. [RAISING HIS VOICE AND POUNDING THE TABLE TO PUNCTUATE HIS COMMENTS]: I've heard those excuses for years and that's just what they are—a crock of you-know-what! This faculty doesn't sound very committed to cultural diversity at all!

SECOND WHITE MALE PROFESSOR: Paul, calm down! Don't let your emotions carry you away. Let's address these issues in a rational manner.

DR. S.: What do you mean? I'm not rational? That pisses me off! All I ever hear is we can't do this, or we can't do that! I want to know where you all are coming from. Are we going to do anything about cultural diversity? [Several faculty members on either side of Dr. S. have shifted away from him. At this point, Dr. S. turns to one of them and speaks.] *Don't worry, I'm not going to hit you!*

> WHITE MALE PROFESSOR: *I don't believe we should discuss this matter further, until we can control our feelings. I'm not going to sit here and be the object of anger and insults.*
>
> DR. S.: *Anger? What are you talking about? Just because I feel strongly about my convictions, you think I'm angry? All I'm asking for is you to tell me how you stand on the issues.*
>
> WHITE MALE PROFESSOR: *I already have.*
>
> DR. S.: *No you haven't! You've just given me a bunch of intellectual bullshit. Where do you stand?*
>
> THIRD WHITE MALE PROFESSOR: *Mr. Chairman, I move we table this discussion.*

The preceding example of a Black-White interaction, witnessed by one of the authors, illustrates some very powerful and important features about cultural communication styles. While we are concerned about the possibility of overgeneralization, this verbal/nonverbal exchange between an African American faculty member and several White colleagues has occurred in sufficient frequency to suggest that many Blacks and Whites have different styles of communication. Let us briefly analyze the example.

First, it is quite obvious from this exchange that the White professor perceived Dr. S. to be angry, out of control, and irrational. How did he arrive at that conclusion? No doubt part of it may have been the language used, but equally important were the nonverbals (raising of the voice, pounding on the table, prolonged eye contact, etc.). In a faculty meeting where White males predominate, the mode of acceptable communication is considered to be low-key, dispassionate, impersonal, and issue-oriented. However, many African Americans not only define the issues differently, but also process them in a manner that is misunderstood by many Whites. African American styles tend to be high-key, animated, confrontational, and interpersonal. The differences in styles of communication are not limited solely to the academic environment.

For example, in the political arena, noticeable differences can be observed between how Black and White politicians debate and communicate. When the Reverend Jesse Jackson gave the keynote address many years ago at a Democratic convention, many supporters characterized his speech as "moving," "coming from the heart," and indicative of his "sincerity and honesty." Yet many television commentators (mainly White newsmen) made observations that Jackson's address was like a "Baptist revival meeting," "pep rally," more "style than substance." They seemed to discredit his message because it was "too emotional."

These characterizations reveal a value judgment and possible misinterpretations occurring as a result of differing communication styles. Often, the presence of affect in a debate is equated with emotion (anger and hostility) and is seen as counter to reason. Statements that Dr. S. should calm down, not be irrational, and address the issues in an objective fashion are reflective of such an interpretation. Likewise, many African Americans may perceive White communication styles in a negative manner. In his attempt to find out where the White male professor was coming from, Dr. S. was disinclined to believe that his colleague does not have an opinion on the matter. Dealing with the issues on an intellectual level (even if the issues raised are legitimate) may be perceived as *fronting*, a Black concept used to denote a person who is purposely concealing how he or she honestly feels or believes.

Second, it is very possible that differences in communication style may be triggered by certain preconceived notions, stereotypes, or beliefs we may have about various minority groups. As we have seen, one of the most dominant White stereotypes is that of the angry, hostile Black male who is prone to violence. African Americans are very aware of these stereotypes, as in the case of Dr. S.'s statement to one White colleague, "Don't worry, I'm not going to hit you!"

Examples of this kind of Black-White interaction and misinterpretation are played out in countless everyday situations. They occur in sufficient frequency and consistency to raise the question, "Do African Americans and Euro-Americans differ not only in the content of a debate, but also in the style by which the disagreement is to be resolved?" Likewise, do different racial/ethnic groups differ in their communication styles? If they do, might not they create misunderstandings and misinterpretations of one another's behavior? What implications do communication styles have for helping styles or therapeutic styles? Do some therapy styles seem more appropriate and effective in working with certain racial/ethnic group members?

Communication Styles

In Chapter 4 we defined therapy as a process of interpersonal interaction, communication, and social influence. For effective therapy to occur, both the therapist and client must be able to send and receive both verbal and non-verbal messages accurately and appropriately. In other words, therapy is a form of communication. It requires that the therapist not only *send* messages (make himself or herself understood) but also *receive* messages (attend to what is going on with the client). The definition for effective therapy also includes *verbal* (content of what is said) and *nonverbal* (how something is said) elements. Furthermore, most therapists seem more concerned with the *accuracy* of communication (let's get to the heart of the matter) than with whether the communication is *appropriate*. As indicated in the last chapter, traditional Asian culture highly prizes a person's subtlety and indirectness in communication. The direct and confrontational techniques in therapy may be perceived by traditional Asian or Native American clients as lacking in respect for the client, a crude and rude form of communication, and a reflection of insensitivity. In most cases, therapists have been trained to tune in to the content of what is said rather than how something is said.

When we refer to communication style, we are addressing those factors that go beyond the content of what is said. Some communication specialists believe that only 30% to 40% of what is communicated conversationally is verbal (Condon & Yousef, 1975; Ramsey & Birk, 1983; Singelis, 1994). What people say and do is usually qualified by other things that they say and do. A gesture, tone, inflection, posture, or degree of eye contact may enhance or negate the content of a message. Communication styles have a tremendous impact on our face-to-face encounters with others. Whether our conversation proceeds with fits or starts, whether we interrupt one another continually or proceed smoothly, the topics we prefer to discuss or avoid, the depth of our involvement, the forms of interaction (ritual, repartee, argumentative, persuasive, etc.), and the channel we use to communicate (verbal-nonverbal vs. nonverbal-verbal) are all aspects of communication style (Douglis, 1987; Wolfgang, 1985). Some refer to these factors as the *social rhythms* that underlie all our speech and actions. Communication styles are strongly correlated with race, culture, and ethnicity. Gender has also been found to be a powerful determinant of communication style (J. C. Pearson, 1985; Robinson & Howard-Hamilton, 2000).

Reared in a Euro-American middle-class society, mental health professionals may assume that certain behaviors or rules of speaking are universal and possess the same meaning. This may create major problems for therapists and other culturally distinct clients. Since differences in communication style are most strongly manifested in nonverbal communication, this chapter concentrates on those aspects of communication that transcend the written or spoken word. First, we explore how race/culture may influence several areas of nonverbal behavior: (a) proxemics, (b) kinesics, (c) paralanguage, and (d) high-low context communication. Second, we briefly discuss the function and importance of nonverbal behavior as it relates to stereotypes and preconceived notions that we may have of diverse groups. Last, we propose a basic thesis that various racial minorities such as Asian Americans, American Indians, African Americans, and Latino/Hispanic Americans possess unique communication styles that may have major implications for mental health practice. These implications suggest that certain therapeutic approaches (person-centered, existential, analytic, cognitive, behavioral, etc.) may be more appropriate helping strategies for certain ethnic groups.

Nonverbal Communication

Although language, class, and cultural factors all interact to create problems in communication between the minority client and therapist, an oft-neglected area is nonverbal behavior (Singelis, 1994; Wolfgang, 1985). What people say can be either enhanced or negated by their nonverbals. When a man raises his voice, tightens his facial muscles, pounds the table violently, and proclaims, "Goddamn it, I'm not angry!" he is clearly contradicting the content of the communication. If we all share the same cultural and social upbringing, we may all arrive at the same conclusion. Interpreting nonverbals, however, is difficult for several reasons. First, the same nonverbal behavior on the part of an American Indian client may mean something quite different than if it were made by a White person. Second, nonverbals often occur outside our levels of awareness. As a result, it is important that therapists begin the process of recognizing nonverbal communications and their possible cultural meanings. It is important to note that our discussion of nonverbal codes will not include all the possible nonverbal cues. Some of the areas excluded are time considerations, olfaction (taste and smell), tactile cues, and artifactual communication (clothing, hairstyle, display of material things, etc.; for more on these areas, see DePaulo, 1992; Douglis, 1987; R. E. Pearson, 1985; Ramsey & Birk, 1983; Robinson & Howard-Hamilton, 2000).

Proxemics
The study of *proxemics* refers to perception and use of personal and interpersonal space. Clear norms exist concerning the use of physical distance in social interactions. Hall (1969) identified four interpersonal distance zones characteristic of U.S. culture: intimate, from contact to 18 in; personal, from 1.5 ft to 4 ft; social, from 4 ft to 12 ft; and public (lectures and speeches), greater than 12 ft.

In this society, individuals seem to grow more uncomfortable when others stand too close rather than too far away (Goldman, 1980). These feelings and reactions associated with a violation of personal space may range from flight, withdrawal, anger, and conflict (J. C. Pearson, 1985). On the other hand, we tend to allow closer proximity or to move closer to people whom we like or feel interpersonal attraction toward. Some evidence exists that personal space can be reframed in terms of dominance and status. Those with greater status, prestige, and power may occupy more space (larger homes, cars, or offices). However, different cultures dictate different distances in personal space. For Latin Americans, Africans, Black Americans, Indonesians, Arabs, South Americans, and French, conversing with a person dictates a much closer stance than is normally comfortable for Euro-Americans (J. V. Jensen, 1985; Nydell, 1996). A Latin-American client's closeness may cause the therapist to back away. The client may interpret the therapist's behavior as indicative of aloofness, coldness, or a desire not to communicate. In some cross-cultural encounters, it may even be perceived as a sign of haughtiness and superiority. On the other hand, the therapist may misinterpret the client's behavior as an attempt to become inappropriately intimate, a sign of pushiness or aggressiveness. Both the therapist and the culturally different client may benefit from understanding that their reactions and behaviors are attempts to create the spatial dimension to which they are culturally conditioned.

Research on proxemics leads to the inevitable conclusion that conversational distances are a function of the racial and cultural background of the conversant (Mindess, 1999; Susman & Rosenfeld, 1982; Wolfgang, 1985). The factor of personal space has major implications for how furniture is arranged, where the seats are located, where you seat the client, and how far you sit from him or her (LaBarre, 1985). Latin Americans, for example, may not feel comfortable with a desk between them and the person they are speaking to. Euro-Americans, however, like to keep a desk between themselves and others. Some Eskimos may actually prefer to sit side by side rather than across from one another when talking about intimate aspects of their lives.

Kinesics

While proxemics refers to personal space, *kinesics* is the term used to refer to bodily movements. It includes such things as facial expression, posture, characteristics of movement, gestures, and eye contact. Again, kinesics appears to be culturally conditioned (Mindess, 1999).

Much of our counseling assessments are based upon expressions on people's faces (J. C. Pearson, 1985). We assume that facial cues express emotions and demonstrate the degree of responsiveness or involvement of the individual.

For example, smiling is a type of expression in our society that is believed to indicate liking or positive affect. People attribute greater positive characteristics to others who smile; they are intelligent, have a good personality, and are pleasant (Singelis, 1994). However, when Japanese smile and laugh, it does not necessarily mean happiness but may convey other meanings (embarrassment, discomfort, shyness, etc.). Such nonverbal misinterpretations also fueled many of the conflicts in Los Angeles directly after the Rodney King verdict when many African Americans and Korean grocery store owners became at odds with one another. African Americans confronted their Korean American counterparts about exploitation of Black neighborhoods. During one particularly heated exchange, African Americans became incensed when many Korean American store owners had a constant "smile" on their faces. They interpreted the facial expression as arrogance, taunting, and lack of compassion for the concerns of Blacks. Little did they realize that a smile in this situation more rightly indicated extreme embarrassment and apprehension.

On the other hand, some Asians believe that smiling may suggest weakness. Among some Japanese and Chinese, restraint of strong feelings (anger, irritation, sadness, and love or happiness) is considered to be a sign of maturity and wisdom. Children learn that outward emotional expressions (facial expressions, body movements, and verbal content) are discouraged except for extreme situations. Unenlightened therapists may assume that their Asian American client is lacking in feelings or out of touch with them. More likely, the lack of facial expressions may be the basis of stereotypes such as the statement that Asians are "inscrutable," "sneaky," "deceptive," and "backstabbing."

A number of gestures and bodily movements have been found to have different meanings when the cultural context is considered (LaBarre, 1985). In the Sung Dynasty in China, sticking out the tongue was a gesture of mock terror and meant as ridicule; to the Ovimbundu of Africa, it means "you're a fool" (when coupled with bending the head forward); a protruding tongue in the Mayan statues of the gods signifies wisdom; and in our own culture, it is generally considered to be a juvenile quasi-obscene gesture of defiance, mockery, or contempt.

Head movements also have different meanings (Eakins & Eakins, 1985; Jensen, 1985). An educated Englishman may consider the lifting of the chin when conversing as a poised and polite gesture, but to Euro-Americans it may connote snobbery and arrogance ("turning up one's nose"). While we shake our head from side to side to indicate "no," Mayan tribe members say "no" by jerking the head to the right. In Sri Lanka, one signals agreement by moving the head from side to side like a metronome (Singelis, 1994).

Most Euro-Americans perceive squatting (often done by children) as improper and childish. In other parts of the world, people have learned to rest by taking a squatting position. On the other hand, when we put our feet up on a desk, it is believed to signify a relaxed and informal attitude. Yet, Latin Americans and Asians may perceive it as rudeness and arrogance, especially if the bottom of the feet is shown to them.

Shaking hands is another gesture that varies from culture to culture and may have strong cultural/historical significance. Latin Americans tend to shake hands more vigorously, frequently, and for a longer period of time. Interestingly, most cultures use the right hand when shaking. Since most of the population of the world is right-handed, this may not be surprising. However, some researchers believe that shaking with the right hand may be a symbolic act of peace, as in older times it was the right hand that generally held the weapons. In some Moslem and Asian countries, touching anyone with the left hand may be considered an obscenity (the left hand aids in the process of elimination and is "unclean," while the right one is used for the intake of food and is "clean"). Offering something with the left hand to a Moslem may be an insult of the most serious type.

Eye contact is, perhaps, the nonverbal behavior most likely to be addressed by mental health providers. It is not unusual for us to hear someone say, "Notice that the husband avoided eye contact with the wife," or "Notice how the client averted his eyes when. . . ." Behind these observations is the belief that eye contact or lack of eye contact has diagnostic significance. We would agree with that premise, but in most cases, therapists attribute negative traits to the avoidance of eye contact: shy, unassertive, sneaky, or depressed.

This lack of understanding has been played out in many different situations when Black-White interactions have occurred. In many cases, it is not necessary for Blacks to look at one another in the eye at all times to communicate (E. J. Smith, 1981). An African American may be actively involved in doing other things when engaged in a conversation. Many White therapists are prone to view the African American client as being sullen, resistant, or uncooperative. E. J. Smith (1981, p. 155) provides an excellent example of such a clash in communication styles:

> *For instance, one Black female student was sent to the office by her gymnasium teacher because the student was said to display insolent behavior. When the student was asked to give her version of the incident, she replied, "Mrs. X asked all of us to come over to the side of the pool so that she could show us how to do the backstroke. I went over with the rest of the girls. Then Mrs. X started yelling at me and said I wasn't paying attention to her because I wasn't looking directly at her. I told her I was paying attention to her (throughout the conversation, the student kept her head down, avoiding the principal's eyes), and then she said that she wanted me to face her and look her squarely in the eye like the rest of the girls [who were all White]. So I did. The next thing I knew she was telling me to get out of the pool, that she didn't like the way I was looking at her. So that's why I'm here."*

As this example illustrates, Black styles of communication may not only be different from their White counterparts, but also may lead to misinterpretations. Many Blacks do not nod their heads or say "uh huh" to indicate they are listening (E. T. Hall, 1976; Kochman, 1981; E. J. Smith, 1981). Going through the motions of looking at the person and nodding the head is not necessary for many Blacks to indicate that they are listening (E. T. Hall, 1974, 1976).

Statistics indicate that when White U.S. Americans listen to a speaker, they make eye contact with the speaker about 80% of the time. When speaking to others, however, they tend to look away (avoid eye contact) about 50% of the time. This is in marked contrast to many Black Americans, who make greater eye contact when speaking and make infrequent eye contact when listening!

Paralanguage

The term *paralanguage* is used to refer to other vocal cues that individuals use to communicate. For example, loudness of voice, pauses, silences, hesitations, rate, inflections, and the like all fall into this category. Paralanguage is very likely to be manifested forcefully in conversation conventions such as how we greet and address others and take turns in speaking. It can communicate a variety of different features about a person, such as age, gender, and emotional responses, as well as the race and sex of the speaker (Banks & Banks, 1993; Lass, Mertz, & Kimmel, 1978; Nydell, 1996).

There are complex rules regarding when to speak or yield to another person. For example, U.S. Americans frequently feel uncomfortable with a pause or silent stretch in the conversation, feeling obligated to fill it in with more talk. Silence is not always a sign for the listener to take up the conversation. While it may be viewed negatively by many, other cultures interpret the use of silence differently. The British and Arabs use silence for privacy, while the Russians, French, and Spanish read it as agreement among the parties (Hall, 1969, 1976). In Asian culture, silence is traditionally a sign of respect for elders. Furthermore, silence by many Chinese and Japanese is not a floor-yielding signal inviting others to pick up the conversation. Rather, it may indicate a desire to continue speaking after making a particular point. Often silence is a sign of politeness and respect rather than a lack of desire to continue speaking.

The amount of verbal expressiveness in the United States, relative to other cultures, is quite high. Most Euro-Americans encourage their children to enter freely into conversations, and teachers encourage students to ask many questions and state their thoughts and opinions. This has led many from other countries to observe that Euro-American youngsters are brash, immodest, rude, and disrespectful (Irvine & York, 1995; Jensen, 1985). Likewise, teachers of minority children may see reticence in speaking out as a sign of ignorance, lack of motivation, or ineffective teaching (Banks & Banks, 1993) when in reality the students may be showing proper respect (to ask questions is disrespectful because it implies that the teacher was unclear). American Indians, for example, have been taught that to speak out, ask questions, or even raise one's hand in class is immodest.

A mental health professional who is uncomfortable with silence or who misinterprets it may fill in the conversation and prevent the client from elaborating further. Even greater danger is to impute incorrect motives to the minority client's silence. One can readily see how therapy, which emphasizes talking, may place many minorities at a disadvantage.

Volume and intensity of speech in conversation are also influenced by cultural values. The overall loudness of speech displayed by many Euro-American visitors to foreign countries has earned them the reputation of being boisterous and shameless. In Asian countries, people tend to speak more softly and would interpret the loud volume of a U.S. visitor to be aggressiveness, loss of self-control, or anger. When compared to Arabs, however, people in the United States are soft-spoken. Many Arabs like to be bathed in sound, and the volumes of their radios, phonographs, and televisions are quite loud. In some countries where such entertainment units are not plentiful, it is considered a polite and thoughtful act to allow neighbors to hear by keeping the volume high. We in the United States would view such behavior as being a thoughtless invasion of privacy.

A therapist or counselor working with clients would be well advised to be aware of possible cultural misinterpretations as a function of speech volume. Speaking loudly may not indicate anger and hostility, and speaking in a soft voice may not be a sign of weakness, shyness, or depression.

Directness of a conversation or the degree of frankness also varies considerably among various cultural groups. Observing the English in their parliamentary debates will drive this point home. The long heritage of open, direct, and frank confrontation leads to heckling of public speakers and quite blunt and sharp exchanges. Britons believe and feel that these are acceptable styles and may take no offense at being the object of such exchanges. However, U.S. citizens feel that such exchanges are impolite, abrasive, and irrational. Relative to Asians, Euro-Americans are seen as being too blunt and frank. Great care is taken by many Asians not to hurt the feelings of or embarrass the other person. As a result, use of euphemisms and ambiguity is the norm.

Since many minority groups may value indirectness, the U.S. emphasis on "getting to the point" and "not beating around the bush" may alienate others. Asian Americans, American Indians, and some Latino/Hispanic Americans may see this behavior as immature, rude, and lacking in finesse. On the other hand, clients from different cultures may be negatively labeled as evasive and afraid to confront the problem.

High-Low Context Communication

Edward T. Hall, author of such classics as *The Silent Language* (1959) and *The Hidden Dimension* (1969), is a well-known anthropologist who has proposed the concept of high-low context cultures (Hall, 1976). A high-context (HC) communication or message is one that is anchored in the physical context (situation) or internalized in the person. Less reliance is placed on the explicit code or message content. A HC communication relies heavily on nonverbals and the group identification/understanding shared by those communicating. For example, a normal-stressed "no" by a U.S. American may be interpreted by an Arab as "yes." A real negation in Arab culture would be stressed much more emphatically. A prime example of the contextual dimension in understanding communication is demonstrated in the following example:

> *I was asked to consult with a hospital that was having a great deal of difficulty with their Filipino nurses. The hospital had a number of them on its staff, and the medical director was concerned about their competence in understanding and*

following directions from doctors. As luck would have it, when I came to the hospital, I was immediately confronted with a situation that threatened to blow up. Dr. K., a Euro-American physician, had brought charges against a Filipino American nurse for incompetence. He had observed her incorrectly using and monitoring life support systems on a critically ill patient. He relates how he entered the patient's room and told the nurse that she was incorrectly using the equipment and that the patient could die if she didn't do it right. Dr. K. states that he spent some 10 minutes explaining how the equipment should be attached and used. Upon finishing his explanation, he asked the nurse if she understood. The Filipino nurse nodded her head slightly and hesitantly said, "Yes, yes, Doctor." Later that evening, Dr. K. observed the same nurse continuing to use the equipment incorrectly; he reported her to the head nurse and asked for her immediate dismissal. While it is possible that the nurse was not competent, further investigation revealed strong cultural forces affecting the hospital work situation. What the medical administration failed to understand was the cultural context of the situation. In the Philippines, it is considered impolite to say "no" in a number of situations. In this case, for the nurse to say "no" to the doctor (a respected figure of high status) when asked whether she understood would have implied that Dr. K. was a poor teacher. This would be considered insulting and impolite. Thus, the only option the Filipino nurse felt open to her was to tell the doctor "yes."

In Filipino culture, a mild, hesitant "yes" is interpreted by those who understand as a "no" or a polite refusal. In traditional Asian society, many interactions are understandable only in light of high context cues and situations. For example, to extend an invitation only once for dinner would be considered an affront because it implies that you are not sincere. One must extend an invitation several times, encouraging the invitee to accept. Arabs may also refuse an offer of food several times before giving in. However, most Euro-Americans believe that a host's offer can be politely refused with just a "no, thank you."

If we pay attention to only the explicit coded part of the message, we are likely to misunderstand the communication. According to E. T. Hall (1976), low-context (LC) cultures place a greater reliance on the verbal part of the message. In addition, LC cultures have been associated with being more opportunistic, more individual rather than group oriented, and as emphasizing rules of law and procedure (E. J. Smith, 1981).

It appears that the United States is a LC culture (although it is still higher than the Swiss, Germans, and Scandinavians in the amount of contexting required). China, perhaps, represents the other end of the continuum; its complex culture relies heavily on context. Asian Americans, African Americans, Hispanics, American Indians, and other minority groups in the United States also emphasize HC cues.

In contrast to LC communication, HC is faster, as well as more economical, efficient, and satisfying. Because it is so bound to the culture, it is slow to change and tends to be cohesive and unifying. LC communication does not unify but changes rapidly and easily.

Twins who have grown up together can and do communicate more economically (HC) than do two lawyers during a trial (LC). Bernstein's (1964) work in language analysis refers to restricted codes (HC) and elaborated codes (LC). Restricted codes are observed in families where words and sentences collapse and are shortened without loss of meaning. However, elaborated codes, where many words are used to communicate the same content, are seen in classrooms, diplomacy, and law.

African American culture has been described as HC. For example, it is clear that many Blacks require fewer words than their White counterparts to communicate the same content (Irvine & York, 1995; Jenkins, 1982; Stanback & Pearce, 1985; Weber, 1985). An African American male who enters a room and spots an attractive woman may stoop slightly in her direction, smile, and tap the table twice while vocalizing a long drawn out "uh huh." What he has communicated would require many words from his White brother! The fact that African Americans may communicate more by HC cues has led many to characterize them as nonverbal, inarticulate, unintelligent, and so forth.

Another example of how HC and LC orientations may lead to misunderstandings was a situation that occurred during a cross-cultural communications conference. Social scientists from Asia, the Pacific, and the mainland United States were invited to attend a conference in Hawaii. It was run very much like most typical sessions. All invitees were to present an original piece of research (45 minutes) on cross-cultural communications, and then a respondent would react to it (10 minutes). Contrasting communication styles became immediately apparent. If the presenters were Asian, they would go through an elaborate ritual of expressing gratitude for being invited, derogating the self, praising those in the audience, and so forth. With slight variations, this behavior occurred consistently whether the Asian person was a presenter or respondent. If the latter, the person would apologize for his or her naïveté, praise the paper, and spend only a short time critiquing it. When the presenter or respondent was someone from the U.S. mainland, the White researcher would usually attend directly to the task. Critiques were direct and to the point.

During mealtimes, many of the participants from the mainland indicated that their Asian counterparts did not seem to realize the weaknesses in some of their colleagues' research papers. On the other hand, many of the Asian participants expressed reluctance to continue because the "Americans" were too blunt in their remarks. As a result, they could be shamed in public and lose face. They did not want to continue with the conference if the respondent to their paper was from the U.S. mainland. Such reactions were due in large part to the HC-LC differences among participants. The LC participant relied heavily on the explicit code (written and spoken word) as the main means of conveying thoughts, ideas, and feelings. The HC participant relied on implicit aspects of the communication. For example, many of the White conferees saw the Asian critiques as wishy-washy and lacking in critical analysis. They did not understand that the praises heaped on the person were more form than substance.

The key to understanding the basis of the Asian critiques was not in the words used, but in factors such as (a) the amount of time used to praise the paper, (b) the amount of time spent to derogate the self, (c) the descriptors used, and (d) the questions that were asked at the end. Consider a response such as, "I would only ask Dr. Yamamoto two questions. First, how did he decide to use the particular research methodology, and second, how did he select the population to be researched?" Those in the audience who understood the context (HC) knew that the questions indicated (a) that the wrong methodology was used and (b) that the population was not representative. These examples indicate how important it is for the therapist to understand racial/cultural communication styles.

Sociopolitical Facets of Nonverbal Communication

There is a common saying among African Americans: "If you really want to know what White folks are thinking and feeling, don't listen to what they say, but how they say it." In most cases, such a statement refers to the biases, stereotypes, and racist attitudes that Whites are believed to possess but that they consciously or unconsciously conceal.

Right or wrong, many minority individuals through years of personal experience operate from three assumptions. The first assumption is that all Whites in this society are racist. Through their own cultural conditioning, they have been socialized into a culture that espouses the superiority of White culture over all others (J. M. Jones, 1997; Parham, 1993; Ridley, 1995). The second assumption is that most Whites find such a concept disturbing and will go to great lengths to deny that they are racist or biased. Some of this is done deliberately and with awareness, but in most cases one's racism is largely unconscious. The last of these assumptions is that nonverbal behaviors are more accurate reflections of what a White person is thinking or feeling than is what they say.

There is considerable evidence to suggest that these three assumptions held by various racial/ethnic minorities are indeed accurate (McIntosh, 1989; Ridley, 1995; D. W. Sue et al., 1998). Counselors and mental health practitioners need to be very cognizant of nonverbal cues from a number of different perspectives.

In the last section we discussed how nonverbal behavior is culture-bound and how the counselor or therapist cannot make universal interpretations about it. Likewise, nonverbal cues are important because they often (a) unconsciously reflect our biases and (b) trigger off stereotypes we have of other people.

Nonverbals as Reflections of Bias

Some time back, a TV program called *Candid Camera* was the rage in the United States. It operated from a unique premise, which involved creating very unusual situations for naive subjects who were then filmed as they reacted to them. One of these experiments involved interviewing housewives about their attitudes toward African American, Latino/Hispanic, and White teenagers. The intent was to select a group of women who by all standards appeared sincere in their beliefs that Blacks and Latinos were no more prone to violence than were their White counterparts. Unknown to them, they were filmed by a hidden camera as they left their homes to go shopping at the local supermarket.

The creator of the program had secretly arranged for an African American, Latino, and White youngster (dressed casually but nearly identically) to pass these women on the street. The experiment was counterbalanced; that is, the race of the youngster was randomly assigned as to which would approach the shopper first. What occurred was a powerful statement on unconscious racist attitudes and beliefs.

All the youngsters had been instructed to pass the shopper on the purse side of the street. If the woman was holding the purse in her right hand, the youngster would approach and pass on her right. If the purse was held with the left hand, the youngster would pass on her left. Studies of the film revealed consistent outcomes. Many women when approached by the Black or Latino youngster (approximately 15 feet away) would casually switch the purse from one arm to the other! This occurred infrequently with the White subject. Why?

The answer appears quite obvious to us. The women subjects who switched their purses were operating from biases, stereotypes, and preconceived notions about what minority youngsters are like: They are prone to crime, more likely to snatch a purse or rob, more likely to be juvenile delinquents, and more likely to engage in violence. The disturbing part of this experiment was that the selected subjects were, by all measures, sincere individuals who on a conscious level denied harboring racist attitudes or beliefs. They were not liars, nor were they deliberately deceiving the interviewer. They were normal, everyday people. They honestly believed that they did not possess these biases, yet when tested, their nonverbal behavior (purse switching) gave them away.

The power of nonverbal communication is that it tends to be least under conscious control. Studies support the conclusion that nonverbal cues operate primarily on an unawareness level (DePaulo, 1992; Singelis, 1994), that they tend to be more spontaneous and difficult to censor or falsify (Mehrabian, 1972), and that they are more trusted than words. In our society, we have learned to use words (spoken or written) to mask or conceal our true thoughts and feelings. Note how our politicians and lawyers are able to address an issue without revealing much of what they think or believe. This is very evident in controversial issues such as gun control, abortion, and issues of affirmative action and immigration.

Nonverbal behavior provides clues to conscious deceptions or unconscious bias. There is evidence that the accuracy of nonverbal communication varies with the part of the body used: Facial expression is more controllable than the hands, followed by the legs and the rest of the body (Hansen, Stevic, & Warner, 1982). The implications for multicultural counseling are obvious. A therapist who has not adequately dealt with his or her own biases and racist attitudes may unwittingly communicate them to a culturally different client.

As mentioned earlier, minority clients will often test the therapist through a series of challenges. Many of these challenges are aimed at getting the helping professional to self-disclose. The intent is to ascertain not only the therapist's level of expertness, but the level of trustworthiness as well: "How open and honest are you about your own racism, and will you allow it to interfere with our relationship?" The minority client, in an attempt to seek an answer to the question, will create situations aimed at getting the counselor to reveal himself or herself. Some very common verbal tests are posed in questions like, "How can you possibly understand the minority experience? Have you ever laughed at racist jokes? How do you feel about interracial relationships? Are you a racist? Do you really care what happens to Blacks (Latinos, etc.)?" How you answer the challenge (verbally and nonverbally) will either enhance or diminish your credibility.

If counselors are unaware of their own biases, the nonverbals are most likely to reveal their true feelings. Studies suggest that women and minorities are better readers of nonverbal cues than are White males (Hall, 1976; Jenkins, 1982; J. C. Pearson, 1985; Weber, 1985). Much of this may be due to their HC orientation, but another reason may be *survival.* For an African American person to survive in a predominantly White society, he or she has to rely on nonverbal cues more often than verbal ones.

One of our male African American colleagues gives the example of how he must constantly be vigilant when traveling in an unknown part of the country. Just to stop at a roadside restaurant may be dangerous to his physical well-being. As a result, when entering a diner, he is quick to observe not only the reactions of the staff (waiter/waitress, cashier, cook, etc.) to his entrance, but the reactions of the patrons as well. Do they stare at him? What type of facial expressions do they have? Do they fall silent? Does he get served immediately, or is there an inordinate delay? These nonverbal cues reveal much about the environment around him. He may choose to be himself or play the role of a "humble" Black person who leaves quickly if the situation poses danger.

Interestingly, this very same colleague talks about tuning in to nonverbal cues as a means of *psychological survival.* He believes it is important for minorities to accurately read where people are coming from in order to prevent invalidation of the self. For example, a minority person driving through an unfamiliar part of the country may find himself or herself forced to stay at a motel overnight. Seeing a vacancy light flashing, the person may stop and knock on the manager's door. Upon opening the door and seeing the Black person, the White manager may show hesitation, stumble around in his or her verbalizations, and then apologize for having forgotten to turn off the vacancy light. The Black person is faced with the dilemma of deciding whether the White manager was telling the truth or is simply not willing to rent to a Black person.

Some of you might ask, "Why is it important for you to know? Why don't you simply find someplace else? After all, would you stay at a place where you were unwelcome?" Finding another place to stay might not be as important as the psychological well-being of the minority person. Racial/ethnic minorities have encountered too many situations in which double messages are given to them. For the African American to accept the simple statement, "I forgot to turn off the vacancy light," may be to deny one's own true feelings at being the victim of discrimination. This is especially true when the nonverbals (facial expression, anxiety in voice, and stammering) may reveal other reasons.

Too often, culturally different individuals are placed in situations where they are asked to deny their true feelings in order to perpetuate *White deception.* Statements that minorities are oversensitive (paranoid?) may represent a form of denial. When a minority colleague makes a statement such as "I get a strange feeling from John; I feel some bias against minorities coming out," White colleagues, friends, and others are sometimes too quick to dismiss it with statements like, "You're being oversensitive." Perhaps a better approach would be to say, "What makes you feel that way?" rather than to negate or invalidate what might be an accurate appraisal of nonverbal communication.

Thus, it is clear that racial/ethnic minorities are very tuned in to nonverbals. For the therapist who has not adequately dealt with his or her own racism, the minority client will be quick to assess such biases. In many cases, the minority client may believe that the biases are too great to be overcome and will simply not continue in therapy. This is despite the good intentions of the White counselor/therapist who is not in touch with his or her own biases and assumptions about human behavior.

Nonverbals as Triggers to Biases and Fears

Often people assume that being an effective multicultural therapist is a straightforward process that involves the acquisition of knowledge about the various racial/ethnic groups. If we know that Asian Americans and African Americans have different patterns of eye contact and if we know that these patterns signify different things, then we should be able to eliminate biases and stereotypes that we possess. Were it so easy, we might have eradicated racism years ago. While increasing our knowledge base about the lifestyles and experiences of minority groups is important, it is not a sufficient condition in itself. Our racist attitudes, beliefs, and feelings are deeply ingrained in our total being. Through years of conditioning they have acquired a strong irrational base, replete with emotional symbolisms about each particular minority. Simply opening a text and reading about African Americans and Latinos/Hispanics will not deal with our deep-seated fears and biases.

Let us return to the example of Black-White interactions given at the beginning of the chapter to illustrate our point. Recall that many of the White faculty members believed that their African American colleague was "out of control," "too emotional," "irrational," and "angry," and that the meeting should be terminated until such time as the topic could be addressed in an objective manner. On the other hand, the Black faculty member denied being angry and believed that the White faculty members were fronting, deliberately concealing their true thoughts and feelings. Much of the confusion seemed to be linked to a difference in communication styles and how these differences trigger off fears and biases we may possess.

One of the major barriers to effective understanding is the common assumption that different cultural groups operate according to identical speech and communication conventions. In the United States, it is often assumed that distinctive racial, cultural, and linguistic features are deviant, inferior, or embarrassing (Kochman, 1981; Singelis, 1994; Stanback & Pearce, 1985). These value judgments then become tinged with beliefs that we hold about Black people (E. J. Smith, 1981): racial inferiority, being prone to violence and crime, quick to anger, and a threat to White folks (Irvine & York, 1995; Weber, 1985). The communication style of Black folks (manifested in nonverbals) can often trigger off these fears. We submit that the situation presented at the beginning of the chapter represents just such an example.

Black styles of communication are often high-key, animated, heated, interpersonal, and confrontational. Many emotions, affects, and feelings are generated (E. T. Hall, 1976; Shade & New, 1993; Weber, 1985). In a debate, Blacks tend to act as advocates of a position, and ideas are to be tested in the crucible of argument (Banks & Banks, 1993; Kochman, 1981). White middle-class styles, however, are characterized as being detached and objective, impersonal and nonchallenging. The person acts not as an *advocate* of the idea, but as a *spokesperson* (truth resides in the idea). A discussion of issues should be devoid of affect because emotion and reason work against one another. One should talk things out in a logical fashion without getting personally involved. African Americans characterize their own style of communication as indicating that the person is sincere and honest, while Euro-Americans consider their own style to be reasoned and objective (Irvine & York, 1995).

Many African Americans readily admit that they operate from a point of view and, as mentioned previously, are disinclined to believe that White folks do not. E. J. Smith (1981, p. 154) aptly describes the Black orientation in the following passage:

> When one Black person talks privately with another, he or she might say: "Look, we don't have to jive each other or be like White folks; let's be honest with one another." These statements reflect the familiar Black saying that "talk is cheap," that actions speak louder than words, and that Whites beguile each other with words. . . . In contrast, the White mind symbolizes to many Black people deceit, verbal chicanery, and sterile intellectivity. For example, after long discourse with a White person, a Black individual might say: "I've heard what you've said, but what do you really mean?"

Such was the case with the African American professor who believed that his White colleagues were fronting and being insincere.

While Black Americans may misinterpret White communication styles, it is more likely that Whites will misinterpret Black styles. The direction of the misunderstanding is generally linked to the activating of unconscious triggers or buttons about racist stereotypes and fears they harbor. As we have repeatedly emphasized, one of the dominant stereotypes of African Americans in our society is that of the hostile, angry, prone-to-violence Black male. The more animated and affective communication style, closer conversing distance, prolonged eye contact when speaking, greater bodily movements, and tendency to test ideas in a confrontational/argumentative format lead many Whites to believe that their lives are in danger. It is not unusual for White mental health practitioners to describe their African Americans clients as being hostile and angry. We have also observed that some White trainees who work with Black clients nonverbally respond in such a manner as to indicate anxiety, discomfort, or fear (leaning away from their African American clients, tipping their chairs back, crossing their legs or arms, etc.). These are nonverbal distancing moves that may reflect the unconscious stereotypes that they hold of Black Americans. While we would entertain the possibility that a Black client is angry, most occasions we have observed do not justify such a descriptor.

It appears that many Euro-Americans operate from the assumption that when an argument ensues, it may lead to a ventilation of anger with the outbreak of a subsequent fight. When the Black professor was told to calm down, such may have been the fear of the White colleague. When the African American professor stated, "Don't worry, I'm not going to hit you!" it was obvious he knew what was going on in the head of his White colleague. What many Whites fail to realize is that African Americans distinguish between an argument used to debate a difference of opinion and one that ventilates anger and hostility (DePaulo, 1992; Irvine & York, 1995; Kochman, 1981; Shade & New, 1993). In the former, the affect indicates sincerity and seriousness; there is a positive attitude toward the material; and the validity of ideas is challenged. In the latter, the affect is more passionate than sincere; there is a negative attitude toward the opponent; and the opponent is abused.

To understand African American styles of communication and to relate adequately to Black communication would require much study in the origins, functions, and manifestations of Black language (Jenkins, 1982). Weber (1985) believes that the historical and philosophical foundations of Black language have led to several verbal styles among Blacks. *Rapping,* not the White usage (rap session), was originally a dialogue between a man and a woman in which the intent was to win over the admiration of the woman. Imaginary statements, rhythmic speech, and creativity are aimed at getting the woman interested in hearing more of the rap. It has been likened to a mating call, an introduction of the male to the female, and a ritual expected by some African American women.

Another style of verbal banter is called *woofing,* which is an exchange of threats and challenges to fight. It may have derived from what African Americans refer to as *playing the dozens,* which is considered by many Blacks to be the highest form of verbal warfare and impromptu speaking (Kochman, 1981; Jenkins, 1983; Weber, 1985). To the outsider, it may appear cruel, harsh, and provocative. Yet to many in the Black community, it has historical and functional meanings. The term *dozens* was used by slave owners to refer to Black persons with disabilities. Because they were considered damaged goods, disabled Black people would often be sold at a discount rate with eleven (one dozen) other damaged slaves (Weber, 1985). It was primarily a selling ploy in which "dozens" referred to the negative physical features. Often played in jest, the game requires an audience to act as judge and jury over the originality, creativity, and humor of the combatants:

> *Say man, your girlfriend so ugly, she had to sneak up on a glass to get a drink of water. . . . Man, you so ugly, yo mamma had to put a sheet over your head so sleep could sneak up on you. (Weber, 1985, p. 248)*

> *A: Eat shit.*
> *B: What should I do with your bones?*
> *A: Build a cage for your mother.*

B: At least I got one.
A: She is the least. (Labov, 1972, p. 321)

A: Got a match?
B: Yeah, my ass and your face or my farts and your breath. (Kochman, 1981, p. 54)

Woofing and playing the dozens seem to have very real functional value. First, they allow training in self-control about managing one's anger and hostility in the constant face of racism. In many situations, it would be considered dangerous by an African American to respond to taunts, threats, and insults. Second, woofing also allows a Black person to establish a hierarchy or pecking order without resorting to violence. Last, it can create an image of being fearless where one will gain respect.

This verbal and nonverbal style of communication can be a major aspect of Black interactions. Likewise, other minority groups have characteristic styles that may cause considerable difficulties for White counselors. One way of contrasting communication style differences may be in the overt activity dimension (the pacing/intensity) of nonverbal communication. Table 5.1 contrasts five different groups along this continuum. How these styles affect the therapist's perception and ability to work with culturally different clients is important for each and every one of us to consider.

Counseling and Therapy as Communication Style

Throughout this text we have repeatedly emphasized that counseling and therapy may be perceived as a process of interpersonal interaction, communication, and social influence. As a result, it is not difficult to assume that *different* theories of counseling and psychotherapy represent *different* communication styles. There is considerable early research support for this statement. The film series *Three Approaches to Psychotherapy* (Shostrom, 1966), which features Carl Rogers, Fritz Perls, and Albert Ellis, and the *Three Approaches to Psychotherapy: II* (Shostrom, 1977), which features Carl Rogers, Everett Shostrom, and Arnold Lazarus, have been the subject of much analysis. In most cases, the studies have focused on the first film and tried to identify differences in verbal response categories among the counselors. While internal consistency of the therapists has been questioned in several cases (Dolliver, Williams, & Gold, 1980; Weinrach, 1987), some general conclusions may be tentatively drawn from all of these studies. Each theoretical orientation (Rogers, person-centered therapy; Perls, existential therapy; Ellis, rational-emotive therapy; Shostrom, actualizing therapy; and Lazarus, multimodal therapy) can be distinguished from one another, and the therapy styles/skills

Table 5.1 **Communication Style Differences (Overt Activity Dimension—Nonverbal/Verbal)**

American Indians	Asian Americans and Hispanics	Whites	Blacks
1. Speak softly/slower	1. Speak softly	1. Speak loud/fast to control listener	1. Speak with affect
2. Indirect gaze when listening or speaking	2. Avoidance of eye contact when listening or speaking to high-status persons	2. Greater eye contact when listening	2. Direct eye contact (prolonged) when speaking, but less when listening
3. Interject less; seldom offer encouraging communication	3. Similar rules	3. Head nods, nonverbal markers	3. Interrupt (turn taking) when can
4. Delayed auditory (silence)	4. Mild delay	4. Quick responding	4. Quicker responding
5. Manner of expression low-keyed, indirect	5. Low-keyed, indirect	5. Objective, task oriented	5. Affective, emotional, interpersonal

exhibited seem to be highly correlated with their theoretical orientations. For example, Rogers's style seemed to emphasize attending skills (encouragement to talk: minimal encouragers, nonverbal markers, paraphrasing, and reflecting feelings); Shostrom relied on direct guidance, providing information, and so forth; while Lazarus took an active, reeducative style. One study, for example, found that Rogers used minimal encouragers 53% of the time; restatements 11% of the time; and interpretation, reflection, and information each 7% of the time (Hill, Thames, & Rardin, 1979). These results are highly consistent with person-centered counseling.

Rogers (1980) believed that clients have the innate capacity to advance and grow on their own. The reason they encounter problems in life is that significant others impose conditions of worth upon them. The result is that individuals try to live up to others' expectations, standards, and values while denying their innate actualizing tendency. Rogers' writings suggest his strong belief that people have the capacity to self-correct or grow in a positive direction if left on their own. It is almost like each of us possesses a genetic blueprint. Counselors must avoid imposing conditions of worth on their clients, telling them what to do or how to solve problems, and imposing their definition of the problem on them. Rather, counselors need to provide a nurturing and nutritious environment for their clients, accept them for what they are, and provide them with a way to view themselves (a mirror) as they are, and as they were meant to be. In this manner, clients will actively begin to change on their own.

The person-centered philosophy would be expected to be evident in the types of skills exhibited by the helping professional. For example, using Ivey's microcounseling language (Ivey, Ivey, & Simek-Downing, 1987), one would clearly see that Rogers would use primarily attending skills (minimal encouragers, paraphrasing, reflection of feelings, summarization, etc.) over influencing skills (giving advice and direction, expressing content/teaching, expressing feelings on the part of the counselor, and interpreting). Attending skills are person-centered and provide a way for the client to see himself or herself. It is highly consistent with Rogerian philosophy. Influencing skills are active attempts to direct the client, and they are considered counterproductive in counseling because their use may impose conditions of worth—the precise dynamics that have led the client to suffer difficulties. Likewise, we see that if a theory assumes that the basis of problems resides in cognitions (irrational thoughts and processes), as does the rational-emotive approach, then the therapist would take a more active approach to attack the basis of the belief system directly and teach the client new ways of thinking. Influencing skills would be highly used, and analysis of Ellis's style indeed confirms this impression.

Differential Skills in Multicultural Counseling/Therapy

Just as race, culture, ethnicity, and gender may affect communication styles, there is considerable evidence that theoretical orientations in counseling will influence helping styles as well. There is strong support for the belief that different cultural groups may be more receptive to certain counseling/communication styles because of cultural and sociopolitical factors (Herring, 1997; D. W. Sue, 1990; Wehrly, 1995). Indeed, the literature on multicultural counseling/therapy strongly suggests that American Indians, Asian Americans, Black Americans, and Hispanic Americans tend to prefer more active-directive forms of helping than nondirective ones (Cheatham et al., 1997; Ivey et al., 1997; D. W. Sue et al., 1998). We briefly describe two of these group differences here to give the reader some idea of their implications.

Asian American clients who may value restraint of strong feelings and believe that intimate revelations are to be shared only with close friends may cause problems for the counselor who is oriented toward insight or feelings. It is entirely possible that such techniques as reflection of feelings, asking questions of a deeply personal nature, and making depth interpretations may be perceived as lacking in respect for the client's integrity. Asian American clients may not value the process of insight into underlying processes. For example, some clients who come for vocational information may be perceived by counselors as needing help in finding out what motivates their actions and decisions. Requests for advice or information from the client are seen as indicative of deeper, more personal conflicts. Although this might be true in some cases, the blind application of techniques that clash with cultural values seriously places many Asian Americans in an uncomfortable and oppressed position. Atkinson, Maruyama, and Matsui (1978) tested this hypothesis with a number of Asian American students. Two tape recordings of a contrived counseling session were prepared in which the client's responses were identical but the counselor's responses differed, being directive in one and nondirective in the other. Their findings indicated that counselors who use the directive approach were rated more credible and approachable than were those using the nondirective counseling approach. Asian Americans seem to prefer a logical, rational, structured counseling approach to an affective, reflective, and ambiguous one. Other researchers have drawn similar conclusions (see the excellent reviews by Atkinson & Lowe, 1995; Leong, 1986).

In a groundbreaking study carried out over 20 years ago, Berman (1979) found similar results with a Black population. The weakness of the previous study was its failure to compare equal responses with a White population. Berman's study compared the use of counseling skills between Black and White male and female counselors. A videotape of culturally varied client vignettes was viewed by Black and White counselor trainees. They responded to the question, "What would you say to this person?" The data were scored and coded according to a microcounseling taxonomy that divided counseling skills into attending and influencing ones. The hypothesis made by the investigator was that Black and White counselors would give significantly different patterns of responses to their clients. Data supported the hypothesis. Black males and females tended to use the more active expressive skills (directions, expression of content, and interpretation) with greater frequency than did their White counterparts. White males and females tended to use a higher percentage of attending skills. Berman concluded that the person's race/culture appears to be a major factor in the counselor's choice of skills, that Black and White counselors appear to adhere to a distinctive style of counseling. Berman also concluded that the more active styles of the Black counselor tend to include practical advice and allow for the introjection of a counselor's values and opinions.

The implications for therapy become glaringly apparent. Mental health training programs tend to emphasize the more passive attending skills. Therapists so trained may be ill equipped to work with culturally different clients who might find the active approach more relevant to their own needs and values.

Implications for Multicultural Counseling/Therapy

Ivey's continuing contributions (Ivey, 1981, 1986; Ivey et al., 1997) in the field of microcounseling, multicultural counseling, and developmental counseling seem central to our understanding of counseling/communication styles. He believes that different theories are concerned with generating different sentences and constructs and that different cultures may also be expected to generate different sentences and constructs. Counseling and psychotherapy may be viewed as special types of temporary cultures. When the counseling style of the counselor does not match the communication style of their culturally diverse clients, many difficulties may arise: premature termination of the session, inability to establish rapport, or cultural oppression of the client. Thus, it becomes clear that effective multicultural counseling occurs when the counselor and client are able to send and receive both verbal and nonverbal messages appropriately and accurately. When the counselor is able to engage in such activities, his or her credibility and attractiveness will be increased (see Chapter 4). Communication styles manifested in the clinical context may either enhance or negate the effectiveness of MCT. Several major implications for counseling can be discerned.

Therapeutic Practice
As practicing clinicians who work with a culturally diverse population, we need to move decisively in educating ourselves about the differential meanings of nonverbal behavior and the broader implications for communication styles. We need to realize that proxemics, kinesics, paralanguage, and high-low context factors are important elements of communication; that they may be highly culture-bound; and that we should guard against possible misinterpretation in our assessment of clients. Likewise, it is important that we begin to become aware of and understand our own communication/helping style: What is my clinical/communication style? What does it say about my values, biases, and assumptions about human behavior? How do my nonverbals reflect stereotypes, fears, or preconceived notions about various racial groups? What nonverbal messages might I be communicating unknowingly to my client? In what way does my helping style hinder my ability to work effectively with a culturally different client? What culturally/racially influenced communication styles cause me the greatest difficulty or discomfort? Why?

We believe that therapists must be able to shift their therapeutic styles to meet the developmental needs of clients. We contend further that effective mental health professionals are those who can also shift their helping styles to meet the cultural dimensions of their clients. Therapists of differing theoretical orientations will tend to use different skill patterns. These skill patterns may be antagonistic or inappropriate to the communication/helping styles of clients. In research cited earlier, it was clear that White counselors (by virtue of their cultural conditioning and training) tended to use the more passive attending and listening skills in counseling/therapy, while racial/ethnic minority populations appear more oriented toward an active influencing approach. There are several reasons why this may be the case.

First, we contend that the use of more directive, active, and influencing skills is more likely to provide personal information about where the therapist is coming from (self-disclosure). Giving advice or suggestions, interpreting, and telling the client how you, the counselor or therapist, feel are really acts of counselor self-disclosure. While the use of attending or more nondirective skills may also self-disclose, it tends to be minimal relative to using influencing skills. In multicultural counseling, the culturally diverse client is likely to approach the counselor with trepidation: "What makes you any different from all the Whites out there who have oppressed me?" "What makes you immune from inheriting the racial biases of your forebears?" "Before I open up to you [self-disclose], I want to know where you are coming from." "How open and honest are you about your own racism, and will it interfere with our relationship?" "Can you really understand what it's like to be Asian, Black, Hispanic, American Indian, or the like?" In other words, a culturally diverse client may not open up (self-disclose) until you, the helping professional, self-disclose first. Thus, to many minority clients, a therapist who expresses his or her thoughts and feelings may be better received in a counseling situation.

Second, minorities' more positive response to the use of influencing skills appears to be related to diagnostic focus. In Chapter 8 we present the concept of locus of responsibility. Studies support the thesis that White therapists are more likely to focus their problem diagnosis in individual, rather than societal, terms (Berman, 1979; Nwachuku & Ivey, 1991; D. W. Sue et al., 1998).

In a society where individualism prevails, it is not surprising to find that Euro-American counselors tend to view their client's problems are residing within the individual rather than society. Thus, the role of the therapist will be person-focused because the problem resides within the individual. Skills utilized will be individual-centered (attending), aimed at changing the person. Many minorities accept the importance of individual contributions to the problem, but they also give great weight to systemic or societal factors that may adversely impact their lives. Minorities who have been the victims of discrimination and oppression perceive that the problem resides externally to the person (societal forces). Active systems intervention is called for, and the most appropriate way to attack the environment (stressors) would be an active approach (Lewis et al., 1998). If the counselor shares their perception, he or she may take a more active role in the sessions, giving advice and suggestions, as well as teaching strategies (becoming a partner to the client).

Unfortunately, our mental health training programs are very deficient in teaching therapists the appropriate influencing skills needed for effective multicultural counseling/therapy. Much of this resides in a philosophical belief that clients should solve problems on their own, that they are ultimately responsible for the outcomes in their lives, and that therapists who dispense advice/suggestions and disclose their thoughts or feelings are adversely influencing their clients or fostering dependency. As one minority client said to us, "I'm not that weak, stupid, or fragile that what advice you give to me will be unquestioningly accepted."

Finally, while it would be ideal if we could effectively engage in the full range of therapeutic responses, such a wish may prove unrealistic. We cannot be all things to everyone. That is, there are personal limits to how much we can change our communication styles to match those of our clients. The difficulty in shifting styles may be a function of inadequate practice, inability to understand the other person's worldview, or personal biases or racist attitudes that have not been adequately resolved. In these cases, the counselor might consider several alternatives: (a) seek additional training/education, (b) seek consultation with a more experienced counselor, (c) refer the client to another therapist, and (d) become aware of personal communication style limitations and try to anticipate their possible impact on the culturally diverse client. Often, a therapist who recognizes the limitations of his or her helping style and knows how it will impact the culturally diverse client can take steps to minimize possible conflicts. Interestingly, one study (Yao, Sue, & Hayden, 1991) found that once rapport and a working relationship are established with a minority client, the counselor may have greater freedom in using a helping style quite different from that of the client. The crucial element appears to be the counselor's ability to acknowledge limitations in his or her helping style and to anticipate the negative impact it may have on the culturally diverse client. In this way, the helping professional may be saying to the client, "I understand your worldview, and I know that what I do or say will appear very Western to you, but I'm limited in my communication style. I may or may not understand where you're coming from, but let's give it a try." For some minority clients, this form of communication may be enough to begin the process of bridging the communication-style gap.

Implications for Clinical Practice

This chapter has made it abundantly clear that communication styles are strongly influenced by such factors as race, culture, ethnicity, and gender. Most of the studies we have reviewed lend support to the notion that various racial groups do exhibit differences in communication styles. If counseling and therapy are seen as subsets of the communication process, then it may have significant implications for what constitutes helping. What is missing is explicit research exploring the interaction of these styles with various theoretical counseling/therapy approaches. Do race and culture affect a client's receptivity to counseling styles? From Chapter 3 we might even ask the question, "How does the style affect a client's perception of therapist expertness, attractiveness, and trustworthiness?" In any case, some general suggestions gleaned from this chapter might prove helpful:

1.   Recognize that no one style of counseling or therapy will be appropriate for all populations and situations. A counselor or therapist who is able to engage in a variety of helping styles and roles is most likely to be effective in working with a diverse population.

2.   Become knowledgeable about how race, culture, and gender affect communication styles. It is especially important to study the literature on nonverbal communication and test it out in a real-life situation by making a concerted and conscious effort to observe the ways in which people communicate and interact. As we have mentioned, the power of nonverbal communication is that it generally is least under conscious control. Your clinical observation skills will be greatly enhanced if you sharpen your nonverbal powers of observation of clients. It will also serve as a check on our tendency to make unwarranted or inaccurate interpretations.

3.   Become aware of your own communication and helping styles. In this case, it means knowing your social impact on others and being able to anticipate how it affects your clients. There are several reasons why this is important. First, how we behave often unconsciously reflects our own beliefs and values. As we have seen, research suggests that racial/ethnic minorities and women are better at reading nonverbal behaviors. It is important for us to realize what we communicate to others. Second, knowing how we affect people allows us to modify our behaviors should our impact be negative. To do this, we need to seek feedback from friends and colleagues about how we impact them. Another helpful approach is to view ourselves on videotape in various situations (including therapy sessions) to learn about how we behave.

4.   Try to obtain additional training and education on a variety of theoretical orientations and approaches. Programs that are primarily psychoanalytically oriented, cognitively oriented, existentially oriented, person-centered oriented, or behaviorally oriented may be doing a great disservice to trainees. The goals and processes espoused by the theories may not be those held by culturally different groups. The theories tend to be not only culture-bound, but also narrow in how they conceptualize the human condition.

5.   Know that each school of counseling and therapy has strengths, but they may be one-dimensional; they concentrate only on feelings, or only on cognitions, or only on behaviors. We need to realize that we are

feeling, thinking, behaving, social, cultural, spiritual, and *political* beings. In other words, try to think holistically rather than in a reductionist manner when it comes to conceptualizing the human condition.

6. It is important for training programs to use an approach that calls for openness and flexibility both in conceptualizing the issues and in actual skill building. In many respects, it represents a metatheoretical and eclectic approach to helping. Rather than being random, haphazard, and inconsistent, the metatheoretical approach is an attempt to use helping strategies, techniques, and styles that consider not only individual characteristics, but cultural and racial factors as well.

To develop relevant and effective culture-specific approaches may require a completely different perspective: Before the advent of Western counseling/therapy approaches, for example, how did members of a particular culture solve their problems? What were the intrinsic, natural, help-giving networks? We need to identify specific helping skills in indigenous cultures and use that as a frame of reference rather than Western concepts of mental health.

Multicultural Family Counseling and Therapy

6

Chapter

Esteban and Carmen O., a Puerto Rican couple, sought help at a community mental health clinic in the Miami area. Mr. O. had recently come to the United States with only a high school education but had already acquired several successful printing shops. Carmen, his wife, was a third-generation Latina raised in Florida. The two had a whirlwind courtship that resulted in marriage after only a three-month acquaintance. She described her husband as handsome, outspoken, confident, and strong person who could be affectionate and sensitive. Carmen used the term machismo *several times to describe Esteban.*

The couple had sought marital counseling after a series of rather heated arguments over Esteban's long work hours and his tendency to "go drinking with the boys" after work. She missed his companionship, which was constantly present during their courtship but now seemed strangely absent. Carmen, who had graduated from the University of Florida with a BA in business, had been working as an administrative assistant when she met Esteban. While she enjoyed her work, Carmen reluctantly resigned the position prior to her marriage, with the urging of Esteban, who stated that it was beneath her and that he was capable of supporting them both. Carmen had convinced Esteban to seek outside help with their marital difficulties, and they had been assigned to Dr. Carla B., a White female psychologist. The initial session with the couple was characterized by Esteban's doing most of the talking. Indeed, Dr. B. was quite annoyed by Esteban's arrogant attitude. He frequently spoke for his wife and interrupted Dr. B. often, not allowing her to finish questions or make comments. Esteban stated that he understood his wife's desire to spend more time with him but that he needed to seek financial security for "my children." While the couple did not have any children at the present time, it was obvious that Esteban expected to have many with his wife. He jokingly stated, "After three or four sons, she won't have time to miss me."

It was obvious that his remark had a strong impact on Carmen, as she appeared quite surprised. Dr. B., who during this session had been trying to give Carmen an opportunity to express her thoughts and feelings, seized the opportunity. She asked Carmen how she felt about having children. As Carmen began to answer, Esteban blurted out quickly, "Of course, she wants children. All women want children."

At this point Dr. B. (obviously angry) confronted Esteban about his tendency to answer or speak for his wife and the inconsiderate manner in which he kept interrupting everyone. "Being a 'macho man' is not what is needed here," stated Dr. B. Esteban became noticeably angry and stated, "No woman lectures Esteban. Why aren't you at home caring for your husband? What you need is a real man." Dr. B. did not fall for Esteban's baiting tactic and refused to argue with him. She was nevertheless quite angry with Esteban and disappointed in Carmen's passivity. The session was terminated shortly thereafter.

During the next few weeks Carmen came to the sessions without her husband, who refused to return. Their sessions consisted of dealing with Esteban's "sexist attitude" and the ways in which Carmen could be her "own person." Dr. B. stressed the fact that Carmen had an equal right in the decisions made at home, that she should not allow anyone to oppress her, that she did not need her husband's approval to return to her former job, and that having children was an equal and joint responsibility.

During Carmen's six months of therapy, the couple separated from one another. It was a difficult period for Carmen, who came for therapy regularly to talk about her need "to be my own person," a phrase used often by Dr. B.

Carmen and Esteban finally divorced after only a year of marriage.

As in individual therapy, family systems therapy may be equally culture-bound and, when inappropriately applied, can have disastrous consequences. Dr. B. failed to understand the gender role relationship between traditional Puerto Rican men and women, unwittingly applied a culture-bound definition of a healthy male-female relationship to Esteban and Carmen, and allowed her own (feminist) values to influence her therapeutic decisions. While we cannot blame her for the divorce of this couple, one wonders whether this would have happened if the therapist had clarified the cultural issues and conflicts occurring between the couple and realized how the values of couple counseling and those manifested in Puerto Rican culture might be at odds with one another.

For example, the egalitarian attitude held by the therapist may be in conflict with Puerto Rican values concerning male-female relationships and the division of responsibilities in the household. Traditional Puerto Rican families are patriarchal, a structure that gives men authority over women and the ability to make decisions without consulting them (Garcia-Preto, 1996; Ramos-McKay, Comas-Diaz, & Rivera, 1988). Encouraging Carmen to be her own person, having a right to make independent decisions and sharing the decision-making process with Esteban, might be violating traditional gender role relationships. These men-women relationships are reinforced by the constructs of *machismo* and *marianismo*. Machismo is a term used in many Latino cultures to indicate maleness, virility, and the man's role as provider and protector of the family. The term denotes male sexual prowess, allows males greater sexual freedom, and dictates a role that makes them responsible for protecting the honor of women in the family. In the United States, machismo has acquired negative connotations, been pathologized, and is often equated with sexist behavior (De La Cancela, 1991).

The construct of marianismo is the female counterpart that is derived from the cult of the Virgin Mary; while men may be sexually superior, women are seen as morally and spiritually superior and capable of enduring greater suffering (Garcia-Preto, 1996). Women are expected to keep themselves sexually pure and to be self-sacrificing in favor of their children and especially the husband; she is the caretaker of the family, and the homemaker. These gender role relationships have existed for centuries within Puerto Rican culture, although intergenerational differences have made these traditional roles an increasing source of conflict.

Dr. B. is obviously unaware that her attempts to interrupt Esteban's dialogue, to encourage Carmen to speak her mind freely, and to derogate machismo may be a violation of Puerto Rican cultural values; it may also be perceived as an insult to Esteban's maleness. The therapist is also unaware that her gender (being a woman) might also be a source of conflict for Esteban. Not only may he perceive Dr. B. as playing an inappropriate role (she should be at home taking care of her husband and children), but also it must be a great blow to his male pride to have a female therapist taking charge of the sessions.

We are not making a judgment about whether the patriarchal nature of a cultural group is good or bad. We are also not taking the position that egalitarian relationships are better than other culturally sanctioned role relationships. What is important, however, is the realization that personal values (equality in relationships), definitions of desirable male-female role relationships, and the goals of marital or family therapy (independence, or becoming one's own person) may be culture-bound and negatively impact multicultural family counseling/therapy. Effective multicultural family therapy is very difficult not only because of these cultural clashes, but also because of the way in which they interact with class issues. Let us use another family counseling case to illustrate the complexity of this interaction.

Several years ago, a female school counselor sought the senior author's advice about a Mexican American family she had recently seen. She was quite concerned about the identified client, Elena Martinez, a 13-year-old student who was referred for counseling because of alleged peddling of drugs on the school premises. The counselor had formed an impression that the parents "did not care for their daughter," "were uncooperative," and "were attempting to avoid responsibility for dealing with Elena's delinquency."

When pressed for how she arrived at these impressions, the counselor provided the following information:

Elena Martinez was the second oldest of four siblings, ages 15, 12, 10, and 7. The father was an immigrant from Mexico and the mother a natural citizen. The family resided in a blue-collar Latino neighborhood in San Jose, California.

Elena had been reported as having minor problems in school prior to the "drug-selling incident." For example, she had "talked back to teachers," refused to do homework assignments, and had "fought" with other students. Her involvement with a group of other Latino students (suspected of being responsible for disruptive school-yard pranks) had gotten her into trouble. Elena was well known to the counseling staff at the school. Because of the seriousness of the drug accusations, the counselor felt that something had to be done and that the parents needed to be informed immediately.

The counselor reported calling the parents in order to set up an interview with them. When Mrs. Martinez answered the telephone, the counselor explained that a police officer had caught Elena selling marijuana on school premises. Rather than arrest her, the officer turned the student over to the vice-principal, who luckily was present at the time of the incident. After the explanation, the counselor had asked that the parents make arrangements for an appointment as soon as possible. The meeting would be aimed at informing the parents about Elena's difficulties in school and coming to some decision about what could be done.

During the phone conversation, Mrs. Martinez seemed hesitant about choosing a time to come in and, when pressed by the counselor, excused herself from the telephone. The counselor reported overhearing some whispering on the other end, and then the voice of Mr. Martinez. He immediately asked the counselor how his daughter was and expressed his consternation over the entire situation. At that point, the counselor stated that she understood his feelings, but it would be best to set up an appointment for the following day and to talk about it then. Several times the counselor asked Mr. Martinez about a convenient time for the meeting, but each time he seemed to avoid the answer and to give excuses. He had to work the rest of the day and could not make the appointment. The counselor strongly stressed how important the meeting was for the daughter's welfare, and that the several hours of missed work were not important in light of the situation. The father stated that he would be able to make an evening session, but the counselor informed him that school policy prohibited evening meetings. When the counselor suggested that the mother could initially come alone, further hesitations seemed present. Finally, the father agreed to attend.

The very next day, Mr. and Mrs. Martinez and a brother-in-law (Elena's godfather) showed up together in her office. The counselor reported being upset at the presence of the brother-in-law when it became obvious that he planned to sit in on the session. At that point, she explained that a third party present would only make the session more complex and the outcome counterproductive. She wanted to see only the family.

The counselor reported that the session went poorly with minimal cooperation from the parents. She reported, "It was like pulling teeth, trying to get the Martinezes to say anything at all."

The case of Elena Martinez exemplifies other major misunderstandings that often occur in working with minority families. Like Dr. B. in the first case, the counselor's obvious lack of understanding concerning Latino cultural values and how they traditionally affect communication patterns are present once again. This lack of knowledge and the degree of insensitivity to the Latino family's experience in the United States can lead to negative impressions such as, "They are uncooperative, avoiding responsibility and not caring for their children." Like the case of Esteban and Carmen, failure to understand cultural differences and the experiences of minority status in the United States compounds the problems. A number of important points need to be made about this case.

First, it is entirely possible that the incidents reported by the counselor mean something different when seen from traditional Mexican American culture. Again, like many Euro-American counselors, this counselor possesses a value system of egalitarianism in the husband-wife relationship. The helping professional must guard against making negative judgments of patriarchal Mexican American roles. In reality, division of roles (husband is protector/provider while wife cares for the home/family) allows both to exercise influence and make decisions. Breaking the role divisions (especially by the woman) is done only out of necessity. A wife would be remiss in publicly making a family decision (setting up an appointment time) without consulting or obtaining agreement from the husband. Mrs. Martinez's hesitation on the phone to commit a meeting time with the counselor may be a reflection of the husband-wife role relationship rather than a lack of concern for the daughter. The counselor's persistence in forcing Mrs. Martinez to decide may actually be asking her to violate cultural dictates about appropriate role behaviors.

Second, the counselor may have seriously undermined the Hispanic concept of the extended family by expressing negativism toward the godfather's attendance at the counseling session. Middle-class White Americans consider the family unit to be nuclear (husband, wife, and children related by blood), while most minorities define the family unit as an extended one. A Hispanic child can acquire a godmother (madrina) and a godfather (padrino) through a baptismal ceremony. Unlike many White Americans, the role of godparents in Hispanic culture is more than symbolic, as they can become coparents (compadre) and take an active part in raising the child. Indeed, the role of the godparents is usually linked to the moral, religious, and spiritual upbringing of the child. Who else would be more appropriate to attend the counseling session than the god-father? Not only is he a member of the family, but the charges against Elena deal with legal and moral/ethical implications as well.

Third, the counselor obviously did not consider the economic impact that missing a couple of hours' work might have on the family. Again, she tended to equate Mr. Martinez's reluctance to take off work for the "welfare of his daughter" as evidence of the parents' disinterest in their child. Trivializing the missing of work reveals major class/work differences that often exist between mental health professionals and their minority clients. Most professionals (mental health practitioners, educators, white-collar workers) are often able to take time off for a dental appointment, teacher conference, or other personal needs without loss of income. Most of us can usually arrange for others to cover for us or make up the lost hours on some other day. If we are docked for time off, only a few hours are lost and not an entire afternoon or day's work. This, indeed, is a middle- or upper-class luxury not shared by those who face economic hardships or who work in settings that do not allow for schedule flexibility.

For the Martinez family, loss of even a few hours' wages has serious financial impact. Most blue-collar workers may not have the luxury or option of making up their work. How, for example, would an assembly-line worker make up the lost time when the plant closes at the end of the day? In addition, the worker often does not miss just a few hours, but must take a half or full day off. In many work situations, getting a worker to substitute for just a few hours is not practical. To entice replacement workers, the company must offer more than a few hours (in many cases, a full day). Thus, Mr. Martinez may actually be losing an entire day's wages! His reluctance to miss work may actually represent *high concern* for the family rather than *lack of care.*

Fourth, the case of Elena and the Martinez family raises another important question: What obligation do educational and mental health services have toward offering flexible and culturally appropriate services to minority constituents? Mr. Martinez's desire for an evening or weekend meeting brings this issue into clear perspective. Does the minority individual or family always have to conform to system rules and regulations? We are not arguing with the school policy itself—in some schools there are very legitimate reasons for not staying after school ends (high crime rate, etc.). What we are arguing for is the need to provide alternative service deliveries to minority families. For example, why not home visits or sessions off the school premises? Social workers have historically used this method with very positive results. It has aided the building of rapport (the family perceives your genuine interest), increased comfort in the family for sharing with a counselor, and allowed a more realistic appraisal of family dynamics. Counselors frequently forget how intimidating it may be for a minority family to come in for counseling. The Martinez's lack of verbal participation may be a function not only of the conflict over the absence of the godfather, but also of the impersonal and formal nature of counseling relative to the personal orientation of the Hispanic family (*personalismo*).

Family Systems Counseling and Therapy

Family systems therapy encompasses many aspects of the family, which may include marital counseling/therapy, parent-child counseling, or work with more than one member of the family (Nichols & Schwartz, 1995). Its main goal is to modify relationships within a family in order to achieve harmony (Becvar & Becvar, 1996; Sanchez, 2001). Family systems therapy is based on several assumptions: (a) It is logical and economical to treat together all those who exist and operate within a system of relationships (in most cases, it implies the nuclear family); (b) the problems of the "identified patient" are only symptoms, and the family itself is the client; (c) all symptoms or problematic behaviors exhibited by a member of the family serves a purpose; (d) the behaviors of family members are tied to one another in powerful reciprocal ways (circular causality emphasized over linear causality); and (e) the task of the therapist is to modify relationships or improve communications within the family system (Corey, 2001; Goldenberg & Goldenberg, 1998; McGoldrick & Giordano, 1996).

There are many family systems approaches, but two characteristics seem to be especially important. One of these, the *communications approach,* is based on the assumption that family problems are communication difficulties. Many family communication problems are both subtle and complex. Family therapists concentrate on improving not only faulty communications but also interactions and relationships among family members (Satir, 1967, 1983). The way in which rules, agreements, and perceptions are communicated among members may also be important (J. Haley, 1967). The therapist's role in repairing faulty communications is active but not dominating. He or she attempts to show family members how they are now communicating with one another; to prod them into revealing what they feel and think about themselves and other family members, and what they want from the family relationship; and to convince them to practice new ways of responding.

The *structural approach* also considers communication to be important, but it emphasizes the interlocking roles of family members (Minuchin, 1974). Most families are constantly in a state of change; they are in the process of structuring and restructuring themselves into systems and subsystems. The health of a family is often linked to the members' abilities to recognize boundaries of the various systems—alliances, communication patterns, and so forth. Often, unhealthy family functioning and the symptoms exhibited by members are caused by boundary disputes.

From a philosophical and theoretical perspective, both approaches appear appropriate in working with various minority groups. For example, they appear to

- Highlight the importance of the family (vs. the individual) as the unit of identity
- Focus on resolving concrete issues
- Be concerned with family structure and dynamics
- Assume that these family structures and dynamics are historically passed on from one generation to another
- Attempt to understand the communication and alliances via reframing
- Place the therapist in an expert position

Many of these qualities, as we have seen, would be consistent with the worldview of racial/ethnic minorities. Many culturally different families favorably view its emphases on the family as the unit of identity and study, understanding the cultural norms and background of the family system, and the need to balance the system.

The problem arises, however, in how these goals and strategies are translated into concepts of "the family" or what constitutes the "healthy" family. Some of the characteristics of healthy families may pose problems in therapy with various culturally different groups. They tend to be heavily loaded with value orientations that are incongruent with the value systems of many culturally different clients (Corey, 2001; McGoldrick, Giordano, & Pearce, 1996). They tend to

- Allow and encourage expressing emotions freely and openly
- View each member as having a right to be his or her own unique self (individuate from the emotional field of the family)
- Strive for an equal division of labor among members of the family
- Consider egalitarian role relationships between spouses desirable
- Hold the nuclear family as the standard

As in the case of Esteban and Carmen and the case of Elena Martinez, these translations in family systems therapy can cause great problems in working with minority clients. It is clear that the culturally effective family systems therapist must escape from his or her cultural encapsulation, necessarily understand the sociopolitical forces that affect minority families, become aware of major differences in the value system that he or she possesses when contrasted with racial/cultural family values, and understand structural family relationships that are different from his or her own concepts of family.

Issues in Working with Ethnic Minority Families

Effective multicultural family counseling and therapy must incorporate the many racial, cultural, economic, and class issues inherent in the two clinical family examples given earlier. While not unique to racial/ethnic minority families, distinguishing quantitative and qualitative life events differentiate the minority experience from middle-class White families. Several factors have been identified as important for culturally sensitive family therapists to take into consideration (Ho, 1987, 1997; McGoldrick & Giordano, 1996; Robinson & Howard-Hamilton, 2000).

Ethnic Minority Reality

This refers to the racism and poverty that dominate the lives of minorities. Lower family income, greater unemployment, increasing numbers falling below the poverty line, and other issues have had major negative effects not only on the individuals, but on family structures as well. The relocation of 120,000 Japanese Americans into concentration camps during World War II, for example, drastically altered the traditional Japanese family structures and relationships (D. W. Sue & Kirk, 1973). By physically uprooting these U.S. citizens, symbols of ethnic identity were destroyed, creating identity conflicts and problems. Furthermore, the camp experience disrupted the traditional lines of authority. The elderly male no longer had a functional value as head of household; family discipline and control became loosened; and women gained a degree of independence unheard of in traditional Japanese families.

Likewise, African American families have been victims of poverty and racism. Nowhere is this more evident than in statistics revealing a higher incidence of Black children living in homes without the biological father present—82%, as compared with 43% for Whites (Wilkinson, 1993). More Black families are classified as impoverished (46%) than are White families (10%). In addition, many more Black males are single, widowed, or divorced (47%), compared with Whites (28%). The high mortality rate among Black males has led some to call them an endangered species in which societal forces have even strained and affected the Black male-female relationship (Gibbs, 1987; Parham et al., 1999). Under slavery, class distinctions were obliterated; the slave husband was disempowered as the head of the household; and the man's inability to protect and provide for kin had a negative effect upon African American family relationships (Wilkinson, 1993).

Conflicting Value Systems

Imposed by White Euro-American society upon minority groups, conflicting value systems have also caused great harm to them. The case of Elena Martinez reveals how the White counselor's conception of the nuclear family may clash with traditional Latino/Hispanic emphasis on extended families. It appears that almost all minority groups place greater value on families, historical lineage (reverence of ancestors), interdependence among family members, and submergence of self for the good of the family (S. C. Kim, 1985; Uba, 1994). African Americans are often described as having a kinship system in which relatives of a variety of blood ties (aunts, uncles, brothers, sisters, boyfriends, preachers, etc.) may act as the extended family (Black, 1996; Hines & Boyd-Franklin, 1996). Likewise, the extended family in the Hispanic culture includes numerous relatives and friends (Falicov, 1996; Garcia-Preto, 1996), as evidenced in the case of Elena Martinez. Perhaps most difficult to grasp for many mental health professionals is the American Indian family network, which is structurally open and assumes village-like characteristics (Herring, 1999; Red Horse, 1983; Sutton & Broken Nose, 1996). This family extension may include several households. Unless therapists are aware of these value differences, they may unintentionally mislabel behaviors that they consider bizarre or make decisions that are detrimental to the family. We have more to say about this important point shortly.

Biculturalism

Biculturalism refers to the fact that minorities in the United States inherit two different cultural traditions. In the next chapter we discuss issues of culture conflict, cultural racism, and the melting-pot concept as it affects identity development. The therapist must understand how biculturalism influences the structures, communications, and dynamics of the family. A 22-year-old Latino male's reluctance to go against the wishes of his parents and marry a woman he loves may not be a sign of immaturity. Rather, it may reflect a conflict between duality of membership in two groups or the positive choice of one cultural dictate over another. A culturally effective therapist is one who understands the possible conflicts that may arise as a result of biculturalism.

Related to biculturalism is the therapist's need to understand the process of acculturation and the stresses encountered by culturally diverse families. While the term was originally used to indicate the mutual influence of two different cultures on one another, biculturalism is best understood in the United States as the interaction between a dominant and nondominant culture. Some questions that need to be addressed by family systems therapists when working with culturally diverse families are: What are the psychological consequences of nondominant families as they encounter the dominant culture? What effects does the dominant culture have on minority family dynamics and structure? What types of issues or problems are likely to arise as a result of the acculturation process? For example, a recently migrated family often has parents who are allied with the culture of the country of origin while their offspring are more likely to adapt to the dominant culture more rapidly. In many cases, children may be more oriented to the culture of the larger society, resulting in intergenerational conflicts (Gushue & Sciarra, 1995). However, it is important for the therapist to understand the sociopolitical dimensions of this process. The problem may not be so much a function of intergenerational conflict as it is the dominant-subordinate clash of cultures (Gushue & Sciarra, 1995; Szapocznik & Kurtines, 1993). The multiculturally skilled family therapist would focus on the problems created by cultural oppression and reframe the goal as one of stressing the benefits of intergenerational collaboration and alliance against a common foe (Gushue & Sciarra, 1995).

Ethnic Differences in Minority Status

These differences refer to the life experiences and adjustments that occur as a result of minority status in the United States. All four racial/ethnic minority groups have been subjected to dehumanizing forces:

- The history of slavery for Black Americans not only has negatively impacted their self-esteem but also has contributed to disruption of the Black male/Black female relationship and the structure of the Black family. Slavery imposed a pathological system of social organization on the African American family, resulting in disorganization and a constant fight for survival and stability. Despite the system of slavery, however, many African Americans overcame these negative forces by sheer force of will, by reasserting their ties of affection, by using extended kinship ties, by their strength of spirit and spirituality, and by their multigenerational networks (Wilkinson, 1993). It would be highly beneficial if the family systems therapist recognized these strengths in the African American family, rather than stressing its instability and problems.

- Racism and colonialism have made American Indians immigrants in their own land, and the federal government has even imposed a definition of race upon them (they must be able to prove they are at least one-quarter Indian "blood"). Such a legal definition of race has created problems among Native Americans by confusing the issues of identity. Like their African American brothers and sisters, Native Americans have experienced conquest, dislocation, cultural genocide, segregation, and coerced assimilation (Herring, 1999; Sutton & Broken Nose, 1996). American Indian family life has been strongly affected by government policies that include using missionaries, boarding schools, and the Bureau of Indian Affairs in an attempt to "civilize" the "heathens." The results have been devastating to Native Americans: learned helplessness; gambling, alcohol, and drug abuse; suicide; and family relationship problems (Tofoya & Del Vecchio, 1996). A family systems therapist must be aware of the multigenerational disruption of the Native American family through 500 years of historical trauma.

- Immigration status among Latino/Hispanics and Asian refugees/immigrants (legal resident to illegal alien) and the abuses, resentments, and discrimination experienced by them are constant stressful events in their lives. Anti-immigrant feelings have never been more pervasive and intense. As mentioned earlier, this negativism was symbolized in California by the 1994 passage of Proposition 187. Mean-spirited and obviously unfair, the initiative sought to expel children from school who were in the United States illegally, leaving them to fend for themselves; in addition, it denied nonemergency health care and other social services and increased fears of deportation and other reprisals. In addition to the hostile climate experienced by recent immigrants, the migration experience can be a source of stress and disappointment. The multicultural family systems therapist must differentiate between the reasons for migration because their impact on the family may be quite different. A family deciding to migrate in search of adventure or wealth (voluntary decision) will experience the change differently than will refugees/immigrants who must leave because of war or religious and political persecution. Attitudes toward assimilation and acculturation might be quite different between the two families.

Skin color and obvious physical differences are also important factors that determine the treatment of minority individuals and their families. These physical differences continue to warp the perception of White America in that persons of color are seen as aliens in their own land. During the 1998 Winter Olympics in Japan, MSNBC posted a Web page covering the participation of Tara Lipinski and Michelle Kwan, two American athletes competing in ice skating. The headline of the article, "American Beats Out Kwan," implied that Tara Lipinsky (White) is an American and Michelle Kwan (Asian American) is not. In the end, MSNBC was forced to issue an apology. Equating physical differences and particularly skin color with being alien, negative, pathological, or less than human has a long history. Travel logs of early European seafarers describe their encounters with Blacks and the images and judgments associated with Africans:

> *And entering in [a river], we see*
> *A number of blacke soules,*
> *Whose likelinesse seem'd men to be,*
> *But all as blacke as coles. (Quoted in Jordan, 1969, pp. 4–5)*

J. M. Jones (1997, 475) pointed out that the *Oxford English Dictionary* definition of the color black prior to the sixteenth century was the following:

Deeply stained with dirt; soiled, dirty, foul. . . . Having dark or deadly purposes, malignant; pertaining to or involving death, deadly; baneful, disastrous, sinister. . . . Foul, iniquitous, atrocious, horrible, wicked. . . . Indicating disgrace, censure, liability to punishment, etc.

It is clear then, that the concept of blackness was associated with being bad, ugly, evil, and nonhuman. J. M. Jones (1997) also observes the relationship between color name and a classic clinical report of multiple personality disorder. In the *Three Faces of Eve* (Thigpen & Cleckley, 1954, p. 476), the two personalities Eve White and Eve Black reflect positive associations with Whiteness and negative ones with Blackness:

Eve Black is lacking in culture but curiously likable. She is playful, childlike, entertaining. Her superego is nonfunctional, which makes her a delight, the one who has all the fun. Black is where the "fun" things go to be. Yet, just as there is a kind of nostalgia and envy directed at Eve Black, there is judgment and castigation, as well. A certain voyeurism makes Eve Black someone one would like to be around, but wouldn't want in one's family. Eve White, by contrast, has "all the right stuff." She is socialized to traditional values, properly "feminine," devoted, even heroic. Her saintliness is admired, but somehow she is repressed, and one's admiration for her is tinged with sadness.

The personality traits associated differentially with Eve White and Eve Black are not pulled from thin air; instead, they suggest the content of cultural beliefs about the races as well as the genders. These cultural beliefs did not, in 1954, depart substantially from the first conclusions about racial differences by Englishmen in 1550!

While skin color is probably the most powerful physical characteristic linked to racism, other physical features and differences may also determine negative treatment by the wider society. External societal definitions of race have often resulted in ideological racism that links physical characteristics of groups (usually skin color) to major psychological traits (Feagin, 1989). For example, golfer Jack Nicklaus's expression in 1996 that Blacks are born with the wrong muscles to play golf at the higher levels (apparently he has never seen Tiger Woods play), as well as Al Campanis's (former Dodger executive) and former sportscaster Jimmy "The Greek" Snyder's comments that Blacks are "great athletes" but "poor scholars" are sentiments which have shaped U.S. treatment of African Americans. Likewise, other physical features such as head form, facial features, color and texture of body hair, and so on all contrast with the ideal image of blond hair, and fair skin. Not only is there an external negative evaluation of those who differ from such "desired" features, but many persons of color may form negative self-images and body images and attempt to become "Westernized" in their physical features. One wonders, for example, at the psychological dynamics that have motivated some Asian American women to seek cosmetic surgery to reshape their eyes in a more "Westernized" fashion.

Ethnicity and Language

These dimensions refer to the "common sense of bonding" among members of a group that contributes to a sense of belonging. The symbols of the group (ethnicity) are manifested primarily in language. Language structures meaning, determines how we see things, is the carrier of our culture, and affects our worldviews. Many minority clients do not possess vocabulary equivalents to standard English and when forced to communicate in English may appear "flat," "nonverbal," "uncommunicative," and "lacking in insight" (Romero, 1985). The problem is linguistic and not psychological. In psychotherapy, where words are the major vehicle for effective change, language has been likened to what a baton is to the conductor and what a scalpel is to the surgeon (Russell, 1988).

Studies in the field of linguistics and sociolinguistics support the fact that language conveys a wealth of information other than the primary content of the message; the cues of background, place of origin, group membership, status in the group, and the relationship to the speaker can all be determined (Kennedy, 1996; Kochman, 1981; Lass et al., 1978; Russell, 1988; Samovar & Porter, 1982). Thus, the gender, race, and social class of the speaker can be accurately identified. More importantly, however, these studies also suggest that the listener utilizes this sociolinguistic information to formulate opinions of the speaker and in the interpretation of the message. Because our society values standard English, the use of nonstandard English, dialects, or accented speech is often associated with undesirable characteristics—being less intelligent, uncouth, lower class, unsophisticated, and uninsightful. Thus, while racial/ethnic minority groups may use their linguistic characteristics to bond with one another and to communicate more accurately, the larger society may invalidate, penalize, or directly punish individuals or groups who exhibit bilingualism or group-idiosyncratic use of language. In Arizona, for example, voters passed a 1996 law requiring that official state and local business be conducted in English only. The law was subsequently ruled unconstitutional by the Arizona Supreme Court in 1998. Unfortunately, in June 1998 California voters voted in favor of Proposition 227, which effectively abolished bilingual education and has had a devastating impact on the 1.4 million students attending public schools who are not fluent in English. These students were given only one year of intensive English immersion before being moved to regular classes. Since its passage, some school districts have refused to implement its mean-spirited policies on the basis of its educational unsoundness. Others have been using loopholes to avoid the devastating consequences. Still others have legally challenged the constitutionality of the measure. It is interesting to note that over 60% of Californians voted in favor of Proposition 227. Proponents of the bill played on the public's fears that the United States would be overrun by "aliens," contributing to the climate of antagonism toward racial/ethnic minorities.

Ethnicity and Social Class

These refer to aspects of wealth, name, occupation, and status. Class differences between mental health professionals and their minority clients can often lead to barriers in understanding and communication. This was clearly evident in the case of Elena Martinez in that the counselor had difficulty relating to a missed day of work. Needless to say, understanding class differences becomes even more important for therapists working with minority families because they are disproportionately represented in the lower socioeconomic classes. Many argue that class may be a more powerful determinant of values and behavior than race or ethnicity. For example, we know that the wealthiest one million people in the United States earn more than the next 100 million combined, that the top 1% own 40% of the nation's wealth, and that the gap between rich and poor is increasing (Thurow, 1995). From a political perspective, some believe that racial conflicts are promulgated by those at the very top, to detract from the real cause of inequities: a social structure that allows the dominant class to maintain power (Bell, 1993). While there is considerable truth to this view, not all differences can be ascribed to class alone. Further, while one cannot change race or ethnicity, changes in social class can occur. We contend that all three are important, and the therapist must understand their interactions with one another.

Multicultural Family Counseling/Therapy: A Conceptual Model

Effective multicultural family counseling/therapy operates under principles similar to that outlined in earlier chapters. First, counselors need to become culturally aware of their own values, biases, and assumptions about human behavior (especially as it pertains to the definition of family). Second, it is important to become aware of the worldview of the culturally different client and how that client views the definition, role, and function of the family. Last, appropriate intervention strategies need to be devised to maximize success and minimize cultural oppression. While in earlier chapters the focus was on individual clients and their ethnic/racial groups, our concern in this chapter is with the family unit as defined from the group's perspective. In attempting to understand the first two goals, we are using a model first outlined by Kluckhohn and Strodtbeck (1961). This model allows us to understand the worldviews of culturally diverse families by contrasting the value orientations of the four main groups we are studying (as illustrated in Table 6.1): Asian Americans, Native Americans, African Americans, and Latino/Hispanic Americans.

People-Nature Relationship

Traditional Western thinking believes in mastery and control over nature. As a result, most therapists operate from a framework that subscribes to the belief that problems are solvable and that both therapist and client must take an active part in solving problems via manipulation and control. Active intervention is stressed in controlling or changing the environment. As seen in Table 6.1, the four other ethnic groups view people as harmonious with nature.

Confucian philosophy, for example, stresses a set of rules aimed at promoting loyalty, respect, and harmony among family members (W. M. L. Lee, 1999; Uba, 1994). Harmony within the family and the environment leads to harmony within the self. Dependence on the family unit and acceptance of the environment seem to dictate differences in solving problems. Western culture advocates defining and attacking the problem directly. Asian cultures tend to accommodate or deal with problems through indirection. In child rearing, many Asians believe that it is better to avoid direct confrontation and to use deflection. A White family may deal with a child who has watched too many hours of TV by saying, "Why don't you turn the TV off and study?" To be more threatening, the parent might say, "You'll be grounded unless the TV goes off!" An Asian parent may respond by saying, "That looks like a boring

Table 6.1   **Cultural Value Preferences of Middle-Class White Euro-Americans and Racial/Ethnic Minorities: A Comparative Summary**

Area of Relationships	Middle-Class White Americans	Asian Americans	American Indians	Black Americans	Hispanic Americans
People to Nature/ Environment	Mastery over	Harmony with	Harmony with	Harmony with	Harmony with
Time Orientation	Future	Past-present	Present	Present	Past-present
People Relations	Individual	Collateral	Collateral	Collateral	Collateral
Preferred Mode of Activity	Doing	Doing	Being-in-becoming	Doing	Being-in-becoming
Nature of Man	Good & bad	Good	Good	Good & bad	Good

Source: From *Family Therapy with Ethnic Minorities* (p. 232) by M. K. Ho, 1987, Newbury Park, CA: Sage. Copyright 1987 by Sage Publications. Reprinted by permission.

program; I think your friend John must be doing his homework now," or, "I think father wants to watch his favorite program." Such an approach stems from the need to avoid conflict and to achieve balance and harmony among members of the family and the wider environment.

In an excellent analysis of family therapy for Asian Americans, S. C. Kim (1985) pointed out how current therapeutic techniques of confrontation and of having clients express thoughts and feelings directly may be inappropriate and difficult to handle. For example, one of the basic tenets of family therapy is that the identified patient (IP) typically behaves in such a way as to reflect family influences or pathology. Often, an acting-out child is symbolic of deeper family problems. Yet most Asian American families come to counseling or therapy for the benefit of the IP and not the family! Attempts to directly focus in on the family dynamics as contributing to the IP will be met with negativism and possible termination. S. C. Kim (1985, p. 346) states,

> *A recommended approach to engage the family would be to pace the family's cultural expectations and limitations by (1) asserting that the IP's problem (therefore not the IP by implication) is indeed the problem; (2) recognizing and reinforcing the family's concerns to help the IP to change the behavior; and (3) emphasizing that each family member's contribution in resolving the problem is vitally needed, and that without it, the problem will either remain or get worse bringing on further difficulty in the family.*

Thus, it is apparent that U.S. values that call for us to dominate nature (i.e., conquer space, tame the wilderness, or harness nuclear energy) through control and manipulation of the universe are reflected in family counseling. Family systems counseling theories attempt to describe, explain, predict, and control family dynamics. The therapist actively attempts to understand what is going on in the family system (structural alliances and communication patterns), identify the problems (dysfunctional aspects of the dynamics), and attack them directly or indirectly through manipulation and control (therapeutic interventions). Ethnic minorities or subgroups that view people as harmonious with nature or believe that nature may overwhelm people ("acts of God") may find the therapist's mastery-over-nature approach inconsistent or antagonistic to their worldview. Indeed, attempts to intervene actively in changing family patterns and relationships may be perceived as the problem because it may potentially unbalance that harmony that existed.

Time Dimension

How different societies, cultures, and people view time exerts a pervasive influence on their lives. U.S. society may be characterized as preoccupied with the future (Katz, 1985; Kluckhohn & Strodtbeck, 1961; J. Spiegel & Papajohn, 1983). Furthermore, our society seems very compulsive about time in that we divide it into seconds, minutes, hours, days, weeks, months, and years. Time may be viewed as a commodity ("time is money" and "stop wasting time") in fixed and static categories rather than as a dynamic and flowing process. It has been pointed out that the United States' future orientation may be linked to other values as well: (a) stress on youth and achievement, in which the children are expected to "better their parents"; (b) controlling one's own destiny by future planning and saving for a rainy day; and (c) optimism and hope for a better future. The spirit of the nation may be embodied in an old General Electric slogan, "Progress is our most important product." This is not to deny that people are concerned about the past and the present as well, but rather to suggest that culture, groups, and people may place greater emphasis on one over the other. Nor do we deny the fact that age, gender, occupation, social class, and other important demographic factors may be linked to time perspective. However, our work with various racial/ethnic minority groups and much of the research conducted (Ho, 1987; Inclan, 1985; Kluckhohn & Strodtbeck, 1961) support the fact that race, culture, and ethnicity are powerful determinants of whether the group emphasizes the past, present, or future.

Table 6.1 reveals that both American Indians and African Americans tend to value a present time orientation, while Asian Americans and Hispanic Americans have a combination past-present focus. Historically, Asian societies have valued the past as reflected in ancestor worship and the equating of age with wisdom and respectability. This contrasts with U.S. culture, in which youth is valued over the elderly and the belief that one's usefulness in life is over once one hits the retirement years. As the U.S. population ages, however, it will be interesting to note whether there will be a shift in the status of the elderly. As compared to Euro-American middle-class norms, Latinos also exhibit a past-present time orientation. Strong hierarchical structures in the family, respect for elders and ancestors, and the value of *personalismo* all combine in this direction. American Indians also differ from their White counterparts in that they are very grounded in the here and now rather than the future. American Indian philosophy relies heavily on the belief that time is flowing, circular, and harmonious. Artificial division of time (schedules) is disruptive to the natural pattern (Ho, 1987). African Americans also value the present because of the spiritual quality of their existence and their history of racism. Several difficulties may occur when the counselor or therapist is unaware of the differences of time perspective (Hines & Boyd-Franklin, 1996).

First, if time differences exist between the minority family and the White Euro-American therapist, it will most likely be manifested in a difference in the pace of time: Both may sense things are going too slowly or too fast. An American Indian family who values being in the present and the immediate experiential reality of being may feel that the therapist lacks respect for them and is rushing them (Herring, 1997; Sutton & Broken Nose, 1996) while ignoring the quality of the personal relationship. On the other hand, the therapist may be dismayed by the "delays," "inefficiency," and lack of "commitment to change" among the family members. After all, time is precious, and the therapist has only limited time to impact upon the family. The result is frequently dissatisfaction among the parties, no establishment of rapport, misinterpretation of the behaviors or situations, and probably discontinuation of future sessions.

Second, Inclan (1985) pointed out how confusions and misinterpretations can arise because Hispanics, particularly Puerto Ricans, mark time differently than do their U.S. White counterparts. The language of clock-time in counseling (50-minute hour, rigid time schedule, once-a-week sessions) can conflict with minority perceptions of time (Garcia-Preto, 1996). The following dialogue illustrates this point clearly:

> *"Mrs. Rivera, your next appointment is at 9:30 A.M. next Wednesday."*
> *"Good, it's convenient for me to come after I drop off the children at school."*
> Or, *"Mrs. Rivera, your next appointment is for the whole family at 3:00 P.M. on Tuesday."*
> *"Very good. After the kids return from school we can come right in." (Inclan, 1985, p. 328)*

Since school starts at 8 A.M., the client is bound to show up very early, while in the second example the client will most likely be late (school ends at 3 P.M.). In both cases, the counselor is most likely to be inconvenienced, but worse yet is the negative interpretation that may be made of the client's motives (anxious, demanding, or pushy in the first case, while resistant, passive-aggressive, or irresponsible in the latter one). The counselor needs to be aware that many Hispanics may mark time by events rather than by the clock.

Third, Ho (1987) suggested that many minorities who are present-time oriented overall would be more likely to seek immediate, concrete solutions than future-oriented, abstract goals. In earlier chapters we noted that goals or processes that are insight oriented assume that the client has time to sit back and self-explore. Career/vocational counseling, in which clients explore their interests, values, work temperaments, skills, abilities, and the world of work, may be seen as highly future oriented. While potentially beneficial to the client, these approaches may pose dilemmas for both the minority family and the counselor.

Relational Dimension

In general, the United States can be characterized as an achievement-oriented society, which is most strongly manifested in the prevailing Protestant work ethic. Basic to the ethic is the concept of *individualism:* (a) The individual is the psychosocial unit of operation; (b) the individual has primary responsibility for his or her own actions; (c) independence and autonomy are highly valued and rewarded; and (d) one should be internally directed and controlled. In many societies and groups within the United States, however, this value is not necessarily shared. Relationships in Japan and China are often described as being lineal, and identification with others is both wide and linked to the past (ancestor worship). Obeying the wishes of ancestors or deceased parents and perceiving your existence and identity as linked to the historical past are inseparable. Almost all racial/ethnic minority groups in the United States tend to be more collateral in their relationships with people. In an individualistic orientation, the definition of the family tends to be linked to a biological necessity (nuclear family), while a collateral or lineal view encompasses various concepts of the extended family. Not understanding this distinction and the values inherent in these orientations may lead the family therapist to erroneous conclusions and decisions. Following is a case illustration of an young American Indian.

> *A younger probationer was under court supervision and had strict orders to remain with responsible adults. His counselor became concerned because the youth appeared to ignore this order. The client moved around frequently and, according to the counselor, stayed overnight with several different young women. The counselor presented this case at a formal staff meeting, and fellow professionals stated their suspicion that the client was either a pusher or a pimp. The frustrating element to the counselor was that the young women knew each other and appeared to enjoy each other's company. Moreover, they were not ashamed to be seen together in public with the client. This behavior prompted the counselor to initiate violation proceedings. (Red Horse, Lewis, Feit, & Decker, 1981, p. 56)*

If an American Indian professional had not accidentally come upon this case, a revocation order initiated against the youngster would surely have caused irreparable alienation between the family and the social service agency. The counselor had failed to realize that the American Indian family network is structurally open and may include several households of relatives and friends along both vertical and horizontal lines. The young women were all first cousins to the client, and each was as a sister, with all the households representing different units of the family.

Likewise, African Americans have strong kinship bonds that may encompass both blood relatives and friends. Traditional African culture values the collective orientation over individualism (J. H. Franklin, 1988; Hines & Boyd-Franklin, 1996; Sudarkasa, 1988). This group identity has also been reinforced by what many African Americans describe as the sense of "peoplehood" developed as a result of the common experience of racism and discrimination. In a society that has historically attempted to destroy the Black family, near and distant relatives, neighbors, friends, and acquaintances have arisen in an extended family support network (Black, 1996). Thus, the Black family may appear quite different from the ideal nuclear family. The danger is that certain assumptions made by a White therapist may be totally without merit or may be translated in such a way as to alienate or damage the self-esteem of African Americans.

For example, the absence of a father in the Black family does not necessarily mean that the children do not have a father figure. This function may be taken over by an uncle or male family friend. M. B. Thomas and Dansby (1985) provided an example of a group-counseling technique that was detrimental to several Black children. Clients in the group were asked to draw a picture of the family dinner table and place circles representing the mother, father, and children in their seating arrangement. They reported that even before the directions for the exercise were finished, a young Black girl ran from the room in tears. She had been raised by an aunt. Several other Black clients stated that they did not eat dinners together as a family except on special occasions or Sundays—according to Willie (1981) a typical routine in some affluent Black families.

The importance of family membership and the extended family system has already been illustrated in the case of Elena Martinez. We give one example here to illustrate that the moral evaluation of a behavior may depend on the value orientation of the subject. Because of their collective orientation, Puerto Ricans view obligations to the family as primary over all other relationships (Garcia-Preto, 1996). When a family member attains a position of power and influence, it is expected that he or she will favor the relatives over objective criteria. Businesses that are heavily weighted by family members, and appointments of family members in government positions, are not unusual in many countries. Failure to hire a family member may result in moral condemnation and family sanctions (Inclan, 1985). This is in marked contrast to what we ideally believe in the United States. Appointment of family members over objective criteria of individual achievement is condemned.

It would appear that differences in the relationship dimension between the mental health provider and the minority family receiving services can cause great conflict. While family therapy may be the treatment of choice for many minorities (over individual therapy), its values may again be antagonistic and detrimental to minorities. Family approaches that place heavy emphasis on individualism and freedom from the emotional field of the family may cause great harm. Our approach should be to identify how we might capitalize on collaterality to the benefit of minority families.

Activity Dimension

One of the primary characteristics of White U.S. cultural values and beliefs is an action (doing) orientation: (a) We must master and control nature; (b) we must always do things about a situation; and (c) we should take a pragmatic and utilitarian view of life. In counseling, we expect clients to master and control their own life and environment, to take action to resolve their own problems, and to fight against bias and inaction. The doing mode is evident everywhere and is reflected in how White Americans identify themselves by what they *do* (occupations), how children are asked what they want to do when they grow up, and how higher value is given to inventors over poets and to doctors of medicine over doctors of philosophy. An essay topic commonly given to schoolchildren returning to school is "What I did on my summer vacation."

It appears that both American Indians and Latinos/Hispanics prefer a being or being-in-becoming mode of activity. The American Indian concepts of self-determination and noninterference are examples. Value is placed on the spiritual quality of being, as manifested in self-containment, poise, and harmony with the universe. Value is placed on the attainment of inner fulfillment and an essential serenity of one's place in the universe. Because each person is fulfilling a purpose, no one should have the power to interfere or impose values. Often, those unfamiliar with Indian values perceive the person as stoic, aloof, passive, noncompetitive, or inactive. In working with families, the counselor role of active manipulator may clash with American Indian concepts of being-in-becoming (noninterference).

Likewise, Latino/Hispanic culture may be said to have a more here-and-now or being-in-becoming orientation. Like their American Indian counterparts, Hispanics believe that people are born with *dignidad* (dignity) and must be given *respecto* (respect). They are born with innate worth and importance; the inner soul and spirit are more important than the body. People cannot be held accountable for their lot in life (status, roles, etc.) because they are born into this life state (Inclan, 1985). A certain degree of *fatalismo* (fatalism) is present, and life events may be viewed as inevitable (*Lo que Dios manda*, what God wills). Philosophically, it does not matter what people have in life or what position they occupy (farm laborer, public official, or attorney). Status is possessed by existing, and everyone is entitled to *respecto*.

Since this belief system deemphasizes material accomplishments as a measure of success, it is clearly at odds with Euro-American middle-class society. While a doing-oriented family may define a family member's worth via achievement, a being orientation equates worth simply to belonging. Thus, when clients complain that someone is not an effective family member, what do they mean? This needs to be clarified by the therapist. Is it a complaint that the family member is not performing and achieving (doing), or does it mean that the person is not respectful and accommodating to family structures and values (being)?

Ho (1987) describes both Asian Americans and African Americans as operating from the doing orientation. However, it appears that "doing" in these two groups is manifested differently than in the White American lifestyle. The active dimension in Asians is related not to individual achievement, but to achievement via conformity to family values and demands. Controlling one's own feelings, impulses, desires, and needs to fulfill responsibility to the family is strongly ingrained in Asian children. The doing orientation tends to be more ritualized in the roles of and responsibilities toward members of the family. African Americans also exercise considerable control (endure the pain and suffering of racism) in the face of adversity to minimize discrimination and to maximize success.

Nature of People Dimension

Middle-class Euro-Americans generally perceive the nature of people as neutral. Environmental influences such as conditioning, family upbringing, and socialization are believed to be dominant forces in determining the nature of the person. People are neither good nor bad but a product of the environment. While several minority groups may share features of this belief with Whites, there is a qualitative and quantitative difference that may affect family structure and dynamics. For example, Asian Americans and American Indians tend to emphasize the inherent goodness of people. We have already discussed the Native-American concept of noninterference, which is based on the belief that people have an innate capacity to advance and grow (self-fulfillment) and that problematic behaviors are the result of environmental influences that thwart the opportunity to develop. Goodness will always triumph over evil if the person is left alone. Likewise, Asian philosophy (Buddhism and Confucianism) believes in peoples' innate goodness and prescribes role relationships that manifest the "good way of life." Central to Asian belief is the fact that the best healing source lies within the family (Ho, 1987) and that seeking help from the outside (e.g., counseling and therapy) is nonproductive and against the dictates of Asian philosophy.

Latinos may be described as holding the view that human nature is both good and bad (mixed). Concepts of *dignidad* and *respecto* undergird the belief that people are born with positive qualities. Yet some Hispanics, such as Puerto Ricans, spend a great deal of time appealing to the supernatural forces so that children may be blessed with a good human nature (Inclan, 1985). Thus, a child's "badness" may be accepted as destiny, so parents may be less inclined to seek help from educators or mental health professionals for such problems. The preferred mode of help may be religious consultations and ventilation to neighbors and friends who sympathize and understand the dilemmas (change means reaching the supernatural forces).

African Americans may also be characterized as having a mixed concept of people, but in general they believe, like their White counterparts, that people are basically neutral. Environmental factors have a great influence on how people develop. This orientation is consistent with African American beliefs that racism, discrimination, oppression, and other external factors create problems for the individual. Emotional disorders and antisocial acts are caused by external forces (system variables) rather than internal, intrapsychic, psychological forces. For example, high crime rates, poverty, and the current structure of the African family are the result of historical and current oppression of Black people. White Western concepts of genetic inferiority and pathology (African American people are born that way) hold little validity for the Black person.

Implications for Clinical Practice

It is extremely difficult to speak specifically about applying multicultural strategies and techniques to minority families because of the great variations not only among Asian Americans, African Americans, Latino/Hispanic Americans, Native Americans, and Euro-Americans, but also within the groups themselves. For example, the term "Asian and Pacific American" covers some 32 distinct subgroups in the United States. To suggest principles of multicultural family systems therapy that would have equal validity to all groups may make our discussion too general and abstract. Worse yet, we may foster overgeneralizations that border on being stereotypes.

Likewise, to attempt an extremely specific discussion would mean dealing with literally thousands of racial, ethnic, and cultural combinations, a task that is humanly impossible. What seems to be required is a balance of these two extremes: a framework that would help us both to understand differences in communication styles/structural alliances in the family and to pinpoint more specifically cultural differences that exist within a particular family. Once that is accomplished, the therapist can turn his or her attention to creatively developing approaches and strategies of family therapy appropriate to the lifestyle of the minority family. To aid therapists in developing competencies in multicultural family therapy, we would like to outline some general guidelines that may be helpful.

1. Know that our increasing diversity presents us with different cultural conceptions of the family. Whether groups value a lineal, collateral, or individualistic orientation has major implications for their and our definitions of the family. One definition cannot be seen as superior to another.

2. Realize that families cannot be understood apart from the cultural, social, and political dimensions of their functioning. The traditional definition of the nuclear family as consisting of heterosexual parents in a long-term marriage, raising their biological children, and with the fa-

ther as sole wage earner is a statistical minority. Extended families, intermarriage, divorce, openly gay/lesbian relationships, commingling of races, single parent and two parents working outside the home makes the conventional "normal family" definition an anomaly.

3. When working with a racial/ethnic group different from you, make a concerted and conscientious effort to learn as much as possible about their definition of family, the values that underlie the family unit, and your own contrasting definition.

4. Be especially attentive to traditional cultural family structure and extended family ties. As seen in the case of Elena Martinez, nonblood relatives may be considered an intimate part of the extended family system. Understanding husband-wife relationships, parent-child relationships, and sibling relationships from different cultural perspectives is crucial to effective work with minority families.

5. Do not prejudge from your own ethnocentric perspective. Be aware that many Asian Americans and Hispanics have a more patriarchal spousal relationship, while Euro-Americans and Blacks have a more egalitarian one. The concept of equal division of labor in the home between husband and wife or working toward a more equal relationship may be a violation of family norms.

6. Realize that most minority families view the *wifely* role as less important than the *motherly* role. For instance, the existence of children validates and cements the marriage; therefore, motherhood is often perceived as a more important role. Therapists should not judge the health of a family on the basis of the romantic egalitarian model characteristic of White culture.

7. Do not overlook the prospect of utilizing the natural help-giving networks and structures that already exist in the minority culture and community. It is ironic that the mental health field behaves as if minority communities never had anything like mental health treatment until it came along and invented it.

8. Recognize the fact that helping can take many forms. These forms often appear quite different from our own, but they are no less effective or legitimate. Multicultural counseling calls for us to modify our goals and techniques to fit the needs of minority populations. Granted, mental health professionals are sometimes hard-pressed in challenging their own assumptions of what constitutes counseling and therapy, or they feel uncomfortable in roles to which they are not accustomed. However, the need is great to move in this most positive direction.

9. Assess the importance of ethnicity to clients and families. Be aware that acculturation is a powerful force and that this is especially important for

the children, since they are most likely to be influenced by peers. Many tensions and conflicts between the younger generation and their elders are related to culture conflicts. These conflicts are not pathological, but normative responses to different cultural forces.

10. Realize that the role of the family therapist cannot be confined to culture-bound rules that dictate a narrow set of appropriate roles and behaviors. Effective multicultural family counseling may include validating and strengthening ethnic identity, increasing one's own awareness and use of client support systems (extended family, friends, and religious groups), serving as a culture broker, becoming aware of advantages and disadvantages in being of the same or different ethnic group as your client, not feeling you need to know everything about other ethnic groups, and avoiding polarization of cultural issues.

11. Accept the notion that the family therapist will need to be creative in the development of appropriate intervention techniques when working with minority populations. With traditional Asian Americans, subtlety and indirectness may be called for rather than direct confrontation and interpretation. Formality in addressing members of the family, especially the father (Mr. Lee rather than Tom), may be more appropriate. For African Americans, a much more interactional approach (as opposed to an instrumental one) in the initial encounter (rather than getting to the goal or task immediately) may be dictated. Approaches are often determined by cultural/racial/system factors, and the more you understand about these areas, the more effective you will become.

Non-Western and Indigenous
Methods of Healing

7

Chapter

Both the postmodern movement in psychology and the changing demographics in the United States have fueled renewed interest in indigenous methods of healing. In the former, the importance of understanding alternative realities, cultural relativism, spirituality, and a holistic perspective have challenged traditional Euro-American science (Fukuyama & Sevig, 1999; Highlen, 1994, 1996). In the latter, the increasing numbers of racial/ethnic minority groups in our society—especially recent Asian, Latin American, and African immigrants—have exposed mental health professionals to a host of different belief systems, some radically different from the Euro-American worldview (Fukuyama & Sevig, 1999). As counselors and therapists will increasingly come into contact with client groups who differ from them in race, culture, and ethnicity, it seems important to study and understand indigenous healing practices in order to (a) understand the worldview of culturally diverse clients, (b) anticipate potential conflicts in belief systems that might hinder our ability to be therapeutically effective, and (c) develop an appreciation for the richness of these older forms of treatment. To prevent our journey from becoming a philosophical and abstract exercise, we make use of multiple case studies to illustrate alternative belief systems and treatments.

Spirit Attacks: The Case of Vang Xiong

Vang Xiong is a former Hmong (Laotian) soldier who, with his wife and child, was resettled in Chicago in 1980. The change from his familiar rural surroundings and farm life to an unfamiliar urban area must have produced a severe culture shock. In addition, Vang vividly remembers seeing people killed during his escape from Laos, and he expressed feelings of guilt about having to leave his brothers and sisters behind in that country. Five months after his arrival, the Xiong family moved into a conveniently located apartment, and that is when Vang's problems began:

Symptoms and Cause

Vang could not sleep the first night in the apartment, nor the second, nor the third. After three nights of sleeping very little, Vang came to see his resettlement worker, a young bilingual Hmong man named Moua Lee. Vang told Moua that the first night he woke suddenly, short of breath, from a dream in which a cat was sitting on his chest. The second night, the room suddenly grew darker, and a figure, like a large black dog, came to his bed and sat on his chest. He could not push the dog off and he grew quickly and dangerously short of breath. The third night, a tall, white-skinned female spirit came into his bedroom from the kitchen and lay on top of him. Her weight made it increasingly difficult for him to breathe, and as he grew frantic and tried to call out he could manage but a whisper. He attempted to turn onto his side, but found he was pinned down. After 15 minutes, the spirit left him, and he awoke, screaming. . . . He was afraid to return to the apartment at night, afraid to fall asleep, afraid he would die during the night, or that the spirit would make it so that he and his wife could never have another child. He told Moua that once, when he was 15, he had had a similar attack; that several times, back in Laos, his elder brother had been visited by a similar spirit; and that his brother was subsequently unable to father children due to his wife's miscarriages and infertility. (Tobin & Friedman, 1983, p. 440)

Moua Lee and mental health workers became very concerned in light of the high incidence of "sudden death syndrome" among Southeast Asian refugees. For some reason, the incidence of unexplained deaths, primarily among Hmong men, would occur within the first two years of residence in the United States. Autopsies produced no identifiable cause for the deaths. All the reports were the same: A person in apparently good health went to sleep and died without waking. Often, the victim displayed labored breathing, screams, and frantic movements just before death. With this dire possibility for Vang, the mental health staff felt that they lacked the expertise for so complex and potentially dangerous a case. Conventional Western means of treatment for other Hmong clients had proved minimally effective. As a result, they decided to seek the services of Mrs. Thor, a 50-year-old Hmong woman who was widely respected in Chicago's Hmong community as a shaman. The description of the treatment is given below:

Shamanic Cure

That evening, Vang Xiong was visited in his apartment by Mrs. Thor, who began by asking Vang to tell her what was wrong. She listened to his story, asked a few questions, and then told him she thought she could help. She gathered the Xiong family around the dining room table, upon which she placed some candles alongside many plates of food that Vang's wife had prepared. Mrs. Thor lit the candles, and then began a chant that Vang and his wife knew was an attempt to communicate with spirits. Ten minutes or so after Mrs. Thor had begun chanting, she was so intensely involved in her work that Vang and his family felt free to talk to each other, and to walk about the room without fear of distracting her. Approximately one hour after she had begun, Mrs. Thor completed her chanting, announcing that she knew what was wrong. He said that she had learned from her spirit that the figures in Vang's dreams who lay on his chest and who made it so difficult for him to breathe were the souls of the apartment's previous tenants, who had apparently moved out so abruptly they had left their souls behind. Mrs. Thor constructed a cloak out of newspaper for Vang to wear. She then cut the cloak in two, and burned the pieces, sending the spirits on their way with the smoke. She also had Vang crawl through a hoop, and then between two knives, telling him that these maneuvers would make it very hard for spirits to follow. Following these brief ceremonies, the food prepared by Vang's wife was enjoyed by all. The leftover meats were given in payment to Mrs. Thor, and she left, assuring Vang Xiong that his troubles with spirits were over. (Tobin & Friedman, 1983, p. 441)

Clinical knowledge regarding what is called the Hmong sudden death syndrome indicates that Vang was one of the lucky victims of the syndrome: He survived it. Indeed, since undergoing the healing ceremony in which the unhappy spirits were released, Vang has reported no more problems with nightmares or with his breathing during sleep.

Such a story might appear unbelievable and akin to mysticism to many people. After all, most of us have been trained in a Western ontology that does not embrace indigenous or alternative healing approaches. Indeed, if anything, it actively rejects such approaches as unscientific and supernatural; mental health professionals are encouraged to rely on sensory information, defined by the physical plane of existence rather than the spiritual plane (Fukuyama & Sevig, 1999; Highlen, 1996). Such a rigid stance is unfortunate and shortsighted because there is much that Western healing can learn from these age-old forms of treatment. Let us briefly analyze the case of Vang Xiong to illustrate what these valuable lessons might be and draw parallels between non-Western and Western healing practices.

The Legitimacy of Culture-Bound Syndromes: Nightmare Deaths and the Hmong Sudden Death Phenomena

The symptoms experienced by Vang and the frighteningly high number of early Hmong refugees who have died from these so-called *nightmare deaths* have baffled mental health workers for years. Indeed, researchers at the Federal Centers for Disease Control and epidemiologists have studied it but remain mystified (D. Sue, Sue, & Sue, 2000; Tobin & Friedman, 1983). Such tales bring to mind anthropological literature describing voodoo deaths and *bangungut,* or Oriental nightmare death. What is clear, however, is that these deaths do not appear to have a primary biological basis and that psychological factors (primarily belief in the imminence of death—either by a curse, as in voodoo suggestion, or some form of punishment and excessive stress) appear to be causative. Belief in spirits and spirit possession is not uncommon among many cultures, especially in Southeast Asia (Eliade, 1972; Fadiman, 1997; Harner, 1990). Such worldview differences pose problems for Western-trained mental health professionals who may quickly dismiss these belief systems and impose their own explanations and treatments on culturally different clients. Working outside of the belief system of culturally different clients might not have a desired therapeutic effect, and the risk of unintentional harm (in this case the potential death of Vang) is great.

That the sudden death phenomenon is a culture-bound reality is being increasingly recognized by Western science (Kamarack & Jenning, 1991). Most researchers now acknowledge that attitudes, beliefs, and emotional states are intertwined and can have a powerful effect on physiological responses and physical well-being. Death from bradycardia (slowing of the heartbeat) seems correlated with feelings of helplessness, as in the case of Vang (there was nothing he could do to get the cat, dog, or white-skinned spirit off his chest). The following case shows the impact of this emotion on heart rate:

> *The patient was lying very stiffly in bed, staring at the ceiling. He was a 56-year-old man who had suffered an anterior myocardial infarction [heart attack] some 2½ days ago. He lay there with bloodshot eyes, unshaven, and as we walked into the room, he made eye contact first with me and then with the intern who had just left his side. The terror in his eyes was reflected in those of the intern. The patient had a heart rate of forty-eight that was clearly a sinus bradycardia. I put my hands on his wrist, which had the effect of both confirming the pulse and making some physical contact with him, and I asked what was wrong.*
>
> *"I am very tired," he said. "I haven't slept in two and one-half days, because I'm sure that if I fall asleep, I won't wake up." I discussed with him the fact that we had been at fault for not making it clear that he was being very carefully*

monitored, so that we would be aware of any problem that might develop. I informed him further that his prognosis was improving rapidly. As I spoke, his pulse became fuller. (Shine, 1984, p. 27)

It is clear that the patient's physiological response was counteracted by the physician's assurance that his situation was not hopeless—in essence, by removing the source of stress. In other words, the patient believed in the power of the doctor and of the monitoring devices attached to him. Likewise, it is apparent that Vang was helped by his belief in the power of Mrs. Thor and the treatment he received. We return to this important point shortly.

The text revision of the fourth edition of the American Psychiatric Association's *Diagnostic and Statistical Manual of Mental Disorders* (DSM-IV-TR; American Psychiatric Association, 1999) has made initial strides in recognizing the importance of ethnic and cultural factors related to psychiatric diagnosis. The manual warns that mental health professionals who work with immigrant and ethnic minorities must take into account (a) the predominant means of manifesting disorders (e.g., possessing spirits, nerves, fatalism, inexplicable misfortune), (b) the perceived causes or explanatory models, and (c) the preferences for professional and indigenous sources of care. Interestingly, the DSM-IV-TR now contains a glossary of culture-bound syndromes in Appendix I (see Table 7.1 for a listing of these disorders). They describe culture-bound syndromes as

recurrent, locality-specific patterns of aberrant behavior and troubling experience that may or may not be linked to a particular DSM-IV diagnostic category. Many of these patterns are indigenously considered to be "illnesses," or at least afflictions, and most have local names. . . . Culture-bound syndromes are generally limited to specific societies or culture areas and are localized, folk, diagnostic categories that frame coherent meanings for certain repetitive, patterned, and troubling sets of experiences and observations. (American Psychiatric Association, 1999, p. 844)

In summary, it is very important for mental health professionals to become familiar not only with the cultural background of their clients, but to be knowledgeable about specific culture-bound syndromes. A primary danger from lack of cultural understanding is the tendency to overpathologize (overestimate the degree of pathology); the mental health professional would have been wrong in diagnosing Vang as a paranoid schizophrenic suffering from delusions and hallucinations. Most might have prescribed powerful antipsychotic medication or even institutionalization. The fact that he was cured so quickly indicates that such a diagnosis would have been erroneous. Interestingly, it is equally dangerous to underestimate the severity or complexity of a refugee's emotional condition as well.

Table 7.1 **Culture-Bound Syndromes from the DSM-IV**

Culture-bound syndromes are disorders specific to a cultural group or society but not easily given a DSM diagnosis. These illnesses or afflictions have local names with distinct culturally sanctioned beliefs surrounding causation and treatment. Some of these are briefly described.

Amok. This disorder was first reported in Malaysia but is found also in Laos, the Philippines, Polynesia, Papua New Guinea, and Puerto Rico, as well as among the Navajo. It is a dissociative episode preceded by introspective brooding and then an outburst of violent, aggressive, or homicidal behavior toward people and objects. Persecutory ideas, amnesia, and exhaustion signal a return to the premorbid state.

Ataque de nervios. This disorder is most clearly reported among Latinos from the Caribbean but is recognized in Latin American and Latin Mediterranean groups as well. It involves uncontrollable shouting, attacks of crying, trembling, verbal or physical aggression, and dissociative or seizure-like fainting episodes. The onset is associated with a stressful life event relating to family (e.g., death of a loved one, divorce, conflicts with children, etc.).

Brain fag. This disorder is usually experienced by high school or university students in West Africa in response to academic stress. Students state that their brains are fatigued and that they have difficulties in concentrating, remembering, and thinking.

Ghost sickness. Observed among members of American Indian tribes, this disorder is a preoccupation with death and the deceased. It is sometimes associated with witchcraft and includes bad dreams, weakness, feelings of danger, loss of appetite, fainting, dizziness, anxiety, and a sense of suffocation.

Koro. This Malaysian term describes an episode of sudden and intense anxiety that the penis of the male or the vulva and nipples of the female will recede into the body and cause death. It can occur in epidemic proportions in local areas and has been reported in China, Thailand, and other South and East Asian countries.

Mal de ojo. Found primarily in Mediterranean cultures, this term refers to a Spanish phrase that means "evil eye." Children are especially at risk, and symptoms include fitful sleep, crying without apparent cause, diarrhea, vomiting, and fever.

Nervios. This disorder includes a range of symptoms associated with distress, somatic disturbance, and inability to function. Common symptoms include headaches, brain aches, sleep difficulties, nervousness, easy tearfulness, dizziness, and tingling sensations. It is a common idiom of distress among Latinos in the United States and Latin America.

Rootwork. This refers to cultural interpretations of illness ascribed to hexing, witchcraft, sorcery, or the evil influence of another person. Symptoms include generalized anxiety, gastrointestinal complaints, and fear of being poisoned or killed (voodoo death). Roots, spells, or hexes can be placed on people. It is believed that a cure can be manifested via a root doctor who removes the root. Such a belief can be found in the southern United States among both African American and European American populations and in Caribbean societies.

Shen-k'uei (Taiwan); Shenkui (China). This is a Chinese described disorder that involves anxiety and panic symptoms with somatic complaints. There is no identifiable physical cause. Sexual dysfunctions are common (premature ejaculation and impotence). The physical symptoms are attributed to excessive semen loss from frequent intercourse, masturbation, nocturnal emission, or passing of "white turbid urine" believed to contain semen. Excessive semen loss is feared and can be life threatening because it represents one's vital essence.

Table 7.1 continued

Susto. This disorder is associated with fright or soul loss and is a prevalent folk illness among some Latinos in the United States as well as inhabitants of Mexico, Central America, and South America. Susto is attributed to a frightening event that causes the soul to leave the body. Sickness and death may result. Healing is associated with rituals that call the soul back to the body and restore spiritual balance.

Zar. This term is used to describe spirits possessing an individual. Dissociative episodes, shouting, laughing, hitting the head against a wall, weeping, and other demonstrative symptoms are associated with it. It is found in Ethiopia, Somalia, Egypt, Sudan, Iran, and other North African and Middle Eastern societies. People may develop a long-term relationship with the spirit, and their behavior is not considered pathological.

Causation and Spirit Possession

Vang believed that his problems were related to an attack by undesirable spirits. His story in the following passage gives us some idea about beliefs associated with the fears:

> The most recent attack in Chicago was not the first encounter my family and I have had with this type of spirit, a spirit we call Chia. My brother and I endured similar attacks about six years ago back in Laos. We are susceptible to such attacks because we didn't follow all of the mourning rituals we should have when our parents died. Because we didn't properly honor their memories we have lost contact with their spirits, and thus we are left with no one to protect us from evil spirits. Without our parents' spirits to aid us, we will always be susceptible to spirit attacks. I had hoped flying so far in a plane to come to America would protect me, but it turns out spirits can follow even this far. (Tobin & Friedman, 1983, p. 444)

Western science remains skeptical of using supernatural explanations to explain phenomena and certainly does not consider the existence of spirits to be scientifically sound. Yet belief in spirits and its parallel relationship to religious, philosophic, and scientific worldviews have existed in every known culture, including the United States (e.g., the witch hunts of Salem, Massachusetts). Among many Southeast Asian groups, it is not uncommon to posit the existence of good and evil spirits, to assume that they are intelligent beings, and to believe that they are able to affect the life circumstance of the living (Fadiman, 1997; E. Lee, 1996). Vang, for example, believed strongly that his problems were due to spirits who were unhappy with him and were punishing him. Interestingly, among the Hmong, good spirits often serve a protective function against evil spirits. Because Vang's parental spirits had deserted him, he was more susceptible to the workings of evil forces. Many cultures believe that a cure can come about only through the aid of a shaman or healer who could reach and communicate with the spirit world via divination skills.

While mental health professionals may not believe in spirits, therapists are similar to the Hmongs in their need to explain the troubling phenomena experienced by Vang and to construe meaning from them. Vang's sleep disturbances, nightmares, and fears can be seen as the result of emotional distress. From a Western perspective, his war experiences, flight, relocation, and survivor stress (not to mention the adjustment to a new country) may all be attributed to combat fatigue (Posttraumatic Stress Disorder, or PTSD) and survivor guilt (Mollica, Wyshak, & Lavelle, 1987; Tobin & Friedman, 1983; Uba, 1994). Studies on the hundreds of thousands of refugees from Southeast Asia suggest that they were severely traumatized during their flight for freedom (Mollica et al., 1987). The most frequent diagnoses for this group were generally Major Affective Disorder and PTSD. In addition to being a combat veteran, Vang is a disaster victim, a survivor of a holocaust that has seen perhaps 200,000 of the approximately 500,000 Hmongs die. Vang's sleeplessness, breathing difficulties, paranoid belief that something attacked him in bed, and symptoms of anxiety and depression are the result of extreme trauma and stress. Tobin and Friedman (1983, p. 443) believed that Vang also suffered from survivor's guilt and concluded,

> *Applying some of the insights of the Holocaust literature to the plight of the Southeast Asian refugees, we can view Vang Xiong's emotional crisis (his breathing and sleeping disorder) as the result not so much of what he suffered as what he did not suffer, of what he was spared. . . . "Why should I live while others died?" so Vang Xiong, through his symptoms, seemed to be saying, "Why should I sleep comfortably here in America while the people I left behind suffer? How can I claim the right to breathe when so many of my relatives and countrymen breathe no more back in Laos?"*

Even though we might be able to recast Vang's problems in more acceptable psychological terminology, the effective multicultural helping professional requires knowledge of cultural relativism and respect for the belief system of culturally different clients. Respecting another's worldview does not mean that the helping professional needs to subscribe to it. Yet the counselor or therapist must be willing and ready to learn from indigenous models of healing and to function as a facilitator of indigenous support systems or indigenous healing systems (Atkinson, Thompson, & Grant, 1993).

The Shaman as Therapist: Commonalities

It is probably safe to conclude that every society and culture has had individuals or groups designated as healers: those who comforted the ailing. Their duties involved not only physical ailments, but those related to psychological distress or behavioral deviance as well (Harner, 1990). While every culture has multiple healers, the shaman in non-Western cultures is perhaps the most powerful of all because only he or she possesses the ultimate magico-religious powers that go beyond the senses (Eliade, 1972). Mrs. Thor was a well-known and respected shaman in the Hmong community of the Chicago area. While her approach to treating Vang (incense, candle burning, newspaper, trance-like chanting, spirit diagnosis, and even her home visit) on the surface might appear like mysticism, there is much in her behavior that is similar to Western psychotherapy. First, as we saw in Chapter 3, the healer's credibility is crucial to the effectiveness of therapy. In this case, Mrs. Thor had all the cultural credentials of a shaman; she was a specialist and professional with long years of training and experience in dealing with similar cases. By reputation and behavior, she acted in a manner familiar to Vang and his family; more important, she shared their worldview as to problem definition. Second, she showed compassion while maintaining a professional detachment, did not pity or make fun of Vang, avoided premature diagnosis or judgment, and listened to his story carefully. Third, like the Western therapist, she offered herself as the chief instrument of cure. She used her expertise and ability to get in touch with the hidden world of the spirits (in Western terms we might call it the unconscious) and helped Vang to understand (become conscious of) the mysterious power of the spirits (unconscious) to effect a cure.

Because Vang believed in spirits, Mrs. Thor's interpretation that the nightmares and breathing difficulties were spiritual problems was intelligible, desired, and ultimately curative. It is important to note, however, that Vang also continued to receive treatment from the local mental health clinic in coming to grips with the deaths of others (his parents, fellow soldiers, and those of other family members).

In the case of Vang Xiong, both non-Western and Western forms of healing were combined with one another for maximum effect. The presence of a mental health treatment facility that employed bilingual/bicultural practitioners, its vast experience with Southeast Asian immigrants, and its willingness to use indigenous healers provided Vang with a culturally appropriate form of treatment that probably saved his life. Not all immigrants, however, are so fortunate. Witness the case of the Nguyen family:

A Case of Child Abuse?

Mr. And Mrs. Nguyen and their four children left Vietnam in a boat with 36 other people. Several days later, they were set upon by Thai pirates. The occupants were all robbed of their belongings; some were killed, including two of the Nguyens' children. Nearly all the women were raped repeatedly. The trauma of the event is still very much with the Nguyen family, who now reside in St. Paul, Minnesota. The event was most disturbing to Mr. Nguyen, who had watched two of his children drown and his wife being raped. The pirates had beaten him severely and tied him to the boat railing during the rampage. As a result of his experiences, he continued to suffer feelings of guilt, suppressed rage, and nightmares.

The Nguyen family came to the attention of the school and social service agencies because of suspected child abuse. Their oldest child, Phuoc (age 12), had come to school one day with noticeable bruises on his back and down the spinal column. In addition, obvious scars from past injuries were observed on the child's upper and lower torso. His gym teacher had seen the bruises and scars and reported them to the school counselor immediately. The school nurse was contacted about the possibility of child abuse, and a conference was held with Phuoc. He denied that he had been hit by his parents and refused to remove his garments when requested to do so. Indeed, he became quite frightened and hysterical about taking off his shirt. Since there was still considerable doubt about whether this was a case of child abuse, the counselor decided to let the matter drop for the moment. Nevertheless, school personnel were alerted to this possibility.

Several weeks later, after four days of absence, Phuoc returned to school. The homeroom teacher noticed bruises on Phuoc's forehead and the bridge of his nose. When the incident was reported to the school office, the counselor immediately called Child Protective Services to report a suspected case of child abuse.

Because of the heavy caseload experienced by Child Protective Services, a social worker was unable to visit the family until weeks later. The social worker, Mr. P., had called the family and visited the home on a late Thursday afternoon. Mrs. Nguyen greeted Mr. P. upon his arrival. She appeared nervous, tense, and frightened. Her English was poor, and it was difficult to communicate with her. Since Mr. P. had specifically requested to see Mr. Nguyen as well, he inquired about his whereabouts. Mrs. Nguyen answered that he was not feeling well and was in the room downstairs. She said he was having "a bad day," had not been able to sleep last night, and was having flashbacks. In his present condition, he would not be helpful.

When Mr. P. asked about Phuoc's bruises, Mrs. Nguyen did not seem to understand what he was referring to. The social worker explained in detail the reason for his visit. Mrs. Nguyen explained that the scars were due to the beating given her children by the Thai pirates. She became very emotional about the topic and broke into tears.

While this had some credibility, Mr. P. explained that there were fresh bruises on Phuoc's body as well. Mrs. Nguyen seemed confused, denied that there were new injuries, and denied that they would hurt Phuoc. The social worker pressed Mrs. Nguyen about the new injuries until she suddenly looked up and said, "Thùôc Nam." It was obvious that Mrs. Nguyen now understood what Mr. P. was referring to. When asked to clarify what she meant by the phrase, Mrs. Nguyen pointed at several thin bamboo sticks and a bag of coins wrapped tightly in a white cloth. It looked like a blackjack! She then pointed downstairs in the direction of the husband's room. It was obvious from Mrs. Nguyen's gestures that her husband had used these to beat her son.

There are many similarities between the case of the Nguyen family and that of Vang Xiong. One of the most common experiences of refugees forced to flee their country is the extreme stressors that they experienced. Constantly staring into the face of death was, unfortunately, all too common an experience. Seeing loved ones killed, tortured, and raped; being helpless to change or control such situations; living in temporary refugee or resettlement camps; leaving familiar surroundings; and encountering a strange and alien culture can only be described as multiple severe traumas. It is highly likely that many Cambodian, Hmong/Laotian, and Vietnamese refugees suffer from serious posttraumatic stress and other forms of major affective disorders. Mr. and Mrs. Nguyen's behaviors (flashbacks, desire to isolate the self, emotional fluctuations, anxiety and tenseness) might all be symptoms of PTSD. Accurate understanding of their life circumstances will prevent a tendency to overpathologize or underpathologize their symptoms (Mollica et al., 1987). These symptoms, along with a reluctance to disclose to strangers and discomfort with the social worker, should be placed in the context of the stressors that they experienced and their cultural background. More important, as in the case of the Nguyen family, behaviors should not be interpreted to indicate "guilt" or "a desire not to disclose the truth" about child abuse.

Second, mental health professionals must consider potential linguistic and cultural barriers when working with refugees, especially when one lacks both experience and expertise. In this case, it is clear that the teacher, school counselor, school nurse, and even the social worker did not have sufficient understanding or experience in working with Southeast Asian refugees. For example, the social worker's failure to understand Vietnamese phrases and Mrs. Nguyen's limited English proficiency place serious limitations on their ability to communicate accurately. The social worker might have avoided much of the misunderstanding if an interpreter had been present. In addition, the school personnel may have misinterpreted many culturally sanctioned forms of behavior on the part of the Vietnamese. Phuoc's reluctance to disrobe in front of strangers (the nurse) may have been prompted by cultural taboos rather than by attempts to hide the "injuries." Traditional Asian culture dictates strongly that family matters are handled within the family. Many Asians believe that family affairs should not be discussed publicly, and especially not with strangers. Disrobing publicly and telling others about the scars or the trauma of the Thai pirates would not be done readily. Yet such knowledge is required by educators and social service agencies that must make enlightened decisions.

Third, both school and social service personnel are obviously unenlightened about indigenous healing beliefs and practices. In the case of Vang Xiong, we saw how knowledge and understanding of cultural beliefs led to appropriate and helpful treatment. In the case of the Nguyen family, lack of understanding led to charges of child abuse. But is this really a case of child abuse? When Mrs. Nguyen said "Thúôc Nam," what was she referring to? What did the fresh bruises along Phuoc's spinal column, forehead, and bridge of the nose mean? And didn't Mrs. Nguyen admit that her husband used the bamboo sticks and bag of coins to beat Phuoc?

In Southeast Asia, traditional medicine derives from three sources: Western medicine (Thùôc Tay), Chinese or Northern medicine (Thúôc Bac), and Southern medicine (Thúôc Nam). Many forms of these treatments continue to exist among Asian Americans and are even more prevalent among the Vietnamese refugees, who brought them to the United States (Hong & Ham, 2001). Thúôc Nam, or traditional medicine, involves using natural fruits, herbs, plants, animals, and massage to heal the body. Massage treatment is the most common cause of misdiagnosis of child abuse because it leaves bruises on the body. Three common forms of massage treatment are Bắt Gió ("catching the wind"), Cao Gió ("scratching the wind," or "coin treatment"), and Giác Hoi ("pressure massage," or "dry cup massage"). The latter involves steaming bamboo tubes so that the insides are low in pressure, applying them to a portion of the skin that has been cut, and sucking out "bad air" or "hot wind." Cao Gió involves rubbing the patient with a mentholated ointment and then using coins or spoons to strike or scrape lightly along the ribs and both sides of the neck and shoulders. Bắt Gió involves using both thumbs to rub the temples and massaging toward the bridge of the nose at least 20 times. Fingers are used to pinch the bridge of the nose. All three treatments leave bruises on the parts of the body treated.

If the social worker could have understood Mrs. Nguyen, he would have known that Phuoc's four-day absence from school was due to illness and that he was treated by the parents via traditional folk medicine. Massage treatments are widespread customs practiced not only by Vietnamese, but also by Cambodians, Laotians, and Chinese. These treatments are aimed at curing a host of physical ailments such as colds, headaches, backaches, and fevers. In the mind of the practitioner, such treatments have nothing to do with child abuse. Yet, the question still remains: Is it considered child abuse when traditional healing practices result in bruises? This is a very difficult question to answer because it raises a larger question: Can culture justify a practice, especially when it is harmful? While unable to answer this last question directly (we encourage you to dialogue about it), we point out that many medical practitioners in California do not consider it child abuse because (a) medical literature reveals no physical complications as a result of Thúôc Nam; (b) the intent is not to hurt the child but to help him or her; and (c) it is frequently used in conjunction with Western medicine. However, we would add that health professionals and educators have a responsibility to educate parents concerning the potential pitfalls of many folk remedies and indigenous forms of treatment.

The Principles of Indigenous Healing

Ever since the beginning of human existence, all societies and cultural groups have developed not only their own explanations of abnormal behaviors but also their culture-specific ways of dealing with human problems and distress (Das, 1987; Harner, 1990; C. C. Lee & Armstrong, 1995). Within the United States, counseling and psychotherapy are the predominant psychological healing methods; in other cultures, however, indigenous healing approaches continue to be widely used. While there are similarities between Euro-American helping systems and the indigenous practices of many cultural groups, there are major dissimilarities as well. Western forms of counseling, for example, rely on sensory information defined by the physical plane of reality (Western science), while most indigenous methods rely on the spiritual plane of existence in seeking a cure. In keeping with the cultural encapsulation of our profession, Western healing has been slow to acknowledge and learn from these age-old forms of wisdom (Highlen, 1996; C. C. Lee, 1996). In its attempt to become culturally responsive, however, the mental health field must begin to put aside the biases of Western science, to acknowledge the existence of intrinsic help-giving networks, and to incorporate the legacy of ancient wisdom that may be contained in indigenous models of healing.

The work and writings of Lee (C. C. Lee, 1996; C. C. Lee & Armstrong, 1995; C. C. Lee, Oh, & Mountcastle, 1992) are especially helpful in this regard. Lee has studied what is called the *universal shamanic tradition,* which encompasses the centuries-old recognition of healers within a community. The anthropological term *shaman* refers to people often called witches, witch doctors, wizards, medicine men or women, sorcerers, and magic men or women. These individuals are believed to possess the power to enter an altered state of consciousness and in their healing rituals journey to other planes of existence beyond the physical world. Such was the case of Mrs. Thor, a shaman who journeyed to the spirit world in order to find a cure for Vang.

A study of indigenous healing in 16 non-Western countries found that three approaches were often used (Lee et al., 1992). First, there is heavy reliance on the use of communal, group, and family networks to shelter the disturbed individual (Saudi Arabia), to problem solve in a group context (Nigeria), and to reconnect them with family or significant others (Korea). Second, spiritual and religious beliefs and traditions of the community are used in the healing process. Examples include reading verses from the Koran and using religious houses or churches. Third, use of shamans (called piris and fakirs in Pakistan and Sudan) who are perceived to be the keepers of timeless wisdom constitutes the norm. In many cases, the person conducting a healing cere-mony may be a respected elder of the community or a family member.

An excellent example that incorporates these approaches is the Native Hawaiian *ho'oponopono* healing ritual (Nishihara, 1978; Shook, 1985). Trans-lated literally, the word means "a setting to right, to make right, to correct." In cultural context, *ho'oponopono* attempts to restore and maintain good rela-tions among family members and between the family and the supernatural powers. It is a kind of family conference (family therapy) aimed at restoring good and healthy harmony in the family. Many Native Hawaiians consider it to be one of the soundest methods of restoring and maintaining good rela-tions that any society has ever developed. Such a ceremonial activity occurs usually among members of the immediate family but may involve the ex-tended family and even nonrelatives if they were involved in the *pilikia* (trouble). The process of healing includes the following:

1. The *ho'oponopono* begins with *pule weke* (opening prayer) and ends with *pule ho'opau* (closing prayer). The pule creates the atmosphere for the healing and involves asking the family gods for guidance. These gods are not asked to intervene but to grant wisdom, understanding, and honesty.

2. The ritual elicits *'oia'i'o* or "truth telling," sanctioned by the gods, and makes compliance among participants a serious matter. The leader states the problem, prays for spiritual fusion among members, reaches out to resistant family members, and attempts to unify the group.

3. Once this occurs, the actual work begins through *mahiki,* a process of getting to the problems. Transgressions, obligations, righting the wrongs, and forgiveness are all aspects of *ho'oponopono.* The forgiving-releasing-severing of wrongs, the hurts, and the conflicts produces a deep sense of resolution.

4. Following the closing prayer, the family participates in *pani,* the termi-nation ritual in which food is offered to the gods and to the participants.

In general we can see several principles of indigenous Hawaiian healing: (a) Problems reside in relationships with people and spirits; (b) harmony and balance in the family and nature are desirable; (c) healing must involve the entire group and not just an individual; (d) spirituality, prayer, and ritual are important aspects of healing; (e) the healing process comes from a respected elder of the family; and (f) the method of healing is indigenous to the culture.

Indigenous healing can be defined as helping beliefs and practices that originate within the culture or society. It is not transported from other regions, and it is designed for treating the inhabitants of the given group. Those who study indigenous psychologies do not make an a priori assumption that one particular perspective is superior to another (U. Kim & Berry, 1993). The Western ontology of healing (counseling/therapy), however, does consider its methods to be more advanced and scientifically grounded than those found in many cultures. Western healing has traditionally operated from several assumptions: First, reality consists of distinct and separate units or objects (the therapist and client, the observer and observed); second, reality consists of what can be observed and measured via the five senses; third, space and time are fixed and are absolute constructs of reality; and fourth, science operates from universal principles and is culture-free (Highlen, 1996). While these guiding assumptions of Western science have contributed much to human knowledge and to the improvement of the human condition, most non-Western indigenous psychologies appear to operate from a different perspective. For example, many non-Western cultures do not separate the observer from the observed and believe that all life-forms are interrelated with one another, including mother nature and the cosmos; that the nature of reality transcends the senses; that space and time are not fixed; and that much of reality is culture-bound (D. W. Sue et al., 1998). Let us briefly explore several of these parallel assumptions and see how they are manifested in indigenous healing practices.

Holistic Outlook, Interconnectedness, and Harmony

The concepts of separation, isolation, and individualism are hallmarks of the Euro-American worldview. On an individual basis, modern psychology takes a reductionist approach to describing the human condition (i.e., id, ego, and superego; belief, knowledge, and skills; cognitions, emotions, and behaviors). In Western science, the experimental design is considered the epitome of methods used to ask and answer questions about the human condition or the universe. The search for cause-effect is linear and allows us to identify the independent variables, the dependent variables, and the effects of extraneous variables that we attempt to control. It is analytical and reductionist in character. The attempt to maintain objectivity, autonomy, and independence in understanding human behavior is also stressed. Such tenets have resulted in separation of the person from the group (valuing of individualism and uniqueness), science from spirituality, and man/woman from the universe.

Most non-Western indigenous forms of healing take a holistic outlook on well-being in that they make minimal distinctions between physical and mental functioning and believe strongly in the unity of spirit, mind, and matter. The interrelatedness of life-forms, the environment, and the cosmos is a given. As a result, the indigenous peoples of the world tend to conceptualize reality differently. As mentioned in Chapter 4, the psychosocial unit of operation for many culturally diverse groups, for example, is not the individual but the group (collectivism). In many cultures, acting in an autonomous and independent manner is seen as the problem because it creates disharmony within the group. The following case description by a Chinese counselor trainee (an international student) reveals just such a difference in worldview perspectives.

Who Has the Problem?

Carol, 29 years of age, blames herself for her family's tension and dissension. Her father is out of work and depressed most of the time; her mother feels overburdened and ineffective. In the past Carol has assumed responsibility for the problems and has done a lot for her parents. She is convinced, however, that if she were more hard working and more competent, most of the family problems would diminish greatly. The fact that she is increasingly unable to effect change bothers her, and she has come to a counselor for help. When my professor asked the class to analyze what the woman's problem was, everybody, except me, said that Carol was too submissive, that she should not continue to put family interests above her own. When the teacher played to the class two model tapes of interviews based on the case, much to my dismay, the student counselors, implicitly or explicitly, encouraged the client to think of her own needs first, leave her family and live alone, and make sure not to let her parents override her wishes. Almost the entire class agreed that the client needed assertiveness training, which I felt was quite unacceptable.

I just cannot understand why putting the family's interest before one's own is not correct or "normal" in the dominant American culture. I believe a morally responsible son or daughter has the duty to take care of his or her parents, whether it means sacrifice on his or her own part or not. . . . What is wrong with this interdependence? To me, it would be extremely selfish for Carol to leave her family when the family is in such need of her.

Although I do not think the client has a significant psychological problem, I do believe that the parents have to become more sensitive to their daughter's needs. It is not very nice and considerate for the parents to think only of themselves at the cost of their daughter's well-being. If I were the counselor of this client, I would do everything in my power to try to help change the parents, rather than the client. I feel strongly that it is the selfish person who needs to change, not the selfless person.

I was criticized by some of my American classmates for being judgmental; I think they are probably right. I would argue, however, that as soon as they defined Carol's problem as one of putting her family's interests before her own and suggested assertiveness training as a way of solving her problem, they had made a judgment, too. No? (Zhang, 1994, pp. 79–80)

The author concludes: "In contemporary China, where submergence of self for the good of the family, community, and country is still valued, and individualism condemned, our beginning counseling practice could fail should we adopt American counseling theories and skills without considerable alteration" (Zhang, 1994, p. 80).

Illness, distress, or problematic behaviors are seen as an imbalance in people relationships, a disharmony between the individual and his or her group, or as a lack of synchrony with internal or external forces. Harmony and balance are the healer's goal. Among American Indians, for example, harmony with nature is symbolized by the circle, or hoop of life (Heinrich, Corbin, & Thomas, 1990; Sutton & Broken Nose, 1996). Mind, body, spirit, and nature are seen as a single unified entity with little separation between the realities of life, medicine, and religion. All forms of nature, not just the living, are to be revered because they reflect the creator or deity. Illness is seen as a break in the hoop of life, an imbalance, or a separation between the elements. Many indigenous beliefs come from a metaphysical tradition. They accept the interconnectedness of cosmic forces in the form of energy or subtle matter (less dense than the physical) that surrounds and penetrates the physical body and the world. Both the ancient Chinese practice of acupuncture and chakras in Indian yoga philosophy involve the use of subtle matter to rebalance and heal the body and mind (Highlen, 1996). Chinese medical theory is concerned with the balance of yin (cold) and yang (hot) in the body, and it is believed that strong emotional states, as well as an imbalance in the type of foods eaten, may create illness (C. C. Lee, 1996; Mullavey-O'Byrne, 1994). As we saw in the case of Phuoc Nguyen, treatment might involve eating specific types or combinations of foods or using massage treatment to suck out "bad" or "hot" air. Such ideas of illness and health can also be found in the Greek theory of balancing body fluids (blood, phlegm, black bile, and yellow bile; Bankart, 1997).

Likewise, the Afrocentric perspective also teaches that human beings are part of a holistic fabric—that they are interconnected and should be oriented toward collective rather than individual survival (Asante, 1987; Hines & Boyd-Franklin, 1996; J. L. White & Parham, 1990). The indigenous Japanese assumptions and practices of Naikan and Morita therapy attempt to move clients toward being more in tune with others and society, to move away from individualism, and to move toward interdependence and connectedness (harmony with others; Bankart, 1997; Walsh, 1995). Naikan therapy, which derives from Buddhist practice, requires the client to reflect on three aspects of human relationships: (a) what other people have done for them, (b) what they have done for others, and (c) how they cause difficulties to others (Ishiyama, 1986; Walsh, 1995). The overall goal is to expand awareness of how much we receive from others, how much gratitude is due them, and how little we demonstrate such gratitude. This ultimately leads to a realization of the interdependence of the parts to the whole. Working for the good of the group ultimately benefits the individual.

Belief in Metaphysical Levels of Existence

Several years ago, two highly popular books—*Embraced by the Light* (Eadie, 1992) and *Saved by the Light* (Brinkley, 1994)—and several television specials described fascinating cases of near death experiences. All had certain commonalities: The individuals who were near death felt like they were leaving their physical bodies, observed what was happening around them, saw a bright beckoning light, and journeyed to higher levels of existence. Although the popularity of such books and programs might indicate that the American public is inclined to believe in such phenomena, science has been unable to validate these personal accounts and remains skeptical of their existence. Yet many societies and non-Western cultures accept, as given, the existence of different levels or planes of consciousness, experience, or existence. The means of understanding and ameliorating the causes of illness or problems of life are often found in a plane of reality separate from the physical world of existence.

Asian psychologies posit detailed descriptions of states of consciousness and outline developmental levels of enlightenment that extend beyond that of Western psychology. Asian perspectives concentrate less on psychopathology and more on enlightenment and ideal mental health (Tart, 1986; Walsh & Vaughan, 1993). The normal state of consciousness, in many ways, is not considered optimal and may be seen as a "psychopathology of the average" (Maslow, 1968). Moving to higher states of consciousness has the effect of enhancing perceptual sensitivity and clarity, concentration, and sense of identity, as well as emotional, cognitive, and perceptual processes. Such movement, according to Asian philosophy, frees one from the negative pathogenic forces of life. Attaining enlightenment and liberation can be achieved through the classic practices of meditation and yoga. Research findings indicate that they are the most widely used of all therapies (Walsh, 1995). They have been shown to reduce anxiety, specific phobias, and substance abuse (Shapiro, 1982; West, 1987; Kwee, 1990); to benefit those with medical problems by reducing blood pressure and aiding in the management of chronic pain (Kabat-Zinn, 1990); to enhance self-confidence, sense of control, marital satisfaction, and so on (Alexander, Rainforth, & Gelderloos, 1991); and to extend longevity (Alexander, Langer, Newman, Chandler, & Davies, 1989). Today, meditation and yoga in the United States have become accepted practices among millions, especially for relaxation and stress management. For practitioners of meditation and yoga, altered states of consciousness are unquestioned aspects of reality.

According to some cultures, nonordinary reality states allow some healers to access an invisible world surrounding the physical one. Puerto Ricans, for example, believe in *espiritismo* (spiritism), a world where spirits can have major impacts on the people residing in the physical world (Ramos-McKay et al., 1988). *Espiritistas,* or mediums, are culturally sanctioned indigenous healers who possess special faculties allowing them to intervene positively or negatively on behalf of the their clients. Many cultures strongly believe that human destiny is often decided in the domain of the spirit world. Mental illness may be attributed to the activities of hostile spirits, often in reaction to transgressions of the victim or the victim's family (C. C. Lee, 1996; Mullavey-O'Byrne, 1994). As in the case of Mrs. Thor, shamans, mediums, or indigenous healers often enter these realities on behalf of their clients in order to seek answers, to enlist the help of the spirit world, or to aid in realigning the spiritual energy field that surrounds the body and extends throughout the universe. Ancient Chinese methods of healing and the Hindu chakra also acknowledge another reality that parallels the physical world (Highlen, 1996). Accessing this world allows the healer to use these special energy centers to balance and heal the body and mind. Occasionally, the shaman may aid the helpee or novice in accessing that plane of reality so that he or she may find the solutions. The *vision quest,* in conjunction with the sweat lodge experience, is used by some American Indians as religious renewal or as a rite of passage (Hammerschlag, 1988; Heinrich et al., 1990). Behind these uses, however, is the human journey to another world of reality. The ceremony of the vision quest is intended to prepare the young man for the proper frame of mind; it includes rituals and sacred symbols, prayers to the Great Spirit, isolation, fasting, and personal reflection. Whether in a dream state or in full consciousness, another world of reality is said to reveal itself. Mantras, chants, meditation, and the taking of certain drugs (peyote) all have as their purpose a journey into another world of existence.

Spirituality in Life and the Cosmos

Native American Indians look on all things as having life, as having spiritual energy and importance. A fundamental belief is that all things are connected. The universe consists of a balance among all of these things and a continuous flow of cycling of this energy. Native American Indians believe that we have a sacred relationship with the universe that is to be honored. All things are connected, all things have life, and all things are worthy of respect and reverence.

> *Spirituality focuses on the harmony that comes from our connection with all parts of the universe in which everything has the purpose and value exemplary of "personhood" including plants (e.g., "tree people"), the land ("Mother Earth"), the winds ("the Four powers"), "Father Sky," "Grandfather Sun," "Grandmother Moon," "The Red Thunder Boys" . . . Spiritual being essentially requires only that we seek our place in the universe; everything else will follow in good time. Because everyone and everything was created with a specific purpose to fulfill, no one should have the power to interfere or to impose on others the best path to follow. (J. T. Garrett & Garrett, 1994, p. 187)*

The sacred Native American beliefs concerning spirituality are a truly alien concept to modern Euro-American thinking. The United States has had a long tradition in believing that one's religious beliefs should not enter into scientific or rational decisions. Incorporating religion in the rational decision-making process or in the conduct of therapy has generally been seen as unscientific and unprofessional. The schism between religion and science occurred centuries ago and has resulted in a split between science/psychology and religion (Fukuyama & Sevig, 1999). This is reflected in the oft-quoted phrase "separation of Church and State." The separation has become a serious barrier to mainstream psychology's incorporating indigenous forms of healing into mental health practice, especially when religion is confused with spirituality. While people may not have a formal religion, indigenous helpers believe that spirituality is an intimate aspect of the human condition. While Western psychology acknowledges the behavioral, cognitive, and affective realms, it only makes passing reference to the spiritual realm of existence. Yet indigenous helpers believe that spirituality transcends time and space, mind and body, and our behaviors, thoughts, and feelings (Lee & Armstrong, 1995).

These contrasting worldviews are perhaps most clearly seen in definitions of "the good life" and how our values are manifested in evaluating the worth of others. In the United States, for example, the pursuit of happiness is most likely manifested in material wealth and physical well-being, while other cultures value spiritual or intellectual goals. The worth of a person is anchored in the number of separate properties he or she owns and in a person's net worth and ability to acquire increasing wealth. Indeed, it is often assumed that such an accumulation of wealth is a sign of divine approval (Condon & Yousef, 1975). In cultures where spiritual goals are strong, the worth of people is unrelated to materialistic possessions, but rather resides within individuals, emanates from their spirituality, and is a function of whether they live the "right life." People from capitalistic cultures often do not understand self-immolations and other acts of suicide in other countries such as India. They are likely to make statements such as "life is not valued there" or, better yet, "life is cheap." These statements indicate a lack of understanding about actions that arise from cultural forces rather than personal frustrations;

they may be symbolic of a spiritual-valuing rather than a material-valuing orientation.

One does not have to look beyond the United States, however, to see such spiritual orientations; many racial/ethnic minority groups in this country are strongly spiritual. African Americans, Asian Americans, Latino/Hispanic Americans, and Native Americans place strong emphasis on the interplay and interdependence of spiritual life and healthy functioning. Puerto Ricans, for example, may sacrifice material satisfaction in favor of values pertaining to the spirit and soul. The Lakota Sioux often say *"Mitakuye Oyasin"* at the end of a prayer or as a salutation. Translated, it means "to all my relations," which acknowledges the spiritual bond between speaker and all people present and extends to forebears, the tribe, the family of man, and mother nature. It speaks to the philosophy that all life forces, mother earth, and the cosmos are sacred beings and that the spiritual is the thread that binds all together.

Likewise, a strong spiritual orientation has always been a major aspect of life in Africa, and this was true also during the slavery era in the United States:

> *Highly emotional religious services conducted during slavery were of great importance in dealing with oppression. Often signals as to the time and place of an escape were given then. Spirituals contained hidden messages and a language of resistance (e.g., "Wade in the Water" and "Steal Away"). Spirituals (e.g., "Nobody Knows the Trouble I've Seen") and the ecstatic celebrations of Christ's gift of salvation provided Black slaves with outlets for expressing feelings of pain, humiliation, and anger. (Hines & Boyd-Franklin, 1996, p. 74)*

The African American church has a strong influence over the lives of Black people and is often the hub of religious, social, economic, and political life. Religion is not separated from the daily functions of the church, as it acts as a complete support system for the African American family with its minister, deacons, deaconesses, and church members operating as one big family. A strong sense of peoplehood is fostered via social activities, choirs, Sunday school, health-promotion classes, day-care centers, tutoring programs, and counseling. To many African Americans the road to mental health and the prevention of mental illness lie in the health potentialities of their spiritual life.

Mental health professionals are becoming increasingly open to the potential benefits of spirituality as a means for coping with hopelessness, identity issues, and feelings of powerlessness (Fukuyama & Sevig, 1999). As an example of this movement, the Association for Counselor Education and Supervision (ACES) recently adopted a set of competencies related to spirituality. They define spirituality as

> *the animating force in life, represented by such images as breath, wind, vigor, and courage. Spirituality is the infusion and drawing out of spirit in one's life. It is ex-*

perienced as an active and passive process. Spirituality is also described as a capacity and tendency that is innate and unique to all persons. This spiritual tendency moves the individual towards knowledge, love, meaning, hope, transcendence, connectedness, and compassion. Spirituality includes one's capacity for creativity, growth, and the development of a values system. Spirituality encompasses the religious, spiritual, and transpersonal. (American Counseling Association, 1995, p. 30)

Interestingly enough, it appears that many in the United States are experiencing a "spiritual hunger" or a strong need to reintegrate spiritual or religious themes into their lives (Gallup, 1995; Thoreson, 1998). For example, it appears that there is a marked discrepancy between what patients want from their doctors and what doctors supply. Often, patients want to talk about the spiritual aspects of their illness and treatment, but doctors are either unprepared or disinclined to do so (Marwick, 1995). Likewise, most mental health professionals feel equally uncomfortable, disinclined, or unprepared to speak with their clients about religious or spiritual matters. Thoresen (1998) reported in a meta-analysis of over 200 published studies that the relationship between spirituality and health is highly positive. Those with higher levels of spirituality have lower disease risk, fewer physical health problems, and higher levels of psychosocial functioning. It appears that people require "faith" as well as reason to be healthy, and that psychology may profit from allowing the "spirit" to rejoin matters of the mind and body (Strawbridge, Cohen, Shema, & Kaplan, 1997).

Conclusions

In general, indigenous healing methods have much to offer to Euro-American forms of mental health practice. The contributions are valuable not only because multiple belief systems now exist in our society, but also because counseling and psychotherapy have historically neglected the spiritual dimension of human existence. Our heavy reliance on science and on the reductionist approach to treating clients has made us view human beings and human behavior as composed of separate noninteracting parts (cognitive, behavioral, and affective). There has been a failure recognize our spiritual being and to take a holistic outlook on life. Indigenous models of healing remind us of these shortcomings and challenge us to look for answers in realms of existence beyond the physical world.

Implications for Clinical Practice

We have repeatedly stressed that worldviews of culturally diverse clients may often be worlds apart from the dominant society. When clients attribute disorders to a cause quite alien from the Euro-American diagnosis, when their definitions of a healer are different from that of conventional therapists, and when the role behaviors (process of therapy) are not perceived as therapeutic, major difficulties are likely to occur in the provision of therapeutic services to culturally diverse groups in the United States. As a Western-trained therapist, for example, how would you treat clients who believed (a) that their mental problems were due to spirit possession, (b) that only a shaman with inherited powers could deal with the problem, and (c) that a cure could only be effected via a formal ritual (chanting, incense burning, symbolic sacrifice, etc.) and a journey into the spirit world? Most of us have had very little experience with indigenous methods of treatment and would find great difficulty in working effectively with such clients. There are, however, some useful guidelines that might help bridge the gap between contemporary forms of therapy and traditional nonwestern indigenous healing.

1. Do not invalidate the indigenous cultural belief systems of your culturally diverse client. On the surface, the assumptions of indigenous healing methods might appear radically different from our own. When we encounter them, we are often "shocked," find such beliefs to be "unscientific," and are likely to negate, invalidate, or dismiss them. Such an attitude will have the effect of invalidating our clients as well, since these beliefs are central to their worldview and reflect their cultural identity. It is important that therapists be open and able to entertain alternative worldviews and to understand that such beliefs reflect the realities of a different culture. Such an orientation does not mean that the therapist must subscribe to that belief system; it does mean, however, that the helping professional must avoid being judgmental. This will encourage and allow the client to share his or her story more readily, to feel validated, and to encourage the building of mutual respect and trust. Remember that one of the key components of multicultural competence is the ability to understand the worldview of your culturally diverse client. This must entail a willingness to hear your client's stories. Cultural storytelling and personal narratives have always been an intimate process of helping in all cultures.

2. Become knowledgeable about indigenous beliefs and healing practices. Therapists have a professional responsibility to become knowledgeable and conversant with the assumptions and practices of indigenous healing so that a process of desensitization and normalization can occur. By becoming knowledgeable and understanding of indigenous helping approaches, the therapist will avoid equating differences with deviance. Furthermore, we have found that therapists must do two things. First, they must understand that there is often a logical consistency between treatment approaches and philosophical explanations of human behav-

ior. If one believes that mental illness is due to biological factors (chemical imbalance, genetic transmission, or malfunction of internal organs), then medication or some other form of medical intervention is called for. If one believes that mental disorders are due to psychological factors (stress, unconscious conflicts, guilt, or abuse), then counseling/therapy may be dictated. Likewise, if one believes that abnormal behavior is a function of a supernatural force, then shamanic practices seem natural. Second, as we indicated in the example of Mrs. Thor, many similarities exist between Western and non-Western healing practices. Rather than perceiving non-Western indigenous forms of healing as abnormal, we can see them as a normal process within a particular cultural context.

3. Realize that learning about indigenous healing and beliefs entails experiential or lived realities. While reading books about non-Western forms of healing and attending seminars and lectures on the topic is valuable and helpful, understanding culturally different perspectives must be supplemented by lived experience. Even when we travel abroad, few of us actively place ourselves in situations that are unfamiliar because it evokes discomfort, anxiety, and a feeling of being different. Nonetheless, this is one of the few means of truly understanding and relating to others. Because the United States has become so diverse, one need not leave the country to experience the richness of different cultures. Opportunities abound. We suggest that you consider attending cultural events, meetings, and activities of the culturally different groups in your community. Such actions allow you to view culturally different individuals interacting in their community and to see how their values are expressed in relationships. Hearing from church leaders, attending open community forums, and visiting community celebrations allow you to sense the strengths of the minority community, observe leadership in action, personalizes your understanding, and identify potential guides and advisors to your own self-enlightenment.

4. Avoid overpathologizing and underpathologizing a culturally diverse client's problems. A therapist or counselor who is culturally unaware and who believes primarily in a universal psychology may often be culturally insensitive and inclined to see differences as deviance. They may be guilty of overpathologizing a culturally different client's problems by seeing it as more severe and pathological than it truly may be. There is also a danger, however, of underpathologizing a culturally diverse client's symptoms. While being understanding of a client's cultural context, having knowledge of culture-bound syndromes, and being aware of cultural relativism are desirable, being oversensitive to these factors may predispose the therapist to minimize problems, thereby underpathologizing disorders.

5. Be willing to consult with traditional healers or make use of their services. Mental health professionals must be willing and able to form partnerships with indigenous healers or develop community liaisons. Such an outreach has several advantages: (a) Traditional healers may provide knowledge and insight into client populations that would prove of value to the delivery of mental health services; (b) such an alliance will ultimately enhance the cultural credibility of therapists; and (c) it allows for referral to traditional healers (shamans, religious leaders, etc.) when treatment is rooted in cultural traditions. To accomplish these goals, therapists must respect the universal shamanic tradition while still being embedded in a Western psychological tradition. Most culturally different clients are open to a blend of both Western and non-Western approaches. For example, in the Asian Community Mental Health Services in Oakland, California, a Buddhist monk serves on the staff. This lends credibility to the service delivery organization, and the monk provides for the spiritual needs of the Asian American/Pacific Islander community as well.

6. Recognize that spirituality is an intimate aspect of the human condition and a legitimate aspect of mental health work. Spirituality is a belief in a higher power that allows us to make meaning of life and the universe. It may or may not be linked to a formal religion, but there is little doubt that it is a powerful force in the human condition. As indicated earlier, many groups accept the prevalence of spirituality in nearly all aspects of life; thus, separating it from one's existence is not possible. A counselor or therapist who does not feel comfortable dealing with spiritual needs of the clients, or who believes in an "artificial" separation of the spirit (soul) from the everyday life of the culturally different client, may not be providing the help needed. Just as therapists might inquire about the physical health of their clients, they should feel free and comfortable to inquire about their client's values and beliefs as they relate to spirituality. We do not, however, advocate indoctrination of the client. Nor do we endorse having the therapist prescribe any particular pathway to embracing, validating, or expressing spirituality and spiritual needs. What we suggest is that a mental health professional be open to exploring this aspect of the human condition and actively seek to integrate it into his or her practice.

7. Be willing to expand your definition of the helping role to community work and involvement. More than anything else, indigenous healing is community oriented and focused. Culturally competent mental health professionals must begin to expand their definition of the helping role to encompass a greater community involvement. The in-the-office setting is often nonfunctional in minority communities. Culturally sensi-

tive helping requires making home visits, going to community centers, and visiting places of worship and areas within the community. The types of help most likely to prevent mental health problems are building and maintaining healthy connections with one's family, one's god(s), and one's universe. It is clear that we live in a monocultural society—a society that invalidates and separates us from one another, from our spirituality, and from the cosmos. There is much wisdom in the ancient forms of healing that stress that the road to mental health is through becoming united and in harmony with the universe. Activities that promote these attributes involve community work. They include client advocacy and consultation, preventive education, and outreach programs, as well as becoming involved in systemic change and aiding in the formation of a public policy that allows for equal access and opportunities for all.

Part IV

WORLDVIEWS IN MULTICULTURAL COUNSELING/THERAPY

8

Chapter

For nearly all my life I have never seriously attempted to dissect my feelings and attitudes about being a Japanese American woman. Aborted attempts were made, but they were never brought to fruition, because it was unbearably painful. Having been born and raised in Arizona, I had no Asian friends. I suspect that given an opportunity to make some, I would have avoided them anyway. That is because I didn't want to have anything to do with being Japanese American. Most of the Japanese images I saw were negative. Japanese women were ugly; they had "cucumber legs," flat yellow faces, small slanty eyes, flat chests, and were stunted in growth. The men were short and stocky, sneaky and slimy, clumsy, inept, "wimpy looking," and sexually emasculated. I wanted to be tall, slender, large eyes, full lips, and elegant looking; I wasn't going to be typical Oriental!

At Cal [University of California, Berkeley], I've been forced to deal with my Yellow-White identity. There are so many "yellows" here that I can't believe it. I've come to realize that many White prejudices are deeply ingrained in me; so much so that they are unconscious. . . . To accept myself as a total person, I also have to accept my Asian identity as well. But what is it? I just don't know. Are they the images given me through the filter of White America, or are they the values and desires of my parents? . . .

Yesterday, I had a rude awakening. For the first time in my life I went on a date with a Filipino boy. I guess I shouldn't call him a "boy" as my ethnic studies teacher says it is derogatory toward Asians and Blacks. I only agreed to go because he seemed different from the other "Orientals" on campus. (I guess I shouldn't use that word either.) He's president of his Asian fraternity, very athletic and outgoing. . . . When he asked me, I figured, "Why not?" It'll be a good experience to see what its like to date an Asian boy. Will he be like White guys who will try to seduce me, or will he be too afraid to make any move when it comes to sex? . . . We went to San Francisco's Fisherman's Wharf for lunch. We were seated and our orders were taken before two other White women. They were, however, served first. This was painfully apparent to us, but I wanted to pretend that it was just a mix-up. My friend, however, was less forgiving and made a public fuss with the waiter. Still, it took an inordinate amount of time for us to get our lunches, and the filets were overcooked (purposely?). My date made a very public scene by placing a tip on the table, and then returning to retrieve it. I was both embarrassed, but proud of his actions.

This incident and others made me realize several things. For all my life I have attempted to fit into White society. I have tried to convince myself that I was different, that I was like all my other White classmates, and that prejudice and discrimination didn't exist for me. I wonder how I could have been so oblivious to prejudice and racism. I now realize that I cannot escape from my ethnic heritage and from the way people see me. Yet I don't know how to go about resolving many of my feelings and conflicts. While I like my newly found Filipino "male" friend (he is sexy), I continue to have difficulty seeing myself married to anyone other than a White man. (excerpts from a Nisei student journal, 1989)

From reading the preceding journal entry, it is not difficult for us to conclude that this Nisei (third-generation) Japanese American female is experiencing a racial awakening that has strong implications for her racial/cultural identity development. Her previous belief systems concerning Euro-Americans and Asian Americans are being challenged by social reality and the experiences of being a visible racial/ethnic minority. As our focus on this chapter is on racial/cultural identity development, let us briefly analyze this case for themes that are important for our understanding of this process.

First and foremost, a major theme involving societal portrayals of Asian Americans is clearly expressed in the student's beliefs about racial/cultural characteristics: She describes the Asian American male and female in a highly insulting fashion. More important, she seems to have internalized these beliefs and to be using "White" standards to judge Asian Americans as being either desirable or undesirable. For the student, the process of incorporating these standards has not only attitudinal but behavioral consequences as well. In Arizona, she would not have considered making Asian American friends even if the opportunity presented itself. In her mind, she was not a "typical Oriental"; she disowned or felt ashamed of her ethnic heritage; and she even concludes that she would not consider marrying anyone but a White male.

Second, her denial that she is not an Asian American is beginning to crumble. Being immersed on a campus in which many other fellow Asian Americans attend forces her to explore ethnic identity issues—a process she has been able to avoid while living in a predominantly White area. In the past when she encountered prejudice or discrimination, she had been able to deny it or to rationalize it away. The differential treatment she received at a restaurant and her male friend's labeling it as "discrimination" makes such a conclusion inescapable. The shattering of illusions is manifest in a realization that (a) despite her efforts to "fit in", it is not enough to gain social acceptance among many White Americans; (b) she cannot escape her racial/cultural heritage; and (c) she has been "brainwashed" into believing that one group is superior over another.

Third, the student's internal struggle to cast off the cultural conditioning of her past and the attempts to define her ethnic identity are both painful and conflicting. When she refers to her "Yellow-White" identity; writes about the negative images of Asian American males but winds up dating one; uses the terms "Oriental" and "boy" (in reference to her Asian male friend) but acknowledges their derogatory racist nature; describes Asian men as "sexually emasculated" but sees her Filipino date as "athletic," "outgoing," and "sexy"; expresses embarrassment at confronting the waiter about discrimination but feels proud of her Asian male friend for doing so; and states that she finds him attractive but could never consider marrying anyone but a White man, we have clear evidence of the internal turmoil she is undergoing. Understanding the process by which racial/cultural identity develops in persons of color is crucial for effective multicultural counseling/therapy.

Fourth, it is clear that the Japanese American female is a victim of ethnocentric monoculturalism. As we mentioned previously, the "problem" being experienced by the student does not reside in her, but in our society. It resides in a society that portrays racial/ethnic minority characteristics as inferior, primitive, deviant, pathological, or undesirable. The resulting damage strikes at the self-esteem and self/group identity of many culturally different individuals in our society; many, like the student, may come to believe that their racial/cultural heritage or characteristics are burdens to be changed or overcome. Understanding racial/cultural identity development and its relationship to therapeutic practice are the goals of this chapter.

Racial/Cultural Identity Development Models

One of the most promising approaches to the field of multicultural counseling/therapy has been the work on racial/cultural identity development among minority groups (Atkinson, Morten, et al., 1998; Casas & Pytluk, 1995; Carter, 1995; Choney, Berryhill-Paapke, & Robbins, 1995; W. E. Cross, 1971, 1995; Helms, 1984, 1985, 1993; Parham, 1989; Parham & Helms, 1981; Vandiver, Fhagen-Smith, Cokley, Cross, & Worrell, 2001). Most would agree that Asian Americans, African Americans, Latino/Hispanic Americans, and American Indians have a distinct cultural heritage that makes each different from the other. Yet such cultural distinctions can lead to a monolithic view of minority group attitudes and behaviors (Atkinson, Morten, et al., 1998). The erroneous belief that all Asians are the same, all Blacks are the same, all Hispanics are the same, or all American Indians are the same has led to numerous therapeutic problems.

First, therapists may often respond to the culturally diverse client in a very stereotypic manner and fail to recognize within-group or individual differences. For example, research indicates that Asian American clients seem to prefer and benefit most from a highly structured and directive approach rather than an insight/feeling-oriented one (Hong & Domokos-Cheng Ham, 2001; S. C. Kim, 1985; Mau & Jepson, 1988; Root, 1998). While such approaches may generally be effective, they are often blindly applied without regard for possible differences in client attitudes, beliefs, and behaviors. Likewise, conflicting findings in the literature regarding whether a minority client prefers a therapist of his or her own race seem to be a function of our failure to make such distinctions. Preference for a racially or ethnically similar therapist may really be a function of the cultural/racial identity of the minority person (within-group differences) rather than of race or ethnicity per se.

Second, the strength of racial/cultural identity models lies in their potential diagnostic value (Helms, 1984; Vandiver, 2001). In a previous chapter we cited statistics indicating that premature termination rates among minority clients may be attributed to the inappropriateness of transactions that occur between the helping professional and the culturally diverse client. Research now suggests that a minority individual's reaction to counseling, the counseling process, and the counselor is influenced by his or her cultural/racial identity and is not simply linked to minority group membership. The high failure-to-return rate of many clients seems to be intimately connected to the mental health professional's inability to assess the cultural identity of the client accurately.

A third important contribution derived from racial identity models is their acknowledgment of sociopolitical influences in shaping minority identity (à la the Nisei Japanese student). As mentioned previously, most therapeutic approaches often neglect their potential sociopolitical nature. The early models of racial identity development all incorporated the effects of racism and prejudice (oppression) upon the identity transformation of their victims. Vontress (1971), for instance, theorized that African Americans moved through decreasing levels of dependence on White society to emerging identification with Black culture and society (Colored, Negro, and Black). Other similar models for Blacks have been proposed (W. E. Cross, 1971; W. S. Hall, Cross, & Freedle, 1972; B. Jackson, 1975; C. W. Thomas, 1970, 1971). The fact that other minority groups such as Asian Americans (Maykovich, 1973; D. W. Sue & S. Sue, 1972; S. Sue & Sue, 1972b), Hispanics (A. S. Ruiz, 1990; Szapocznik, Santisteban, Kurtines, Hervis, & Spencer, 1982), women (Downing & Roush, 1985; K. McNamara & Rickard, 1989), lesbians/gays (Cass, 1979), and disabled individuals (Olkin, 1999) have similar processes may indicate experiential validity for such models as they relate to various oppressed groups.

Black Identity Development Models

Early attempts to define a process of minority identity transformation came primarily through the works of Black social scientists and educators (W. E. Cross, 1971; B. Jackson, 1975; C. W. Thomas, 1971). While there are several Black identity development models, the Cross model of psychological nigrescence (the process of becoming Black) is perhaps the most influential and well documented (W. E. Cross, 1971, 1991, 1995; W. S. Hall et al., 1972). The original Cross model was developed during the Civil Rights movement and delineates a five-stage process in which Blacks in the United States move from a White frame of reference to a positive Black frame of reference: *preencounter, encounter, immersion-emersion, internalization, and internalization-commitment.* The *preencounter* stage is characterized by individuals (African Americans) who consciously or unconsciously devalue their own Blackness and concurrently value White values and ways. There is a strong desire to assimilate and acculturate into White society. Blacks at this stage evidence self-hate, low self-esteem, and poor mental health (Vandiver, 2001). In the encounter stage, a two-step process begins to occur. First, the individual encounters a profound crisis or event that challenges his or her previous mode of thinking and behaving; second, the Black person begins to reinterpret the world, resulting in a shift in worldviews. Cross points out how the slaying of Martin Luther King Jr. was such a significant experience for many African Americans. The person experiences both guilt and anger over being brainwashed by White society. In the third stage, immersion-emersion, the person withdraws from the dominant culture and becomes immersed in African American culture. Black pride begins to develop, but internalization of positive attitudes toward one's own Blackness is minimal. In the emersion phase, feelings of guilt and anger begin to dissipate with an increasing sense of pride. The next stage, internalization, is characterized by inner security as conflicts between the old and new identities are resolved. Global anti-White feelings subside as the person becomes more flexible, more tolerant, and more bicultural/multicultural. The last stage, internalization-commitment, speaks to the commitment that such individuals have toward social change, social justice, and civil rights. It is expressed not only in words, but also in actions that reflect the essence of their lives. It is important to note, however, that Cross's original model makes a major assumption: The evolution from the preencounter to the internalization stage reflects a movement from psychological dysfunction to psychological health (Vandiver, 2001).

Confronted with evidence that the "stages" may mask multiple racial identities, questioning his original assumption that all Blacks at the preencounter stage possess low self-esteem and self-hatred, and aware of the complex issues related to race salience, in his book *Shades of Black* W. E. Cross

(1991) revised his theory of nigrescence. His changes, which are based on a critical review of the literature on Black racial identity, have increased the model's explanatory powers and promise high predictive validity (Vandiver et al., 2001; Worrell, Cross, & Vandiver, 2001). In essence, the revised model contains nearly all the features from the earlier formulation, but it differs in several significant ways. First, Cross introduces the concept of race salience, the degree to which race is an important and integral part of a person's approach to life. The Black person may either function with "race" consciousness playing a large role in his or her identity or a minimal one. In addition, salience for Blackness can possess positive (pro-Black) or negative (anti-Black) valence. Instead of using the term "pro-White" in the earlier preencounter stage, Cross now uses the term race salience. Originally, Cross believed that the rejection of Blackness and the acceptance of an American perspective were indicative of only one identity characterized by self-hate and low self-esteem. His current model now describes two identities: (a) preencounter assimilation and (b) preencounter anti-Black. The former has low salience for race and a neutral valence toward Blackness, while the latter describes individuals who hate Blacks and hate being Black (high negative salience). In other words, it is possible for a Black person at the preencounter stage who experiences the salience of race as very minor and whose identity is oriented toward an "American" perspective not to be filled with low self-esteem or self-hate.

The sense of low self-esteem, however, is linked to the preencounter anti-Black orientation. According to Cross, such a psychological perspective is the result of miseducation and self-hatred. The miseducation is the result of the negative images about Blacks portrayed in the mass media, among neighbors, friends, and relatives, and in the educational literature (Blacks are unintelligent, criminal, lazy, and prone to violence). The result is an incorporation of such negative images into the personal identity of the Black person. Interestingly, the female Nisei student described earlier in this chapter, though Japanese American, would seem to possess many of the features of Cross' preencounter anti-Black identity.

Several other changes were made by Cross in his later stages. First, the immersion-emersion stage once described one fused identity (anti-White/ pro-Black) but is now divided into two additional ones: anti-White alone and anti-Black alone. While Cross speaks about two separate identities, it appears that there are three possible combinations: anti-White, pro-Black, and an anti-White/pro-Black combination. Second, Cross has collapsed the fourth and fifth stages (internalization and internalization-commitment) into one: internalization. He observed that minimal differences existed between the two stages but one of "sustained interest and commitment." This last stage is characterized by Black self-acceptance and can be manifested in three types of identities: Black nationalist (high Black positive race salience), biculturalist (Blackness and fused sense of Americanness), and multiculturalist (multiple identity formation including race, gender, sexual orientation, etc.).

While Cross' model has been revised significantly and the newer version is more sophisticated, his original 1971 nigrescense theory continues to dominate the racial identity landscape. Unfortunately, this has created much confusion among researchers and practitioners. We encourage readers to familiarize themselves with his most recent formulation (W. E. Cross, 1991, 1995).

Asian American Identity Development Models

Asian American identity development models have not advanced as far as those relating to Black identity. One of the earliest heuristic, "type" models was developed by S. Sue and Sue (1971b) to explain what they saw as clinical differences among Chinese American students treated at the University of California Counseling Center: (a) *traditionalist*—a person who internalizes conventional Chinese customs and values, resists acculturation forces, and believes in the "old ways"; (b) *marginal person*—a person who attempts to assimilate and acculturate into White society, rejects traditional Chinese ways, internalizes society's negativism toward minority groups, and may develop racial self-hatred (à la the Japanese Nisei student); and (c) *Asian American*—a person who is in the process of forming a positive identity, who is ethnically and politically aware, and who becomes increasingly bicultural.

Kitano (1982) also proposed a type model to account for Japanese American role behaviors with respect to Japanese and American cultures: (a) positive-positive, in which the person identifies with both Japanese and White cultures without role conflicts; (b) negative-positive, in which there is a rejection of White culture and acceptance of Japanese American culture with accompanying role conflicts; (c) positive-negative, in which the person accepts White culture and rejects Japanese culture with concomitant role conflict; and (d) negative-negative, in which one rejects both.

These early type models suffered from several shortcomings (F. Y. Lee, 1991). First, they failed to provide a clear rationale for why an individual develops one ethnic identity type over another. While they were useful in describing characteristics of the type, they represented static entities rather than a dynamic process of identity development. Second, the early proposals seem too simplistic to account for the complexity of racial identity development. Third, these models were too population specific in that they described only one Asian American ethnic group (Chinese American or Japanese American), and one wonders whether they are equally applicable to Korean Americans, Filipino Americans, Vietnamese Americans, and so on. Last, with the exception of a few empirical studies (F. Y. Lee, 1991; D. W. Sue & Frank, 1973), testing of these typologies is seriously lacking.

In response to these criticisms, theorists have begun to move toward the development of stage/process models of Asian American identity development (J. Kim, 1981; F. Y. Lee, 1991; Sodowski, Kwan, & Pannu, 1995). Such models view identity formation as occurring in stages from less healthy to more healthy evolutions. With each stage there exists a constellation of traits and characteristics associated with racial/ethnic identity. They also attempt to explain the conditions or situations that might retard, enhance, or impel the individual forward.

After a thorough review of the literature, J. Kim (1981) used a qualitative narrative approach with third-generation Japanese American women to posit a progressive and sequential stage model of Asian American identity development: ethnic awareness, White identification, awakening to social political consciousness, redirection to Asian American consciousness, and incorporation. Her model integrates the influence of acculturation, exposure to cultural differences, environmental negativism to racial differences, personal methods of handling race-related conflicts, and the effects of group or social movements on the Asian American individual.

1. The *ethnic awareness* stage begins around the ages of 3 to 4, when the child's family members serve as the significant ethnic group model. Positive or neutral attitudes toward one's own ethnic origin are formed depending on the amount of ethnic exposure conveyed by the caretakers.

2. The *White identification* stage begins when children enter school, where peers and the surroundings become powerful forces in conveying racial prejudice that negatively impacts their self-esteem and identity. The realization of "differentness" from such interactions leads to self-blame and a desire to escape racial heritage by identifying with White society.

3. The *awakening to social political consciousness* stage means the adoption of a new perspective, often correlated with increased political awareness. J. Kim (1981) believed that the civil rights and women's movements and other significant political events often precipitate this new awakening. The primary result is an abandoning of identification with White society and a consequent understanding of oppression and oppressed groups.

4. The *redirection* stage means a reconnection or renewed connection with one's Asian American heritage and culture. This is often followed by the realization that White oppression is the culprit for the negative experiences of youth. Anger against White racism may become a defining theme with concomitant increases of Asian American self-pride and group pride.

5. The *incorporation* stage represents the highest form of identity evolution. It encompasses the development of a positive and comfortable identity

as Asian American and consequent respect for other cultural/racial heritages. Identification for or against White culture is no longer an important issue.

Latino/Hispanic American Identity Development Models

While a number of ethnic identity development models have been formulated to account for Hispanic identity (Bernal & Knight, 1993; Casas & Pytluk, 1995; Szapocznik et al., 1982), the one most similar to those of African Americans and Asian Americans was proposed by A. S. Ruiz (1990). His model was formulated from a clinical perspective via case studies of Chicano/Latino subjects. Ruiz made several underlying assumptions. First, he believed in a culture-specific explanation of identity for Chicano, Mexican American, and Latino clients. While models about other ethnic group development or the more general ones were helpful, they lacked the specificity of Hispanic cultures. Second, the marginal status of Latinos is highly correlated with maladjustment. Third, negative experiences of forced assimilation are considered destructive to an individual. Fourth, having pride in one's cultural heritage and ethnic identity is positively correlated with mental health. Last, pride in one's ethnicity affords the Hispanic greater freedom to choose freely. These beliefs underlie the five-stage model.

1. *Causal stage.* During this period messages or injunctions from the environment or significant others either affirm, ignore, negate, or denigrate the ethnic heritage of the person. Affirmation about one's ethnic identity is lacking, and the person may experience traumatic or humiliating experiences related to ethnicity. There is a failure to identify with Latino culture.

2. *Cognitive stage.* As a result of negative/distorted messages, three erroneous belief systems about Chicano/Latino heritage become incorporated into mental sets: (a) Ethnic group membership is associated with poverty and prejudice; (b) assimilation to White society is the only means of escape; and (c) assimilation is the only possible road to success.

3. *Consequence stage.* Fragmentation of ethnic identity becomes very noticeable and evident. The person feels ashamed and is embarrassed by ethnic markers such as name, accent, skin color, cultural customs, and so on. The unwanted self-image leads to estrangement and rejection of Chicano/Latino heritage.

4. *Working through stage.* Two major dynamics distinguish this stage. First, the person becomes increasingly unable to cope with the psychological distress of ethnic identity conflict. Second, the person can no longer be a "pretender" by identifying with an alien ethnic identity. The person is

propelled to reclaim and reintegrate disowned ethnic identity fragments. Ethnic consciousness increases.

5.   *Successful resolution stage.* This last stage is exemplified by greater acceptance of one's culture and ethnicity. There is an improvement in self-
esteem and a sense that ethnic identity represents a positive and suc-
cess-promoting resource.

The Ruiz model has a subjective reality that is missing in many of the
empirically based models. This is expected since it was formulated through a
clinical population. It has the added advantage of suggesting intervention focus and direction for each of the stages. For example, the focus of counseling
in the causal stage is disaffirming and restructuring of the injunctions; for the
cognitive stage it is the use of cognitive strategies attacking faulty beliefs; for
the consequence stage it is reintegration of ethnic identity fragments in a positive manner; for the working through stage ethnocultural identification issues are important; and for the successful resolution stage the promotion of
a positive identity becomes important.

A Racial/Cultural Identity Development Model

Earlier writers (Berry, 1965; Stonequist, 1937) have observed that minority
groups share similar patterns of adjustment to cultural oppression. In the past
several decades, Asian Americans, Hispanics, and American Indians have experienced sociopolitical identity transformations so that a *Third World consciousness* has emerged with cultural oppression as the common unifying
force. As a result of studying these models and integrating them with their
own clinical observations, Atkinson, Morten, and Sue (1979, 1989, 1998)
proposed a five-stage Minority Identity Development model (MID) in an attempt to pull out common features that cut across the population-specific
proposals. D. W. Sue & Sue (1990, 1999) later elaborated on the MID, re-
naming it the Racial/Cultural Identity Development model (R/CID) to encompass a broader population. As discussed shortly, this model may be applied to White identity development as well.

The R/CID model proposed here is not a comprehensive theory of personality, but rather a conceptual framework to aid therapists in understanding their culturally different clients' attitudes and behaviors. The model defines five stages of development that oppressed people experience as they
struggle to understand themselves in terms of their own culture, the dominant culture, and the oppressive relationship between the two cultures: *conformity, dissonance, resistance and immersion, introspection,* and *integrative awareness.* At each level of identity, four corresponding beliefs and attitudes that
may help therapists better understand their minority clients are discussed.

These attitudes/beliefs are an integral part of the minority person's identity and are manifest in how he or she views (a) the self, (b) others of the same minority, (c) others of another minority, and (d) majority individuals. Table 8.1 outlines the R/CID model and the interaction of stages with the attitudes and beliefs.

Conformity Stage

Similar to individuals in the preencounter stage (W. E. Cross, 1991), minority individuals are distinguished by their unequivocal preference for dominant cultural values over their own. White Americans in the United States represent their reference group, and the identification set is quite strong.

Table 8.1 **The Racial/Cultural Identity Development Model**

Stages of Minority Development Model	Attitude toward Self	Attitude toward Others of the Same Minority	Attitude toward Others of a Different Minority	Attitude toward Dominant Group
Stage 1— Conformity	Self-depreciating or neutral due to low race salience	Group-depreciating or neutral due to low race salience	Discriminatory or neutral	Group-appreciating
Stage 2— Dissonance and appreciating	Conflict between self-depreciating and group-appreciating	Conflict between group-depreciating views of minority hierarchy and feelings of shared experience	Conflict between dominant-held and group depreciating	Conflict between group-appreciating
Stage 3— Resistance and immersion	Self-appreciating	Group-appreciating experiences and feelings of culturocentrism	Conflict between feelings of empathy for other minority	Group-depreciating
Stage 4— Introspection	Concern with basis of self-appreciation	Concern with nature of unequivocal appreciation	Concern with ethnocentric basis for judging others	Concern with the basis of group-depreciation
Stage 5— Integrative Awareness	Self-appreciating	Group-appreciating	Group-appreciating	Selective appreciation

Source: From Donald R. Atkinson, George Morten, and Derald Wing Sue, *Counseling American Minorities: A Cross Cultural Perspective,* 5th ed. Copyright © 1998 Wm. C. Brown Publishers, Dubuque, IA. All rights reserved. Reprinted by permission.

Lifestyles, value systems, and cultural/physical characteristics that most resemble White society are highly valued, while those most like their own minority group may be viewed with disdain or may hold low salience for the person. We agree with Cross that minority people at this stage can be oriented toward a pro-American identity without subsequent disdain or negativism toward their own group. Thus, it is possible for a Chinese-American to feel positively about U.S. culture, values, and traditions without evidencing disdain for Chinese culture or feeling negatively about oneself (absence of self-hate). Nevertheless, we believe that they represent a small proportion of persons of color at this stage. Research on their numbers, on how they have handled the social-psychological dynamics of majority-minority relations, on how they have dealt with their minority status, and on how they fit into the stage models (progression issues) needs to be conducted.

We believe that the conformity stage continues to be most characterized by individuals who have bought into societal definitions about their minority status in society. Because the conformity stage represents, perhaps, the most damning indictment of White racism, and because it has such a profound negative impact on nearly all minority groups, we spend more time discussing it than the other stages. Let us use a case approach to illustrate the social-psychological dynamics of the conformity process.

Who Am I? White or Black

A 17-year-old White high school student, Mary, comes to counseling for help in sorting out her thoughts and feelings concerning an interracial relationship with an African American student. Although she is proud of the relationship and feels that her liberal friends are accepting and envious, Mary's parents are against it. Indeed, the parents have threatened to cut off financial support for her future college education unless she terminates the affair immediately.

During counseling, Mary tells of how she has rid herself of much bigotry and prejudice from the early training of her parents. She joined a circle of friends who were quite liberal in thought and behavior. She recalls how she was both shocked and attracted to her new friends' liberal political beliefs, philosophies, and sexual attitudes. When she first met John, a Black student, she was immediately attracted to his apparent confidence and outspokenness. It did not take her long to become sexually involved with him and to enter into an intense relationship. Mary became the talk of her former friends, but she did not seem to care. Indeed, she seemed to enjoy the attention and openly flaunted her relationship in everyone's face.

Because Mary requested couple counseling, the counselor saw them together. John informs the counselor that he came solely to please Mary. He sees few problems in their relationship that cannot be easily resolved. John seems to feel that he has overcome many handicaps in his life and that this represents just another obstacle to be conquered. When asked about his use of the term "handicap," he responds, "It's not easy to be Black, you know. I've proven to my parents and friends in high school, including myself, that I'm worth something. Let them disapprove—I'm going to make it into a good university." Further probing revealed John's resentment over his own parents' disapproval of the relationship. While his relations with them had worsened to the point of near-physical assaults, John continued to bring Mary home. He seemed to take great pride in being seen with a "beautiful blond-haired, blue-eyed White girl."

In a joint session, Mary's desire to continue therapy and John's apparent reluctance becomes obvious. Several times when John mentions the prospect of a "permanent relationship" and their attending the same university, Mary does not seem to respond positively. She does not seem to want to look too far into the future. Mary's constant coolness to the idea and the counselor's attempt to focus on this reluctance anger John greatly. He becomes antagonistic toward the counselor and puts pressure on Mary to terminate this useless talk "crap." However, he continues to come for the weekly sessions. One day his anger boils over, and he accuses the counselor of being biased. Standing up and shouting, John demands to know how the counselor feels about interracial relationships.

There are many approaches to analyzing the above case, but we have chosen to concentrate on the psychological dynamics evidenced by John, the African American student. However, it is clear from a brief reading of this case that both John and Mary are involved in an interracial relationship as a means of rebellion and as attempts to work out personal and group identity issues. In Mary's case, it may be rebellion against conservative parents and parental upbringing, as well as the secondary shock value it has for her former friends and parents (appearing liberal). John's motivation for the relationship is also a form of rebellion. There are many clues in this case to indicate that John identifies with White culture and feels disdain for Black culture. First, he seems to equate his Blackness with a handicap to be overcome. Is it possible that John feels ashamed of who and what he is (Black)? While feeling proud of one's girlfriend is extremely desirable, does Mary's being White, blond-haired, and blue-eyed have special significance? Would John feel equally proud if the woman were beautiful and Black? Being seen in the company of a White woman may represent affirmation to John that he has "made it" in White society. Perhaps he has been sold a false bill of goods and is operating under the belief that White ways are better.

While John's anger in counseling is multidimensional, much of it seems misdirected toward the counselor. John may actually be angry toward Mary because she seems less than committed to a long-term or permanent relationship. Yet to acknowledge that Mary may not want a permanent relationship will threaten the very basis of John's self-deception (that he is not like the other Blacks and is accepted in White society). It is very easy to blame John for his dilemma and to call him an Oreo (Black outside and White inside). However, lest we fall prey to blaming the victim, let us use a wider perspective in analyzing this case.

John (and even Mary) is really a victim of larger social psychological forces operating in our society. The key issue here is the dominant-subordinate relationship between two different cultures (Atkinson, Morten, et al., 1998; Carter, 1995; Freire, 1970; B. Jackson, 1975). It is reasonable to believe that members of one cultural group tend to adjust themselves to the group possessing the greater prestige and power in order to avoid feelings of inferiority. Yet it is exactly this act that creates ambivalence in the minority individual. The pressures for assimilation and acculturation (melting-pot theory) are strong, creating possible culture conflicts. John is the victim of ethnocentric monoculturalism (D. W. Sue et al., 1998): (a) belief in the superiority of one group's cultural heritage—its language, traditions, arts-crafts, and ways of behaving (White) over all others; (b) belief in the inferiority of all other lifestyles (non-White); and (c) the power to impose such standards onto the less powerful group.

The psychological costs of racism on minorities are immense, and John exemplifies this process. Constantly bombarded on all sides by reminders that Whites and their way of life are superior and that all other lifestyles are inferior, many minorities begin to wonder whether they themselves are not somehow inadequate, whether members of their own group are not to blame, and whether subordination and segregation are not justified. K. B. Clark and Clark (1947) first brought this to the attention of social scientists by stating that racism may contribute to a sense of confused self-identity among Black children. In a study of racial awareness and preference among Black and White children, they found that (a) Black children preferred playing with a White doll over a Black one, (b) the Black doll was perceived as being "bad," and (c) approximately one-third, when asked to pick the doll that looked like them, picked the White one.

It is unfortunate that the inferior status of minorities is constantly reinforced and perpetuated by the mass media through television, movies, newspapers, radio, books, and magazines. This contributes to widespread stereotypes that tend to trap minority individuals: Blacks are superstitious, childlike, ignorant, fun loving, or dangerous, and criminal; Hispanics are dirty, sneaky, and criminal; Asian Americans are sneaky, sly, cunning, and passive; Indians are primitive savages. Such portrayals cause widespread harm to the self-esteem of minorities who may incorporate them. That preconceived expectations can set up self-fulfilling prophecies has been demonstrated by Rosenthal and Jacobson (1968). The incorporation of the larger society's standards may lead minority group members to react negatively toward their own racial and cultural heritage. They may become ashamed of who they are, reject their own group identification, and attempt to identify with the desirable "good" White minority. In the *Autobiography of Malcolm X* (A. Haley, 1966), Malcolm X relates how he tried desperately to appear as White as possible. He went to painful lengths to straighten and dye his hair so that he would appear more like White males. It is evident that many minorities do come to accept White standards as a means of measuring physical attractiveness, attractiveness of personality, and social relationships. Such an orientation may lead to the phenomenon of racial self-hatred, in which people dislike themselves for being Asian, Black, Hispanic, or Native American. Like John, individuals operating from the conformity stage experience racial self-hatred and attempt to assimilate and acculturate into White society. People at the conformity stage seem to possess the following characteristics.

1. *Attitudes and beliefs toward the self (self-depreciating attitudes and beliefs).* Physical and cultural characteristics identified with one's own racial/cultural group are perceived negatively, as something to be avoided, denied, or changed. Physical characteristics (black skin color, "slant-shaped eyes" of Asians), traditional modes of dress and appearance, and behavioral characteristics associated with the minority group are a source of shame. There may be attempts to mimic what is perceived as White mannerisms, speech patterns, dress, and goals. Low internal self-esteem is characteristic of the person. The fact that John views his own Blackness as a handicap, something bad, and something to deny is an example of this insidious, but highly damaging, process.

2. *Attitudes and beliefs toward members of the same minority (group-depreciating attitudes and beliefs).* Majority cultural beliefs and attitudes about the minority group are also held by the person in this stage. These individuals may have internalized the majority of White stereotypes about their group. In the case of Hispanics, for example, the person may believe that members of his or her own group have high rates of unemployment because "they are lazy, uneducated, and unintelligent." Little thought or validity is given to other viewpoints, such as unemployment's being a function of job discrimination, prejudice, racism, unequal opportunities, and inferior education. Because persons in the conformity stage find it psychologically painful to identify with these negative traits, they divorce themselves from their own group. The denial mechanism most commonly used is, "I'm not like them; I've made it on my own; I'm the exception."

3. *Attitudes and beliefs toward members of different minorities (discriminatory).* Because the conformity-stage person most likely strives for identification with White society, the individual shares similar dominant attitudes and beliefs not only toward his or her own minority group, but toward other minorities as well. Minority groups most similar to White cultural groups are viewed more favorably, while those most different are viewed less favorably. For example, Asian Americans may be viewed more favorably than African Americans or Latino/Hispanic Americans in some situations. While a stratification probably exists, we caution readers that such a ranking is fraught with hazards and potential political consequences. Such distinctions often manifest themselves in debates over which group is more oppressed and which group has done better than the others. Such debates are counterproductive when used to (a) negate another group's experience of oppression; (b) foster an erroneous belief that hard work alone will result in success in a democratic society; (c) shortchange a minority group (i.e., Asian Americans) from receiving the necessary resources in our society, and (d) pit one minority against another (divide and conquer) by holding one group up as an example to others.

4. *Attitude and beliefs toward members of the dominant group (group-appreciating attitude and beliefs).* This stage is characterized by a belief that White cultural, social, and institutional standards are superior. Members of the dominant group are admired, respected, and emulated. White people are believed to possess superior intelligence. Some individuals may go to great lengths to appear White. Consider again the example from the *Autobiography of Malcolm X,* in which the main character would straighten his hair and primarily date White women (as in the case of John and the Nisei female student). Reports that Asian women have undergone surgery to reshape their eyes to conform to White female standards of beauty may (but not in all cases) typify this dynamic.

Dissonance Stage

No matter how much one attempts to deny his or her own racial/cultural heritage, an individual will encounter information or experiences that are inconsistent with culturally held beliefs, attitudes, and values. An Asian American who believes that Asians are inhibited, passive, inarticulate, and poor in people relationships may encounter an Asian leader who seems to break all these stereotypes (e.g., the Nisei student). A Latino who feels ashamed of his cultural upbringing may encounter another Latino who seems proud of his or her cultural heritage. An African American who believes that race problems are due to laziness, untrustworthiness, or personal inadequacies of his or her own group may suddenly encounter racism on a personal level. Denial begins to break down, which leads to a questioning and challenging of the attitudes/beliefs of the conformity stage. This was clearly what happened when the Nisei Japanese American student encountered discrimination at the restaurant.

In all probability, movement into the dissonance stage is a gradual process. Its very definition indicates that the individual is in conflict between disparate pieces of information or experiences that challenge his or her current self-concept. People generally move into this stage slowly, but a traumatic event may propel some individuals to move into dissonance at a much more rapid pace. W. E. Cross (1971) stated that a monumental event such as the assassination of a major leader like Martin Luther King Jr. can often push people quickly into the ensuing stage.

1. *Attitudes and beliefs toward the self (conflict between self-depreciating and self-appreciating attitudes and beliefs).* There is now a growing sense of personal awareness that racism does exist, that not all aspects of the minority or majority culture are good or bad, and that one cannot escape one's cultural heritage. For the first time the person begins to entertain the possibility of positive attributes in the minority culture and, with it, a sense of pride in self. Feelings of shame and pride are mixed in the individual, and a sense of conflict develops. This conflict is most likely to be brought to the forefront quickly when other members of the minority group may express positive feelings toward the person: "We like you because you are Asian, Black, American Indian, or Latino." At this stage, an important personal question is being asked: "Why should I feel ashamed of who and what I am?"

2. *Attitudes and beliefs toward members of the same minority (conflict between group-depreciating and group-appreciating attitudes and beliefs).* Dominant-held views of minority strengths and weaknesses begin to be questioned as new, contradictory information is received. Certain aspects of the minority culture begin to have appeal. For example, a Latino/Hispanic male who values individualism may marry, have children, and then suddenly realize how Latino cultural values that hold the family as the psychosocial unit possess positive features. Or the minority person may find certain members of his group to be very attractive as friends, colleagues, lovers, and so forth.

3. *Attitudes and beliefs toward members of a different minority (conflict between dominant-held views of minority hierarchy and feelings of shared experience).* Stereotypes associated with other minority groups are questioned, and a growing sense of comradeship with other oppressed groups is felt. It is important to keep in mind, however, that little psychic energy is associated with resolving conflicts with other minority groups. Almost all en-

ergies are expended toward resolving conflicts toward the self, the same minority, and the dominant group.

4. *Attitudes and beliefs toward members of the dominant group (conflict between group-appreciating and group-depreciating attitudes).* The person experiences a growing awareness that not all cultural values of the dominant group are beneficial. This is especially true when the minority person experiences personal discrimination. Growing suspicion and some distrust of certain members of the dominant group develops.

Resistance and Immersion Stage

The minority person tends to endorse minority-held views completely and to reject the dominant values of society and culture. The person seems dedicated to reacting against White society and rejects White social, cultural, and institutional standards as having no personal validity. Desire to eliminate oppression of the individual's minority group becomes an important motivation of the individual's behavior. During the resistance and immersion stage, the three most active types of affective feelings are *guilt, shame,* and *anger.* There are considerable feelings of guilt and shame that in the past the minority individual has sold out his or her own racial and cultural group. The feelings of guilt and shame extend to the perception that during this past "sellout" the minority person has been a contributor and participant in the oppression of his or her own group and other minority groups. This is coupled with a strong sense of anger at the oppression and feelings of having been brainwashed by the forces in White society. Anger is directed outwardly in a very strong way toward oppression and racism. Movement into this stage seems to occur for two reasons. First, a resolution of the conflicts and confusions of the previous stage allows greater understanding of social forces (racism, oppression, and discrimination) and his or her role as a victim. Second, a personal questioning of why people should feel ashamed of themselves develops. The answer to this question evokes feelings of guilt, shame, and anger.

1. *Attitudes and beliefs toward the self (self-appreciating attitudes and beliefs).* The minority individual at this stage is oriented toward self-discovery of one's own history and culture. There is an active seeking out of information and artifacts that enhance that person's sense of identity and worth. Cultural and racial characteristics that once elicited feelings of shame and disgust become symbols of pride and honor. The individual moves into this stage primarily because he or she asks the question, "Why should I be ashamed of who and what I am?" The original low self-esteem engendered by widespread prejudice and racism that was most characteristic of the conformity stage is now actively challenged in

order to raise self-esteem. Phrases such as "Black is beautiful" represent a symbolic relabeling of identity for many Blacks. Racial self-hatred begins to be actively rejected in favor of the other extreme: unbridled racial pride.

2. *Attitudes and beliefs toward members of the same minority (group-appreciating attitudes and beliefs).* The individual experiences a strong sense of identification with and commitment to his or her minority group as enhancing information about the group is acquired. There is a feeling of connectedness with other members of the racial and cultural group, and a strengthening of new identity begins to occur. Members of one's group are admired, respected, and often viewed now as the new reference group or ideal. Cultural values of the minority group are accepted without question. As indicated, the pendulum swings drastically from original identification with White ways to identification in an unquestioning manner with the minority group's ways. Persons in this stage are likely to restrict their interactions as much as possible to members of their own group.

3. *Attitudes and beliefs toward members of a different minority (conflict between feelings of empathy for other minority group experiences and feelings of culturocentrism).* While members at this stage experience a growing sense of comradeship with persons from other minority groups, a strong culturocentrism develops as well. Alliances with other groups tend to be transitory and based on short-term goals or some global shared view of oppression. There is less an attempt to reach out and understand other racial-cultural minority groups and their values and ways, and more a superficial surface feeling of political need. Alliances generally are based on convenience factors or are formed for political reasons such as combining together as a large group to confront an enemy perceived to be larger.

4. *Attitudes and beliefs toward members of the dominant group (group-depreciating attitudes and beliefs).* The minority individual is likely to perceive the dominant society and culture as an oppressor and as the group most responsible for the current plight of minorities in the United States. Characterized by both withdrawal from the dominant culture and immersion in one's cultural heritage, there is also considerable anger and hostility directed toward White society. There is a feeling of distrust and dislike for all members of the dominant group in an almost global anti-White demonstration and feeling. White people, for example, are not to be trusted because they are the oppressors or enemies. In extreme form, members may advocate complete destruction of the institutions and structures that have been characteristic of White society.

Introspection Stage

Several factors seem to work in unison to move the individual from the resistance and immersion stage into the introspection stage. First, the individual begins to discover that this level of intensity of feelings (anger directed toward White society) is psychologically draining and does not permit one to really devote more crucial energies to understanding themselves or to their own racial-cultural group. The resistance and immersion stage tends to be a reaction against the dominant culture and is not proactive in allowing the individual to use all energies to discover who or what he or she is. Self-definition in the previous stage tends to be reactive (against White racism), and a need for positive self-definition in a proactive sense emerges.

Second, the minority individual experiences feelings of discontent and discomfort with group views that may be quite rigid in the resistance and immersion stage. Often, in order to please the group, the individual is asked to submerge individual autonomy and individual thought in favor of the group good. Many group views may now be seen as conflicting with individual ones. A Latino individual who may form a deep relationship with a White person may experience considerable pressure from his or her culturally similar peers to break off the relationship because that White person is the "enemy." However, the personal experiences of the individual may, in fact, not support this group view.

It is important to note that some clinicians often confuse certain characteristics of the introspective stage with parts of the conformity stage. A minority person from the former stage who speaks against the decisions of his or her group may often appear similar to the conformity person. The dynamics are quite different, however. While the conformity person is motivated by global racial self-hatred, the introspective person has no such global negativism directed at his or her own group.

1. *Attitudes and beliefs toward the self (concern with basis of self-appreciating attitudes and beliefs).* While the person originally in the conformity stage held predominantly to majority group views and notions to the detriment of his or her own minority group, the person now feels that he or she has too rigidly held onto minority group views and notions in order to submerge personal autonomy. The conflict now becomes quite great in terms of responsibility and allegiance to one's own minority group versus notions of personal independence and autonomy. The person begins to spend more and more time and energy trying to sort out these aspects of self-identity and begins increasingly to demand individual autonomy.

2. *Attitudes and beliefs toward members of the same minority (concern with the unequivocal nature of group appreciation).* While attitudes of identification are

continued from the preceding resistance and immersion stage, concern begins to build up regarding the issue of group-usurped individuality. Increasingly, the individual may see his or her own group taking positions that might be considered quite extreme. In addition, there is now increasing resentment over how one's group may attempt to pressure or influence the individual into making decisions that may be inconsistent with the person's values, beliefs, and outlooks. Indeed, it is not unusual for members of a minority group to make it clear to the member that if they do not agree with the group, they are against it. A common ploy used to hold members in line is exemplified in questions such as "How Asian are you?" and "How Black are you?"

3. *Attitudes and beliefs toward members of a different minority (concern with the ethnocentric basis for judging others).* There is now greater uneasiness with culturocentrism, and an attempt is made to reach out to other groups in finding out what types of oppression they experience and how this has been handled. While similarities are important, there is now a movement toward understanding potential differences in oppression that other groups might have experienced.

4. *Attitudes and beliefs toward members of the dominant group (concern with the basis of group depreciation).* The individual experiences conflict between attitudes of complete trust for the dominant society and culture and attitudes of selective trust and distrust according to the dominant individual's demonstrated behaviors and attitudes. Conflict is most likely to occur here because the person begins to recognize that there are many elements in U.S. American culture that are highly functional and desirable, yet there is confusion as to how to incorporate these elements into the minority culture. Would the person's acceptance of certain White cultural values make the person a sellout to his or her own race? There is a lowering of intense feelings of anger and distrust toward the dominant group but a continued attempt to discern elements that are acceptable.

Integrative Awareness Stage

Minority persons in this stage have developed an inner sense of security and now can own and appreciate unique aspects of their culture as well as those in U.S. culture. Minority culture is not necessarily in conflict with White dominant cultural ways. Conflicts and discomforts experienced in the previous stage become resolved, allowing greater individual control and flexibility. There is now the belief there are acceptable and unacceptable aspects in all cultures, and that it is very important for the person to be able to examine and accept or reject those aspects of a culture that are not seen as desirable. At the integrative awareness stage, the minority person has a strong commitment and desire to eliminate all forms of oppression.

1. *Attitudes and beliefs toward the self (self-appreciating attitudes and beliefs).* The culturally diverse individual develops a positive self-image and experiences a strong sense of self-worth and confidence. Not only is there an integrated self-concept that involves racial pride in identity and culture, but the person develops a high sense of autonomy. Indeed, the client becomes bicultural or multicultural without a sense of having "sold out one's integrity." In other words, the person begins to perceive his or her self as an autonomous individual who is unique (individual level of identity), a member of one's own racial-cultural group (group level of identity), a member of a larger society, and a member of the human race (universal level of identity).

2. *Attitudes and beliefs toward members of same minority (group-appreciating attitudes and beliefs).* The individual experiences a strong sense of pride in the group without having to accept group values unequivocally. There is no longer the conflict over disagreeing with group goals and values. Strong feelings of empathy with the group experience are coupled with awareness that each member of the group is also an individual. In addition, tolerant and empathic attitudes are likely to be expressed toward members of one's own group who may be functioning at a less adaptive manner to racism and oppression.

3. *Attitudes and beliefs toward members of a different minority (group-appreciating attitudes).* There is now literally a reaching-out toward different minority groups in order to understand their cultural values and ways of life. There is a strong belief that the more one understands other cultural values and beliefs, the greater is the likelihood of understanding among the various ethnic groups. Support for all oppressed people, regardless of similarity to the individual's minority group, tends to be emphasized.

4. *Attitudes and beliefs toward members of the dominant group (attitudes and beliefs of selective appreciation).* The individual experiences selective trust and liking from members of the dominant group who seek to eliminate oppressive activities of the group. The individual also experiences openness to the constructive elements of the dominant culture. The emphasis here tends to be on the fact that White racism is a sickness in society and that White people are also victims who are also in need of help.

Therapeutic Implications of the R/CID Model

Let us first point out some broad general clinical implications of the R/CID model before discussing specific meanings within each of the stages. First, an understanding of cultural identity development should sensitize therapists and counselors to the role that oppression plays in a minority individual's development. In many respects, it should make us aware that our role as helping professionals should extend beyond the office and should deal with the many manifestations of racism. While individual therapy is needed, combating the forces of racism means a proactive approach for both the therapist and the client. For the therapist, systems intervention is often the answer. For culturally diverse clients, it means the need to understand, control, and direct those forces in society that negate the process of positive identity. Thus, a wider sociocultural approach to therapy is mandatory.

Second, the model will aid therapists in recognizing differences between members of the same minority group with respect to their cultural identity. It serves as a useful assessment and diagnostic tool for therapists to gain a greater understanding of their culturally different client (Atkinson, Morten, et al., 1998; Helms, 1985; D. W. Sue et al., 1998; Vandiver et al., 2001). In many cases, an accurate delineation of the dynamics and characteristics of the stages may result in better prescriptive treatment. Therapists who are familiar with the sequence of stages are better able to plan intervention strategies that are most effective for culturally different clients. For example, a client experiencing feelings of isolation and alienation in the conformity stage may require a different approach than he or she would in the introspection stage.

Third, the model allows helping professionals to realize the potentially changing and developmental nature of cultural identity among clients. If the goal of multicultural counseling/therapy is intended to move a client toward the integrative awareness stage, then the therapist is able to anticipate the sequence of feelings, beliefs, attitudes, and behaviors likely to arise. Acting as a guide and providing an understandable end point will allow the client to understand more quickly and work through issues related to his or her own identity. We now turn our attention to the R/CID model and its implications for the therapeutic process.

Conformity Stage: Therapeutic Implications

For the vast majority of those in the conformity stage (belief in the superiority of White ways and the inferiority of minority ways), several therapeutic implications can be derived. First, persons of color are most likely to prefer a White therapist over a minority therapist. This flows logically from the belief that Whites are more competent and capable than are members of one's own race. Such a racial preference can be manifested in the client's reaction to a minority therapist via negativism, resistance, or open hostility. In some instances, the client may even request a change in therapist (preferably someone White). On the other hand, the conformity individual who is seen by a White therapist may be quite pleased about it. In many cases, the minority client, in identifying with White culture, may be overly dependent on the White therapist. Attempts to please, appease, and seek approval from the helping professional may be quite prevalent.

Second, most conformity individuals will find attempts to explore cultural identity or to focus in upon feelings very threatening. Clients in this stage generally prefer a task-oriented, problem-solving approach because an exploration of identity may eventually touch upon feelings of low self-esteem, dissatisfaction with personal appearance, vague anxieties, and racial self-hatred and challenge the client's self-deception that he or she is not like the other members of his or her own race. Recall, for example, the case of John, who, when threatened by the idea that Mary may not want a "permanent" relationship, uses the counselor as a scapegoat for his feelings of anger toward Mary. To recognize that he is really angry at Mary means a breakdown in his denial system and the need to confront his feelings of racial self-hatred, along with the realization that he is a Black person!

Whether you are a White or minority counselor working with a conformity individual, the general goal may be the same. There is an obligation to help the client sort out conflicts related to racial/cultural identity through some process of reeducation. Somewhere in the course of counseling or therapy, issues of cultural racism, majority-minority group relations, racial self-hatred, and racial cultural identity need to be dealt with in an integrated fashion. We are not suggesting a lecture or solely a cognitive approach, to which clients at this stage may be quite intellectually receptive, but exercising good clinical skills that take into account the client's socio-emotional state and readiness to deal with feelings. Only in this manner will the client be able to distinguish the difference between positive attempts to adopt certain values of the dominant society and a negative rejection of one's own cultural value (a characteristic of the integrative awareness stage).

While the goals for the White and minority therapist are the same, the way a therapist works toward them may be different. For example, a minority therapist will likely have to deal with hostility from the racially and culturally similar client. The therapist may symbolize all that the client is trying to reject. Because therapy stresses the building of a coalition, establishment of rapport, and to some degree a mutual identification, the process may be especially threatening. The opposite may be true of work with a White therapist. The culturally different client may be overeager to identify with the White professional in order to seek approval. However, rather than being detrimental to multicultural counseling/therapy, these two processes may be used quite effectively and productively. If the minority therapist can aid the client in working through his or her feelings of antagonism, and if the majority therapist can aid the client in working through his or her need to over-identify, then the client will be moved closer to awareness than to self-deception. In the former case, the therapist can take a nonjudgmental stance toward the client and provide a positive minority role model. In the latter, the White therapist needs to model positive attitudes toward cultural diversity. Both need to guard against unknowingly reinforcing the client's self-denial and rejection.

Dissonance Stage: Therapeutic Implications

As individuals become more aware of inconsistencies between dominant-held views and those of their group, a sense of dissonance develops. Preoccupation and questions concerning self, identity, and self-esteem are most likely brought in for therapy. More culturally aware than their conformity counterparts, dissonance clients may prefer a counselor or therapist who possesses good knowledge of the client's cultural group, although there may still be a preference for a White helper. However, the fact that minority helping professionals are generally more knowledgeable of the client's cultural group may serve to heighten the conflicting beliefs and feelings of this stage. Since the client is so receptive toward self-exploration, the therapist can capitalize on this orientation in helping the client come to grips with his or her identity conflicts.

Resistance and Immersion Stage: Counseling Implications

Minority clients at this stage are likely to view their psychological problems as products of oppression and racism. They may believe that only issues of racism are legitimate areas to explore in therapy. Furthermore, openness or self-disclosure to therapists not of one's own group is dangerous because White therapists are "enemies" and members of the oppressing group.

Clients in the resistance and immersion stage believe that society is to blame for their present dilemma and actively challenge the establishment. They are openly suspicious of institutions, such as mental health services, because they view them as agents of the establishment. Very few of the more ethnically conscious and militant minorities will use mental health services because of its identification with the status quo. When they do, they are usually suspicious and hostile toward the helping professional. Before therapy can proceed effectively, the therapist will have to deal with certain challenges from these students, such as the following:

> LATINO/HISPANIC CLIENT: *First of all, I don't believe in therapy. I think it's a lot of bullshit. You [therapists] are always trying to adjust people to a sick society, and what is needed is to overthrow these damned oppressive institutions.*

I feel the same way about those stupid tests you want me to take. Cultural bias—they aren't applicable to minorities. The only reason I came in here was—well, I heard your lecture in Psychology 160, and I think I can work with you.

The male client in this case happened to be hostile and depressed over the recent death of his father. Although he realized he had some need for help, he still did not trust the counseling process.

CLIENT: *Psychologists see the problem inside of people when the problem is in society. Don't you think White society has made all minorities feel inferior and degraded?*

COUNSELOR: *Yes, your observations appear correct. White society has done great harm to minorities.*

Here, the client was obviously posing a direct challenge to the counselor. Any defense of White society or explanations of the value of counseling might have aroused greater hostility and mistrust. It would have been extremely difficult to establish rapport without some honest agreement on the racist nature of American society. Later, the counselee revealed that his father had just died. He was beginning to realize that there was no contradiction in viewing society as being racist and in having personal problems. Often, growing pride in self-identity in the extreme makes it difficult for clients who are having emotional problems to accept their personal difficulties.

A therapist working with a client at this stage of development needs to realize several important things. First, he or she will be viewed by the culturally different client as a symbol of the oppressive society. If you become defensive and personalize the attacks, you will lose your effectiveness in working with the client. It is important not to be intimidated or afraid of the anger that is likely to be expressed; often, it is not personal and is quite legitimate. White guilt and defensiveness can only serve to hinder effective multicultural counseling/therapy. We have more to say about this in the next chapter. It is not unusual for clients at this stage to make sweeping negative generalizations about White Americans. The White therapist who takes a nondefensive posture will be better able to help the client explore the basis of his or her racial tirades. In general, clients at this stage prefer a therapist of their own race. However, the fact that you share the same race or culture as your client will not insulate you from the attacks. For example, an African American client may perceive the Black counselor as a sellout of his or her own race or as an Uncle Tom. Indeed, the anger and hostility directed at the minority therapist may be even more intense than that directed at a White one.

Second, realize that clients in this stage will constantly test you. In earlier chapters we described how minority clients will pose challenges to therapists in order to test their sincerity, openness, nondefensiveness, and competencies. Because of the active nature of client challenges, therapy sessions may become quite dynamic. Many therapists frequently find this stage the most difficult to deal with because counselor self-disclosure is often necessary for establishing credibility.

Third, individuals at this stage are especially receptive to approaches that are more action oriented and aimed at external change (challenging racism). Also, group approaches with persons experiencing similar racial/cultural issues are well received. It is important that the therapist be willing to help the culturally different client explore new ways of relating to both minority and White persons.

Introspection Stage: Therapeutic Implications

Clients at the introspection stage may continue to prefer a therapist of their own race, but they are also receptive to help from therapists of other cultures as long as they understand their worldview. Ironically, clients at this stage may on the surface appear similar to conformity persons. Introspection clients are in conflict between their need to identify with the minority group and their need to exercise greater personal freedom. Exercising personal autonomy may occasionally mean going against the wishes or desires of the minority group. This is often perceived by minority persons and their group as a rejection of their own cultural heritage. This is not unlike conformity persons, who also reject their racial/cultural heritage. The dynamics between the two groups, however, are quite dissimilar. It is very important for therapists to distinguish the differences. The conformity person moves away from his or her own group because of perceived negative qualities associated with it. The introspection person wants to move away on certain issues but perceives the group positively. Again, self-exploration approaches aimed at helping the client integrate and incorporate a new sense of identity are important. Believing in the functional values of U.S. society does not mean that a person is selling out or going against his or her own group.

Integrative Awareness Stage: Therapeutic Implications

Clients at this stage have acquired an inner sense of security as to self-identity. They have pride in their racial/cultural heritage but can exercise a desired level of personal freedom and autonomy. Other cultures and races are appreciated, and there is a development toward becoming more multicultural in perspective. While discrimination and oppression remain a powerful part of their existence, integrative awareness persons possess greater psychological resources to deal with these problems. Being action or systems oriented, clients respond positively to the designing and implementation of strategies aimed at community and society change. Preferences for therapists are not based on race, but on those who can share, understand, and accept their worldviews. In other words, attitudinal similarity between therapist and client is a more important dimension than membership-group similarity.

Implications for Clinical Practice

We have already given considerable space to outlining specific therapeutic suggestions, so a repeat of these would be redundant. Rather, in proposing the R/CID model, we have been very aware of some major cautions and possible limitations that readers should take into account in working with minority clients.

1. Be aware that the R/CID model should not be viewed as a global personality theory with specific identifiable stages that serve as fixed categories. The process of cultural identity development is dynamic, not static. One of the major dangers is to use these stages as fixed entities. In actuality, the model should serve as a conceptual framework to help us understand development.

2. Do not fall victim to stereotyping in using these models. Most minority clients may evidence a dominant characteristic, but there are mixtures from other stages as well. Furthermore, situations and the types of presenting problems may make some characteristics more manifest than others. It is possible that minority clients may evidence conformity characteristics in some situations but resistance and immersion characteristics in others.

3. Know that minority development models are conceptual aids and that human development is much more complex. A question often raised in the formulation of cultural identity development models is whether identity is a linear process. Do individuals always start at the beginning of these stages? Is it possible to skip stages? Can people regress? In general, our clinical experience has been that minority and majority individuals in this society do tend to move at some gross level through each of the identifiable stages. Some tend to move faster than others; some tend to stay predominately at only one stage; and some may regress.

4. Know that identity development models begin at a point that involves interaction with an oppressive society. Most of these are weak in formulating a stage prior to conformity characteristics. Recent Asian immigrants to the United States are a prime example of the inadequacy of cultural identity development models. Many of the Asian immigrants tend to hold very positive and favorable views of their own culture and

possess an intact racial/cultural identity already. What happens when they encounter a society that views cultural differences as being deviant? Will they or their offspring move through the conformity stage as presented in this model?

5. Be careful of the implied value judgment given in almost all development models. They assume that some cultural resolutions are healthier than others. For example, the R/CID model obviously does hold the integrative awareness stage as a higher form of healthy functioning.

6. Take into consideration sociocultural forces that impact on identity development. Many of the early Black identity development models arose as a result of perceived and real experiences of oppression in our society. The Third World movement (Black power movement, Yellow power movement, Red power movement, and Brown power movement) occurred in a period of our society that was characterized by heightened racial/cultural pride and awareness. In other words, identity transformations are seen as being triggered by social movements that have powerful effects on the identity of persons of color. Does this mean that if social situations change, many of the cultural identity development models would also change? We still need to explore and investigate how interpersonal, institutional, societal, and cultural factors may either facilitate or impede cultural identity development.

7. Be aware that racial/cultural identity development models seriously lack an adequate integration of gender, class, sexual orientation, and other sociodemographic group identities. William Cross has made some beginning attempts to do so.

8. Know that racial/cultural identity is not a simple, global concept. A great deal of evidence is mounting that while identity may sequentially move through identifiable stages, affective, attitudinal, cognitive, and behavioral components of identity may not move in a uniform manner. For example, it is entirely possible that the emotions and affective elements associated with certain stages do not have a corresponding one-to-one behavioral impact.

9. Begin to look more closely at the possible therapist and client stage combinations. As mentioned earlier, therapeutic processes and outcomes are often the function of the identity stage of both therapist and client. White identity development of the therapist can either enhance or retard effective therapy.

White Racial Identity Development: Therapeutic Implications

What does being White mean? Have you ever asked yourself that question? If not, why haven't you? If you have, what was your answer? The following is taken from *You Are a Racist!* (in progress).

What Does It Mean to Be White?

42-year-old White businessman

> *Q: What does it mean to be White?*
> *A: Frankly, I don't know what you're talking about!*
> *Q: Aren't you White?*
> *A: Yes, but I come from Italian heritage. I'm Italian, not White.*
> *Q: Well then, what does it mean to be Italian?*
> *A: Pasta, good food, love of wine* [obviously agitated]. *This is getting ridiculous!*

OBSERVATIONS: *Denial and/or conflicted about being White. Claims Italian heritage, but unable to indicate more than superficial understanding of ethnic meaning. Expresses annoyance at the question.*

26-year-old White female college student

> *Q: What does it mean to be White?*
> *A: Is this a trick question?* [pause] *I've never thought about it. Well, I know that lots of Black people see us as being prejudiced and all that stuff. I wish people would just forget about race differences and see one another as human beings. People are people and we should all be proud to be Americans.*

OBSERVATIONS: *Seldom thinks about being White. Defensive about prejudicial associations with Whiteness. Desires to eliminate or dilute race differences.*

235

65-year-old White male retired construction worker

> *Q: What does it mean to be White?*
> *A: That's a stupid question* [sounds irritated]*!*
> *Q: Why?*
> *A: Look, what are you . . . Oriental? You people are always blaming us for stereotyping, and here you are doing the same to us.*
> *Q: When you say "us," to whom are you referring?*
> *A: I'm referring to Americans who aren't colored. We are all different from one another. I'm Irish but there are Germans, Italians, and those Jews. I get angry at the colored people for always blaming us. When my grandparents came over to this country, they worked 24 hours a day to provide a good living for their kids. My wife and I raised five kids, and I worked every day of my life to provide for them. No one gave me nothing! I get angry at the Black people for always whining. They just have to get off their butts and work rather than going on welfare. At least you people [reference to Asian Americans] work hard. The Black ones could learn from your people.*

OBSERVATIONS: Believes question stereotypes Whites and expresses resentment with being categorized. Views White people as ethnic group. Expresses belief that anyone can be successful if they work hard. Believes African Americans are lazy and that Asian Americans are successful. Strong anger directed toward minority groups.

34-year-old White female stockbroker

> *Q: What does it mean to be White?*
> *A: I don't know* [laughing]. *I've never thought about it.*
> *Q: Are you White?*
> *A: Yes, I suppose so* [seems very amused].
> *Q: Why haven't you thought about it?*
> *A: Because it's not important to me.*
> *Q: Why not?*
> *A: It doesn't enter into my mind because it doesn't affect my life. Besides, we are all unique. Color isn't important.*

OBSERVATIONS: Never thought about being White because it's unimportant. People are individuals, and color isn't important.

These are not atypical responses given by White Euro-Americans when posed with this question. When people of color are asked the same question, their answers tended to be more specific:

29-year-old Latina administrative assistant

> *Q: What does it mean to be White?*
> *A: I'm not White; I'm Latina!*
> *Q: Are you upset with me?*
> *A: No. . . . Its just that I'm light, so people always think I'm White. Its only when I speak that they realize I'm Hispanic.*
> *Q: Well, what does it mean to be White?*
> *A: Do you really want to know? . . . Okay, it means you're always right. It means you never have to explain yourself or apologize. . . . You know that movie [Love Story, which features the line, "Love is never having to say you're sorry]? Well, being White is never having to say you're sorry. It means they think they're better than us.*

OBSERVATIONS: Strong reaction to being mistaken for being White. Claims that being White makes people feel superior and is reflected in their disinclination to admit being wrong.

39 year-old Black male salesman

> *Q: What does it mean to be White?*
> *A: Is this a school exercise or something? Never expected someone to ask me that question in the middle of the city. Do you want the politically correct answer or what I really think?*
> *Q: Can you tell me what you really think?*
> *A: You won't quit, will you [laughing]? If you're White, you're right. If you're Black, step back.*
> *Q: What does that mean?*
> *A: White folks are always thinking they know all the answers. A Black man's word is worth less than a White man's. When White customers come into our dealership and see me standing next to the cars, I become invisible to them. Actually, they may see me as a well-dressed janitor [laughs], or actively avoid me. They will search out a White salesman. Or when I explain something to a customer, they always check out the information with my White colleagues. They don't trust me. When I mention this to our manager, who is White, he tells me I'm oversensitive and being paranoid. That's what being White means. It means having the authority or power to tell me what's really happening even though I know it's not. Being White means you can fool yourself into thinking that you're not prejudiced, when you are. That's what it means to be White.*

OBSERVATIONS: Being White means you view minorities as less competent and capable. You have the power to define reality. You can deceive yourself into believing you're not prejudiced.

21-year-old Chinese American male college student (majoring in ethnic studies)

Q: What does it mean to be White?
A: My cultural heritage class was just discussing that question this week.
Q: What was your conclusion?
A: Well, it has to do with White privilege. I read an article by a professor at Wellesley. It made a lot of sense to me. Being White in this society automatically guarantees you better treatment and unearned benefits and privileges than minorities. Having white skin means you have the freedom to choose the neighborhood you live in. You won't be discriminated against. When you enter a store, security guards won't assume you will steal something. You can flag down a cab without the thought they won't pick you up because you're a minority. You can study in school and be assured your group will be portrayed positively. You don't have to deal with race or think about it.
Q: Are White folks aware of their White privilege?
A: Hell no! They're oblivious to it.

OBSERVATIONS: Being White means having unearned privileges in our society. It means you are oblivious to the advantages of being White.

The Invisible Whiteness of Being

The responses given by White Euro-Americans and persons of color are radically different from one another. Yet the answers given by both groups are quite common and representative of the range of responses students give in our diversity and multicultural classes. White respondents would rather not think about their Whiteness, are uncomfortable or react negatively to being labeled "White," deny its importance in affecting their lives, and seem to believe that they are unjustifiably accused of being bigoted simply because they are White.

Strangely enough, Whiteness is most visible to people of color when it is denied, evokes puzzlement/negative reactions, and is equated with normalcy. Few people of color react negatively when asked what it means to be Black, Asian American, Latino, or a member of their race. Most could readily inform the questioner about what it means to be a person of color. There seldom is a day, for example, in which we (the authors) are not reminded of being racially and culturally different from those around us. Yet Whites often find the question about Whiteness quite disconcerting and perplexing.

It appears that the denial and mystification of Whiteness for White Euro-Americans are related to two underlying factors. First, most people seldom think about the air that surrounds them and about how it provides an essential life-giving ingredient, oxygen. We take it for granted because it appears plentiful; only when we are deprived of it does it suddenly become frighteningly apparent. Whiteness is transparent precisely because of its everyday occurrence—its institutionalized normative features in our culture—and because Whites are taught to think of their lives as morally neutral, average, and ideal. To people of color, however, Whiteness is not invisible because it may not fit their normative qualities (values, lifestyles, experiential reality, etc.). Persons of color find White culture quite visible because even though it is nurturing to White Euro-Americans, it may invalidate the lifestyles of multicultural populations.

Second, Euro-Americans often deny that they are White, seem angered by being labeled as such, and often become very defensive. "I'm not White, I'm Irish." "You're stereotyping, because we're all different." "There isn't anything like a White race." In many respects, these statements have validity. Nonetheless, many White Americans would be hard pressed to describe their Irish, Italian, German, or Norwegian heritage in any but the most superficial manner. One of the reasons is related to the processes of assimilation and acculturation. While there are many ethnic groups, being White allows for assimilation.

While persons of color are told to assimilate, this psychological process is meant for Whites only. Assimilation and acculturation are processes that assume a receptive society. Racial minorities are told in no uncertain terms that they are allowed only limited access to the fruits of our society. Thus, the accuracy of whether Whiteness defines a race is largely irrelevant. What is more relevant is that Whiteness is associated with unearned privilege—advantages conferred on White Americans but not on persons of color. It is our contention that much of the denial associated with being White is related to the denial of White privilege, an issue we explore in a moment.

Understanding the Dynamics of Whiteness

Our analysis of the responses from both Whites and persons of color leads us to the inevitable conclusion that part of the problem of race relations (and by inference multicultural counseling and therapy) lies in the different worldviews of both groups. Which group, however, has the more accurate assessment related to this topic? The answer seems to be contained in the following series of questions: If you want to understand oppression, should you ask the oppressor or the oppressed? If you want to learn about sexism, do you ask men or women? If you want to understand homophobia, do you ask straights or gays? If you want to learn about racism, do you ask Whites or persons of color? It appears that the most accurate assessment of bias comes not from those who enjoy the privilege of power, but from those who are most disempowered (D'Andrea & Daniels, 2001; Dovidio, in press; Hanna, Talley, & Guindon, 2000; Neville et al., 2001). Taking this position, the following assumptions are made about the dynamics of Whiteness.

First, it is clear that most White folks perceive themselves as unbiased individuals who do not harbor racist thoughts and feelings; they see themselves as working toward social justice and possess a conscious desire to better the life circumstances of those less fortunate than they. While admirable qualities, this self-image serves as a major barrier to recognizing and taking responsibility for admitting and dealing with one's own prejudices and biases. To admit to being racist, sexist, or homophobic requires people to recognize that the self-images that they hold so dear are based on false notions of the self.

Second, being a White person in this society means chronic exposure to ethnocentric monoculturalism as manifested in White supremacy (D. W. Sue et al., 1998). It is difficult, if not impossible, for anyone to avoid inheriting the racial biases, prejudices, misinformation, deficit portrayals, and stereotypes of their forebears. To believe that they are somehow immune from inheriting such aspects of White supremacy is to be naive or to engage in self-deception. Such a statement is not intended to assail the integrity of White folks, but to suggest that they also have been victimized. It is clear to us that no one was born wanting to be racist, sexist, or homophobic. Misinformation is not acquired by free choice, but is imposed upon White folks through a painful process of cultural conditioning. In general, lacking awareness of their biases and preconceived notions, counselors may function in a therapeutically ineffective manner.

> *The development of White identity in the United States is closely intertwined with the development and progress of racism in this country. The greater the extent that racism exists and is denied, the less possible it is to develop a positive White identity. (Carter, 1995, p. 39)*

Third, if White helping professionals are ever able to become effective multicultural counseling/therapy therapists, they must free themselves from the cultural conditioning of their past and move toward the development of a nonracist White identity. Unfortunately, many White Euro-Americans seldom consider what it means to be "White" in our society. Such a question is vexing to them because they seldom think of "race" as belonging to them— nor of the privileges that come their way by virtue of their white skin. Katz (1985, pp. 616–617) points out a major barrier blocking the process of White Euro-Americans investigating their own cultural identity and worldview:

> *Because White culture is the dominant cultural norm in the United States, it acts as an invisible veil that limits many people from seeing it as a cultural system. . . . Often, it is easier for many Whites to identify and acknowledge the different cul-*

tures of minorities than accept their own racial identity. . . . The difficulty of accepting such a view is that White culture is omnipresent. It is so interwoven in the fabric of everyday living that Whites cannot step outside and see their beliefs, values, and behaviors as creating a distinct cultural group.

Ridley (1995, p. 38) asserts that this invisible veil can be manifested in therapy unintentionally with harmful consequences to minority clients:

Unintentional behavior is perhaps the most insidious form of racism. Unintentional racists are unaware of the harmful consequences of their behavior. They may be well-intentioned, and on the surface, their behavior may appear to be responsible. Because individuals, groups, or institutions that engage in unintentional racism do not wish to do harm, it is difficult to get them to see themselves as racists. They are more likely to deny their racism.

The conclusion drawn from this understanding is that White counselors and therapists may be unintentional racists: (a) They are unaware of their biases, prejudices, and discriminatory behaviors; (b) they often perceive themselves as moral, good, and decent human beings and find it difficult to see themselves as racist; (c) they do not have a sense of what their Whiteness means to them; and (d) their therapeutic approaches to multicultural populations are likely to be more harmful (unintentionally) than helpful. These conclusions are often difficult for White helping professionals to accept because of the defensiveness and feelings of blame they are likely to engender. Nonetheless, we ask that White therapists and students not be "turned off" by the message and lessons of this chapter. We ask you to continue your multicultural journey in this chapter as we explore the question, "What does it mean to be White?"

Models of White Racial Identity Development

A number of multicultural experts in the field have begun to emphasize the need for White therapists to deal with their concepts of Whiteness and to examine their own racism (Carter, 1995; Corvin & Wiggins, 1989; Helms, 1984, 1990; Ponterotto, 1988; D. W. Sue et al., 1998). These specialists point out that while racial/cultural identity development for minority groups proves beneficial in our work as therapists, more attention should be devoted toward the White therapist's racial identity. Since the majority of therapists and trainees are White middle-class individuals, it would appear that White identity development and its implication for multicultural counseling/therapy would be important aspects to consider, both in the actual practice of clinical work and in professional training.

For example, research has found that the level of White racial identity awareness is predictive of racism (Carter, 1990; Pope-Davis & Ottavi, 1994): (a) The less aware subjects were of their White identity, the more likely they were to exhibit increased levels of racism; and (b) women were less likely to be racist. It was suggested that this last finding was correlated with women's greater experiences with discrimination and prejudice. Evidence also exists that multicultural counseling/therapy competence is correlated with White racial identity attitudes (Neville, Worthington, & Spanierman, 2001; Ottavi, Pope-Davis, & Dings, 1994). Other research suggests that a relationship exists between a White Euro-American therapist's racial identity and his or her readiness for training in multicultural awareness, knowledge, and skills (Carney & Kahn, 1984; Helms, 1990; Ponterotto, 1988; Sabnani, Ponterotto, & Borodovsky, 1991; D. W. Sue & Sue, 1990). Since developing multicultural sensitivity is a longterm developmental task, the work of many researchers has gradually converged toward a conceptualization of the stages/levels/ statuses of consciousness of racial/ethnic identity development for White Euro-Americans (Bennett, 1986; E. J. Smith, 1991). A number of these models describe the salience of identity for establishing relationships between the White therapist and the culturally different client, and some have now linked stages of identity with stages for appropriate training (Bennett, 1986; Carney & Kahn, 1984; Sabnani et al., 1991).

The Hardiman White Racial Identity Development Model

One of the earliest integrative attempts at formulating a White racial identity development model is that of Rita Hardiman (1982). Intrigued with why certain White individuals exhibit a much more nonracist identity than do other White Americans, Hardiman studied the autobiographies of individuals who had attained a high level of racial consciousness. This led her to identify five White developmental stages: (a) naïveté—lack of social consciousness (b) acceptance, (c) resistance, (d) redefinition, and (e) internalization.

1. The *naïveté stage* (lack of social consciousness) is characteristic of early childhood, when we are born into this world innocent, open, and unaware of racism and the importance of race. Curiosity and spontaneity in relating to race and racial differences tend to be the norm. A young White child who has almost no personal contact with African Americans, for example, may see a Black man in a supermarket and loudly comment on the darkness of his skin. Other than the embarrassment and apprehensions of adults around the child, there is little discomfort associated with this behavior for the youngster. In general, awareness and the meaning of race, racial differences, bias, and prejudice are either absent or minimal. Such an orientation becomes less characteristic of the child as the socialization process progresses. The negative reac-

tions of parents, relatives, friends, and peers toward issues of race, however, begin to convey mixed signals to the child. This is reinforced by the educational system and mass media, which instill racial biases in the child and propel him or her into the acceptance stage.

2. The *acceptance stage* is marked by a conscious belief in the democratic ideal: that everyone has an equal opportunity to succeed in a free society and that those who fail must bear the responsibility for their failure. White Euro-Americans become the social reference group, and the socialization process consistently instills messages of White superiority and minority inferiority into the child. The underemployment, unemployment, and undereducation of marginalized groups in our society are seen as support that non-White groups are lesser than Whites. Because everyone has an equal opportunity to succeed, the lack of success of minority groups is seen as evidence of some negative personal or group characteristic (low intelligence, inadequate motivation, or biological/cultural deficits). Victim blaming is strong as the existence of oppression, discrimination, and racism is denied. Hardiman believes that while the naïveté stage is brief in duration, the acceptance stage can last a lifetime.

3. Over time, the individual begins to challenge assumptions of White superiority and the denial of racism and discrimination. Moving from the acceptance stage to the *resistance stage* can prove to be a painful, conflicting, and uncomfortable transition. The White person's denial system begins to crumble because of a monumental event or a series of events that not only challenge but also shatter the individual's denial system. A White person may, for example, make friends with a minority coworker and discover that the images he or she has of "these people" are untrue. They may have witnessed clear incidents of unfair discrimination toward persons of color and may now begin to question assumptions regarding racial inferiority. In any case, the racial realities of life in the United States can no longer be denied. The change from one stage to another might take considerable time, but once completed, the person becomes conscious of being White, is aware that he or she harbors racist attitudes, and begins to see the pervasiveness of oppression in our society. Feelings of anger, pain, hurt, rage, and frustration are present. In many cases, the White person may develop a negative reaction toward his or her own group or culture. While they may romanticize people of color, they cannot interact confidently with them because they fear that they will make racist mistakes. This discomfort is best exemplified in a passage by Sara Winter (1977, p. 1):

We avoid Black people because their presence brings painful questions to mind. Is it OK to talk about watermelons or mention "black coffee"? Should we use

Black slang and tell racial jokes? How about talking about our experiences in Harlem, or mentioning our Black lovers? Should we conceal the fact that our mother still employs a Black cleaning lady? . . . We're embarrassedly aware of trying to do our best but to "act natural" at the same time. No wonder we're more comfortable in all-White situations where these dilemmas don't arise.

According to Hardiman (1982), the discomfort in realizing that one is White and that one's group has engaged in oppression of racial/ethnic minorities may propel the person into the next stage.

4. Asking the painful question of who one is in relation to one's racial heritage, honestly confronting one's biases and prejudices, and accepting responsibility for one's Whiteness are the culminating marks of the *redefinition stage.* New ways of defining one's social group and one's membership in that group become important. The intense soul searching is most evident in Winter's (1977, p. 2) personal journey as she writes,

    In this sense we Whites are the victims of racism. Our victimization is different from that of Blacks, but it is real. We have been programmed into the oppressor roles we play, without our informed consent in the process. Our unawareness is part of the programming: None of us could tolerate the oppressor position, if we lived with a day-to-day emotional awareness of the pain inflicted on other humans through the instrument of our behavior. . . . We Whites benefit in concrete ways, year in and year out, from the present racial arrangements. All my life in White neighborhoods, White schools, White jobs and dealing with White police (to name only a few), I have experienced advantages that are systematically not available to Black people. It does not make sense for me to blame myself for the advantages that have come my way by virtue of my Whiteness. But absolving myself from guilt does not imply forgetting about racial injustice or taking it lightly (as my guilt pushes me to do).

    There is realization that Whiteness has been defined in opposition to people of color—namely, by standards of White supremacy. By being able to step out of this racist paradigm and redefining what her Whiteness meant to her, Winter is able to add meaning to developing a nonracist identity. The extremes of good/bad or positive/negative attachments to "White" and "people of color" begin to become more realistic. The person no longer denies being White, honestly confronts one's racism, understands the concept of White privilege, and feels increased comfort in relating to persons of color.

5. The *internalization stage* is the result of forming a new social and personal identity. With the greater comfort in understanding oneself and the development of a nonracist White identity comes a commitment to social action as well. The individual accepts responsibility for effecting per-

sonal and social change without always relying on persons of color to lead the way. As Winter (1977, p. 2) explains,

To end racism, Whites have to pay attention to it and continue to pay attention. Since avoidance is such a basic dynamic of racism, paying attention will not happen naturally. We Whites must learn how to hold racism realities in our attention. We must learn to take responsibility for this process ourselves, without waiting for Blacks' actions to remind us that the problem exists, and without depending on Black people to reassure us and forgive us for our racist sins. In my experience, the process is painful but it is a relief to shed the fears, stereotypes, immobilizing guilt we didn't want in the first place.

The racist-free identity, however, must be nurtured, validated, and supported in order to be sustained in a hostile environment. Such an individual is constantly bombarded by attempts to be resocialized into the oppressive society.

There are several potential limitations to the Hardiman (1982) model: (a) The select and limited sample that she uses to derive the stages and enumerate the characteristics makes potential generalization suspect; (b) the autobiographies of White Americans are not truly representative, and their experiences with racism may be bound by the era of the times; (c) the stages are tied to existing social identity development theories, and the model proposes a naïveté stage that for all practical purposes exists only in children ages 3 to 4 years (it appears tangential in her model and might better be conceptualized as part of the acceptance stage of socialization); and (d) there have been no direct empirical or other postmodern methods of exploration concerning the model to date. Despite these cautions and potential limitations, Hardiman has contributed greatly to our understanding of White identity development by focusing attention on racism as a central force in the socialization of White Americans.

The Helms White Racial Identity Model

Working independently of Hardiman, Janet Helms (1984, 1990, 1994, 1995) created perhaps the most elaborate and sophisticated White racial identity model yet proposed. Helms is arguably the most influential White identity development theorist. Not only has her model led to the development of an assessment instrument to measure White racial identity, but it also has been scrutinized empirically (Carter, 1990; Helms & Carter, 1990) and has generated much research and debate in the psychological literature. Like Hardiman (1982), Helms assumes that racism is an intimate and central part of being a White American. To her, developing a healthy White identity requires movement through two phases: (a) abandonment of racism and (b) defining a nonracist White identity. Six specific racial identity statuses are distributed equally in the two: contact, disintegration, reintegration, pseudoindependence, immersion/emersion, and autonomy. Originally, Helms used the term "stages" to refer to the six, but because of certain conceptual ambiguities and the controversy that ensued, she has abandoned its usage.

1. *Contact status.* People in this status are oblivious to and unaware of racism, believe that everyone has an equal chance for success, lack an understanding of prejudice and discrimination, have minimal experiences with persons of color, and may profess to be colorblind. Such statements as "People are people," "I don't notice a person's race at all," and "You don't act Black" are examples. While there is an attempt to minimize the importance or influence of race, there is a definite dichotomy of Blacks and Whites on both a conscious and unconscious level regarding stereotypes and the superior/inferior dimensions of the races. Because of obliviousness and compartmentalization, it is possible for two diametrically opposed belief systems to coexist: (a) Uncritical acceptance of White supremacist notions relegates minorities into the inferior category with all the racial stereotypes, and (b) there is a belief that racial and cultural differences are considered unimportant. This allows Whites to avoid perceiving themselves as "dominant" group members, or of having biases and prejudices. Such an orientation is aptly stated by Peggy McIntosh (1989, p. 8) in her own White racial awakening:

   My schooling gave me no training in seeing myself as an oppressor, as an unfairly advantaged person, or as a participant in a damaged culture. I was taught to see myself as an individual whose moral state depended on her individual moral will. . . . Whites are taught to think of their lives as morally neutral, normative, and average, and also ideal, so that when we work to benefit others, this is seen as work which will allow "them" to be more like "us."

2. *Disintegration status.* While in the previous status the individual does not recognize the polarities of democratic principles of equality and the unequal treatment of minority groups, such obliviousness may eventually break down. The White person becomes conflicted over irresolvable racial moral dilemmas that are frequently perceived as polar opposites: believing one is nonracist, yet not wanting one's son or daughter to marry a minority group member; believing that "all men are created equal," even though society treats Blacks as second-class citizens; and not acknowledging that oppression exists, and then witnessing it (e.g., the beating of Rodney King). Conflicts between loyalty to one's group

and "humanistic ideals" may manifest themselves in various ways. The person becomes increasingly conscious of his or her Whiteness and may experience dissonance and conflict, resulting in feelings of guilt, depression, helplessness, or anxiety. Statements such as, "My grandfather is really prejudiced, but I try not to be" and "I'm personally not against interracial marriages, but I worry about the children," are representative of personal struggles occurring in the White person. This type of conflict is best exemplified in the following passage from Winter (1977, p. 24):

When someone pushes racism into my awareness, I feel guilty (that I could be doing so much more); angry (I don't like to feel like I'm wrong); defensive (I already have two Black friends. . . . I worry more about racism than most whites do— isn't that enough?); turned off (I have other priorities in my life with guilt about that thought); helpless (the problem is so big—what can I do?). I HATE TO FEEL THIS WAY. That is why I minimize race issues and let them fade from my awareness whenever possible.

While a healthy resolution might be to confront the "myth of meritocracy" realistically, the breakdown of the denial system is painful and anxiety provoking. Attempts at resolution, according to Helms, may involve (a) avoiding contact with persons of color, (b) not thinking about race, and (c) seeking reassurance from others that racism is not the fault of Whites.

3. *Reintegration status.* This status can best be characterized as a regression in which the pendulum swings back to the most basic beliefs of White superiority and minority inferiority. In their attempts to resolve the dissonance created from the previous process, there is a retreat to the dominant ideology associated with race and one's own socioracial group identity. This ego status results in idealizing the White Euro-American group and the positives of White culture and society; there is a consequent negation and intolerance of other minority groups. In general, a firmer and more conscious belief in White racial superiority is present. Racial/ethnic minorities are blamed for their own problems.

I'm an Italian grandmother. No one gave us welfare or a helping hand when we came over [immigrated]. My father worked day and night to provide us with a decent living and to put all of us through school. These Negroes are always complaining about prejudice and hardships. Big deal! Why don't they stop whining and find a job? They're not the only ones who were discriminated against, you know. You don't think our family wasn't? We never let that stop us. In America everyone can make it if they are willing to work hard. I see these Black welfare mothers waiting in line for food stamps and free handouts. You can't convince me they're starving. Look at how overweight most of them are. . . . Laziness—that's what I see. (quoted from a workshop participant)

4. *Pseudoindependence status.* This status represents the second phase of Helms's model, which involves defining a nonracist White identity. As in the Hardiman model, a person is likely to be propelled into this phase because of a painful or insightful encounter or event that jars the person from the reintegration status. The awareness of other visible racial/ethnic minorities, the unfairness of their treatment, and a discomfort with the racist White identity may lead a person to identify with the plight of persons of color. There is an attempt to understand racial, cultural, and sexual orientation differences and a purposeful and conscious decision to interact with minority group members. However, the well-intentioned White person at this status may suffer from several problematic dynamics: (a) While intending to be socially conscious and helpful to minority groups, the White individual may unknowingly perpetuate racism by helping minorities adjust to the prevailing White standards; and (b) choice of minority individuals is based on how "similar" they are to him or her, and the primary mechanism used to understand racial issues is intellectual and conceptual. As a result, understanding has not reached the experiential and affective domains. In other words, understanding Euro-American White privilege, sociopolitical aspects of race, and issues of bias, prejudice, and discrimination tend to be more an intellectual exercise.

5. *Immersion/emersion status.* If the person is reinforced to continue a personal exploration of him- or herself as a racial being, questions become focused on what it means to be White. Helms states that the person searches for an understanding of the personal meaning of racism and the ways in which one benefits from White privilege. There is an increasing willingness to confront one's own biases, to redefine Whiteness, and to become more activistic in directly combating racism and oppression. This status is different from the previous one in two major ways: It is marked by (a) a shift in focus from trying to change Blacks to changing the self and other Whites and (b) increasing experiential and affective understanding that was lacking in the previous status. This later process is extremely important. Indeed, Helms believes that a successful resolution of this stage requires an emotional catharsis or release that forces the person to relive or reexperience previous emotions that were denied or distorted. The ability to achieve this affective/experiential upheaval leads to a euphoria or even a feeling of rebirth and is a necessary condition to developing a new nonracist White identity. As Winter (1977, p. 3) states,

Let me explain this healing process in more detail. We must unearth all the words and memories we generally try not to think about, but which are inside us all the time: "nigger," "Uncle Tom," "jungle bunny," "Oreo"; lynching, cattle prods, castrations, rapists, "black pussy," and black men with their huge penises, and hundreds more. (I shudder as I write.). We need to review three different kinds of material: (1) All our personal memories connected with blackness and black people including everything we can recall hearing or reading; (2) all the racist images and stereotypes we've ever heard, particularly the grossest and most hurtful ones; (3) any race-related things we ourselves said, did or omitted doing which we feel bad about today. . . . Most whites begin with a good deal of amnesia. Eventually the memories crowd in, especially when several people pool recollections. Emotional release is a vital part of the process. Experiencing feelings seems to allow further recollections to come. I need persistent encouragement from my companions to continue.

6.   *Autonomy status.* Increasing awareness of one's own Whiteness, reduced feelings of guilt, acceptance of one's role in perpetuating racism, and renewed determination to abandon White entitlement lead to an autonomy status. The person is knowledgeable about racial, ethnic, and cultural differences; values the diversity; and is no longer fearful, intimated, or uncomfortable with the experiential reality of race. Development of a nonracist White identity becomes increasingly strong. Indeed, the person feels comfortable with his or her nonracist White identity, does not personalize attacks on White supremacy, and can explore the issues of racism and personal responsibility without defensiveness. A person in this status "walks the talk" and actively values and seeks out interracial experiences. Characteristics of the autonomy status can be found in the personal journey of Kiselica (1998, pp. 10–11):

I was deeply troubled as I witnessed on a daily basis the detrimental effects of institutional racism and oppression on ethnic-minority groups in this country. The latter encounters forced me to recognize my privileged position in our society because of my status as a so-called Anglo. It was upsetting to know that I, a member of White society, benefited from the hardships of others that were caused by a racist system. I was also disturbed by the painful realization that I was, in some ways, a racist. I had to come to grips with the fact that I had told and laughed at racist jokes and, through such behavior, had supported White racist attitudes. If I really wanted to become an effective, multicultural psychologist, extended and profound self-reckoning was in order. At times, I wanted to flee from this unpleasant process by merely participating superficially with the remaining tasks . . . while avoiding any substantive self-examination.

Table 9.1   **White Racial Identity Ego Statuses and Information-Processing Strategies**

1. *Contact status:* satisfaction with racial status quo, obliviousness to racism and one's participation in it. If racial factors influence life decisions, they do so in a simplistic fashion. Information-processing strategy (IPS): Obliviousness.

Example: "I'm a White woman. When my grandfather came to this country, he was discriminated against, too. But he didn't blame Black people for his misfortunes. He educated himself and got a job: That's what Blacks ought to do. If White callers [to a radio station] spent as much time complaining about racial discrimination as your Black callers do, we'd never have accomplished what we have. You all should just ignore it" (quoted from a workshop participant).

2. *Disintegration status:* disorientation and anxiety provoked by irresolvable racial moral dilemmas that force one to choose between own-group loyalty and humanism. May be stymied by life situations that arouse racial dilemmas. IPS: Suppression and ambivalence.

Example: "I myself tried to set a nonracist example [for other Whites] by speaking up when someone said something blatantly prejudiced—how to do this without alienating people so that they would no longer take me seriously was always tricky—and by my friendships with Mexicans and Blacks who were actually the people with whom I felt most comfortable" (Blauner, 1993, p. 8).

3. *Reintegration status:* idealization of one's socioracial group, denigration, and intolerance for other groups. Racial factors may strongly influence life decisions. IPS: Selective perception and negative out-group distortion.

Example: "So what if my great-grandfather owned slaves. He didn't mistreat them and besides, I wasn't even here then. I never owned slaves. So, I don't know why Blacks expect me to feel guilty for something that happened before I was born. Nowadays, reverse racism hurts Whites more than slavery hurts Blacks. At least they got three square [meals] a day. But my brother can't even get a job with the police department because they have to hire less-qualified Blacks. That [expletive] happens to Whites all the time" (quoted from a workshop participant).

4. *Pseudoindependence status:* intellectualized commitment to one's own socioracial group and deceptive tolerance of other groups. May make life decisions to "help other racial groups." IPS: Reshaping reality and selective perception.

Example: "Was I the only person left in American who believed that the sexual mingling of the races was a good thing, that it would erase cultural barriers and leave us all a lovely shade of tan? . . . Racial blending is inevitable. At the very least, it may be the only solution to our dilemmas of race" (Allen, 1994, p. C4).

5. *Immersion/emersion status:* search for an understanding of the personal meaning of racism and the ways by which one benefits and a redefinition of Whiteness. Life choices may incorporate racial activism. IPS: Hypervigilance and reshaping.

Example: "It's true that I personally did not participate in the horror of slavery, and I don't even know whether my ancestors owned slaves. But I know that because I am White, I continue to benefit from a racist system that stems from the slavery era. I believe that if White people are ever going to understand our role in perpetuating racism, then we must begin to ask ourselves some hard questions and be willing to consider our role in maintaining a hurtful system. Then, we must try to do something to change it" (quoted from a workshop participant).

Table 9.1 **continued**

6. *Autonomy status:* informed positive socioracial group commitment, use of internal standards for self-definition, capacity to relinquish the privileges of racism. May avoid life options that require participation in racial oppression. IPS: Flexibility and complexity.

Example: "I live in an integrated [Black-White] neighborhood and I read Black literature and popular magazines. So, I understand that the media presents a very stereotypic view of Black culture. I believe that if more of us White people made more than a superficial effort to obtain accurate information about racial groups other than our own, then we could help make this country a better place for all peoples" (quoted from a workshop participant.

Source: Helms (1995, p. 185).

Helm's model is by far the most widely cited, researched, and applied of all the White racial identity formulations. Part of its attractiveness and value is the derivation of "defenses," "protective strategies," or what Helms (1995) formally labels *information-processing strategies* (IPSs), which White people use to avoid or assuage anxiety and discomfort around the issue of race. Each status has a dominant IPS associated with it: contact = obliviousness or denial, disintegration = suppression and ambivalence, reintegration = selective perception and negative out-group distortion, pseudoindependence = reshaping reality and selective perception, immersion/emersion = hypervigilance and reshaping, and autonomy = flexibility and complexity. Table 9.1 lists examples of IPS statements likely to be made by White people in each of the six ego statuses. Understanding these strategic reactions is important for White American identity development, for understanding the barriers that must be overcome in order to move to another status, and for potentially developing effective training or clinical strategies.

The Helms model, however, is not without its detractors. In an article critical of the Helms model and of most "stage" models of White racial identity development, Rowe, Bennett, and Atkinson (1994) raised some serious objections. First, they claim that Helms's model is erroneously based on racial/ethnic minority identity development models (discussed in the previous chapter). Because minority identity development occurs in the face of stereotyping and oppression, it may not apply to White identity, which does not occur under the same conditions. Second, they believe that too much emphasis is placed on the development of White attitudes toward minorities and that not enough is placed on the development of White attitudes toward themselves and their own identity. Third, they claim that there is a conceptual inaccuracy in putting forth the model as developmental via stages (linear) and that the progression from less to more healthy seems to be based on the author's ethics.

It is important to note that the critique of the Helms (1984) model has not been left unanswered. Thompson (1995) believes that these criticisms are based on a misrepresentation of Helms's writings and research; that she does emphasize White identity and minority identity development in different contexts; that the task of developing a positive White identity is central to the model; and that the model does meet criteria for a developmental theory that is not necessarily linear. In subsequent writings, Helms (1994, 1995) has also disclaimed the Rowe et al. (1994) characterization of her model and has attempted to clarify her position.

The continuing debate has proven beneficial for two reasons. First, the Helms model has evolved and changed (whether because of these criticism or not) so that it has become even more intricate and clear. For example, Helms denies ever being a "stage theorist," but to prevent continuing future confusion, she now prefers the term "status" and describes her thinking on this issue in detail (Helms, 1995). Second, in responding to the Helms model, Rowe et al. (1994) offered an alternative means of conceptualizing White identity that has contributed to the increasing understanding of White identity development.

Briefly, Rowe et al. (1994) prefer to conceptualize White racial identity as one of "types" or "statuses" rather than "stages." They take care in explaining that these types are not fixed entities but are subject to experiential modification. They propose two major groupings with seven types of racial consciousness: unachieved (avoidant, dependent, and dissonant) and achieved (dominative, conflictive, reactive, and integrative). Movement from type to type is dependent on the creation of dissonance, personal attributes, and the subsequent environmental conditions encountered by the person. As a result, the primary gateway for change involves the dissonant type. Persons can move between all types except the two unachieved ones, avoidant and dependent. These latter two are characterized by lack of internalized attitudes. Space does not permit an extended discussion of the model; we have chosen to summarize these types and their characteristics in Table 9.2. A more detailed discussion of the model can be found in Rowe et al. (1994).

The Process of White Racial Identity Development: A Descriptive Model

Analysis of the models just discussed reveals some important differences. First, the identity development models seem to focus on a more definite and sequential movement through stages or statuses. They differ, however, in where they place the particular stages or statuses in the developmental process. Given that almost all models now entertain the possibility that development can vary (looping and recycling), the consciousness development model allows greater latitude conceptually for movement to various types. Rowe et al. (1994) seem to offer a more fluid process of racial experience by

Table 9.2 **Rowe, Bennett, and Atkinson's Model of White Racial Consciousness Types and Their Characteristics**

I. Unachieved

    A. Avoidant types ignore, avoid, deny, or minimize racial issues. They do not consider their own racial identity, nor are they seemingly aware of minority issues.

    B. Dependent types have minimal racial attitudes developed through person experience or consideration. They most often follow the lead of significant others in the life, such as would a child with his or her parent.

    C. Dissonant types often feel conflict between their belief systems and contradictory experiences. This type may break away from these attitudes depending on the degree of support or the intensity of the conflict. As such, it is a transitory status for the person.

II. Achieved

    A. Dominative types are very ethnocentric and believe in White superiority and minority inferiority. They may act out their biases passively or actively.

    B. Conflictive types oppose direct and obvious discrimination but would be unwilling to change the status quo. Most feel that discrimination has been eliminated and that further efforts constitute reverse racism.

    C. Reactive types have good awareness that racism exists but seem unaware of their personal responsibility in perpetuating it. They may overidentify with or be paternalistic toward minorities.

    D. Integrative types "have integrated their sense of Whiteness with a regard for racial/ethnic minorities . . . [and] integrate rational analysis, on the one hand, and moral principles, on the other, as they relate to a variety of racial/ethnic issues" (Rowe, Bennett, & Atkinson, 1994, p. 141).

White people. Consequently, the model is also less bound by the context or era of the times (identity formed during the Civil Rights movement vs. current times). The addition of nonachieved statuses is missing in the development theories and may capture more closely the "passive" feel that White folks experience in their racial identity development.

However, the essential concept of developing a positive White identity is conspicuously absent from the consciousness model. It lacks richness in allowing White folks to view their developmental history better and to gain a sense of their past, present, and future. Struggling with racial identity and issues of race requires a historical perspective, which development theories offer. It is with this in mind that we have attempted to take aspects of White racial identity/consciousness development into formulating a descriptive model with practical implications.

In our work with White trainees and clinicians, we have observed some very important changes through which they seem to move as they work toward multicultural competence. We have been impressed with how Whites seem to go through parallel racial/cultural identity transformations. This is especially true if we accept the fact that Whites are as much victims of societal forces (i.e., they are socialized into racist attitudes and beliefs) as are their minority counterparts. No child is born wanting to be a racist! Yet White people do benefit from the dominant-subordinate relationship in our society. It is this factor that Whites need to confront in an open and honest manner.

Using the formulation of D. W. Sue & Sue (1990) and D. W. Sue et al. (1998), we propose a five-stage process that integrates many characteristics from the other formulations. Furthermore, we make some basic assumptions with respect to those models: (a) Racism is an integral part of U.S. life, and it permeates all aspects of our culture and institutions (ethnocentric monoculturalism); (b) Whites are socialized into the society and therefore inherit all the biases, stereotypes, and racist attitudes, beliefs, and behaviors of the larger society; (c) how Whites perceive themselves as racial beings follows an identifiable sequence that can occur in a linear or nonlinear fashion; (d) the status of White racial identity development in any multicultural encounter affects the process and outcome of interracial relationships; and (e) the most desirable outcome is one in which the White person not only accepts his or her Whiteness but also defines it in a nondefensive and nonracist manner.

1. *Conformity phase.* The White person's attitudes and beliefs in this stage are very ethnocentric. There is minimal awareness of the self as a racial being and a strong belief in the universality of values and norms governing behavior. The White person possesses limited accurate knowledge of other ethnic groups, but he or she is likely to rely on social stereotypes as the main source of information. As we saw, Hardiman (1982) described this stage as an acceptance of White superiority and minority inferiority. Consciously or unconsciously, the White person believes that White culture is the most highly developed and that all others are "primitive" or inferior. The conformity stage is marked by contradictory and often compartmentalized attitudes, beliefs, and behaviors. A person may believe simultaneously that he or she is not racist but that minority inferiority justifies discriminatory and inferior treatment, and that minority persons are different and deviant but that "people are people" and differences are unimportant (Helms, 1984). As with their minority counterparts at this stage, the primary mechanism operating here is one of denial and compartmentalization. For example, many Whites deny that they belong to a race that allows them to avoid personal responsibility for perpetuating a racist system. Like a fish in water, White folks either have difficulty seeing or are unable to see the invisible veil of cultural assumptions, biases, and prejudices that guide their perceptions and actions. They tend to believe that White Euro-American culture is superior and that other cultures are primitive, infe-

rior, less developed, or lower on the scale of evolution. It is important to note that many Whites in this phase of development are unaware of these beliefs and operate as if they are universally shared by others. They believe that differences are unimportant and that "people are people," "we are all the same under the skin," "we should treat everyone the same," "problems wouldn't exist if minorities would only assimilate," and discrimination and prejudice are something that others do. The helping professional with this perspective professes color blindness and views counseling/therapy theories as universally applicable and does not question their relevance to other culturally different groups.

Wrenn's (1962, 1985) reference to and description of the "culturally encapsulated counselor" fulfills characteristics of conformity. The primary mechanism used in encapsulation is denial—denial that people are different, denial that discrimination exists, and denial of one's own prejudices. Instead, the locus of the problem is seen to reside in the minority individual or group. Minorities would not encounter problems if they would only assimilate and acculturate (melting pot), value education, or work harder.

2. *Dissonance phase.* Movement into the dissonance stage occurs when the White person is forced to deal with the inconsistencies that have been compartmentalized or encounters information/experiences at odds with denial. In most cases, a person is forced to acknowledge Whiteness at some level, to examine their own cultural values, and to see the conflict between upholding humanistic nonracist values and their contradictory behavior. For example, a person who may consciously believe that "all men are created equal" and that he or she "treats everyone the same" suddenly experiences reservations about having African Americans move next door or having their son or daughter involved in an interracial relationship. These more personal experiences bring the individual face to face with his or her own prejudices and biases. In this situation, thoughts that "I am not prejudiced," "I treat everyone the same regardless or race, creed, or color," and "I do not discriminate" collide with the denial system. Additionally, some major event (the assassination of Martin Luther King Jr., the Rodney King beating, etc.) may force the person to realize that racism is alive and well in the United States.

The increasing realization that one is biased and that Euro-American society does play a part in oppressing minority groups is an unpleasant one. Dissonance may result in feelings of guilt, shame, anger, and depression. Rationalizations may be used to exonerate one's own inactivity in combating perceived injustice or personal feelings of prejudice: for example, "I'm only one person—what can I do?" or

"Everyone is prejudiced, even minorities." As these conflicts ensue, the White person may retreat into the protective confines of White culture (encapsulation of the previous stage) or move progressively toward insight and revelation (resistance and immersion stage).

Whether a person regresses is related to the strength of positive forces pushing an individual forward (support for challenging racism) and negative forces pushing the person backward (fear of some loss). For example, challenging the prevailing beliefs of the times may mean risking ostracism from other White relatives, friends, neighbors, and colleagues. Regardless of the choice, there are many uncomfortable feelings of guilt, shame, anger, and depression related to the realization of inconsistencies in one's belief systems. Guilt and shame are most likely related to the recognition of the White person's role in perpetuating racism in the past. Guilt may also result from the person's being afraid to speak out on the issues or take responsibility for his or her part in a current situation. For example, the person may witness an act of racism, hear a racist comment, or be given preferential treatment over a minority person but decide not to say anything for fear of violating racist White norms. Many White people rationalize their behaviors by believing that they are powerless to make changes. Additionally, there is a tendency to retreat into White culture. If, however, others (which may include some family and friends) are more accepting, forward movement is more likely.

3. *Resistance and immersion phase.* The White person who progresses to this stage will begin to question and challenge his or her own racism. For the first time, the person begins to realize what racism is all about, and his or her eyes are suddenly open. Racism is seen everywhere (advertising, television, educational materials, interpersonal interactions, etc.). This phase of development is marked by a major questioning of one's own racism and that of others in society. In addition, increasing awareness of how racism operates and its pervasiveness in U.S. culture and institutions are the major hallmark of this level. It is as if the person has awakened to the realities of oppression; sees how educational materials, the mass media, advertising, and other elements portray and perpetuate stereotypes; and recognizes how being White granted certain advantages denied to various minority groups.

There is likely to be considerable anger at family and friends, institutions, and larger societal values, which are seen as having sold him or her a false bill of goods (democratic ideals) that were never practiced. Guilt is also felt for having been a part of the oppressive system. Strangely enough, the person is likely to undergo a form of racial self-hatred at this stage. Negative feelings about being White are present, and the accompanying feelings of guilt, shame, and anger toward oneself and other Whites may develop. The "White liberal syndrome" may develop and be manifested in two complementary styles: the paternalistic protector role or the overidentification with another minority group (Helms, 1984; Ponterotto, 1988). In the former, the White person may devote his or her energies in an almost paternalistic attempt to protect minorities from abuse. In the latter, the person may actually want to identify with a particular minority group (Asian, Black, etc.) in order to escape his or her own Whiteness. The White person will soon discover, however, that these roles are not appreciated by minority groups and will experience rejection. Again, the person may resolve this dilemma by moving back into the protective confines of White culture (conformity stage), again experience conflict (dissonance), or move directly to the introspective stage.

4. *Introspective phase.* This phase is most likely a compromise of having swung from an extreme of unconditional acceptance of White identity to a rejection of Whiteness. It is a state of relative quiescence, introspection, and reformulation of what it means to be White. The person realizes and no longer denies that he or she has participated in oppression and benefited from White privilege, or that racism is an integral part of U.S. society. However, individuals at this stage become less motivated by guilt and defensiveness, accept their Whiteness, and seek to define their own identity and that of their social group. This acceptance, however, does not mean a less active role in combating oppression. The process may involve addressing the questions, "What does it mean to be White?" "Who am I in relation to my Whiteness?" and "Who am I as a racial/cultural being?"

   The feelings or affective elements may be existential in nature and involve feelings disconnectedness, isolation, confusion, and loss. In other words, the person knows that he or she will never fully understand the "minority experience" but feels disconnected from the Euro-American group as well. In some ways, the introspective phase is similar in dynamics to the dissonance phase in that both represent a transition from one perspective to another. The process used to answer the previous questions and to deal with the ensuing feelings may involve a searching, observing, and questioning attitude. Answers to these questions involve dialoging and observing one's own social group and actively creating and experiencing interactions with various minority group members as well.

5. *Integrative awareness phase.* Reaching this level of development is most characterized as (a) understanding the self as a racial/cultural being, (b) being aware of sociopolitical influences regarding racism, (c) appre-

ciating racial/cultural diversity, and (d) becoming more committed toward eradicating oppression. The formation of a nonracist White Euro-American identity emerges and becomes internalized. The person values multiculturalism, is comfortable around members of culturally different groups, and feels a strong connectedness with members of many groups. Most important, perhaps, is the inner sense of security and strength that needs to develop and that is needed to function in a society that is only marginally accepting of integrative aware White persons.

Implications for Multicultural Counseling/Therapy Training

If we acknowledge, as suggested by theorists of White racial identity development, that becoming aware of one's own White identity is an important attribute of multicultural competence, then this means several important things in the helping professions. Graduate training programs, for example, would be advised to assess the phase of development for White trainees with respect to identity development. The characteristics associated with one level may dictate the types of objectives and techniques most successful in use with trainees. Linking specific stages of development with ideas for training, Carney and Kahn (1984) described a fivestage development model for trainees who, while not explicitly described as such, are taken to be White. They identified appropriate learning-environment features related to each (unnamed) stage of development and discussed points at which it might be important to use sameculture, mixed-culture, and otherculture trainers.

Especially important is the work of Ponterotto and his colleagues (Ponterotto, 1988; Sabnani et al., 1991), who have focused on integrating general models of White racial identity into a developmental training model specifically designed for White counselors and therapists. Sabnani et al. (1991) integrated and collapsed the models of Hardiman (1982), Helms (1984), and Ponterotto (1988) into a fivestage developmental model. Stage one, preexposure/precontact, is characterized by a general lack of awareness of self as a racial being. In stage two, conflict, there is an expansion of knowledge regarding racial matters incurred through interactions with nonWhite persons or through exposure during training (e.g., a required multicultural course). This stage is characterized by conflict between the desire to conform to majority-group norms and the wish to represent humanistic, nonracist values. The emotions of guilt, depression, and anger are common in this stage and result from the aforementioned conflict or from an increasing awareness that racism continues in American society.

In stage three, pro-minority/antiracism, the White individual develops a strong prominority stance concomitant with the rejection of internalized racist beliefs and anger directed at the White status quo. This affective reaction serves to alleviate the guilt common to stage two. Stage four, retreat into White culture, occurs when a White person perceives rejection from non-White persons or from the minority community. This retreat into the familiarity of samerace relations may occur also in response to a White person's lack of selfassuredness in interracial situations. Feelings of defensiveness, anger, and fear are associated with this stage. Finally, stage five, redefinition and integration, is characterized by a movement toward the clear development of White racial identity and a culturally transcendent worldview.

Emphasizing the developmental nature of their identity model and acknowledging that different majority-group therapists are at varied stages of readiness for incorporating multicultural training, Sabnani et al. (1991) outlined detailed and specific training exercises designed to facilitate movement through the stages. The authors organized their training regiments for each racial identity stage within the context of both training goals and tasks for each of the competency areas (beliefs/attitudes, knowledge, and skills) endorsed by the Division of Counseling Psychology (D. W. Sue et al., 1982). Table 9.3 summarizes the stage-specific training exercises.

Whatever the White racial identity of the therapist, it makes sense that his or her awareness is likely to have major implications for the client and the process of counseling and therapy (Carter, 1995; Helms, 1984; Ponterotto, 1988). A White therapist at the conformity level, for example, may cause great harm to culturally different clients at their levels of identity development. The therapist may intentionally and unintentionally (a) reinforce a conformity client's feelings of racial self-hatred, (b) prevent or block a dissonance client from looking at inconsistent feelings/attitudes/beliefs, (c) dismiss and negate the resistance and immersion client's anger about racism (he or she is a radical), and (d) perceive the integrative awareness individual as having a confused sense of self-identity.

Other combinations of cross-status relationships can lead to even greater confusion in clinical work. What would therapy be like, for example, if the culturally different client was at the conformity level while the White therapist was at the resistance and immersion level? Would the White therapist feel negatively toward the minority client because he or she views the person as having sold out? We are obviously dealing with a highly complex and speculative area that requires greater research and investigations (see Helms's excellent 1984 analysis of dyad combinations). Earlier admonitions for helping professionals to "know thyself" and grow culturally aware of their own biases, values, and assumptions about human behavior become more important.

Table 9.3 Stages of White Identity Development and Training Implications

	Beliefs/attitudes		Knowledge		Skills	
	Goals	Tasks	Goals	Tasks	Goals	Tasks
Stage 1 Preexposure/ Precontact	Awareness of one's own cultural heritage Awareness of the cultural heritage of minority groups	Awareness group experience[ab] "Ethnic dinners"[b] Tours/exhibits of other cultures' crafts/areas Intercultural sharing[c] Multicultural action planning (low level of active involvement)[c] Free drawing test[h] Public and private self-awareness exercise[g] Value statements exercise[g] Decision awareness exercise[g]	Knowledge of the cultural heritage of other minority groups	Research into the history of other cultures Intercultural sharing[c] Multicultural action planning (low level of active involvement)[c] Ethnic literature reviews Field trips Case studies[c] Culture assimilator[ijk]	Beginning development of counseling skills	Regular counselor training tasks (microskills training)[def]

Table 9.3 continued

	Beliefs/attitudes		Knowledge		Skills	
	Goals	Tasks	Goals	Tasks	Goals	Tasks
Stage 2 Conflict	Awareness of one's stereotypes and prejudicial attitudes and the impact of these on minorities Awareness of the conflict between wanting to conform to White norms while upholding humanitarian values Dealing with feelings of guilt and depression or anger	Critical incidents exercise[h] Implicit assumptions checklist exercise[h] We and you exercises[h] Exercise for experiencing stereotypes[c] Stereotypes awareness exercise[c] Less structured cross-cultural encounter groups	More extensive knowledge of other cultures Knowledge of the concepts of prejudice and racism Knowledge of the impact of racism on minorities and the privileges of being White	MAP-investigative[e] Tours to other communities Research on racism in the past and present Classes in multicultural issues presenting survey data on minorities Films	Develop more client-specific methods of intervention	Critical incidents method[l] Role-playing exercise[h] Role-playing a problem in a group[h]
Stage 3 Pro-minority Antiracism	Awareness of over-identification and of paternalistic attitudes, and the impact of these on minorities	Interracial encounters[m] Cross-cultural encounter groups Responsible feedback exercise[h] Anonymous feedback from the group exercise[h]	Further immersion into other cultures	Guided self-study Exposure to audiovisual presentations[g] Interviews with consultants and experts[g] Lectures Minority student panels[b] Research into the impact of race on counseling	Continue developing cultural emic and etic approaches to counseling	Role-playing exercises Communication skills training Facilitating interracial groups (FIG)[b] Counseling ethnic minorities (CEM)[b]

Table 9.3 continued

	Beliefs/attitudes		Knowledge		Skills	
	Goals	Tasks	Goals	Tasks	Goals	Tasks
Stage 4 Retreat into White culture	Awareness of and dealing with one's own fear and anger	Cross-cultural encounter groups / Lump sum[h]	Knowledge of the development of minority identity and White identity	Research into minority identity development models / Research into White identity development models	Building culturally etic (transcendent) approaches	Microskills / Ponterotto and Benesch (1988)
Stage 5 Redefinition and Integration	Develop an identity that claims Whiteness as a part of it	Feedback-related exercises (see Stage 3)	Expand knowledge on racism in the real world / Expand knowledge on counseling methods more appropriate to minorities	Visits to communities with large minority populations / Research on ways to transform White-based counseling methods to one more credible to minorities	Deepen more culturally emic approaches / Face more challenging cross-cultural counseling interactions	Facilitating interracial groups (FIG)[b] / Counseling ethnic minorities individually (CEMI)[b] / Triad model[g] / Cross-cultural practica

Note: References for exercises suggested in Table 16.2 are indicated by letters, as follows: a. Parker & McDavis, 1979; b. McDavis & Parker, 1977; c. Parker, 1988; d. Ivey & Authier, 1978; e. Egan, 1982; f. Clarkhuff & Anthony, 1979; g. Pedersen, 1988; h. Weeks et al., 1977; i. Brislin et al., 1986; j. Albert, 1983; k. Merta, Stringham, & Ponterotto, 1988; l. Sue, 1981; m. Katz & Ivey, 1977. From White racial identity development and cross-cultural counselor training. *The Counseling Psychologist,* 1991, *19,* 76–102 by Sabnani, H.B., Ponterotto, J.G., & Borodovsky, L.G. (1991). Copyright 1991 by Sage Publications, Inc. Reprinted by permission of Sage Publications.

Implications for Clinical Practice

It is important to stress again the need for White Euro-American counselors to understand the assumptions of White racial identity development models. We ask readers to consider seriously the validity of these assumptions and engage one another in a dialogue about them. Ultimately, the effectiveness of White therapists is related to their overcoming sociocultural conditioning and making their Whiteness visible. To do so, the following guidelines/suggestions are given.

1. Accept the fact that racism is a basic and integral part of U.S. life and permeates all aspects of our culture and institutions. Know that as a White person you are socialized into U.S. society and, therefore, inherit the biases, stereotypes, and racist attitudes, beliefs, and behaviors of the society. In other words, all White Euro-Americans are racist—whether knowingly or unknowingly.

2. Understand that the level of White racial identity development in a cross-cultural encounter (working with minorities, responding to multicultural training, etc.) affects the process and outcome of an interracial relationship (including counseling/therapy).

3. Work on accepting your own Whiteness, but define it in a nondefensive and nonracist manner. How you perceive yourself as a racial being seems to be correlated strongly with how you perceive and respond to racial stimuli.

4. Spend time with healthy and strong people from another culture or racial group. As a counselor, the only contact we usually have comes from working with only a narrow segment of the society. Thus, the knowledge we have about minority groups is usually developed from working with troubled individuals.

5. Know that becoming culturally aware and competent comes through lived experience and reality. Identify a cultural guide, someone from the culture who is willing to help you understand his or her group.

6. Attend cultural events, meetings, and activities led by minority communities. This allows you to hear from church leaders, attend community celebrations, and participate in open forums so that you may sense the strengths of the community, observe leadership in action, personalize your understanding, and develop new social relationships.

7. When around persons of color, pay attention to feelings, thoughts, and assumptions that you have when race-related situations present themselves. Where are your feelings of uneasiness, differentness, or outright fear coming from? Do not make excuses for these thoughts or feelings,

dismiss them, or avoid attaching meaning to them. Only if you are willing to confront them directly can you unlearn the misinformation and nested emotional fears.

8. Dealing with racism means a personal commitment to action. It means interrupting other White Americans when they make racist remarks and jokes or engage in racist actions, even if it is embarrassing or frightening. It means noticing the possibility for direct action against bias and discrimination in your everyday life.

Dimensions of Worldviews

10

Chapter

Felix Sanchez is a 19-year-old second-generation Hispanic freshman attending a major university in northern California. He is the oldest of five siblings, all currently residing in Colorado. Felix's father works as a delivery driver for a brewery, and his mother is employed part-time as a housekeeper. Both parents have worked long and hard to make ends meet and have been instrumental in sending their eldest son to college.

Felix is the first in his entire family (including relatives) ever to have attended an institution of higher education. It is generally understood that the parents do not have the financial resources to send Felix's other brothers and sisters to college. If they are to make it, they would need to do it on their own or obtain help elsewhere. Out of a sense of obligation, Felix obtained a part-time job without the knowledge of his parents in order to save money for his siblings' future education.

During the last two quarters, however, Felix has been experiencing academic difficulties in many of his classes. Felix's inability to obtain grades better than Cs or Ds has greatly discouraged him. Last quarter, he was placed on academic probation, and the thought of failing evoked a great sense of guilt and shame in him. While he had originally intended to become a social worker and had looked forward to his course work, he now felt depressed, lonely, alienated, and guilt-ridden. It was not so much his inability to do the work, but the meaninglessness of his courses and of the materials in the texts, as well as the manner in which his courses were taught. Worse yet, he just could not relate to the students in his dormitory and to all the rules and regulations.

At the beginning of his last quarter, Felix was referred by his Educational Opportunity Program adviser to the University Counseling Center. Felix's counselor, Dr. Blackburne, seemed sincere enough, but the counseling sessions only made Felix feel worse. Besides spending time explaining his situation to the counselor, Felix was asked to take a series of vocational interest tests. According to Dr. Blackburne, the tests were "non-definitive" in that no clear-cut interest pattern seemed to emerge. The counselor had strongly implied several possible reasons for Felix's inability to do well in school. First, it was possible that he was "not college material" and had to face that fact. After all, Felix was admitted to the university only because the affirmative action program allowed less qualified minority students in. Second, the vocational tests supported Dr. Blackburne's belief that Felix lacked the motivation to pursue work in higher education and that this was evident in his lack of desire to pursue social work. Third, his constant "sacrificing" of his time (part-time work) to help his siblings contributed to his poor grades. Fourth, Felix's depression and alienation were symptomatic of serious acculturation problems; he needed to "fit in" and "adjust better to the academic environment," to learn English better, and to "think about himself more," rather than doing what he thought would please his parents and family.

In the last chapter we indicated how White racial identity could influence how a White person perceives the world. While there is a strong relationship between racial/cultural identity development and worldviews, the latter concept is more global and encompassing. Each of us possesses a worldview that affects how we perceive and evaluate situations and how we derive appropriate actions based on our appraisal; the nature of clinical reality is very much linked to worldviews (Ivey et al., 1997; Trevino, 1996). In this vignette, Dr. Blackburne's worldview affects his assessment and definition of the problem and his proposed solutions. Let us analyze this vignette to illustrate some of the points to be made in this chapter.

First, we would like to acknowledge the fact that Dr. Blackburne is a well-intentioned helping professional. His worldview, however, contains certain philosophical assumptions that may prove detrimental to his culturally different clients. If we look at the reasons entertained by the counselor for why Felix is doing poorly in school (not being college material, lacking motivation, sacrificing study time, and needing to assimilate more), they all imply several things: (a) Success or failure in life is due to individual effort or lack of it; (b) we are all personally responsible for the outcomes in our life; and (c) changing ourselves and our life circumstances is totally within our control. The counselor tends to attribute Felix's academic difficulties to personal deficiencies. Interestingly enough, the reasons are significantly correlated also with stereotypes about many racial/ethnic minorities: "not being college material" = not very bright; unmotivated = lazy; "need to think about himself more" = dependent; and "need to fit in" = problems in acculturation.

Such a worldview is related to perceiving the individual as the psychosocial unit of operation and involves an implicit valuing of individualism. The causes of behaviors are sought within the individual. As a result, there is a proclivity toward "person blame." Such a worldview tends to give lesser weight to external explanations as the causes of behavior. The danger here is that we overlook legitimate systemic (as opposed to individual) factors affecting Felix's feelings of loneliness, isolation, depression, and meaninglessness.

Is it possible, for example, that the academic cultural climate is to blame for Felix's difficulties, rather than some personal deficiency? Is it possible that the feelings of alienation and meaninglessness are related to the content of the courses taught and the texts used? It is not unusual for many students of color to complain that course content is taught from only one (Euro-American) perspective and that they do not "see themselves" portrayed in texts, nor in a realistic fashion. Also, how might White middle-class learning/teaching styles clash with those from a Latino/Hispanic perspective? Likewise, how may institutional rules and regulations clash with Hispanic values of *personalismo*? In many Hispanic groups, human relationships take precedence over institutional policies. Simply put, this traditional Latino concept holds that people are more important than formal rules and regulations and that personal interactions take precedence over such impersonal aspects of existence. In addition, is the counselor failing to understand the traditional Hispanic family structures and responsibilities, which place great importance on the eldest son and his ensuing responsibilities and obligations? When the counselor uses the word "sacrifice," has he not turned a cultural value into a deficiency? The counselor may be unintentionally communicating to Felix that his values are outdated and pathological.

If we answer in the affirmative to many of these questions, then we must begin to entertain the notion that contributors to Felix's dilemma lie in the educational system and not in him. We have radically shifted our worldview! There are times when systemic forces may be so overpowering and stacked against culturally diverse clients that they are truly not responsible for their fate and cannot exercise enough systemic control to change or alter the outcome. High unemployment among African American workers, for example, may not be due to some inherent deficits (laziness or stupidity), but to systemic forces (bias, prejudice, and discrimination). The system is to blame, not the person. From this perspective, the therapeutic solution is to change the system rather than the person (acculturate). We submit that the worldview exemplified by Dr. Blackburne is representative of traditional theories of counseling and psychotherapy.

It has become increasingly clear that many minority persons hold worldviews that differ from members of the dominant culture. In Chapters 8 and 9 we examined one specific aspect of worldviews—racial/cultural identity. In a broader sense, we can define a worldview (D. W. Sue, 1977a, 1977b, 1978) as how a person perceives his or her relationship to the world (nature, institutions, other people, etc.). Worldviews are highly correlated with a person's cultural upbringing and life experiences (Katz, 1985; Ibrahim, 1985; Trevino, 1996). Ivey et al. (1997) refer to worldviews as "the way you frame the world and what it means to you," "one's conceptual framework," or "how you think the world works." Ibrahim (1985) refers to worldviews as "our philosophy of life" or "our experience within social, cultural, environmental, philosophical, and psychological dimensions." Put in a much more practical way, not only are worldviews composed of our attitudes, values, opinions, and concepts, but also they may affect how we think, define events, make decisions, and behave.

For minorities in America, a strong determinant of worldviews is very much related to racism and the subordinate position assigned to them in society. While the intent of this chapter is to discuss racial and ethnic minorities, it must be kept in mind that economic and social class, religion, sexual orientation, and gender are also interactional components of a worldview. Thus, Asian Americans, African Americans, Hispanic/Latino Americans, and Native Americans from differing socioeconomic classes do not necessarily have identical views of the world.

Helping professionals who hold a worldview different from that of their clients and who are unaware of the basis for this difference are most likely to impute negative traits to clients. Constructs used to judge "normality" and "healthy" or "abnormality" and "unhealthy" may be inadvertently applied to clients (Ibrahim, Roysircar-Sodowsky, & Ohnishi, 2001). In most cases, culturally different clients are more likely to have worldviews that differ from those of therapists. Yet many therapists are so culturally unaware that they respond according to their own conditioned values, assumptions, and perspectives of reality without regard for other views. Therapists need to become culturally aware—to act on the basis of a critical analysis and understanding of their own conditioning, the conditioning of their clients, and the sociopolitical system of which they and their clients are both a part. Without this awareness, counselors who work with the culturally different may be engaging in cultural oppression. Let us begin our exploration of worldviews by continuing with the value orientation model proposed by Kluckhohn and Strodtbeck (1961).

Value Orientation Model of Worldviews

One of the most useful frameworks for understanding differences among individuals and groups is the Kluckhohn and Strodtbeck (1961) model presented in Chapter 6. It assumes a set of core dimensions (human questions) that are pertinent for all peoples of all cultures. Differences in value orientations can be ascertained by how we answer them. These questions and the three possible responses to them are given in Table 10.1.

Kluckhohn and Strodtbeck (1961) clearly recognized that racial/ethnic groups vary in how they perceive *time*. Cultures may emphasize history and tradition, the here and now, or the distant future. For example, Puerto Ricans

Table 10.1 **Value-Orientation Model**

Dimensions	Value Orientations		
1. *Time Focus* What is the temporary focus of human life?	*Past* The past is important. Learn from history.	*Present* The present moment is everything. Don't worry about tomorrow.	*Future* Plan for the future: Sacrifice today for a better tomorrow.
2. *Human Activity* What is the modality of human activity?	*Being* It's enough just to be.	*Being & In-Becoming* Our purpose in life is to develop our inner self.	*Doing* Be active. Work hard and your efforts will be rewarded.
3. *Social Relations* How are human relationships defined?	*Lineal* Relationships are vertical. There are leaders and followers in this world.	*Collateral* We should consult with friends/families when problems arise.	*Individualistic* Individual autonomy is important. We control our own destiny.
4. *People/Nature Relationship* What is the relationship of people to nature?	*Subjugation to Nature* Life is largely determined by external forces (God, fate, genetics, etc.).	*Harmony with Nature* People and nature coexist in harmony.	*Mastery over Nature* Our challenge is to conquer and control nature.

Source: Adapted from "Effective Cross-Cultural Counseling and Psychotherapy: A Framework," by F. A. Ibrahim, 1985, *The Counseling Psychologist, 13,* 625–638. Copyright 1985 by *The Counseling Psychologist.* Adapted by permission. Adapted from *Variations in Value Orientations* by F. R, Kluckhohn and F. L. Strodtbeck, 1961, Evanston, IL: Row, Patterson & Co. Copyright 1961 by Row, Patterson & Co. Adapted by permission. Adapted from *Handbook for Developing Multicultural Awareness* (p. 256) by Pedersen, 1988, Alexandria, VA: AACD Press. Copyright 1988 by AACD Press. Adapted by permission.

tend to exhibit present time value orientation behaviors that differ from the Euro-American future orientation (Garcia-Preto, 1996; Inclan, 1985). Puerto Ricans frequently comment on how Euro-Americans do not seem to know how to have fun because they will leave a party in order to prepare for a meeting tomorrow. Likewise, Euro-Americans will often comment on how Puerto Ricans are "poor and disorganized planners." They may notify their boss at the last minute that they need to travel home for the holidays. Worse yet, they may attempt to make airline reservations for the Christmas holidays on December 20, only to be forced to fly standby because of "poor planning." As we saw in the chapter on family therapy, Puerto Ricans and Euro-Americans mark time differently.

Cultures differ also in their attitudes toward activity. In White culture, doing is valued over being, or even being-in-becoming. There is a strong belief that one's own worth is measured by task accomplishments. In White culture, statements such as "do something" indicate the positive value placed on action. Likewise, when someone is involved in being, it may be described as "hanging out" or "killing time." In most cases these represent pejorative statements. In counseling and therapy, the perceived "inaction" of a client who may adhere to a "being" orientation is usually associated with some form of personal inadequacy.

Another dimension of importance is our relationships with others. In some cultures, relationships tend to be more lineal, authoritarian, and hierarchical (traditional Asian cultures), and the father is the absolute ruler of the family. Some cultures may emphasize a horizontal, equal, and collateral relationship, while others value individual autonomy, as in U.S. society. In earlier chapters we pointed out how a counseling relationship that tends to be more equal and individualistic (I-thou) may prove uncomfortable for clients who adhere to a much more formal hierarchical relationship.

The nature of people has often been addressed in psychology and philosophy. In theories of personality, for example, Freud saw humans as basically evil or bad; Rogers saw them as innately good; and behaviorists tended to perceive human nature as neutral. There is no doubt that cultures, societies, and groups may socialize people into a trusting or suspicious mode. Third World groups, by virtue of their minority status in the United States, may develop a healthy suspiciousness toward institutions and people. Unfortunately, because many mental health professionals operate from a different value orientation (man is basically neutral or good), they may see the minority clients as evidencing paranoid traits.

The value-orientation model also states that people make assumptions about how they relate to nature. Many American Indians, for example, perceive themselves as harmonious with "Mother Earth" and nature (J. T. Garrett & Garrett, 1994). Poor Puerto Ricans are governed more by a value of subjugation to nature (Nieto, 1995). White Euro-Americans, however, value conquering and controlling nature (Pedersen, 1988; Ivey et al., 1997). Such an orientation by the therapist may lead to difficulties: This aspect of the value dimension presumes that barriers to personal success or happiness may be overcome through hard work and perseverance. Minority or poor clients, however, may perceive this strategy as ineffective against many problems created by racism or poverty. Clients who fail to act in accordance with their therapist's values may be diagnosed as being the source of their own problems. It is precisely this value dimension that we feel has been severely neglected in the mental health field. The reason may lie in its sociopolitical nature.

The remaining part of this chapter deals with a discussion of worldviews as they relate to this central concept. It discusses how race and culture-specific factors may interact in such a way as to produce people with different worldviews, and it presents a conceptual model that integrates research findings with the clinical literature.

First, we discuss two factors identified as important in understanding persons with different psychological orientations: (a) locus of control and (b) locus of responsibility. Second, we look at how these variables form four different psychological outlooks in life and their consequent characteristics, dynamics, and implications for the clinician. Last, we set forth some conclusions and precautions.

Locus of Control

Rotter's (1966) historic work in the formulation of the concepts of internal-external control and the internal-external (I-E) dimension has contributed greatly to our understanding of human behavior. *Internal control* (IC) refers to people's beliefs that reinforcements are contingent on their own actions and that they can shape their own fate. *External control* (EC) refers to people's beliefs that reinforcing events occur independently of their actions and that the future is determined more by chance and luck. Rotter conceived this dimension as measuring a generalized personality trait that operated across several different situations.

Based on past experience, people learn one of two worldviews: The locus of control rests with the individual or with some external force. Early researchers (Lefcourt, 1966; Rotter, 1966, 1975) have summarized the research findings that correlated high internality with (a) greater attempts at mastering the environment, (b) superior coping strategies, (c) better cognitive processing of information, (d) lower predisposition to anxiety, (e) higher achievement motivation, (f) greater social action involvement, and (g) greater value on skill-determined rewards. As can be seen, these attributes are highly valued by U.S. society and constitute the core features of mental health.

Early research on generalized expectancies of locus of control suggests that ethnic group members (Hsieh, Shybut, & Lotsof, 1969; Levenson, 1974; B. Strickland, 1973; Tulkin, 1968; Wolfgang, 1973), people from low socioeconomic classes (Battle & Rotter, 1963; Crandall, Katkovsky, & Crandall, 1965; Garcia & Levenson, 1975; Lefcourt, 1966; B. Strickland, 1971), and women (Sanger & Alker, 1972) score significantly higher on the external end of the locus-of-control continuum. Using the I-E dimension as a criterion of mental health would mean that minority, poor, and female clients would be viewed as possessing less desirable attributes. Thus, a clinician who encounters a minority client with a high external orientation ("It's no use trying," "There's nothing I can do about it," and "You shouldn't rock the boat") may interpret the client as being inherently apathetic, procrastinating, lazy, depressed, or anxious about trying. As we see in the next section, all these statements tend to blame the individual for his or her present condition.

The problem with an unqualified application of the I-E dimension is that it fails to take into consideration the different cultural and social experiences of the individual. This failure may lead to highly inappropriate and destructive applications in therapy (Lewis et al., 1998; Ibrahim et al., 2001). While the social-learning framework from which the I-E dimension is derived may be very legitimate, it seems plausible that different cultural groups, women, and people from lower classes have learned that control operates differently in their lives than how it operates for society at large. In the case of persons of color, the concept of external control takes on a wider meaning (Carter, 1995; Ridley, 1995).

We believe that the locus-of-control continuum must make clearer distinctions on the external end. For example, externality related to impersonal forces (chance and luck) is different from that ascribed to cultural forces and from that ascribed to powerful others. Chance and luck operate equally across situations for everyone. However, the forces that determine locus of control from a cultural perspective may be viewed by the particular ethnic group as acceptable and benevolent. In this case, externality is viewed positively. Two ethnic groups may be used as examples to illustrate this point.

For example, we have always known that Chinese, American-born Chinese, and Euro-Americans vary in the degree of internal control they feel (Hsieh et al., 1969). The first group scores lowest in internality, followed next by Chinese Americans and then Euro-Americans. It is believed that the "individual-centered" American culture emphasizes the uniqueness, independence, and self-reliance of each individual. It places a high premium on self-reliance, individualism, and status achieved through one's own efforts. In contrast, the "situation-centered" Chinese culture places importance on the group (an individual is not defined apart from the family), on tradition, social roles-expectations, and harmony with the universe (Root, 1998). Thus, the cultural orientation of the more traditional Chinese tends to elevate the external scores. Note, however, that the external orientation of the Chinese is highly valued and accepted (Leong, 1985; Root, 1998; Uba, 1994).

Likewise, one might expect Native Americans to score higher on the external end of the I-E continuum on the basis of their own cultural values. Several writers (J. T. Garrett & Garrett, 1995; LaFromboise, 1998) have pointed to American Indian concepts of "noninterference" and "harmony with nature" that may tend to classify them as high externals. Euro-Americans are said to be concerned with attempts to control the physical world and to assert mastery over it. To American Indians, accepting the world (harmony) rather than changing it is a highly valued lifestyle.

Support for the fact that Rotter's I-E distinction is not a one-dimensional trait has come also from a number of past studies (Gurin, Gurin, Lao, & Beattie, 1969; Mirels, 1970) that indicate the presence of a political influence (powerful others). For example, a major force in the literature dealing with locus of control is that of powerlessness. *Powerlessness* may be defined as the expectancy that a person's behavior cannot determine the outcomes or reinforcements that he or she seeks. Mirels (1970) feels that a strong possibility exists that externality may be a function of a person's opinions about prevailing social institutions. For example, lower-class individuals and Blacks are not given an equal opportunity to obtain the material rewards of Western culture (Carter, 1988, 1995; Lewis et al., 1998). Because of racism, African Americans may be perceiving, in a realistic fashion, a discrepancy between their ability and attainment.

In this case, externality may be seen as a malevolent force to be distinguished from the benevolent cultural ones just discussed. It can be concluded that while high external people are less effectively motivated, perform poorly in achievement situations, and evidence greater psychological problems, this does not necessarily hold for minorities and low-income persons (Gurin et al., 1969; J. L. White & Parham, 1990). Focusing on external forces may be motivationally healthy if it results from assessing one's chances for success against systematic and real external obstacles rather than unpredictable fate. Three factors of importance for our discussion can be identified.

The first factor, called control ideology, is a measure of general belief about the role of external forces in determining success and failure in the larger society. It represents a cultural belief in the Protestant ethic: Success is the result of hard work, effort, skill, and ability. The second factor, personal control, reflects a person's belief about his or her own sense of personal efficacy or competence. While control ideology represents an ideological belief, personal control is more related to actual control. Apparently, African Americans can be equally internal to Whites on the control ideology, but when a personal reference (personal control) is used, they are much more external. This indicates that African Americans may have adopted the general cultural beliefs about internal control, but find that these cannot always be applied to their own life situations (because of racism and discrimination). It is interesting to note that Whites endorse control ideology statements at the same rate as they endorse personal control ones. Thus, the disparity between the two forms of control does not seem to be operative for White Americans. A third interesting finding is that personal control, as opposed to ideological control, is more related to motivational and performance indicators. A student high on personal control (internality) tends to have greater self-confidence, higher test scores, higher grades, and so on. Individuals who are high on the ideological measure are not noticeably different from their externally oriented counterparts.

The I-E continuum is useful for therapists only if they make clear distinctions about the meaning of the external control dimension. High externality may be due to (a) chance/luck, (b) cultural dictates that are viewed as benevolent, and (c) a political force (racism and discrimination) that represents malevolent but realistic obstacles. In each case, it is a mistake to assume that the former is operative for a culturally different client. To do so would be to deny the potential influence of cultural values and the effects of prejudice and discrimination. The problem becomes more complex when we realize that both cultural and discriminatory forces may be operative. That is, American Indian cultural values that dictate an external orientation may be compounded by their historical experience of prejudice and discrimination in America. The same may be true for poor Puerto Ricans who often perceive a subjugation to nature because of their poverty and religious beliefs (Inclan, 1985).

Locus of Responsibility

Another important dimension in world outlooks was formulated from attribution theory (J. M. Jones, 1997; E. E. Jones et al., 1972) and can be legitimately referred to as *locus of responsibility*. In essence, this dimension measures the degree of responsibility or blame placed on the individual or system. In the case of African Americans, their lower standard of living may be attributed to their personal inadequacies and shortcomings, or the responsibility for their plight may be attributed to racial discrimination and lack of opportunities (Chen, Froehle, & Morran, 1997). The former orientation blames the individual, while the latter explanation blames the system.

The degree of emphasis placed on the individual as opposed to the system in affecting a person's behavior is important in the formation of life orientations. Such terms as "person-centered" or "person-blame" indicate a focus on the individual. Those who hold a person-centered orientation (a) emphasize the understanding of a person's motivations, values, feelings, and goals; (b) believe that success or failure is attributable to the individual's skills or personal inadequacies; and (c) believe that there is a strong relationship between ability, effort, and success in society. In essence, these people adhere strongly to the Protestant ethic that idealizes "rugged individualism." On the other hand, "situation-centered" or "system-blame" people view the sociocultural environment as more potent than the individual. Social, economic, and political forces are powerful; success or failure is generally dependent on the socioeconomic system and not necessarily on personal attributes (Lewis et al., 1998; D. W. Sue et al., 1998).

The causes of social problems in Western society are seen as residing in individuals who are thus responsible for them. Such an approach has the effect of labeling that segment of the population (racial and ethnic minorities) that differs in thought and behavior from the larger society as "deviant." Defining the problem as residing in the person enables society to ignore situationally relevant factors and to protect and preserve social institutions and belief systems. Caplan and Nelson (1973, pp. 200–201) stated this point well:

What is done about a problem depends on how it is defined. The way a social problem is defined determines the attempts at remediation—problem definition determines the change strategy, the selection of a social action delivered system, and the criteria for evaluation. . . . Problem definitions are based on assumptions about the causes of the problem and where they lie. If the causes of delinquency, for example, are defined in person-centered terms (e.g., inability to delay gratification, or incomplete sexual identity), then it would be logical to initiate person-change treatment techniques and intervention strategies to deal with the problem. Such treatment would take the form of counselor or other person-change efforts to "reach" the delinquent, thereby using his potential for self-control to make his behavior more conventional. . . .

If, on the other hand, explanations are situation centered, for example, if delinquency were interpreted as the substitution of extra legal paths for already preempted, conventionally approved pathways for achieving socially valued goals, then efforts toward corrective treatment would logically have a system-change orientation. Efforts would be launched to create suitable opportunities for success and achievement along conventional lines; thus, existing physical, social, or economic arrangements, not individual psyches, would be the targets for change.

A person-centered problem definition has characterized clinical practice (Chen et al., 1997; D'Andrea, Daniels, Arredondo, et al., 2001; McNamee, 1996; M. White, 1993). Definitions of mental health, the assumptions of vocational guidance, and most therapy theories stress the uniqueness and importance of the individual. As a result, the onus of responsibility for change in counseling tends to rest on the individual. It reinforces a social myth about a person's ability to control his or her own fate by rewarding the members of the middle class who "made it on their own" and increases complacency about those who have not made it on their own.

Thus, the individual system-blame continuum may need to be viewed differentially for minority groups. An internal response (acceptance of blame for one's failure) might be considered normal for the White middle class, but for minorities it may be extreme and intrapunitive.

For example, an African American male client who has been unable to find a job because of prejudice and discrimination may blame himself ("What's wrong with me?" "Why can't I find a job?" "Am I worthless?"). Thus, an external response may be more realistic and appropriate ("Institutional racism prevented my getting the job"). Early research indicates that African Americans who scored external (blame system) on this dimension (a) more often aspired to nontraditional occupations, (b) were more in favor of group rather than individual action for dealing with discrimination, (c) engaged in more civil rights activities, and (d) exhibited more innovative coping behavior (Gurin et al., 1969). It is important to note that the personal control dimension discussed in the previous section was correlated with traditional measures of motivation and achievement (grades), while individual system-blame was a better predictor of innovative social action behavior. This latter dimension has been the subject of speculation and studies about its relationship to militancy and racial identity.

Formation of Worldviews

The two psychological orientations, locus of control (personal control) and locus of responsibility, are independent of one another. As shown in Figure 10.1, both may be placed on the continuum in such a manner that they intersect, forming four quadrants: internal locus of control–internal locus of responsibility (IC-IR), external locus of control–internal locus of responsibility (EC-IR), internal locus of control–external locus of responsibility (IC-ER), and external locus of control–external locus of responsibility (EC-ER). Each quadrant represents a different worldview or orientation to life. Theoretically, then, if we know the individual's degree of internality or externality on the two loci, we could plot them on the figure. We would speculate that various ethnic and racial groups are not randomly distributed throughout the four quadrants. The previous discussion concerning cultural and societal influences on these two dimensions would seem to support this speculation. Indeed, several studies on African Americans (Helms & Giorgis, 1980; Oler, 1989) and therapists (Latting & Zundel, 1986) offer partial support for this hypothesis. Because our discussion focuses next on the political ramifications of the two dimensions, there is an evaluative "desirable-undesirable" quality to each worldview.

Internal Locus of Control (IC)–Internal Locus of Responsibility (IR)

As mentioned earlier, high internal personal control (IC) individuals believe that they are masters of their fate and that their actions do affect the outcomes. Likewise, people high in internal locus of responsibility (IR) attribute their

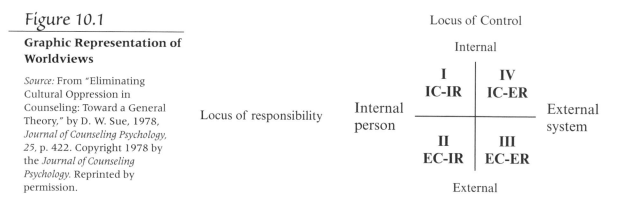

Figure 10.1

Graphic Representation of Worldviews

Source: From "Eliminating Cultural Oppression in Counseling: Toward a General Theory," by D. W. Sue, 1978, *Journal of Counseling Psychology,* 25, p. 422. Copyright 1978 by the *Journal of Counseling Psychology.* Reprinted by permission.

Locus of Control

Internal

Locus of responsibility

| | Internal person | | | External system |

| I
IC-IR | IV
IC-ER |
| II
EC-IR | III
EC-ER |

External

current status and life conditions to their own unique attributes; success is due to one's own efforts, and the lack of success is attributed to one's shortcomings or inadequacies. Perhaps the greatest exemplification of the IC-IR philosophy is U.S. society. U.S. American culture can be described as the epitome of the individual-centered approach that emphasizes uniqueness, independence, and self-reliance (Herring, 1997; D. W. Sue, 2001; D. W. Sue et al., 1998). A high value is placed on personal resources for solving all problems: self-reliance, pragmatism, individualism, status achievement through one's own effort, and power or control over others, things, animals, and forces of nature. Democratic ideals such as "equal access to opportunity," "liberty and justice for all," "God helps those who help themselves," and "fulfillment of personal destiny" all reflect this worldview. The individual is held accountable for all that transpires. Constant and prolonged failure or the inability to attain goals leads to symptoms of self-blame (depression, guilt, and feelings of inadequacy). Most White middle-class members would fall within this quadrant.

Five American patterns of cultural assumptions and values can be identified (E. C. Stewart, 1971; Pedersen, 1988; Wehrly, 1995). These are the building blocks of the IC-IR worldview and typically guide our thinking about mental health services in Western society. As we have seen in the Kluckhohn and Strodtbeck model (1961), these values are manifested in the generic characteristics of counseling. The five systems of assumptions may be described as follows.

1. *Definition of activity.* Western culture stresses an activity modality of doing, and the desirable pace of life is fast, busy, and driving. A being orientation that stresses a more passive, experimental, and contemplative role is in marked contrast to American values (external achievement, activity, goals, and solutions). Existence is in acting, not being. Activism is seen most clearly in the mode of problem solving and decision making. Learning is active and not passive. American emphasis is on planning behavior that anticipates consequences.

2. *Definition of social relations.* Americans value equality and informality in relating to others. Friendships tend to be many, of short commitment, nonbinding, and shared. In addition, the person's rights and duties in a group are influenced by one's own goals. Obligation to groups is limited, and value is placed on one's ability to influence the group actively. In contrast, many cultures stress hierarchical rank, formality, and status in interpersonal relations. Friendships are intense, of long term, and exclusive. Acceptance of the constraints on the group and the authority of the leader dictate behavior in a group.

3. *Motivation.* Achievement and competition are seen as motivationally healthy. The worth of an individual is measured by objective, visible,

and material possessions. Personal accomplishments are more important than place of birth, family background, heritage, or traditional status. Achieved status is valued over ascribed status.

4.   *Perception of the world.* The world is viewed as distinctly separate from humankind and is physical, mechanical, and follows rational laws. Thus, the world is viewed as an object to be exploited, controlled, and developed for the material benefit of people. It is assumed that control and exploitation are necessary for the progress of civilized nations.

5.   *Perception of the self and individual.* The self is seen as separate from the physical world and others. Decision making and responsibility rest with the individual and not the group. Indeed, the group is not a unit but an aggregate of individuals. The importance of a person's identity is reinforced in socialization and education. Autonomy is encouraged, and emphasis is placed on solving one's own problems, acquiring one's own possessions, and standing up for one's own rights.

J. Katz (1985) converted many of these characteristics into the components of counseling (and therapy) in Table 10.2.

Therapeutic Implications

It becomes obvious that Western approaches to clinical practice occupy the quadrant represented by IC-IR characteristics. Most therapists are of the opinion that people must take major responsibility for their own actions and that they can improve their lot in life by their own efforts. The epitome of this line of thought is represented by the numerous self-help approaches currently in vogue in our field.

Clients who occupy this quadrant tend to be White middle-class clients, and for these clients such approaches might be entirely appropriate. In working with clients from different cultures, however, such an approach might be inappropriate. Diaz-Guerrero (1977), in his attempt to build a Mexican psychology, presented much data on how Mexicans and U.S. Americans differ with respect to their views of life. To be actively self-assertive is more characteristic of Euro-American sociocultural premises than of the Mexican. Indeed, to be actively self-assertive in Mexican socioculture clinically forecasts adjustment difficulties. Counselors with a quadrant I orientation are often so culturally encapsulated that they are unable to understand their minority client's worldview. Thus, cultural oppression in therapy becomes an ever-present danger.

Table 10.2 The Components of White Culture: Values and Beliefs

Rugged Individualism
Individual is primary unit
Individual has primary responsibility
Independence and autonomy highly valued and
    rewarded
Individual can control environment

Competition
Winning is everything
Win/lose dichotomy

Action Orientation
Must master and control nature
Must always do something about a situation
Pragmatic/utilitarian view of life

Communication
Standard English
Written tradition
Direct eye contact
Limited physical contact
Control of emotions

Time
Adherence to rigid time
Time is viewed as a commodity

Holidays
Based on Christian religion
Based on White history and male leaders

History
Based on European immigrants' experience in the
    United States
Romanticize war

Protestant Work Ethic
Working hard brings success

Progress & Future Orientation
Plan for future
Delayed gratification
Value continual improvement and progress

Emphasis on Scientific Method
Objective, rational, linear thinking
Cause and effect relationships
Quantitative emphasis

Status and Power
Measured by economic possessions
Credentials, titles, and positions
Believe "own" system
Believe better than other systems
Owning goods, space, property

Family Structure
Nuclear family is the ideal social unit
Male is breadwinner and the head of the household
Female is homemaker and subordinate to the
    husband
Patriarchal structure

Esthetics
Music and art based on European cultures
Women's beauty based on blonde, blue-eyed, thin,
    young
Men's attractiveness based on athletic ability, power,
    economic status

Religion
Belief in Christianity
No tolerance for deviation from single god concept

Source: From *The Counseling Psychologist* (p. 618) by Katz, 1985, Beverly Hills, CA: Sage. Copyright 1985 by Sage Publications, Inc. Reprinted by permission.

External Locus of Control (EC)–Internal Locus of Responsibility (IR)

Individuals who fall into this quadrant are most likely to accept the dominant culture's definition for self-responsibility but to have very little real control over how they are defined by others. The term "marginal man" (person) was first coined by Stonequist (1937) to describe a person living on the margins of two cultures and not fully accommodated to either. Although there is nothing inherently pathological about bicultural membership, J. M. Jones (1997) feels that Western society has practiced a form of cultural racism by imposing its standards, beliefs, and ways of behaving onto minority groups. Marginal individuals deny the existence of racism; believe that the plight of their own people is due to laziness, stupidity, and a clinging to outdated traditions; reject their own cultural heritage and believe that their ethnicity represents a handicap in Western society; evidence racial self-hatred; accept White social, cultural, and institutional standards; perceive physical features of White men and women as an exemplification of beauty; and are powerless to control their sense of self-worth because approval must come from an external source. As a result, they are high in person-focus and external control. The same dynamics and characteristics of the conformity stage (see Chapter 9) seem to operate here.

In the past, mental health professionals have assumed that marginality and self-hatred were internal conflicts of the person almost as if they arise from the individual. In challenging the traditional notion of marginality, Freire (1970, pp. 10–11) stated,

> *Marginality is not by choice, marginal man has been expelled from and kept outside of the social system and is therefore the object of violence. In fact, however, the social structure as a whole does not "expel," nor is marginal man a "being outside of" . . . [Marginal persons] are "beings for another." Therefore the solution to their problem is not to become "beings inside of," but men freeing themselves; for, in reality, they are not marginal to the structure, but oppressed men within it.*

It is quite clear that marginal persons are oppressed, have little choice, and are powerless in the face of the dominant-subordinate relationship between the middle-class Euro-American culture and their own minority culture. According to Freire (1970), if this dominant-subordinate relationship in society were eliminated, the phenomenon of marginality would also disappear. For if two cultures exist on the basis of total equality (an ideal for biculturalism), then the conflicts of marginality simply do not occur in the person.

Therapeutic Implications
The psychological dynamics for the EC-IR minority client are likely to reflect his or her marginal and self-hate status. For example, White therapists might be perceived as more competent and preferred than are therapists of the client's own race. To EC-IR minority clients, focusing on feelings may be very threatening because it ultimately may reveal the presence of self-hate and the realization that clients cannot escape from their own racial and cultural her-

itage. A culturally encapsulated White counselor or therapist who does not understand the sociopolitical dynamics of the client's concerns may unwittingly perpetuate the conflict. For example, the client's preference for a White therapist, coupled with the therapist's implicit belief in the values of U.S. culture, becomes a barrier to effective counseling. A culturally sensitive helping professional needs to help the client (a) understand the particular dominant-subordinate political forces that have created this dilemma and (b) distinguish between positive attempts to acculturate and a negative rejection of one's own cultural values.

External Locus of Control (EC)–External Locus of Responsibility (ER)

The inequities and injustices of racism seen in the standard of living tend to be highly damaging to minorities. For example, the standard of living for African Americans, Hispanic Americans, and American Indians is much below that enjoyed by Whites. Discrimination may be seen in the areas of housing, employment, income, and education. In American cities, African Americans are by far the most segregated of the minorities, and the inferior housing to which they are confined is not the result of free choice or poverty, but discrimination. This inequity in housing is applicable to other minorities as well. Contrary to popular belief, Chinatowns in San Francisco and New York City represent ghetto areas with high rates of unemployment, suicide, juvenile delinquency, poverty, and tuberculosis. Inferior jobs, high unemployment rates, and a much lower income than their White counterparts are also characteristics of the plight suffered by other minorities. Lower income cannot be attributed primarily to less education. African Americans also suffer from segregated and inferior education: Class size, qualification of teachers, physical facilities, and extracurricular activities all place them at a disadvantage. Furthermore, extreme acts of racism can wipe out a minority group. American Indians have witnessed widespread massacres that destroyed their leadership and peoples.

A person high in system-blame and external control feels that there is very little one can do in the face of such severe external obstacles as prejudice and discrimination. In essence, the EC response might be a manifestation of (a) having given up or (b) attempting to placate those in power. In the former, individuals internalize their impotence even though they are aware of the external basis of their plight. In its extreme form, oppression may result in a form of "learned helplessness" (Seligman, 1982). Seligman believes that humans exposed to helplessness (underemployment, unemployment, poor quality of education, poor housing) via prejudice and discrimination may exhibit passivity and apathy (poor motivation), may fail to learn that there are events that can be controlled (cognitive disruption), and may show anxiety and depression (emotional disturbance). When minorities learn that their responses have minimal effects from the environment, the resulting phenomenon can best be described as an expectation of helplessness. People's susceptibility to helplessness depends on their experience with controlling the environment. In the face of continued racism, many may simply give up in their attempts to achieve personal goals. The basic assumption in the theory of learned helplessness is that organisms exposed to prolonged noncontrol in their lives develop expectations of helplessness in later situations. Unfortunately, this expectation occurs even in situations that are now controllable.

The dynamics of the placater, however, are not related to the giving-up response. Rather, social forces in the form of prejudice and discrimination are seen as too powerful to combat at that particular time. The best one can hope to do is to suffer the inequities in silence for fear of retaliation. "Don't rock the boat," "keep a low profile," and "survival at all costs" are the phrases that describe this mode of adjustment. Life is viewed as relatively fixed, and there is little that the individual can do. Passivity in the face of oppression is the primary reaction of the placater.

Slavery was one of the most important factors shaping the sociopsychological functioning of African Americans. Interpersonal relations between Whites and Blacks were highly structured and placed African Americans in a subservient and inferior role. Those Blacks who broke the rules or did not show proper deferential behavior were severely punished. The spirits of most African Americans, however, were not broken. Conformance to White Euro-American rules and regulations was dictated by the need to survive in an oppressive environment. Direct expressions of anger and resentment were dangerous, but indirect expressions were frequent.

Therapeutic Implications
EC-ER African Americans are very likely to see the White therapist as symbolic of any other Black-White relations. They are likely to show "proper" deferential behavior and not to take seriously admonitions by the therapist that they are the masters of their own fate. As a result, an IC-IR therapist may perceive the culturally different client as lacking in courage and ego strength and as being passive. A culturally effective therapist, however, would realize the bases of these adaptations. Unlike EC-IR clients, EC-ER individuals do understand the political forces that have subjugated their existence. The most helpful approach on the part of the therapist would be (a) to teach the clients new coping strategies, (b) to have them experience successes, and (c) to validate who and what they represent.

Internal Locus of Control (IC)–External Locus of Responsibility (ER)

Individuals who score high in internal control and system-focus believe that they are able to shape events in their own life if given a chance. They do not accept the fact that their present state is due to their own inherent weakness. However, they also realistically perceive that external barriers of discrimination, prejudice, and exploitation block their paths to the successful attainment of goals. There is a considerable body of evidence to support this contention. Recall that the IC dimension was correlated with greater feelings of personal efficacy, higher aspirations, and so forth, and that ER was related to collective action in the social arena area. If so, we would expect that IC-ER people would be more likely to participate in civil rights activities and to stress racial identity and militancy.

Racial Pride and Identity

Pride in one's racial and cultural identity is most likely to be accepted by an IC-ER person. The low self-esteem engendered by widespread prejudice and racism is actively challenged by these people. There is an attempt to redefine a group's existence by stressing consciousness and pride in their own racial and cultural heritage. Such phrases as "Black is beautiful" represent a symbolic relabeling of identity from Negro and colored to Black or African American. To many African Americans, "Negro" and "colored" are White labels symbolic of a warped and degrading identity given them by a racist society. As a means of throwing off these burdensome shackles, the Black individual and African Americans as a group are redefined in a positive light. Many racial minorities have begun the process in some form and banded together into what is called the *Third World movement* (Asian Americans, African Americans, Hispanic/Latino Americans, American Indians, and others). Since all minorities share the common experience of oppression, they have formed alliances to expose and alleviate the damage that racism has done. Problems such as poverty, unemployment, housing, education, and juvenile delinquency, as well as emotional problems, are seen as arising from racism in society. Persons of color have attempted to enhance feelings of group pride by emphasizing the positive aspects of their cultural heritage.

Militancy

Another area seemingly in support of the IC-ER worldview was intimately related to the concept of militancy and collective social action. Between 1964 and 1968 there were 239 violent riots involving racial overtones, resulting in 8,000 casualties and 191 dead, mostly Black (National Commission on the Causes and Prevention of Violence, 1969). These events occurred in epidemic proportions that left the American people dazed and puzzled. Rochester in

1964, Chicago in 1965, Los Angeles in 1965, Cleveland in 1966, Detroit in 1967, and Newark in 1967, to name a few, were all struck by a seemingly senseless wave of collective violence in the Black ghettos. Confrontations between the police and Blacks, looting, sniping, assaults, and the burning of homes and property filled the television screens in every American home. In light of these frightening events, many people searched for explanations for what had happened. The basis of the riots did not make sense in terms of rising income, better housing, and better education for Blacks in America. After all, reasoned many, conditions have never been better for Black Americans. Why should they riot?

When the riots of the 1960s are studied, two dominant explanations seem to arise. The first, called the *riffraff theory,* explained the riots as the result of the sick, criminal elements of the society (person-blame): emotionally disturbed individuals, deviants, communist agitators, criminals, or unassimilated migrants. These agitators were seen as peripheral to organized society and possessing no broad social or political concerns. The agitators' frustrations and militant confrontations were seen as part of their own personal failures and inadequacies.

A second explanation, referred to as the *blocked-opportunity theory,* views riot participants as those with high aspirations for their own lives and belief in their ability to achieve these goals (system-blame). However, environmental forces rather than their own personal inadequacies prevent them from advancing in the society and bettering their condition. The theory holds that riots are the result of massive discrimination against African Americans that has frozen them out of the social, economic, and political life of America. Caplan and Paige (1968) found that more rioters than nonrioters reported experiencing job obstacles and discrimination that blocked their mobility. Further probing revealed that it was not lack of training or education that accounted for the results. Fogelson (1970) presented data in support of the thesis that the ghetto riots are manifestations of grievances within a racist society. In referring to the riots Fogelson (1970, p. 145) stated that the rioting

> was triggered not only because the rioters issued the protest and faced the danger together but also because the rioting revealed the common fate of Blacks in America. For most Blacks, and particularly northern Blacks, racial discrimination is a highly personal experience. They are denied jobs, refused apartments, stopped-and-searched, and declared uneducable (or so they are told), they are inexperienced, unreliable, suspicious, and culturally deprived, and not because they are Black.

The recognition that ghetto existence is a result of racism and not the result of some inherent weakness, coupled with the rioters' belief in their ability to control events in their own lives, made a situation ripe for the venting of frustration and anger. Several studies support the contention that those who rioted have an increased sense of personal effectiveness and control (R. P. Abeles, 1976; Caplan, 1970; Caplan & Paige, 1968; Forward & Williams, 1970; Gore & Rotter, 1963; Marx, 1967). Indeed, a series of studies concerning characteristics of the rioters and nonrioters failed to confirm the riffraff theory (Caplan, 1970; Caplan & Paige, 1968; Forward & Williams, 1970; Turner & Wilson, 1976). In general, the following emerged of those who engaged in rioting during the 1960s: (a) Rioters did not differ from nonrioters in income and rate of unemployment, so they appear to be no more poverty stricken, jobless, or lazy; (b) those who rioted were generally better educated, so rioting cannot be attributed to the poorly educated; (c) rioters were better integrated than nonrioters in social and political workings of the community, so the lack of integration into political and social institutions cannot be used as an explanation; (d) long-term residents were more likely to riot, so rioting cannot be blamed on outside agitators or recent immigrants; (e) rioters held more positive attitudes toward Black history and culture (feelings of racial pride) and thus were not alienated from themselves. Caplan (1970) concluded that militants are not more socially or personally deviant than are their nonmilitant counterparts. Evidence tends to indicate they are more healthy along several traditional criteria for measuring mental health. Caplan also believes that attempts to use the riffraff theory to explain riots have an underlying motive. By attributing causes to individual deficiencies, the users of the riffraff theory relieve White institutions of the blame. Such a conceptualization means that psychotherapy, social work, mental hospitalization, or imprisonment should be directed toward the militants. Demands for systems-change are declared illegitimate because the riots are the products of "sick" or "confused" minds. Maintenance of the status quo rather than needed social change (social therapy) is reaffirmed.

Therapeutic Implications

There is much evidence to indicate that minority groups are becoming increasingly conscious of their own racial and cultural identities as they relate to oppression in U.S. society (Atkinson, Morten, et al., 1998; Carter, 1995; Helms, 1995; D. W. Sue et al., 1998). If the evidence is correct, it is also probable that more and more minorities are most likely to hold an IC-ER worldview. Thus, therapists who work with the culturally different will increasingly be exposed to clients with an IC-ER worldview. In many respects, these clients pose the most difficult problems for the White IC-IR therapist. These clients are likely to raise challenges to the therapist's credibility and trustworthiness. The helping professional is likely to be seen as a part of the Establishment that has oppressed minorities. Self-disclosure on the part of the client is not likely to come quickly, and more than any other worldview, an IC-ER orientation means that clients are likely to play a much more active part in the therapy process and to demand action from the therapist.

The theory being proposed here predicts several things about the differences between IC-IR and IC-ER worldviews in counseling and therapy. First, these two worldviews may dictate how a clinician and client define problems and how they use and are receptive to different styles of counseling and therapy. For example, IC-IR people will tend to see the problem as residing in the person, while IC-ER people will see the problem as being external to the individual. Furthermore, IC-ER therapists may use and are most receptive to therapy skills, styles, or approaches that are action oriented. This is in contrast to IC-IR clinicians, who may be more nondirective in their interactions with clients. Two early studies seem to bear out these predictions.

Berman (1979) cited the example of a study that compared African American and White counselor trainees viewing video vignettes of African American and White clients. The clients presented problems related to vocational choice. To a question of "What would you say next?" White males tended to ask questions, White females tended to reflect feelings and to paraphrase, and African Americans tended to give advice and directions. More important, African Americans identified the problem as being in society rather than in the individual, whereas Whites tended to focus more on the individual. The assumption being made is that the Blacks in this study are most likely IC-ER counselor trainees. A similar study conducted by Atkinson et al. (1978) with Asian Americans also revealed consistent findings. The more politically conscious Asian American (IC-ER) rated the counselor as more credible and approachable when using a directive (structure, advice, suggestions) rather than nondirective (reflection and paraphrase) approach.

Some Cautions

In closing, some precautions should be taken in using this model. First, the validity of this model has not been directly established through research, although preliminary inquiries are promising (Helms & Giorgis, 1980; Latting & Zundel, 1986; Oler, 1989) and much of the research literature on racial/cultural identity development also supports it. While much empirical and clinical evidence is consistent with the model, many of the assertions in the chapter remain at the speculative level. Second, the behavior manifestations of each quadrant have not been specifically identified. Regardless of a person's psychological orientation, we would suspect that individuals can adapt and use behaviors associated with another worldview. This, indeed, is the basis of training therapists to work with the culturally different. Third, each style represents conceptual categories. In reality, while people might tend to hold one worldview in preference to another, it does not negate them from holding variations of others. Most Persons of Color represent mixes of each rather than a pure standard. Fourth, whether this conceptual model can be applied to groups other than minorities in America has yet to be established. Last, we must remember that it is very possible for individuals from different cultural groups to be more similar in worldviews than are those from the same culture. While race and ethnicity may be correlated with one's outlook in life, the correspondence certainly is not one to one.

Implications for Clinical Practice

The conceptual model presented in this chapter concerning worldviews and identity development among persons of color is consistent with many of the formulations discussed in the last two chapters. Racial/cultural identity for minorities in America is intimately related to racism and oppression. Using this model in working with culturally different clients has many practical and research-oriented implications.

1.   Be aware that counseling/therapy in the United States falls into the IC-IR quadrant. Clients are seen as able to initiate change and are held responsible for their current plights. If you operate from this framework, you will most likely be person-centered. While such a view is not necessarily incorrect or bad, it may be applied inappropriately to clients who do not share your perception. Avoid being culturally/sociopolitically unaware and imposing your worldview on clients without regard for the legitimacy of their worldviews. Otherwise, you may be engaging in a form of cultural oppression.

2.   Become culturally aware, understand the basis of the worldviews of others, and understand and accept the possibility of their legitimacy. Only when graduate training programs begin to incorporate multicultural concepts in their training (not from a White perspective, but from the perspective of each culture) will therapy be able to lose its oppressive orientation.

3.   Use the theory of worldviews to understanding possible psychological dynamics of persons of color. Figure 10.2 presents a transactional analysis of the four quadrants. For example, an EC-IR client who experiences self-hatred and marginality may be a victim of the dominant-subordinate relationship fostered in American society. The problem is not inherent or internal, and counseling may be aimed at a reeducative process to help that client become aware of the wider sociopolitical forces at the basis of his or her plight.

     An EC-IR person, whether he or she has given up or is placating, must be taught new coping skills to deal with people and institutions. Experiences of success are critically important for clients in this quadrant. IC-ER clients are especially difficult for therapists to handle,

Figure 10.2

Transactional Analysis of Cultural Identity Quadrants

Source: From *Counseling and Development in a Multicultural Society* (p. 399), by J. A. Axelson. Copyright © 1993 by Wadsworth, Inc. Reprinted by permission of Brooks/Cole Publishing Company, Pacific Grove, California 93950, a division of Wadsworth, Inc.

IC-IR	IC-ER
I. (Assertive/Passive) I'm O.K. and have control over myself. Society is o.k., and I can make it in the system.	*IV. (Assertive/Assertive)* I'm O.K. and have control, but need a chance. Society is not o.k., and I know what's wrong and seek to change it.
EC-IR	**EC-ER**
II. (Marginal/Passive) I'm O.K. but my control comes best when I define myself according to the definition of the dominant culture. Society is o.k. the way it is; it's up to me.	*III. (Passive/Aggresive)* I'm not O.K. and don't have much control; might as well give up or please everyone. Society is not o.k. and is the reason for my plight; the bad system is all to blame.

because they will likely challenge that counseling and therapy are acts of oppression. A therapist who is not in touch with these wider socio-political issues will quickly lose credibility and effectiveness. In addition, IC-ER clients are externally oriented and will likely demand that the therapist take external action (setting up a job interview, helping the client fill out forms, etc.). While most of us have been taught not to intervene externally on behalf of the client, all of us must look seriously at the value base of this dictate.

4. Know that problem definitions and specific therapy skills are differentially associated with a particular worldview. One reason why culturally diverse clients may prematurely terminate therapy is that therapists not only differ in worldviews but also use clinical skills inappropriate to their clients' lifestyles. Our next step would be to research the following questions: Are there specific counseling or therapy goals, techniques, and skills best suited for a particular worldview? If so, the implications for clinical training are important.

5. There is an overwhelming need to teach trainees the importance of being able to understand and share the worldviews of their clients. It is no longer enough for you to learn a limited number of therapy skills. The culturally effective therapist is one who is able to generate the widest repertoire of responses (verbal/nonverbal) consistent with the lifestyles and values of the culturally different client. Particularly for minorities, the passive approaches of asking questions, reflecting feelings, and par-

aphrasing must be balanced with directive responses (giving advice and suggestions, disclosing feelings, etc.) on the part of the therapist.

6. You need to understand that each worldview has much to offer that is positive. While these four psychological orientations have been described in a highly evaluative manner, positive aspects of each can be found. For example, the individual responsibility and achievement orientation of quadrant I; the biculturalism and cultural flexibility of quadrant II; the ability to compromise and adapt to life conditions of quadrant III; and collective action and social concern of quadrant IV need not be at odds with one another. Your role may be to help the client integrate aspects of each worldview that will maximize his or her effectiveness and psychological well-being. To accomplish this goal means you are able to share the worldviews of your clients. In essence, your ultimate goal as a culturally competent therapist is that of a functional integrator.

COUNSELING AND THERAPY WITH RACIAL/ ETHNIC MINORITY POPULATIONS

Counseling African Americans

The gap in Black-White views appears to be growing. While 85% of Whites believe that Black children have the same educational opportunities as White children, only 52% of Blacks agree with that statement (Tilove, 2001).

A human rights commission successfully brought a civil lawsuit against two Klan groups for harassing and threatening African Americans who had moved into an all-White housing project. (Baldauf & Johnson, 1998)

The Supreme Court agreed to decide whether a suit involving "environmental racism" could be brought in federal courts. Chester, Pennsylvania, is a town of 42,000 (65% of which is African American) and has five major waste facilities. The rest of the county, which is 91% white, has 500,000 people but has only two waste facilities. (Watson, 1998)

The African American population numbers 34,658,190, or about 12.3% of the U.S. population (U.S. Bureau of the Census, 2001). Of the increase since 1980, 16% was due to immigration. The poverty rate for African Americans remains nearly three times higher than that of White Americans (33.1% versus 12.2%), and the unemployment rate twice as high (11% versus 5%; U.S. Bureau of the Census, 1995). Their disadvantaged status, as well as racism and poverty, contribute to the following statistics. About one third of African American men in their 20s are in jail, on probation, or on parole. This rate has increased by over one third during the past five years (Freeberg, 1995). Over 20% of Black males are temporarily or permanently banned from voting in Texas, Florida, and Virginia because of felony convictions (Cose et al., 2000). The lifespan of African Americans is five to seven years shorter than that of White Americans (N. B. Anderson, 1995; Felton, Parson, Misener, & Oldaker, 1997).

Other health statistics are equally dismal. Twenty percent of African Americans have no health insurance (Giachello & Belgrave,

1997). About 40% of new AIDS cases in 1995 were African Americans (Talvi, 1997). Rates of hypertension (National Center for Health Statistics, 1996) and obesity (Kumanyika, 1993) are higher than those of the White population. Although hypertension has been thought to be primarily biological in African Americans, psychological factors may also be involved. African Americans exposed to videotaped or imaginal depictions of racism showed increases in heart rate and digital blood flow (D. R. Jones, Harrell, Morris-Prather, Thomas, Omowale, 1996). Systolic blood pressure also appears to be influenced by response to discrimination. African Americans who responded by accepting discrimination showed higher blood pressure than did those who challenged the situation (Krieger & Sidney, 1996). Medical researchers (Ayanian, Udvarhelyi, Gatsonis, Pashos, & Epstein, 1993; Harris, Andrews, & Elixhauser, 1997) have found that compared to White patients, African American patients were less likely to undergo corrective surgeries or major therapeutic procedures. Since all had insurance coverage, the reason for the difference in care is unclear, although race-based decisions remain one possibility.

Although these statistics are grim, Ford (1997) pointed out that much of the literature is based on individuals of the lower social class who are on welfare or unemployed, and not enough is based on other segments of the African American population. This focus on one segment of African Americans masks the great diversity that exists among African Americans, who may vary greatly from one another on factors such as socioeconomic status, educational level, cultural identity, family structure, and reaction to racism. More than one third of African Americans are now middle-class or higher. They tend to be well-educated, married homeowners. In 1989, one out of seven African American families had an income of $50,000 or higher (Hildebrand, Phenice, Gray, & Hines, 1997). These are important distinctions. Many middle- and upper-class African Americans are receptive to the values of the dominant society, believe that advances can be made through hard work, feel that race has a relative rather than a pervasive influence in their lives, and embrace their heritage. However, they may feel bicultural stress. As Leanita McClain, the first African American elected to the Board of Directors of the Chicago Tribune, reported,

> *I run a gauntlet between two worlds, and I am cursed and blessed by both. I travel, observe, and take part in both; I can also be used by both. I am a rope in a tug of war. . . . Whites won't believe that I remain culturally different; Blacks won't believe that I remain culturally the same. (Ford, 1997, p. 93)*

However, middle-class African Americans are also exposed to feelings of guilt for having "made it," frustrations by the limitations imposed by the "glass ceiling," and feelings of isolation. Often, upward mobility can produce unintentional effects, as shown in the following case study.

A 14-year-old African American boy, Joseph, came into counseling because of feelings of depression and anger. His parents are professionals and moved to a predominantly White suburb. Prior to the move, Joseph attended a mainly Black school, where he received many awards for academic achievement. Since his enrollment in a primarily White school, Joseph's performance has fallen. His teachers report him to be disruptive, off-task, and argumentative—particularly on issues of justice and minority groups. Joseph complains that they are insensitive and resents being the "expert" on Blacks. He has been asked why Blacks commit so many crimes and why they are so good in sports. He is also teased when he visits friends at his first school for speaking "proper English." Joseph has stolen money from his parents in an attempt to "buy" friendship with his white peers. (Ford, 1997)

The move from his predominantly Black school to one that is primarily White has exposed Joseph to issues of racism and the feeling of being different from both White Americans and African Americans. Issues of racial identity are also evident. It is also apparent that Joseph's parents are not aware of the racial issues that have surfaced with the change in schools. These factors need to be addressed with both the parents and Joseph.

Ford (1997) believes that middle- and upper-class African Americans may suffer a negative impact on mental health from issues such as believing a double standard exists (having to work twice as hard to succeed); feelings of isolation (being the only African American in the organization); powerlessness (given responsibility only on tasks pertaining to minorities); being an "expert" or a "representative" on minority issues (e.g., African American professors might be asked to teach multicultural classes even if it is not their area of expertise); and "survival guilt" in moving to a higher class and neighborhood. Because of this, middle- and upper-class African Americans may occupy a marginal status in which they are not fully accepted by White Americans and are rejected by African Americans.

The African American population is becoming increasingly heterogeneous in terms of social class, educational level, and political orientation. In this chapter we discuss value differences exhibited by many African Americans, issues of racism and discrimination, research findings, and their implications for treatment as they apply to this population.

African American Values, Research, and Implications for Counseling and Therapy

Family Characteristics

Increasingly larger percentages of African American families are headed by single parents. In 1994, 47% of all African American families involved married couples, as compared to 68% in 1970 and 56% in 1980 (U.S. Bureau of the Census, 1995). The African American family has been generally described as matriarchal and is blamed for many of the problems faced by Black Americans today. Among lower-class African American families, over 70% are headed by women. Black females who are unmarried account for nearly 60% of births, and of these mothers the majority are teenagers.

However, these statistics lack an acknowledgment of the strengths in the African American family structure. For many, there exists an extended family network that provides emotional and economic support. Among families headed by females, the rearing of children is often undertaken by a large number of relatives, older children, and close friends. Within the Black family are an adaptability of family roles, strong kinship bonds, a strong work and achievement ethic, and strong religious orientation (Hildebrand et al., 1996; McCollum, 1997). African American men and women value behaviors such as assertiveness; within a family, males are more accepting of women's work roles and are more willing to share in the responsibilities traditionally assigned to women, such as picking up children from school. Despite the challenges of racism and prejudice, many African American families have been able to instill positive self-esteem in their children.

Implications. Our reaction to African American families is due to our Eurocentric nuclear family orientation. Many assessment forms and evaluation processes are still based on the middle-class Euro-American perspective of what constitutes a family. The different family structures indicate the need to consider various alternative treatment modes and approaches in working with Black Americans. In working with African American families, the counselor often has to assume various roles, such as advocate, case manager, problem solver, and facilitating mentor (Ahai, 1997). In many cases the counselor not only has to intervene in the family but also has to deal with community interventions. A number of African American families who go into counseling are required to do so by the schools, courts, or police. Issues that may need to be dealt with are feelings about differences in ethnicity between the client and counselor and clarification of the counselor's relationship to the referring agency.

For family therapy to be successful, counselors must first identify their own set of beliefs and values regarding appropriate roles and communication patterns within a family. One must be careful not to impose these beliefs on a family. For example, African American parents, especially those of the working class, are more likely than White parents to use physical punishment to discipline their children (E. E. Pinderhughes, Dodge, Bates, Pettit, & Zelli, 2000). However, while some types of physical discipline have been related to more acting-out behavior in White children, this was not found in African American children (Deater-Deckard, Dodge, Bates, & Pettit, 1996). Physical discipline should not be seen as necessarily indicative of a lack of parental warmth or negativity. Parent education approaches based on White, intact, nuclear families are often inappropriate for African American families. In fact, they may perpetuate the view that minorities have deficient child-rearing skills. Attempts are being made to develop culturally sensitive parent education programs for African Americans that focus on responses to racism by the family, culture conflicts, single parenting, drug abuse, and different types of discipline. Differences in family functioning should not be automatically seen as deficits (Gorman & Balter, 1997).

Family therapy can be particularly difficult for many African American families who feel that the counselor may react negatively to issues such as out-of-wedlock births, marital status of adult members of a family, and the paternity of children. These are in addition to other trust issues that may be involved. Knowledge of the family structure can aid in therapy. In addition, the impact of racism, economic difficulties, and identity issues in the family should also be explored.

Kinship Bonds and Extended Family and Friends

A mother, Mrs. J., brought in her 13-year-old son, Johnny, who she said was having behavioral problems at home and in school. During the interview, the therapist found out that Johnny had five brothers and sisters living in the home. In addition, his stepfather, Mr. W., also lived in the house. The mother's sister, Mary, and three children had recently moved in with the family until their apartment was repaired. The question "Who is living in the home?" caught this. The mother was also asked about other children not living at home. She had a daughter living with an aunt in another state. The aunt was helping the daughter raise her child. When asked, "Who helps you out?" the mother responded that a neighbor watches her children when she has to work and that both groups of children had been raised together. Mrs. J.'s mother also assisted with her children.

Further questioning revealed that Johnny's problem developed soon after his aunt and her children moved in. Before this, Johnny had been the mother's primary helper and took charge of the children until the stepfather returned home from work. The changes in the family structure that occurred when the sister and her children moved in produced additional stress on Johnny. Treatment included Mrs. J. and her children, Mr. W., Mary and her children, and Mrs. J.'s mother. Pressures on Johnny were discussed, and alternatives were considered. Mrs. J.'s mother agreed to take in Mary and her children temporarily. To deal with the disruption in the family, follow-up meetings were conducted to help clarify roles in the family system. Within a period of months, behavioral problems in the home and school had stopped for Johnny. He once again assumed a parental role to help out his mother and stepfather.

Implications. Montague (1996) pointed out several important considerations to make in working with Black families. Because of the possibility of an extended or nontraditional family arrangement, questions should be directed toward finding out who is living in the home and who helps out. It is also important to work to strengthen the original family structure and try to make it more functional rather than change it. One of the strengths of the African American family is that men, women, and children are allowed to adopt multiple roles within the family. An older child like Johnny could adopt a parental role while the mother might take on the role of the father. The grandmother may be a very important family member who also helps raise the children. Her influence and help should not be eliminated, but the goal should be to make more efficient the working alliance with the other caregivers. A family therapist should remember that flexibility of roles is a strength but that it can produce problems if roles conflict with one another.

Educational Orientation

African American parents encourage their children to develop career and educational goals at an early age in spite of the obstacles produced by racism and economic conditions. The gap in educational attainment between Black and White children is gradually narrowing. The high school dropout rate for African Americans declined from 11% in 1970 to 5% in 1994 and now does not differ significantly from that of Whites. The number of African Americans earning a bachelor's degree was 103,874, which was an increase of 8.75% over the 1997–1998 figures. A disturbing trend continues in historically Black colleges and universities: Women account for two thirds or more of the graduates (Brotherton, 2001). However, problems are still found in academic performance. Especially at risk are African American boys, who show a tendency toward disidentification (the disengagement of academic performance from self-esteem), subsequently losing interest in academics during middle and high school. In a longitudinal study Osbourne (1997) examined Hispanic and African American students and found that African American males were the only group to show no relationship between academic performance and global self-esteem. This may lead to lower academic performance. Unfortunately, low academic and social skills are predictors for delinquency and substance use in African American adolescents (J. H. Williams, Ayers, Abbott, Hawkins, & Catalano, 1999).

Implications. Factors associated with school failure, especially in African American males, must be identified, and intervention strategies must be applied. This might involve systems, family, and individual interventions. Many school systems have predominantly White teaching staffs, but the student population has changed from being predominantly White to predominantly minority. Because of this, teaching skills that were effective in the past may no longer work. For example, many African American youths display an animated, persuasive, and confrontational communication style, while schools have norms of conformity, quietness, teacher-focused activities, and individualized, competitive activities. Indeed mainstream teachers may see communication patterns, nonstandard movements, and walking style as aggression or misbehavior (Duhaney, 2000). Many teachers are not sensitive to these cultural differences and may respond inappropriately to minority group members. Curricula and classroom styles may need to be changed to take cultural factors into consideration.

Spirituality

> *D is a 42-year-old African American woman who was married for 20 years and recently divorced. She presented with depressive-like symptoms—feelings of loneliness, lack of energy, lack of appetite, and crying spells. She was raising two children with very little support from her ex-husband. . . . Although part of the treatment focused on traditional psychological interventions such as cognitive restructuring, expression of feelings, and changing behaviors, D's treatment also consisted of participating in two church-related programs. D's treatment involved participating in the women's ministry of her church to decrease her emotional and social isolation and to develop a support network. Treatment also involved participation in "The Mother to Son Program." The purpose of this program is to provide support to single mothers parenting African American boys. The program provides support for parents and rites of passage programs and mentors for Black boys. (Queener & Martin, 2001, p. 120).*

Spirituality and religion play an important role in many African American families and provide comfort in the face of oppression and economic support. Participation in religious activities allows for opportunities for self-expression, leadership, and community involvement (Kane, 1998). Among a sample of low-income African American children, those whose parents regularly attended church had fewer problems (Christian & Barbarin, 2001).

Implications. If the family is heavily involved in church activities or has strong religious beliefs, the counselor could enlist resources (e.g., the pastor or minister) to deal with problems involving conflicts within the family, school, or community. For many African American families, spiritual beliefs play an important role and may have developed as part of a coping strategy to deal with stressors. Churches should be considered as much a potential source of information as are clinics, schools, hospitals, or other mental health professionals. The church personnel may have an understanding of the family dynamics and living conditions of the parishioners. A pastor or minister can help create sources of social support for family members and help them with social and economic issues. In addition, programs for the enrichment of family life may be developed jointly with the church.

Ethnic or Racial Identity

Many believe that minorities go through a sequential process of racial identity or consciousness. For African Americans, the process involves a transformation from a non-Afrocentric identity to one that is Afrocentric (although some African Americans already have a Black identity through early socialization). The W. E. Cross (1991, 1995) model, which was described in detail in Chapter 8, identifies several of these stages: preencounter, encounter, immersion-emersion, and internalization.

Implications. Those who are at the preencounter level are less likely to report racial discrimination, while those in the immersion stage tend to be younger and least satisfied with societal conditions (Hyers, 2001). Additionally, African American preferences for counselor ethnicity are related to the stage of racial identity (Atkinson & Lowe, 1995). Similarly, Parham and Helms (1981) found that African Americans at the preencounter stage preferred a White counselor, while those in the other stages preferred a Black counselor. Pomales, Claiborn, and LaFromboise (1986), however, found that the most important counselor characteristic for African American students was cultural sensitivity. A culturally sensitive counselor (one who acknowledges the possibility that race or culture might play a role in the client's problem) is seen as more competent than is a culture-blind counselor (one who focuses on factors other than culture and race when dealing with the presenting problem). In the study, stage of racial identity played only a minor role in preference for counselor ethnicity. An assessment of racial identity may be useful for a counselor to hypothesize the types of conflict that the client may be undergoing and the way the world is viewed.

African American Youth

For many urban Black adolescents, life is complicated by problems of poverty, illiteracy, and racism. The homicide rate for African American youth between the ages of 15 and 24 was nearly 10 times that of White youth in 1989; their suicide rate increased to over twice that of other teenagers between 1980 and 1992; and they are more likely to contract sexually transmitted diseases than other groups of teenagers (Harvey & Rauch, 1997). Unemployment can range from 37% to nearly 50% among Black teenagers. Most African American youth feel strongly that race is still a factor in how people are judged (Gannett News Service, 1998).

Issues presented in counseling may differ to some extent between males and females. African American adolescent females, like other females, are burdened by living in a male-dominated society, face issues with racial identity and negative stereotypes, and strive to succeed in relationships and careers. They often undertake adult responsibilities such as the care of younger siblings and household duties at an early age. As a group, although they encounter both racism and sexism, they display higher self-confidence, lower levels of substance use, and more positive body images than do White female adolescents (Belgrave, Chase-Vaughn, Gray, Addison, & Cherry, 2000). Their awareness of racial and gender issues is reflected in the following comments:

Well, in this time I think it's really hard to be an African American woman . . . we are what you call a double negative; we are Black and we are a woman and it's really hard. . . .

I'd rather say I'm African-American than I'm Black because of the connection with the land, knowing that I come from somewhere. . . .

[Racial identity] is important to me because society sees African-American females as always getting pregnant and all that kind of thing and being on welfare. (Shorter-Gooden & Washington, 1996, p. 469)

In this sample of young African American females, Shorter-Gooden and Washington (1996) found that the struggle over racial identity was a more salient factor than was gender identity in establishing self-definition. These adolescents believed that they had to be strong and determined to overcome the obstacles in being Black. About half had been raised by their mother, and most indicated the importance of the mother-daughter relationship. Careers were also important to two thirds of the females; most felt that the motivation to succeed academically was instilled by their parents. In counseling young African American women, issues involving racial identity and conflict should be explored, and their sense of internal strength should be increased because it appears to serve as a buffer to racism and sexism.

African American females often have to deal with the double issue of being both Black and female. They have to fight against negative images to prevent their being incorporated into their own belief systems; simultaneously, they must develop pride and dignity in Black womanhood (Jordan, 1997).

Black youth often do not come to counseling willingly. Often they come because they have been referred or brought in by their parents. Because of this, cooperation may be difficult:

Michael is a 19-year-old African American male who was brought to counseling by his aunt, Gloria, with whom he has lived for the past 2 years. Gloria is concerned about Michael's future as a result of his being present during a recent drug raid at the home of some friends. . . . Although Michael graduated from high school and is employed part-time at a fast food restaurant, he is frustrated with this work and confused about his future. He believes that Black men "don't get a fair shake" in life, and therefore is discouraged about his prospects about getting ahead. . . . Michael's aunt . . . is concerned that Michael's peers are involved in gangs and illegal activities. She thinks the rap music he listens to is beginning to fill his head with hate and anger. . . . Michael's major issues center around developing a positive identity as an African American man and discovering his place in the world. (Frame & Williams, 1996, p. 22).

Implications. The type of socialization that African American children and teenagers receive from their parents has been found to be related to social anxiety. Facing racism, African American parents may (a) address racism and prejudice directly and help their children identify with their own race; (b) discuss race only when the issue is brought up by their children and consider it to be of minor importance; (c) focus on human values and ignore the role of race. Neal-Barnett & Crowther (2000) found that the third approach was related to higher levels of social anxiety, particularly with African American peers. Ignoring racial issues in socialization left children vulnerable to anxiety when Black peers accused them of "acting White." They had not had the opportunity to develop coping strategies. Racial socialization of children by African American families helped to buffer the negative effects of racist discrimination (Fischer & Shaw, 1999). Protective factors have included increasing positive feelings about self and enhancing the sense of culture for African American youth (Belgrave et al., 2000).

In the case of Michael, Frame and Williams (1996) suggested several strategies for working with Black youth. The first involves the use of metaphors and is based on the African tradition of storytelling. Instead of just responding to "Black men don't get a fair shake," the counselor could get Michael to help identify family phrases or Biblical stories that instill hope. Additional metaphors could be generated from the writings of contemporary African American figures. The second strategy could be support for Michael's struggle with societal barriers. He could envision himself as a crusader for human rights and learn how to direct his anger in appropriate ways. Third, Michael could be asked to bring in his rap music and discuss what is appealing about it. Issues addressed in the lyrics could be explored, and the counselor could help with decisions regarding healthy outlets for his feelings of anger or despair. Fourth, family and community support systems could be generated. Members of the extended family, the pastor, teachers, and other important individuals in Michael's life could be asked to meet together in Aunt Gloria's home. All the members could share information about their struggles and search for identity. Use of these techniques, derived from African American experiences, can lead to personal empowerment.

Paster (1985) makes several recommendations in working with Black youth. First, the youth's expectations about the usefulness of counseling should be discussed. Second, a negotiated contract on counseling duration and goals should be obtained. Paster recommends making it a short-term (6- to 8-week) trial period. Third, the counselor should set firm limits, especially when dealing with verbal abuse. A streetwise youth might deliberately attempt to frighten or shock the counselor by describing drug use and sexual behaviors in graphic detail. Others might adopt a highly confrontational and aggressive stance or tell tales as a means of testing out the therapist. In addition, Paster feels that it is important for the counselor to act as an advocate for the youth and deal as an intermediary with agencies such as the school and the court. When possible, community resources should be utilized.

Racism and Discrimination

The existence of racism has produced a variety of defensive and survival mechanisms among Black Americans. This cultural mistrust, or "healthy cultural paranoia," acts as a coping strategy (Phelps, Taylor, & Gerard, 2001). A lack of trust and feelings of discrimination exist for social services and medical support, especially among the youth (Miller, Seib, & Dennie, 2001). Only 9% of African Americans believe that they are treated the same as White Americans (Tilove, 2001). The experience of perceived racial discrimination leads to lower levels of mastery and higher levels of psychological distress (Broman, Mavaddat, & Hsu, 2000). Discriminatory practices may also account for the fact that African Americans are less likely than their White counterparts to receive an antidepressant for depression and less likely to receive the newer selective serotonin reuptake inhibitor (SSRI) medications (Blazer, Hybels, Somonsick, & Hanlon, 2000; Melfi, Croghan, Hanna, & Robinson, 2000).

Implications. Since the mental health environment is a microcosm of the larger society, the mental health professional should be willing to address and anticipate possible mistrust from African American clients (Whaley, 2001). If the problem is due to discriminatory practices by an institution, the therapist may have to operate at the institutional level by making certain that clinics evaluate their procedures to ensure prescribing appropriate medications for African American clients. In other cases, the therapist may have to examine the African American client's response to the problem situation. The client may have only a limited or reflexive problem-solving capability. In counseling a client about dealing with situations in which racism plays a part, the counselor must assist the client in developing a wider range of options and encourage the development of a more conscious, problem-solving mode. The client must consider the way he or she usually deals with racism and consider other options that might be more productive. The following case study demonstrates this approach.

> *A recently divorced, 25-year-old African American medical student sought therapy for migraine headaches that were stress related. He felt that the racist environment of the training school and a particular professor were responsible for his problem. He proposed to deal with the problem by directly confronting his professor and accusing him of racism. It did appear that the professor had engaged in prejudicial behavior. However, it is very possible that directly confronting the professor in this manner would have led to the student's dismissal from the school. The therapist also found that the client's choice of this strategy was at least partially related to his unresolved feeling of anger over his recent divorce. This event had made him feel more vulnerable, and the resulting bitter feelings helped in his choice of directly confronting the professor. As the client understood the impact of his divorce, he was able to consider a wider range of options. He decided that it would be best to file a complaint with the minority affairs office. Although the tension between the student and the professor remained high, the student felt that he had chosen the best option and remained in school.*

A. C. Jones (1985) feels that four sets of interactive factors must be considered in working with an African American client (see Figure 11.1). The first factor involves the reaction to racial oppression. Most African Americans have faced racism, and the possibility that this factor might play a role in the present problem should be examined. Vontress and Epp (1997) described this factor as "historical hostility," a reaction in response to current and past suffering endured by the group. Because of this, problems are often perceived through this filter. The second factor is the influence of African American culture on the client's behavior. Clients may vary greatly in their identification with African American traditions. The third factor involves the degree of adoption of majority culture values. The task of the therapist is to help the client understand his or her motivation and make conscious, growth-producing choices. The fourth factor involves the personal experiences of the individual. African Americans differ significantly in their family and individual experiences. For some, this last category may be much more significant than racial identity.

Although all four factors may influence an African American client, the degree of overlap or importance of each of the factors may vary greatly from individual to individual. A middle-class African American living in a predominantly White neighborhood may show a pattern that differs from that of a lower-class African American living in a Black neighborhood. The advantage of this model is that it includes the elements involved in the studies on identity and forces the counselor to assess more completely the external and internal influences on a Black American's problem.

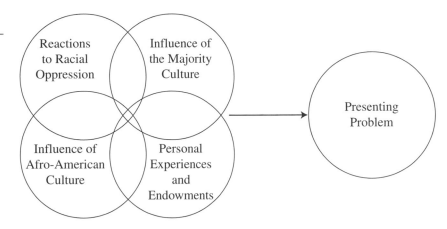

Figure 11.1

The Interaction of Four Sets of Factors in the Jones Model

Source: From "Psychological Functioning in Black Americans: A Conceptual Guide for Use in Psychotherapy," by A. C. Jones, 1985, *Psychotherapy, 22,* p. 367. Copyright 1982 by *Psychotherapy.* Reprinted by permission of the Editor, *Psychotherapy.*

Value Differences and Consultation

In consultation, as in counseling, we have to be aware of our own values and realize that they provide the lenses through which we view other cultural groups. We may have to alter our paradigm to make it appropriate for our consultees. In doing so, we need to have an understanding of their values and behavior (D. Brown, 1997; Warner & Morris, 1997). Gibbs (1980) described some of her experiences in school consultation. She observed that African Americans tend to focus more on interpersonal factors, while White Americans respond more to the instrumental skills demonstrated by the consultant. Her observations are based on a presentation of a proposed school project made to both Black and White teachers at an inner-city school. She found that the same five-stage consultation sequence occurred but that each group focused on separate issues.

1. *Appraisal stage.* During this stage, both African American and White teachers evaluated the consultant. Gibbs observed that African American teachers tended to be aloof and cool. They responded minimally and did not indicate interest through questions about the project. They wanted to know about the potential harm the project could have on the African American children in the school. White teachers were much more attentive and asked questions related to the methods and goals of the project.

2. *Investigation stage.* During this stage, the consultant was checked out. The African American consultees focused on the consultant's personal life and her background and values. For example, the African American principal asked Gibbs personal questions and then also related her own

experiences with teaching. After this discussion, the African American principal said that she would support Gibbs because she "liked her." Another African American teacher, who was initially critical about the project, became friendlier and supportive after a discussion that revealed areas of commonality with the consultant. White teachers continued to focus on the technical aspects of the project and did not seek personal information except about the expertise and experiences of the consultant.

3. *Involvement stage.* If a favorable evaluation occurred during stages 1 and 2, the consultees became involved. For African American teachers it revolved around whether a personal relationship had been established. Part of their involvement included exchanges of personal information and social interactions during coffee breaks and lunch. White teachers maintained a formal professional relationship and were interested in what they would gain from their involvement. One teacher indicated that the approach could be used in working with emotionally disturbed children. Another indicated the belief that the project might help the school achieve goals.

4. *Commitment stage.* During this stage, African American teachers exhibited more interest in the goals of the project and less in the consultant's personality. White consultees also expressed willingness to participate.

5. *Engagement stage.* Final commitment was made by the teachers to support the project. For African American teachers this commitment was based on interpersonal qualities of the consultant; for White teachers it was based on the instrumental competence displayed.

Because African American teachers focused on interpersonal relationships, Gibbs (1980) felt that it is important for the consultant to be genuine and down to earth, and to establish an equal relationship. The consultant must also be open to interpersonal approaches and questioning by Black consultees. Gibbs's observations are useful in (a) helping understand the ways African American and White individuals differ during the consultation stages, (b) pointing out the differences between instrumental and interpersonal orientations, (c) providing training models for consultants who will work with African Americans, and (d) providing a cross-cultural orientation useful in training both African American and White consultants to work with different cultural groups.

Guidelines for Clinical Practice

In working with African American youth and adults in counseling situations, certain suggestions can be made about the elements necessary during the vital first few sessions. The first sessions are crucial in determining whether the client will return. The following steps below by explaining what counseling is and by enlisting the assistance of the client. Prior experiences may render issues of trust very important. The counselor can deal with these issues by discussing them directly and by being open, authentic, and empathetic. The African American client will often make a decision based on his or her interpersonal evaluation of the counselor. The role of the counselor may have to be much broader for the African American client than for the White client. He or she may have to be more directive, serve in an educative function, and help the client deal with agencies or with issues involving employment and health. Although the order of these elements can be modified and some can be omitted, these steps may be helpful to the counselor and client:

1. During the first session, it may be beneficial to bring up the reaction of the client to a counselor of a different ethnic background. (Although African Americans show a same-race preference, being culturally competent has been shown to be even more important.) A statement such as, "Sometimes clients feel uncomfortable working with a counselor of a different race; would this be a problem for you?" or a variant can be used.

2. If the clients are referred, determine their feelings about counseling and how it can be made useful for them. Explain your relationship with the referring agency and the limits of confidentiality.

3. Identify the expectations and worldviews of the African American clients, find out what they believe counseling is, and explore their feelings about counseling. Determine how they view the problem and the possible solutions.

4. Establish an egalitarian relationship. In contrast to other ethnic groups, most African Americans tend to establish a personal commonality with the counselor. This may be accomplished by self-disclosure. If the client appears hostile or aloof, discussing some noncounseling topics may be useful.

5. Determine whether and how the client has responded to discrimination and racism both in unhealthy and healthy ways. Also examine issues around racial identity (many clients at the preencounter stage will not believe that race is an important factor). For some, the identification with Afrocentricity may be important in establishing a positive self-identity. In these cases, elements of African/African American culture should be incorporated in counseling. This can be achieved through readings, movies, music, and discussions of African American mentors.

6. Assess the positive assets of the client, such as family (including relatives and nonrelated friends), community resources, and the church.

7. Determine the external factors that might be related to the presenting problem. This may involve contact with outside agencies for financial and housing assistance. Do not dismiss issues of racism as "just an excuse"; instead, help the client identify alternative means of dealing with the problems.

8. Help the client define goals and appropriate means of attaining them. Assess ways in which the client, family members, and friends have handled similar problems successfully.

9. After the therapeutic alliance has been formed, apply problem-solving and time-limited approaches.

Counseling American Indians and Alaskan Natives

12

Chapter

The U.S. Government had judged that Indians were incapable of managing their own land, so they placed the property in a trust in 1887 and promised that the Indians would receive the income from their land. They never did. On December 1999, a Federal judge ruled that the government had breached its sacred trust duties. (Maas, 2001)

Of the 175 Indian languages spoken in the United States, only about 20 are passed on from mothers to babies. James Jackson Jr. remembered his experience in a boarding school when a teacher grabbed him when he was speaking his native language and threatened to wash out his mouth with soap: "That's where we lost it [our language]." (Brooke, 1998)

At a U.S. Senate hearing, an elder sang and beat a drum while hundreds of American Indians stood. On the other side of the aisle, a similar number of Euro-Americans rose and sang "The Star-Spangled Banner." Thus began a hearing regarding whether tribal immunity should be terminated from lawsuits from members of the outside community. American Indians believe that conflicts over fishing rights, gambling restrictions on reservations, and the rights of tribal courts to deal with Indian affairs have been attempts to break further the "solemn promises" made in treaties. (Shukovsky, 1998)

In North America, wars and diseases that resulted from contact with Europeans decimated the American Indian population. It is estimated that the large population of American Indians had decreased to only 10% of its original number by the end of the eighteenth century. The experience of American Indians in America is not comparable to that of any other ethnic group. In contrast to immigrants who arrived with few resources and struggled to gain equality, American Indians had resources. They had land and status that were gradually eroded by imperial, colonial, and then federal and state policies (K. W. Johnson et al., 1995). Extermination and seizure of lands seemed to be the primary

309

policy of the North Americans. Experience with this type of contact prompted this observation from a Delaware warrior: "I admit that there are good White men, but they bear no proportion to the bad; the bad must be the strongest, for they rule." Indians suffered massive losses of their land.

During the 1930s, over 125,000 Indians from different tribes were forced from their homes in many different states to a reservation in Oklahoma. The move was traumatic for Indian families and, in many cases, disrupted their cultural traditions. Assaults against the Indian culture occurred in attempts to "civilize" the Indians. Many Indian children were forced to be educated in English-speaking boarding schools. They were not allowed to speak their own language and had to spend eight continuous years away from their families and tribes. Children were also removed from their homes and placed with non-Indian families until the Indian Child Welfare Act of 1978 (Blanchard, 1983; Choney et al., 1995; K. W. Johnson et al., 1995). These practices had a great negative impact on family and tribal cohesion and prevented the transmission of cultural values from parents to children. The following case study illustrates some of the disruptions caused by a boarding school experience.

> *Mary was born on the reservation. She was sent away to school when she was 12 and did not return to the reservation until she was 20. By the time she returned, her mother had died from pneumonia. She didn't remember her father, who was the medicine man of the tribe, very well. Shortly after she returned, she became pregnant by a non-Indian man she met at a bar.*
>
> *Mary's father . . . looked forward to teaching and leaving to his grandson John the ways of the medicine man. . . . John felt his grandfather was out of step with the 20th century. . . . Mary . . . could not validate the grandfather's way of life . . . she remembered having difficulty fitting in when she returned to the reservation. . . . In response to the growing distance between the two men, she became more and more depressed and began to drink heavily. (Sage, 1997, p. 48)*

In the past, the tribe, through the extended family, was responsible for the education and training of the children. The sense of identity developed through this tradition has been undermined. In addition, even recent history is full of broken treaties, the seizure or misuse of Indian land, and battles (often led by the U.S. government) to remove or severely limit fishing and hunting rights. These acts have made the American Indians very suspicious of the motives of the majority culture, and most of them do not expect to be treated fairly by non-Indian agencies (K. W. Johnson et al., 1995).

> *One of the most serious failings of the present system is that Indian children are often removed from the custody of their natural parents by nontribal government authorities who have no basis for intelligently evaluating the cultural and social*

premises underlying Indian home life and childrearing. Many of the individuals who decide the fate of our children are at best ignorant of our cultural values, and at worst contemptuous of the Indian way and convinced that removal, usually to a non-Indian household or institution, can only benefit an Indian child. (Congressional Record, 1997)

Chief Calvin Isaac of the Mississippi Band of Choctaw Indians spoke these words during the house hearings of 1978 in support of the Indian Child Welfare Act. Statistics were cited that indicated that over 90% of American Indian children were being placed by state courts and child welfare workers into non-Indian homes (Congressional Record, 1997). Such placements weakened the cultural identity of the children and weakened the tribes as well since values could not be passed on to the children. The passage of the act dramatically reduced this type of placement, although amendments to strengthen or weaken it continue to be brought up.

Implications. When working with American Indian children and families, the mental health professional should be aware of the political relationship as it exists between American Indians, the different states, and the U.S. government. The Indian Child Welfare Act has important implications for child protective services, runaways, and adoption procedures. In general, decisions regarding the placement of American Indian children are to be held in tribal courts. If they are to be removed from their parents, the first placements to be considered should be with extended family members, other tribal members, or other Indian families. Testimony from expert witnesses who are familiar with the specific Indian cultural group must be obtained before children can be removed from their homes. The counselor should understand the history of oppression that has existed and understand local issues and specific tribal history (Dana, 2000).

The American Indian and the Alaskan Native

American Indians/Alaskan Natives form a highly heterogeneous group composed of over 512 distinct tribes, some of which consist of only four or five members (Hamby, 2000). The American Indian, Eskimo, and Aleut population grew rapidly to 2,475,956 in the year 2000. An additional 1.6 million claim to have Indian roots (U.S. Bureau of the Census, 2001). The population is young, with 39% under 29 years of age as compared to 29% of the total U.S. population. About 6 in 10 were married-couple families, versus 8 in 10 of the nation's families overall. Female householders with no husband present represented 27% of families versus 17% of the U.S. average. Fewer American Indians are high school graduates than the general U.S. population

(66% versus 75%). Their income level is only 62% of the U.S. average, and the poverty rate is nearly three times as high (U.S. Bureau of the Census, 1995). Of the American Indians living on or near a reservation, 50% are unemployed (Juntunen et al., 2001). Health statistics also paint a dismal picture. The alcoholism mortality rate is six times higher than that for the U.S. population as a whole (Frank, Moore, & Ames, 2000). Because of the sedentary reservation lifestyle, the rates of obesity and diabetes are much higher in this group than in the U.S. population (Balderas, 2000).

There are large within-group and between-group differences among the different tribes in customs, language, and type of family structure. Although tribes differ from one another in customs and values, they all share the history of having lost their ancestral lands, forced education in boarding schools, systematic attempts to eradicate their language and religion, and restrictions on their traditional means of obtaining a livelihood (I. M. Norton & Manson, 1996). Over 60% of American Indians are of mixed heritage, having Black, White, and Hispanic backgrounds. In addition, American Indians differ in their degree of acculturation (Trimble, Fleming, Beauvais, & Jumper-Thurman, 1996). The majority of American Indians do not live on reservations, in part because of the lack of economic opportunities (K. W. Johnson et al., 1995), although many are returning because of casino jobs or a more nurturing environment. One man who returned described his need for a more "friendly place, friendly face, and friendly greetings" (Shukovsky, 2001, p. A1).

What constitutes an Indian is often an area of controversy. The U.S. Census depends on self-report of racial identity; some tribes have developed their own criteria and specify either tribal enrollment or blood quantum levels. Ken Hansen, chairman of the Samish tribe, stated, "It is a fundamental right of any nation, including tribal nations, to define their own membership. If a person meets the criteria for membership in a tribe, they are Indian" (Shukovsky, 2001, p. A13). Congress has formulated a legal definition. An individual must have an Indian blood quantum of at least 25% to be considered an Indian. This definition has caused problems both within and outside the Indian community. Some believe that belonging to a tribe should be the most important criterion and that those that do not have a tribal affiliation are "wanna-bes."

Indians are often thought to have specific physical characteristics such as black hair and eyes, brown skin, and high cheekbones. However, American Indians display a wide range of phenotypic characteristics in terms of body size, skin and hair color, and facial features. Conflicts in identity are often great for individuals who do not fit the traditional physical stereotypes. They may meet with prejudice and rejection from Indians and non-Indians alike.

Tribe and Reservation

For the many Indians living on reservations and for those living in urban areas, the tribe is of fundamental importance. The relationship that Indians have with their tribes is different from that between non-Indians and their societies. Indians see themselves as an extension of their tribe.

Implications. The tribe and reservation provide American Indians with a sense of belonging and security, forming an interdependent system. Status and rewards are obtained by adherence to tribal structure. Indians judge themselves in terms of whether their behaviors are of benefit to the tribe. Personal accomplishments are honored and supported if they serve to benefit the tribe. Interventions with American Indian families and individuals should include an assessment of the importance of tribal relationships in any decision-making process. The reservation itself is very important for many American Indians, even among those who do not reside there. Many use the word "here" to describe the reservation and the word "there" to describe everything that is outside. The reservation is a place to conduct ceremonies and social events and to maintain cultural identity. Indians who leave the reservation to seek greater opportunities often lose their sense of personal identity, since they lose their tribal identity (M. J. Anderson & Ellis, 1995; Lone-Knapp, 2000). Some American Indians who have left the reservations can reestablish their cultural identity by participating in social and ceremonial activities on reservations.

American Indian/Alaskan Native Characteristics, Values, and Implications on Behavior

Family Structure

It is difficult to describe "the Indian family." It varies from matriarchal structures seen in the Navajo, where women govern the family, to patriarchal structures, in which men are the primary authority figures. Some generalizations can be made, however. American Indians are characterized by a high fertility rate, a large percentage of out-of-wedlock births, and strong roles for women. For most tribes, the extended family is the basic unit. Children are often raised by relatives such as aunts, uncles, and grandparents who live in separate households (Hildebrand et al., 1996). Living conditions for most American Indians are poor, especially for those on reservations. The per capita income in 1989 for all American Indians living on reservations or trust lands was $4,478, versus $8,328 for all American Indians. Between 1979 and 1989, the poverty rate for American Indians increased from 24% to 27%, and the median family income declined by 5%. Of the families maintained by females with no husband present, 50% were poor, compared with 31% of all families maintained by women with no husbands present (U.S. Bureau of the Census, 1995). In one tribe, over 90% of the grandparents lived in separate households but were involved and fulfilled traditional family roles on a daily basis with their children, grandchildren, and great-grandchildren. The existence of high unemployment on reservations has forced many to move into urban areas. However, cultural conflict and the loss of contact with the extended family and tribe may be responsible for the fact that many are returning to the reservation.

Implications. The concept of the extended family is often misunderstood by those in the majority culture who operate under the concept of the nuclear family. The extended family often stretches through the second cousin. It is not unusual to have youngsters stay in a variety of different households. Misinterpretations can be made if one thinks that only the parents should raise and be responsible for the children. Y. Red Horse (1982) presented a case of a 15-year-old girl who was doing very well in school. However, she chose not to live with her parents, who had problems with alcohol, but lived instead in five different households of relatives during a 3-year period. The White caseworker felt that this pattern of moving around was an indication of irresponsibility on the part of the girl and neglect on the part of the parents. If the girl were a member of the majority culture, such an interpretation would not be out of line. At the age of 17, Linda requested a place of her own. This request was resisted by the social worker, who believed that that Linda was behaving irresponsibly and was displaying a pattern of instability. However, Indian professionals pointed out that Linda was doing very well in school and that many members of her extended family lived within an eight-block radius of her apartment. Further, she had the support of the school counselor and Indian professionals. It was also pointed out that living in the households of the extended family was not uncommon.

There are several factors to note in this example. First, the pattern of behavior has to be considered in a cultural context. Second, the decision regarding Linda's request was based not only on cultural knowledge but also on her individual strengths and weaknesses. If she had not done well in school or had not displayed responsible behavior, the decision would most likely have been different. Red Horse (1983) cautioned that in working with American Indians, the consideration of Indian values as well as specific problem behaviors should be reviewed before a treatment plan is developed. In working with American Indian children, the counselor should determine the roles of other family members so that interventions can include appropriate individuals. If the other family members play important roles, they should be invited to attend the sessions. The emphasis on collectivism is strong. If the goals or techniques of therapy lead to discord with the family or tribe, they will not be utilized. Interventions may have to be developed with the help of the family, relatives, friends, elders, or tribal leaders.

American Indian Values

Because of the great diversity and variation among American Indians/ Alaskan Natives, it is difficult to describe a set of values that encompasses all groups. However, certain generalizations can be made regarding Indian values (Garwick & Auger, 2000; Herring, 1997; Swinomish Tribal Mental Health Project, 1991).

1. *Sharing.* Among Indians, honor and respect are gained by sharing and giving, while in the dominant culture, status is gained by the accumulation of material goods.

Implications. Once enough money is earned, Indians may stop working and spend time and energy in ceremonial activities. The accumulation of wealth is not a high priority but is a means to enjoy the present with others. Refusing to accept an invitation to share drinks or substances with a member of the same tribe would be considered an affront to the individual making the offer and a violation of the value of sharing and giving. Strategies to deal with alcohol and drug use have to take into consideration the value of sharing.

2. *Cooperation.* Indians believe that the tribe and family take precedence over the individual. Indian children tend to display sensitivity to the opinions and attitudes of their peers. They will actively avoid disagreements or contradictions. Most do not like to be singled out and made to perform in school unless the whole group would benefit.

Implications. Indian children may be seen as unmotivated in schools because of reluctance to compete with peers in the classroom. To compete could be seen as an expression of individuality that suggests that the student is better than the tribe. Because of this value, American Indian students may also feel it is necessary to show their answers to another tribe member. Instead of going to an appointment, they may assist a family member needing help. Indians work hard to prevent discord and disharmony. In a counseling setting, they may find it easy to agree with the counselor but not follow through with the suggestions. In contrast to the majority culture, individual achievement and competition are not seen as important.

3. *Noninterference.* Indians are taught not to interfere with others and to observe rather than react impulsively. Rights of others are respected. This value influences parenting style.

Implications. It is important to be aware of how cultural influences have shaped our perception of what is right or wrong in parent-child relationships. American Indians are more indulgent and less punitive to their children than are parents from other ethnic groups (MacPhee, Fritz, & Miller-Heyl, 1996). Euro-American parenting styles may conflict with American Indian values. A culturally sensitive parent education program has been developed for American Indians that involves (a) use of the oral tradition by storytelling to teach lessons to children; (b) understanding of the spiritual nature of child rearing and the spiritual value of children; and (c) use of the extended family in child rearing. The eight-session program involves a half-hour social time for parents and children before each session. Storytelling and a potluck meal are included. The focus is the application of traditional teaching methods (nurturing, use of nature to teach lessons, and use of harmony as a guiding principle for family life; Gorman & Baiter, 1997).

For traditionally oriented or even marginally identified American Indian parents, a culturally adapted approach may be more appropriate than mainstream methods of parent education. Even among family members, children are rarely told what to do but are encouraged to make their own decisions. Few rules exist, and the father is considered an administrator of the family, not a rule-giver. Consequently, American Indian parents may be seen as "permissive in child rearing" or may even be accused of "child neglect." The majority culture values action and taking charge. A mental health professional working with a family must determine if the child-rearing practices are culturally consistent.

4. *Time orientation.* Indians are very much involved in the present rather than the future. Ideas of punctuality or planning for the future may be unimportant. Life is to be lived in the here and now.

Implications. Long-term plans such as going to college are seen as acts of egoism rather than future planning. Things get done according to a rational order and not according to deadlines. In the majority culture, delay of gratification and planning for future goals are seen as important qualities. In working with these issues, the counselor should acknowledge the value differences and their potential conflict and help the individual or family develop possible strategies to deal with these.

5. *Spirituality.* The spirit, mind, and body are all interconnected. Wellness is a disharmony between these elements.

Implications. Traditional curative approaches attempt to restore the harmony of these systems. The sweat lodge and vision quest are often used to reestablish the connections between the mind, body, and spirit. To treat a problem successfully, all of these elements have to be considered and addressed. Positive emotions can be curative. Medicine is in each event, memory, place, or person such as talking to an old friend on the phone or watching children play (M. T. Garrett & Wilbur, 1999). The counselor should help the client identify the factors involved in disharmony; determine curative events, behaviors, and feelings; and utilize client-generated solutions so that a balance is obtained.

6. *Nonverbal communication.* Learning occurs by listening rather than talking. Direct eye contact with an elder is seen as a sign of disrespect. Indian families tend to ask few direct questions.

Implications. Differences in nonverbal communication can lead to misunderstandings. Several families reported misunderstandings with teachers. An American Indian child who did not look directly at the teacher talking to her was accused of being disrespectful (Garwick & Auger, 2000). This interpretation was premature, since the teacher was not aware that among many Indian groups, eye contact between a child and an elder indicates a lack of respect. The mother explained that this was the way her child was brought up. There have been reported cases in which the lack of eye contact has been regarded as a deficit. For example, a behavior modification procedure was employed to shape eye contact in a Navaho girl (Everett, Proctor, & Cortmell, 1989). It is important to determine whether specific behaviors are due to cultural values or are actual problems. Since American Indians may not ask for services, mental health professionals should let the families know of programs and services that are available. They expect to hear from someone who can provide them with information.

Specific Problem Areas for American Indians/Alaskan Natives

Education

American Indian children appear to do well during the first few years of school. However, by the fourth grade, a pattern of decline and dropouts develops. Due to a variety of factors, a significant drop in achievement motivation occurs around the seventh grade. Some students are ridiculed for pursuing higher education and are called "wanna-bes" by their peers, who believe that achievers are just trying to "act White." There also may be a lack of family support for education. Few American Indians who pursue higher education graduate (Juntunen et al., 2001). In addition, many youth can find jobs on the reservation, so they do not see the necessity for "White man's education." The inability to complete an education perpetuates the cycle of poverty and lack of opportunities and may contribute to the high suicide rate among American Indian adolescents (Keane, Dick, Bechtold, & Manson, 1996).

Implications. At a systems level, changes need to be made in public schools and higher education to accommodate some of the social and cultural differences of American Indian and Alaskan Native students. In the Seattle School District, nearly 59% of American Indian students in middle school had a grade point average (GPA) below 2.00 (9% had GPAs above 3.00), compared to 21% of White students. American Indian students were also more likely to be suspended (34%) than White students (17%; Seattle Public Schools, 1986). The reasons for this statistic must be determined and remedied. Some tribes have given up on the public school system and have developed their own learning centers and community colleges. Schools must help students bridge the two worlds of Native American and White cultures. To maintain their cultural identity and feeling of connectedness with their tribe, several strategies have been identified or utilized by American Indians attending higher education programs. Some utilized a "powwow fix" to stay connected. Others reminded themselves of who they are (Juntunen et al., 2001). Reestablishing contact with the tribe and reservation may help students retain a sense of connection and cultural identity. For American Indians, barriers to higher education include a sense of cultural incongruity, an unreceptive or nonsupportive university environment, and college stress. In one study, the most important factors in college success for American Indians were social support networks and faculty or staff mentors. Other important variables for success were positive self-esteem, self-efficacy, and a strong sense of identity (Gloria & Kurpius, 2001). Culturally consistent cognitive strategies were also useful. Some American Indians found self-talk that encouraged persistence in traditional ways to be helpful. For example, conventional wisdom that was carried down from tribes or families was identified. Culture conflict and persistence were reduced by using the "inner voice" (e.g., "Keep looking for the light"; "Remember where you came from"; Montgomery, Milville, Winterowd, Jeffries, & Baysden, 2000). These culturally consistent cognitive strategies helped American Indian students persist in their educational experiences.

Acculturation Conflicts

Not only do Indian children and adolescents face the same developmental problems that all young people do, but they are also in a state of conflict over exposure to two very different cultures. They are caught between expectations of their parents to maintain traditional values and the necessity to adapt to the majority culture. In one study of American Indian adolescents, the most serious problems identified involved family relationships, grades, and concerns about the future. In addition, boys frequently cited their Indianness or being Indian as a problem. Surprisingly, one third of the girls reported feeling that they did not want to live (Bee-Gates, Howard—Pitney, LaFramboise, & Rowe, 1996). These and other stressors may account for the fact that truancy, delinquency and arrest rates, school failure, drug use, and suicide are high among Indian youth.

Although some of the value differences between Indians and non-Indians have been presented, many Indians are acculturated and hold the values of the larger society. The degree of Indian identity versus acculturation and assimilation should always be considered, since it influences receptivity in counseling (Trimble et al., 1996). Five cultural orientation types were formulated by M. T. Garrett and Pichette (2000):

1. *Traditional.* The individual may speak little English, thinks in the native language, and practices traditional tribal customs and methods of worship.
2. *Marginal.* The individual may speak both languages but has lost touch with his or her cultural heritage and is not fully accepted in mainstream society.
3. *Bicultural.* The person is conversant with both sets of values and can communicate in a variety of contexts.
4. *Assimilated.* The individual embraces only the mainstream culture's values, behaviors, and expectations.
5. *Pantraditional.* Although the individual has only been exposed to or adopted mainstream values, he or she has made a conscious effort to return to the "old ways."

Implications. It is clear that within-group differences have to be considered in working with American Indians. Because of differences in acculturation, approaches that might be appropriate for a given individual might not be appropriate for all Indians (Choney et al., 1995). For example, the types of problems and the therapeutic process and goals appropriate for an American Indian living on a rural reservation may be very different from those appropriate for an urbanized Indian who retains few of the traditional beliefs. An American Indian with a traditional orientation may be unfamiliar with the expectations of the dominant culture. In contrast, assimilated or marginal American Indians may face issues such as (a) the denial and lack of pride in being a Native American; (b) pressure to adopt the majority cultural values; (c) guilty feelings over not knowing or participating in his or her culture; (d) negative views of Native Americans; and (e) a lack of a support and belief system. The mental health professional should assess for tribal affiliation if any, languages spoken, self-identity, and where the individual grew up and if there is current relationship to a tribe or tribal culture (M. T. Garrett & Pichette, 2000). Different strategies would have to be developed according to the degree of cultural identity. Those who are traditionally oriented may need to develop the skills and resources to deal with mainstream society. Acculturated individuals may need to examine value and self-identity conflicts.

In working with American Indian adolescents, ethnic identity issues should be explored. For many, Indianness, or the emphasis one places on being Indian, is a very important feature in the development of self-identity (BigFoot-Sipes, Dauphinais, LaFromboise, Bennett, & Rowe, 1992). Considering identity issues serves several purposes. First, it allows the client to be aware of potential problems if the therapist is of different ethnicity. Second, it gets the client to consider his or her own feelings about values, self-identity, and relationship with the majority society. Problems involving identity formation may be great and swing back and forth, with the Indian youths sometimes seeing themselves as primarily Indian, and sometimes moving in the direction of White values. The therapist should help the client recognize and clarify the conflicts so that the client can make an individual resolution. Many Indians do not prefer assimilation or individuality, as they see themselves as an extension of the tribe. Harmony, cooperation, and the prevention of discord are important (M. J. Anderson & Ellis, 1995).

Domestic Violence

Domestic violence, along with physical and sexual assault, is quite high in many native communities. American Indian women suffer a higher rate of violence (3½ times higher) than the national average (Bhungalia, 2001). This may be an underestimate. Many do not report assaults because of the tension that exists between law enforcement and women. This level of domestic violence may be a result of the loss of traditional status and roles for both men and women as well as social and economic marginalization.

Implications. During counseling, it may be difficult to determine whether domestic violence is occurring in a family or couple. American Indian women who are abused may remain silent because of cultural barriers, a high level of distrust with White dominated agencies, fear of familial alienation, and a history of the inadequacy of state and tribal agencies to prosecute domestic crimes (Bhungalia, 2001). Jurisdictional struggles between state and tribal authorities may result in a lack of help for women. Many tribes acknowledge the problem of family violence and have developed community-based domestic violence interventions. Strategies need to be developed from the American Indian perspective; using material or resources from the majority culture can raise issues of domination (Hamby, 2000). In working with a domestic violence issue with an American Indian woman, tribal issues, tribal programs, and family support should be identified.

Suicide

Robert Jaycob Jensen was first. The lanky 17-year-old Sioux Indian, who'd been drinking heavily and having run-ins with police all summer, slipped into his family's dank basement last Aug. 30. Over toward the corner, past the rusted-out furnace and broken sewer line, he threaded a braided leather belt over a board nailed between floor beams, buckled it around his neck and hanged himself.

On Nov. 16, in the same basement with the same type of belt, Robert's 16-year-old cousin and best friend, Charles Gerry, hanged himself. Three other Indian youths have since taken their lives. . . . In the five months since Robert's death, 43 reservation boys and girls have attempted suicide. ("Rash of Indian," 1998, p. A5)

The suicide epidemic is thought to be the result of alcohol abuse, poverty, boredom, and family breakdown. American Indian youth have twice the rate of attempted and completed suicide as other youth. Adolescence to adulthood is the time of greatest risk for suicide, especially among young males (EchoHawk, 1997; Middlebrook, LeMaster, Beals, Novins, & Manson, 2001).

Implications. It is difficult to address many of the societal and economic issues that face American Indians. For those who live on a reservation or identify with a tribe, community involvement or programs may exist or may need to developed. Any program developed should be culturally consistent. A promising culturally tailored suicide intervention program was implemented by LaFromboise and Howard-Pitney (1995) at the request of the Zuni Tribal High School. The participants were involved in either an intervention or a no-intervention condition. Scores on a suicide probability measure indicated that 81% of the students were in the moderate to severe risk ranges. Of the participants, 18% reported having attempted suicide, and 40% reported knowing of a relative or friend who had committed suicide. The program involved the development of suicide intervention skills through role-playing. Other components included self-esteem building, identifying emotions and stress, recognizing and eliminating negative thoughts or emotions, receiving information on suicide and intervention strategies, and setting personal and community goals. The program was effective in reducing feelings of hopelessness and suicidal probability ratings. However, scores on depression did not change. In addition, the students in the intervention condition could behaviorally demonstrate problem-solving and suicide intervention strategies. Although the long-term effects of the program are not known, the approach seems promising in the prevention of suicide. Other programs for American Indians involve alcohol and drug abuse education as well as developing more effective communication with others (Middlebrook et al., 2001).

Alcohol and Substance Abuse

Substance abuse is one of the greatest problems faced by American Indians. They are six times more likely to die of alcohol-related causes than the general U.S. population (Frank et al., 2000). In Indian Health Service hospitals approximately 21% of hospitalizations are for alcohol-related problems (*Morbidity and Mortality Weekly Report,* 1994). In Alaska, 32% of American Indians/ Alaskan Natives of childbearing age reported heavy drinking, which is responsible for the disproportionately high percentage of cases of fetal alcohol syndrome reported in this population (*Morbidity and Mortality Weekly Report,* 1994). In addition, drug abuse and dependence are very high among young Indian clients. However, it must be remembered that many American Indians/Alaskan Natives do not drink or only drink moderately. Abstinence is high among certain tribes such as the Navajo (Myers, Kagawa-Singer, Kumanyika, Lex, & Markides, 1995).

A variety of explanations have been put forth to indicate possible reasons for the rise in alcohol abuse (see Figure 12.1). Substance abuse is often related to low self-esteem, cultural identity conflicts, lack of positive role models, abuse history, social pressure to use substances, hopelessness about life, and a breakdown in the family (Swinomish Tribal Mental Health Project, 1991; Yee et al., 1995). The use of illicit substances is related to the 50% dropout rate from school by American Indian youth (Beauvais, Chavez, Oetting, Deffenbacher, & Cornell, 1996). Heavy alcohol use is associated with both low general self-efficacy and feelings of powerlessness in life (Taylor, 2000). Drinking alcoholic beverages may initially have been incorporated into cultural practices as an activity of sharing, giving, and togetherness (Swinomish Tribal Mental Health Project, 1991). Turning down an offered drink is considered to be an act of individual autonomy and that is disruptive to group harmony. Other explanations have focused on (a) the release of feelings of frustration and boredom, allowing Indians to express emotions that are normally under control; (b) drinking of alcohol as a social event; and (c) the acceptance of drinking in many tribal groups (M. J. Anderson & Ellis, 1995). Manson, Tatum, and Dinges (1982) indicated that among many American Indians drinking is an accepted practice and is encouraged among family members. Parents are often heavy drinkers and allow their children to drink. Manson and his colleagues felt that a major etiologic component of childhood abuse of alcohol is the Indian respect for autonomy and permissiveness, which then allows a child to determine how much alcohol to consume.

Figure 12.1

Strands in the Web of Alcohol Abuse

Source: From *A Gathering of Wisdoms*, Swimonish Tribal Mental Health Project, 1991. Reprinted by permission.

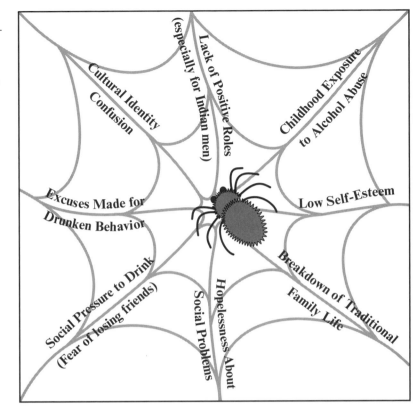

Implications. Successful residential drug treatment programs have incorporated appropriate cultural elements. If alcohol use has been incorporated into tribal or family customs or traditions, the problem would have to be addressed at both the systems and the individual level. Because of the history of conflicts between tribal and state and federal agencies, one must be careful not to be seen as imposing "White solutions" to problems on the reservation. One tribal community reduced the alcoholism rate from 95% to 5% in 10 years by creating a community culture in which alcoholism was not tolerated while revitalizing traditional culture (Thomason, 2000). Work within the resources of the tribes. Many have developed programs to deal with alcohol and substance abuse issues. Gutierres and Todd (1997) found that including the use of a sweat lodge and a talking circle with American Indian substance abuse increased successful treatment completion. Schinke et al. (1985) proposed that prevention and treatment of substance abuse are best accomplished in groups of Indian youth, preferably led by Indian social workers, teachers, or school counselors. The process involves six steps. The first provides the students with accurate information on drugs and alcohol. Respected elders and older youth might be invited to talk about some of the dangers of drug use. Suggestions can be made that natural highs can be reached by spirit dancing, singing, and dancing. Second, problem-solving skills in rejecting alcohol are developed. Schinke and his colleagues gave an example of a teenager who shared a six-pack of beer with friends during the school lunch hour. He did not like feeling sleepy in class after consuming the beer. He was asked to brainstorm solutions. Suggestions that he came up were that he could drink only a little, pretend to drink, stay in class during the lunch break, pretend that he had a stomachache, or not drink at all. He chose the last solution but decided to stand beside his cousin, who would not pressure him to drink. The development of alternative responses can be very helpful in reducing the chances of abuse. The third step would be to develop a cognitive rehearsal strategy. Coping statements can be thought of, expressed subvocally, and then said aloud. The individual thinks of what he or she can say to refuse to participate and then rehearses it aloud. The fourth step involves behavioral rehearsal with coaching and reinforcement. For example, a student might be told to consider a situation such as, "A friend of yours wants you to smoke pot with her. How would you indicate that you do not wish to do so?" In this situation another American Indian student supports and reinforces the student who is practicing refusal skills. The fifth step involves establishing a positive social network. Family and friends who will support not drinking are identified and brought into the social network. Involvement in alternative activities such as dance, intertribal sports, and clan activities is encouraged. Pairs and groups of individuals are formed to assist one another in rejecting the use of alcohol and other drugs in the last step.

Guidelines for Clinical Practice

1. Before working with American Indians, explore ethnic differences and values. It is important to be aware of our own cultural biases and how they might hinder the counseling relationship and the development of appropriate goals.

2. Determine the cultural identity of the client and family members and their association with a tribe or a reservation. Many American Indians adhere completely to mainstream values; others, especially those on or near reservations, are more likely to hold to traditional values.

3. Understand the history of oppression, and be aware of or inquire about local issues associated with the tribe or reservation for traditionally oriented American Indians. Many may be distrustful of agencies.

4. Begin with a client-centered listening style and gradually provide more

structure and questions. Try not to hurry the individual. Allow them time to finish statements and thoughts. Confrontation is considered rude and should be kept to a minimum.

5. Assess the problem from the perspective of the individual, family, extended family, and, if appropriate, the tribal community. Try to determine the cultural experiential aspects.

6. If necessary, address basic needs first, such as problems involving food, shelter, child care, and employment. Identify possible resources such as Indian Health Services or tribal programs.

7. Be careful not to overgeneralize, but evaluate for problems such as domestic violence, substance abuse, depression, and suicidality during assessment. In addition, determine the appropriateness of a mind-body-spirit emphasis.

8. Identify possible environmental contributors to problems such as racism, discrimination, poverty, and acculturation conflicts.

9. Help children and adolescents determine whether cultural values or an unreceptive environment contribute to their problem. Strategize different ways of dealing with the conflicts.

10. Help determine concrete goals that incorporate cultural, family, extended family, and community perspectives.

11. Remember that in American Indian families, there is a great deal of independence in the behavior of members. Families typically are not hierarchical, and children are afforded a great deal of freedom. Determine whether child-rearing practices are consistent with traditional Indian methods and how they may conflict with mainstream methods.

12. In family interventions, identify extended family members, determine their roles, and request their assistance.

13. Be prepared to work at the systems level to produce change if the school, community, or workplace contributes to the presenting problem.

14. Generate possible solutions with the clients and consider their consequences from the individual, family, and community perspectives. Include strategies that may involve cultural elements and that focus on holistic factors (mind, body, spirit).

15. Recognize that culturally modified brief interventions based on cognitive-behavioral psychology can be useful. Identify helpful cognitions, ceremonies, and traditions utilized by the tribe or family.

16. Evaluate the intervention from the perspective of the individual, family, and community.

Counseling Asian Americans

A 16-year old immigrant girl writes, "I know my parents had come to this country to provide a better environment for my education. . . . They sacrificed a lot for me. . . . That's why I must do an excellent job in school. . . . I do not want to let my parents down. (Ying, Coombs, & Lee, 1999, p. 350)

Eric Liu, the son of immigrants from Taiwan, graduated from Yale and had written speeches for President Clinton and doesn't feel like an "Asian American." He believes the identity is contrived and unnecessary. (Chang, 1998)

A recent poll found that approximately 25% of Americans hold very strong negative stereotypes of Chinese Americans. Henry S. Tang, whose organization sponsored the poll, responded to the findings by stating, "What these numbers do is force us into a realization that we're always having to earn our recognition over and over again." (Richardson & MacGregor, 2001, p. E1)

The Asian American population is growing rapidly and is currently 10,242,988. An additional 1,655,840 checked Asian and one other ethnic group (U.S. Department of Commerce, 2001). The large increase is due to the changes in immigration laws that occurred in 1965 and to the entry of over 1.5 million Southeast Asian refugees since 1975 (Chung, Bemak, & Okazaki, 1997). With the relaxation of immigration laws, the population of Asian Americans increased fivefold from 1973 to 1993. The immigration pattern has changed the characteristics of the Asian American population. The majority of Asian Americans are foreign born (nearly two thirds of Filipinos and Chinese and three fourths of Asian Indians, Koreans, and Southeast Asians; Hing, 1993; Population Reference Bureau, 1998). In fact, with the exception of Japanese Americans, Asian American populations are now principally composed of foreign-born individuals.

Between-group differences within the Asian American population may be quite large, since the population is composed of at least 40 distinct subgroups that differ in language, religion, and values (Sandhu, 1997). They include the larger Asian groups in the United States (Chinese, Filipinos, Koreans, Asian Indians, and Japanese), refugees and immigrants from Southeast Asia (Vietnamese, Laotians, Cambodians, and Hmongs), and Pacific Islanders (Hawaiians, Guamanians, and Samoans). Compounding the difficulty in making any generalization about the Asian American population are within-group differences. Individuals diverge on variables such as migration or relocation experiences, degree of assimilation or acculturation, identification with the home country, facility in their native languages and in English, family composition and intactness, amount of education, and degree of adherence to religious beliefs.

Asian Americans: A Success Story?

In contrast to that for many Third World groups, the contemporary image of Asian Americans is that of a highly successful minority that has "made it" in society (Yin, 2000). For example, the belief that Asian Americans represent a "model" minority has been played up by the popular press in such headlines as "Asian! To America with Skills" (Doerner, 1985) and "The Oriental Express" (McLeod, 1986). Indeed, a close analysis of census figures (Population Reference Bureau, 1998) seems to support this contention. In 1997, of those individuals over 25, 42% of Asians/Pacific Islanders had at least a bachelor's degree versus 26% by their White counterparts. Approximately 10% of all students at Harvard, 22% of those at Berkeley, and 19% of those at MIT are Asian Americans (Sandhu, 1997). Words such as "intelligent," "hardworking," "enterprising," and "disciplined" are frequently applied to this population (Morrissey, 1997).

A closer analysis of the status of Asian Americans reveals disturbing truths that contrast with popular views of their success story. First, in terms of economics, references to the higher median income of Asian Americans do not take into account (a) the higher percentage of Asian American families having more than one wage earner, (b) a higher prevalence of poverty despite the higher median income (14% vs. 8% for the U.S. population), and (c) the discrepancy between education and income. The poverty rate of certain Southeast Asian groups is in fact five times higher than that of the general population. Due to a lack of job skills or English proficiency, Southeast Asians are three times more likely to be on welfare than is the general population (Sandhu, 1997).

Second, in the area of education, Asian Americans show a disparate picture of extraordinary high educational attainment and a large undereducated mass. Among the Hmong, only 31% have completed high school, and fewer than 6% of Tongans, Cambodians, Laotians, and Hmongs 25 years and older have a bachelor's degree (U.S. Bureau of the Census, 1995). When averaged out, this bimodal distribution indicates how misleading statistics can be.

Third, there is now widespread recognition that, apart from being tourist attractions, Chinatowns, Manilatowns, and Japantowns in San Francisco and New York represent ghetto areas with prevalent unemployment, poverty, health problems, and juvenile delinquency. People outside these communities seldom see the deplorable social conditions that exist behind the bright neon lights, restaurants, and quaint shops. Over one third of the residents in these areas complain of depression and emotional tension (S. Sue, Sue, Sue, & Takeuchi, 1995). Mass murders committed over the years have been traced to Chinese juvenile gangs operating in Chinatowns, and recent news reports show this trend to be on the increase.

Fourth, although Asian Americans underutilize mental health services, it is not clear if this is due to low rates of socioemotional adjustment difficulties, discriminatory mental health practices, or cultural values inhibiting self-referral. It is possible that much of the mental illness, the adjustment problems, and the juvenile delinquency among Asians is hidden. The discrepancy between official and real rates may be due to cultural factors such as the shame and disgrace associated with admitting to emotional problems, the handling of problems within the family rather than relying on outside resources, and the manner of symptom formation, such as a low prevalence of acting-out disorders. Many Southeast Asian refugees show psychiatric symptoms associated with past traumas and current resettlement problems. Very high levels of Posttraumatic Stress Disorder (PTSD) and major depression have been discovered in this population (S. Sue et al., 1995).

Fifth, Asian Americans have been exposed to discrimination and racism throughout history and continue to face anti-Asian sentiments. In 1995, the number of hate crimes against Asian Americans rose with assaults increasing by 11% and aggravated assaults by 14% (Matthee, 1997). Although some are fourth- and fifth-generation Americans, many are still identified as "foreign" and are regarded with suspicion. In a survey of a representative sample of 1,216 adults to determine their attitudes toward Asian Americans, several disturbing findings were reported (Committee of 100, 2001). About one fourth of the respondents reported that they would be "uncomfortable" having an Asian American as president of the United States versus 15% if the individual was African American or 14% if it were a woman. Nearly one third indicated that Chinese Americans would be more loyal to China than the United States, and nearly half of all the people surveyed believed that Chinese Americans would pass secret information to China. About a quarter of the sample would disapprove if someone in their family married an Asian American, and 17% would be upset if a "substantial" number of Asian Americans moved into their neighborhoods. As Henry Tang, chairman of the Committee of 100, noted, "What these numbers do is to force us into a realization that we're always having to earn our recognition over and over again. . . . No matter how educated we are, or how well we do, it doesn't matter" (Richardson & MacGregor, 2001, E1).

It is important for counselors, academic advisors, and educators who work with Asian Americans to look behind the success myth and to understand the historical and current experiences of Asians in America. The matter is even more pressing for counselors when we realize that Asian Americans underutilize counseling and other mental health facilities and are more likely to seek help at a counseling service rather than at a psychiatric facility. The approach of this chapter is twofold. First, we attempt to indicate how the interplay of social and cultural forces have served to shape and define the lifestyle of recent immigrants/refugees and American-born Asians. Second, we explore how an understanding of Asian American values and social experiences necessitate the need for modifications in counseling and psychotherapeutic practices in working with this population.

Traditional Asian Cultural Values, Behavior Patterns, and Implications for Therapy

In the following section we present some of the cultural values, behavioral characteristics, and expectations about therapy of Asian Americans as well as their implications for counseling. Much of the following consists of group generalizations whose accuracy must be determined for each individual client or family and which are not to be applied in a stereotypic manner. Although cultural knowledge is important in helping the counselor identify potential conflict areas, one must be careful not to apply cultural information rigidly. It must be remembered that within- and between-group differences are quite large: Some individuals and families are quite acculturated, and others retain a more traditional cultural orientation. Cultural differences, such as the degree of assimilation, socioeconomic background, family experiences, and educational level, impact each individual in a unique manner. Knowledge of cultural values can help generate hypotheses about the way an Asian might view a disorder and his or her expectations of treatment. It must also be remembered that values and behavior patterns evolve and change over time. The therapist's task is to help the clients identify or develop a variety of ways of dealing with problems within cultural constraints and to develop the skills to negotiate cultural differences with the larger society.

Collectivistic Orientation

I was born and raised in Korea and came to the United States in 1968. . . . I must move back to Seoul to take care of my aging mother. I am a man of Asian values (filial piety), and they {his children} are young college graduates of American values (career advancement and development). (Choi, 1999, p. 7)

Instead of promoting individual needs and personal identity, Asian families tend to have a family and group orientation. Children are expected to strive for family goals and not to engage in behaviors that would bring dishonor to the family. Asian American adolescents appear to retain the expectation to assist, support, and respect their family even when exposed to a society that emphasizes adolescent autonomy and independence (Fuligni et al., 1999). While Euro-American parents rated being "self-directed" as the most important attribute in children's social competence, Japanese American parents chose "behaves well" (O'Reilly, Tokuno, Ebata, 1986). Chinese American parents also believe that politeness and calmness were more important to inculcate in their children than did Euro-American parents (Jose, Huntsinger, Huntsinger, & Liaw, 2000). Asian American families differ in the degree in which they place individual needs over family needs. In the case just given, Choi (1999) has accepted the fact that his adult children will not stay with his wife (their mother) while he is in Korea to take care of his mother. He decries American society, in which individualism prevails over collectivism. However, he acknowledges that his children have honored the family by being successful. He understands that they define family obligations in a different manner.

Implications. Because of a possible collectivistic orientation, it is important to consider the family and community context during assessment and problem definition. After doing an individual analysis, you might also ask questions such as, "How does your family see the problem?" For traditionally oriented Asian Americans, a focus on individual client needs and wishes may run counter to the value of collectivism. Determining whether the client is aware of conflicting expectations is also important. Goals and treatment approaches may have to include a family focus (e.g., "How important are considerations of your family in deciding how to deal with the problem?" and "How would achieving the different goals affect you, your family, friends, and social community?"). Questions such as these allow the therapist to assess the degree of collectivism in the client. Acculturated Asian Americans with an individualistic orientation can often benefit from traditional counseling approaches, but the family should still be assessed since conflicts due to acculturation differences are common.

Hierarchical Relationships

Traditional Asian American families tend to be hierarchical and patriarchal in structure, with males and older individuals occupying a higher status. Communication flows down from the parent to the child, who is expected to defer to the adults. The sons are expected to carry on the family name and tradition. Even when they are married, their primary allegiance is to the parents. In general, the mother serves to mediate communication within the family. Second-generation Chinese American high school students place a higher priority on filial piety and obedience to their parents and authorities than do their Euro-American counterparts (Feldman & Rosenthal, 1990). Third-generation Japanese Americans still feel the pressure of parental obligations (Ina, 1997). Between-group differences do exist. Among Asian American groups, Japanese Americans are the most acculturated. The majority are third- to fourth-generation Americans. Filipino American families tend to be more egalitarian, while Korean, Southeast Asian, and Chinese American families tend to be more patriarchal and traditional in orientation (Blair & Qian, 1998).

Implications. In family therapy it is important to determine the family structure and communication pattern. It is generally most productive to address the father first and then the mother. If English is a problem, use an interpreter with the parents. Having children interpret for the parents can be counterproductive because it upsets the hierarchical structure. For very traditionally oriented families, having communication from members directed to the therapist is more congruent with cultural values than having the family members address one another. It is also important to assess for status change within the family. It is not uncommon among Asian immigrants for women to retain their occupational status while men are either underemployed or unemployed. A loss of male status may result in family conflict. The father may become even more authoritarian to maintain his status. In such cases, it is helpful to cast societal factors as the "identified patient."

Parenting Styles

> *When she does something wrong, I think, something like misbehavior, something not good, I will sit down first, think about how to solve this problem. If I have difficulty, I will consult an expert on how to solve this problem. (Kass, 1998, p. 3)*
>
> *Hou-Lin Li and his wife, Luying Deng, had completed a parent education course after being accused of slapping their 8-year-old daughter for lying and forging their signature on a disciplinary note from a teacher. For this, the state prosecutor, Richard Devine, charged the parents with child abuse and threatened them with deportation back to China. (Kass, 1998)*

Asian American parenting style tends to be more authoritarian and directive than in Euro-American families, although a relaxed style is used with children younger than the age of 6 or 7 (Jose et al., 2000; Meston, Heiman, Trapnell, & Carlin, 1999). Problem behavior in children is thought to be due to a lack of discipline. In one sample of undergraduates, Asian American students reported a somewhat higher level of physical and emotional punishment from their parents than did their Euro-American counterparts (Meston et al., 1999). However, differences in parenting style between Asian American groups have been found. Japanese and Filipino American families tend to have the most egalitarian relationships, while Korean, Chinese, and Southeast Asian Americans are more authoritarian (Blair & Qian, 1998).

Implications. Egalitarian or Western-style parent effectiveness training strategies may run counter to traditional rearing patterns. Traditional Asian American families may feel that their parenting skills are being criticized when exposed to Western techniques or styles. Instead of attempting to establish egalitarian relationships, there can be a focus on identifying different aspects of parenting. Rather than just punishment, Asian parenting styles typically include caretaking, teaching, modeling, and playing. The therapist can help refocus parenting to utilize the more positive aspects of Asian child-rearing strategies. These would be couched in terms of helping the children with problems rather than altering poor parenting. It is also important to commiserate with parents in terms of raising children in a society with different cultural standards.

Emotionality

Strong emotional displays, especially in public, are considered to be signs of immaturity or a lack of control. In many Asian families there is generally less open display of emotions, especially to older children. Care and concern are shown by attending to the physical needs of family members. The father maintains an authoritative and distant role and is generally not emotionally demonstrative or involved with his children. His role is to provide for the economic and physical needs of the family. Shame and guilt are used to control and train the children. Mothers are more responsive to the children but use less nurturance and more verbal and physical punishments than do Euro-American mothers (Kelly & Tseng, 1992). However, mothers are expected to meet the emotional needs of the children and often serve as the intermediary between the father and the children. When the children are exposed to more open displays of emotions from Western society, they may begin to question the comparative unemotionality of their parents. Chang-Rae Lee (1995, p. 58), in a novel, describes his father as "unencumbered by the needling questions of existence and self-consciousness. . . . I wasn't sure he had the capacity to love."

Implications. Counseling microskills that focus directly on emotions may be uncomfortable and produce shame for traditional Asian Americans. Emotional behavior can be recognized in a more indirect manner. For example, if an individual shows discomfort, the therapist could respond by saying either "You look uncomfortable" or "This situation would make someone uncomfortable." In both cases the discomfort would be recognized, but we have found that Asian American students are more responsive to the second, more indirect acknowledgment of emotions. C.-R. Lee's (1995) reaction to his father's lack of emotional responsiveness could lead to a discussion of value conflicts and how to deal with them instead of blame. It is also helpful to focus more on behaviors than emotions and identify how family members are meeting each other's needs. In one study (Juang & Tucker, 1991), care and concern between an Asian couple were shown more by taking care of the physical needs of the partner than by expressing care verbally. Western marital therapy, which emphasizes verbal and emotional expressiveness as the main goal, may not be adequate in dealing with some Asian couples or families.

Holistic View on Mind and Body

A female client complained about all kinds of physical problems such as dizziness, loss of appetite, an inability to complete household chores, and insomnia. She asked the therapist if her problem could be due to "nerves." The therapist suspected depression since these are some of the physical manifestations of the disorder and asked the client if she felt depressed and sad. At this point, the client paused and looked confused. She finally stated that she feels very ill and that these physical problems are making her sad. Her perspective is that it was natural for her to feel sad when sick. As the therapist followed up by attempting to determine if there was a family history of depression, the client displayed even more discomfort and defensiveness. Although the client never directly contradicted the therapist, she did not return for the following session. (Tsui & Schultz, 1985)

Because the mind and body are considered inseparable, Asian Americans may present emotional difficulties through somatic complaints. Physical complaints are a common and culturally accepted means of expressing psychological and emotional stress. It is believed that physical problems cause emotional disturbances and that these will disappear as soon as there is appropriate treatment of the physical illness. Instead of talking about anxiety and depression, the mental health professional will often hear complaints involving headaches, fatigue, restlessness, and disturbances in sleep and appetite (D. Sue, 1997; Toarmino & Chun, 1997). Even psychotic patients typically made somatic complaints and sought treatment for those physical ailments (S. D. Nguyen, 1985).

Implications. Treat somatic complaints as real problems. Inquire about medications or other physical treatments they may use. To determine if psychological factors are also involved, inquire in the following manner: "Dealing with headaches and dizziness can be quite troublesome; how are these affecting your mood, relationships, etc.?" This approach legitimizes the physical complaints but allows an indirect way to assess psychosocial factors. Develop an approach that would deal both with somatic complaints and with the consequences of being "ill."

Academic and Occupational Goals

I want to write. I have to write. . . . This is not the choice my parents would make, and surely not the choice they would wish me to make. . . . I must not let it deter my progress or shut down my dreams, my purpose. (Ying et al., 1999, p. 357)

There is great pressure for children to succeed academically and to have a successful career since both would be indicative of a good family upbringing. As a group, Asian Americans perform better academically than do their Euro-American counterparts. Although Asian American students have high levels of academic achievement, they also have more fear of academic failure compared to their Euro-American peers. They spend twice as much time each week on academics as their non-Asian counterparts do (Eaton & Dembo, 1997). However, this is often accompanied with a price. Asian American adolescents report feeling isolated, depressed, and anxious and reported little praise for the accomplishments from their parents (Lorenzo, Pakiz, Reinherz, & Frost, 1995). Asian American parents often have specific career goals in mind for their children (generally in technical fields or the hard sciences). Deviations from either academic excellence or "appropriate" career choices can produce conflict among family members.

Implications. Have parents recognize other positive behaviors and contributions made by their children, not just academic performance. Some may not do well academically. Indicate that there are many ways that parents can feel proud of their children. For career or occupational conflicts, acknowledge that the parents are seeking success for their children but that there are many new career options. Give them information about areas other than technical fields. For individual clients, discuss the conflict between academic goals defined by the parents and individual desires. Present this as a culture conflict issue and identify the best way of presenting the child's side to the parents.

Racism and Prejudice

Asian Americans continue to face issues of racism and discrimination. Very negative stereotypes of this group are still held by a large number of American adults. Asian Americans report significantly more workplace discrimination than Caucasian counterparts (M. P. Bell, Harrison, & McLaughlin, 1997), and Southeast Asian refugees who experienced racial discrimination reported high rates of depression (Noh, Beiser, Kaspar, Hou, & Rummens, 1999).

Implications. A therapist must assess the effects of possible environmental factors such as racism on mental health issues in Asian Americans. A client should not internalize an issue that is based on discriminatory practices. Instead, the focus should be on how to deal with racism and on possible efforts to change the environment. If a problem occurs in school, the therapist should determine the receptivity of the Asian American's peers and the school's academic and social environment to this ethnic group. The same would be done with the place of employment. Intervention may have to occur at a systems level, and the therapist may have to be an advocate for the client.

Acculturation Conflicts between Parents and Children

> *Children with Asian parents encounter a unique challenge because they must deal with cultural differences. Children are raised with two conflicting viewpoints—an American culture that calls for active parental involvement, and a home life that demands individual and community responsibility. (Ulep & Ulep, 2001, p. 1)*

Children of Asian descent who are exposed to different cultural standards often attribute psychological distress to their parent's backgrounds and different values. The issue of not quite fitting in with their peers and being considered "too Americanized" by their parents is common. The inability to resolve differences in acculturation results in misunderstandings, miscommunication, and conflict (R. M. Lee, Choe, Kim, & Ngo, 2000). Parents may feel at loss in terms of how to deal with their children. Some respond by becoming more rigid. One Asian Indian daughter described her parents as displaying a "museumization of practices." On a trip to India, she discovered that there was a wide difference between the parents' version of "Indian" and what Indians in India actually did. Her parents' version was much more restrictive (Das Gupta, 1997).

Implications. To prevent interpersonal exchanges between parents and their children, the problem should be reframed or conceptualized as acculturation conflicts. In this way both the parents and the children can discuss cultural standards and the expectations from larger society.

Identity Issues

As Asians become progressively more exposed to the standards, norms, and values of the wider society, increasing assimilation and acculturation are frequently the result. Bombarded on all sides by peers, schools, and the mass media, which uphold Western standards as better than their own, Asian Americans are frequently placed in situations of extreme culture conflict that may lead to much pain and agony regarding behavioral and physical differences. Asian American college women report lower self-esteem and less satisfaction with their racially defined features than do their Caucasian counterparts (Mintz & Kashubeck, 1999). C.-R. Lee (1995) described his experiences as "straddling two worlds and at home in neither." He felt alienated from both American and Korean cultures. As with other adolescents, those of Asian American descent also struggle with the question of "Who am I?" Individuals undergoing acculturation conflicts may respond in the following manner (Huang, 1994):

1. *Assimilation.* Seeks to become part of the dominant society to the exclusion of his or her own cultural group
2. *Separation.* Identifies exclusively with the Asian culture
3. *Integration/biculturalism.* Retains many Asian values but adapts to the dominant culture by learning necessary skills and values
4. *Marginalization.* Perceives one's own culture as negative but is unable to adapt to majority culture

Implications. Identity issues are a problem for some Asian Americans and not for others. Some believe that ethnic identity is not salient or important. Assessing the ethnic identity of clients is important because it can impact problem definition and the choice of techniques used in therapy. Assimilated Asian clients are generally receptive to Western styles of counseling and may not want reminders of their ethnicity. (S. J. Lee, 1994, described a group of students called "New Wavers" who rejected Asian values and instead cut classes to be "more American" or "more cool.") Traditionally identified Asians are more likely to be recent immigrants or refugees, and they tend to retain strong cultural values and be more responsive to culturally adapted counseling approach. Bicultural Asian Americans adhere to some traditional values but have also incorporated many Western ones.

Special Problems of Refugees and Immigrants

Mrs. N. is a 48-year-old Vietnamese woman who sought help at a mental health clinic for depression and frequent nightmares of atrocities and the death of her husband. She and her two daughters fled Vietnam in 1982. During the escape, one of her daughters died. She spent two and a half years in a refugee camp in Thailand before relocating to the United States.

Although Mrs. N.'s daughter is now a teenager and appears to have adjusted well, Mrs. N. continues to suffer from suicidal thoughts and disturbed memories involving her husband and dead daughter. She has a few Vietnamese women friends and works as a janitor. Her "only reason for living" appears to be to take care of her remaining daughter. (Chung et al., 1997)

Some 1.5 million refugees from Southeast Asia have arrived in the United States since 1975. The majority are Vietnamese, Cambodian or Khmer, and Laotian (Chung et al., 1997). In general, refugees are under more stress than immigrants. As Bemak, Chung, and Bornemann (1996) pointed out, immigrants are individuals who have had time to prepare their move to the United States. However, refugees are often not in control of their own fates. For example, the vast majority of Vietnamese, who left just before the fall of Saigon in 1975, had only a few days to decide whether to leave their country. Refugees often had to wait in camps for years before immigrating to countries such as the United States, Australia, and France. Many Cambodians have experienced death by starvation in their immediate family or conflict with the Vietcong since they had worked with the Central Intelligence Agency (L.-R. L. Cheung, 1987). Over 92% of the Hmong have stress-related illnesses. In fact, 75% are unemployed, and 86% indicate that they would return to Laos if possible (Smalley, 1984). Refugees and immigrants face culture shock when exposed to Western society. Many report feelings of homesickness and concerns over the breakup of family and community ties. There are often worries about the future, difficulties communicating in English, and unemployment. Refugees and their family members have high rates of PTSD and depression (Chun, Eastman, Wang, & Sue, 1998).

Implications. Assessment of the previous country experiences, possible trauma, and difficulties in adjustment of these individuals are important. The therapist may have to help refugee or immigrant clients with the necessities of life, such as contacts with agencies that can provide food, shelter, health care, and employment. Many refugees have few social contacts. In the case of Mrs. N., it would be important to help her establish contact with other Vietnamese immigrants or refugees. A sense of family needs to be reestablished. Many communities have programs for refugees and immigrants that offer resources such as the Asian Counseling and Referral Service in Seattle, Washington.

Shame

In Asian American groups, public discussion of family problems is considered to be a source of embarrassment and an indication of the family's failure.

Implications. Discuss issues regarding confidentiality. Since problem behaviors are seen as a source of shame for the entire family, knowing that the information obtained will be confidential will offer some relief. Acknowledge the difficulty involved in sharing private information but indicate that it is a necessary process to develop solutions. To determine the possibility that cultural constraints exist, the counselor might also state something like the following: "Sometimes people in counseling believe that family issues should stay in the family. How do you feel about this belief?" Concerns over feelings of betrayal or shame need to be addressed before counseling can begin. When possible, "normalize" the presenting problem by indicating that it is not an unusual individual or family issue or externalize it by casting it as an acculturation issue. If family conflicts are apparent, the counselor could say, "Parents and their offspring often differ in terms of expectations. This could be due to generational or value differences. In counseling we try to come up with solutions to these common but difficult issues." It is important not to minimize the problem but to offer hope for change.

Psychotherapy Is a Foreign Concept to Many Asian Americans

Explain the nature of the counseling and therapy process and the necessity of obtaining information.

Implications. Describe the client's role. Indicate that the problems may be individual, relational, environmental, or a combination of these and that you will perform an assessment of each of these areas. Introduce the concept of *coconstruction*—that the problem and solutions are developed with the help of the client and the counselor. Coconstruction reduces the chance that the therapist will impose his or her theoretical framework on the client. For example, the therapist might explain, "In counseling we try to understand the problem as it affects you, your family, friends, and community, so I will ask you questions about these different areas. With your help we will also consider possible solutions that you can try out."

Expectations of Counseling

Counselors often believe that they should adopt an authoritarian or highly directive stance with Asian American clients. What is actually expected by

Asian clients is an active role by the counselor in structuring the session and guidelines on the types of responses that they will be expected to make.

Implications. The counselor should be directive but ensure the full participation from the clients in developing goals and intervention strategies. Suggestions can be given and different options presented for consideration by the client. The client can select the option that he or she believes will be the most useful in dealing with the problem. Also encourage the client to develop his or her own solutions. The consequences for any action should also be considered, not only for the individual clients but also for the possible impact on the family and community. Even among acculturated Asian American college students, the preference for a helper role involves advice, consultation, and the facilitation of family and community support systems (Atkinson, Kim, & Caldwell, 1998). The opportunity for Asian American clients to try interventions on their own promotes the cultural value of self-sufficiency.

Counseling Interventions

Asian American clients expect concrete goals and strategies focused on solutions. Mental health professionals must be careful not to impose techniques or strategies.

Implications. Focus on the specific problem brought in by the client, and help the client develop his or her goals for therapy. This allows the client to present his or her concerns and reduces the chance that the therapist's worldview will be imposed on the client. Determine what needs to be done if cultural or family issues are involved. Therapy should be time limited, focus on concrete resolution of problems, and deal with the present or immediate future. Cognitive-behavioral and other solution-focused strategies are useful in working with Asian Americans. However, as with other Eurocentric approaches, these approaches need to be altered because the focus is on the individual, whereas the unit of treatment for Asian Americans may actually be the family, community, or society. Modify cognitive-behavioral approaches to incorporate a collectivistic rather than an individualistic perspective. For example, assertiveness training can be altered for Asian clients who have difficulty in asserting themselves. First, consider possible cultural and social factors that may affect assertiveness (values placed on modesty, minority status, etc.). Then identify situations where assertiveness might be functional, such as in class or seeking employment, and ones where a traditional cultural style might be more appropriate (with elders or parents). Next, determine anxiety-producing cognitions and possible cultural or societal influences. Finally, substitute appropriate thoughts and employ role-playing to increase assertiveness in specific situations. This alteration of a cognitive-behavioral approach takes cultural factors into consideration and is concrete, allowing clients to establish self-control.

Family Therapy

Although family therapy would seem to be the ideal medium in which to deal with problems for Asian Americans, certain difficulties exist. Most therapy models are based on Euro-American perspectives of egalitarian relationships and require verbal and emotional expressiveness. Some models assume that a problem in a family member is reflective of dysfunction among family members. In addition, the use of direct communication from child to parents, confrontational strategies, and nonverbal techniques such as "sculpting" may be an affront to the parents.

Implications. Assess the structure of the Asian American family. Is it hierarchical or more egalitarian? What is their perception of "healthy" family functioning? How are decisions made in the family? How are family members showing respect and contributing to the family? Focus on the positive aspects of the family and reframe conflicts to reduce confrontation. Expand systems theory to include societal factors such as prejudice, discrimination, poverty, and conflicting cultural values. Issues revolving around the pressures of being an Asian American family in this society need to be investigated. Describe the session as a solution-oriented one and explain that family problems are not uncommon. Have communication from family members come through the therapist. Function as a culture-broker in helping the family negotiate conflicts with the larger society.

Guidelines for Clinical Practice

In working with Asian Americans and other diverse groups, the goal is to help clients achieve the ability to "formulate plans, act on many possibilities existing in a culture, and reflect on these actions" (Ivey et al., 1997, p. 15). Although Asian culture dictates general principles and values, there is a range of responses in dealing with situations. Helping Asian American clients formulate different culturally acceptable practices for specific problems can improve their problem-solving abilities. In addition, they can evaluate the effectiveness of their approach. Asian Americans also must develop skills to interact with the larger society and to achieve a balance when conflicting values are involved. The following guidelines are based on Asian American cultural values, but the therapist or counselor must be aware of the large differences in degree of acculturation in this population. Many of the counseling skills learned in traditional programs will be effective with modifications.

1. Be aware of cultural differences between the therapist and the client as regarding counseling, appropriate goals, and process. How would they affect work with Asian Americans who have a collectivistic, hierarchical, and patriarchal orientation?

2. Build rapport by discussing confidentiality and explaining the client role and the need to coconstruct the problem definition and solutions.

3. Assess not just from an individual perspective but include family, community, and societal influences on the problem. Obtain the worldview and ethnic identity of the Asian American client.

4. Conduct a positive assets search. What strengths, skills, problem-solving abilities, and social supports are available to the individual or family?

5. Consider or reframe the problem when possible as one in which issues of culture conflict or acculturation are involved.

6. Determine whether somatic complaints are involved and assess their influence on mood and relationships.

7. Take an active role but allow Asian Americans to choose and evaluate suggested interventions.

8. Use problem-focused, time-limited approaches that have been modified to incorporate possible cultural factors.

9. With family therapy, the therapist should be aware that western based theories and techniques may not be appropriate for Asian families. Determine the structure and communication pattern among the members. It may be helpful to address the father first and to initially have statements by family members directed to the therapist. Focus on positive aspects of parenting such as modeling and teaching. Use a solution-focused model.

10. In couples counseling, assess for societal or acculturation conflicts. Determine the way that caring, support or affection is shown. Among traditional Asians, providing for the needs of the other is as or more important than verbalizations of affection. Obtain their perspective on the goals for better functioning.

11. With Asian children and adolescents, common problems involve acculturation conflicts with parents, feeling guilty or stressful over academic performance, negative self-image or identity issues, and struggle between interdependence and independence.

12. Among recent immigrants or refugees, assess for living situation, culture conflict and social or financial condition. Case management skills may be needed to obtain help in obtaining food and other community resources.

13. Consider the need to act as an advocate or engage in systems-level intervention in cases of institutional racism or discrimination.

Counseling Hispanic/Latino Americans

I can remember having to hide when I was a kid. . . . I would come home and my parents would be maybe 20 or 30 minutes late, and I would cry until they got home because I was afraid they had been deported. (Modie, 2001, A6)

It was sometimes hard to adjust. When I went outside, I was in America, but inside my house, it was Mexico. My father was the leader of the house. It wasn't that way for some of my American friends. (Middleton, Arrendondo, & D'Andrea, 2000, p. 24)

A thick scar below his right elbow reminds him of his first days in the fields, when he slipped and fell on some sharp farming tools. . . . Like many farm-worker children, Gonzales went to work to help his family pay the bills. He was a good student until he dropped out at age 15. He hasn't given up hope . . . but his family comes first. (Kramer, 1998, p. A6)

14
Chapter

In this chapter, the terms *Latino* and *Hispanic* encompass individuals living in the United States with ancestry from Mexico, Puerto Rico, Cuba, El Salvador, the Dominican Republic, and other Latin American countries. However, the terms are not accepted by all groups; some individuals prefer to be referred to as "Latinos" or "la raza" (the race). Even within specific subgroups, there are different opinions on the appropriate terms of identification. Some Hispanics from Mexico may refer to themselves as "Mexicano," "Mexican American," "Chicano," or "Spanish American" (Comas-Diaz, 2001; G. M. Gonzales, 1997). The designation "Chicano" often produces a mixed reception. It is used by some Mexican Americans to indicate racial pride and consciousness, but it is rejected by others, primarily older Mexican Americans, who consider it to be an insulting term that refers to uneducated, exploited farmhands. Even the term "Hispanic" is controversial because it does not indicate the influence of the indigenous cultures. However, the term will be employed in this chapter to indicate the common back-

343

ground of Spanish language and customs. Although Hispanics share many characteristics, there are distinct differences between and within the different groups.

In physical characteristics, the appearance of Hispanics varies greatly and may include resemblance to North American Indians, Blacks, Asians, or Latins and Europeans depending on their country of origin (Casas & Vasquez, 1996). Mexican Americans are mostly of Mestizo ancestry (mixed Spanish and native Aztec-Indian blood). In Mexico it is estimated that 55% are Mestizo, 29% are Indian, and 15% are of European background. Among Cuban Americans, most are of Spanish decent, and the rest are of Black or mixed ancestry. In Latin America, the immigration of African and Asian populations has resulted in a wide range of physical characteristics. Puerto Ricans generally are of Spanish descent, but influences from Indians and Blacks can also be seen.

According to the U.S. Census (U.S. Bureau of the Census, 2001), Hispanic Americans comprise a population of 35,305,818, of whom nearly 60% are of Mexican descent, 10% are from Puerto Rico (Puerto Rico became a commonwealth on July 25, 1952, and its residents are U.S. citizens who can move between the island and the mainland without any restrictions), 3.58% are Cuban, and the remaining 28% are primarily from Latin American countries. Because of the high birthrate and ongoing immigration patterns, Hispanics are currently the largest minority group in the United States. Hispanic Americans are a highly heterogeneous population with large between-group and within-group differences. Some individuals are oriented toward their ethnic group, while others are quite acculturated to mainstream values. Some have lived for generations within the United States, while a large proportion are recent immigrants (Moore, 2001). In addition, it is estimated that there are also about 7 million illegal Mexican immigrants living in the country. Being undocumented, they occupy the lowest rung of the labor pool and are often taken advantage of because they have no legal status. Almost half of the migrant farm workers are here illegally. The illegal immigrants rarely see doctors because of the cost and the fear of discovery of their status (*New York Times* News Service, 2001).

As a group, Hispanic Americans are a very young population; their average age is almost 9 years younger than that of White Americans. However, the median age of the subpopulations differ, ranging from the Cuban population (43.6 years) to the Mexican population (24.6 years). Because of their religious background as well as strong emphasis on large families and youth, nearly twice as many Hispanic households (54%) are composed of four or more people, compared to 28% for the country as a whole.

The majority of Hispanic Americans is situated in metropolitan areas of the United States, but Hispanic Americans populate every state, including Alaska and Hawaii. In certain states and cities, they make up a substantial percentage of the population. The population of Arizona is 16% Hispanic; of New Mexico, 36%; of Denver, Colorado, 19%; of Hartford, Connecticut, 20%; and of Miami, Florida, 64%. Mexican Americans reside primarily in the Southwest and Great Lakes regions and in various metropolitan areas throughout the United States. Cubans populate the Miami Beach area and other large cities in Florida. Puerto Ricans reside primarily in the large northeastern cities. In 1990 the majority of Mexican Americans lived in California; they made up about one fourth of the population of California and Texas. They number 619,000 in Arizona, 612,000 in Illinois, and 329,233 in New Mexico (G. M. Gonzalez, 1997).

Hispanics are overrepresented among the poor, have high unemployment, and often live in substandard housing. Most are blue-collar workers and hold semiskilled or unskilled occupations. There is a significant discrepancy between the annual incomes of Hispanics and Caucasians. In 1992 the median annual salary for a full-time Hispanic worker was $20,054 for males and $17,124 for females, compared to $31,765 for White males and $21,930 for White females. Nearly 40% of Hispanic children live in poverty, compared to 13.2% of White children (U.S. Bureau of the Census, 1995). Puerto Ricans appear to have the highest rate of poverty, while Cubans have the highest incomes. About half of the native Hispanic families in Southern California are middle-class, and two thirds of those in the United States live above the poverty line (Robinson, 1998).

Hispanic Americans have disproportionately high rates of tuberculosis, AIDS, and obesity. Nearly 40% of men and 48% of women are overweight, which increases the risk for developing diabetes and other physical conditions. Among Hispanic farm workers, infant mortality rates are reported as to be as high as 25%, and they are 50 times more likely than the general population to have parasitic infections (K. W. Johnson et al., 1995). Among Puerto Ricans, death rates for heart disease, pneumonia, asthma, liver disease, and homicide exceed those of other Hispanic groups (Flack et al., 1995). Asthma, especially in children, occurs at a higher than expected rate (Christiansen et al., 1996). Among recent immigrants and migrant workers, health information is often inaccurate or inadequate. In one sample of infected Hispanic immigrants enrolled in a county health department program, 50% did not know how tuberculosis is contracted (Ailinger, 1997). In one study, between one third to one half of female migrant workers surveyed believed that individuals could contract AIDS from mosquito bites, by using public restrooms, by kissing, and by being tested for AIDS (Organista, Organista, & Soloff, 1998). Thirty percent of Hispanic American children are not covered by health insurance as compared to 4% of Whites and 20% of African Americans. In addition, the highest rates of out-of-wedlock births occur in Hispanic Americans (Moore, 2001).

Traditional Hispanic Values, Characteristics, Behavior Patterns, and Implications for Therapy

In the following sections we consider the values, characteristics, and issues faced by Hispanic families and individuals and consider their implications in treatment. Remember that these are generalizations and their applicability needs to be assessed for particular Hispanic clients and families.

Family Values

Family tradition is an important aspect of life for Hispanic Americans. Family unity (*familismo*) is seen as very important, as are respect for and loyalty to the family. Cooperation rather than competition among family members is stressed. Interpersonal relationships are maintained and nurtured within a large network of family and friends. For the family, a critical element is to develop and maintain interpersonal relationships. There is deep respect and affection among friends and family. Hispanic American students are more likely to endorse the following items than are White students: loyalty to the family, strictness of child rearing, religiosity, and respect to adults (Negy, 1993). For many Hispanic Americans, the extended family includes not only relatives but often nonblood "relatives" such as the best man (*padrino*), maid of honor (*madrina*), and godparents (*compadre* and *comadre*). Each member of the family has a role: grandparents (wisdom), mother (abnegation), father (responsibility), children (obedience), and godparents (resourcefulness; P. Ruiz, 1995).

Implications. Because of these familial and social relationships, outside help is generally not sought until resources from the extended family and close friends are exhausted. Even in cases of severe mental illness, many Hispanic families waited two or more months before seeking treatment (Urdaneta, Saldana, & Winkler, 1995). Although there are many positive features of the extended family, emotional involvement and obligations with a large number of family and friends may function as additional sources of stress. Since family relationships are so important, decisions may be made that impact the individual negatively. Allegiance to the family is of primary importance, taking precedence over any outside concerns, such as school attendance or work (Avila & Avila, 1995). For example, older children may be kept at home in order to help care for ill siblings or parents. They may be absent from school to attend family functions (Hildebrand et al., 1996) or to meet a family financial obligation (Headden, 1997). Under these circumstances, not only must the problematic behavior issue be addressed, but it must also be characterized as a conflict between cultural and societal expectations. Possible solutions are then sought that acknowledge cultural expectations but at the same time meet the demands of societal requirements such as school attendance. Problem definition and solution may need to incorporate the perspectives of the nuclear and extended family members.

Cultural differences can also impact the most effective way of mediating family disputes. In a study of mediation services for a community with a large Hispanic population, Weller, Martin, and Lederach (2001) found the following differences between Hispanic and White Americans. For White Americans, the procedure generally involve contact with an official agency and the use of a mediator who has formal training; does not have personal relationships with the people involved in the dispute; and is expected to be neutral. The information obtained from the parties is confidential, with one person talking at a time. The conflict is defined, and issues are addressed one at a time with the easiest ones addressed first. A written agreement is obtained, and the mediator's role ends. In contrast, Hispanic Americans responded more favorably to the following in the resolution of a domestic conflict: The meeting is held in a church or school within the neighborhood. The mediator is an older, respected member of the community and may be acquainted with the parties. Perspectives are gathered from extended family members, including godparents, and venting is considered a part of the process. There is emphasis on respect, honor, and saving face. The mediator generates options and may remain involved after an agreement is reached. These differences indicate the need to adapt mediation procedures to better fit the culture of Hispanic Americans, especially recent immigrants or those with a traditional cultural orientation. Although these findings apply to family mediation services, they also have implications for altering individual and family therapy.

Family Structure

In 1994 about 71% of Hispanics had two married parents, while 25% of Hispanic families have a female head of household (G. M. Gonzalez, 1997). Traditional Hispanic families are hierarchical in form with special authority given to the elderly, the parents, and males. Within the family, the father assumes the role of the primary authority figure. Sex roles are clearly delineated (Avila & Avila, 1995; Mejia, 1983; Mizio, 1983). The sexual behaviors of adolescent females are severely restricted, while male children are afforded greater freedom to come and go as they please. Children are expected to be obedient, are usually not consulted on family decisions, and are expected to contribute financially to the family when possible. Parents reciprocate by providing for them through young adulthood and even during marriage. This type of reciprocal relationship is a lifelong expectation. Older children are expected to take care of and protect their younger siblings when away from home, and the older sister may function as a surrogate mother. Even though they may be adolescents, many think of themselves and function as young adults. Marriage and parenthood are entered into early in life and are seen as stabilizing influences.

Implications. When conducting individual or family session with Hispanic clients, assess the structure of the family. Determine the degree of hierarchical structure. In a traditionally oriented family, the father should be addressed first and his comments given weight. The mother is also considered as superordinate to children. The pattern of mothers talking more and children listening may be comfortable and expected in the traditional culture (Lefkowitz, Romo, Corona, Au, & Sigman, 2000). Deviations from this cultural pattern may produce conflict in family functioning. For families, determine how decisions are made. If conflicts arise over the cultural roles and expectations for family members, assess and treat the problem as a clash between cultural values and mainstream society expectations. Often the conflicts among family members involve differences in acculturation. In less acculturated families, Paniagua (1994) recommended interviewing the father for a few minutes during the beginning of the first session. This would show recognition of the father's authority and indicate that the counselor is sensitive to cultural factors in counseling. In a more acculturated family, the father could still be addressed first and then the mother and the children. It also must be remembered that in traditionally oriented Hispanic American families, less importance is placed on shared interests and joint activities between husband and wife, although a great deal of socialization occurs during social events involving families and friends (Negy & Woods, 1992). Szapocznik and Kurtines (1993) recommend that acculturation play the role of the "identified patient" and solutions be obtained that involve the reframing and negotiation of the conflicting cultural norms and values. Determine different ways in which family members can still demonstrate their allegiance to the family structure and resolve conflicts. One such approach is demonstrated in the following case:

> *During family therapy, a Puerto Rican mother indicated to her son, "You don't care for me anymore. You used to come by every Sunday and bring the children. You used to respect me and teach your children respect. Now you go out and work, you say, always doing this or that. I don't know what spirit* [que diablo] *has taken over you." (Inclan, 1985, p. 332)*

In response the son indicated that he was working hard and sacrificing for the children—that he wanted to be a success in the world and an individual of whom his children could be proud. In examining the case, it is clear that the mother is expressing disappointment. She defines love as being with her, having the family gather together, and subordinating individual desires for the family. The son has adopted a middle-class set of values stressing individual achievement, doing, and the future. The clash in value differences was at the root of the problem.

In working with the family, the therapist provided an alternative way of viewing the conflict instead of using terms such as right or wrong. He explained that our views are shaped by the values that we hold. He asked about the socialization process that the mother had undergone. She emphasized the "good old days" and the socialization and values of her childhood. The son indicated the pain he felt in losing the understanding of the parents, but he felt he had to change in order to succeed in the United States. The therapist pointed out that different adaptive styles may be necessary for different situations and that what is right is dependent on the social context. Both of them began to acknowledge that they still loved one another but might have to show it in different ways. As a result of the sessions, the mother and son accepted one another and understood the nature of the original conflict.

Sex Role Expectations

In working with Hispanic Americans, the counselor will often face problems dealing with conflicts over sex roles. In their traditional culture, men are expected to be strong, dominant, and the provider for the family (machismo), whereas women are expected to be nurturant, submissive to the male, and self-sacrificing (marianismo). As head of the family, the male expects the members to be obedient to him. Those with higher levels of ethnic identity are more likely to subscribe to traditional male and female roles (Abreu, Goodyear, Campos, & Newcomb, 2000). Areas in which males may have sex-role conflicts include the following (Avila & Avila, 1995; Carillo, 1982; Hildebrand et al., 1996)

1. *Submissiveness or assertion in the area of authority.* The Hispanic male may have difficulty interacting with agencies and individuals outside of the family and may feel that he is not fulfilling his role. In addition, changes involving greater responsibility of the wife and children may produce problems related to his authority.

2. *Feelings of isolation and depression because of the need to be strong.* Talking about or sharing views of problems with others may be seen as a sign of weakness. With the additional stress of living in a very different culture, the inability to discuss feelings of frustration and anxiety produces isolation.

3. *Conflicts over the need to be consistent in his role.* As ambiguity and stresses increase, the need to adjust and to seek security in a more rigid adherence to the role produces anxiety.

4. *Anxiety over questions of sexual potency.*

For females, conflicts may involve (a) expectations to meet the require-ments of her role, (b) anxiety or depression over not being able to live up to these standards, and (c) the inability to act out her feelings of anger (Avila & Avila, 1995). Espin (1985) feels that Hispanic women are socialized to feel that they are inferior and that suffering and being a martyr are characteristics of a good woman. With greater exposure to the dominant culture, such views may be questioned. Certain roles may change more than others. For example, Espin indicated that some women are very modern in their views of educa-tion and employment but remain traditional in the area of sexual behavior and personal relationships. Others remain very traditional in all areas. Other writers (G. M. Gonzalez, 1997; McCurdy & Ruiz, 1980; A. Ruiz, 1981) cau-tion that Hispanic sex roles are not as inflexible and rigid as has often been described. For example, the concept of masculinity or machismo includes be-ing a good provider. Egalitarian decision making appears to be increasing with later generations of Mexican Americans (G. M. Gonzalez, 1997). Also, many Hispanic women assert their influence indirectly and "behind the scenes," thus preserving the appearance of male control (L. L. Hayes, 1997).

Implications. The double standard is decreasing rapidly in the urban class. Part of the reason for the change is that many women are required to act inde-pendently in the work setting and to deal with schools and other agencies. In some cases, the woman may become the wage earner, which produces prob-lems since this role traditionally belongs to the male. Conversely, as the wife becomes more independent, the husband may feel anxiety. Both may feel that the man is no longer fulfilling his role. The counselor must be able to help the family deal with the anxiety and suspiciousness associated with role change. For both males and females, role conflict is likely to occur if the male is unemployed, if the female is employed, or both. In addition, it may be eas-ier for the female to obtain a job than for the male to do so. Since both feel that the male should be the provider for the family, an additional source of stress can occur.

In dealing with sex-role conflicts, the counselor faces a dilemma and po-tential value conflict. If the counselor believes in equal relationships, should he or she move the clients in this direction? Therapists working with cultural values different from their own must be particularly careful not to impose their views on the clients. Instead, they must try not only to help the client achieve their goals of greater independence but to accomplish this within a cultural framework as well. The consequences of change also must be con-sidered. Any counselor who works to help a female client achieve more in-dependence without apprising her of potential problems within her family and community is not fulfilling his or her obligations. Again, the conflicts in sex roles in both men and women can be cast as involving differing expecta-tions from their ethnic group and mainstream values. Reframing the problem as an external issue that the couple or family can face jointly can reduce intrafamily conflicts and result in problem-solving approaches to deal with the different sets of expectations.

Spirituality and Religiosity

> *Mrs. Lopez, age 70, and her 30-year-old daughter sought counseling because they had a very conflictual relationship. . . . The mother was not accustomed to a counseling format. . . . At a pivotal point in one session, she found talking about emotional themes overwhelming and embarrassing. . . . In order to reengage her, the counselor asked what resources she used when she and her daughter quarreled. She . . . prayed to Our Lady of Guadalupe. (Zuniga, 1997, p. 149)*

The therapist employed a culturally adapted strategy of having Mrs. Lopez use prayer to understand her daughter and to find solutions for the counseling sessions. This format allowed Mrs. Lopez to discuss spiritual guidance and possible solutions to the problem. The use of a cultural perspective allowed the sessions to continue. The Catholic religion has a major influence in Hispanic groups and is a source of comfort in times of stress. There is strong belief in the importance of prayer, and most participate in Mass. This religious belief is related to the view that (a) sacrifice in this world is helpful to salvation, (b) being charitable to others is a virtue, and (c) you should endure wrongs done against you (Yamamoto & Acosta, 1982). The consequences of these beliefs are that many Hispanics have difficulty behaving assertively. Life's misfortunes are seen as inevitable, and Hispanics often feel resigned to their fate (*fatalismo*). In addition to the Catholic perspective, some Hispanics believe that evil spirits cause mental health problems.

Implications.   During assessment, it is important to determine the possible influence of religious or spiritual beliefs. If there is a strong belief in fatalism, instead of attempting to change it, the therapist might acknowledge this attitude and help the individual or family determine the most adaptive response to the situation. A therapist might say, "Given that the situation is unchangeable, how can you and your family deal with this?" You are still attempting to have the client develop problem-solving skills within certain parameters. The strong reliance on religion can be a resource. Sometimes a priest can help deal with counseling issues. Acosta and Evans (1982) reported the case of a 35-year-old, Spanish-speaking Mexican American, José, who came into the clinic complaining of anxiety attacks. The precipitating event appeared to be his impending marriage, which would necessitate reducing the amount of money he could send to his parents in Mexico. He felt that it would be a sin to reduce his financial assistance. The counselor suggested that José talk to his priest about this issue. With short-term counseling, along with assurance from the priest that he would not be committing a sin, José was able to marry and reconcile sending less to his parents. The belief in evil spirits should also be assessed and may require consultation with a *curandero* or spiritual healer.

Acculturation Conflicts

As with many ethnic minority groups, Hispanic Americans are faced with a society that has a different set of values. Some maintain their traditional orientation, whereas others assimilate and exchange their native cultural practices and values for those of the host culture. A bicultural orientation allows individuals to maintain some components of the native culture and to incorporate some practices and beliefs of the host culture. Miranda and Umhoefer (1998a, 1998b) believed that a bicultural orientation may be the "healthiest" resolution to acculturation conflicts. In their study, they found that both high- and low-acculturated Mexican Americans scored high on social dysfunction, alcohol consumption, and acculturative stress. Bicultural individuals appeared to fare much better because of an ability to accept and negotiate aspects of both cultures. Perhaps additional stressors are involved with either the complete rejection or acceptance of the values of the host culture (Milville, Koonce, Darlington, & Whitlock, 2000; Miranda & Umhoefer, 1998a, 1998b). Some of the issues involved in culture conflict are evident in the following:

> *A teenager, Mike, was having difficulty knowing who he was or what group he belonged with. His parents had given him an Anglo name to ensure his success in American society. They only spoke to him in English because they were fearful that he might have an accent. During his childhood, he felt estranged from his relatives. His grandparents, aunts, and uncles could speak only Spanish, so they were able to communicate only through nonverbal means. At school, he did not fit in with his African American peers, and he also felt different from the Mexican American students who would ask him why he was unable to speak Spanish. The confusion over his ethnic identity was troublesome for him. He attempted to learn Spanish in college but was unable to do so. (Avila & Avila, 1995)*

During middle school Hispanic children begin to have questions about their identity. Should they adhere to mainstream values? Few role models exist for Hispanic Americans. The representation of Hispanic Americans on television has actually decreased over the last 30 years. They account for only 2% of characters in 139 prime-time series. In depictions, they are more likely to behave criminally or to be violent (Espinosa, 1997). The mixed heritage of many Hispanic Americans raises additional identity questions. If they are of Mexican/Indian heritage, should they call themselves "Mexican American," "Chicano," "Latino," or "Spanish American"? What about mixtures involving other racial backgrounds? An ethnic identity provides a sense of belonging and group membership. Many Hispanic youngsters undergo this process of searching for an identity. This struggle may be responsible for such problems as the following: (a) Mexican American adolescents report more depressive symptoms and conduct disorders than White youth; (b) small-town Mexican American youth have more severe and elevated rates of alcohol and drug abuse; and (c) suicidal behaviors are high in Hispanic female adolescents and Puerto Rican males (Roberts & Sobhan, 1992).

Implications. Ethnic identity issues should be recognized and incorporated within the school curriculum with modules on ethnicity, focusing on what it means to be Hispanic, Chicano, or Spanish speaking. Case studies of contributions made by different ethnic group members can be presented. Conflicts between mainstream values and ethnic group values can be discussed, and students can engage in brainstorming for methods to bridge the differences. Teaching styles can be altered to accommodate different cultural learning styles. It should be stressed that ethnic identity is part of the normal development process. In many cases, a bicultural perspective may be the most functional, since such a perspective does not involve the wholesale rejection of either culture (Galan, 1998; Gay, 1998). In psychotherapy, the degree of acculturation should be assessed because it has implications for treatment. Hispanic Americans with minimal acculturation rarely present mental health issues to counselors and may believe that counseling will take only one session (G. M. Gonzalez, 1997). Second-generation Hispanic Americans are usually bilingual, but frequently with only functional use of English. They are often exposed to Spanish at home and exposed to English in the school and on television. Second-generation Hispanic Americans are often marginal in both native and majority cultures. Acculturation also may influence perceptions of counseling and responses to counseling. Mexican Americans with a strong traditional orientation may have more difficulty being open and self-disclosing than are those with a strong orientation toward the dominant culture (G. M. Gonzalez, 1997).

Because knowledge of the acculturation level is important, a variety of acculturation measures have been developed. One formal assessment measure is the Acculturation Rating Scale for Mexican Americans (Cuellar, Harris, & Jasso, 1980). Scores on this 20-item questionnaire allow categorizing on a five-point scale: "Very Mexican," "Bicultural, Mexican oriented," "True Bicultural," "Bicultural, Anglo oriented," and "Very Anglicized." Measures of acculturation also exist for Puerto Ricans (Inclan, 1979) and Cubans (Szapocznik, Scopetta, Kurtines, & Aranalde, 1978). If the counselor feels uncomfortable using a formal measure, it is also possible to inquire about the specific Hispanic group that they are from, the length of time spent in the country or generational status, primary language, religious orientation and strength of religious beliefs, whether they live in a barrio, the reason for immigration (if immigrants), if they are in an extended family situation, and other information related to acculturation.

Educational Characteristics

> *Peer pressure to drop out can be nearly overwhelming in the Hispanic community, as DeAnza Montoya, a pretty Santa Fe teen, can attest. In her neighborhood, it was considered "anglo" and "nerdy" to do well in school. . . . "In school they make you feel like a dumb Mexican," she says, adding that such slights only bring Hispanics closer together. (Headden, 1997, p. 64)*

Educationally, Hispanic Americans have not been faring well in the public schools. Hispanic students have a very high dropout rate. Over one third drop out before completing high school. This is nearly double the rate for Blacks and nearly four times higher than the rate for White students (Moore, 2001). Only 10% of children of migrant workers complete school. Twenty-five percent of Hispanic eighth graders have repeated one grade, and over 15% have been retained two or more times in their school careers (Gersten & Woodward, 1994). Among Hispanic groups, Puerto Rican students have the highest dropout rate. Although there has been a great deal of emphasis on the importance of nondiscriminatory assessment, in Texas Mexican Americans are overrepresented by 300% in the special education programs under the learning disabilities classification. Many of these students were placed in these programs because of their lack of English proficiency (tests were conducted in English, or they were unable to perform adequately from classroom material in a language they were just beginning to learn; Gersten & Woodward, 1994).

A number of problems contribute to the high dropout rate of Hispanic students. As was mentioned earlier, many of the educational difficulties faced by Hispanics relate to their varied proficiency with English. Spanish is the primary language spoken in the homes of over half of Hispanic Americans, and a much larger percentage regularly listen to or speak Spanish on a more limited basis. Second-generation Hispanics are often bilingual. However, their command of the English language is often limited. Many are exposed first to Spanish in the home and then to English in the school. Immigrant parents may speak in Spanish, and their child may respond in a combination of Spanish and English. Of the Hispanic eighth graders who scored poorly on an academic test, almost half had parents who had not completed high school (Gersten & Woodward, 1994). The poor performance of Hispanic Americans has often been blamed on their culture or the parents for failing to prepare or to motivate their children academically. However, their parents do have high aspirations for their children. Most want their children to complete college

(Retish & Kavanaugh, 1992). Hispanic children also lack role models. Hispanic Americans constitute just 1.5% of all college faculty and 1.1% of all tenured faculty (Kavanaugh & Retish, 1991).

Implications. In general, schools have been poorly equipped to deal with large numbers of Spanish-speaking students. The move against bilingual education and rapid immersion of Spanish-speaking students in English may increase their already excessive numbers in special education classrooms. This would be a disservice to students who are placed there merely because of poor English skills, the use of tests not standardized for Spanish-speaking populations, or the improper administration of tests (Middleton et al., 2000). Teachers who do not have proficiency in Spanish have a difficult time preparing understandable lessons for students and have no means of effectively evaluating their performance. The inability to communicate with Hispanic parents compounds the problem and hampers information passed through parent-teacher conferences. Many low-income Hispanic parents feel that they have no right to question the teacher or school decisions. Some are unable to attend conferences because of work requirements. This may be interpreted as a lack of caring or parental involvement in the child's education. To engage parents, the conferences should be scheduled at flexible hours. Child care should be made available, as well as interpreters if the teacher is not bilingual. Face-to-face communication or other personal contact is more successful than written material (even if written in Spanish). Trust develops slowly, and it is important to identify and support the family's strengths rather than focusing on the shortcomings (Espinosa, 1997). Altering instructional strategies to fit cultural values is important. Instead of saying to a child, "Good work, you should be proud of yourself," the teacher could respond, "Good work, your family will be proud of you" and have the child bring the work home to show the parents. Teachers often do not know how to respond when they observe cultural characteristics in children. J. A. Vasquez (1998) has a three-step procedure to modify instructional strategy (See Figure 14.1).

Immigration, Racism, Discrimination, and Other Societal Factors

Complex interaction of stressors such as racism, acculturation conflicts, and fatalism can lead to a number of mental disorders. The high level of acculturative stress found among adult Mexican immigrants results in depressive symptoms and suicidal ideation. The severing of ties to family and friends in Mexico, the loss of coping and financial resources, language inadequacy, unemployment, and culture conflict all function as stressors to recent immigrants (Hovey, 2000). Acculturation conflicts with the family and perceived

Figure 14.1

Three-Step Procedure for Adapting Instruction to Cultural Traits

Source: J. A. Vasquez, 1998, *The Prevention Researcher,* 5(1), p. 3. Reprinted by permission of the Editor, *The Prevention Researcher.*

THREE-STEP PROCEDURE FOR ADAPTING INSTRUCTION TO CULTURAL TRAITS

Step 1 — Teacher observes/identifies student trait.

Step 2 — Trait is passed through "filter" of three questions to identify which aspect of teaching (content, context, mode) should be affected.

Step 3 — Teacher verbalizes/writes out the new instruction strategy.

1. Carlos is very concerned about pleasing his family.

2. Sammy and Joanna seem disinterested when given individual work and more "turned on" when interacting with others.

3. Ben seems intimidated and shy when I ask him questions to which he may not know the answer.

4. Charlotte does better when the material I teach involves people interacting with one another; she is not strongly "object" oriented.

Content

a. Does any aspect of the trait suggest the kind of material I should be teaching?

Context

b. Does any aspect of the trait suggest the physical or psychological setting I should create in the classroom?

Mode

c. Does any aspect of the trait suggest the manner in which I should be teaching?

1. I'll tell Carlos that I'll inform his parents when he does really good work. (Carlos should work with great effort and expectation and thus for him the context is changed).

2. I'll provide more activities that allow Sammy and Joanna to work on projects with others in small groups. (Mode is changed since the means of instruction has shifted to include more student input.)

3. I'll ask Ben questions in class that I'm fairly sure he can answer correctly, and work with him individually in areas in which he is less knowledgeable. (This strategy affects both the mode of instruction and the psychological context for Ben.)

4. I'll teach more math concepts in the context of people dealing with one another, as in buying, trading, borrowing. (The mode is basically changed to suit Charlotte's preferred style of learning.)

societal racism also impact Hispanic adolescents. In a national poll, 16% of Hispanic Americans indicated that prejudice was the most important issue facing them (Krupin, 2001). Possibly because of issues such as these, Hispanic students (11%) are at a greater risk for depression and are more likely than are Euro-American students (6%) to attempt suicide (Tortolero & Roberts, 2001). Many youths attempt to deal with family distress, discrimination in the school and community, feelings of hopelessness, and a lack of family support by involvement in gang activities (Baca & Koss-Chioino, 1997).

Implications. A clinician must assess not only for intrapsychic issues but also for the degree that external conditions are involved with mental health issues. Because many suffer from poverty, stressors attributable to inadequate food and shelter or from dealing with bureaucracies and unemployment have to be dealt with (De La Cancela, 1985; J. M. Vazquez, 1997). "If extrapsychic conflict is predominant, therapy aimed at social action and the alleviation of discrimination and poverty may be appropriate. If intrapsychic conflict is more basic, introspective or behavioral therapy is the treatment of choice" (LeVine & Padilla, 1980, p. 256). Careful assessment of the source of emotional disturbance is necessary before appropriate action can be taken, and this should be done very early in the counseling session. One case involved a married migrant worker in his mid-50s who came into therapy complaining that he heard threatening voices. He was afraid to leave his home. In working with him, A. Ruiz (1981) recommended an analysis of external causes first. In this case, it is suggested that the worker undergo a complete physical with special attention to exposure to pesticides and other agricultural chemicals that might result in mental symptoms. It is also possible that the feelings of fear displayed by the individual stem from factors such as suspiciousness of outside authorities, fear of deportation of self or others in the family, or recent encounters with creditors. External factors that are specific to the experience of Hispanic Americans must be examined along with intrapsychic mental health issues.

For troubled Hispanic American youths who are members of or attracted to gangs, Baca and Koss-Chioino (1997) offered several suggestions for counseling and therapy:

1. Talk about the needs that gangs fulfill and consider alternative ways of having these met. Bring in the cultural themes of family (*familia*) and respect (*respecto*) and consider different ways they can be obtained.

2. Discuss cultural or ethnic identity and problems with acculturation. The lack of an ethnic identity leads to low self-esteem and a lack of social or personal responsibility, resulting in consequences such as AIDS or unplanned pregnancy.

3. Recognize that low self-esteem leads to an intense involvement with peers and therefore a diminished sense of self-care.

4. Suggest new patterns of self-care and caring for others.

5. Confront issues around drug use, negative peer pressure, sexuality, sexism, discrimination, and death.

6. Empower the client by increasing self-awareness and skills in dealing with family, school, neighborhood, and societal issues. This approach offers a cultural context in problem solving.

Assessment Issues

> *Sandra G is a 24-year-old female college student. . . . She identified herself as "Mexican" although she has lived in this country for about 11 years. . . . She reported a very negative experience in adjusting to life in this country . . . especially in the area of friendships with U.S. born Chicanos or Mexican Americans (whom she considered to be sexist). . . . Sandra sought treatment . . . for several issues, including chronic depression, anxiety, low self-esteem, and a "combative relationship" with her boyfriend. . . . She had no history of mental illness . . . and displayed no symptoms of psychosis. (Velasquez et al., 1997, pp. 115–116)*

During the counseling sessions, Sandra would use Spanish when discussing issues that involved emotional content. Because she used English primarily, the English version of the Minnesota Multiphasic Personality Inventory–Second Edition (MMPI-2) was given to her. Her profile appeared valid and showed peaks on schizophrenia, psychasthenia, and paranoia. Such a profile might result in neuroleptic medication or hospitalization. However, this pattern did not seem indicative of the mental status of the client, so the Spanish version of the MMPI-2 was given. The new profile indicated maladjustments more suggestive of dysthymia (depression) and personality disorder, which had a better fit with the clinical impressions. She was successfully treated with cognitive and interpersonally based therapies. It appears that in choosing between the English and Spanish versions of the MMPI-2 for bilingual clients, the selection should be based on the language employed for emotional issues. Assessments should always be interpreted within a sociocultural context and be supported by additional data.

Implications. Traditional assessments do not place much emphasis on language differences, validity of tests for ethnic minorities, or the influence of cultural or social factors. Acculturation issues accompany many disorders in Hispanic Americans and can be used as a modifier or specifier to mental disorders. It is important to attend to all the Axes in the *Diagnostic and Statistical Manual of*

Mental Disorders–Fourth Edition, Text Revision (DSM-IV-TR). Axis 4 can help identify psychosocial and environmental issues such as language barriers, discrimination, immigration stress, and poverty (M. Gonzales et al., 1997).

Because of the lack of bilingual counselors, problems in diagnosis can occur with Hispanic clients who are not conversant in English. For example, Marcos (1973) found that Mexican American patients were seen as suffering from greater psychopathology when interviewed in English than when interviewed in Spanish. However, interpreters themselves may present difficulties in the counseling process. They are often responsible for distortions in communication. Personal relationships may also develop between the interpreter and the client. In one case, a client offered to care for the translator's child (Cooper & Costas, 1994). Marcos (1979) found that distortions may result from (a) the interpreter's language competence and translation skills, (b) the interpreter's lack of psychiatric knowledge, and (c) the attitudes of the counselor. For example, relatives used as interpreters often answer the questions put to the client without waiting for a response. The following example occurred in an actual exchange:

> CLINICIAN [TO SPANISH-SPEAKING PATIENT]: *What about worries; do you have many worries?*
> INTERPRETER [TO PATIENT]: *Is there anything that bothers you?*
> PATIENT: *I know; I know that God is with me; I'm not afraid. They cannot get me.* [pause] *I'm wearing these new pants and feel protected. I feel good, I don't get headaches anymore.*
> INTERPRETER [TO CLINICIAN]: *He says he is not afraid; he feels good; he doesn't have headaches anymore. (Marcos, 1979, p. 173)*

To reduce some of these errors, Marcos (1979) and Cooper and Costas (1994) recommended that the mental health professional meet with the interpreter to discuss goals, areas to be assessed, and possible sensitive areas that may need to be explored. The language proficiency of the interpreter should also be assessed. In addition, it might be helpful to have as part of the team an indigenous worker who is knowledgeable about the community and can provide help in contacting social service agencies or assistance when this is needed in working with a client.

Guidelines for Clinical Practice

Several writers (Padilla & DeSnyder, 1985; Paniagua, 1994; Ruiz, 1995; Velasquez et al., 1997; Yamamoto & Acosta, 1982) have made suggestions regarding how to conduct the initial session with Hispanic Americans.

1. It is important to engage in a respectful, warm, and mutual introduction with the client. Less acculturated Hispanic Americans expect a more formal relationship. The counselor will be seen as an authority figure and should be formally dressed.

2. Give a brief description of what counseling is and the role of each participant. Less acculturated Hispanic Americans often expect medication and to meet for only one or two sessions.

3. Explain the notion of confidentiality. Even immigrants with legal status have inquired about whether the information shared during counseling would "end up in the hands of the Border Patrol or other immigration authorities" (Velasquez et al., 1997, p. 112). Immigrant families may also be uncertain about the limits of confidentiality, especially as it applies to child abuse or neglect issues. Physical discipline is used more often in Hispanic families (this is also the case for lower-class Whites) than in middle-class White families. They may be fearful about how their child-rearing practices will be perceived.

4. Have the client state in his or her own words the problem or problems as he or she sees it. Determine the possible influence of religious or spiritual beliefs.

5. Assess the acculturation level.

6. Consider whether there are cultural or societal aspects to the problem. What are the impacts of racism, poverty, and acculturative stress on the problem?

7. Determine whether a translator is needed. Be careful not to interpret slow speech or long silences as indicators of depression or cognitive dysfunction. The individual may just have problems with English.

8. Determine the positive assets and resources available to the client and his or her family. Have they, other family members, or friends dealt with similar problems? How was a successful outcome defined? Use paraphrasing to summarize the problem as you understand it and make sure that the client knows you understand it.

9. Help the clients prioritize the problems and determine what they perceive as the important goals. What are their expectations? How will they know when the goals have been achieved?

10. Discuss possible consequences of achieving the goals for the individual, family, and community.

11. Discuss the possible participation of family members and consider family therapy. Within the family, determine the hierarchical structure as well as the degree of acculturation of the different members. Focus on the problems produced by conflicting values.

12. Assess possible problems from external sources, such as need for food, shelter, or employment, or stressful interactions with agencies. Provide necessary assistance in developing and maintaining environmental supports.

13. Explain the treatment to be used, why it was selected, and how it will help achieve the goals.

14. With the client's input, determine a mutually agreeable length of treatment. It is better to offer time-limited, solution-based therapies.

15. Remember that *personalismo* is a basic cultural value of Hispanic Americans. Although the first meetings may be quite formal, once trust has developed, the clients may develop a close personal bond with the counselor. He or she may be perceived as a family member or friend and may be invited to family functions and given gifts. These behaviors are not evidence of dependency or a lack of boundaries.

16. Evaluate the effectiveness of the therapy.

Counseling Individuals of Multiracial Descent

15

Chapter

Pro Golfer Tiger Woods stood on the fairway green surrounded by reporters and fans. He was peppered with questions after another outstanding tournament, when one reporter asked how he felt to be the first Black superstar golfer. Tiger, however, described himself as "Cablinasian" because he was a racial mixture of Caucasian, Black, Indian, and Asian ancestry. Despite his constant correction to the press, Woods is nearly always referred to as an African American. (Eddings, 1997)

Society has made up nothing for the biracial child. I would buy these Golden Books by the stackful. . . . There were none with biracial children in them at that time, but I found myself looking for ones that were illustrated with black children. . . . When you look into a book and you're a little child, it would be nice sometimes to see a brown daddy and a pink mom. (Rosenblatt, Karis, & Powell, 1995, p. 202)

Lester Dixon, an AC Transit bus driver from Alameda, Ca., is Black and Filipino. His brother and sisters, including his 10 children and 10 grandchildren are also of mixed racial heritage. In all the U.S. Census until now, they have had to check just one box to define their race for the national head count. For Dixon, that meant denying either his Filipino mother or his African American father. He had a choice, however, of checking the often alienating and uninformative "other box." (San Francisco Chronicle, 2001, A1, A17).

For years, many multiracial individuals have fought for the right to identify themselves as belonging to more than one racial group. Our society, however, is a monoracially oriented one that forces people to choose one racial identity over another (e.g., Lester Dixon) or imposes a singular racial identity upon them (e.g., Tiger Woods). People of mixed race heritage are often ignored, neglected, and considered nonexistent in our educational materials, media portrayals, and psychological literature (Root, 1992, 1996; Torres, 1998). Such dynamics may lead to major psychological and social stressors for multiracial individuals in identity formation, lowered self-esteem, and an existence between the margins of two or more cultures (Root, 2001). Further, mental health professionals receive little training in working with multiracial clients victimized by having monoracial categories imposed upon them. Indeed, many counselors have conscious and unconscious attitudes, biases, and stereotypes similar to the layperson regarding race mixing (miscegenation) and racial contamination (hypodescent).

In more ways than one, the 2000 census set in motion a complex psychological and political debate for the first time because it allowed people to check more than one box for their racial identities and to be counted as multiracial. Proponents have argued that it is unfair to force one identity on multiracial people, that it creates alienation and identity confusions, that it denies racial realities, that there should be pride in being multiracial, and that there are strong medical reasons for knowing one's racial heritage. Custom, history, and prejudices, however, continue to affect perceptions regarding a singular racial identity. Further, many civil rights organizations, including the National Association for the Advancement of Colored People (NAACP), believe that such counts will dilute the strength of their constituencies because census numbers on race and ethnicity figure into many calculations involving antidiscrimination laws, voting, and dispersal of funds for minority programs. Caught in the struggle—and often victimized—are persons of mixed racial heritage.

Facts and Figures Related to Biracial/Multiracial Populations

Mental health professionals would benefit from awareness and knowledge related to the following facts (taken from J. J. Johnson, 1992; Root, 1992; Rosenblatt et al., 1995; U.S. Bureau of the Census, 2001; Wehrly, Kenney, & Kenney, 1999; Wright, 1994).

- The biracial baby boom in the United States started in 1967 when the last laws against race mixing (antimiscegenation) were repealed. As a result, there has been a rapid increase in interracial marriage and a subsequent rise in the number of biracial children in the United States. The number of children living in families where one parent is White and the other is Black, Asian, or American Indian has tripled from 1970 to 1990. This does not include children of single parents or children whose parents are divorced.

- Prior to 2000, estimation of the multiracial population was difficult because it contained only monoracial categories. It was hoped that the

2000 census would correct the situation. However, only 2.4% (6.8 million) of respondents checked more than one box to represent their race. Private estimates place the true number at closer to 6% (16.5 million), although this may also be a gross underestimation in light of the fact that many monoracial individuals choose to self-identify with only one race.

- Compounding accurate counting is the fact that 30% to 70% of African Americans are multiracial by multigenerational history; virtually all Latinos and Fillipinos are multiracial, as are the majority of American Indians and Native Hawaiians.

- In the 2000 census, 93% of multiracial individuals reported membership in exactly two racial combinations in the following percentages: "White and Some Other Race," 32%; "White and American Indian and Alaska Native," 16%; "White and Asian," 13%; and "White and Black or African American," 11%.

- Consistent with the most frequent biracial combinations, interracial marriages occur more frequently among Euro-Americans and Asians. Black-White marriages make up the smallest percentage of interracial unions: about 3.4% of first marriages.

- When gender is taken into consideration, Latinas and Asian American and Native American women are more likely than their male counterparts to marry interracially; Black and White men have a higher interracial marriage rate. The highest rate of interracial marriage is between White men and Asian women, and the lowest is between White men and Black women.

Implications. These statistics raise major questions regarding the monoracial and multiracial climate of our society. For example, why are the offspring of a Black-White union considered "Black" by our society? Why not White? Why is it easier for us to accept the notion that children of certain mixed couples (Asian/White, Native American/White, etc.) are multiracial, while other combinations that involve African Americans are not? Why do some people of mixed-race heritage perceive or choose to identity themselves with only one race? Are certain interracial relationships more acceptable than others? Why? What accounts for the fact that Asian American women and Latinas are more likely than their male counterparts to marry out?

Mental health professionals who work with multiracial clients need to understand the implications to these questions if they are to be effective with their racially mixed clients. In our journey to understand the implications of the issues confronting multiracial individuals, we concentrate on several themes that have been identified as important in working with this population.

Hypodescent: "The One Drop of Blood Rule"

Several years ago, Alvin Poussaint, an African American Harvard psychiatrist and consultant to the *Cosby Show,* stood before a packed audience and posed a pointed question to them: "Do you know how powerful Black blood is?" After an awkward silence, he answered, "It is so powerful that one tiny drop will contaminate the entire bloodstream of a White person!" What Poussaint was referring to is called hypodescent or the "one drop rule": a social system that maintains the myth of monoracialism by assigning the person of mixed racial heritage to the least desirable racial status (Root, 1996). In essence, hypodescent has even more insidious and devious motives.

First, it was an attempt by White European immigrants to maintain racial purity and superiority by passing laws against interracial marriages (antimiscegenation) primarily directed at Blacks and Native Americans. As early as the 1660s, laws were passed making it a crime for "Negro slaves" to marry "freeborn English women" (Wehrly et al., 1999). Interestingly, such laws were clear evidence of gender bias because they were based on property rights (women perceived as property) and (a) men of color could not have access to valued property while (b) White men could have sexual access to Black women as property (Pascoe, 1991). If White women were caught in a sexual liaison with a Black man, she also could be considered the property of the master. Second, not only could racial purity be maintained, but also hypodescent thinking and laws generated additional property for slave owners. Africans were brought over as slave laborers; the more slaves an owner possessed, the greater his/her wealth (free labor). Thus, economically, it was beneficial to classify offspring of a Black-White union as "Negro" because it increased property. Third, the prevalent beliefs of the time were that "Negroes and Indians" were subhuman creatures, uncivilized, lower in intellect, and impulsively childlike. One drop of Black blood in a person would make him or her contaminated and Black. Indeed, in 1894 in the case of *Plessy v. Ferguson* the Supreme Court ruled that a person who was seven-eighths White and one-eighth Black and "maintained that he did not look Negro" was nonetheless to be classified as Negro (Davis, 1994).

The rule of hypodescent applies to other racial/ethnic minority groups as well, but it appears to fluctuate more widely than for African Americans. While groups of color are often averse to discussing a social desirability ranking among them, conventional wisdom and some data suggest that African Americans are often considered less desirable than are their Asian American counterparts (Jackson et al., 1996), although the latter is still considered significantly less desirable than Whites. It also appears that whether one is a man or a woman of a minority group affects how society perceives them. For example, images of Asian American women are much more favorable (domestic, petite, exotic, and sexually pleasing) than are their male counterparts (passive, emasculated, inhibited, and unattractive; D. W. Sue & Sue, 1999). These findings offer an explanation for why interracial marriages between Asian Americans and European Americans occur more frequently than between Blacks and Whites; why mixed-race children of a former union are more likely to be considered multiracial while unions of the latter are still more likely to be considered Black; and why Asian American women are more likely than their male counterparts to marry out (Lewandowski & Jackson, 2001; Jackman, Wagner, & Johnson, 2001). This not only has often been the basis of hard feelings and resentments between African Americans and Asian Americans but also has created friction among men and women within the Asian American population as well as other racial minority groups. It is important to understand that the issue of antagonisms between racial/ethnic minority groups and between the sexes of a group is the result of a biased sociopolitical process and is not inherent in race or gender. The true cause is society's differential acceptance and stereotyping of minority groups and the role that men and women play in the process.

Implications. Many multiracial individuals face forces that impose a racial identity upon them, and that identity is likely to be among the lowest statuses defined by the society. Even if their mixed racial heritage is acknowledged, it is generally considered lesser than that of a "White person." As indicated by W. E. Cross (1991), multiracial children, when asked their heritage, may answer one way internally and another way to the questioner. The external answer may be an attempt to "fit in," not to violate the expectations of the interrogator, or to take the path of least resistance. For example, answering that one is biracial may not be satisfactory to the questioner and will result in further probing. The child or adolescent is often unable to identify his or her conflicts and feelings about being multiracial and settles for the answer most likely to end the questions: a monoracial answer that may result in internal disharmony, a false sense of self, social marginality, and guilt (Gibbs & Moskowitz-Sweet, 1991; Winn & Priest, 1993).

Racial/Ethnic Ambiguity, or "What Are You?"

Racial/ethnic ambiguity refers to the inability of people to distinguish the monoracial category of the multiracial individual from phenotypic characteristics. These traits play a major role in how people perceive the person. If African American traits are dominant, the one drop rule will automatically classify the person as Black, despite the answer of the multiracial individual: "She says she's mixed, but she is really Black." For those multiracial individuals with ambiguous features, the "What are you?" question becomes a constant dilemma. Possessing a volume of racial components, the multiracial person may not possess the language or sophistication to answer properly. Our society, for example, places a continuing negative association with the process and dynamics that produce a multiracial child (interracial marriages and relationships) and the language associated with offspring are often unfamiliar and undesirable in usage. Such terms as "Mulatta(o)" (African/European), "Afroasian" (African/Asian), "Mestiza(o)" (Indian/Spanish), and so on are confusing to most people, including the multiracial child (Root 1992, 1996). Second, the "What are you?" question almost asks a biracial child to justify his or her existence in a world rigidly built on the concepts of racial purity and monoracialism. This is reinforced by a multiracial person's attempt to answer such a question by discerning the motives of the interrogator: "Why is the person asking?" "Does it really matter?" "Are they really interested in the answer, or am I going to violate their expectations?" "Do they see me as an oddity?" If the person answers "American," this will only lead to further inquiry (Ramirez, 1996). If the answer is "mixed," the interrogator will query further: "What ethnicity are you?" If the answer is "part White and Black," other questions follow: "Who are your parents?" "Which is Black?" "Why did they marry?" The multiracial person begins to feel picked apart and fragmented when questioned about the components of his or her race (Root, 1990). The problem with giving an answer is that it is never "good enough." The communication from our society is quite clear: "You do not belong in this world, and there is something wrong with you." We cannot stress enough how often multiracial persons face a barrage of questions about their racial identities from childhood to adulthood (Houston, 1997; Wehrly et al., 1999). The inquisition can result in invalidation, conflicting feelings of loyalties to the racial/ethnic identities of parents, internal trauma, and confused identity development.

Implications. Multiracial children often feel quite isolated and find little support even from their parents. This is especially true for monoracial parents who themselves are not multiracial. How, for example, does a White mother married to a Black husband raise her child? White? Black? Mixed? Other? Parents of interracial marriages may fail to understand the challenges encountered by their children, gloss over differences, or raise the child as if he or she were monoracial. The child may therefore lack a role model and feel even greater loneliness. Even being a multiracial parent may not result in greater empathy or understanding of the unique challenges faced by their multiracial children, especially if parents (themselves victims of a monoracial system) have not adequately resolved their own sense of identity conflicts. The problem is compounded by the gender of the parents and the multiracial child. One clinical study of ten families found that when the mother is White and the father Black, daughters are more likely to identify with the mother's racial background; and when the mother is Black and the father White, boys and girls will likely identify with being Black (Bowles, 1993). In almost all of these cases, the children expressed shame in not being able to include their father's heritage as part of their identity and experienced anxiety, depression, and difficulty in coping. Interestingly, it was found that the one child raised as biracial seemed to be the healthiest of the entire group.

The Marginal Syndrome, or Existing between the Margins

Root (1990) asserted that mixed-race people begin life as "marginal individuals" because society refuses to view the races as equal and because their ethnic identities are ambiguous. They are often viewed as fractionated people— composed of fractions of a race, culture, or ethnicity. A person who is Asian, White European, and African may not be acceptable to any group. None of these groups may view the multiracial person as being truly Asian, White, or Black. They will encounter prejudice and discrimination not only from the dominant group, but from secondary ethnic groups as well (Brown, 1990). One study of Black and Japanese biracials found that half felt that not belonging to one racial group was the true negative aspect of their identity struggles (C. C. I. Hall, 1980). Stonequist (1937) first coined the term *identity purgatory* to describe an existence of a person of mixed race who exists on the margins of one or several worlds, not fully included in any.

In Chapter 8 we spent considerable time discussing racial/cultural identity development among minority groups. Several major criticisms have been leveled at these theories: (a) They were developed from a monoracial perspective (African Americans, Asian Americans, etc.) rather than a multiracial one; (b) they falsely assume that multiracial individuals will be accepted by their parent culture or cultures; and (c) their linear nature is inadequate to describe the complexity of the many possible multiracial resolutions (Root, 1990, 1992, 1996; Kerwin & Ponterotto, 1995; Poston, 1990). In an early biracial identity development model, Poston (1990) described five stages.

At the *personal identity* stage, biracial children's sense of self is largely independent of ethnic heritage; at the *choice of group categorization* stage, the youngster feels pressures to identify with one racial orientation by either parents, peers or societal forces; at the *enmeshment/denial* stage, there are likely to be considerable negative feelings, whether conscious or unconscious, regarding the denial of one of the racial heritages; at the *appreciation* stage, the person begins to value the racial roots of both parents; and at the *integration* stage, wholeness and integration of both identities occur.

Multiracial individuals confront the process of resolving marginality and developing a healthy identity throughout their entire lives. Perhaps the most sophisticated of the multiracial identity development models is the one proposed by Root (1990, 1998). We focus here on Root's descriptions of the four possible healthy resolutions of marginality.

1. The multiracial individual may accept the identity assigned by society. Thus, a product of a Black-Japanese union may be considered Black by his or her friends, peers, and family. Root believes that this can be a positive choice if the person is satisfied with the identity, receives family support, and is active rather than passive in evidencing the identity. Of all the identities, however, this is the most likely to be fluid and to change radically in different situations. If the person, for example, moves to another community or part of the country, the assigned racial identity may become Japanese or even "mixed."

2. The person may choose to resolve marginality through the ability to identify with both groups. In this case, the person is very much like the "protean person," able to shift from one identity (Japanese American) when with one group and another identity (African American) when with a different group. The method of adaptation is healthy as long as the person does not lose his or her sense of self-integrity, views the ability to move in two worlds as positive, and can relate well to positive aspects of both identities and cultures.

3. The person may decide to choose a single racial identity in an active manner. While it may appear similar to the first option, it differs in two ways: (a) The person makes the choice of racial group identity (not society), and (b) the identity is less prone to shifting when the situational context changes. Again, this is a healthy identity when the group with whom the individual chooses to identify does not marginalize the person and if the individual does not deny his or her other racial heritage.

4. Identification with a new "mixed-race heritage" is another option. There is equal valuing of all aspects of one's racial/cultural heritage, good ability to relate to both groups, and feelings of being well integrated. While not directly addressed, it appears that this identification has many options and alternatives. For example, individuals who choose this route may appear quite different from one another. In other words, there are many ways to be of mixed race.

Root's contribution to understanding multiracial identity development has had a profound impact also on monoracial models. She has challenged the linear models of racial identity; increased our understanding that identity is fluid and not fixed; produced a more ecological model that integrates gender, class, racism, and so on; and reminded us that there are many types of healthy adjustments to racial identity. This has led her to state that the multiracial experience is allowing us to cross racial borders and to discover a new frontier in race relations (Root, 1996).

Implications. While not unlike monoracial identity development models, several important distinctions are made. First, resolutions occur not only between dominant-subordinate group relations (culture-conflicts), but often within racial identities as well (White-Asian, Native American–Black, etc.). Second, resolutions can involve more than a conflict between two racial groups (Black, White, and Asian). Third, the complexity of multiple resolutions may be different depending on the type of multiracial combination, gender, and other group identity factors such as socioeconomic status, age, and sexual orientation. Fourth, identities may shift and are fluid depending on the situational context. Last, multiracial identity development models entertain the notion that there is more than one resolution that can lead to a healthy adjustment.

Stereotypes and Myths of Multiracial Individuals and Interracial Couples

There is considerable evidence that the myths and stereotypes associated with multiracial individuals and interracial couples are attempts to prevent the mixing of races through stigmatizing them (Wehrly et al., 1999). Unfortunately, it appears that sociopsychological research on this topic has often perpetuated and reinforced these beliefs and has carried over into our everyday beliefs about race mixing and mixed-race people. It is not unusual, for example, to discern beliefs suggesting that multiracial children are inferior to monoracial ones and that they are more prone to major social and psychological problems (Jackman et al., 2001). Further, interracial unions are filled with images of unhappy and unstable couples or deficiencies in partners who choose to marry out of their race.

Early research and writings on the characteristics and dynamics of interracial relationships and marriages focused primarily on negative attributes. Most prevalent were beliefs that individuals who chose to marry out were possessed of low self-esteem, filled with self-loathing and feelings of inferiority (Beigel, 1966); rebelling against parental authority (Saxton, 1968); and evidencing mental problems (Brayboy, 1966). Stereotypes fluctuate depending on the race and the gender of the person marrying out. A White person who violated social norms against interracial marriages would be seen as experimenting with the "exotic," attempting to express a liberal view, possessing very low self-esteem, or being a social/occupational failure unable to attract a member of his or her own race (Rosenblatt et al., 1995). Members of a minority group would often be seen as trying to "elevate" themselves socially, economically, and psychologically.

Sexual stereotypes also play a major role in the perception of men and women who are involved in interracial relationships/marriages. Asian American women are often perceived by the wider society as "exotic" and "erotic" creatures, eager to please men, domestically oriented, and likely to be submissive; their male counterparts, however, are seen as sexually emasculated, passive and unassertive, inhibited, and lacking in social confidence (S. Sue & Sue, 1971a). These are quite pervasive beliefs whether conscious or unconscious. Some suggest that the higher rate of marrying out for Asian American women may be due to these myths. Regardless, there does seem to be greater positive associations with Asian American women, and they are more socially acceptable than are their male counterparts. On the other hand, Black men and women are often described as possessing "primitive sexuality," "animalistic," passionate, potent, and sexually virile (Frankenberg, 1993). While Asian American men may not be seen as a competitive threat, African American men with their "aggressive and promiscuous sexual behaviors" are seen as a danger to "White women." History is replete with incidents of the wider society's hostility and antagonisms toward Black men.

Stereotypes of multiracial individuals are also largely negative. Due to legal (until as recently as 1967) and social prohibitions against interracial relationships, it is not difficult to see why multiracial children may also be subjected to negative perceptions. Products of an "unholy and immoral union," multiracial individuals are seen as being doomed to an immoral or troubled existence, likely to suffer identity problems and low self-esteem and be marginal persons who are socially isolated. On the other hand, multiracial individuals are also described as inordinately beautiful and handsome in a physical sense, but even then it is associated with promiscuity and the sexual myths of this population.

Implications. In general, the myths about mixed marriages and multiracial people imply that these unions are the result of unhealthy motives by the partners and that offspring are doomed to suffer many deficiencies and pathologies. The early studies cited and the assumptions they made suffer from several problems. First, if partners in mixed marriages and multiracial individuals suffer from greater identity issues, conflicts, and psychological problems, then they are more often the result of an intolerant and hostile society. They are caused from the bias, discrimination, and racism of people rather than inherent in the marriage or the "unhealthy" qualities of those involved. Second, we already know that to a large extent research is influenced and reflects societal views. It seems likely, therefore, that early researchers most likely asked questions and designed studies that attributed a "problem-oriented" definition of multiracial people. The focus becomes identifying pathology, rather than the healthy and functional traits of a group. Third, in the case of interracial relationships/marriages, current research now suggests that these marriages are based on the same ingredients as are intraracial marriages: love, companionship, and compatible interests and values (Lewandowski & Jackson, 2001; Porterfield, 1982; Rosenblatt et al., 1995). Last, the image of multiracial individuals is an unbalanced one. Increasingly, research reveals that beneficial sociopsychological traits may be the outcome of a multiracial heritage: increased sense of uniqueness, better ability to relate to more diverse groups, greater tolerance and understanding of people, ability to deal with racism, enjoying what many groups have to offer, greater variety in one's life, and better ability to build alliances with many diverse people and groups (Root, 1996; Rosenblatt et al., 1995; Wehrly et al., 1999).

A Multiracial Bill of Rights

> *Countless number of times I have fragmented and fractionalized myself in order to make the other more comfortable in deciphering my behavior, my words, my loyalties, my choice of friends, my appearance, my parents, and so on. And given my multiethnic history, it was hard to keep track of all the fractions, to make them add up to one whole. It took me over 30 years to realize that fragmenting myself seldom served a purpose other than to preserve the delusions this country has created around race.*
>
> *Reciting the fractions to the other was the ultimate act of buying into the mechanics of racism in this country. Once I realized this, I could ask myself other questions. How exactly does a person be one fourth, one eighth, or one half something? To fragment myself and others, "she is one half Chinese and one half white," or "he is one quarter Native, one quarter African American, and one half Spanish" was to unquestioningly be deployed to operate the machinery that disenfranchised myself, my family, my friends, and others I was yet to meet. (Root, 1996, pp. 4–5)*

These words were written by Maria Root, a leading psychologist in the field of multiracial identity and development. She believes that our society has relegated multiracial persons to deviant status, minimized their contributions to society, and ignored their existence because they do not fit into our monoracial classification. In her personal and professional journey, Root (1996) has developed a "Bill of Rights for Racially Mixed People" that is composed of three major affirmations: resistance, revolution, and change.

1. Resistance refers to the multiracial individual's right to resist the belief system imposed by society, the data on which they are based, and the rationalizations used to justify the status quo regarding race relations. It

means refusing to fragment, marginalize or disconnect from others and the self. Four assertions embody resistance:
  I have the right not to

- Justify my existence in this world
- Keep the races separate within me
- Be responsible for people's discomfort with my physical ambiguity
- Justify my ethnic legitimacy

2. Revolution refers to multiracial people or anyone who enters into an interracial relationship who chooses to "cross the boundaries" of race relations. According to Root, these individuals are often seen as "race traitors" who can create an emotional/psychic earthquake that challenges the reality of our oppressive racial system. Four assertions embody revolution:
  I have the right to

- Identify myself differently than strangers expect me to
- Identify myself differently than how my parents identify me
- Identify myself differently than my brothers and sisters
- Identify myself differently in different situations

3. Change refers to the active attempt to build connections, wholeness, and a sense of belonging to one another. While the two other sets of assertions are attempts to free one from the racialized existence of a monoracial system, connections acknowledge that our social fates are intertwined and dependent on one another. According to Root, this sense of belonging serves as a force against perpetrating atrocities against fellow human beings. Four assertions embody change:
  I have the right to

- Create a vocabulary to communicate about being multiracial
- Change my identity over my lifetime—and more than once
- Have loyalties and identify with more than one group of people
- Choose freely whom I befriend and love

Implications. Root's Bill of Rights is much more complex and meaningful than is described here. It has major implications for the mental health provider because it challenges our notions of a monoracial classification system, reorients our thoughts about the many myths of multiracial persons, makes us aware of the systemic construction and rationalizations of race, warns us about the dangers of fractionating identities, and advocates freedom of choice for the multiracial individual. For the mental health provider, much of importance can be derived from the twelve assertions contained in the Bill of Rights.

Guidelines for Clinical Practice

While monoracial minority groups have many similarities with multiracial ones, the latter are likely to experience unique stressors related to their multiple racial/ethnic identities in addition to dealing with racism. For example, most monoracial minorities find their own groups receptive and supportive of them. Multiracial individuals may be placed in an awkward situation where none of their groups of origin accept them. Likewise, an African American youngster can expect psychological and emotional support from his or her parents. The parents share common experiences with their sons and daughters, can act as mentors, and relate to the experiences their children encounter with respect to minority status. However, multiracial children may be the products of monoracial parents. In any case, some helpful guidelines include the following:

1. Become aware of your own stereotypes and preconceptions regarding interracial relationships and marriages. When you see a racially mixed couple, do you pay extra attention to them? What thoughts and images do you have? Only when you are able to become aware of your biases will you be able to avoid imposing them upon your clients.

2. When working with multiracial clients, avoid stereotyping. Like interracial relationships, all of us have been culturally conditioned to believe certain things about racially mixed people. In general, these images are based on mistaken beliefs that deny the mixed-race heritage of the person and his or her uniqueness.

3. See multiracial people in a holistic fashion rather than as fractions of a person. This means being careful when dealing with the "What are you?" question. In most cases, it is important to emphasize the positive qualities of the total person rather than seeing the person as parts.

4. Remember that being a multiracial person often means coping with marginality, isolation, and loneliness. These feelings are not the result of internal problems but are generally brought about by external factors related to prejudice. Nevertheless, mixed-race persons often experience strong feelings of loneliness, rejection, forced choice situations, guilt/shame from not fully integrating all aspects of their racial heritage, differentness, and anger. These feelings have often been submerged and hidden because there is no one to share them with who understands. As

mentioned earlier, mixed-race children often come from homes with monoracial parents.

5. With mixed-race clients, emphasize the freedom to choose one's identity. Root's Bill of Rights is helpful here. There is no one identity suitable for everyone. The racial identity models discussed in this chapter all have limitations, and it is important to note that identities are both changing and fluid, rather than fixed.

6. Take an active psychoeducational approach. Multiracial individuals are often subjected to a rigid monoracial system that stereotypes and fits them into rigid categories. Oftentimes, children may learn to internalize the stereotypes and accept an identity imposed upon them. Somewhere in the counseling process, clients can be helped to understand the forces of oppression, and the counselor can empower them to take an active part in formulating their identities.

7. Since mixed race people are constantly portrayed as possessing deficiencies, stress their positive attributes and the advantages of being multiracial and multicultural.

8. Recognize that family counseling may be especially valuable in working with mixed-race clients, especially if they are children. Frequently, parents (themselves often monoracial) are unaware of the unique conflicts related to their child's multiracial journey. Parents can be taught to empower their children, convey positive aspects of being multiracial, and help them integrate a healthy identity. Root (1998), for example, suggested things like giving mixed-race children a first and/or middle name that connects them to their heritage, developing answers to the "What are you?" question, being positive about one's multiple heritage, attending community events of the family's heritage, and avoiding negative remarks about people of color.

9. When working with multiracial clients, ensure that you possess basic knowledge of the history and issues related to hypodescent (the one drop rule), ambiguity (the "What are you?" question, marginality, and racial/cultural identity. The knowledge cannot be superficial but must entail a historical, political, social, and psychological understanding of the treatment of race, racism, and monoracialism in this society. In essence, these four dynamics form the context that the multiracial individual deals with on a continuing basis.

Part VI

COUNSELING OTHER CULTURALLY DIVERSE POPULATIONS

Counseling Sexual Minorities

Jerry Falwell, on the Pat Robertson program The 700 Club, *indicated his belief that the September 11, 2001, terrorist attack that took thousands of innocent lives was partly due to the growing influence of gay and lesbian groups. Jerry Falwell was later forced to apologize for his remarks.*

Jacob Williams, a preschool student, was playing when a little girl who had been observing him asked where his dad was. Jacob responded by saying he didn't have a father but had two moms. The little girl was confused but later walked up to one of the two mothers and said she had "figured it out." She had two granddads, so Jacob could have two moms. (Wingert & Kantrowitz, 2000)

At Lane Community College in Oregon, a janitor's closet has been converted into a private shower for Michael May (he has already changed his name to Amy), who is planning to undergo a male to female sex-change operation. May is taking female hormones to increase breast size and feels that he may be invading others' privacy in the men's locker room. (Associated Press, 2001)

Homosexuality involves the affectional and/or sexual orientation to a person of the same sex. In self-definitions, most males prefer the term *gay* to homosexual, and most females prefer the term *lesbian*. It is difficult to get an accurate estimate on the number of gay, lesbian, and bisexual individuals in the United States. It is estimated that approximately 4% to 10% of the U.S. population are homosexual (J. L. Norton, 1995). Approximately 7% of a national sample of 6,254 boys and 5,686 girls reported having a same-sex attraction or relationship (Russell & Joyner, 2001). Transgender individuals include transsexuals and others who cross-dress for a variety of reasons. Most gay/lesbian/bisexual/transgender (GLBT) individuals live in the states of California, Florida, New York, and Texas (Cohn, 2001).

The mood of the country seems to exhibit contradictory attitudes and actions toward sexual minorities. In some cases, there appears to be a greater acceptance of GLBT individuals and their lifestyles. Even with progress occurring on these fronts, however, discrimination and violence against these populations remain high.

Positive developments include the following:

- In New Jersey, two gay men were awarded custody of a 3-year-old boy after a 2-year effort. They successfully challenged the state law that did not allow adoption by same-sex couples (Smothers, 1998).

- The Washington Supreme Court held that gays might be entitled to the estates of partners who have died even without a will. The unanimous decision overturned a lower court that had ruled the claim invalid because same-sex marriage is illegal in Washington (Skolnik, 2001).

- Antidiscrimination laws have been passed in 28 local governments to protect transgender individuals and give them the right to file civil complaints and lawsuits.

- The city of San Francisco decided on February 2001 to expand health care benefits to include psychotherapy, medical treatment, and surgery for sex-conversion operations for transgender city employees.

- A court decision in Massachusetts allowed a transgender female to wear women's clothing to high school (M. McNamara, 2001).

Examples of continuing prejudice include the following:

- In a Newsweek poll of the U.S. public, 83% supported job protection, 78% supported antidiscrimination in housing, and 58% were for health benefits for gays and lesbians. However, the same poll indicated that 57% are still opposed to gay or lesbian marriage, 50% against adoption for gay or lesbian individuals, 35% against serving in the military, and 36% against teaching in elementary school.

- Currently, over 32 states ban same-sex marriages (Leland, 2000). Denise Penn, a bisexual, feels this contradiction. While her neighbors are quite accepting of her partners or friends of either sex, she felt shaken over the battle on Proposition 22, which banned gay marriage. Her "accepting" neighbors displayed signs reading "PROTECT MARRIAGE" (Leland, 2000).

- A transgender woman being treated at the scene of a car accident by paramedics was denied further assistance when her penis was discovered (Wright, 2001). Transgender individuals also are not fully accepted among gay, lesbian, and bisexual groups (Cada, 2000).

- Gay men and lesbians still constitute one of the least liked groups in the country (Goldberg, 1998).

- In Los Angeles in 1994, there were 332 reported incidents of hate crimes ranging from harassment to murder directed at gay men and lesbians, a 53% increase from the previous year (Boxall, 1995).

    Gay bashing is hard to understand and is often described as an extreme homophobic reaction. One victim, Arthur Dong, responded: "I was stunned. I was never attacked as an Asian man, and I'm obviously an Asian man. . . . But I was attacked as a gay man. . . . Why do people do this?" (Graham, 1997, p. D11). Dong was so disturbed by this that he produced *License to Kill,* an award-winning film that showed interviews with six men explaining why they had murdered gay men. One of the cases involved a man who had murdered two gay men. He was raised in a strict, religious household where his father denounced homosexuality. Jay Johnson, the killer, was himself gay!

Same Sex Relationships Are Not Signs of Mental Disorders

Although the American Psychiatric Association and the American Psychological Association no longer consider homosexuality to be a mental disorder, some individuals still harbor the belief that it is. Trent Lott, the Senate majority leader, recently described homosexuality as a disorder akin to alcoholism, kleptomania, and sexual addiction—a condition that should be treated (Mitchell, 1998). Dr Laura, a talk-show host, described homosexuality as a "biological error," gay sex as "deviant," and she supports reparative therapy. The American Psychiatric Association first voted in 1973 to remove homosexuality from the *Diagnostic and Statistical Manual of Mental Disorders* (DSM). However, it did create a new category, ego-dystonic homosexuality, in the third edition of the DSM (American Psychiatric Association, 1980) for individuals with (a) a lack of heterosexual arousal that interferes with heterosexual relationships and (b) persistent distress from unwanted homosexual arousal. This category was eliminated in the face of the argument that societal pressure and prejudice created the condition.

The American Psychological Association took an even stronger stand and adopted a official policy statement that "homosexuality per se implies no impairment in judgment, stability, reliability, or general social or vocational capabilities" and indicated that mental health professionals should take the lead in removing the stigma of mental illness that has long been associated with homosexual orientations (Conger, 1975). A number of studies (Berube, 1990; Gonsiorek, 1982; Hooker, 1957; Reiss, 1980) have demonstrated few adjustment differences between individuals with a homosexual or heterosexual orientation. As one researcher concluded, "Homosexuality in and of itself is unrelated to psychological disturbance or maladjustment. Homosexuals as a group are not more psychologically disturbed on account of their homosexuality" (Gonsiorek, 1982, p. 74). However, exposure to societal discrimination may be responsible for the recent findings that lesbian and gay youth report elevated rates of major depression, generalized anxiety disorder, and substance abuse. Gay men also reported high rates of major depression. Lesbian women appeared to fare better and reported mental health equal to that of their heterosexual counterparts as well as higher self-esteem (DeAngelis, 2002). Gender identity issues and cross-dressing can be characterized as mental disorders according to the mental health organizations. However, transgender individuals are hoping that they can follow the success and path taken by the gay liberation movement and eliminate these as mental disorders.

A number of research studies reveal that bias continues to exist among mental health professionals. In one study, 97 counselors read a fictitious intake report about a bisexual woman seeking counseling with no indication that the problem involved her sexual orientation. The problems involved career choice, issues with parents over independence, ending a two-year relationship with another woman, and problems with her boyfriend. Thus, issues involved were boundary with parents, career choice, and romantic relationships. Counselors with the most negative attitude regarding bisexuality believed that the problems stemmed from her bisexuality and rated her lower in psychosocial functioning (Mohr, Israel, & Sedlacek, 2001). Similarly, another study found that therapists who possess even low levels of homophobia tended to blame the clients for problems (J. A. Hayes & Erkis, 2000).

Garnets, Hancock, Cochran, Goodchilds, and Peplau (1998) conducted a survey of instances of biased or beneficial responses that therapists heard of or knew of from other therapists or clients in counseling gay or lesbian clients. The following biased or inappropriate practices were reported:

1. Believing that homosexuality is a form of mental illness. Some therapists continue to believe that homosexuality represents a personality disorder or other mental disturbance and is not just a different lifestyle.

2. Failing to understand that a client's problem, such as depression or low self-esteem, can be a result of the internalization of society's view of homosexuality.

3. Assuming that the client is heterosexual, thereby making it harder to bring up issues regarding sexual orientation.

4. Focusing on sexual orientation when it is not relevant. Problems may be completely unrelated to sexual orientation, but some therapists continue to focus on it as the major contributor to all presented problems.

5. Attempting to have clients renounce or change their sexual orientation. For example, a lesbian was asked by the therapist to date men.

6. Trivializing or demeaning homosexuality. A therapist responded to a lesbian who brought up that she was "into women" that he didn't care, since he had a client who was "into dogs."

7. Transferring clients to another therapist without dealing with the emotional aspects of the change.

8. Lacking an understanding of identity development in lesbian women and gay men or viewing homosexuality solely as sexual activity.

9. Not understanding the impact of possible internalized negative societal pressures or homophobia on identity development.

10. Underestimating the consequences of "coming out" for the client. Such suggestion should be provided only after a careful discussion of the pros and cons of this disclosure.

11. Misunderstanding or underestimating the importance of intimate relationships for gay men and lesbians. One therapist reportedly advised a lesbian couple who were having problems in their relationship to not consider it a permanent relationship and consider going to a gay bar to meet others.

12. Using the heterosexual framework inappropriately when working with lesbian and gay male relationships. One couple was given a book to read dealing with heterosexual relationships.

13. Presuming that clients with a different sexual orientation cannot be good parents and automatically assuming that their children's problems are a result of the orientation.

14. Being insensitive to the degree of prejudice and discrimination faced by lesbians and gay males and their children.

15. Displaying inaccurate or insufficient information about gay and lesbian issues.

Implications. Although mental health organizations have acknowledged that homosexuality is not a mental disorder, it is recognized that a "need for better education and training of mental health practitioners" exists (Division 44/ Committee on Lesbian, Gay, and Bisexual Concerns Joint Task Force, 2000). Curriculum changes and the infusion of information about gay and lesbian concerns and lifestyles are needed in mental health programs. Research on GLBT populations has focused on a "sickness" model and can be characterized as victim blaming (Martin & Knox, 2000). We also need to address the positive characteristics and relationships found in these groups. Heterosexist bias in therapy has to be acknowledged and changed.

Many still consider the departure from heterosexual norms as repugnant or a sign of psychological maladjustment. We have to examine possible stereotypes that we have of GLBT clients. Certain changes in the provision of mental health services have been found to be helpful. GLBT perceived counselors more positively, indicated a greater willingness to disclose personal information, and reported greater comfort in disclosing sexual orientation when a counseling interview was free of heterosexist language (e.g., using the term partner or spouse instead of "boyfriend or girlfriend," "husband and wife"; Dorland & Fischer, 2001). Workshops and training in the use of nondiscriminatory intake forms and identifying psychological and health issues faced by many GLBT clients are helpful means of increasing the effectiveness of health care providers (Blake, Ledsky, Lehman, & Goodenow, 2001). Certain issues have been identified as helpful in working with GLBT clients. Liddle (1996) summarized the reports of 392 lesbian women and gay men who reported their experiences with 923 therapists. Gay and lesbian therapists, bisexual therapists of both genders, and heterosexual female therapists were all rated more helpful than were heterosexual male therapists (although 30% of heterosexual males were rated very helpful). Issues that were identified as important to the client included (a) understanding the effects of societal prejudice on development and health, (b) recognizing and dealing with the issue of internalized homophobia, (c) assisting the client in developing a positive gay or lesbian identity, and (d) being aware of community resources. However, respondents warned that counselors should not focus on sexual orientation if it is not a present issue.

Mental health professionals should also not adopt a "color-blind" stance—that everyone is the same. Although this would seem to be a democratic strategy, GLBT individuals face unique sets of stressors, life experiences, stigmatization, and identity crises that have a profound impact on their lives. Mental health professionals need to educate themselves on the special concerns faced by GLBT clients. Experiences with harassment, victimization, and fear of or actual losses of friends and family due to their sexual orientation needs to assessed and addressed.

GLBT Couples and Families

About 1.2 million people are part of gay and lesbian couples in the United States, representing a 300% increase since 1990. There are about as many lesbian as gay male couples (Cohn, 2001). The intimate relationships of gay and lesbian couples appear to be similar to those of heterosexual individuals. However, among lesbian couples there is a more egalitarian relationship. Household chores and decision making are equally shared. Also, many GLBT couples and individuals are showing increasing interest in becoming parents. Gays and lesbians can adopt children in every state except Florida (Wingert & Kantrowitz, 2000). Children of GLBT couples show healthy cognitive and behavioral functioning. It has been concluded that heterosexual family structures are not necessary for healthy child development (B. R. Strickland,

1995). Because of the large increase in the number of GLBT couples and families, mental health professional are likely to encounter them as clients. Mental health professionals may be asked to evaluate the suitability of prospective GLBT individuals to be parents. Before service can be provided, mental health professionals must determine whether they have a heterosexist bias regarding relationships and families.

Implications. Along with problems that are faced by heterosexual couples and families, GLBT individuals also face prejudice and discrimination from society. In relationships, each may differ in internalized homophobia or the extent to which they are "out" to others in their social, work, or family networks. They may be uncomfortable showing public displays of affection or feel the need to hide their sexual orientation (Blando, 2001). In evaluating GLBT parents or determining suitability as adoptive parents, mental health professionals should determine their attitudes and beliefs regarding GLBT individuals. The empirical data indicate that GLBT parenting styles and child-rearing practices do not differ from that of their heterosexual counterparts. One concern commonly expressed has been the impact of GLBT parenting on the sexual orientation of the children. Research shows that children raised by gay and lesbian parents do not have problems with gender identity, gender role behavior, sexual orientation, or sexual adjustment (Crawford, McLeod, Zamboni, & Jordan, 1999). Problems faced by gay and lesbian couples may include legal issues with adoption, medical benefits for same-sex couples, and prejudice. In addition to normal developmental issues, children of GLBT parents may face having to explain to peers or classmates their nontraditional family with two dads, two moms, or dads dressed as women. Family and parenting resources available for both therapists and gay and lesbian parents include *Social Services for Gay and Lesbian Couples* by Kurdek (1994), *Lesbians and Gays in Couples and Families* by Laird and Green (1996), *Lesbian Step Families* by Wright (1998), and *Out of the Ordinary: Essays on Growing Up with Gay, Lesbian, and Transgender Parents* (Howey & Samuels, 2000).

GLBT Youth

As compared to heterosexual adolescents, GLBT youth report more substance use, high-risk sexual behaviors, suicidal thoughts or attempts, and personal safety issues (Blake et al., 2001; R. Lee, 2000). They are more likely to have been involved in a fight that needed medical attention (Russell, Franz, & Driscoll, 2001). Gay and lesbian youths face discrimination and harassment in schools. In a study of Massachusetts high school students, gay, lesbian, and bisexual students were more likely than their peers to be confronted with a weapon at school (32.7% vs. 7.1%) or not attend school because of safety concerns (25.1% vs. 5.1%). In addition, they were more likely to have attempted suicide during the past year than were their heterosexual-identified counterparts. The suicide rate does not appear to be because of their sexual orientation but because their school, home, and social environments have been compromised (Russell & Joyner, 2001). However, recent studies show little difference in suicide rates between GLBT and heterosexual youth (DeAngelis, 2002). The murder of Brandon Teena, who was the inspiration for the movie *Boys Don't Cry,* illustrates the problems faced by transgender youth.

Implications. Mental health professionals need to address the problems of GLBT youth at both the systems and individual levels. To improve the school environment, inclusion of gay and transgender issues in the curriculum, addressing self-management and social skills relevant to GLBT youth, providing adequate social services, and a nondiscriminatory school environment can be advocated. It is important to have policies that protect GLBT youth from harassment and violence. School staff should be trained on sexual orientation issues. Support groups for GLBT and heterosexual students to discuss GLBT issues in a safe and confidential environment are also important. Counseling services should be provided for GLBT students and family members (Blake et al., 2001). Approximately 700 gay-straight alliance groups in schools have started since the 1998 murder of Matthew Shepherd. These groups were formed for gay and straight students to work against homophobia. GLBT youth need safe places to meet others and to socialize. Community-based supports involving hotlines and youth clubs can be helpful. Such organizations defuse possible harassment and violence in school and allow gay students to gain support and create openly gay lives (Peyser & Lorch, 2000). A useful resource for both the counselor and GLBT youth is *Queer Kids: The Challenge and Promise for Lesbian, Gay, and Bisexual Youth* by Owens (1998). The book discusses how children and adolescents cope with emerging sexual orientation. In individual counseling sessions, assess for substance use, suicidality, social support, and self-esteem issues. Appropriate coping skills and support groups can be identified and strengthened.

Identity Issues

The slow discovery of being different is agonizing. As one individual observed, "Imagine learning about love and sexuality in a heterosexual world when your preference is for people of the same gender" (Parker & Thompson, 1990). Awareness of the sexual orientation of gay males and lesbian females tends to occur in the early teens with sexual self-identification during the mid-teens, same-sex experience in the mid-teens, and same-sex relationships in the late teens (Blake et al., 2001). Disclosure to parents tends to occur by the age of 30, although even at that age over half have not disclosed

(J. L. Norton, 1995). The struggle for identity involves one's internal perceptions, in contrast to the external perceptions or assumptions of others about one's sexual orientation. The individual must learn to accept his or her internal identity, often struggling with the society's definition of what is "healthy." To come to an appropriate resolution, the individual ceases struggling to be "straight" and begins to establish a new identity and self-concept and understanding of what constitutes a good life. Often during this period, individuals must deal with issues of grief over letting go of the old identity (Browning, Reynolds, & Dworkin, 1998; Parker & Thompson, 1990).

Individuals with gender identity issues also report feeling "different" at an early age. One activist described gender dysphoria as "one of the greatest agonies . . . when your anatomy doesn't match who you are inside" (Wright 2001). Cross-sex behaviors and appearance are highly stigmatized in school and society.

Implications. Adolescence is a time of exploration and experimentation. Heterosexual activity does not mean one is a heterosexual, nor does same sex activity indicate homosexuality. Overly interpreting sexual behavior in adolescents should be avoided. In one study of junior and senior high students, 88% indicated they were predominantly heterosexual, 1% bisexual or predominantly homosexual, but 10% were unsure (Ryan & Futterman, 2001a). Many GLBT youth describe feeling "different" from early childhood. When their sexual identity is acknowledged, they must deal with a stigmatized identity. Many feel alone and isolated, having no one to talk to. They feel emotionally disconnected to others since the discovery of their "secret" may lead to rejection. Accurate information about homosexuality is lacking (Ryan & Futterman, 2001b). Many pretend to be straight or avoid discussing sexuality. Because of this they lack the ability to obtain support and nurturance from parents, families, or peer groups. The mental health professional must help GLBT youth develop coping and survival skills and to expand environmental supports. Several online resources exist: American Psychological Association (APA), www.apa.org; Gay, Lesbian, and Straight Education Network (GLSEN), www.glsen.org; Parents, Family, and Friends of Lesbians and Gays (PFLAG), www.pflag.org; and Youth Resource, www.youthresource.com. These provide accurate information and resources for GLBT youth. If you work in schools, indicate availability by displaying posters supporting diversity including sexual orientation.

Coming Out

The discovery that one's sexual orientation is different from that accepted by society can produce a profound feeling of loss. One woman who discovered her sexual orientation after 25 years of marriage writes,

Several years ago my husband and I attended the 50th birthday for one of our oldest friends. Everyone was sharing anecdotes about the guest of honor, Jeff, as he stood arm in arm with his wife, Sherry. She looked at him lovingly: Suddenly my eyes filled with tears and I fled the room . . . during my 25th year of marriage, I fell in love with my best friend. . . . My confession to her destroyed our friendship. . . . My tears were for . . . the isolation my silence condemned me to, my internalized homosexuality. (Strock, 1998, p. 16)

For this individual, the heterosexual ideal of a picture-perfect relationship was lost forever. Gay men and lesbian women, after realizing their sexual orientation, may feel isolated from their families and friends who adhere to the heterosexual standard. Many no longer feel welcome in churches and are concerned about having their orientation discovered in the workplace. The counselor must help the client discover new sources of support.

The decision to *come out* is extremely difficult and is often influenced by the overwhelming sense of isolation the individual feels. In maintaining the secret, relationships with friends and family may be seriously affected. Coming out is especially difficult for adolescents who are emotionally and financially dependent on their family. They have less access to appropriate role models and to support systems in the gay and lesbian community (Browning et al., 1998). Coming out to parents and friends can lead to rejection, anger, and grief. Most recipients of the information will also experience grief at the loss of the individual they thought they knew. Parents may feel a loss for their children in terms of the picture that society has painted of appropriate relationships. They may worry that their parenting was the cause of the sexual orientation (Shannon & Woods, 1998).

Implications. The decision of when to come out should be carefully considered. To whom does the individual want to reveal the information? What are the possible effects and consequences of the self-disclosure for the individual and the recipient of the information? What new sources of support among family, friends, or community are available for them? If the individual is already in a relationship, how will the disclosure affect his or her partner? Have they also considered the consequences? In many cases, it may be best not to tell. If the individual has considered the implications of coming out and still desires to do so, the counselor should offer specific help and preparation in determining how this should be accomplished. Role-plays and the discussion of possible reactions should be practiced. If parents were open, counseling sessions would be helpful for them to obtain accurate information. Many parents will also have to deal with grief (past goals for their children, weddings, and grandchildren) and guilt issues (whether their parenting was responsible). They will have to deal with the societal stigma of having a homosexual family member and may benefit from receiving information and education regarding myths and stereotypes of homosexuality. If the parents are reject-ing, the individual must strengthen other sources of social support. Also, the mental health professional should help the client identify the external sources for their issues over identity rather than allow self-blame to occur.

Aging

The two older women often sit next to each other in identical recliners. . . . Evenings they hold hands under a blanket on the sofa watching TV. . . . They've been partners for 18 years. More than anything, they want to stay together in old age. (King, 2001, B1)

The two women—Selma Kannel, 75, and Nancy King, 67—are worried about their remaining years. If one needs to go to a nursing home, will the partner be allowed to make health care decisions for the other, and will people respond to their relationship negatively? It is estimated that up to 3 million GLBT individuals in the United States are over the age of 65 (King, 2001). The elderly gay are less likely to have revealed their sexual orienta-tions to others when compared to the younger generations. If still in the closet, the individual may be hesitant to reveal his or her sexual orientation and attempt to hide it when dealing with health or government agencies. One man accompanied his partner, who was dying of cancer, to see the surgeon. Initially the physician was surprised to see the male patient accompanied by a man and became hostile, but he later talked to him as if he were the next of kin (King, 2001). In addition, as with other segments of U.S. society, ageism exists in gay and lesbian communities. All of these can produce a great deal of concern among the GLBT elderly in obtaining health care and responding to a diminishing social support system.

Implications. With GLBT elderly, issues of coming out may have to be ad-dressed as need for health care or social services increases. The mental health counselor can assist them in developing additional coping skills, expand their social support system, and advocate or help locate services for the elderly gay. Advocacy groups exist for older gay men and lesbians, and their number is in-creasing. One organization, Senior Action in a Gay Environment (SAGE), provides counseling, educational and recreational activities, and discussion groups for older GLBT individuals. In addition, teleconferences exist for homebound seniors. For example, the Friend and Visitor's program that con-nects volunteers with elderly GLBT individuals. In Seattle, the Rainbow Train gives caregivers and medical practitioners the skills they need for working with older GLBT patients. Communities geared toward retired gay and les-bian residents have been developed. Many organizations have added the transgender community to their mission statements. The mental health professional needs to aware of these resources and advocate changes in laws regarding GLBT partners' rights to participate in health care decision.

Other Issues Faced by GLBT Individuals

Substance abuse issues need to be assessed among GLBT populations. GLBT individuals are at higher risk for substance- and alcohol-related problems (Cochran, Keenan, Schober, & Mays, 2000). Issues involving safe sex also need to be addressed. Minority GLBT individuals face additional problems. Gay Latino men who engage is high-risk sexual behaviors had been subjected to racial and antihomosexual slurs as compared to those engaging in low-risk behavior. However, high-risk sexual behavior among gay males is relatively high (Hayasaki, 2001). The rate of HIV infection among transgender individuals is high and may surpass that of bisexual and homosexual men. Many transgender women are at risk primarily because of risky sexual behavior and also the sharing of needles during injections of hormones or drugs. Among these groups, African American transgender individuals had the highest risk of positive HIV test results and may be a very high-risk group. However, few resources have been devoted to this group. Even in a city such as San Francisco, there is evidence of discrimination against transgender individuals in HIV/AIDS programs (Lombardi, 2001). Many GLBT individuals also face discrimination from places of employment, schools, or church. A schoolteacher, Dana Rivers, was fired in Sacramento because she discussed her transition with students. She received a settlement of $150,000, although a student who supported the dismissal stated, "Seeing a man in a dress would be a distraction" (M. McNamara, 2001, A1). At the level of employment, discrimination can prevent an individual from being hired or can cause employees to receive fewer rewards, resources, or opportunities for salary increases or support from supervisors (Burton, 2001). A helpful resource is *A Providers Introduction to Substance Abuse Treatment for Lesbian, Gay, Bisexual and Transgender Individuals* (2001).

Implications. Therapists working with GLBT clients should be aware of the special issues faced by these clients. To provide adequate service, sexual orientation, behavior, or attraction questions should be included during the assessment. Special concerns such as mental health issues, substance use, and high-risk sexual behaviors may need to be addressed. Unfortunately, GLBT youth are less likely to get information about sexually transmitted diseases and AIDS than are straight teenagers. Substance use and high-risk sexual behaviors may also be a result of a reaction to prejudice, discrimination, and societal standards. Some gay individuals may engage in unsafe sex as an exaggerated adherence to masculinity. Male to female transgender individuals may engage in sexual activity to demonstrate their sexual attractiveness. Unhealthy reactions to prejudice have to be identified and changed. Mental health professionals should also advocate for changes in discriminatory policies both at the governmental and private levels. Companies that have policies affirming sexual diversity in the work force are associated with high levels of satisfaction and commitment between lesbian and gay employees. A policy and public affirmation of nondiscrimination that includes sexual diversity in an organization enhances the atmosphere of the working place. Some organizations have adopted same-sex health coverage for employees, and a few permit informal lesbian and gay networks within the company (Burton, 2001).

Guidelines for Clinical Practice

1. Examine your own views regarding heterosexuality and determine their impact on work with GLBT clients. A way to personalize this perspective is to assume that some of your coworkers may be GLBT.

2. Read the "Guidelines for Psychotherapy with Lesbian, Gay, and Bisexual Clients" (Division 44/Committee on Lesbian, Gay, and Bisexual Concerns, 2000).

3. Develop partnerships, consultation, or collaborative efforts with local and national GLBT organizations.

4. Assure that your intake forms, interview procedures, and language are free of heterosexist bias and include a question on sexual behavior, attraction, or orientation.

5. Do not assume that the presenting problems necessarily are the result of sexual orientation but be willing to address possible societal issues and their role in the problems faced by GLBT clients.

6. Remember that common mental health issues may include stress due to prejudice and discrimination; internalized homophobia; the coming out process; a lack of family, peer, school, and community supports; being a victim of assault; suicidal ideation or attempts; and substance abuse.

7. Realize that GLBT couples may have problems similar to those of their heterosexual counterparts but may also display unique concerns such differences in the degree of comfort with public demonstrations of their relationship or reactions from their family of origin.

8. Assess spiritual and religious needs. Many GLBT individuals have a strong faith in religion but encounter exclusion. Religious support is available. The Fellowship United Methodist Church accepts all types of diversity and is open to a gay congregation.

9. Because many GLBT clients have internalized the societal belief that

they cannot have long-lasting relationships, have materials available that portray healthy and satisfying GLBT relationships.

10. Recognize that a large number of GLBT clients have been subject to hate crimes. Depression, anger, posttraumatic stress, and self-blame may result. They may believe the attack was deserved and exhibit a low sense of mastery (Herek, Gillis, & Cogan, 1999). These need to be assessed and treated.

11. For clients still dealing with internalized homosexuality, help them establish a new affirming identity. Some deal with possible discrimination by assuming a heterosexual identity and avoiding the issue of sexuality with others, while some are able to reveal their true identity. The consequences of each of these reactions need to be considered both from the individual and environmental perspective.

12. Remember that in group therapy, a GLBT individual may have specific concerns over confidentiality and different life stressors as compared with their heterosexual counterparts. In these situations, a decision has to be made to determine if the group can be restructured to be helpful to GLBT clients.

13. A number of therapeutic strategies can be useful with internalized homophobia, prejudice, and discrimination. They can include identifying and correcting cognitive distortions, coping skills training, assertiveness training, and utilizing social supports.

14. If necessary, take systems-level intervention to schools, employment, and religious organizations. Diversity workshops can help organizations acquire accurate information regarding sexual diversity.

15. Conduct research on the mental health needs of the GLBT communities and the effectiveness of current programs.

Counseling Elderly Clients

We are an ageist society where the young are valued much more than the old; youth is glorified and older people are seen as incompetent, inflexible, wedded to the past, desexed, uncreative, poor, sick, and slow. (Dychtwald, 1989, p. 26)

For Mrs. B., things got worse before they got better. . . . For a time, she was taking multiple psychoactive medications and her cognitive function deteriorated at a rapid rate. Medication washout was instituted, and her orientation and memory rebounded. A year later, after an intervening small stroke, her memory function is slightly worse, but her mood is brighter, she communicates well. (La Rue & Watson, 1998)

17

Chapter

The population of older individuals in the United States is growing. The increase in the number of the elderly (those aged 65 and over) has exceeded the growth rate of the population as a whole. During the past decade the 85-year-old and older group has increased by 38%, while those between 75 and 84 increased by 23%. There are about 35 million people living in the United States who are over 65, and the population is expected to number 70 million by the year 2030 (U.S. Department of Commerce, 2001). The elderly population included 29.8 million Euro-Americans, 2.7 million African Americans, 1.5 million Hispanic Americans, 615,000 Asian Americans and Pacific Islanders, and 137,000 American Indians/Alaskan Natives. By the year 2030, those over 65 years of age will constitute 20% of the population. Those 85 years and older are the fastest growing part of the elderly population, and this trend will continue into the next century. Because females live longer than males, at age 65 there are only 39 elderly men for every 100 women. This ratio increases with increasing age (U.S. Bureau of the Census, 1995).

As with other minority groups, elderly individuals are subject to negative stereotypes and discrimination. The media described 54-year-old Mick Jagger of the Rolling Stones as "defying nature" during a recent concert; a 16-year-old commented, "I honestly thought, you know, all those granddads looking disgusting up there, but they bowled me over" (Currie, 1997, p. 7115). Ageism has been defined as negative attitudes toward the process of aging or toward elderly people. Older women are even more likely to be viewed negatively by society as a whole. Our visual entertainment, news, and advertising media are dominated by youth, with few exceptions. Information about older people often comes from youthful interviewers who do not have the appropriate perspective for the experiences of the older generation. One exception is 73-year-old Donald M. Murray, a Boston columnist who covers issues of age and some of its positive aspects. In his column, he often corrects the misperceptions of the young about older adults:

> *I am not elderly, I am old and proud of it. I am aged, like a good cheese. I am a walking history book, an elder of the tribe, tested, tempered, wise. . . . I can leave parties early. . . . I enjoy melancholy, even revel in it. (Frankel, 1998, p. 16)*

Implications. Ageism influences how both the general public and mental health professionals perceive the elderly. In a review of attitudes towards older individuals, Atkinson and Hackett (1998) found that elderly persons were thought to be rigid and not adaptable in their thought processes, in poor health and not very intelligent or alert, and either having no sexual interest or that the activity was not thought to be appropriate for this population. Jokes about old age abound and are primarily negative in nature. Many medical staff members feel uncomfortable around elderly patients. These negative stereotypes lead to the elderly being viewed as less valued members of society. As a result of ageism, elderly individuals may come to accept these views and suffer a loss of self-esteem. In fact, they also believe that they will suffer mental decline. When a group of older individuals were asked if they felt that there was a strong possibility that they would become senile, 90% responded affirmatively (Grant, 1996).

Unfortunately, studies have found that mental health professionals also display age bias. As a group they expressed reluctance to work with older adults, perceived them as less interesting, having a poorer prognosis, more set in their ways, and less likely to benefit from mental health services. Mental health problems in older adults are attributed to aging. The view appears to be that mental illness is normal for older clients but abnormal for younger ones (Danzinger & Welfel, 2000). Stereotyping and ageism have limited the access of older adults to needed services. We are an aging society, yet we are poorly prepared to handle our currently aged population and certainly not equipped for the coming baby boomer generation (Ponzo, 1992). The elderly population is underserved and little understood. Few resources have been devoted to determine their needs. A. U. Kim and Atkinson (1998) noted that few training programs in counseling deal with older populations. Information is lacking on therapies and medications for older individuals. As a group, they are less likely to receive new treatments for heart attacks or other illnesses, and elderly women are less likely to receive radiation and chemotherapy after breast cancer surgery. This is surprising, since a healthy 70-year-old individual can be expected to live at least 10 years more (People's Medical Society Newsletter, 1998).

There is an increasing need for mental health professionals to work with older Americans. It is important that the necessary education and skills development be obtained from resources such as graduate courses, self-guided study, or continuing education. It is important to be aware of the changes (biological, psychological, and social) that generally accompany aging as well as the types of psychopathology that are experienced by older adults (Qualls, 1998a). A number of journals can provide needed information on issues retarding mental health and aging: *Psychology and Aging, Journal of Gerontology, Journal of Clinical Geropsychology, International Journal of Aging and Human Development, The Gerontologist,* and *Aging and Mental Health.*

Problems of the Elderly Individual

Physical and Economic Health

Older people are more likely than younger populations to suffer from physical impairments such as some degree of loss of hearing or vision and cardiovascular diseases. About one fourth of adults between the ages of 65 and 74 suffer from some hearing impairment, and this is increased to about two out of five for those over the age of 75 (Desselle & Proctor, 2000). Half of older adults have difficulties falling asleep or insomnia (APA, 2001c). Most older individuals, however, are quite healthy and able to live independent lives, requiring only minimal assistance. Only 5% of people 65 and over live in nursing homes; this increases to only 22% by age 85 (Heller, 1998). Approximately 9% of those between the ages of 65 and 69 require personal assistance for daily activities; at the age of 85 and over, about 50% require assistance. In all age categories, women are more likely to need assistance than are men (U.S. Bureau of the Census, 1995).

The rate of poverty for elderly individuals has been decreasing, from 25% in 1970 to 13% in 1992. However, economic difficulties remain for many older individuals, especially women and minority members. Elderly women are more likely to be poor than are elderly men (16% versus 9%). Among elderly minority group members, rates of poverty for African Americans were 27% for men and 38% for women; for Hispanic Americans, 27% for men and 25% for women (U.S. Bureau of the Census, 1995).

Implications. In providing mental health services for older adults, the possibility that physical limitations exist should be considered. Make sure that the environment is receptive for the older client. The room should be adequately lighted and any limiting physical condition identified. Determine the mode of communication that is most comfortable for the individual. If older clients have or have used eyeglasses or hearing aids, make sure they are present in the session. Because comorbid physical conditions often exist such as cardiovascular disease and hypertension, rule out the possibility that the mental health problem may be a result of multiple medications or their interactions. Side effects are particularly troublesome for the elderly, especially since they have decreased lean muscle mass and total body water along with a decrease in liver mass. Because of these changes, patients should be on lower dosages of certain drugs such as phenothiazines and bezodiazepines (Masand, 2000). A physician or psychiatrist should have evaluated the individual to determine if the mental symptoms may have physical causes. Some cases of delirium (disturbances in consciousness) are caused by urinary tract infections, electrolyte abnormalities, hyper- or hypoglycemia, liver or kidney failure, or fever (Tune, 2001).

Among poor and minority older Americans, there are delays in seeking mental health services and high rates of noncompliance with treatment. Some of these problems involve a lack of understanding of the medications, cultural or folk beliefs regarding illness, or a lack of financial resources. The mental health professional should assess the reasons for noncompliance. Environmental issues also need to be identified. Many of the mental health problems of the older poor and minority adults are due to poverty, unemployment, poor living conditions, discrimination, and the lack of receptivity of health care providers. Case management or advocacy skills may be needed to address these issues.

Mental Health

There is a perception that rates of mental illness are high among elderly persons. This may be due to observation of the small number of mentally ill adults living in nursing homes. In actuality, elderly individuals have rates of affective disorders lower than that of younger adults, although their rates for anxiety disorders approximate that of the general population (APA Working Group, 1999). Although rates of mental illness appear to be lower among older adults, the rates are higher among those in nursing homes and other kinds of senior housing. Only about 6% of older adults are in the community mental health system, which is far below the proportion predicted according to their percentage in the population (Heller, 1998). Part of the problem may be that both the health providers and elderly individuals conceptualize mental health issues or symptoms as due to physical health or aging rather than psychological factors (Heller, 1998). The consequences are that older adults are not very likely to be referred for treatment by physicians to mental health professionals.

Mental Deterioration or Incompetence

> *After 49 years of teaching in Whatcom County schools, including the last 26 as a substitute, Mitch Evich has come across all kinds of students. "Recently I've worked in classes that were lovely, you can't beat them," Evich said. "Of course other classes, I wish I could," he said with a laugh. Evich, now 81, has no immediate plans on ending his substitute teaching career. (Lane, 1998, p. A1)*

A common view of elderly persons is that they are mentally incompetent. Words such as "senile" reflect this perspective. However, only a minority of elderly persons has dementia. Most are still mentally sharp and benefit from the store of knowledge that they have acquired over a lifetime. Some 5% to 10% of individuals over the age of 65 have mild to moderate dementia; this increases to 15% to 20% for those over 75 years of age and 25% to 50% of those over 85 (American Psychiatric Association, 1997; Saunders, 1998). By the year 2040, it is estimated that 7 million people in the United States will have Alzheimer's disease (Freeborne, 2000). Even with cognitive problems, Saunders found that patients with dementia attempt to maintain a sense of competence and dignity. They would blame their confusion on external events, such as being pressured too much. Older persons with dementia can still show varied aspects of themselves. One woman responded to an inability to recall her husband's name humorously, by using a metaphor, stating that her brain was "off key." Another responded to memory problems by joking that "my brain is gone on strike, I think" (Saunders, 1998, p. 67). Despite their memory impairment, older individuals often use humor and demonstrate their competence and verbal sophistication through their use of metaphors.

Implications. Most older adults will show some declines in certain cognitive abilities, which are considered to be part of the normal developmental process. A substantial minority of the very old will show declines that are greater than would be expected to the point of taking away their ability to communicate or to recognize even loved ones. Alzheimer's disease is the leading cause of progressive dementia. Some older adults show an intermediate cognitive decline between those typically found associated with normal aging and dementia. This decline may or may not be progressive (APA, Presidential Task Force, 1998). Because the prevalence of cognitive disorders does increase with age, this possibility should be assessed in older adults. The mental status exam can give some indication of problem areas, but the most frequently used assessment is the Mini-Mental State Examination (MMSE). This test takes about 5 to 10 minutes to administer and has normative and validity data. It is comprised of eleven items and assesses orientation, registration, attention and calculation, recall, language, and visual motor integrity. Early detection allows for treatment and advance planning (wills, estate and other legal matters, and dealing with potential problems such as driving).

Steps in evaluating dementia and other cognitive changes (APA, Presidential Task Force, 1998) include the following:

- Obtain self-report from client regarding possible changes in memory or cognitive functions.

- Be aware that reported memory problems or lack thereof might be due to lack of awareness or denial.

- Obtain reports from family members and friends on estimations of cognitive performance. Be especially alert to discrepancies.

- Take a careful history of the onset and progression of the cognitive changes.

- Remember to assess for possible side effects of medication or other physical conditions that may be related to cognitive declines.

- Assess for depression since it can also result in dementia-like performance or the overreporting of cognitive problems. Remember that depression and dementia can also occur together.

Family Intervention

Although dementia has a gradual progression, the effects of this disorder impact both the afflicted individual and family members. Family members often do not understand that patients with dementia may not retain what they are told. They may attempt to offer corrected statements and be frustrated when the individual with the disorder has forgotten it again. Some may believe the behavior is willful or may try to assume responsibility over all behaviors even when the older person can perform effectively in some areas. Guilt is often expressed in terms of statements such as, "Am I doing the right thing?" (LaRue & Watson, 1998). Another frequent problem is that adult children may infantilize or dominate their parent with the cognitive decline. They assume that their actions are in the best interest of their parent but fail to take the parent's own preferences or values into consideration. Adult children tend to overemphasize values related to physical or mental health, whereas parents expressed preference for values related to self-identity and autonomy. In general, the focus is on the family's point of view of disability rather than parent's (Orel, 1998).

Caregiving responsibility differs between the different ethnic groups. Forty-two percent of Asian Americans provide care for their aging parents or other older relatives versus 34% of Hispanic Americans, 28% of African Americans, and 19% of White Americans. Guilt in not doing enough for the extended family is reported by 72% of Asian Americans, 65% of Hispanic Americans, 54% of African Americans, and 44% of White Americans. For all ethnic groups, resources for coping involve religious faith, family connections and their siblings, physicians, and government agencies. Asian Americans report the greatest amount of stress caused by pressures of caring for older family members or parents, and they are the group most likely to expect that their children will care for them in their old age. White Americans feel less stress and guilt about their caregiving roles. Caregiving demands are especially high for women. Caregiving may be stressful and increase conflict among family members. In working with family members who care for a relative with dementia, a mental health professional should address the following issues (American Psychiatric Association, 1997):

1. The need for patience and understanding in working with individuals with dementia.

2. The potential stresses on family members and the need to develop more coping strategies.

3. Education of family members regarding the neurological problems, how they are manifested in behavior, and available treatments. In the early stages, memory problems are primary symptoms. Language and spatial dysfunction tend to occur later. Delusions and hallucinations may also occur in the late stage.

4. Practical solutions for problems such as how to deal with agitation, wandering, and other safety issues. Exercise is helpful but should be supervised. Identification on clothing and medical alert bracelets is helpful if unsupervised departures do occur. In the beginning stages of dementia, the individual should be advised not to drive.

5. The family dynamics as they relate to the caregiving situation and how responsibilities should be allocated.

6. Improving communication of the family members.

7. Cultural factors involving caregiving responsibilities and guilt need to be addressed.

8. Community resources such as the Alzheimer's Association and other support groups.

9. Financial and legal matters involving the patient, such as the power of attorney.

10. Decisions that may need to be made, such as under what circumstance the afflicted person would need to be cared for in a nursing home or other outside agency.

Elder Abuse and Neglect

Agnes, 85 years old, lost her husband last year. Because of her own problems with arthritis and congestive heart failure, Agnes moved in with her 55-year-old daughter, Emily. The situation is difficult for all of them. Sometimes Emily feels as if she's at the end of her rope, caring for her mother, worrying about her college-age son and her husband, who is about to be forced into early retirement. Emily has caught herself calling her mother names and accusing her mother of ruining her life. (APA, 2001b, p. 1)

Over 2 million older Americans are victims of psychological or physical abuse and neglect. This statistic is probably only about 20% of actual cases because underreporting of abuse or neglect generally occurs in the family home, although a minority is reported in nursing homes. The family circumstances that are associated with abuse and neglect are (a) a pattern and history of violence in family, (b) stress and life adjustment in accommodating an older parent or relative, (c) financial burdens, (d) overcrowded quarters, and (e) marital stress due to changes in living arrangements (U.S. Department of Health and Human Services, 1998). In addition, caregiver stress has been directly related to the time spent in providing assistance (Bookwala & Schulz, 2000).

Implications. To reduce the prevalence of elder abuse and neglect, several steps can be taken with the general public and those caring for older adults (APA, 2001b). First, continued public education can bring the problem out in the open and increase awareness of the risk factors involved in abuse. Second, respite care or having someone else such as family members, friends, or hired workers take over can be quite helpful. Even having a few hours per week away or a "vacation" from the responsibility can reduce stress. Third, increasing social contact and support is also likely to help keep stress manageable. Assistance may also be possible from religious or community organizations. Specific disease organization and support groups can furnish both needed information and support. Mental health professionals working with an older adult should identify and interview caregivers and determine whether family members live in the same household with the older adult client. The mental health professional can provide a source of support for the family members and demonstrate an understanding of the stress involved in caregiving. Counseling and treatment can be encouraged for problems that can lead to abuse or burnout. Many caregivers place their own needs behind those of their ill parent, relative, or spouse. Solutions can be developed to address their mental and physical health.

Substance Abuse

"I wouldn't get up in the morning," she said. "I realized I was using alcohol to raise my spirits. It raises your spirits for a little while, and then you become depressed. . . . With people dying around you, you feel more lonely and isolated." (Wren, 1998, p. 12)

Alcohol abuse can begin after a loss. Genevieve May, a psychiatrist, started abusing alcohol after the death of her husband. Finding that this was not the solution, Dr. May entered the Betty Ford Center and was successfully treated at age 83. She is now 88 and has been sober for 5 years. It is estimated that 17% of adults aged 60 and older abuse alcohol or prescription drugs; some of the misuse of prescription drugs may involve confusion over or misunderstanding of the directions. Because older adults take an average of five different prescription drugs a day, the chance of negative drug interactions or reactions with alcohol increases dramatically (Guerra, 1998). Often these reactions resemble psychological or organic conditions. Elderly problem drinkers are more likely to be unmarried, report more stress, have more financial problems, report persistent interpersonal conflicts with others, and have fewer social resources (Brennan & Moos, 1996). About 30% started drinking after the age of 60 because of depression and negative life changes (Guerra, 1998).

Implications. Older adults rarely seek treatment for substance abuse problems because of shame and perhaps because they may feel uncomfortable in programs that also deal with drugs such as heroin or crack cocaine. One 74-year-old woman who was in group therapy with younger drug abusers asked, "What is crack?" She was successfully treated only after entering a program for older adults (Wren, 1998). As compared to younger substance abusers, older patients responded better to more structured program policies, more flexible rules regarding discharge, more comprehensive assessment, and more outpatient mental health aftercare (Moos, Mertens, & Brennan, 1995). Late-onset alcohol and drug abuse problems seem to be related to stressors such as the death of family members, spouses, or friends; retirement issues; family conflicts; physical health problems; or financial concerns. Some of these stressors are developmental issues of later life and need to be identified and treated (APA Working Group on the Older Adult Brochure, 1998). Programs developed specifically for older adults generally have more beneficial outcomes. Older adults who receive appropriate treatment respond well and return to their previous lifestyle.

Depression and Suicide

The rate for depression increases for males with age, while the higher rate of depression in women decreases after the age of 60. In men, depression is associated with vascular disease, erectile dysfunction, and decreased testosterone. Depression needs to be identified and treated since it is also seen as an independent risk factor for cardiovascular and cerebrovascular disease. Suicide rates are also high among older adults. Especially at risk are white men 85 and older whose suicide rate is about six times the national rate. Suicides in individuals 65 and older accounted for 19% of all suicides in 1997. Among the elderly, men are seven times more likely to commit suicide than women (Roose, 2001). Factors associated with suicide included being separated, divorced, or alone; suffering depression; having an anxiety disorder; having physical or medical problems; and dealing with family conflict or loss of a relationship. Caucasian men were at greater risk for suicide than were non-Caucasian men or women (Florio, Hendryx, Jensen, & Rockwood, 1997). Although rates of depression are lower among older individuals than in the population as a whole, depression still plays a role in many suicides. In women, depression is related to financial loss; for men, the loss of health is the greatest stressor (Ponzo, 1992). Healthy, normally functioning older adults do not appear to be at greater risk for depression than younger adults. What seems to be age-related depression is often depression over physical health problems and the related disability. Aging, independent of declining health problems, does not increase the risk of depression (Roberts, Kaplan, Shema, & Strawbridge, 1997). Reynolds, Dew, Frank, and Begley (1998) found that both early onset (first-time major depression at 59 or less) and late onset (first-time major depression after age 60) responded well to a combination of psychotherapy and antidepressants. However, individuals in the early onset group required 5 to 6 weeks longer to achieve remission.

Implications. It is very important to assess for depression and suicidality in older adults. The best instrument for depression is the Geriatric Depression Scale, which was specifically developed for older adults. It has age-related norms and omits somatic symptoms that may be associated with physical problems and not depression. Major depression tends to be unrecognized in older adults and is a significant predictor of suicide. Because depression often co-occurs with physical illnesses such as cardiovascular disease, stroke, diabetes, and cancer, health providers and patients often believe that the mood disturbance is a normal consequence of problems, so it goes untreated. Many who commit suicide visited a primary care physician very close to the time of suicide (20% on the same day, 40% within one week, and 70% within one month; National Institute of Mental Health, 2001). There is an urgent need to detect and adequately treat depression in order to reduce suicide among the elderly. A number of biological and psychological treatments have been effective in treating depression in older adults. Newer antidepressants such as the selective serotonin reuptake inhibitors (SSRIs) have fewer side effects, making them more likely to be adhered to by older adults. Cognitive-behavioral therapy and interpersonal therapy are also useful in reducing depression with this population. Approximately 80% of older adults with depression overcome it if they are given appropriate treatment. Especially effective is the combination of drug and psychotherapy.

Sexuality in Old Age

The topic of sexuality and the aging process appears to be given even less consideration now than it was 10 years ago. Underlying this neglect is the belief that sexuality should not be considered in the aged. One physician notes,

> *I recently worked in an infectious disease clinic where I met a patient in her late 60s who was infected with the human immunodeficiency virus (HIV). My surprise at seeing an older woman with an infection associated with unprotected sex or injecting drug use, made me realize I had preconceptions about aging and the elderly. . . . My attitudes could be construed as sexist in nature. (McCray, 1998, pp. 1035–1036)*

In our youth-oriented society, sexual activity among older persons is thought rare and even considered to be inappropriate. Older adults are not expected to be interested in sex. However, sexual interest and activity continue well into the 80s and 90s for many individuals (Diokno, Brown, & Herzog, 1990; Kun & Schwartz, 1998). In a study of 1,216 elderly people with a mean age of 77.3, nearly 30% had participated in sexual activity during the past month, and 67% were satisfied with their current level of sexual activity. Men were more sexually active than women but less satisfied with their level of sexual activity. Age did not appear to be related to sexual satisfaction (Matthias, Lubben, Atchison, & Schweitzer, 1997). Most respondents voiced positive reactions to their sexual experiences such as, "Physical satisfaction is not the only aim of sex. . . . It is the nearness of someone throughout the lonely nights of people in their 70s and 80s" and "I believe sex is a wonderful outlet for love and physical health and worth trying to keep alive in advancing age. . . . It makes one feel youthful and close to one's mate and pleased to 'still work'" (B. Johnson, 1995, p. A23). Of the more than 600 older women surveyed, 35% said that their present level of sexual interest had decreased. However, Johnson found that two thirds said that they were very interested in sexual intercourse and that most believed they had liberal sexual attitudes.

Changes do occur in sexual functioning in both older men and women

(A. U. Kim & Atkinson, 1998). In men, erections occur more slowly and need more continuous stimulation, but they can be maintained for longer periods of time without the need for ejaculation. The refractory period increases so that it may take a day or two for the man to become sexually responsive again. Antihypertensive drugs, vascular diseases of the penile arteries, and diabetes are common causes of impotence in men. For women, aging is associated with a decline of estrogens, and vaginal lubrication decreases. However, sexual responsiveness by the clitoris is similar to that of younger women. Sexual activities remain important for older men and women. Medical and psychological methods have been successful in treating sexual dysfunctions in older adults.

Implications. As with younger adults, sexual concerns and functioning should be assessed in older adults because it is considered an important activity. One psychology intern remarked, "You just never think the same about your older clients [or your grandparents] after you have an 80-year-old woman telling you how much she enjoys oral sex" (Zeiss, 2001, p. 1). Treatments and medications such as Viagra are now available to improve sexual functioning in older adults. Knowledge of these advances is important in counseling older adults. Emotional stressors (retirement, caregiving, and lifestyle changes) as well as physical changes can produce problems in sexual functioning and should also be assessed. The mental health professional should determine the reason for the difficulties and employ or suggest appropriate interventions. Mental health professionals can obtain a number of journal articles dealing with sexuality in older adults and successful forms of treatment from the APA *Aging and Human Sexuality Resource Guide* (APA, 2001a). Client information on sexuality can also be obtained from the National Institute on Aging and *Love and Life: A Healthy Approach to Sex for Older Adults* (a kit that contains brochures, training materials, and videotapes for use by older adult organizations) from the National Council on Aging.

Multiple Discrimination

Minority status in combination with older age can produce a double burden. For example, older lesbian women may still encounter discrimination on the basis of their sexual orientation. Some remain distressed over their lack of acceptance from the heterosexual community and even family members. They observe that neighbors interact with them but do not invite them over. In addition, they may feel isolated from the lesbian community:

> *I was shocked and hurt when one of them [a young lesbian] who considers herself quite liberated didn't want to dance with me at a local lesbian bar, but she did dance with others. (Jacobson & Samdahl, 1998, p. 242)*

The woman attributed this rejection to her being older than the other women. She points out that in lesbian newsletters or activities, there was seldom anything about older women. Unfortunately, even minority members who have experienced discrimination themselves can display ageism.

Implications. The therapist should assess for potential problems of multiple discrimination when working with older adults who have disabilities or are from different cultural groups, social classes, or sexual minorities. An individual can come to terms with factors associated with ageism and find different sources or social support or actively work to change the negative societal attitudes.

Guidelines for Clinical Practice

Older adults have to deal with issues such as the loss of friends and other significant individuals, the cultural devaluation of their group, health and physical problems, forced isolation, and having more limited financial resources (Butler & Lewis, 1983; Moye & Brown, 1995). However, many develop alternative support systems in the community and have contact with extended family members. Social contacts are important, and engaging in either paid or volunteer work enhances the self-esteem and life satisfaction of older individuals (Acquino, Russell, Cutrona, & Altmaier, 1996). Issues that older adults face may include chronic illness and disability, loss of loved ones, caregiving for a loved one, and change of roles (Knight & McCallum, 1998).

The following are suggestions (APA Working Group, 1998; Butler & Lewis, 1983; Knight & McCallum, 1998; Qualls, 1998a) in offering mental health services to older adults:

1. Obtain specific knowledge and skills in counseling older adults. Critically evaluate your own attitudes about aging and quality of life.

2. Be knowledgeable about legal and ethical issues that arise when working with older adults (e.g., competency issues).

3. Determine the reason for evaluation and the social aspects related to the problem, such as recent losses, financial stressors, and family issues.

4. Determine the older adult's views of the problem, belief system, stage of life issues, educational background, and social and ethnic influences.

5. Identify medical conditions and prescription and over-the-counter medications because mental conditions are often a result of physical problems or drug interactions or side effects.

6. Presume competence in older adult clients unless the contrary is obvious.

7. If necessary, slow the pace of therapy to accommodate cognitive slowing.

8. Provide information in a manner that approximates the client's level of reading and comprehension, using alternative methods such as simplified visuals or videotapes if necessary.

9. Involve older adults in decisions as much as possible. If there are cognitive limitations, it may be necessary to use legally recognized individuals.

10. Use multiple assessments and include relevant sources (client, family members, significant others, and health care providers).

11. Determine the role of family caregivers, educate them about the disorder, and help them develop strategies to reduce burnout.

12. When working with an older couple, help negotiate issues regarding time spent alone and together (especially after retirement). Arguments over recreation are common. There is too much "couple time" and no "legitimate" reason for separateness.

13. Recognize that it is important to help individuals who are alone establish support systems in the community.

14. Help the older adult develop a sense of fulfillment in life by discussing the positive aspects of their experiences. "Success" can be defined as having done one's best or having met and survived challenges. A life review is often helpful.

15. Assist in interpreting the impact of cultural issues such as ethnic group membership, gender, and sexual orientation on their lives.

16. For adults very close to the end of their lives, help them deal with a sense of attachment to familiar objects by having them decide how heirlooms, keepsakes, and photo albums will be distributed and cared for. Counseling can improve the quality of life for older adults or help them resolve late-life issues.

Counseling Women

Congresswoman Patricia Schroeder won a seat to the Armed Services Committee along with Ron Dellums, an African American. According to Pat Schroeder, the chairperson of the committee was not pleased with the new members. "He said that women and blacks were worth only half of one 'regular' member, so he added only one seat to the committee room and made Ron and me share it. . . . Nobody else objected." (Mann, 1998, p. E3)

A new study in the Journal of the American Medical Association *reports that girls in their teens are almost as likely as adult women to experience abuse in relationships. One in five girls reported physical or sexual abuse in a relationship. These girls were also more likely to report eating disorders, drug use, suicidal thoughts and risky sexual behavior." (K. S. Palmer, 2001, p. A17)*

When I was in college I considered a career in medicine. Due to lack of support from family members and future husband, I didn't pursue it. I would have at least tried it if I were 20 today. (A. J. Stewart & Ostrove, 1998, p. 1188)

Although women make up 51% of the United States population, they are underrepresented in positions of power and are victimized by stereotyping and discrimination. Some progress has been made in promoting gender equality, but inequities continue. The National Coalition for Women and Girls in Education (1998) published a report indicating that (a) girls and women continue to be underrepresented in areas such as math and sciences; (b) women continue to predominate in low-wage, traditional female tracks; (c) women comprise 73% of elementary and secondary school teachers but only 35% of principals; (d) pay disparities between male and female educators persist at all levels; (e) female students continue to receive less attention, encouragement, and praise than male students; and (f) sexual harassment of females continues to be pervasive. Studies indicate that 81% of 8th through 11th graders, 30% of undergraduates, and 40% of graduate students have been sexually harassed, a situation that often negatively impacts interest in academics and school. Teachers are often unaware that they may be promoting sexism by providing differential responses to male and female students. A number of studies indicate that teachers view mathematics as a male domain and have higher expectations and a positive attitude toward male students in this area. Male success is explained in terms of ability, while that of females is explained as effort. In one study of third grade teachers who believed they had a gender-free style, the following were observed: (a) Accommodations were made for boys to stop disagreements rather than confronting them; (b) boys were allowed to speak out of turn while girls were not; and (c) when girls spoke out of turn, they were reminded to raise their hands (Garrahy, 2001).

Implications. In the educational areas, mental health professionals need to be involved in advocating for changes at the system levels involving curriculum and staffing. Coursework for future teachers should include demonstrations and discussion of responses that may inadvertently convey gender-restrictive messages. Attitudes do affect performance. In a series of studies, R. P. Brown and Josephs (1999) found that gender-specific performance concerns affect performance. Women who believed a math test would indicate where they were especially weak in math performed worse than women who believed it would indicate whether they were exceptionally strong in this area. Thus, the stereotype that women are bad at math affected their performance. Attitudes and expectations regarding stereotyped personality characteristics and appropriate career choices need to be addressed in educational programs. In the academic community, certain recommendations have been made to increase the success of women faculty (APA Public Interest, 2001):

1. Monitor equity in participation, compensation, course assignments, and resources.
2. Seek out women for positions of leadership.
3. Ensure lines of communication between women faculty and the administration.
4. Provide continuing education of gender equality and sexual harassment.
5. Support institutional aids such as faculty women's groups and committees on the status of women.
6. Encourage administrators who will not tolerate sexism or racism.
7. Support courses related to the psychology of women and gender issues.
8. Have a campus-wide policy against sexism or sexual harassment. Hav-

ing an institution become aware and supportive of gender issues can impact both teacher and students in the educational process.

Problems Faced by Women

Economic Status

Forty-one percent of families headed by single women live in poverty, making under $12,500 annually (Kantrowitz & Wingertt, 2001). In terms of income, females make less than their male counterparts across all racial groups; this disparity is most pronounced between White women and White men, with women earning less than three fourths of the salaries earned by men (U.S. Bureau of the Census, 1995). Nontraditional career fields are often not hospitable to women, resulting in the larger percentage of women who remain in "feminine" careers. Females are overrepresented in occupations such as secretary (98.5%), cashier (78.3%), nurse's aide (89.4%), elementary school teacher (83.9%), and receptionist (96.5%), and they are underrepresented in administrative positions (U.S. Department of Labor, 1998). Even in occupations where women represent the numerical majority, they earn less than men in the same field (Atkinson & Hackett, 1998). Many women on welfare report mental health problems or issues. Over 50% report experiencing domestic violence and having symptoms of Posttraumatic Stress Disorder (PTSD; Women's Program Office, 1998).

Implications. Women in poverty often need assistance with economic issues, housing, and food. Mental health professionals may need to use case management skills to obtain needed resources for the client. Due to financial considerations, mental health services should be provided in convention locations such as family planning clinics, primary health care provider offices, and government assistant offices. Child care and other onsite programs for family members as the mother receives counseling can increase participation in the mental health system.

Barriers to Career Choices

College women perceive more obstacles to their career choices than do males. They believe that they will have a more difficult time getting hired, experience discrimination, be treated differently, and experience negative sexual comments from superiors or coworkers. Minority college women perceived even higher career barriers because of both gender and ethnic background issues (Luzzo & McWhirter, 2001). The underrepresentation of women in certain fields is due in part to gender role stereotypes. Some jobs require characteristics not generally associated with females. Femininity includes the qualities of emotionality, sensitivity, nurturance, and interdependence (E. P. Cook, 1990). When a woman behaves in a manner that is not considered to be "feminine," negative consequences may result. If a woman displays a task-oriented style of leadership that violates the gender norm of modesty, she is rated as competent but incurs cost in low social attraction and likability ratings. Men displaying the same leadership style are rated high in competence and are better liked (Rudman, 1998). Forsyth, Heiney, and Wright (1997) found similar results in a comparison of responses to male and female group leaders displaying task-oriented or relationship-oriented leadership styles. Group members favored men over women when selecting leaders and evaluating leaders, even when the leadership behaviors were held constant. However, group members with a liberal attitude toward women's roles responded positively to either leadership style by women. It was also interesting to observe that biases against the task-oriented style for women leaders was not restricted to male group members.

Even successful businesswomen report barriers to advancement on the corporate ladder (Lyness & Thompson, 2000). These were manifested in the following manner:

1. Women were made to feel that they are tokens, not a good fit at senior management levels, and that they need to change in some way. They perceived discomfort from the men working with them, did not have the same gender role models, and felt they had to perform at a higher level than men.

2. Men heightened cultural boundaries by emphasizing camaraderie and differences from women, thus excluding them from the information necessary for job performance. This was exemplified in the male use of the "old boys" network. Informal networking was more useful to male managers than to female managers for getting promoted.

3. Women received less or less effective mentoring than male executives. Some of the problems were limited access to potential mentors, mentors unwilling to work with them, and the misinterpreting of a mentorship request as a sexual invitation.

4. Because of stereotyped views, women found it difficult to obtain developmental assignments needed for career advancement.

The influences on career are somewhat different with African American women, who face the issues of both racism and sexism. Among these women, the most important variables related to a successful career included the promotion of education by the family, positive relationships with family members, family gender socialization (androgynous sex roles), and values toward work. One African American woman attributed her success to her extended family. She stated, "Learning and academics were very important to my grandmother. She taught us: if you can't learn you can't change things. That has carried over to my work life in the corporate world, because there it is all about change. And people who can't learn or aren't academically gifted either fail or become dated and useless" (Pearson & Bieschke, 2001, p. 305). The family appears to be very important in the career success of African American women.

Implications. Mental health professionals should help expand the career choices available to women. In doing so, a comprehensive approach must be involved. One program (Sullivan & Mahalik, 2000) increased the career self-efficacy of college women by having them:

- Identify successful performance accomplishments.
- Participate in vicarious or observational learning. This was accomplished by interviewing women outside the groups about their career decision-making processes, discussing observations about their career decision-making insights, and reading material on women's unique career development.
- Attend to emotional arousal and learning to manage anxiety through relaxation and adaptive self-talk. The women learned to identify and challenge self-defeating thoughts.
- Experience verbal persuasion and encouragement. Positive affirmation was encouraged by talking about past mastery experiences, and discussions were focused on self-esteem issues and the lack of role models as they affected women's assessments of their skills and abilities. Career goals were identified, and the participants learned to use campus resources to help them with networking, developing resumes and interviewing skills, and exploring jobs.

Career self-efficacy was increased in this group of women by developing self-evaluation skills, identifying career paths by successful women, promoting skills to deal with anxiety, and helping them understand the impact of gender socialization issues in their careers.

Discrimination and Victimization

Approximately 20% of female students report being physically or sexually abused by their dating partner. The abuse is associated with increased use of drugs, binge drinking, considering and attempting suicide, unhealthy or disordered eating patterns, and intercourse before the age of 15 (Silverman, Raj,

Mucci, & Hathaway, 2001). It is clear that victims of abuse often suffer from depression and other emotional difficulties. The majority of women who are in treatment for childhood sexual abuse suffer from PTSD (Rodriguez, Ryan, Vande Kemp, & Foy, 1997). Sexual harassment is also quite prevalent in the work environment.

> *One woman who suffered six years of harassment from her male colleagues that included lewd behavior and suggestive comments finally threatened to report them. They responded by saying, "Fine. We know where your car is, and we know where you live." (Lewis 1998, p. D5)*

As with many women in the same circumstances, the woman decided not to fight back. Over 70% of women office workers have reported harassment at their place of employment (Piotrkowski, 1998). Women respond to the harassment by attempting to ignore it, taking a leave of absence, or using alcohol to cope. Lower job satisfaction, poorer physical health, and higher levels of depression and anxiety can be the result of harassment (Fitzgerald, Drasgow, Hulin, Gelfand, & Magley, 1997). Even low-frequency sexual harassment has been found to have a significant negative impact on the psychological well-being of the victims (Schneider, Swan, & Fitzgerald, 1997).

Implications. Violence and sexual harassment against girls and women are highly prevalent and lead to a number of mental health problems. Even among adolescents, screening should be performed for dating abuse, especially in cases where suicidal thought, use of drugs, or disordered eating patterns exist. Prevention strategies should be developed that are appropriate to school settings. The APA Policy Office (2001) recommends support for policy initiatives, including legal and legislative reform addressing the issue of violence against women; improved training for mental health workers to recognize and treat victims; the dissemination of information on violence against women to church and community groups, educational institutions, and the general public; and the exploration of psychoeducational and sociocultural intervention to change male objectification of women.

Gender Issues

The stereotyped standards of beauty expressed through advertisement and the mass media have had an impact on the health and self-esteem of girls and women. Societal pressure for females to be thin has led to the internalization of an unrealistic body shape as the ideal and has resulted in body dissatisfaction and disordered eating patterns and dieting (Stice, Shaw, & Nemeroff, 1998). It is estimated that 35% of women engage in disordered eating, and many attempt to control their weight through self-induced vomiting and the use of laxatives (Kendler et al., 1991). Bulimia nervosa is 10 times more common in females than in males and affects up to 3% of women between the ages of 13 and 20 (McGilley & Pryor, 1998). The need to meet societal standards for thinness or beauty becomes more intense when girls at the ages of 12 and 13 begin to date and to experience the physical changes associated with puberty. They become more concerned about their physical appearance and are more likely to start dieting (Heatherton, Mahamedi, Striepe, Field, & Keel, 1997). Interestingly, African American females appear to have a different standard for attractiveness than do White females. Nearly three fourths of African American females in one study were satisfied with their current weight or body shape. Most had a broad definition of beauty that included being well groomed, demonstrating the right attitude and personality, and style. They also felt that they would become more beautiful with age (Parker, Nichter, Vuckovic, Sims, & Ritenbaugh, 1995).

Implications. Programs need to address the influence of societal emphasis on thinness as the standard by which girls and women should judge themselves. Several programs have been developed to prevent the internalization of the superthin body image. In the YMCA's leadership camp, middle school girls perform community service projects, are exposed to women in leadership roles, and participate in communication and problem-solving exercises. Part of the discussion involves the feelings of inadequacy produced by the body image portrayed by the mass media and deviations from that standard. The camp is useful in helping participants to realize that they have similar reactions to societal pressures and to learn to develop internal standards that they can feel good about (Steinberg, 1998). In another program, marketing students from different high schools have approached several large department stores requesting that the displays show a more diverse range of body types than just the superthin image. The students pointed out to store managers that half of the teens and adult women in the United States wear a size 14 or larger and that the mannequins and models were size 8 or less. In support of their position, they cited a survey done at their schools that indicated that 93% of the students wanted to see more diverse body types in advertisements and in magazines. Only one department store, Union Bay, advertised using a range of body types or "healthy looking" models (Cronin, 1998). Programs directed at changing the unrealistically thin female image promoted by advertisers, magazines, and other mass media may be effective ways of reducing body dissatisfaction in females.

In individual counseling, Sands (1998) suggested the following in working with females with disordered eating patterns. First, encourage them to identify the cultural and social context for the behavior so that they do not engage in self-blame. A gender role analysis identifies messages that they receive from society (girls must be thin, pretty, and sexy). Second, determine the consequences of the gender-related messages and the self-statements associated with them. Third, choose an appropriate message (e.g., "Being healthy is important, so I will eat and exercise appropriately") and develop a plan to implement the change.

Affective Disorders

Up to 7 million women currently have depression, which is twice the rate found in men (Schwartzman & Glaus, 2000). The same ratio has been found between African American women and men. However, no clear-cut gender differences for affective disorders have been found for Hispanic Americans (Robins & Regier, 1991). Factors contributing to depression in women include poor socioeconomic status, unhealthy societal gender standards, and posttraumatic stress (Culbertson, 1997). Women feel the pressure to fulfill stereotyped feminine social roles in which they are evaluated according to physical beauty, modesty, and marriageability. Deviating from these standards can lead to self-doubt, poor self-image, and depression (Sands, 1998). Poor body image and eating disturbance predict increases in depressive symptoms in adolescent girls. Depression stems from body dissatisfaction, failure to obtain a superslim body by exercising or dieting, and guilt from the use of vomiting or laxatives to control weight (Stice & Bearman, 2001). E. P. Cook (1990) believed also that women devalue their relationship capabilities. Depression may result from their socialization to try to maintain relationships at the cost of their own needs and wishes. Failures in relationships are often seen as personal failures, compounding stress and affecting mood.

Approximately 20% of women have had an abortion. In general, they report more symptoms of depression and lower life satisfaction than other groups of women. Is abortion related to depression? In a study, Russo and Denious (2001) found that after controlling for a history of abuse and partner characteristics, abortion was not related to poorer mental health. It was physical or sexual abuse, partner violence, and rape or sexual assault that were related to suicidal ideation, depression, and anxiety.

Minority women have multiple characteristics that are subject to discrimination and prejudice and see additional obstacles to achieving their life goals. African American teenagers who were interviewed concerning their multiple minority status were quite aware of the discrimination that they face.

I'm a black female and black females are the lowest. The black female has a hard time, for one, because she's black, two, because she's a female, and I think it would take more for me to strive to get what I want. . . . (Olsen, 1996, p. 113)

African American teenagers in this study were aware of the negative messages regarding their ethnicity and also the disparagement of the female gender role. Although they acknowledged the disadvantages of their gender, not one of them wanted to be a boy.

Implications. Assess for environmental factors such as poverty, racism, economic conditions, and poor or abusive relationships. Identify the possible impact of sexism or gender messages on the individual's well-being. Some believe that depression is an extreme version of society's prescribed female role (passivity, low self-esteem, dependence on others; Sands, 1998). During adolescence, gender intensification becomes stronger, and there is increased societal pressure to be pretty, popular, and feminine. Deviations from this standard result in isolation from others and rejection from the peer group. In therapy it is important to address the stressors faced by females and identify the societal and cultural factors as well as individual influences. Women may need to understand the power differential in society, the expectations for their gender, and the impact they may have on their mood states. Identifying cognitions based on stereotypes and developing more realistic coping self-statements can reduce depression. Learning to act assertively can counteract the patterns of helplessness and low self-esteem (Sands, 1998).

Depression in women is associated with an increased risk of cardiovascular disease, which is the leading cause of death in women. Consequently, the mental health professional should also educate women about the risk and likelihood of developing coronary heart disease (CHD). Other health risk factors such as smoking, high fat diet, sedentary lifestyle, and obesity should be addressed, and psychological intervention should be used to modify these. A woman should also know the symptoms of CHD (e.g., fatigue, dizziness, and fainting, in addition to the more classic signs involving pain or pressure in the chest or sweating or pain radiating to the neck, jaw, arm, or back; Schwartzman & Glaus, 2000).

Aging

With the emphasis on youth and the sexism that exists in our society, older women are viewed more negatively than older men. Some women believed that age discrimination was evidenced by younger people not relating to them socially; by preference given to younger females in stores, restaurants, and other public establishments; by reduced dating opportunities; and by being "invisible" to men (Committee on Women in Psychology, 1999). Women increasingly outnumber men as they age, and there are five women for every two men over the age of 75. There are relatively few positive images of older women. In addition, older women are thought to face additional stressors such as the "empty nest" syndrome and menopause (Lippert, 1997). About 53 million women are over the age of 45 and are experiencing or have experienced menopause. Responses to it may be impacted by ageism and sexism, depending on the meaning that is ascribed to it. Some may believe that sexual attractiveness and youth are lost at menopause. Younger women have more negative attitudes toward menopause than do menopausal and postmenopausal women (Huffman & Myers, 1999).

However, many of these midlife stressors do not appear to be difficult transitions for most women. Of a group of women ages 40 to 59 asked about how they felt about "this time in life," nearly three fourths felt "very happy" or "happy" and nearly two thirds found it "not very confusing" or "not confusing at all." Only 13.7% felt "unhappy" or "very unhappy." Most were enjoying midlife because of increased independence, freedom from worrying about what others think, freedom from parenting, and the ability to define their own identity based on their own interests (McQuaide, 1998). Similar findings were reported for several groups of well-educated women. Instead of being concerned about a midlife crisis, aging, the empty nest syndrome, or menopause, the middle-aged women were involved in a midlife review, had a strong sense of identity, were confident, and felt a sense of power over their lives. Some showed regret. One college-educated woman responded during a midlife review, "I would not have let my husband take sole responsibility for determining the course of our lives. His career has always been a deciding factor in our lives, which has not been fair to me or our children" (A. J. Stewart & Ostrove, 1998, p. 1188). After engaging in a life review, many women would make changes or corrections in their life decisions. However, two thirds of the women made major changes in their education or work lives between the age of 37 and 43 to pursue educational or work opportunities more extensively. These findings indicate that transitions through midlife for older women are easier than was previously assumed—at least among well-educated women. Differences in transition may be found with women of other generations, minority women, or those from other social classes.

Implications. Mental health professionals must be careful not to make assumptions about the so-called midlife crisis in women and how such transitions are affecting clients. Some women are grandmothers in graduate school; others are new mothers at 40; and some have multiple careers (Lippert, 1997). Women may need to become aware of contradictory feelings that may be associated with various midlife transitions such as a simultaneous sense of loss and sense of freedom when children leave home. The personal meaning and reaction to these events should be understood. Support loss of roles by affirming new commitments in life. Assist in developing personal meaning through self-exploration. Help them understand that some anxiety is to be expected in going through transitions and that it is an opportunity to achieve greater personal development. For women who are depressed after menopause, discuss the impact of sociocultural attitudes toward women and aging. Determine what their fears and expectations of the process are. Provide information on the process and the availability of support groups. An excellent resource is menopause.org.

Feminist Identity Theory

An identity development model comparable to that for ethnic minority members has been developed for women. Feminist therapists believe that the patriarchal aspect of U.S. society is responsible for many of the problems faced by women. They believe that women show a variety of reactions to their subordinate status in society. The following stages represent an evolution of consciousness of societal subjugation of women and the development of the feminist identity (McNamara & Rickard, 1998).

1. *Passive-acceptance.* During this stage, the female accepts traditional gender roles, sees them as advantageous to her, and considers men to be superior to women. She is unaware of or denies prejudice or discrimination. Male contributions to the arts, business, and theater are valued more than those of women.

2. *Revelation.* Events involving sexism occur in a way that cannot be denied or ignored. The individual becomes personally awakened to prejudice, becomes angry, and feels guilty at being previously unaware. There is intense self-examination and dichotomous thinking. All men are seen as oppressive and all women as positive.

3. *Embeddedness-emanation.* The woman begins to form close emotional relationships with other women. With their help she is able to express her emotions in a supportive environment. Her feminist identity is becoming solidified, and she engages in more relativistic rather than dualistic thinking regarding males.

4. *Synthesis.* During this stage, a positive feminist identity is fully developed. Sexism is no longer considered the cause of all social and personal problems, and other causal factors are considered. The woman can take a stance different from that of other feminists and still maintain her feminist identity.

5. *Active commitment.* The woman is now interested in turning her attention toward making societal changes.

Although some women go through these stages, it is not clear how applicable this model is to most women. This theory is based on W. E. Cross's 1971 view of the development of African American identity. Cross has since revised his model (W. E. Cross, 1995), particularly as it applies to the passive-acceptance stage (preencounter). Individuals at this stage may feel that characteristics of race (gender) are of low salience or are not more important than other things such as religion, lifestyle, or social status. They may see progress as due to personal effort and motivation. Many individuals at this stage who have this attitude are mentally healthy. Feminist identity theory is of fairly recent origin, and there is need for further research to determine whether it is applicable to most women.

Therapy for Women

Feminist therapists have been instrumental in pointing out the sexist nature of our society, even in the counseling process. It is important for counselors to be aware of possible biases in working with female clients. For example, what are the attributes believed to be aspects of a "healthy" female? In past research, qualities such as submissiveness and being more emotional and relationship-oriented were seen as positive qualities in women (Atkinson & Hackett, 1998). If counselors adhere to these standards, consciously or unconsciously, these attitudes may be conveyed to clients in the counseling session. One study of family therapy sessions revealed that counselors interrupted women more often than they interrupted men (Werner-Wilson, Price, Zimmerman, & Murphy, 1997). Even though the therapists were not aware of this behavior, they were subtly conveying gender role expectations to the family. Female counselor trainees have also been shown to demonstrate bias in counseling men and women who seem to be seeking nontraditional roles. For example, a greater number of questions regarding parenting were posed to women than to male clients (Seem & Johnson, 1998). Gender role expectations are difficult to eliminate.

Biases can also exist for certain diagnostic categories. Some of the personality disorders may be based on exaggerated gender characteristics. Self-dramatization and exaggerated emotional expressions; intense fluctuations in mood, self-image, and interpersonal relationships; and reliance on others and the inability to assume responsibilities are aspects of Histrionic, Borderline, and Dependent Personality Disorders, respectively. Not surprisingly, women are more likely to be diagnosed with these disorders. Another problematic category is Premenstrual Dysphoric Disorder, which is included in the *Diagnostic and Statistical Manual of Mental Disorders–Fourth Edition, Text Revision* (DSM-IV-TR) as a diagnosis that requires "further study." The essential features include marked change in mood, anger, and depression or anxiety accompanied by complaints of breast tenderness and bodily aches that interfere with work or social activities. The symptoms occur one week before menses and remit a few days afterwards. Critics of this category acknowledge that many women have some of these symptoms but argue that the symptoms should be accepted as a physical reaction. Labeling premenstrual symptoms as a psychological disorder promotes the view that women are emotional and controlled by "raging" hormones (D. Sue, Sue, & Sue, 1997).

Many of our theories are male-oriented. Granello and Beamish (1998) argued that the concept of codependency needs to reconceptualized since many women would receive this label. Codependency in women may reflect a sense of connectedness, nurturance, the role of placing the needs of the family over themselves, and devoting their energies to the home and relationships. Three problems exist with this concept in the family systems model. First, there is no acknowledgement of the unequal distribution of power within families. Codependent behavior may be a result of a power imbalance between men and women. Second, several key concepts such as differentiation of self and anxiety due to emotional fusion are reflective of male stereotypic characteristics. Third, disturbances are always interpreted on the system rather than individual members. Under this scenario, women who are abused can be seen as contributors to the problem. Fourth, the problematic relationship can be interpreted as not one from the woman but rather the inability or unwillingness of the male to relate in a mutually empathetic manner. Thus, in many cases, a woman's desire for connectedness is not pathological but a strength that may be an important part of her self-concept.

Guidelines for Clinical Practice

Both male and female counselors must be careful not to foster traditional sex roles and must be aware of sexist assumptions. Presenting problems need to be understood within a societal context in which devaluation of women is a common occurrence; gender conceptualizations need to be considered integral aspects of counseling and mental health. Both traditional and nontraditional gender roles can be confining. Each female client must choose what is best for her, despite gender conceptions or political correctness (Good, Gilbert, & Scher, 1990).

As DeVoe (1998) pointed out, both feminist and nonsexist counseling approaches may be helpful for women clients. Feminist counseling can be especially useful in working with women who are dissatisfied with gender role restrictions and interested in effecting societal changes. However, the feminist perspective should not be imposed on a client who believes that her problem is not related to gender. Nonsexist counseling incorporates less of the feminist philosophy but attempts to reduce the impact of sexism when counseling women. Fitzgerald and Nutt (1998) identified some guidelines for counselors who counsel women. These guidelines indicate the importance of incorporating features of feminist and nonsexist components in all our counseling programs:

1. Possess up-to-date information regarding the biological, psychological, and sociological issues that impact women. For example, knowledge about menstruation, pregnancy, birth, infertility and miscarriage, gender roles and health, and discrimination, as well as their impact on women, is important.

2. Recognize that most counseling theories are male-centered and require modification when working with women. For example, cognitive approaches can focus on societal messages.

3. Attend workshops to explore gender-related factors in mental health and be knowledgeable about issues related to women.

4. Maintain awareness of all forms of oppression and understand how they interact with sexism.

5. Employ skills that may be particularly appropriate for the needs of women, such as assertiveness training, gender role analysis, and consciousness-raising groups. As with any approach in which traditional perspectives are challenged, clients need to understand the consequences of making changes.

6. Assess sociocultural factors to determine their role in the presenting problem.

7. Assess for attitudes of benevolent sexism, in which women are seen as creatures to be protected, supported, and adored, and which results in the attitude that they should be weak and passive. These attitudes are often used to justify gender inequality and are a subtle form of sexism (Glick & Fiske, 2001).

8. Help clients realize the impact of gender expectations and societal definitions of attractiveness on the mental health of women so that they do not engage in self-blame.

9. Prepare clients for sexism in school, relationships, and careers.

10. Be ready to take an advocacy role in initiating systems-level changes as they relate to sexism in education, business, and other endeavors.

11. Assess for the possible impact of abuse or violence in all women.

12. Refrain from expressing counseling attitudes that constrain life goals or careers for women. Determine when a female counselor may be the most appropriate match for a female client. For example, a male counselor should be aware of when a female client is best served by a female counselor (rape, pregnancy issues, domestic violence).

Counseling Individuals with Disabilities

19
Chapter

In 1988 I became obviously disabled. I walk with crutches and a stiff leg. Since that time I no longer fulfill our cultural standard of physical attractiveness. But worse, there are times when people who know me don't acknowledge me. When I call their name and say, "Hello," they often reply, "Oh, I didn't see you." I have also been mistaken for people who do not resemble me. For example, I was recently asked, "Are you a leader in the disability movement?" While I hope to be that someday, I asked her, "Who do you believe I am?" She had mistaken me for a taller person with a different hair color, who limps but does not use a walking aid. The only common element was our disability. My disability had become my persona. This person saw it and failed to see me. (Buckman, 1998, p. 19)

A 77-year-old woman has been on hemodialysis for 10 years and also has seizures, arthritis, and strokes. Communication with the social worker is not going well since the patient has impaired hearing. The daughter explains that her mother has hearing aids but does not wear them, complaining that they hurt her ears. The social worker directs all her questions to the daughter, leaving the mother wondering what is being discussed. (Desselle & Proctor, 2000).

Danielle Buckman, the woman in the first vignette, is a psychotherapist who teaches university courses on counseling people with disabilities and, due to her own struggle with multiple sclerosis, has firsthand experiences with discriminatory reactions from the general public. Since Ms. Buckman is in midlife, she also expresses concern about the triple whammy involving gender, disability, and aging issues. Attitudes toward individuals with disabilities run the gamut from ignorance to lack of understanding to being overprotective or overly sympathetic. People without handicaps often do not know how to respond to people with disabilities. In the second vignette, the social worker was talking to the daughter as if the mother were not present. The daughter felt frustrated and responded,

> *You are not even trying to communicate with my mother. . . . She can understand you if you look at her and speak slowly and clearly. . . . Imagine how you would feel if you and your spouse went to the doctor to consult about a major surgery you were scheduled for and the doctor directed the conversation only to your spouse as if you were not intelligent enough to know what was being discussed.* (Desselle & Proctor, 2000, p. 277)

Mental health professionals need to understand the nature of disabilities and treat individuals with dignity. For example, most people without hearing loss do not understand that hearing aids can amplify all sounds, resulting in jumbled hearing, which is why many do not wear them. The public often has low expectations for individuals with disabilities. Kerry Clifford, who has a physical disability, believes that the public's reaction is similar to that of Samuel Johnson's to a dog walking on two legs. He is reported to have said, "It is not done well, but you are surprised to see it done at all" (Vacc & Clifford, 1995). Most people without disabilities assume that disability in one area also affects others. One example is responding to an individual who is mute by speaking more loudly or making exaggerated facial and hand gestures (Taggart, 2001).

Implications. Mental health professionals need to address their discomfort with disabilities in clients and to recognize that they are also subject to disability prejudice. Several suggestions from APA (2001a) are helpful:

1. Instead of thinking about a "disabled woman," change the emphasis by using the phrase "a woman with a disability." This emphasizes the individual rather than the limitation.

2. Do not sensationalize disability by referring to the achievements by some as "superhuman" or "extraordinary." It creates unfair expectations. Most have the same range of skills as do nondisabled individuals. Avoid the use of phrases such as "afflicted with" or "a victim of." They evoke pity and conjure up a nonfunctional status.

3. Respond to an individual with a disability according to their skills, personality, and other personal attributes rather than to his or her disability. It is also important to get specific information about disabilities either by reading the literature or consulting with mental health professionals with disabilities. See Table 19.1 for additional suggestions when working with individuals with physical disabilities.

The most common forms of disabling conditions are arthritis and rheumatism, back and spine problems, and cardiovascular disease (*Journal of the American Medical Association*, 2001). A national survey (National Organization on Disability, 1998) reported dismal statistics on the well-being of Americans with disabilities. Of adults with disabilities, only 29% have any type of

Table 19.1 **Things to Remember in Interactions with Individuals with Disabilities**

1. **People with physical disabilities (arthritis, mobility problems, wheelchair users, limited or no use of limbs).**

   a. Do not use or move items such as wheelchairs, crutches, and canes without permission. They are considered part of the individual's "personal space."

   b. Ask if assistance is required before providing it; if your offer is accepted, ask for instructions and follow them.

   c. Address the individual directly rather than a person who accompanies the client.

   d. Sit at eye level to facilitate comfort in communication.

   e. Make certain access from parking to your office is possible.

2. **People with vision loss.**

   a. Identify yourself and anyone else who is present when greeting them. If the individual does not extend a hand, offer a verbal welcome.

   b. Offer the use of your arm and guide—rather than steer or push—the individual. Give verbal instructions.

   c. If a service dog is present, do not pet or play with it.

   d. Determine the best way of presenting information. Some are able to read large text, while others may use Braille or audiotapes. Ask about preference at the beginning.

   e. Let the individual know if you are moving about or if the conversation is to end.

   f. Give verbal cues when offering a seat. Place the individual's hand on the back of the chair, and they will not need further help.

3. **People who are deaf or hard of hearing.**

   a. Ask about the individual's preferred communication (some use American Sign Language and identify culturally with the deaf community, while others may prefer to communicate orally, read lips, or rely on residual hearing).

   b. Address the individual directly rather than a person accompanying the client.

   c. Realize that talking very loud does not enhance communication.

   d. To get attention, call the person by name. If there is no response, lightly touch the individual on the arm or shoulder.

   e. Do not pretend to understand if you do not.

   f. Do not include interpreters in the conversation. They are to relay information.

   g. Make direct eye contact and keep your face and mouth visible.

   h. If there is extreme difficulty communicating orally, ask if writing is acceptable.

continued

Table 19.1 continued

4. People with speech impediments

a. Allow the individual to finish speaking before you speak.

b. Realize that communication may take longer and plan accordingly. Do not rush through.

c. Face the individual and give full eye contact.

d. Address the individual directly.

e. Do not pretend to understand if you do not.

f. When appropriate, use yes or no questions.

g. Repeat to demonstrate or check for understanding, but remember that speech impediments do not indicate limited intelligence.

Source: Adapted from United Cerebral Palsy (2001).

employment, compared to 79% of the general public. This 50-point difference is not due to a lack of interest in working; in fact, 72% of individuals with disabilities want to work. Over one third of adults with disabilities have incomes of $15,000 or less, compared to 12% of those without disabilities. Only about one third of adults with disabilities are very satisfied with life, compared to 61% of the nondisabled public. Worse, 20% of adults with disabilities have not finished high school, compared to 9% of those without disabilities—a ratio of more than two to one. Individuals with disabilities earn only two-thirds the income of coworkers without disabilities; minorities with disabilities have an even lower income than Whites with disabilities (Atkinson & Hackett, 1998). It was in part due to dismal statistics like these that Congress passed the Americans with Disabilities Act.

Implications. Mental health professionals need to be in the forefront of assisting individuals with disabilities to obtain employment and to complete education to their potential. Some of the work might involve educating employers about specific disabilities. Greatest prejudice is displayed to hidden disabilities such as HIV. Education about this condition and the remote chances of getting HIV through casual contact can work to allay fears (A. Thomas, 2001). About 6% of students enrolled in postsecondary educational institutions had disabilities. Most involve visual, hearing, or orthopedic problems (Palmer & Roessler, 2000). Mental health professionals can prepare them for success at the college level by teaching them to be self-advocates, for example, by identifying and requesting accommodations when applying to and attending college. Communication and negotiation skills can be developed through role-play. Independence can be encouraged from managing money, doing laundry, eating appropriately, or performing other daily living skills (Ericksen-Radtke & Beale, 2001).

The Americans with Disabilities Act

The Americans with Disabilities Act (ADA) was signed into law in 1990, extending the federal mandate of nondiscrimination toward individuals with disabilities to state and local governments and the private sector. Congress defined disability as "a physical or mental impairment that substantially limits one or more of the major life activities of such individual." It includes individuals with mental retardation, hearing impairment or deafness, orthopedic impairments, learning disabilities, speech impairment, and other health or physical impairments. Psychiatric disorders covered include major depression, bipolar disorder, panic and obsessive-compulsive disorders, personality disorders, schizophrenia, and rehabilitation from drug use or addiction. Conditions not covered include sexual behavior disorders, compulsive gambling, kleptomania, pyromania, and current substance abuse (Sleek, 1998). Under this definition, there are 49 million to 54 million Americans with disabilities, of whom 24 million have a severe form. While more than 60% of the people 65 and over have a disability, the largest number of this population are of working age (Wellner, 2001). The prevalence of disability ranges from 5.8% for children under 18 to 53.9% for those 65 and over (U.S. Bureau of the Census, 1995). The number recognized by the ADA is in fact now higher, since HIV has recently been added as a disability.

The ADA has had an impact on businesses with employees with disabilities. Many have made adjustments and accommodations:

> Mike Johnson wasn't asking for special treatment at work, but his bosses thought they'd better provide it anyway. Two months after being hospitalized for bipolar disorder, Johnson, an accomplished, 35-year-old sales executive, told his boss that he was feeling "stressed out." The boss also noticed that Johnson overbooked his schedule during his manic phases and would wake up late and miss appointments during depressive periods. (Sleek, 1998, p. 15)

Mike Johnson's employer was able to retain a valuable executive with bipolar disorder by developing a flexible work schedule that allowed him to have time off for therapy.

Implications. Mental health professionals working with individuals with disabilities should know the federal and state laws applicable to these individuals. They should know the rights of individuals with disabilities in school and work settings. Under the ADA, employers cannot discriminate against an individual with a disability during employment or promotion if they are otherwise qualified, cannot inquire about a disability but only about the ability to perform the job, are required to make "reasonable" accommodation for people with disabilities, and cannot use tests that will cause individuals to be screened out due to disabilities (Vacc & Clifford, 1995). The counselor should also be aware of problems in using standardized assessment tools with individuals who have disabilities. Finally, it is important for counselors to understand that individuals with the same disability may show a wide range of functional difficulties and accomplishments.

Congress passed the ADA in 1990 to address the following issues:

1. Historically, society has tended to isolate and segregate individuals with disabilities, and despite some improvements, such forms of discrimination against individuals with disabilities continue to be a serious and pervasive social problem.

2. Unlike individuals who have experienced discrimination on the basis of race, color, sex, national origin, religion, or age, individuals who have experienced discrimination on the basis of disability have often had no legal recourse to redress such discrimination.

3. Individuals with disabilities continually encounter various forms of discrimination, including intentional exclusion; the discriminatory effects of architectural, transportation, and communication barriers; overprotective rules and policies; failure to make modifications to existing facilities and practices; exclusionary qualification standards and criteria; segregation; and relegation to lesser services, programs, activities, benefits, jobs, or other opportunities.

4. Census data, national polls, and other studies have documented that people with disabilities, as a group, occupy an inferior status in our society and are severely disadvantaged socially, vocationally, economically, and educationally.

5. The nation's goals regarding individuals with disabilities are to ensure equality of opportunity, full participation, independent living, and economic self-sufficiency. The act prohibits discrimination in employment, telecommunications, transportation, and public services and accommodations (Atkinson & Hackett, 1998).

Implications. Mental health professionals need to ensure that the services they provide address these legal and ethical standards (APA, 1999). Do not separate out or give unequal service to clients with disabilities unless you must do so to provide a service that is as effective as that provided to those without disabilities.

- Do not deny your services to a client with a disability. You may refer him or her if that individual requires treatment outside your area of specialization.

- Watch for criteria that screen out clients with disabilities. For instance, do not require a driver's license for payment by check. Use policies, practices, and procedures in your office that can be modified for those with disabilities, such as making sure service guide animals are permitted in your office.

- You may need to provide auxiliary aids and services, such as readers, sign-language interpreters, Braille materials, large-print materials, videotapes and audiotapes, and computers when necessary to communicate with your clients with disabilities. You may have to use alternative forms of communication, such as notepads and pencils, when these forms are appropriate.

- Evaluate your office for structural and architectural barriers that prevent individuals with disabilities from getting the services they need from you. Change these barriers when they can be readily changed (without much difficulty or expense). Look at ramps, parking spaces, curbs, shelving, elevator control buttons, widths of doorways, and heights of toilet seats.

- When remodeling or building new offices, hire an architect or contractor familiar with ADA requirements.

Myths about People with Disabilities

There are many myths associated with people with disabilities (American Friends Service Committee, 1998):

1. *Most are in wheelchairs.* Of the 49 million individuals with disabilities, only about 10% use wheelchairs, crutches, or walkers. Most have disabilities related to cardiovascular problems, blindness, developmental disabilities, or "invisible" disabilities such as asthma, learning disabilities, or epilepsy.

2. *People with disabilities are a drain on the economy.* It is true that 71% of working-age persons with disabilities are not working. However, 72% of those want to work. Discrimination has kept them out of the workforce.

3. *The greatest barriers to people with disabilities are physical ones.* In actuality, negative attitudes and stereotypes are the greatest impediments and the most difficult to change.

4. *Businesses dislike the ADA.* Actually, 82% of executives surveyed believe that it is worth implementing and note that implementation expenses are minimal.

5. *Government health insurance covers people with disabilities.* Of the 29.5 million individuals with disabilities between the ages of 15 and 64, 18.4 million have private insurance, Medicaid covers 4.4 million, and 5.1 million have no health insurance.

Programs for Individuals with Disabilities

In the past, programs for persons with disabilities focused on rehabilitation rather than assisting them to develop independent living skills. There has been gradual recognition that deficiencies in experiences and opportunities limit the individual's development. The services received by individuals with disabilities are most effective when they enable independence, self-determination, and productive participation in society (Humes, Szymanski, & Hohenshil, 1989). However, the statistics on the outcome of educational programs have not been very positive. One survey found that only 27% of individuals with disabilities go to college, compared to 68% of those without disabilities; 30% drop out of high school. Three to five years after graduation from high school, only 57% are employed, compared to 69% of youth without disabilities (Wagner & Blackorby, 1996). Clearly, new approaches are needed. Several programs have obtained promising results.

Ted Stabelfeldt is a 19-year-old male, paralyzed from the shoulders down, who discovered the DO-IT program at the University of Washington. This program links high school students with disabilities who are interested in science and math with computer technology that is designed to work from their areas of strength. Todd is able to operate his computer with a hollow mouth wand. He types by pointing the wand to letters on the screen and blowing into the wand to make it operate like a computer mouse. One puff represents a single click and two puffs represent a double-click. Todd has learned to operate the computer efficiently but admits that the most difficult part was not learning the new technology but getting over his own negative attitudes toward disability: "When I attended DO-IT, that all changed. I met 40 other gimps—that's what I call them. I realized, hey, man, they're cool. They're real people too" (H. T. George, 1998, p. B2).

Todd's computer skills helped him obtain a job writing medical software. Of the 136 students who participated in the program, over 50% are going into technical schools or colleges, and over 25% have found employment. There has been a shift in the orientation of programs for people with disabilities from remediation or "making them as normal as possible" to identifying and strengthening skills that they possess.

The Bridges from School to Work program, which involved 2,258 students, was also successful. The disabilities included learning disability (52%), mental retardation (22%), emotional disability (14%), and other disabilities (12%); the last category included epilepsy, sensory impairments, head injury, and orthopedic and mobility impairments. Participants had moderate to severe disabilities. The program involved prevocational orientation for both the family and the student. Information on job preparation, job expectations, and skills training was followed by internship placement in local businesses. The 12-week internship involved job skills training and monitoring of performance by the employers. Of the participants who completed their internships, 71% were offered jobs by the same or a different employer. In a 6-month follow-up, 84% of the participants were employed or had enrolled in college. The program was successful both in helping youths with disabilities make the transition to employment or further education and in opening doors in the business community (Fabian, Lent, & Willis, 1998).

Implications. Mental health professionals working with individuals with disabilities should be aware of the number of different programs offering employment and educational assistance. The National Library Service for the Blind and Physically Handicapped produces talking books and magazines on cassette for readers who are legally blind or cannot read printed material. Books and magazines are available free of charge to patrons, and most titles are offered on loan by postage-free mail to library patrons (Lazzaro, 2001). The American Printing House for the Blind offers a database for audio-books, large print, computer disk, and Braille. Books can also be downloaded into talking handheld readers. The National Association of the Deaf operates the captioned media program, and the National Braille Press offers a selection of Braille books and magazines. Software programs can turn text into Braille through the use of a Braille printer, and scanners can convert print from books into speech. It is important for mental health professions to be aware of current technology in enhancing the quality of life and employment opportunities for people with disabilities. Vocational and support group information can also be obtained over the Internet.

Counseling Issues with Individuals with Disabilities

Many counselors and other mental health professionals do not know how to deal with clients who have disabilities.

A 33-year-old client with hearing difficulties has problems at work. Her employer claims that she does not follow orders and inquires about attention or memory problems. The psychologist administers the Wechsler Adult Intelligence Scale—Revised (WAIS-R), the Wechsler Memory Scale—Revised, and the Min-

nesota Multiphasic Personality Inventory (MMPI) and finds no evidence of memory or attentional deficits. The MMPI results suggest mild paranoid and depressive tendencies. (Leigh, Corbett, Gutman, & Morere, 1996)

In this case the psychologist concluded that the problems at work were a result of the woman's depression and paranoid tendencies. There is no mention in his report of the possible impact of her hearing loss on either the results of the assessments or her ability to adapt to the work environment. In fact, it is likely that the woman's hearing impairment accounted for the majority of the presenting symptoms.

Implications. Helping professionals often display the same attitude as the general public toward individuals with disabilities and may feel uncomfortable or experience guilt or pity when working with them. As when working with other oppressed groups, the counselor must examine his or her view of clients with disabilities and identify and question prejudicial assumptions. A client's disability should not be the sole focus for counseling. Environmental contributions to problems should also be identified. Issues involving frustrations with architectural barriers or with negative stereotypes or prejudices against individuals with disabilities need to be addressed in counseling (Vacc & Clifford, 1995).

Kemp and Mallinckrodt (1996) pointed out some of the errors that can occur in counseling relationships with individuals with disabilities. First, errors involving omission may be made. The counselor may fail to ask questions about critical aspects of the client's life because the assumption is made that the issue is unimportant due to the presence of the disability. For example, sexuality and relationship issues may be ignored because of the belief that the individual lacks the ability or interest in pursuing these intimacies. Affective issues may also be avoided, since the counselor may be uncomfortable addressing the impact of the disability on the client. The counselor may display a lowered expectation of the client's capabilities. Second, errors of commission may be made. In this case, the counselor assumes without justification that certain issues should be important because of the disability, when they are not. Personal problems faced by the client are all assumed to be a result of the disability. Career and academic counseling may become a focus even when it is not the client's interest. Other errors identified by Kemp and Mallinckrodt that may be made in working with clients with disabilities are not addressing the disability at all, encouraging dependency and the "sick" role, countertransference in wanting to "rescue" the client, and having a lowered expectation of the client's capabilities.

First, it is generally appropriate to ask a client about a disability and its nature. In doing so, it is important not to succumb to the "spread" phenomenon that often exists with disabilities. This refers to believing that the disability encompasses unrelated aspects of the individual. For example, a person in a wheelchair may also be thought to have a cognitive problem. Second, you might ask if there are ways that the disability is part of the presenting problem (Olkin, 1999). Such an approach allows the therapist to address the disability directly. If the disability is of recent origin, assess factors such as coping style, whether they blame themselves or others for the injury, and the amount of social support available (Rabasca, 1999).

Models of Disability

Olkin (1999) believed that there are three models of disability affecting the way the condition is perceived. First, the *moral model* focuses on the "defect" as representing some form of sin or moral lapse. Feelings of shame occur for both the individuals with the disability and family members who feel responsible. The disability is perceived as a test of faith. Second, the *medical model* is paternalistic in nature. Disability represents a defect or loss of function that resides in the individual. Action is taken to cure or rehabilitate the conditions. Its advantage over the moral model is that it removes the notion of sin for the disability. In addition, the medical model has been responsible for many technological advances. Third, the *minority model* is a relatively new model in which disability is seen as an external problem involving an environment that fails to accommodate the needs of individuals with disabilities and is filled with negative societal attitudes. As such, there are many similarities between the experiences of individuals who are disabled and those of other minority groups.

Implications. The mental health professional needs to identify the way the disability is viewed by the particular individual involved and by family members, since this will likely influence problem definition and intervention strategies. Much of the research indicates that empowering individuals and caregivers increases life satisfactions. This may need to be done within the model adhered to by the family. If the moral model is involved, the source for the interpretation of the disability as due to sin or a test of faith must be identified. Religious support may offer meaningful relief. Within this context, different alternative strategies can be generated. The goal would be to reduce guilt, give meaning to the experience, generate support from the religious community, and develop problem-solving approaches. With the medical model, the focus is on a physical condition that lies within the disabled individual. The "rehabilitation" approach attempts to use technology and training to "normalize" the individual and to have him or her fit into the existing environment. The patient is passive and receives treatment. Lately, there has been increasing emphasis on independent functioning within this model.

Mental health professionals can help clients and family members not only to obtain technological resources but also to develop more strongly independent living skills and to advocate for appropriate accommodations in the school and work environments. The minority model is useful in that societal attitudes are seen as a large part of the problem faced by individuals with disabilities. The focus is to change the environment to facilitate the potential of individuals who have disabilities. "Inoculating" them to societal prejudices and discrimination protects their self-esteem. The emphasis is on self-empowerment and self-advocacy.

Life Satisfaction and Suicide

As was indicated earlier, ratings of life satisfaction among individuals with disabilities tended to be lower than those for people without disabilities. However, these ratings depend on the type of disability and when the ratings were given. Some individuals adjust well, while others remain chronically distressed. In one study of the life satisfaction of people with traumatic spinal cord injuries, 37% indicated they were "very satisfied" and 31% "somewhat satisfied." This compares to 50% "very satisfied" and 40% "somewhat satisfied" among the general population. An interesting aspect of the study was that those who perceived themselves as in control were the most satisfied (Chase, Cornille, & English, 2000). Individuals with disabilities often rate satisfactions such as communication, thinking, and relating socially as more important than being able to walk or to dress oneself. Unfortunately, many mental health professionals display a negative attitude toward disability. In one study, only 18% of physicians and nurses imagined that they would be glad to be alive if they had a high-level spinal cord injury. Of 128 persons with this condition, 92% were glad to be alive.

Implications. Mental health and health care providers often underestimate the quality of life for individuals with disabilities and attempt to have them become content with their condition. Signs of depression or suicidal thoughts among individuals with disabilities might be accepted as normal because of a low quality of life. Interventions may be considered useless. The research seems to show that many individuals with disabilities feel quite satisfied with their lives and that increasing their sense of control is important. Individuals with disabilities can develop self-efficacy by learning or being encouraged to direct their own personal assistance services and to make decisions over important aspects of their lives. As with other conditions, suicidal thoughts or wishes may surface and should be treated. Some support the right of individuals with disabilities to assisted suicide. However, disability organizations argue that individuals with disabilities are an oppressed group and could be coerced to end their lives (Batavia, 2000).

Sexuality and Reproduction

Men and women with disabilities often express concerns over sexual functioning and reproduction. They worry about their sexual attractiveness and how to relate to or find a partner. Some may not know if it is still possible to have children. Mental health professionals who are uncomfortable with these topics may overlook these areas, especially as it may apply to individuals with disabilities.

Implications. Clearly, both clients and therapists need to be educated on these subjects as they relate to the specific disabilities. Many individuals who have a disability receive the societal message that they should not be sexual or that they are sexually unattractive. This concern should be addressed and assessed both individually and to the couple, if applicable. Sexual relationships are based on communication and emotional responsiveness to one another. The mental health professional could help individuals or couples develop new ways of achieving sexual satisfaction. Old messages regarding sexuality may have to be replaced with new ones. Sexual pleasure is possible even with a loss of sensation in the genitals (e.g., with spinal cord injuries). Many women with spinal cord injuries are still capable of orgasms and sexual pleasure from stimulation of the genitals or other parts of the body. The injury also does not preclude the ability to become pregnant or deliver a child. Problems with lubrication may occur, but they can be treated with water-based lubricants such as K-Y jelly. Many women with spinal cord injuries are even able to have a vaginal delivery. Among men with spinal cord injuries, many are able to attain an erection and ejaculate, although they may have to learn new forms of stimulation. Sensate focus exercises can help individuals increase awareness of the areas of the body that may be open to sexual stimulation (Tepper, 2001). Online resources for sexual information include the following:

- *PeopleNet DisAbility DateNet (members.aol.com/bobezwriter/pnet.htm).* This site provides information and the opportunity to participate in discussions on dating, sexuality, and relationships.
- *Through the Looking Glass (lookingglass.org).* This site provides resources for adults and parents with disabilities and parents of children with disabilities.
- *DisAbled Women's Network (DAWN; serv1.thot.net/~dawn/who.html).* This site also provides information on parenting and a feminist perspective.

Spirituality and Religiosity

Spirituality and religious beliefs can be a source of inner strength and support. One woman with a disability wrote, "It sort of helps me to identify myself, thinking I am a woman created by God and I am so precious and I am so loved and I have so much beauty inside of me" (Nosek & Hughes, 2001, p. 23).

Implications. The mental health professional should determine the role, if any, that religious beliefs or spirituality plays in the life of a client with a disability. The woman in the previous example was able to have a positive sense of self partly through her spirituality. The vast majority of Americans believe in God and indicate that their approach to life is grounded in faith (Elliot, Kilpatrick, & McCullough, 1999). Such beliefs could be a source of support for both the caregivers and the patients. In other cases, individuals may believe that their disability is a punishment from God or may blame God for not preventing the injury. These issues should be also addressed and resolved. In any event, the importance of religious beliefs to the clients should be determined.

Family Counseling

Family caregivers now operate as integral parts of the health care system and provide services that were once performed by professional health care providers. They will probably assume even greater caregiving roles in the future. It is therefore important to help them reduce the impact of stressors both on them and on the family member with the disability. With family members, emotional issues such as distress, guilt, self-punishment, or anger may need to be dealt with. Family members may feel responsible for the condition and have a primarily negative focus.

Implications. Individuals with the disability and their family members can decide to withdraw from others or to make positive changes. Hulnick and Hulnick (1989) suggested focusing on choices that can be made. For example, the counselor can ask questions such as "What are you doing that perpetuates the situation?" and "Are you aware of other choices that would have a different result?" These questions are empowering, since clients realize that they have the ability to make choices. Instead of viewing disability as a problem, reframing can be used to identify opportunities through questions such as "In what ways could you use this situation to your advancement?" or "What can you learn from this experience?" Among family caregivers, several attributes led to greater satisfaction both in them and in the individuals with the disability (Elliot, Shewchuk, & Richards, 1999). The first involved employing problem-solving strategies by defining the problem, generating alternatives, evaluating alternatives, implementing solutions, and evaluating outcomes. This helped increase the self-efficacy of the family members and increased their ability to develop coping strategies. The second consisted of developing a more positive orientation toward their ability to meet the demands of the situation. These approaches can improve the emotional health of both the caregivers and family members with disabilities. Reframing can also be useful. One psychologist who is blind believes that he may be less threatening to clients who are self-conscious or that they might respect the fact that he has faced and overcome difficult issues (Clay, 1999). Albert Ellis, the founder of rational-emotive therapy, has experienced the disabilities of diabetes, tired eyes, deficient hearing, and other physical handicaps but has successfully utilized cognitive approaches, such as reframing, to deal with his disabilities. For example, because he cannot keep his eyes open for any length of time, he focuses on the positive aspects of conducting therapy sessions with his eyes closed. He tells himself that with his eyes shut he can (a) focus "unusually well" on his clients' verbalizations (tone of voice, hesitations, etc.), (b) identify more easily their irrational thoughts, (c) help clients feel more relaxed, and (d) serve as a healthy model of an individual with a disability (Ellis, 1997). Ellis has thus been able to redefine his disability as a useful feature in conducting therapy.

Guidelines for Clinical Practice

1. Identify your beliefs, assumptions, and attitudes about individuals with disabilities.
2. Understand the prejudice, discrimination, inconveniences, and barriers faced by individuals with disabilities.
3. Redirect internalized self-blame for the disability to societal attitudes.
4. Employ the appropriate communication format and address the client directly rather than an accompanying individual.
5. Determine if the disability is related to the presenting problem or if it will impact treatment strategies. If it is not an issue, continue with your usual assessments.
6. If the disability is related to the problem, identify whether the client adheres to the moral model (disability is a result of moral lapse or a sin), medical model (disability is a physical limitation), or minority model (disability is the result of a lack of accommodation by the environment).
7. If formal tests are employed, provide appropriate accommodations. Interpret the results with care since most are not standardized with members of this population.
8. Recognize that family members and other social supports are important. Include them in your assessment, goal formation, and selection of techniques. It is also important to determine their model of disability.
9. Identify environmental changes or accommodations that are associated with the problem and assist the family in changing them.

10. Help family members reframe the problem so that positives can be identified. Strengthen positive attributes.

11. Develop self-advocacy skills for both the individual with the disability and the family members.

12. Note that counseling strategies that focus on problem identification, developing and implementing changes, and evaluating effectiveness are useful.

13. Realize that mental health professionals may have to serve as advocates or consultants to initiate changes in academic and work settings.

Part VII

ORGANIZATIONS AND INSTITUTIONS AS CLIENTS

Counseling Monocultural Organizations

Several years after receiving my doctorate in counseling psychology, I accepted a position at a well known private university on the West Coast. The university was located in an area with a large Latino population, but the student body was over 90% White. Having previously been employed at a university in northern California, I had been exposed to the aftermath of the Free Speech Movement and had been involved with the Third World Strike, a movement begun in the late 1960s aimed at multicultural curriculum reform and increasing representation of minorities in students, faculty, and staff alike.

With these goals in mind, several colleagues and I confronted the university administration with the low numbers of Hispanic/Latino American students on the college campus: I (a) suggested that there was bias in the admission criteria, (b) asked for a change in the standards used to admit students of minority cultural background, (c) demanded the placement of minority faculty members on admissions committees, (d) requested the formation of outreach groups to recruit minority students, and (e) asked for the creation of an ethnic studies department.

Being a very conservative institution, the university strongly resisted all of our demands. I recall countless hours of meetings, debates, and even community demonstrations concerning the underrepresentation of minority student admissions to the university. Academic senate meetings became very emotional with the majority of faculty and administrators claiming that our group wanted to "lower the standards" of the university. We, in turn, took the position that current admission criteria were biased toward minority applicants and that what we sought was not a lowering but a changing of standards that could be fairly applied to a culturally diverse student population. Indeed, many of our other requests such as curriculum reform, increased minority faculty and staff, culturally relevant student services, and so on soon were dropped as the battleground was fought on the frontiers of traditional admission criteria (GPA, SAT scores, recommendations, extracurricular activities, etc.).

After nearly a year of sustained debate on this issue, the university administration relented to community pressures and developed what was called a "special accommodated category," which allowed the admission of large numbers of primarily Latino students onto the campus. While many of us celebrated this development, our victory was short-lived. By the end of the first quarter, nearly 50% of the minority students admitted under the new standard were placed on academic probation. By the end of the academic year, many of those on probation had failed, and even those students who had maintained a C average had decided not to return to the university. Fueled by these results, our opponents used them to buttress their arguments: "Minority students were not qualified to undertake college-level work unless they met the same standards as their White counterparts." The next year, the university dropped the special category provision. I also left the following year and accepted a position at another higher education institution.

This incident has always haunted me for several reasons. First, I was filled with guilt at having started a movement that suddenly backfired and left all those involved (proponents and opponents alike) with negative feelings toward concepts of affirmative action and diversity. Second, for years after my departure, I could not fully understand what had happened to derail our movement. I was left with a bitter taste in my mouth; I was confused about what had gone wrong; and I was at a loss as to what else we might have done to effect a more positive outcome. It was only years later, as I became increasingly involved with multicultural organizational development, that I came to fully understand some of the reasons for our downfall.

Why Mental Health Professionals Must Understand Organizational Dynamics

The previous case demonstrates strongly the need for purveyors of institutional change to understand systemic principles and forces. Counseling/clinical practice has too long accepted an extremely narrow view of helping, leaving us with tunnel vision and ill-prepared to work with organizations and larger social systems. For example, it does little good to be culturally competent in clinical work when the very organizations that employ us are not receptive to multicultural practice or directly punish counselors when they choose to exercise those helping skills. Systems forces can be powerful and oppressive; the previous case illustrates how a failure to understand systemic dynamics may derail productive change regardless of the good intentions involved or the willingness to push a multicultural agenda. As we noted earlier, becoming multiculturally competent requires not only changes at an individual practice level, but changes associated with how we define our helping role as well. That role is significantly different from the conventional counselor/therapist one and entails roles that directly impact the system rather than solely the individual. Let us briefly discuss why this change in focus is needed.

1. There is a common belief supported by actual practices that therapists work primarily with individuals or small groups (Atkinson, Morten, et al., 1998). The practice of counseling and psychotherapy has arisen from the study of individual differences and reflects the value of individualism in U.S. society. Traditional Euro-American schools of counseling and therapy have implicitly or explicitly glamorized and defined the clinician as one who conducts his or her trade, working with individuals, in an office environment. While the development of individual intervention skills has been the main focus in graduate training programs, little emphasis is given to other roles, activities, or settings. Thus, not only are therapists lacking in systems-intervention knowledge and skills, but also they are unaccustomed to, and uncomfortable about, leaving their offices (D. W. Sue et al., 1996). Yet work with racial/ethnic minority groups suggests that out-of-office sites/activities (client homes, churches, volunteer organizations, etc.) and alternative helping roles (ombudsman, advocates, consultants, organizational change agents, facilitators of indigenous healing systems, etc.) may prove more therapeutic and effective (Atkinson et al., 1993).

2. Related to the previous point is the belief that clinical work should be concerned primarily with internal or intrapsychic dynamics and conflicts. When the focus of therapy is on the individual, however, there is a strong tendency to see the locus of the problem as residing solely in the person (Lewis et al., 1998) rather than in the organization or social structures. As a result, well-intentioned counselors may mistakenly blame the victim (e.g., "The problem is a deficiency of the person") when, in actuality, it may reside in the environment. For example, African Americans who are unemployed are often perceived as being lazy, unmotivated, or lacking the skills to acquire a job when the actual reasons may be due to prejudice and discrimination. When the problems and practices of an organization (employer) are biased toward minority groups, shouldn't attempts at change be directed toward the "discriminating" organizational structures?

3. Training programs often imbue trainees with the belief that the role of mental health professionals is relatively free of organizational influences or pressures. In the privacy of their offices, counselors may be under the illusion that they are free to help clients attain their full potential—that their allegiance is to the individual client seeking help. Yet it is becoming clear that what we can or cannot do is often dictated by the rules and regulations of our employing agencies (length of sessions, maximum number of sessions, types of problems treated, definition of counseling role, limits of confidentiality, etc.). The managed health care environment has forced us to confront this reality much more than ever

before. The policies of an organization or a superordinate group (insurance carriers, HMOs, state and professional organizations, etc.) may conflict with the therapeutic help needed that our clients need. This is especially true in an organization that lacks sensitivity toward culturally different groups.

In addition, clinicians may find themselves in conflict when the needs of their clients differ from those of the organization or employer. The fact that a therapist's livelihood depends on the employing agency creates additional pressures to conform. How do therapists handle such conflicts? Who truly are their clients? Organizational knowledge and skills become a necessity if the therapist is to be truly effective.

4. Conventional therapy continues to be oriented toward remediation rather than prevention. While no one would deny the important effects of biological and internal psychological factors on personal problems, more research now acknowledges the importance of sociocultural factors (inadequate or biased education, poor socialization practices, biased values, and discriminatory institutional policies) in creating many of the difficulties encountered by individuals. As helping professionals, we are frequently placed in a position of treating clients who represent the aftermath of failed and oppressive policies and practices (D. W. Sue, 1991a, 1991b, 1994). We have been trapped in the role of remediation (attempting to cure clients once they have been damaged by sociocultural biases). While treating troubled clients (remediation) is a necessity, our task would be an endless and losing venture unless the true sources of the problem (stereotypes, prejudice, discrimination and oppression) are changed. Would it not make more sense to take a proactive and preventative approach by attacking the cultural and institutional bases of the problem?

5. Many of us behave as if the main focus of therapy should be on individual or small-group change; organizational change is the province of industrial/organizational (I/O) psychologists. The arguments presented thus far challenge this point of view; acquiring organizational knowledge and skills is a therapeutic necessity. Intraprofessional divisions (territorial turf) should not prevent us from developing and adopting organizational development strategies in our work. We can profit much from I/O principles developed in the business world. Indeed, many counseling and clinical psychologists have recently advocated increasing roles for professionals in business and industry. As psychologists move into the areas of occupational health (Osipow, 1982; Toomer, 1982) and diversity training (Katz & Miller, 1988; D. W. Sue, 1991a, 1991b, 1994), the artificial distinctions between the roles of I/O and clinicians may become blurred.

Organizational Change Principles

Let us briefly return to the opening case study to analyze how unenlightened knowledge of organizational dynamics may lead to failure and derive some basic systems change principles.

Principle One: A Realistic Assessment of the Level of Multicultural Development Is Needed

Before advocating a change in admission standards at the university for prospective minority students, proponents should have conducted a thorough assessment of the institutional climate with respect to multiculturalism. All organizations differ in their receptivity to diversity concepts, and premature intervention may result in devastating consequences. They should have known that not only are institutions conservative (e.g., they resist change), but in this case it was downright hostile to multicultural concerns. Indeed, most multicultural organizational development (MOD) models would have characterized the university as monocultural: (a) Cultural diversity issues are either ignored or purposefully undermined; (b) most workers (faculty and staff) are either ethnocentric or highly assimilated tokens; (c) hiring and admission practices are highly discriminatory; (d) the curriculum is taught from a Eurocentric perspective without regard for other cultural views; and (e) there is a strong organizational belief that there is only one best way to run a University.

Under these conditions, it is little wonder that attempts to implement change met with such devastating results. Their tunnel vision and narrow focus prevented them from seeing the larger picture. The proponents were motivated by naive idealism without a full understanding of systems intervention. Their task was much larger than getting the university to adopt different admissions criteria. It was much greater than trying to convince key members of committees to accept their suggestions. As novices, they failed to realize that the effective introduction of change depends not only on how and what is introduced, but on the readiness and commitment of an organization as well. The stage of MOD of an organization (to be presented shortly) often dictates the type of interventions deemed most effective.

Principle Two: The Interrelationships of Subsystems Need to Be Understood

In family therapy, students are often warned that treating the "identified patient" without intervening in the family system may prove to be futile. The assumption is that the problems or pathology observed in one member of the family is not necessarily due to internal conflicts, but to unhealthy values and pressures of family life (D. W. Sue, 2001). Treating a child in individual sessions, for example, may appear to eradicate the symptoms as long as the child remains outside of the family. Once the child reenters the family, however, he or she may again be forced to play the "sick" role because the subsystems and rules of the family remain unchanged. Treating the child has unbalanced the family homeostasis, and family dynamics will again strive for balance.

Like a family system, organizations are also composed of many interacting subsystems (Levinson, 1994). Over time, these subsystems have worked out a homeostatic relationship held together by institutional policies and practices (formal and informal) governing their relationship to one another. These rules and regulations seemingly attain a "functional autonomy" that dictates what we can or cannot do in an organization (D. W. Sue, 1994). Changing only one aspect of a system does not guarantee change in others. For example, in a very simplistic manner, the university can be seen as having three major functions: recruitment, retention, and graduation of students. Within each of these three functions are multiple systems that theoretically support the activities. Student support services, grading standards and processes, teaching and learning styles, curriculum content, and campus culture may all be seen as subsystems. One very important subsystem is that of the admissions process and the criteria used to select students. Attempts to get the university to change one of these subsystems (standards for admission) were doomed to fail because advocates for diversity did not have the understanding or foresight to recognize that the other systems did not change. Indeed, these other subsystems worked against the changes (attempts to reestablish equilibrium) and eventually succeeded in reinstituting the original monocultural standards. The low enrollment of Latino students at the university may initially have been due to biased admissions criteria (the recruitment system), but failure to consider the influence of other university systems led to the loss of minority students. The subsequent high dropout rates were due largely to characteristics of a monocultural university: Curricula alienated many minority students; the teaching styles were culturally biased; grading practices emphasized individual competition; the campus climate was hostile to minority students (they were also perceived as less qualified); support services (counseling, study skills, etc.) were not geared toward nontraditional students; and there was a lack of role models (minority faculty, staff, and administrators).

The Latino students who were admitted were subjected to all these antagonistic systems that eventually took their toll. What advocates should have done was to make existing systems more sensitive and receptive to multicultural issues (curriculum reform and introducing varying teaching styles that recognize diversity) or to create new subsystems that supported the students. Organizational change must occur throughout to be effective.

Principle Three: Commitment Must Come from the Top

Diversity implementation is most effective when strong leadership is exerted on behalf of multiculturalism. For private businesses, the board of directors, CEO, and management team are the principles; for governmental agencies, it is often the head of the service or unit (e.g., Secretary of Labor, Housing, etc.); for education, it is the school board, superintendent, principal, and so on; and for our nation it is the president of the United States, the Congress, judiciary, and local, state, and federal leaders.

In the case vignette, the University administrators were either publicly or privately resentful or antagonistic to the goals of multiculturalism. The deans and department chairs were usually adamant in their vocal opposition to proposed changes, while those in the higher echelons of the University (president, academic vice president, and governing board) kept silent. The old saying "silence can be deafening" was heard throughout. Even when the changed standards were adopted, many leaders in the University voiced only lukewarm support.

It also is important to note that faculty, staff, and students alike are most likely to watch the actions (not just words) of their leaders. Commitment must be manifested in action. It is more than a written policy statement of affirmative action or statements that one is an "equal opportunity employer." What specific steps has the leadership taken to implement diversity goals at the university? It was clear that the university was not prepared to make any other adjustments in its operation to accommodate minority students. The message was quite clear: "Minority students are not wanted on this campus." Such a message from the leadership gave permission for those in the lower ranks (faculty, staff, and even White students) to resist or sabotage proposed changes.

Principle Four: Premature Introduction of Change May Only Support the Mistaken/Biased Beliefs of the Opposition

One of the greatest lessons learned from this incident was that lack of an overarching plan for change may backfire with devastating consequences. Many of the more well-meaning and receptive colleagues harbored grave doubts about changing admission standards. Advocates for change felt that attempts to work on those who were adamantly opposed was a waste of time, so they concentrated their efforts on the former group. With such a high drop-out rate among the minority students, the "we told you so" cry was used by the opposition in reaffirming three points: (a) The standards of the University had been lowered; (b) less qualified students were admitted solely because of their race; and (c) these students were incapable of handling university work. All of these beliefs became reinforced, and even their borderline allies finally concluded that reinstituting traditional admission criteria was necessary. Thus, the negative beliefs regarding minority students and implementing diversity became more firmly entrenched as a result of the "good intentions" of proponents for change. It might have been better if they had not attempted any intervention at all!

Principle Five: White People Are Also Victims and Are under Strong Institutional Pressures to Conform

Even the most well intentioned White educators or administrators are not immune from inheriting the racial biases, stereotypes, and prejudices of the larger society. During the brief time the senior author was in the psychology department of the university in the case study, he had made a number of friends. When the issue of accepting more minority students came up, he was quite surprised to find that many of his faculty friends expressed biases toward various minority groups. Subsequently, proponents saw these individuals as enemies and unfortunately grouped them in a good or bad dichotomy. This artificial category failed to recognize a simple fact that was learned later in life. While minorities are often seen as being the victims of prejudice and discrimination, White people may be victims as well. Their victimization is different, however, because they were socialized into oppressor roles. It is our belief that no one is ever born wanting to be racist, sexist, or prejudiced. White people are programmed into roles without their informed consent (D. W. Sue, 1992, 1993). While this does not absolve them from taking responsibilities for their biases, this understanding may make it easier to avoid seeing them as "evil beings." Many educators who might have been enlightened with some effort on the part of the proponents were pushed away and dismissed as potential allies.

Furthermore, the advocates' failure to understand the power of institutional forces (forced compliance) led to continued loss of potential allies. For example, in many informal discussions with White faculty and staff, things were said that often suggested their sympathies with the cause of diversity. When asked for their support, they would often readily agree (in private). Yet when more formal meetings were held with committees and university representatives, these very same White faculty members would either say nothing or couch their responses in a very ambiguous or guarded manner. When votes were taken, they would vote against diversity proposals, abstain, or not show for the meetings (always with a very convenient excuse). Advocates were enraged by their actions and saw this as deceit, insincerity, and hypocrisy. Years later, the senior author has gained greater clarity on such behaviors. Again, these were not bad people, but individuals exposed to a punitive system. They may personally have believed in our cause, but the institution had great ability to reward or punish them (promotion, tenure, treatment at the University, etc.). Indeed, it is not much different from a person who hears a racist joke told by a group of friends. While personally offended, the individual fails to voice any objections for fear of losing friends or being ridiculed. This indifference, fear, and lack of action on the part of well-meaning individuals are major mechanisms used by institutional forces to preserve the status quo.

Developing Multicultural Organizational Competence

Just as multicultural counseling/therapy has become a "fourth force" in individual and group counseling/therapy (Pedersen, 1991b), so too must it increasingly influence organizational development. If our society truly is to value diversity and to become multicultural, then our organizations (mental health care delivery systems, businesses, industries, schools, universities, governmental agencies, and even our professional organizations like the American Counseling Association and the American Psychological Association) must move toward becoming multicultural.

The lessons learned from the painful incident described at the beginning of the chapter have taught the senior author the importance of developing organization knowledge and skills. Multicultural organizational development is different from traditional work in that it (a) takes a social justice perspective (ending of oppression and discrimination in organizations); (b) believes that inequities that arise within organizations may not be primarily due to poor communication, lack of knowledge, poor management, person-organization fit problems, and so on but to monopolies of power; and (c) assumes that conflict is inevitable and not necessarily unhealthy. Diversity trainers, consultants, and mental health practitioners increasingly ascribe to MOD, which is based on the premise that organizations vary in their awareness of how racial, cultural, ethnic, sexual orientation, and gender issues impact their clients or workers. Institutions that recognize and value diversity in a pluralistic society will be in a better position to avoid many of the misunderstandings and conflicts characteristic of monocultural organizations. They will also be in a better position to offer culturally relevant services to their multicultural populations and allow mental health professionals to engage in organizationally sanctioned roles and activities without the threat of punishment. Moving from a monocultural to a multicultural organization requires the counselor or change agent to understand their characteristics. Ascertaining what the organizational culture is like, what policies or practices either facilitate or impede cultural diversity, and how to implement change is crucial.

Models of Multicultural Organizational Development

Some of the more helpful MOD models have arisen from a variety of areas including the business sector (Adler, 1986; Foster, Jackson, Cross, Jackson, & Hardiman, 1988; B. W. Jackson & Holvino, 1988; D. W. Sue, 1991a), education (Barr & Strong, l987; Highlen, l994). Interestingly, nearly all of these models seem to describe a stage or process similar to the White racial identity development models in Chapter 8.

In comparing a number of these MOD models, D. W. Sue et al. (1998) noted some very strong similarities. First, most describe a developmental stage process by which organizations move from a primarily monocultural orientation to a more multicultural one. The labels or terms for the stages differ, but their descriptors are primarily the same (see Table 20.1). The following characteristics of organizations as they move toward diversity implementation have been distilled from Adler (1986); Katz and Miller (1988); Foster et al., (1988); Barr and Strong (1987); T. L. Cross, Bazron, Dennis, and Isaacs (1989); D'Andrea, Daniels, and Heck (1991); D. W. Sue (1991a); and Highlen (1994).

1. *Monocultural organizations.* At the one extreme are organizations that are primarily Eurocentric and ethnocentric. They believe in the following premises and practices:

   - There is an implicit or explicit exclusion of racial minorities, women, and other oppressed groups.
   - Many organizations are rigged to the advantage of dominant majority. In this case, Whites are privileged.
   - There is only one best way to deliver health care, manage, teach, or administrate.
   - Culture does not impact management, mental health, or education.
   - Clients, workers, or students should assimilate.
   - Culture-specific ways of doing things are neither recognized nor valued. Everyone should be treated the same.
   - There is strong belief in the melting pot concept.

2. *Nondiscriminatory organizations.* As organizations become more culturally aware and enlightened, they enter this stage. The following premises and practices characterize these organizations:

   - The organization has inconsistent policies and practices regarding multicultural issues. Certain departments or mental health practitioners/managers/teachers are becoming sensitive to minority issues, but it is not an organizational priority.

Table 20.1 **Stages of Multicultural Organizational Development**

Author	Stages					
Adler (1986)	Parochial		Ethnocentric		Synergistic	
Foster, Jackson, Cross, Jackson, and Hardiman (1988)	Monocultural		Nondiscriminatory		Multicultural	
Barr and Strong (1987)	Traditional		Liberal, Managing Diversity		Radical	
Cross, Bazron, Dennis, and Isaacs (1989)	Cultural Destructiveness	Cultural Incapacity	Cultural Blindness	Cultural Precompetence	Cultural Competence	Cultural Proficiency
Characteristics typical of organizations at particular stages	Cultural diversity is either deliberately ignored or destroyed. Organization members are monocultural or highly assimilated "tokens." Hiring practices are discriminatory, and services or products are inadequate or inappropriate for cultural minorities. Organizations believe there is only one right way to do things.		Organizations acknowledge that diversity exists and have "good intentions," but operate from a sense that "our way is the best way." Focus is on meeting affirmative action and EEO goals, with a legalistic approach to nondiscrimination. There may be attempts at cross-cultural sensitivity training for individuals, but no focus on organizational change. Staff may be culturally diverse but are judged by traditional (White, male) standards.		Organizations value diversity, view it as an asset rather than a problem. Staff diversity is evident at all levels, and staff are evaluated and promoted for meeting diversity criteria. Training focuses on the personal and organizational dynamics of racism, sexism, and so on. Planning is creative, flexible, to accommodate ongoing cultural change.	

Note. From *Multicultural Counseling Competencies: Individual and Organizational Development* (p. 101), by D.W. Sue et al., 1998, Thousand Oaks, CA: Sage Publications. Reprinted with permission.

- Leadership may recognize the need for some action, but leaders lack a systematic program or policy addressing the issue of prejudice and bias.
- There is an attempt to make the climate or services of an organization less hostile or different, but these changes are superficial and often without conviction. They are more for public relations or perception.
- Equal employment opportunity (EEO), affirmative action, and

numerical symmetry of minorities and women are implemented grudgingly.

3. *Multicultural organizations.* As organizations become progressively more multicultural, they begin to value diversity and evidence continuing attempts to accommodate ongoing cultural change. An organization at this level

    - Is in the process of working on a vision that reflects multiculturalism.

    - Reflects the contributions of diverse cultural and social groups in its mission, operations, products, or services.

    - Values diversity and views it as an asset.

    - Actively engages in visioning, planning, and problem-solving activities that allow for equal access and opportunities.

    - Realizes that equal access and opportunities are not equal treatment.

    - Values diversity (does not simply tolerate it) and works to diversify the environment.

These models are helpful as heuristic devices, but they still beg the questions what a culturally competent system of care should look like and how best to move an organization toward multiculturalism.

Culturally Competent Mental Health Organizations

The many issues identified in the earlier part of this book constitute the various motivations for mental health organizations to become multicultural, and the unmet needs of minority populations are foremost among them. To meet those needs, not only must a mental health organization employ individuals with multicultural counseling skills, but the agency itself will need to have a "multicultural culture," if you will.

Alvarez et al. (1976, p. 69) offered a general description of a mental health system that would meet community needs, including those of a multicultural population:

A system that is more effective in reaching people and in allocating resources because of improved organization, redefined relationships, continued evaluation, and improved communications will be the hallmark of a functioning [health care] system. This can be successful only if the system's staff and board will engage in education of and by the community and its own affiliates for under-

standing the system and its potential. Comprehensive community mental health has value only if, beyond the concept, program implementation is compatible with the community's understanding of mental health and its interpretation of mental illness. There must be a meaningful relationship between the center's practices, consumers' problems, and community concerns. The programs and services must have the potential to provide solutions that the community accepts as valid. In the center's effort to respond to problems in subunits of a community, it must also explore the consequences of implementing a partial solution to a large community problem.

T. L. Cross et al. (1989) have incorporated the insights of many researchers and gone beyond the three-stage business models to describe a detailed, sixstage developmental continuum of cultural competence for caregiving organizations such as mental health agencies. These have been given the names (a) cultural destructiveness, (b) cultural incapacity, (c) cultural blindness, (d) cultural precompetence, (e) cultural competence, and (f) advocacy.

1. *Cultural destructiveness.* Cross et al. acknowledged the checkered history of organizations and research ostensibly designed to "help" certain racial/ethnic groups by identifying the first stage of (in)competence as cultural destructiveness. Programs that have participated in culture/race based oppression, forced assimilation, or even genocide represent this stratum. Historically, many federal government programs aimed at American Indians fit this description, as do the infamous Tuskegee experiments, in which Black men with syphilis were deliberately left untreated, or the Nazi sponsored medical experiments that singled out Jews, Gypsies, gays/lesbians, and the disabled, among other groups, for systematic torture and death under the guise of medical research.

2. *Cultural incapacity.* At this stage, organizations may not be intentionally culturally destructive, but they may lack the capacity to help minority clients or communities because the system remains extremely biased toward the racial/cultural superiority of the dominant group. The characteristics of cultural incapacity include discriminatory hiring and other staffing practices; subtle messages to people of color that they are not valued or welcome, especially as manifested by environmental cues (building location, decoration, publicity that uses only Whites as models, etc.); and generally lower expectations of minority clients based on unchallenged stereotypical beliefs.

3. *Cultural blindness.* The third stage is one in which agencies provide services with the express philosophy that all people are the same, and the belief that helping methods used by the dominant culture are universally applicable. Despite the agency's good intentions, services are so

ethnocentric as to make them inapplicable for all but the most assimilated minority group members. "Such services ignore cultural strengths, encourage assimilation, and blame the victim for their problems. . . . Outcome is usually measured by how closely a client approximates a middleclass, nonminority existence. Institutional racism restricts minority access to professional training, staff positions, and services" (T. L. Cross et al., 1989, p. 15). Foster et al.'s (1988) nondiscriminatory stage fits here, and they note that organizations at this stage may have more of a fixation on "getting the numbers right" and eliminating any apparent signs of hostility towards new groups. While there may be a sincere desire to eliminate a majority group's unfair advantages, the focus may end up on limited and legalistic attempts to comply with equal employment or affirmative action regulations. It is difficult for organizations to move past this stage if Whites or other cultural majority members are not willing to confront the ways they have benefited from institutional racism, and risk trying on new ways of sharing power (Barr & Strong, 1987).

4. *Cultural precompetence.* Agencies at this stage have, as Schein (1990) might say, at least looked at the "artifacts" and values of their organization to recognize their weaknesses in serving minorities and developing a multicultural staff. They may experiment with hiring more minority staff beyond the minimal numbers required to comply with EEO goals, may recruit minorities for boards of directors or advisory committees, might work cooperatively to perform needs assessments with minority groups in their service area, and might institute cultural sensitivity training for staff, including management. They may propose new programs specifically for a particular ethnic/cultural group, but if planning is not done carefully, this program may end up marginalized within the agency.

    It is at this stage that the level of individuals' racial/ethnic identity awareness comes more clearly to the forefront: Individuals who are less aware of their stage of development may remain unchallenged within a system that overall is pleased with its accomplishments. "One danger at this level is a false sense of accomplishment or of failure that prevents the agency from moving forward along the continuum. . . . Another danger is tokenism" (T. L. Cross et al., 1989, p.16), when minority professionals are expected to raise the agency's level of cross-cultural efficacy by simply being present in slightly greater numbers. However, minority staff may lack training in many of the skills or knowledge areas that would allow them to translate their personal experience into effective counseling, not to mention training of coworkers.

    If the task of developing cultural awareness has been given to minority staff (or motivated majority staff) who do not have the clout to involve all elements of the agency, then "this pattern of program development allows for the phony embracing of multiculturalism because the dominant group can remain on the sidelines judging programs and helping the institution to continue on its merry way" (Barr & Strong, 1987, p. 21). These staff members may sacrifice job performance in other areas and then be criticized, or work doubly hard because they are taking on the extra burden of cultural awareness activities, and then may not receive any acknowledgment, in patterns that continue the oppression of minorities (Gallegos, 1982).

5.   *Cultural competence.* Agencies at this stage show "continuing selfassessment regarding culture, careful attention to the dynamics of difference, continuous expansion of cultural knowledge and resources, and a variety of adaptations to service models in order to better meet the needs of culturally diverse populations" (T. L. Cross et al., 1989, p.17).

Organizations at this stage will have a diverse staff at all levels, and most individuals will have reached the higher stages of individual racial/cultural identity awareness: They are aware of and able to articulate their cultural identity, values, and attitudes toward cultural diversity issues. This will be true for both majority and minority culture members. Staff will regularly be offered or seek out opportunities to increase their crosscultural skills and knowledge. There is recognition that minority group members have to be at least bicultural in U.S. society and that this creates its own mental health issues concerning identity, assimilation, values conflicts, and so on, for staff as well as clients. There will be enough multilingual staff available to offer clients choices in relating to service providers. If the agency has culturespecific programs under its umbrella, agency staff and clients perceive these programs as integral to the agency, and not just as junior partners.

6.   *Cultural proficiency.* This stage encompasses the highest goals of Adler's (1986) synergistic and Foster et al.'s (1988) multicultural stages. As Adler notes, these organizations are very uncommon, given that both the organizational culture and individuals within it are operating at high levels of multicultural competence, having overcome many layers of racism, prejudice, discrimination, and ignorance.

Organizations at this stage seek to add to the knowledge base of culturally competent practices by "conducting research, developing new therapeutic approaches based on culture, and disseminating the results of demonstration projects" (T. L. Cross et al., 1989, p. 17), and follow through on their "broader social responsibility to fight social discrimination and advocate social diversity" in all forums (Foster et al., 1988, p. 3).

Staff members are hired who are specialists in culturally competent practices, or are trained and supervised systematically to reach competency. Every level of an agency (board members, administrators, counselors, and consumers) regularly participates in evaluations of the agency's crosscultural practices and environment and is able to articulate the agency's values and strategies concerning cultural diversity. If the agency runs culture-specific programs, these programs are utilized as resources for everyone in the agency and community, and not perceived as belonging just to that ethnic community (Muñoz & Sanchez, 1996).

Implications for Clinical Practice

As can be seen, the task before us is immense. Being successful means getting organizations to review their policies, practices, and organizational structures to remove potential barriers. They may need to create new policies, practices, and internal structures that will support and advance cultural diversity. To truly value diversity, however, means altering the power relations in organizations to minimize structural discrimination. This may mean the following goals and responsibilities on your part:

1. All organizations must include minorities in decision-making positions and share power with them.

2. Constructing diversity programs and practices with the same economic and maintenance priorities as other valued aspects of the organization is important.

3. Programs need to be implemented that directly attack the biases, prejudices, and stereotypes of mental health administrators, staff, and professional workers.

4. Diversity initiatives must contain a strong antiracism component, or they will not be successful. Eliminating prejudice and discrimination is not simply an acquisition of new knowledge and information (cognitive exercise). If that were the case we would have eradicated racism years ago.

5. Euro-American mental health professionals need to realize that they have directly or indirectly benefited from individual, institutional, and cultural racism. While many Whites may acknowledge that minorities and women are placed at a disadvantage in the current system, few realize or recognize White privilege (i.e., invisible systems that confer dominance on Whites).

6. While no one was ever born wanting to be a biased or prejudiced, White Euro-Americans have been socialized in a racist society and need to accept responsibility for their own racism and to deal with it in a nondefensive, guilt-free manner.

7. Movement toward valuing and respecting differences, becoming aware of one's own values and biases, becoming comfortable with differences that exist in terms of race and culture, among other characteristics, is essential.

8. Receive training in organizational development; broaden your definition of the helping role to include systems intervention.

9. Understand that not only are your clients potentially affected by oppressive systems, but you and other mental health practitioners are likewise affected.

10. Finally, develop a repertoire of system intervention skills. Don't get trapped into only the narrowly defined roles of "clinical work."

References

Abad, V., Ramos, J., & Boyce, E. (1974). A model for delivery of mental health services to Spanish-speaking minorities. *American Journal of Orthopsychiatry, 44, 584–595.*

Abeles, R. P. (1976). Relative deprivation, rising expectations and black militancy. *Journal of Social Issues, 32,* 119–137.

Abreu, J. M., Goodyear, R. K., Campos, A., & Newcomb, M. D. (2000). Ethnic belonging and traditional masculinity ideology among African Americans, European Americans and Latinos. *Psychology of Men and Masculinity, 1,* 75–86.

Acosta, F. X., & Evans, L. A. (1982). Effective psychotherapy for low-income and minority patients. In F. X. Acosta, J. Yamamoto, & L. A. Evans (Eds.), *Effective psychotherapy for low-income and minority patients* (pp. 51–82). New York: Plenum Press.

Acquino, J. A., Russell, D. W., Cutrona, C. E., & Altmaier, E. M. (1996). Employment status, social support, and life satisfaction among the elderly. *Journal of Counseling Psychology, 43,* 480–489.

Adler, N. J. (1986). Cultural synergy: Managing the impact of cultural diversity. *The 1986 annual: Developing human resources.* San Diego, CA: University Associates.

Ahai, C. E. (1997). A cultural framework for counseling African Americans. In C. C. Lee (Ed.), *Multicultural issues in counseling* (2nd ed., pp. 73–80). Alexandria, VA: American Counseling Association.

Ahuvia, A. (2001). Well-being in cultures of choice: A cross-cultural perspective. *American Psychologist, 56* (1), 77.

Ailinger, R. L. (1997). Latino immigrants' explanatory models of tuberculosis infection. *Qualitative Health Research, 7,* 521–526.

Alexander, C., Langer, E., Newman, R., Chandler, H., & Davies, J. (1989). Transcendental meditation, mindfulness and longevity: An experimental study with the elderly. *Journal of Personality and Social Psychology, 57,* 950–964.

Alexander, C., Rainforth, M., & Gelderloos, P. (1991). Transcendental meditation, self actualization and psychological health: A conceptual overview and statistical meta-analysis. *Journal of Social Behavior and Personality, 6,* 189–247.

Allen, A. (1994, May 29). Black unlike me: Confessions of a white man confused by racial etiquette. *Washington Post,* p. C1.

Allison, K. W., Crawford, I., Echemendia, R., Robinson, L., & Knepp, D. (1994). Human diversity and professional competence: Training in clinical and counseling psychology revisited. *American Psychologist, 49,* 792–796.

Allport, G. W. (1961). *Pattern and growth in personality.* New York: Holt, Rinehart & Winston.

Alvarez, A., Batson, R. M., Carr, A. K., Parks, P., Peck, H. B., Shervington, W., Tyler, R. B., & Zwerling, I. (1976). *Racism, elitism, professionalism: Barriers to community mental health.* New York: Aronson.

American Counseling Association. (1995). Summit results in formation of spiritual competencies. *Counseling Today,* p. 30.

American Friends Service Committee. (1998). *People with disabilities.* Philadelphia, PA: Affirmative Action Office.

American Psychiatric Association. (1980). *Diagnostic and Statistical Manual of Mental Disorders–Third Edition.* Washington, DC: Author.

American Psychiatric Association. (1997). Practice guidelines for the treatment of patients with Alzheimer's disease and other dementias of late life. *American Journal of Psychiatry, 154,* 1–39.

American Psychiatric Association. (1999). *Diagnostic and Statistical Manual of Mental Disorders–Fourth Edition, Text Revision.* Washington, DC: Author.

American Psychological Association. (1993). Guidelines for providers of psychological services to ethnic, linguistic, and culturally diverse populations. *American Psychologist, 48,* 45–48.

American Psychological Association. (1999). *Compliance issues.* Washington, DC: Author.

American Psychological Association. (2001a). *Aging and human sexuality resource guide.* Washington, DC: Author.

American Psychological Association. (2001b). *Elder abuse and neglect: In search of solutions.* Washington, DC: Author.

American Psychological Association. (2001c). *Older adults and Insomnia Resource Guide.* Washington, DC: Author.

American Psychological Association, Presidential Task Force on the Assessment of Age Consistent Memory Decline and Dementia. (1998). *Guidelines for the evaluation of dementia and age-related cognitive decline.* Washington, DC: Author.

APA Public Interest. (2001). *Women in academe: Two steps forward, one step back.* Washington, DC: American Psychological Association.

APA Public Policy Office. (2001). *Resolution on male violence against women.* Washington, DC: American Psychological Association.

APA Working Group on the Older Adult Brochure. (1998). *What practitioners should know about working with older adults.* Washington, DC: American Psychological Association.

Anderson, M. J., & Ellis, R. (1995). On the reservation. In N. A. Vacc, S. B. DeVaney, & J. Wittmer (Eds.), *Experiencing and counseling multicultural and diverse populations* (3d ed., pp. 179–198). Bristol, PA: Accelerated Development.

Anderson, N. B. (1995). Behavioral and sociocultural perspectives on ethnicity and health: Introduction to the special issue. *Health Psychology, 14,* 589–591.

Arredondo, P., Toporek, R., Brown, S. P., Jones, J., Locke, D. C., Sanchez, J., & Stadler, H. (1996). Operationalization of the multicultural counseling competencies. *Journal of Multicultural Counseling and Development, 24,* 42–78.

Asante, M. (1987). *The Afrocentric idea.* Philadelphia: Temple University Press.

Associated Press. (2001, May 19). College builds shower for transgender student. *Columbian,* p. C5.

Atkinson, D. R. (1983). Ethnic similarity in counseling psychology: A review of research. *The Counseling Psychologist, 11,* 79–92.

Atkinson, D. R. (1985). Research on cross-cultural counseling and psychotherapy: A review and update of reviews. In P. B. Pederson (Ed.), *Handbook of cross-cultural counseling and therapy* (pp. 191–197). Westport, CT: Greenwood Press.

Atkinson, D. R., Bui, U., & Mori, S. (2001). Multiculturally sensitive empirically supported treatments—an oxymoron? In J. G. Ponterotto, J. M. Casas, L. A. Suzuki, & C. M. Alexander (Eds.), *Handbook of multicultural counseling* (pp. 542–574). Thousand Oaks, CA: Sage.

Atkinson, D. R., & Hackett, G. (1998). *Counseling diverse populations* (2nd ed.). Boston: McGraw-Hill.

Atkinson, D. R., Kim, B. S. K., & Caldwell, R. (1998). Ratings of helper roles by multicultural psychologists and Asian American students: Initial support for the three-dimensional model of multicultural counseling. *Journal of Counseling Psychology, 45,* 414–423.

Atkinson, D. R., & Lowe, S. M. (1995). The role of ethnicity, cultural knowledge, and conventional techniques in counseling and psychotherapy. In J. G. Ponterotto, J. M. Casas, L. A. Suzuki, & C. M. Alexander (Eds.), *Handbook of Multicultural Counseling* (pp. 387–414). Thousand Oaks, CA: Sage.

Atkinson, D. R., Maruyama, M., & Matsui, S. (1978). The effects of counselor race and counseling approach on Asian Americans' perceptions of counselor credibility and utility. *Journal of Counseling Psychology, 25,* 76–83.

Atkinson, D. R., Morten, G., & Sue, D. W. (1979). *Counseling American minorities: A cross-cultural perspective.* Dubuque, IA: Brown.

Atkinson, D. R., Morten, G., & Sue, D. W. (1989). A minority identity development model. In D. R. Atkinson, G. Morten, & D. W. Sue (Eds.), *Counseling American Minorities* (pp. 35–52). Dubuque, IA: W. C. Brown.

Atkinson, D. R., Morten, G., & Sue, D. W. (1998). *Counseling American minorities* (5th ed.). Boston: McGraw-Hill.

Atkinson, D. R., & Schein, S. (1986). Similarity in

counseling. *The Counseling Psychologist, 14,* 319–354.

Atkinson, D. R., Thompson, C. E., & Grant, S. K. (1993). A three-dimensional model for counseling racial/ethnic minorities. *The Counseling Psychologist, 21,* 257–277.

Avila, D. L., & Avila, A. L. (1980). The Mexican-American. In N. A. Vacc & J. P. Wittmer (Eds.), *Let me be me* (pp. 225–281). Muncie; IN: Accelerated Development.

Avila, D. L. & Avila, A. L. (1995). Mexican Americans. In N. A. Vacc, S. B. DeVaney, & J. Wittmer Eds.), *Experiencing and counseling multicultural and diverse populations* (3rd ed., pp. 119–146). Bristol, PA: Accelerated Development.

Axelson, J. A. (1993). *Counseling and Development in a Multicultural Society.* Pacific Grove, CA: Brooks/Cole.

Ayanian, J. Z., Udvarhelyi, I. S., Gatsonis, C. A., Pashos, C. L., & Epstein, A. M. (1993). Racial differences in the use of revascularization procedures after coronary angiography. *JAMA, 269,* 2642–2646.

Baca, L. M., & Koss-Chioino, J. D. (1997). Development of a culturally responsive group counseling model for Mexican American adolescents. *Journal of Multicultural Counseling and Development, 25,* 130–141.

Baldauf, S., & Johnson, K. (1998, June 11). Texas case highlights US problem race hate. *Christian Science Monitor,* p. 1.

Balderas, J. B. (2001, August 12). American Indians' enemy: Diabetes, lifestyle, diets blamed as 50% of Native Americans over 45 are affected. *The Washington Post,* p. A2.

Bankart, C. P. (1997). *Talking cures: A history of Western and Eastern psycho therapies.* Pacific Grove, CA: Brooks/Cole.

Banks, J. A., & Banks, C. A. (1993). *Multicultural Education.* Boston: Allyn & Bacon.

Barak, A., & Dell, D. M. (1977). Differential perceptions of counselor behavior: Replication and extension. *Journal of Counseling Psychology, 24,* 288–292.

Barak, A., & La Crosse, M. B. (1975). Multidimensional perception of counselor behavior. *Journal of Counseling Psychology, 22,* 471–456.

Barongan, C., Bernal, G., Comas-Diaz, L., Iijima Hall, C. C., Nagayama Hall, G. C., LaDue, R. A., Parham, T. A., Pedersen, P. B., Porche-Burke, L. M., Rollock, D., & Root, M. P. P. (1997). Misunderstandings of multiculturalism: Shouting fire in crowded theaters. *American Psychologist, 52,* 654–655.

Barr, D. J., & Strong, L. J. (1987, May). Embracing multiculturalism: The existing contradictions. *ACU-I Bulletin,* pp. 20–23.

Batavia, A. I. (2000). The relevance of data on physician and disability on the right of assisted suicide. *Psychology, Public Policy, and Law, 6,* 546–558.

Battle, E., & Rotter, J. (1963). Children's feelings of personal control as related to social class and ethnic group. *Journal of Personality, 31,* 482–490.

Beauvais, E., Chavez, E. L., Oetting, E. R., Deffenbacher, J. L., & Cornell, G. R. (1996). Drug use, violence, and victimization among white American, Mexican American, and American Indian dropouts, students with academic problems, and students in good academic standing. *Journal of Counseling Psychology, 43,* 292–299.

Becvar, D. S., & Becvar, R. J. (1996). *Family therapy: A systemic integration* (3rd ed.). Needham Heights, MA: Allyn & Bacon.

Bee-Gates, D., Howard-Pitney, B., LaFromboise, T., & Rowe, W. (1996). Help-seeking behavior of Native American Indian high school students. *Professional Psychology: Research and Practice, 27,* 495–499.

Beigel, H. G. (1966). Problems and motives in interracial relationships. *Journal of Sex Research, 2,* 185–205.

Belgrave, F. Z., Chase-Vaughn, G., Gray, F., Addison, J. D., & Cherry, V. R. (2000). The effectiveness of a culture- and gender-specific intervention for increasing resiliency among African American preadolescent females. *Journal of Black Psychology, 26,* 133–147.

Bell, D. (1993). *Faces at the bottom of the well: The permanence of racism.* New York: Basic Books.

Bell, M. P., Harrison, D. A., & McLaughlin, M. E. (1997). Asian American attitudes towards affirmative action in employment: Implications for the model minority myth. *Journal of Applied Behavioral Science, 33,* 356–377.

Bemak, F., Chung, R. C.-Y., & Bornemann, T. (1996). Counseling and psychotherapy with refugees. In P. Pedersen, J. Draguns, W. Lonner, & J. Trimble (Eds.), *Counseling across cultures* (4th ed., pp. 243–265). Thousand Oaks, CA: Sage.

Bennett, M. J. (1986). A developmental approach to training for intercultural sensitivity. *International Journal of Intercultural Relations, 10,* 179–196.

Berman, J. (1979). Counseling skills used by Black and White male and female counselors. *Journal of Counseling Psychology, 26,* 81–84.

Bernal, M. E., & Castro, F. G. (1994). Are clinical psychologists prepared for service and research with ethnic minorities? A report of a decade of progress. *American Psychologist, 49,* 797–805.

Bernal, M. E., & Knight, G. P. (1993). *Ethnic identity: Formation and transmission among Hispanics and other minorities.* Albany, NY: State University of New York Press.

Bernstein, B. (1964). Elaborated and restricted codes: Their social origins and some consequences. In J. J. Gumperz & D. Hymes (Eds.), The ethnography of communication, *American Anthropologist, 66,* 55–69.

Berry, B. (1965). *Ethnic and race relations.* Boston: Houghton Mifflin.

Berube, A. (1990). *Coming out under fire: The history of gay men and women in World War II.* New York: Free Press.

Bhungalia, L. (2001). Native American women and violence. *National NOW Times, 33,* pp. 5, 13.

BigFoot-Sipes, D. S., Dauphinais, P., LaFromboise, T. D., Bennett, S. K., & Rowe, W. (1992). American Indian secondary school students preferences for counselor. *Journal of Multicultural Counseling and Development, 20,* 113–122.

Billingsley, A. (1970). Black families and White social science. *Journal of Social Issues, 26,* 127–142.

Black, L. (1996). Families of African origin: An overview. In M. McGoldrick, J. Giordano, & J. K. Pearce (Eds.), *Ethnicity and Family Therapy* (pp. 57–65). New York: Guilford.

Blair, S. L., & Qian, Z. (1998). Family and Asian students' educational performance. *Journal of Family Issues, 19,* 355–374.

Blake, S. M., Ledsky, R., Lehman, T., & Goodenow, C. (2001). Preventing sexual risk behaviors among gay, lesbian, and bisexual adolescents: The benefits of gay-sensitive HIV instruction in schools. *American Journal of Public Health, 91,* 940–946.

Blanchard, E. L. (1983). The growth and development of American Indians and Alaskan Native children. In G. J. Powell, J. Yamamoto, A. Romero, & A. Morales (Eds.), *The psychosocial development of minority group children.* New York: Brunner/Mazel.

Blando, J. A. (2001). Twice hidden: Older gay and lesbian couples, friends, intimacy. *Generations, 25,* 87–89.

Blauner, B. (1993). But things are much worse for the negro people: Race and radicalism in my life and work. In J. H. Stanfield II (Ed.), *A history of race relations research: First generation recollections* (pp. 1–36). Newbury Park: Sage.

Blazer, D. G., Hybels, C. F., Somonsick, E. M., & Hanlon, J. T. (2000). Marked differences in antidepressant use by race in an elderly community sample: 1986–1996. *American Journal of Psychiatry, 157,* 1089–1094.

Bookwala, J., & Schulz, R. (2000). A comparison of primary stressors, secondary stressors, and depressive symptoms between elderly caregiving husbands and wives. *Psychology and Aging, 15,* 607–616.

Bowles, D. D. (1993). Bi-racial identity: Children born to African-American and White couples. *Clinical Social Work Journal, 21,* 417–427.

Boxall, G. (1995, March 7). Report shows 53% rise in anti-gay hate crimes in L.A. *The Los Angeles Times,* p. 3.

Brayboy, T. L. (1966). Interracial sexuality as an expression of neurotic conflict. *Journal of Sex Research, 2,* 179–184.

Brecher, R., & Brecher, E. (1961). The happiest creatures on earth? *Harpers, 222,* 85–90.

Brennan, P. L., & Moos, R. H. (1996). Late-life drinking behavior. *Alcohol Health and Research World, 20,* 197–204.

Brinkley, D. (1994). *Saved by the light.* New York: Villard Books.

Broman, C. L., Mavaddat, R., & Hsu, S.-Y. (2000). The experience and consequences of perceived racial discrimination: A study of African Americans. *Journal of Black Psychology, 26,* 165–180.

Brooke, J. (1998, April 9). Indians strive to save their languages. *The New York Times,* p. 1.

Brotherton, P. (2001). Minority bachelor's degrees on the rise: Number of African American bachelor's degree holders tops 100,000. *Black Issues in Higher Education, 18,* 34–38.

Brown, D. (1997). Implications of cultural values for cross-cultural consultation with families. *Journal of Counseling and Development, 76,* 29–35.

Brown, R. P., & Josephs, R. A. (1999). A burden of proof: Stereotype relevance and gender differences in math performance. *Journal of Personality and Social Psychology, 76,* 246–257.

Browning, C., Reynolds, A. L., & Dworkin, S. H. (1998). Affirmative psychotherapy for lesbian women. In D. R. Atkinson & G. Hackett (Eds.), *Counseling diverse populations* (2nd ed., pp. 317–334). Boston: McGraw-Hill.

Buckman, D. F. (1998). The see-through syndrome. *Inside MS, 16,* p. 19.

Burton, S. B. (2001). Organizational efforts to affirm sexual diversity: A cross-level examination. *Journal of Applied Psychology, 86,* 17–28.

Butler, R. N., & Lewis, M. I. (1983). *Aging and mental health.* St. Louis, MO: C. V . Mosby.

Cada, C. (2000, April 23). Issue of transgender rights divides many gay activists. *Boston Globe,* p. A8.

Caplan, N. (1970). The new ghetto man: A review of recent empirical studies. *Journal of Social Issues, 26,* 59–73.

Caplan, N., & Nelson, S. D. (1973). On being useful—the nature and consequences of psychological research on social problems. *American Psychologist, 28,* 199–211.

Caplan, N., & Paige, J. M. (1968, August). A study of ghetto rioters. *Scientific American, 219,* 15–21.

Carillo, C. (1982). Changing norms of Hispanic families. In E. E. Jones & S. J. Korchin (Eds.), *Minority mental health* (pp. 250–266). New York: Praeger.

Carney, C. G., & Kahn, K. B. (1984). Building competencies for effective cross-cultural counseling: A developmental view. *The Counseling Psychologist, 12,* 111–119.

Carter, R. T. (1988). The relationship between racial identity attitudes and social class. *Journal of Negro Education, 57,* 22–30.

Carter, R. T. (1990). The relationship between racism and racial identity among White Americans: An exploratory investigation. *Journal of Counseling and Development, 69,* 46–50.

Carter, R. T. (1995). *The influence of race and racial identity in psychotherapy* New York: Wiley.

Carter, R. T., & Qureshi, A. (1995). A typology of philosophical assumptions in multicultural counseling and training. In J. G. Ponterotto, J. M. Casas, L. A. Suzuki, & C. M. Alexander (Eds.), *Handbook of multicultural counseling* (pp. 239–262). Thousand Oaks, CA: Sage.

Casas, J. M., Pavelski, R., Furlong, M. J., & Zanglis, I. (2001). Advent of systems of care: Practice and research perspectives and policy implications. In J. G. Ponterotto, J. M. Casas, L. A. Suzuki, & C. M. Alexander, *Handbook of multicultural counseling* (pp. 222–253). Thousand Oaks, CA: Sage.

Casas, J. M., & Pytluk, S. D. (1995). Hispanic identity development. In J. G. Ponterotto, J. M. Casas, L. A. Suzuki, & C. M. Alexander (Eds.), *Handbook of multicultural counseling* (pp. 155–180). Thousand Oaks, CA: Sage.

Casas, J. M., & Vasquez, M. J. T. (1996). Counseling the Hispanic. In P. B. Pedersen, J. G. Draguns, W. J. Lonner, & J. E. Trimble (Eds.), *Counseling across cultures* (4th ed., pp. 146–176). Thousand Oaks, CA: Sage Publications.

Cass, V. C. (1979). Homosexual identity formation: A theoretical model. *Journal of Homosexuality, 4,* 219–235.

Chang, Y. (1998, June 22). Asian identity crisis. *Newsweek,* p. 68.

Chase, B. W., Cornille, T. A., & English, R. W. (2000). Life satisfaction among persons with spinal cord injuries. *Journal of Rehabilitation, 66,* 14–20.

Cheatham, H., Ivey, A. E., Ivey, M. B., Pedersen, P.,

Rigazio-DiGilio, S., Simek-Morgan, L., & Sue, D. W. (1997). Multicultural counseling and therapy I: Metatheory—Taking theory into practice. In A. E. Ivey, M. B. Ivey, & L. Simek-Morgan (Eds.), *Counseling and psychotherapy: A multicultural perspective* (pp. 133–169). Boston: Allyn & Bacon.

Cheek, D. (1987). *Assertive White . . . puzzled White.* San Luis Obispo, CA: Impact.

Chen, M., Froehle, T., & Morran, K. (1997). Deconstructing dispositional bias in clinical inference: Two interventions. *Journal of Counseling and Development. 76,* 74–81.

Chen, Z. (2001). Chinese American children's ethnic identity: Measurement and implications. *Communication Studies, 51,* 74–95.

Cheung, F. K., & Snowden, L. R. (1990). Community mental health and ethnic minority populations. *Community Mental Health Journal, 26,* 277–291.

Cheung, L.-R. L. (1987). *Assessing Asian language performance.* Rockville, IL: Aspen.

Choi, Y. H. (1999, September 7). Commentary: Asian values meet western realities. *The Los Angeles Times,* p. 7.

Choney, S. K., Berryhill-Paapke, E., & Robbins, R. R. (1995). The acculturation of American Indians: Developing frameworks for research and practice. In J. G. Ponterotto, J. M. Casas, L. A. Suzuki, & C. M. Alexander (Eds.), *Handbook of multicultural counseling* (pp. 73–92). Thousand Oaks, CA: Sage.

Christian, M. D., & Barbarin, O. A. (2001). Cultural resources and psychological adjustment of African American children: Effects of spirituality and racial attribution. *Journal of Black Psychology, 27,* 43–63.

Christiansen, S. C., Martin, S. B., Schleicher, N. C., Koziol, J. A., Mathews, K. P., & Zuraw, B. L. (1996). Current prevalence of asthma-related symptoms in San Diego's predominantly Hispanic inner-city children. *Journal of Asthma, 33,* 17–26.

Chun, K. M., Eastman, K. L., Wang, G. C. S., & Sue, S. (1998). Psychopathology. In L. C. Lee & N. W. S. Zane (Eds.), *Handbook of Asian American psychology* (pp. 457–484). Thousand Oaks, CA: Sage.

Chung, R. C.-Y., Bemak, F., & Okazaki, S. (1997). Counseling Americans of Southeast Asian descent. In C. C. Lee (Ed.), *Multicultural issues in counseling* (2nd ed., pp. 207–231). Alexandria, VA: American Counseling Association.

Clark, K. B. (1963). Educational stimulation of racially disadvantaged children. In A. H. Passow (Ed.), *Education in depressed areas* (pp. 142–162). New York: Teachers College Press.

Clark, K. B., & Clark, M. K. (1947). Racial identification and preference in Negro children. In T. M. Newcomb & E. L. Hartley (Eds.), *Readings in social psychology* (pp. 169–178). New York: Holt, Reinhart & Winston.

Clark, K. B., & Plotkin, L. (1972). A review of the issues and literature of cultural deprivation theory. In K. B. Clark (Ed)., *The educationally deprived* (pp. 47–73). New York: Metropolitan Applied Research Center.

Clay, R. A. (1999). Four psychologists help others to see. *APA Monitor, 30,* 1–4.

Cochran, S. D., Keenan, C., Schober, C., & Mays, V. M. (2000). Estimates of alcohol use and clinical treatment needs among homosexually active men and women in the U.S. population. *Journal of Consulting and Clinical Psychology, 68,* 1062–1071.

Cohn, D. (2001, August 23). Count of gay couples up 300 percent. *The Washington Post,* pp. 1–3.

Collins, B. E. (1970). *Social Psychology.* Reading, MA: Addison-Wesley.

Comas-Diaz, L. (2001). Hispanics, Latinos, or Americanos: The evolution of identity. *Cultural Diversity and Ethnic Minority Psychology, 7,* 115–120.

Committee of 100. (2001). *American attitudes toward Chinese Americans and Asian Americans.* New York: Author.

Committee on Women in Psychology. (1999). *Older psychologists survey.* Washington, DC: American Psychological Association.

Condon, J. C., & Yousef, F. (1975). *An introduction to intercultural communication.* New York: Bobbs-Merrill.

Conger, J. (1975). Proceedings of the American Psychological Association, Incorporated, for the year 1974: Minutes of the annual meeting of

Council of Representatives. *American Psychologist, 30,* 620–651.

Congressional Record. (1997). *Indian Child Welfare Act Amendments of 1997—Hon. George Miller.* Washington, DC: Author.

Cook, E. P. (1990). Gender and psychological distress. *Journal of Counseling and Development, 68,* 371–375.

Cooper, C., & Costas, L. (1994). Ethical challenges when working with Hispanic/Latino families: Personalismo. *The Family Psychologist, 10,* 32–34.

Corey, G. (2001). *Theory and practice of counseling and psychotherapy* (6th ed.). Belmont, CA: Brooks Cole.

Corrigan, J. D., Dell, D. M., Lewis, K. N., & Schmidt, L. D. (1980). Counseling as a social influence process: A review. *Journal of counseling Psychology, 27,* 391–441.

Corvin, S., & Wiggins, F. (1989). An antiracism training model for White professionals. *Journal of Multicultural Counseling and Development, 17,* 105–114.

Cose, E., Smith, V. E., Figueroa, A., Stefanakos, V. S., & Contreras, J. (2000, November 13). American's prison generation. *Newsweek,* 42–49.

Crandall, V., Katkovsky, W., & Crandall, V. (1965). Children's beliefs in their own control of reinforcements in intellectual achievement situations. *Child Development, 36,* 91–109.

Crawford, I., McLeod, A., Zamboni, B. D., & Jordan, M. B. (1999). Psychologists' attitudes toward gay and lesbian parenting. *Professional Psychology: Research and Practice, 30,* 394–401.

Cronin, M. E. (1998, June 11). Body type–body hype—local high-school students challenge marketing of super-thin image. *Seattle Times,* p. E1.

Cross, T. L., Bazron, B. J., Dennis, K. W., & Isaacs, M. R. (1989). *Towards a culturally competent system of care.* Washington, DC: Child and Adolescent Service System Program Technical Assistance Center.

Cross, W. E. (1971). The Negro-to-Black conversion experience: Towards a psychology of Black liberation. *Black World, 20,* 13–27.

Cross, W. E. (1991). *Shades of Black: Diversity in African American identity.* Philadelphia: Temple University Press.

Cross, W. E. (1995). The psychology of Nigrescence: Revising the Cross model. In J. G. Ponterotto, J. M. Casas, L. A. Suzuki, & C. M. Alexander (Eds.), *Handbook of multicultural counseling* (pp. 93–122). Thousand Oaks, CA: Sage.

Cuellar, I., Harris, L. C., & Jasso, R. (1980). An acculturation scale for Mexican American normal and clinical populations. *Hispanic Journal of Behavioral Sciences, 2,* 199–217.

Culbertson, F. M. (1997). Depression and gender. *American Psychologist, 52,* 25–31.

Currie, C. (1997). Old fools, lovers, and sages. *British Medical Journal, 315,* 7115.

Dana, R. H. (1993). *Multicultural assessment perspectives for professional psychology.* Needham Heights, MA: Allyn & Bacon.

Dana, R. H. (2000). The cultural self as a locus for assessment and intervention with American Indian/Alaska Natives. *Journal of Multicultural Counseling and Development, 28,* 66–82.

D'Andrea, M., & Daniels, J. (1995). Promoting multiculturalism and organizational change in the counseling profession: A case study. In J. G. Ponterotto, J. M. Casas, L. A. Suzuki, & C. M. Alexander (Eds.), Handbook of Multicultural Counseling (pp. 17–33). Thousand Oaks, CA: Sage.

D'Andrea, M., & Daniels, J. (2001). Expanding our thinking about White racism: Facing the challenge of multicultural counseling in the 21st century. In J. G. Ponterotto, J. M. Casas, L. A. Suzuki, & C. M. Alexander (Eds.), *Handbook of multicultural counseling* (pp. 289–310). Thousand Oaks, CA: Sage.

D'Andrea, M., Daniels, J., Arredondo, P., Ivey, M. B., Ivey, A. E., Locke, D. C., O'Bryant, B., Parham, T. A., & Sue, D. W. (2001). Fostering organizational changes to realize the revolutionary potential of the multicultural movement. In J. G. Ponterotto, J. M. Casas, L. A. Suzuki, & C. M. Alexander (Eds.), *Handbook of multicultural counseling* (pp. 222–253). Thousand Oaks, CA: Sage.

D'Andrea, M., Daniels, J., & Heck, R. (1991). Evaluating the impact of multicultural counseling training. *Journal of Counseling and Development, 70,* 143–150.

Danzinger, P. R., & Welfel, E. R. (2000). Age, gender and health bias in counselors: An empirical analysis. *Journal of Mental Health Counseling, 22,* 135–149.

Darwin, C. (1859). *On the origin of species by natural selection.* London: Murray.

Das, A. K. (1987). Indigenous models of therapy in traditional Asian societies. *Journal of Multicultural Counseling and Development, 15,* 25–37.

Das Gupta, M. (1997). "What is Indian about you?": A gendered, transnational approach to ethnicity. *Gender and Society, 11,* 572–596.

Davis, R. J. (1994). *Who is Black? One nation's definition.* University Park: Pennsylvania State University Press.

DeAngelis, T. (2002). New data on lesbian, gay, and bisexual mental health. *APA Monitor, 33,* 46–47.

Deater-Deckard, K., Dodge, K. A., Bates, J. E., & Pettit, G. S. (1996). Physical discipline among African American and European American mothers: Links to children's externalizing behaviors. *Developmental Psychology, 32,* 1065–1072.

de Gobineau, A. (1915). *The inequality of human races.* New York: Putnam.

De La Cancela, V. (1985). Toward a sociocultural psychotherapy for low-income ethnic minorities. *Psychotherapy, 22,* 427–435.

De La Cancela, V. (1991). Working affirmatively with Puerto Rican men: Professional and personal reflections. In M. Bograd (Ed.), *Feminist approaches for men and women in family therapy* (pp. 195–211). New York: Harrington Park Press.

Dell, B. M. (1973). Counselor power base, influence attempt, and behavior change in counseling. *Journal of Counseling Psychology, 20,* 399–405.

DePaulo, B. M. (1992). Nonverbal behavior and self-presentation. *Psychological Bulletin, 111,* 203–243.

Desselle, D. C., & Proctor, T. K. (2000). Advocating for the elderly hard-of-hearing population: The deaf people we ignore. *Social Work, 45,* 277–281.

DeVoe, D. (1998). Feminist and nonsexist counseling: Implications for the male counselor. In D. R. Atkinson & G. Hackett (Eds.), *Counseling diverse populations* (2nd ed., pp. 283–291). Boston: McGraw-Hill.

Diaz-Guerrero, R. (1977). A Mexican psychology. *American Psychologist, 32,* 934–944.

Diokno, A. C., Brown, M. B., & Herzog, A. R. (1990). Sexual functioning in the elderly. *Archives of Internal Medicine, 150,* 197–200.

Division 44/Committee on Lesbian, Gay, and Bisexual Concerns Task Force. (2000). Guidelines for psychotherapy with lesbian, gay, and bisexual clients. *American Psychologist, 55,* 1440–1451.

Doerner, J. (1985, July 8). To America with skills. *Time,* pp. 42–44.

Dolliver, R. H., Williams, E. L., & Gold, D. C. (1980). The art of Gestalt therapy or: What are you doing with your feet now? *Psychotherapy: Theory, Research & Practice, 17,* 136–142.

Dorland, J. M., & Fischer, A. R. (2001). Gay, lesbian, and bisexual individuals' perceptions: An analogue study. *Counseling Psychologist, 29,* 532–547.

Dorfman, D. D. (1978). The Cyril Burt question: New findings. *Science, 201,* 1177–1186.

Douglis, R. (1987, November). The beat goes on. *Psychology Today.*

Dovidio, J. (in press). Why can't we all get along? *Cultural Diversity and Ethnic Minority Psychology.*

Downing, N. E., & Roush, K. L. (1985). From passive acceptance to active commitment: A model of feminist identity development for women. *Counseling Psychologist, 13,* 695–709.

Draguns, J. G. (1985). Psychological disorders across cultures. In P. Pedersen (Ed.), *Handbook of cross-cultural counseling and therapy* (pp. 55–62). Westport, CT: Greenwood.

Duhaney, L. M. G. (2000). Culturally sensitive strategies for violence prevention. *Multicultural Education, 7,* 10–19.

Dumas, J. E., Rollock, D., Prinz, R. J., Hops, H., & Blechman, E. A. (1999). Cultural sensitivity: Problems and solutions in applied and preventive intervention. *Applied and Preventive Psychology, 8,* 175–196.

Dychtwald, K. (1989). *Age Wave.* Los Angeles: J. P. Tarcher.

Eadie, B. J. (1992). *Embraced by the light.* Carson City, NV: Gold Leaf Press.

Eakins, B. W., & Eakins, R. G. (1985). Sex differences in nonverbal communication. In L. A.

Samovar & R. E. Porter (Eds.), *Intercultural communication: A reader* (pp. 290–307). Belmont, CA: Wadsworth.

Eaton, M. J., & Dembo, M. H. (1997). Differences in the motivational beliefs of Asian Americans. *Journal of Educational Psychology, 89,* 433–440.

EchoHawk, M. (1997). Suicide: The scourge of Native American people. *Suicide and Life Threatening Behavior, 27,* 60–67.

Eddings, J. (1997). Counting a "new" type of American. *U.S. News & World Report, 123,* 22–23.

Eliade, M. (1972). *Shamanism: Archaic techniques of ecstasy.* New York: Pantheon.

Elliott, T. R., Kilpatrick, S. D., & McCullough, M. E. (1999). Religion and spirituality in rehabilitation psychology. *Rehabilitation Psychology, 44,* 388–402.

Elliott, T. R., Shewchuk, R. M., & Richards, J. S. (1999). Caregiver social problem-solving abilities and family member adjustment to recent-onset physical disability. *Rehabilitation Psychology, 44,* 104–123.

Ellis, A. (1997). Using rational emotive behavior therapy techniques to cope with disability. *Professional Psychology: Research and Practice, 28,* 17–22.

Ericksen-Radtke, M. M., & Beale, A. V. (2001). Preparing students with learning disabilities for college: Pointers for parents–part 2. *Exceptional Parent, 31,* 56–57.

Espin, O. M. (1985). Psychotherapy with Hispanic women. In P. B. Pedersen (Ed.), *Handbook of cross-cultural counseling and therapy* (pp. 165–171). Westport, CT: Greenwood Press.

Espinosa, P. (1997). School involvement and Hispanic parents. *The Prevention Researcher, 5,* 5–6.

Everett, F., Proctor, N., & Cortmell, B. (1989). Providing psychological services to American Indian children and families. In D. R. Atkinson, G. Morten, & D. W. Sue (Eds.), *Counseling American minorities* (3rd ed., pp. 53–71). Dubuque, IA: W. C. Brown.

Fabian, E. S., Lent, R. W., & Willis, S. P. (1998). Predicting work transition outcome for students with disabilities: Implications for counselors. *Journal of Counseling and Development, 76,* 311–316.

Fadiman, A. (1997). *The spirit catches you and you fall down.* New York: Farrar, Straus & Giroux.

Falicov, C. J. (1996). Mexican families. In M. McGoldrick, J. Giordano, & J. K. Pearce (Eds.), *Ethnicity and family therapy* (pp. 169–182). New York: Guilford.

Feagin, J. R. (1989). *Racial and ethnic relations.* Englewood Cliffs, NJ: Prentice-Hall.

Feldman, S. S., & Rosenthal, D. A. (1990). The acculturation of autonomy expectations in Chinese high schoolers residing in two western nations. *International Journal of Psychology, 25,* 259–281.

Felton, G. M., Parson, M. A., Misener, T. R., & Oldaker, S. (1997). Health promoting behavior of black and white college women. *Western Journal of Nursing Research, 19,* 654–664.

Fernando, S. (1988). *Race and culture in psychiatry.* London: Croom Helm.

Festinger, L. (1957). *A theory of cognitive dissonance.* Evanston, IL: Row & Peterson.

Fischer, A. R., & Shaw, C. M. (1999). African Americans' mental health and perceptions of racist discrimination: The moderating effects of racial socialization experiences and self-esteem. *Journal of Counseling Psychology, 46,* 395–407.

Fitzgerald, L. F., Drasgow, F., Hulin, C. L., Gelfand, M. J., & Magley, V. J. (1997). Antecedents and consequences of sexual harassment in organizations: A test of an integrated model. *Journal of Applied Psychology, 82,* 578–589.

Fitzgerald, L. F., & Nutt, R. (1998). The Division 17 principles concerning the counseling/psychotherapy of women: Rationale and implementation. In D. R. Atkinson & G. Hackett (Eds.), *Counseling diverse populations* (2nd ed., pp. 239–270), Boston: McGraw-Hill.

Flack, J. M., Amaro, H., Jenkins, W., Kunitz, S., Levy, J., Mixon, M., and Yu, E. (1995). Panel I: Epidemiology of mental health. *Health Psychology, 14,* 592–600.

Florio, E. R., Hendryx, M. S., Jensen, J. E., & Rockwood, T. H. (1997). A comparison of suicidal and nonsuicidal elders referred to a community mental health center program. *Suicide and Life, 27,* 182–193.

Fogelson, R. M. (1970). Violence and grievances:

Reflections on the 1960's riots. *Journal of Social Issues, 26,* 141–163.

Ford, D. Y. (1997). Counseling middle-class African Americans. In C. C. Lee (Ed.), *Multicultural issues in counseling* (2nd ed., pp. 81–108). Alexandria, VA: American Counseling Association.

Forsyth, D. R., Heiney, M. M., & Wright, S. S. (1997). Biases in appraisals of women leaders. *Group Dynamics: Theory, Research, and Practice, 1,* 98–103.

Forward, J. R., & Williams, J. R. (1970). International external control and Black militancy. *Journal of Social Issues, 26,* 74–92.

Foster, B. G., Jackson, G., Cross, W. E., Jackson, B., & Hardiman, R. (1988). Workforce diversity and business. Alexandria, VA: American Society for Training and Development. (Reprinted from *Training and Development Journal,* April 1988).

Fraga, E. D., Atkinson, D. R., & Wampold, B. E. (2002). *Ethnic group preferences for multicultural counseling competencies.* Manuscript submitted for publication.

Frame, M. W., & Williams, C. B. (1996). Counseling African Americans: Integrating spirituality in therapy. *Counseling and Values, 41,* 16–28.

Frank, J. W., Moore, R. S., & Ames, G. M. (2000). Historical and cultural roots of drinking problems among American Indians. *American Journal of Public Health, 90,* 344–351.

Frankel, M. (1998, May 24). The oldest bias. *New York Times Magazine,* p. 16–17.

Frankenberg, R. (1993). *Euro-American women: Race matters.* Minneapolis: University of Minnesota Press.

Franklin, J. H. (1988). A historical note on black families. In H. P. McAdoo (Ed.), *Black families* (pp. 3–14). Newbury Park, CA: Sage.

Freeberg, L. (1995, October 5). 1 of 3 blacks in 20s has had trouble with law. *Seattle Post-Intelligencer,* pp. A1, A8.

Freeborne, N. (2000). Alzheimer's disease: The possibility of prevention and early treatment. *Journal of the American Academy of Physician Assistants, 13,* 32–38.

Freire, P. (1970). *Cultural action for freedom.* Cambridge: Harvard Educational Review Press.

Freud, S. (1960). Psychopathology of everyday life. In J. Strachey (Ed. and Trans.), *The standard edition of the complete psychological works of Sigmund Freud* (6th ed.). London: Hogarth Press.

Fukuyama, M. A., & Sevig, T. D. (1999). *Integrating spirituality into multicultural counseling.* Thousand Oaks, CA: Sage.

Fuligni, A. J., Burton, L., Marshall, S., Perez-Febles, A., Yarrington, J., Kirsh, L. B., & Merriwether-DeVries, C. (1999). Attitudes toward family obligations among American adolescents with Asian, Latin American, and European backgrounds. *Child Development, 70,* 1030–1044.

Galan, F. J. (1998). An empowerment prevention approach for Hispanic youth. *The Prevention Researcher, 5,* 10–12.

Gallegos, J. S. (1982). Planning and administering services for minority groups. In M. J. Austin & W. E. Hershey (Eds.), *Handbook on mental health administration* (pp. 87–105). San Francisco: Jossey-Bass.

Gallup, G. (1995). *The Gallup poll: Public opinion 1995.* Wilmington, DE: Scholarly Resources.

Galton, F. (1869). *Hereditary genius: An inquiry into its laws and consequences.* London: Macmillan.

Gannett News Service. (1998, May 26). Young Americans optimistic, but face deep racial divisions. *The Bellingham Herald,* p. A7.

Garcia, D., & Levenson, H. (1975). Differences between Black's and White's expectations of control by chance and powerful others. *Psychological Reports, 37,* 563–566.

Garcia-Preto, N. (1996). Puerto Rican Families. In M. McGoldrick, J. Giordano, & J. K. Pearce (Eds.), *Ethnicity and Family Therapy* (pp. 183–199). New York: Guilford.

Garfield, J. C., Weiss, S. L., & Pollock, E. A. (1973). Effects of a child's social class on school counselors' decision making. *Journal of Counseling Psychology, 20,* 166–168.

Garnets, L., Hancock, K. A., Cochran, S. D., Goodchilds, J., & Peplau, L. A. (1998). Issues in psychotherapy with lesbians and gay men: A survey of psychologists. In D. R. Atkinson & G. Hackett (Eds.), *Counseling diverse populations* (2nd ed., pp. 297–316). Boston: McGraw-Hill.

Garrahy, D. A. (2001). Three third-grade teachers'

gender-related beliefs and behavior. *Elementary School Journal, 102,* 81–94.

Garrett, J. T., & Garrett, M. W. (1994). The path of good medicine: Understanding and counseling Native American Indians. *Journal of Multicultural Counseling and Development, 22,* 134–144.

Garrett, M. T., & Pichette, E. F. (2000). Red as an apple: Native American acculturation and counseling with or without reservation. *Journal of Counseling and Development, 78,* 3–13.

Garrett, M. T., & Wilbur, M. P. (1999). Does the worm live in the ground? Reflections on Native American spirituality. *Journal of Multicultural Counseling and Development, 27,* 193–206.

Garwick, A., & Auger, S. (2000). What do providers need to know about American Indian culture? Recommendations from urban Indian family caregivers. *Families, Systems & Health, 18,* 177–190.

Gay, G. (1998). Coming of age ethnically: Teaching young adolescents of color. *The Prevention Researcher, 5,* 7–9.

George, H. T. (1998, July 14). Young quadriplegic has a dream. *Seattle Post-Intelligencer,* p. B2.

Gersten, R., & Woodward, J. (1994). The language-minority student and special education: Issues, trends, and paradoxes. *Exceptional Children, 60,* 310–308.

Giachello, A. L., & Belgrave, F. (1997). Task group VI: Health care systems and behavior. *Journal of Gender, Culture, and Health, 2,* 163–173.

Gibbs, J. T. (1980). The interpersonal orientation in mental health consultation: Toward a model of ethnic variations in consultation. *American Journal of Orthopsychiatry, 45,* 430–445.

Gibbs, J. T. (1987). Identity and marginality: Issues in the treatment of biracial adolescents. *American Journal of Orthopsychiatry, 57,* 265–278.

Gibbs, J. T., & Moskowitz-Sweet, G. (1991). Clinical and cultural issues in the treatment of biracial and bicultural adolescents. *Families in Society: The Journal of Contemporary Human Services, 72,* 579–591.

Gillie, D. (1977). The IQ issue. *Phi Delta Kappan, 58,* 469.

Glick, P., & Fiske, S. T. (2001). An ambivalent alliance: Hostile and benevolent sexism as complementary justifications for gender equality. *American Psychologist, 56,* 109–118.

Gloria, A. M., & Kurpius, S. E. R. (2001). Influences of self-beliefs, social support, and comfort in the university environment on the academic nonpersistence decisions of American Indian undergraduates. *Cultural Diversity and Ethnic Minority Psychology, 7,* 88–102.

Goldberg, C. (1998, May 31). Acceptance of gay men and lesbians is growing, study says. *New York Times,* p. 21.

Goldenberg, I., & Goldenberg, H. (1998). *Family therapy: An overview* (3rd ed.). Pacific Grove, CA: Brooks/Cole.

Goldman, M. (1980). Effect of eye contact and distance on the verbal reinforcement of attitude. *The Journal of Social Psychology, 111,* 73–78.

Gonsiorek, J. C. (1982). Results of psychological testing on homosexual populations. *American Behavioral Scientist, 25,* 385–396.

Gonzalez, G. M. (1997). The emergence of Chicanos in the twenty-first century: Implications for counseling, research, and policy. *Journal of Multicultural Counseling and Development, 25,* 94–106.

Gonzales, M., Castillo-Canez, I., Tarke, H., Soriano, F., Garcia, P., & Velasquez, R. J. (1997). Promoting the culturally sensitive diagnosis of Mexican Americans: Some personal insights. *Journal of Multicultural Counseling and Development, 25,* 156–161.

Good, G. E., Gilbert, L. A., & Scher, M. (1990). Gender aware therapy: A synthesis of feminist therapy and knowledge about gender. *Journal of Counseling and Development, 68,* 376–380.

Gore, P. M., & Rotter, J. B. (1963). A personality correlate of social action. *Journal of Personality, 31,* 58–64.

Gorman, J. C., & Balter, L. (1997). Culturally sensitive parent education: A critical review of quantitative research. *Review of Educational Research, 67,* 339–369.

Gossett, T. F. (1963). *Race: The history of an idea in America.* Dallas, TX: Southern Methodist University Press.

Gottesfeld, H. (1995). Community context and the underutilization of mental health services by minority patients. *Psychological Reports, 76,* 207–210.

Gould, S. J. (1996). *The mismeasure of man.* New York: Norton.

Graham, R. (1997, May 4). Speaking with the enemy, Arthur Dong's film about gay bashing. *Boston Globe,* p. D, 11:3.

Granello, D. H., & Beamish, P. M. (1998). Reconceptualizing codependency in women: A sense of connectedness, not pathology. *Journal of Mental Health Counseling, 20,* 344–358.

Grant, L. D. (1996). Effects of ageism on individual and health care providers' responses to healthy aging. *Health and Social Work, 21,* 9–14.

Greene, B. A. (1985). Considerations in the treatment of Black patients by White therapists. *Psychotherapy, 22,* 389–393.

Grieger, I., & Toliver, S. (2001). Multiculturalism on predominantly White campuses: Multiple roles and functions for the counselor. In J. G. Ponterotto, J. M. Casas, L. A. Suzuki, & C. M. Alexander, *Handbook of multicultural counseling* (pp. 825–848). Thousand Oaks, CA: Sage.

Grier, W., & Cobbs, P. (1968). *Black rage.* New York: Basic Books.

Grier, W., & Cobbs, P. (1971). *The Jesus bag.* San Francisco: McGraw-Hill.

Guerra, P. (1998, July). Older adults and substance abuse: Looking at the "invisible epidemic." *Counseling Today,* pp. 38,43.

Gurin, P., Gurin, G., Lao, R., & Beattie, M. (1969). Internal-external control in the motivational dynamics of negro youth. *Journal of Social Issues, 25,* 29–54.

Gushue, G. V., & Sciarra, D. T. (1995). Culture and families: A multidimensional approach. In J. G. Ponterotto, J. M. Casas, L. A. Suzuki, & C. M. Alexander (Eds.), *Handbook of multicultural counseling* (pp. 586–606). Thousand Oaks, CA: Sage.

Guthrie, R. V. (1976). *Even the rat was White: A historical view of psychology.* New York: Harper and Row.

Guthrie, R. V. (1997). *Even the rat was White: A historical view of psychology* (2nd ed.). New York: Harper and Row.

Gutierres, S. F., & Todd, M. (1997). The impact of childhood abuse on treatment outcomes. *Professional Psychology: Research and Practice, 28,* 348–354.

Habemann, L., & Thiry, S. (1970). The effect of socioeconomic status variables on counselor perception and behavior. Unpublished master's thesis, University of Wisconsin, Madison.

Haley, A. (1966). *The autobiography of Malcolm X.* New York: Grove Press.

Haley, J. (1967). Marriage therapy. In H. Greenwald (Ed.), *Active psychotherapy* (pp. 189–223). Chicago: Aldine.

Hall, C. C. I. (1997). Cultural malpractice. The growing obsolescence of psychology with the changing U.S. population. *American Psychologist, 52,* 642–651.

Hall, C. C. I. (1980). *The ethnic identity of racially mixed people: A study of Black Japanese.* Unpublished doctoral dissertation, University of California, Los Angeles.

Hall, E. T. (1959). *The silent language.* Greenwich, CT: Premier Books.

Hall, E. T. (1969). *The hidden dimension.* Garden City, New York: Doubleday.

Hall, E. T. (1974). *Handbook for proxemic research.* Washington, DC: Society for the Ontology of Visual Communications.

Hall, E. T. (1976). *Beyond culture.* New York: Anchor Press.

Hall, G. C. N. (2001). Psychotherapy research with ethnic minorities: Empirical, ethical, and conceptual issues. *Journal of Counseling and Clinical Psychology, 69,* 502–510.

Hall, W. S., Cross, W. E., & Freedle, R. (1972). Stages in the development of Black awareness: An exploratory investigation. In R. L. Jones (Ed.), *Black Psychology* (pp. 156–165). New York: Harper & Row.

Halleck, S. L. (1971, April). Therapy is the handmaiden of the status quo. *Psychology Today, 4,* 30–34, 98–100.

Hamby, S. L. (2000). The importance of community in a feminist analysis of domestic violence among American Indians. *American Journal of Community Psychology, 28,* 649–669.

Hammerschlag, C. A. (1988). *The dancing healers.* San Francisco: Harper & Row.

Hanna, F. J., Talley, W. B., & Guindon, M. H. (2000). The power of perception: Toward a model of cultural oppression and liberation. *Journal of Counseling and Development, 78,* 430–446.

Hansen, J. C., Stevic, R. R., & Warner, R. W. (1982). *Counseling: Theory and process.* Toronto: Allyn-Bacon.

Hardiman, R. (1982). White identity development: A process oriented model for describing the racial consciousness of White Americans. *Dissertation Abstracts International, 43,* 104A. (University Microfilms No. 82–10330).

Harner, M. (1990). *The way of the shaman.* San Francisco: Harper and Row.

Harris, D. R., Andrews, R., & Elixhauser, A. (1997). Racial and gender differences in use of procedures for black and white hospitalized adults. *Ethnicity and Disease, 7,* 91–105.

Harvey, A. R., & Rauch, J. B. (1997). A comprehensive Afrocentric rites of passage program- for Black male adolescents. *Health and Social Work, 22,* 32–37.

Hatfield, D. (1996, July/August). The Jack Nicklaus syndrome. *The Humanist,* p. 38.

Hayasaki, E. (2001, July 13). Los Angeles: Effects of poverty, racism on gay Latinos studied. *The Los Angeles Times,* p. B3.

Hayes, J. A., & Erkis, A. J. (2000). Therapist homophobia, client sexual orientation, and source of client HIV infection as predictors of therapist reactions to clients with HIV. *Journal of Counseling Psychology, 47,* 71–78.

Hayes, L. L. (1997, August). The unique counseling needs of Latino clients. *Counseling Today,* pp. 1, 10.

Headden, S. (1997). The Hispanic dropout mystery. *US. News & World Report, 123,* 64–65.

Heatherton, T. F., Mahamedi, F., Striepe, M., Field, A. E., & Keel, P. (1997). A 10-year longitudinal study of body weight, dieting, and eating disorders. *Journal of Abnormal Psychology, 106,* 117–125.

Heesacker, M., & Carroll, T. A. (1997). Identifying and solving impediments to the social and counseling psychology interface. *The Counseling Psychologist, 25,* 171–179.

Heesacker, M., Conner, K., & Pritchard, S. (1995). Individual counseling and psychotherapy: Allocations from the social psychology of attitude change. *The Counseling Psychologist, 23,* 611–632.

Heinrich, R. K., Corbin, J. L., & Thomas, K. R. (1990). Counseling Native Americans. *Journal of Counseling & Development, 69,* 128–133.

Heller, K. (1998). Prevention activities for older adults: Social structures and personal competencies that maintain useful social roles. In D. R. Atkinson & G. Hackett (Eds.), *Counseling diverse populations* (2nd ed., pp. 183–198). Boston: McGraw-Hill.

Helms, J. E. (1984). Toward a theoretical explanation of the effects of race on counseling: A Black and White model. *The Counseling Psychologist, 12,* 153–165.

Helms, J. E. (1985). Cultural identity in the treatment process. In P. B. Pedersen (Ed.), *Handbook of cross-cultural counseling and therapy* (pp. 239–245). Westport, CT: Greenwood Press.

Helms, J. E. (1986). Expanding racial identity theory to cover counseling process. *Journal of Counseling Psychology, 33,* 62–64.

Helms, J. E. (1990). *Black and White racial identity: Theory, research, and practice.* New York: Greenwood Press.

Helms, J. E. (1993). I also said, "White racial identity influences White researchers" [reaction]. *The Counseling Psychologist, 21,* 240–243.

Helms, J. E. (1994). How multiculturalism obscures racial factors in the therapy process: Comment on Ridley et al. (1994), Sodowsky et al. (1994), Ottavi et al. (1994), and Thompson et al. (1994). *Journal of Counseling Psychology, 41,* 162–165.

Helms, J. E. (1995). An update of Helms's White and people of color racial identity models. In J. G. Ponterotto, J. M. Casas, L. A. Suzuki, & C. M. Alexander (Eds.), *Handbook of multicultural counseling* (pp. 181–191). Thousand Oaks, CA: Sage.

Helms, J. E., & Carter, R. T. (1990). Development of the White racial identity attitude inventory. In J. E. Helms (Ed.), *Black and White racial identity: Theory, research and practice* (pp. 67–80). Westport, CT: Greenwood.

Helms, J. E., & Giorgis, T. W. (1980, November). A

comparison of the locus of control and anxiety level of African, Black American, and White American college students. *Journal of College Student Personnel,* pp. 503–509.

Helms, J. E., & Richardson, T. Q. (1997). How multiculturalism obscures race and culture as different aspects of counseling competency. In D. B. Pope-Davis & H. L. K. Coleman (Eds.), *Multicultural counseling competencies* (pp. 60–79). Thousand Oaks, CA: Sage.

Henkin, W. A. (1985). Toward counseling the Japanese in America: A cross-cultural primer. *Journal of Counseling & Development, 63,* 500–503.

Heppner, P. P., & Claiborn, C. D. (1989). Social influence research in counseling: A review and critique. *Journal of Counseling Psychology, 36,* 365–387.

Heppner, P. P., & Frazier, P. A. (1992). Social psychological processes in psychotherapy: Extrapolating basic research to counseling psychology. In S. D. Brown & R. W. Lent (Eds.), *Handbook of counseling psychology* (2nd ed., pp. 141–175). New York: Wiley.

Herek, G. M., Gillis, J. R., & Cogan, J. C. (1999). Psychological sequelae of hate-crime victimization among lesbian, gay, and bisexual adults. *Journal of Consulting and Clinical Psychology, 67,* 945–951.

Herlihy, B., & Corey, G. (1997). *Boundary issues in counseling.* Alexandria, VA: American Counseling Association.

Herring, R. D. (1997). *Counseling diverse ethnic youth.* Fort Worth, TX: Harcourt Brace.

Herring, R. D. (1999). *Counseling with Native American Indians and Alaskan Natives.* Thousand Oaks, CA: Sage.

Hernstein, R. (1971). IQ. *Atlantic Monthly,* pp. 43–64.

Hernstein, R., & Murray, C. (1994). *The bell curve: Intelligence and class structure in American life.* New York: Free Press.

Highlen, P. S. (1994). Racial/ethnic diversity in doctoral programs of psychology: Challenges for the twenty-first century. *Applied and Preventive Psychology, 3,* 91–108.

Highlen, P. S. (1996). MCT theory and implications for organizations/systems. In D. W. Sue, A. E. Ivey, & P. B. Pedersen (Eds.), *A theory of multi-*

cultural counseling and therapy (pp. 65–85). Pacific Grove, CA: Brooks/Cole.

Hildebrand, V., Phenice, L. A., Gray, M. M., & Hines, R. P. (1996). *Knowing and serving diverse families.* Englewood Cliffs, NJ: Prentice-Hall.

Hill, C. E., Thames, T. B., & Rardin, D. K. (1979). Comparison of Rogers, Perls, and Ellis on the Hill Counselor Verbal Response Category System. *Journal of Counseling Psychology, 26,* 198–203.

Hills, H. I., & Strozier, A. A. (1992). Multicultural training in APA approved counseling psychology programs: A survey. *Professional Psychology: Research and Practice, 23,* 43–51.

Hines, P. M., & Boyd-Franklin, N. (1996). *African American families.* In M. McGoldrick, J. Giordano, & J. K. Pearce (Eds.), *Ethnicity and family therapy* (pp. 66–84). New York: Guilford Press.

Hing, B. O. (1993). Immigration policy. In *State of Asian Pacific America* (pp. 127–140). Los Angeles: LEAP Asian Pacific American Public Policy Institute and UCLA Asian American Studies Center.

Ho, M. K. (1987). *Family therapy with ethnic minorities.* Newbury Park, CA: Sage.

Ho, M. K. (1997). *Family therapy with ethnic minorities.* (2nd ed). Thousand Oaks, CA: Sage.

Hollingshead, A. R., & Redlich, E. C. (1968). Social class and mental health. New York: Wiley.

Hong, G. K., & Domokos-Cheng Ham, M. (2001). *Psychotherapy and counseling with Asian American clients.* Thousand Oaks, CA: Sage.

Hooker, E. (1957). The adjustment of the male overt homosexual. *Journal of Projective Techniques, 21,* 18–31.

Hoshmand, L. S. T. (1989). Alternate research paradigms: A review and teaching proposal. *The Counseling Psychologist, 17,* 3–79.

Houston, H. R. (1997). "Between two cultures": A testimony. *Amerasia Journal, 23,* 149–154.

Hovey, J. D. (2000). Acculturative stress, depression, and suicidal ideation in Mexican immigrants. *Cultural Diversity and Ethnic Minority Psychology, 6,* 134–151.

Howard, R. (1992). Folie á deux involving a dog. *American Journal of Psychiatry, 149,* 414.

Howey, N., & Samuels, E. (Eds.). (2000). *Out of the*

ordinary: Essays on growing up with gay, lesbian, and transgender parents. New York: St. Martin.

Hsieh, T., Shybut, J., & Lotsof, E. (1969). Internal versus external control and ethnic group membership: A cross-cultural-comparison. *Journal of Consulting and Clinical Psychology, 33,* 122–124.

Huang, L. N. (1994). An integrative approach to clinical assessment and intervention with Asian-American adolescents. *Journal of Clinical Child Psychology, 23,* 21–31.

Huffman, S. B., & Myers, J. E. (1999). Counseling women in midlife: An integrative approach to menopause. *Journal of Counseling and Development, 77,* 258–266.

Hulnick, M. R., & Hulnick, H. R. (1989). "Life's challenges: Curse or opportunity?" Counseling families of persons with disabilities. *Journal of Counseling and Development, 68,* 166–170.

Humes, C. W., Szymanski, E. M., & Hohenshil, T. H. (1989). Roles of counseling in enabling persons with disabilities. *Journal of Counseling and Development, 68,* 145–150.

Hyers, L. L. (2001). A secondary survey analysis study of African American ethnic identity orientation in two national samples. *Journal of Black Psychology, 27,* 139–171.

Ibrahim, F. A. (1985). Effective cross-cultural counseling and psychotherapy: A framework. *The Counseling Psychologist, 13,* 625–638.

Ibrahim, F. A., Roysircar-Sodowsky, G., & Ohnishi, H. (2001). Worldview. In J. G. Ponterotto, J. M. Casas, L. A. Suzuki, & C. M. Alexander (Eds.). *Handbook of multicultural counseling* (pp. 425–456). Thousand Oaks, CA: Sage.

Ina, S. (1997). Counseling Japanese Americans. In C. C. Lee (Ed.), *Multicultural issues in counseling* (2nd ed., pp. 189–206). Alexandria, VA: American Counseling Association.

Inclan, J. (1979). Adjustment to migration: Family organization, acculturation, and psychological symptomatology in Puerto Rican women of three socioeconomic class groups. Unpublished doctoral dissertation. New York: New York University.

Inclan, J. (1985). Variations in value orientations in mental health work with Puerto Ricans. *Psychotherapy, 22,* 324–334.

Irvine, J. J., & York, D. E. (1995). Learning styles and culturally diverse students: A literature review. In J. A. Banks & C. A. McGee Banks (Eds.), *Handbook of Research on Multicultural Education* (pp. 484–497). New York: McMillan.

Ishiyama, F. (1986). Morita therapy. *Psychotherapy, 23,* 375–380.

Ivey, A. E. (1981). Counseling and psychotherapy: Toward a new perspective. In A. J. Marsella and P. B. Pedersen (Eds.), *Cross-cultural counseling and psychotherapy.* New York: Pergamon.

Ivey, A. E. (1986). *Developmental therapy.* San Francisco: Jossey-Bass.

Ivey, A. E., Ivey, M. B., & Simek-Downing, L. (1987). *Counseling and psychotherapy: Skills, theories, and practice.* Englewood Cliffs, NJ: Prentice-Hall.

Ivey, A. E., Ivey, M. B., & Simek-Morgan, L. (1997). *Counseling and psychotherapy: A multicultural perspective* (4th ed.). Boston: Allyn & Bacon.

Jackman, C. F., Wagner, W. G., & Johnson, J. T. (2001). The attitudes toward multiracial children scale. *Journal of Black Studies, 27,* 86–99.

Jackson, B. (1975). Black identity development. *Journal of Educational Diversity, 2,* 19–25.

Jackson, B. W., & Holvino, E. (1988). Developing multicultural organizations. *Journal of Religion and the Applied Behavioral Sciences, 9,* 14–19.

Jackson, L. A., Hodge, C. N., Gerard, D. A., Ingram, J. M., Ervin, K. S., & Sheppard, L. A. (1996). Cognition, affect and behavior in the prediction of group attitudes. *Personality and Social Psychology Bulletin, 22,* 306–316.

Jackson, M. L. (1995). Multicultural Counseling: Historical Perspectives. In J. G. Ponterotto, J. M. Casas, L. A. Suzuki, & C. M. Alexander (Eds.), *Handbook of multicultural counseling* (pp. 3–16). Thousand Oaks, CA: Sage.

Jacobson, S., & Samdahl, D. M. (1998). Leisure in the lives of old lesbians: Experiences with and responses to discrimination. *Journal of Leisure Research, 30,* 233–255.

Jenkins, A. H. (1982). *The psychology of the Afro-American.* New York: Pergamon.

Jensen, A. (1969). How much can we boost IQ and school achievement? *Harvard Educational Review, 39,* 1–123.

Jensen, J. V. (1985). Perspective on nonverbal intercultural communication. In L. A. Samovar & R. E. Porter (Eds.), *Intercultural communication: A reader* (pp. 256–272). Belmont, CA: Wadsworth.

Johnson, B. (1995, January 19). Elderly women need not abandon sexuality. *Seattle Post-Intelligencer.*

Johnson, J. J. (1992). Developmental pathways: Toward an ecological theoretical formulation of race identity in Black-White biracial children. In M. P. P. Root (Ed.), *Racially mixed people in America* (pp. 37–49). Newbury Park, CA: Sage.

Johnson, K. W., Anderson, N. B., Bastida, E., Kramer, B. J., Williams, D., & Wong, M. (1995). Macrosocial and environmental influences on minority health. *Health Psychology, 14,* 601–612.

Jones, A. C. (1985). Psychological functioning in Black Americans: A conceptual guide for use in psychotherapy. *Psychotherapy, 22,* 363–369.

Jones, D. R., Harrell, J. P., Morris-Prather, C. E., Thomas, J., & Omowale, N. (1996). Affective and physiological responses to racism: The roles of afrocentrism and mode of presentation. *Ethnicity and Disease, 6,* 109–122.

Jones, E. E., Kanouse, D., Kelley, H. H., Nisbett, R. E., Valins, S., & Weiner, B. (Eds.). (1972). *Attribution: Perceiving the causes of behavior.* Morristown, NJ: General Learning Press.

Jones, J. M. (1972). *Prejudice and racism.* Reading, MA: Addison Wesley.

Jones, J. M. (1997). *Prejudice and racism* (2nd ed.). New York: McGraw-Hill.

Jordan, J. M. (1997). Counseling African American women from a cultural sensitivity perspective. In C. C. Lee (Ed.), *Multicultural issues in counseling* (2nd ed., pp. 109–122). Alexandria, VA: American Counseling Association.

Jordan, W. D. (1969). *White over Black: American attitudes toward the Negro, 1550–1812.* Baltimore: Penguin Books.

Jose, P. E., Huntsinger, C. S., Huntsinger, P. R., & Liaw, L. (2000). Parental values and practices relevant to young children's social development in Taiwan and the United States. *Journal of Cross-Cultural Psychology, 31,* 677–702.

Jourard, S. M. (1964). *The transparent self.* Princeton, NJ: D. Van Nostrand.

Journal of the American Medical Association. (2000). Prevalence of disabilities and associated health conditions among adults—United States, 1999. *Journal of the American Medical Association, 285,* 1571–1572.

Juang, S.-H., & Tucker, C. M. (1991). Factors in marital adjustment and their interrelationships: A comparison of Taiwanese couples in America and Caucasian American couples. *Journal of Multicultural Counseling and Development, 19,* 22–31.

Jung, C. G. (1960). The structure and dynamics of the psyche. In Collected Works, 8. Princeton, NJ: Princeton University Press.

Juntunen, C. L., Barraclough, D. J., Broneck, C. L., Seibel, G. A., Winrow, S. A., & Morin, P. M. (2001). American Indian perspectives on the career journey. *Journal of Counseling Psychology, 48,* 274–285.

Kabat-Zinn, J. (1990). *Full catastrophe living.* New York: Delacorte.

Kamarack, T., & Jennings, J. R. (1991). Biobehavioral factors in sudden cardiac death. *Psychological Bulletin, 109,* 42–75.

Kamin, L. (1974). *The science and politics of I.Q.* Potomac, MD: Erlbaum.

Kantrowitz, B., & Wingert, P. (2001, May 28). Unmarried with children. *Newsweek,* pp. 46–55.

Kass, J. (1998, May 11). State's attorney needs some sense knocked into him. *Chicago Tribune,* p. 3.

Katz, J. H. (1985). The sociopolitical nature of counseling. *The Counseling Psychologist, 13,* 615–624.

Katz, J. H., & Miller, F. A. (1988). Between monoculturalism and multiculturalism: Traps awaiting the organization. *O.D. Practitioner, 20,* 1–5.

Kavanaugh, P. C., & Retish, P. M. (1991). The Mexican American ready for college. *Journal of Multicultural Counseling and Development, 19,* 136–144.

Keane, E. M., Dick, R. W., Bechtold, D. W., & Manson, S. M. (1996). Predictive and concurrent validity of the Suicide Ideation Questionnaire among American Indian Adolescents. *Journal of Abnormal Child Psychology, 24,* 735–747.

Kelly, M., & Tseng, H. (1992). Cultural differences in childrearing: A comparison of immigrant Chinese and Caucasian American mothers. *Journal of Cross-Cultural Psychology, 23,* 444–455.

Kemp, N. T., & Mallinckrodt, B. (1996). Impact of professional training on case conceptualization of clients with a disability. *Professional Psychology: Research and Practice, 27,* 378–385.

Kendler, K. S., MacLean, C., Neal, M., Kessler, R., Heath, A., & Eaves, L. (1991). The genetic epidemiology of bulimia nervosa. *American Journal of Psychiatry, 148,* 1627–1637.

Kennedy, J. L. (1996). *Job interviews for dummies.* Foster City, CA: IDG Books Worldwide.

Kerwin, C., & Ponterotto, J. G. (1995). Biracial identity development: Theory and research. In J. Ponterotto, J. M. Casas, L. A. Suzuki, & C. M. Alexander (Eds.). *Handbook of multicultural counseling* (pp. 199–217). Newbury Park, CA: Sage.

Kim, A. U., & Atkinson, D. R. (1998). What counselors need to know about aging and sexuality. In D. R. Atkinson & G. Hackett (Eds.), *Counseling diverse populations* (2nd ed., pp. 217–233). Boston: McGraw-Hill.

Kim, J. (1981). The process of Asian American identity development: A study of Japanese-American women's perceptions of their struggle to achieve personal identities as Americans of Asian ancestry. *Dissertation Abstracts International, 42,* 155 1A. (University Microfilms No.81–18080)

Kim, S. C. (1985). Family therapy for Asian Americans: A strategic structural framework. *Psychotherapy, 22,* 342–356.

Kim, U., & Berry, J. W. (1993). *Indigenous psychologies.* Newbury Park, CA: Sage.

King, M. (2001, October 7). Concerns of elder gays. *Seattle Times,* p. B1, 9.

Kiselica, M. S. (1998). Preparing anglos for the challenges and joys of multiculturalism. *The Counseling Psychologist, 26,* 5–21.

Kitano, H. H. L. (1982). Mental health in the Japanese American community. In E. E. Jones & S. J. Korchin (Eds.), *Minority mental health* (pp. 149–164). New York: Praeger.

Kleinke, C. L. (1994). *Common principles of psychotherapy.* Pacific Grove, CA: Brooks/Cole.

Kluckhohn, F. R., & Strodtbeck, F. L. (1961). *Variations in value orientations.* Evanston, IL: Row, Patterson, & Co.

Knight, B. G., & McCallum, T. J. (1998). Adapting psychotherapeutic practice for older clients: Implications of the contextual, cohort-based, maturity, specific challenge model. *Professional Psychology: Research and Practice, 29,* 15–22.

Kochman, T. (1981). *Black and White styles in conflict.* Chicago: University of Chicago Press.

Korman, M. (1973). National conference on levels and patterns of professional training in psychology. *American Psychologist, 29,* 441–449.

Kramer, F. (1998, May 24). On nation's farms, some workers give up childhood—"I just want to go back to school," a youngster tells child-labor forum. *Seattle Times,* p. A6.

Krieger, N., & Sidney, S. (1996). Racial discrimination and blood pressure: the CARDIA study of young black and white adults. *American Journal of Public Health, 86,* 1370–1308.

Krupin, S. (2001, July 25). Prejudice, schools key concerns of Hispanics. *Seattle Post Intelligencer,* p. A7.

Kumanyika, S. K. (1993). Special issues regarding obesity in minority populations. *Annuals of Internal Medicine, 119,* 650–654.

Kun, K. E., & Schwartz, R. W. (1998). Older Americans with HIV/AIDS. *SIECUS Report, 26,* 12–14.

Kurdek, L. A. (Ed.). (1994). *Social services for gay and lesbian couples.* Binghampton, NY: Hayworth Press.

Kwee, M. (1990). *Psychotherapy, meditation and health.* London: East-West.

LaBarre, W. (1985). Paralinguistics, kinesics and cultural anthropology. In L. A. Samovar & R. E. Porter (Eds.), *Intercultural communication: A reader* (pp. 272–279). Belmont, CA: Wadsworth.

Labov, W. (1972). *Language in the inner city: Studies in the Black English vernacular.* Philadelphia: University of Pennsylvania Press.

La Crosse, M. B., & Barak, A. (1976). Differential perception of counselor behavior. *Journal of Counseling Psychology, 23,* 170–172.

LaFromboise, T. (1998). American Indian mental health policy. In D. A. Atkinson, G. Morten, & D. W. Sue (Eds.), *Counseling American minorities: A cross-cultural perspective* (pp. 137–158). Boston: McGraw-Hill.

LaFromboise, T., & Howard-Pitney, B. (1995). The Zuni Life Skills Development Curriculum. *Journal of Counseling Psychology, 42,* 479–486.

LaFromboise, T. D., & Dixon, D. N. (1981). American Indian perception of trustworthiness in a counseling interview. *Journal of Counseling Psychology, 28,* 135–139.

Laing, R. D. (1967). *The divided self.* New York: Pantheon.

Laing, R. D. (1969). *The politics of experience.* New York: Pantheon.

Laird, J., & Green, R. (1996). *Lesbians and gays in couples and families.* San Francisco: Jossey-Bass.

Lane, M. (1988, June 22). At age 81, teacher's lessons are timeless. *Bellingham Herald,* p. A1.

La Rue, A., & Watson, J. (1998). Psychological assessment of older adults. *Professional Psychology: Research and Practice, 29,* 5–14.

Lass, N. J., Mertz, P. J., & Kimmel, K. (1978). The effect of temporal speech alterations on speaker race and sex identification. *Language and Speech, 21,* 279–290.

Latting, J. E. & Zundel, C. (1986). Worldview differences between clients and counselors. *Social Casework, 12,* 66–71.

Lazzaro, J. (2000). Electric books: SF publishers embrace alternative formats such as audio, large print, braille, e-books, and descriptive and captioned video. *Science Fiction Chronicle, 22,* 24–25.

Lee, C. C. (1996). MCT Theory and implications for indigenous healing. In D. W. Sue, A. E. Ivey, & P. B. Pedersen (Eds.), *A theory of multicultural counseling and therapy* (pp. 86–98). Pacific Grove, CA: Brooks/Cole.

Lee, C. C., & Armstrong, K. L. (1995). Indigenous models of mental health intervention: Lessons from traditional healers. In J. G. Ponterotto, J. M. Casas, L. A. Suzuki, & C. M. Alexander (Eds.), *Handbook of Multicultural Counseling* (pp. 441–456). Thousand Oaks, CA: Sage.

Lee, C. C., Oh, M. Y., & Mountcastle, A. R. (1992). Indigenous models of helping in nonwestern countries: Implications for multicultural counseling. *Journal of Multicultural Counseling and Development, 20,* 1–10.

Lee, C.-R. (1995). *Native speaker.* New York: Berkley Publishing Group.

Lee, E. (1988). Cultural factors in working with Southeast Asian refugee adolescents. *Journal of Adolescents, 11,* 167–179.

Lee, E. (1996). Chinese Families. In M. McGoldrick, J. Geordano, & J. K. Pearce (Eds.), *Ethnicity and Family Therapy* (pp. 249–267). New York: Guilford.

Lee, F. Y. (1991). *The relationship of ethnic identity to social support, self-esteem, psychological distress, and help-seeking behavior among Asian American college students.* Unpublished doctoral dissertation, University of Illinois, Urbana-Champaign.

Lee, R. (2000). Health care problems of lesbian, gay, bisexual, and transgender patients. *Western Journal of Medicine, 172,* 403–408.

Lee, R. M., Choe, J., Kim, G., & Ngo, V. (2000). Construction of the Asian American Family Conflicts Scale. *Journal of Counseling Psychology, 47,* 211–222.

Lee, S. J. (1994). Behind the model-minority stereotype: Voices of high- and low-achieving Asian American students. *Anthropology and Education Quarterly, 25,* 413–429.

Lee, W. M. L. (1999). *An introduction to multicultural counseling.* Philadelphia, PA: Taylor & Francis.

Lee, Y. T. (1993). Psychology needs no prejudice but the diversity of cultures. *American Psychologist, 48,* 1090–1091.

Lefcourt, H. (1966). Internal versus control of reinforcement: A review. *Psychological Bulletin, 65,* 206–220.

Lefkowitz, E. S., Romo, L. F. L., Corona, R., Au, T. K.-F., & Sigman, M. (2000). How Latino American and European American adolescents discuss conflicts, sexuality, and AIDS with their mothers. *Developmental Psychology, 36,* 315–325.

Leigh, I. W., Corbett, C. A., Gutman, V., & Morere, D. A. (1996). Providing psychological services to deaf individuals: A response to new perceptions of diversity. *Professional Psychology: Research and Practice, 27,* 364–371.

Leland, J. (2000, March 20). Shades of gray. *Newsweek,* 46–49.

Lent, R. W., & Maddux, J. E. (1997). Self efficacy: Building a sociocognitive bridge between social and counseling psychology. *The Counseling Psychologist, 25,* 240–255.

Leong, F. T. L. (1985). Career development of Asian Americans. *Journal of College Student Personnel, 26,* 539–546.

Leong, F. T. L. (1986). Counseling and psychotherapy with Asian-Americans: Review of literature. *Journal of Counseling Psychology, 33,* 196–206.

Leong, F. T. L. (1994). Asian Americans' differential patterns of utilization of inpatient and outpatient public mental health services in Hawaii. *Journal of Community Psychology, 22,* 82–96.

Leong, F. T. L., Wagner, N. S., & Kim, H. H. (1995). Group counseling expectations among Asian American students: The role of culture-specific factors. *Journal of Counseling Psychology, 42,* 217–222.

Leong, F. T. L., Wagner, N. S., & Tata, S. P. (1995). Racial and ethnic variations in help-seeking attitudes. In J. G. Ponterotto, J. M. Casas, L. A. Suzuki, & C. M. Alexander (Eds.), *Handbook of multicultural counseling* (pp. 415–438). Thousand Oaks, CA: Sage.

Levenson, H. (1974). Activism and powerful others. *Journal of Personality Assessment, 38,* 377–383.

LeVine, E. S., & Padilla, A. M. (1980). *Crossing cultures in therapy: Pluralistic counseling for the Hispanic.* Monterey, CA: Brooks/Cole.

Levinson, H. (1994). Why the behemoths fell: Psychological roots of corporate failure. *American Psychologist, 49,* 428–436.

Lewandowski, D. A., & Jackson, L. A. (2001). Perceptions of interracial couples: Prejudice at the dyadic level. *Journal of Black Psychology, 27,* 288–303.

Lewis, J. A., Lewis, M. D., Daniels, J. A., & D'Andrea, M. J. (1998). *Community Counseling.* Pacific Grove, CA: Brooks/Cole.

Liddle, B. J. (1996). Therapist sexual orientation, gender, and counseling practices as they relate to ratings of helpfulness by gay and lesbian clients. *Journal of Counseling Psychology, 43,* 394–401.

Lippert, L. (1997). Women at midlife: Implications for theories of women's adult development. *Journal of Counseling and Development, 76,* 16–22.

Locke, D. C. (1998). *Increasing multicultural understanding.* Thousand Oaks, CA: Sage.

Lombardi, E. (2001). Enhancing transgender health care. *American Journal of Public Health, 91,* 869–872.

London, P. (1988). *Modes and morals of psychotherapy.* New York: Holt, Rinehart & Winston.

Lone-Knapp, F. (2000). Rez talk: How reservation residents describe themselves. *American Indian Quarterly, 24,* 635–640.

Lorenzo, M. K., Pakiz, B., Reinherz, H. Z., & Frost, A. (1995). Emotional and behavioral problems of Asian American adolescents: A comparative study. *Child and Adolescent Social Work Journal, 12,* 197–212.

Lorion, R. P. (1973). Socioeconomic status and treatment approaches reconsidered. *Psychological Bulletin, 79,* 263–280.

Lorion, R. P. (1974). Patient and therapist variables in the treatment of low-income patients. *Psychological Bulletin, 81,* 344–354.

Lum, R. G. (1982). Mental health attitudes and opinions of Chinese. In E. E. Jones & S. J. Korchin (Eds.), *Minority mental health.* New York: Praeger.

Luzzo, D. A., & McWhirter, E. H. (2001). Sex and ethnic differences in the perception of educational and career-related barriers and levels of coping efficacy. *Journal of Counseling and Development, 79,* 61–67.

Lyness, K. S., & Thompson, D. E. (2000). Climbing the corporate ladder: Do female and male executives follow the same route? *Journal of Applied Psychology, 85,* 86–101.

Maas, P. (2001, September 9). The broken promise. *Parade Magazine,* 4–6.

Mackler, B., & Giddings, M. G. (1965). Cultural deprivation: A study in mythology. *Teachers College Record, 66,* 608–613.

MacPhee, D., Fritz, J., & Miller-Heyl, J. (1996). Ethnic variations in personal social networks and parenting. *Child Development, 67,* 3278–3295.

Mann, J. (1998, July 10). A proud pioneer looks back. *The Washington Post,* p. E03.

Manson, S. M., Tatum, E., & Dinges, N. G. (1982). Prevention research among American Indian and Alaska Native communities: Charting further courses for theory and practice in mental health. In S. M. Manson (Ed.), *New directions in prevention among American Indian and Alaska Native Communities* (pp. 1–61). Portland, OR: Oregon Health Sciences University.

Marcos, L. R. (1973). The language barrier in evaluating Spanish-American patients. *Archives of General Psychiatry, 29,* 655–659.

Marcos, L. R. (1979). Effects of interpreters on the evaluation of psychopathology in non-English speaking patients. *American Journal of Psychiatry, 136,* 171–174.

Martin, J. I., & Knox, J. (2000). Methodological and ethical issues in research on lesbians and gay men. *Social Work Research, 24,* 51–59.

Marwick, C. (1995). Should physicians prescribe prayer for health? Spiritual aspects of well-being considered. *Journal of the American Medical Association, 273,* 1561–1562.

Marx, G. T. (1967). *Protest and prejudice: A study of belief in the Black community.* New York: Harper & Row.

Masand, P. S. (2000). Side effects of antipsychotics in the elderly. *Journal of Clinical Psychiatry, 61,* 43–51.

Maslow, A. H. (1968). *Toward a psychology of being.* Princeton: Van Nostrand.

Matthee, I. (1997, Sept 9). Anti-Asian hate crimes on rise in U.S. but state sees decline in such offenses. *Seattle Post-Intelligencer,* p. A3.

Matthias, R. E., Lubben, J. E., Atchison, K. A., & Schweitzer, S. O. (1997). Sexual satisfaction among very old adults: Results from a community-dwelling Medicare population survey. *The Gerontologist, 37,* 6–14.

Mau, W. C., & Jepson, D. A. (1988). Attitudes toward counselors and counseling processes: A comparison of Chinese and American graduate students. *Journal of Counseling and Development, 67,* 189–192.

Maykovich, M. H. (1973). Political activation of Japanese American youth. *Journal of Social Issues, 29,* 167–185.

Mays, V. M. (1985). The Black American and psychotherapy: The dilemma. *Psychotherapy, 22,* 379–388.

McCollum, V. J. C. (1997). Evolution of the African American family personality: Considerations for family therapy. *Journal of Multicultural Counseling and Development, 25,* 219–229.

McCray, C. C. (1998). Ageism in the preclinical years. *Journal of the American Medical Association, 279,* 1035. Copyright 1998. American Medical Association.

McCurdy, P. C., & Ruiz, R. A. (1980). Sex role and marital agreement. In R. A. Ruiz & R. E. Cromwell (Eds.), *Anglo, Black, and Chicano families in the urban community.*

McGilley, B. M., & Pryor, T. L. (1998). Assessment and treatment of bulimia nervosa. *American Family Physician, 57,* 2743–2750.

McGoldrick, M., & Giordano, J. (1996). Overview: Ethnicity and Family Therapy. In M. McGoldrick, J. Giordano, & J. K. Pearce (Eds.), *Ethnicity and family therapy* (2nd ed., pp. 1–27). New York: Guilford Press.

McGoldrick, M., Giordano, J., & Pearce, J. K. (1996). *Ethnicity and family therapy.* New York: Guilford.

McIntosh, P. (1989, July/August). White privilege: Unpacking the invisible knapsack. *Peace and Freedom,* pp. 8–10.

McLeod, B. (1986). The Oriental express. *Psychology Today,* 48–52.

McNamara, K., & Rickard, K. M. (1989). Feminist identity development: Implications for feminist therapy with women. *Journal of Counseling and Development, 68,* 184–193.

McNamara, K., & Rickard, K. M. (1998). Feminist identity development: Implications for feminist therapy with women. In D. R. Atkinson & G. Hackett (Eds.), *Counseling diverse popula-tions* (2nd ed., pp. 271–282). Boston: McGraw-Hill.

McNamara, M. (2001, February 27). Era of the gender crosser. *Los Angeles Times,* p. A1.

McNamee, S. (1996). Psychotherapy as a social construction. In H. Rosen & K. T. Kuehlwein (Eds.), *Constructing realities: Meaning-making perspective for psychotherapists* (pp. 115–137). San Francisco: Jossey-Bass.

McQuaide, S. (1998). Women at midlife. *Social Work, 43,* 21–31.

Mehrabian, A. (1972). *Nonverbal communication.* Chicago: Aldene-Atherton.

Mejia, D. (1983). The development of Mexican-American children. In G. J. Powell, J. Yamamoto, A. Romero, & A. Morales (Eds.), *The psychosocial development of minority group children* (pp. 77–114). New York: Brunner/Mazel.

Melfi, C. A., Croghan, T. W., Hanna, M. P., & Robinson, R. L. (2000). Racial variation in antidepressant treatment in a Medicaid population. *Journal of Clinical Psychiatry, 61,* 16–21.

Menacker, J. (1971). *Urban poor students and guidance.* Boston: Houghton Mifflin.

Mercer, J. R. (1971). Institutionalized anglocentrism. In P. Orleans & W. Russel (Eds.), *Race, change, and urban society.* Los Angeles: Sage.

Meston, C. M., Heiman, J. R., Trapnell, P. D., & Carlin, A. S. (1999). Ethnicity, desirable responding, and self-reports of abuse: A comparison of European- and Asian-ancestry undergraduates. *Journal of Counseling and Clinical Psychology, 67,* 139–144.

Meyers, H., Echemedia, F., & Trimble, J. E. (1991). American Indians and the counseling process. In P. B. Pedersen (Ed.), *Handbook of cross-cultural counseling* (pp. 3–9). Westport, CT: Greenwood.

Middlebrook, D. L., LeMaster, P. L., Beals, J., Novins, D. K., & Manson, S. M. (2001). Suicide prevention in American Indian and Alaska Native communties: A critical review of programs. *Suicide and Life-Threatening Behavior, 31,* 132–149.

Middleton, R., Arrendondo, P., & D'Andrea, M. (2000, December). The impact of Spanish-speaking newcomers in Alabama towns. *Counseling Today,* 24.

Miller, S. T., Seib, H. M., & Dennie, S. P. (2001). African American perspectives on health care: The voice of the community. *Journal of Ambulatory Care Management, 24,* 37–42.

Milville, M. L., Koonce, D., Darlington, P., & Whitlock, B. (2000). Exploring the relationship between racial/cultural identity and ego identity among African Americans and Mexican Americans. *Journal of Multicultural Counseling and Development, 28,* 208–224.

Mindess, A. (1999). *Reading between the signs.* Yarmouth, ME: Intercultural Press.

Mintz, L. B., Bartels, K. M., & Rideout, C. A. (1995). Training in counseling ethnic minorities and race-based availability of graduate school resources. *Professional Psychology: Research and Practice, 26,* 316–321.

Mintz, L. B., & Kashubeck, S. (1999). Body image and disordered eating among Asian American and Caucasian college students: An examination of race and gender differences. *Psychology of Women Quarterly, 23,* 781–796.

Minuchin, S. (1974). *Families and family therapy.* Cambridge, MA: Harvard University Press.

Mio, J. S., & Iwamasa, G. (1993). To do, or not to do: That is the question for White cross-cultural researchers. *The Counseling Psychologist, 21,* 197–212.

Mio, J. S., & Morris, D. R. (1990). Cross-cultural issues in psychology training programs: An invitation for discussion. *Professional Psychology: Theory and Practice, 21,* 434–441.

Miranda, A. O., & Umhoefer, D. L. (1998a). Acculturation, language use, and demographic variables as predictors of the career self-efficacy of Latino career counseling clients. *Journal of Multicultural Counseling and Development, 26,* 39–51.

Miranda, A. O. & Umhoefer, D. L. (1998b). Depression and social interest differences between Latinos in dissimilar acculturation stages. *Journal of Mental Health Counseling, 20,* 159–171.

Mirels, H. (1970). Dimensions of internal versus external control. *Journal of Consulting and Clinical Psychology, 34,* 226–228.

Mitchell, A. (1998, June 17). Controversy over Lott's view of homosexuality. *New York Times,* p. 24.

Mizio, E. (1983). The impact of macro systems on Puerto Rican families. In G. J. Powell, J. Yamamoto, A. Romero, & A. Morales (Eds.), *The psychosocial development of minority group children* (pp. 216–236). New York: Brunner/Mazel.

Modie, N. (2001, July 25). New hope for the immigrants in limbo. *Seattle Post-Intelligencer,* pp. A1, A6.

Mohr, J. J., Israel, T., & Sedlacek, W. E. (2001). Counselors' attitudes regarding bisexuality as predictors of counselors' clinical responses: An analogue study of a female bisexual client. *Journal of Counseling Psychology, 48,* 212–222.

Mollica, R. F., Wyshak, G., & Lavelle, J. (1987). The psychosocial impact of war trauma and torture on Southeast Asian refugees. *American Journal of Psychiatry, 144,* 1567–1572.

Montague, J. (1996). Counseling families from diverse cultures. A nondeficit approach. *Journal of Multicultural Counseling and Development, 24,* 37–41.

Montgomery, D., Milville, M. L., Winterowd, C., Jeffries, B., & Baysden, M. F. (2000). American Indian college students: An exploration into resiliency factors revealed through personal stories. *Cultural Diversity and Ethnic Minority Psychology, 6,* 387–398.

Moore, K. A. (2001). Time to take a closer look at Hispanic children and families. *Policy & Public Human Services, 59,* 8–9.

Moos, R. H., Mertens, J. R., & Brennan, P. L. (1995). Program characteristics and readmission among older substance abuse patients: Comparisons with middle-aged and younger patients. *Journal of Mental Health Administration, 22,* 332–346.

Morbidity and Mortality Weekly Report. (1992). Alcohol-related hospitalizations–Indian Health Service and Tribal Hospitals, United States, *May 1992, 41,* 757–760.

Morbidity and Mortality Weekly Report. (1994). Prevalence and characteristic of alcohol consumption and fetal alcohol awareness– Alaska, 1991 and 1993, *43,* 3–6.

Morrissey, M. (1997, October). The invisible minority: Counseling Asian Americans. *Counseling Today,* pp. 1, 21–22.

Moye, J., & Brown, E. (1995). Postdoctoral training in geropsychology: Guidelines for formal programs and continuing education. *Professional Psychology: Research and Practice, 26,* 591–597.

Moynihan, D. P. (1965). Employment, income and the ordeal of the Negro family. *Daedalus,* pp. 745–770.

Mullavey-O'Byrne, C. (1994). Intercultural Communication for Health Care Professionals. In R. W. Brislin & T. Yoshida (Eds.), *Improving intercultural interactions* (pp. 171–196). Thousand Oaks, CA: Sage.

Muñoz, R. H., & Sanchez, A. M. (1996). *Developing culturally competent systems of care for state mental health services.* Boulder, CO: Western Interstate Commission for Higher Education.

Myers, H. F., Kagawa-Singer, M., Kumanyika, S. K., Lex, B. W., & Markides, K. S. (1995). Panel III:

Behavioral risk factors related to chronic diseases in ethnic minorities. *Health Psychology, 14,* 613–621.

National Asian Pacific American Legal Consortium. (1997). *Audit of violence against Asian Pacific Americans.* Washington, DC: NAPA.

National Coalition of Anti-Violence Programs. (2001, April 13). *San Francisco Chronicle,* A19, A24.

National Coalition for Women and Girls in Education. (1998). *Title IX at 25; Report card on gender equity.* Washington, DC: National Coalition for Women and Girls in Education.

National Center for Health Statistics. (1996). *Health, United States, 1995.* Hyattsville, MD: Public Health Service.

National Commission on the Causes and Prevention of Violence. (1969). *To establish justice, to insure domestic tranquility.* New York: Award Books.

National Institute of Mental Health. (2000). *Older adults: Depression and suicide facts.* Bethesda, MD: Author.

National Organization on Disability/Louis Harris Survey. (1998). Americans with disabilities still face sharp gaps in securing jobs, education, transportation, and in many areas of daily life. National Organization on Disability.

Neal-Barnett, A. M., & Crowther, J. H. (2000). To be female, middle class, anxious, and Black. *Psychology of Women Quarterly, 24,* 129–136.

Negy, C. (1993). Anglo- and Hispanic-Americans' performance on the Family Attitude Scale and its implications for improving measurements of acculturation. *Psychological Reports, 73,* 1211–1217.

Negy, C., & Woods, D. J. (1992). The importance of acculturation in understanding research with Hispanic-Americans. *Hispanic Journal of Behavioral Sciences, 14,* 224–247.

Neighbors, H. W., Caldwell, C. H., Thompson, E., & Jackson, J. S. (1994). Help-seeking behavior and unmet need. In Sriedman (Ed.), *Disorders in African Americans* (pp. 26–39). New York: Springer.

Neville, H. A., Worthington, R. L., & Spanierman, L. B. (2001). Race, power, and multicultural counseling psychology: Understanding White privilege and color-blind racial attitudes. In J. Ponterotto, J. M. Casas, L. A. Suzuki, & C. M. Alexander (Eds.), *Handbook of multicultural counseling* (pp. 257–288). Thousand Oaks, CA: Sage.

New York Times News Service. (2001, May 13). Fear keeps migrant workers from doctors. *The Bellingham Herald,* p. A8.

Nguyen, S. D. (1985). Mental health services for refugees and immigrants in Canada. In T. C. Owen (Ed.), *Southeast Asian mental health: Treatment, prevention, services, training, and research* (pp. 261–282). Washington, DC: National Institute of Mental Health.

Nichols, M. P., & Schwartz, R. C. (1995). *Family therapy: Concepts and methods* (3rd ed.). Boston: Allyn & Bacon.

Nieto, S. (1995). A history of the education of Puerto Rican students in U.S. mainland schools: "Losers," "Outsiders," or "Leaders"? In J. A. Banks & C. A. McGee Banks (Eds.), *Handbook of research on multicultural education* (pp. 388– 411). New York: McMillan.

Nishihara, D. P. (1978). Culture, counseling, and ho'oponopono: An ancient model in a modem context. *Personnel and Guidance Journal, 56,* 562–566.

Noh, S., Beiser, M., Kaspar, V., Hou, F., & Rummens, J. (1999). Perceived racial discrimination, depression, and coping: A study of Southeast Asian refugees in Canada. *Journal of Health and Social Behavior, 40,* 193–207.

Norton, I. M., & Manson, S. M. (1996). Research in American Indian and Alaskan Native communities: Navigating the cultural universe of values and process. *Journal of Consulting and Clinical Psychology, 64,* 856–860.

Norton, J. L. (1995). The gay, lesbian, bisexual populations. In N. A. Vacc, S. B. DeVaney, & J. Wittmer (Eds.), *Experiencing and counseling multicultural and diverse populations* (3rd ed., pp. 147–177). Bristol, PA: Accelerated Development.

Nosek, M. A., & Hughes, R. B. (2001). Psychospiritual aspects of sense of self in women with physical disabilities. *Journal of Rehabilitation, 67,* 20–25.

Nwachuku, U., & Ivey, A. (1991). Culture specific counseling: An alternative approach. *Journal of Counseling and Development, 70,* 106–111.

Nydell, M. K. (1996). *Understanding Arabs: A guide for westerners.* Yarmouth, ME: Intercultural Press.

Oler, C. H. (1989). Psychotherapy with Black clients' racial identity and locus of control. *Psychotherapy, 26,* 233–241.

Olkin, R. (1999). *What psychotherapists should know about disability.* New York:Guilford.

Olsen, C. S. (1996). African-American adolescent women: Perceptions of gender, race, and class. *Marriage and Family Review, 24,* 105–121.

O'Reilly, J. P., Tokuno, K. A., & Ebata, A. T. (1986). Cultural differences between Americans of Japanese and European ancestry in parental valuing of social competence. *Journal of Comparative Family Studies, 17,* 87–97.

Orel, N. A. (1998). Ethical considerations in assessing the competency of older adults: A provision of informed consent. *Journal of Mental Health Counseling, 20,* 189–201.

Organista, P. B., Organista, K. C., & Soloff, P. R. (1998). Exploring AIDS-related knowledge, attitudes, and behaviors of female Mexican migrant workers. *Health and Social Work, 23,* 96–103.

Ornstein, R. E. (1972). *The psychology of consciousness.* San Francisco: Freeman.

Osbourne, J. W. (1997). Race and academic disidentification. *Journal of Educational Psychology, 89,* 728–735.

Osipow, S. H. (1982). Counseling psychology: Applications in the world of work. *The Counseling Psychologist, 10,* 19–25.

Ottavi, T. M., Pope-Davis, D. B., & Dings, J. G. (1994). Relationship between White racial identity attitudes and self-reported multicultural counseling competencies. *Journal of Counseling Psychology, 41,* 149–154.

Owens, R. E., Jr. (1998). *Queer kids: The challenges and promise for lesbian, gay, and bisexual youth.* New York: Harrington Park Press.

Padilla, A. M., & DeSnyder, N. S. (1985). Counseling Hispanics: Strategies for effective intervention. In P. B. Pedersen (Ed.), *Handbook of cross-*

cultural counseling and therapy (pp. 157–164). Westport, CT: Greenwood Press.

Palmer, C., & Roessler, R. T. (2000). Requesting classroom accommodations: Self-advocacy and conflict resolution training for college students with disabilities. *Journal of Rehabilitation, 66,* 38–43.

Palmer, K. S. (2001, September 10). Younger women turn wrong way to escape abusive boyfriends. *USA Today,* p. A17.

Paniagua, F. A. (1994). *Assessing and treating culturally diverse clients.* Thousand Oaks, CA: Sage.

Paniagua, F. A. (1998). *Assessing and treating culturally diverse clients* (2nd ed.). Thousand Oaks, CA: Sage.

Paniagua, F. A. (2001). *Diagnosis in a multicultural context.* Thousand Oaks, CA: Sage.

Parham, T. A. (1989). Cycles of psychological nigrescence. *The Counseling Psychologist, 17,* 187–226.

Parham, T. A. (1993). White researchers conducting multi-cultural counseling research: Can their efforts be "Mo Betta"? [Reaction]. *The Counseling Psychologist, 21,* 250–256.

Parham, T. A. (1997). An African-centered view of dual relationships. In B. Herlihy & G. Corey (Eds.), *Boundary issues in counseling* (pp. 109–112). Alexandria, VA: American Counseling Association.

Parham, T. A., & Helms, J. E. (1981). The influence of black students' racial attitudes on preferences for counselor's race. *Journal of Counseling Psychology, 28,* 250–257.

Parham, T. A., & Helms, J. E. (1985). Relation of racial identity attitudes to self-actualization and affective status of Black students. *Journal of Counseling Psychology, 32,* 431–440.

Parham, T. A., White, J. L., & Ajamu, A. (1999). *The psychology of Blacks: An African centered perspective* (3rd ed.). Englewood Cliffs, NJ: Prentice-Hall.

Parker, S., Nichter, M., Vuckovic, N., Sims, C., & Ritenbaugh, C. (1995). Body image and weight concerns among African American and White adolescent females: Differences that make a difference. *Human Organization, 54,* 103–114.

Parker, S., & Thompson, T. (1990). Gay and bisexual men: Developing a healthy identity. In D.

Moore & F. Leafgren (Eds.), *Men in conflict* (pp. 113–121). Alexandria, VA: American Counseling Association.

Pascoe, P. (1991). Race, gender, and intercultural relations: The case of interracial marriage. *Frontiers: A Journal of Women Studies, 12,* 5–18.

Paster, V. S. (1985). Adapting psychotherapy for the depressed, unacculturated, acting-out, Black male adolescent. *Psychotherapy, 22,* 408–417.

Pavkov, T. W., Lewis, D. A., & Lyons, J. S. (1989). Psychiatric diagnosis and racial bias: An empirical investigation. *Professional Psychology: Research & Practice, 20,* 364–368.

Pearson, J. C. (1985). *Gender and communication.* Dubuque, IA: W. C. Brown.

Pearson, R. E. (1985). The recognition and use of natural support systems in cross-cultural counseling. In P. B. Pedersen (Ed.), *Handbook of cross-cultural counseling and therapy* (pp. 299–306). Westport, CT: Greenwood Press.

Pearson, S. M., & Bieschke, K. J. (2001). Succeeding against the odds: An examination of familial influences on the career development of professional African women. *Journal of Counseling Psychology, 48,* 301–309.

Pedersen, P. B. (1988). *Handbook for developing multicultural awareness.* Alexandria, VA: American Association for Counseling and Development Press.

Pedersen, P. B. (1991a). Multiculturalism as a generic approach to counseling. *Journal of Counseling and Development, 70*(1), 6–12.

Pedersen, P. B. (1991b). Multiculturalism as a fourth force in counseling [Special issue]. *Journal of Counseling and Development, 70.*

Pedersen, P. B. (1994). *A handbook for developing multicultural awareness* (2nd ed.). Alexandria, VA: American Counseling Association.

Pedersen, P. B. (1999). *Multiculturalism as a fourth force.* Philadelphia, PA: Brunner/Mazel.

Pedersen, P. B. (2000). *A handbook for developing multicultural awareness.* Alexandria, VA: American Counseling Association.

People's Medical Society Newsletter. (1998). Are seniors being shortchanged? *People's Medical Society Newsletter, 17,* p. 1, 6.

Peyser, M., & Lorch, D. (2000). High school controversial. *Newsweek,* 54–56.

Phelps, R. E., Taylor, J. D., & Gerard, P. A. (2001). Cultural mistrust, ethnic identity, racial identity, and self-esteem among ethnically diverse Black university students. *Journal of Counseling and Development, 79,* 209–216.

Pinderhughes, C. A. (1973). Racism in psychotherapy. In C. Willie, B. Kramer, & B. Brown (Eds.), *Racism and mental health* (pp. 61–121). Pittsburgh, PA: University of Pittsburgh Press.

Pinderhughes, E. E., Dodge, K. A., Bates, J. E., Pettit, G. S., & Zelli, A. (2000). Discipline responses influences of parents' socioeconomic status, ethnicity, beliefs about parenting, stress, and cognitive-emotional processes. *Journal of Family Psychology, 14,* 380–400.

Pine, G. J. (1972). Counseling minority groups: A review of the literature. *Counseling and Values, 17,* 35–44.

Piotrkowski, C. S. (l998) Gender harassment, job satisfaction, and distress among employed White and minority women. *Journal of Occupational Health Psychology, 3,* 33–43.

Plomin, R. (1989). Environment and genes: Determinants of behavior. *American Psychologist, 44,* 105–111.

Plous, S., & Williams, T. (1995). Racial stereotypes from the days of American slavery: A continuing legacy. *Journal of Applied Social Psychology,* 795–817.

Pomales, J., Claiborn, C. D., & LaFromboise, T. D. (1986). Effects of Black students' racial identity on perceptions of White counselors varying in cultural sensitivity. *Journal of Counseling Psychology, 34,* 123–131.

Ponterotto, J. G. (1988). Racial consciousness development among white counselors' trainees: A stage model. *Journal of Multicultural Counseling and Development, 16,* 146–156.

Ponterotto, J. G., & Casas, J. M. (1987). In search of multicultural competence within counselor education programs. *Journal of Counseling and Development, 65,* 430–434.

Ponterotto, J. G., & Casas, J. M. (1991). *Handbook of racial/ethnic minority counseling research.* Springfield, IL: Charles C. Thomas.

Ponzo, Z. (1992). Promoting successful aging: Problems, opportunities, and counseling guidelines. *Journal of Counseling and Development, 71,* 210–213.

Pope-Davis, D. B., & Ottavi, T. M. (1994). Examining the association between self-reported multicultural counseling competencies and demographic and educational variables among counselors. *Journal of Counseling and Development, 72,* 651–654.

Population Reference Bureau. (1998). *Population bulletin.* Washington, DC: U.S. Government Printing Office.

Porterfield, E. (1982). *African American-American intermarriages in the United States.* New York: Haworth.

Poston, W. S. (1990). The biracial identity development model: A needed addition. *Journal of Counseling and Development, 69,* 152–155.

President's Commission on Mental Health. (1978). *Report from the President's Commission on Mental Health.* Washington, DC: U.S. Government Printing Office.

A provider's introduction to substance abuse treatment for lesbian, gay, bisexual, and transgender individuals. (2001). DHHS Publication SMA 01 3498. Washington, DC: U.S. Government Printing Office.

Qualls, S. H. (1998a). Marital therapy with later life couples. In D. R. Atkinson & G. Hackett (Eds.), *Counseling diverse populations* (2nd ed., pp. 199–216). Boston: McGraw-Hill.

Qualls, S. H. (1998b). Training in geropsychology: Preparing to meet the demand. *Professional Psychology: Research and Practice, 29,* 23–28.

Queener, J. E., & Martin, J. K. (2001). Providing culturally relevant mental health services: Collaboration between psychology and the African American church. *Journal of Black Psychology, 27,* 112–122.

Rabasca, L. (1999). Guidelines for spinal cord injuries don't go far enough. *APA Monitor, 30,* 1–2.

Ramirez, D. A. (1996). Multiracial identity in a color-conscious world. In M. P. P. Root (Ed.). *The multiracial experience: Racial borders as the new frontier* (pp. 49–62). Newbury Park, CA: Sage.

Ramos-McKay, J. M., Comas-Diaz, L., & Rivera, L. A. (1988). Puerto Ricans. In L. Comas-Diaz & E. E. H. Griffith (Eds.), *Clinical Guidelines in*

Cross-Cultural Mental Health (pp. 204–232). New York: Wiley.

Ramsey, S., & Birk, J. (1983). Preparation of North Americans for interaction with Japanese: Considerations of language and communication style. In D. Landis & R. W. Brislin (Eds.), *Handbook of intercultural training: Volume III* (pp. 227–259). New York: Pergamon.

Rash of Indian teen suicides. (1998, Feb. 8). *The Bellingham Herald*, p. A5.

Red Horse, J. G. (1983). Indian family values and experiences. In G. J. Powell, J. Yamamoto, A. Romero, & A. Morales (Eds.), *The psychosocial development of minority group children* (pp. 258–272). New York: Brunner/Mazel.

Red Horse, J. G., Lewis, R., Feit, M., & Decker, J. (1981). In R. H. Dana (ed.), *Human services for cultural minorities*. Baltimore: University Park Press.

Red Horse, Y. (1982). A cultural network model: Perspectives for adolescent services and paraprofessional training. In S. M. Manson (Ed.), *New directions in prevention among American Indian and Alaska Native Communities* (pp. 173–184). Portland, OR: Oregon Health Sciences University.

Reiss, B. F. (1980). Psychological tests in homosexuality. In J. Marmor (Ed.), *Homosexual behavior: A modern reappraisal* (pp. 296–311). New York: Basic Books.

Retish, P. & Kavanaugh, P. (1992). Myth: America's public schools are educating Mexican American students. *Journal of Multicultural Counseling and Development, 20,* 89–96.

Reynolds, A. L. (2001). Multidimensional cultural competence: Providing tools for transforming psychology. *The Counseling Psychologist, 29,* 833–841.

Reynolds, C. F., III, Dew, M. A., Frank, B., & Begley, A. E. (1998). Effects of age at onset of first life-time episode of recurrent major depression on treatment response and illness course in elderly patients. *American Journal of Psychiatry, 155,* 795–799.

Richardson, L., & MacGregor, H. E. (2001, April 30). To be Chinese in America: A poll finds that Chinese Americans are still viewed in a "very negative" light. *The Los Angeles Times,* p. E1.

Ridley, C. R. (1984). Clinical treatment of the nondisclosing Black client. *American Psychologist, 39,* 1234–1244.

Ridley, C. R. (1995). *Overcoming unintentional racism in counseling and therapy: A practitioner's guide to intentional intervention.* Thousand Oaks, CA: Sage.

Riessman, F. (1962). *The culturally deprived child.* New York: Harper & Row.

Ritter, K. Y., & O'Neill, C. W. (1989). Moving through loss: The spiritual journey of gay men and lesbian women. *Journal of Counseling and Development, 68,* 9–15.

Rivera, A. N. (1984). *Toward a psychotherapy for Puerto Ricans.* Rio Piederis, PR: CEDEPP.

Roberts, R. E., Kaplan, G. A., Shema, S. J., & Strawbridge, W. J. (1997). Does growing old increase the risk for depression? *American Journal of Psychiatry, 154,* 1384–1390.

Roberts, R. E., & Sobhan, M. (1992). Symptoms of depression in adolescence: A comparison of Anglo, African, and Hispanic Americans. *Journal of Youth and Adolescents, 21,* 639–650.

Robins, L. N., & Regier, D. A. (1991). *Psychiatric disorders in America.* New York: The Free Press.

Robinson, L. (1998, May 11). "Hispanics" don't exist. *US. News & World Report, 124,* 26–32.

Robinson, T. L., & Howard-Hamilton, M. F. (2000). *The convergence of race, ethnicity, and gender.* Columbus, OH: Merrill.

Rodriguez, N., Ryan, S. W., Vande Kemp, H., & Foy, D. W. (1997). Posttraumatic stress disorder in adult female survivors of child sexual abuse: A comparison study. *Journal of Consulting and Clinical Psychology, 65,* 53–59.

Rogers, C. (1980). *A way of being.* Boston: Houghton Mifflin.

Rogers, C. R. (1961). *On becoming a person.* Boston: Houghton Mifflin.

Rogler, L. H., Malgady, R. G., Constantino, G., & Blumenthal, R. (1987). What do culturally sensitive mental health services mean? The case of Hispanics. *American Psychologist, 42,* 565–570.

Romero, D. (1985). Cross-cultural counseling: Brief reactions for the practitioner. *The Counseling Psychologist, 13,* 665–671.

Roose, S. P. (2001). Men over 50: An endangered species. Psychiatry Clinical Updates. Medscape Inc.

Root, M. P. P. (1990). Resolving "other" status: Identity development of biracial individuals. In L. S. Borwn & M. P. P. Root (Eds.), *Diversity and complexity in feminist therapy* (pp. 185–205). New York: Haworth.

Root, M. P. P. (Ed.). (1992). *Racially mixed people in America.* Thousand Oaks, CA: Sage.

Root, M. P. P. (Ed.). (1996). *The multiracial experience.* Thousand Oaks, CA: Sage.

Root, M. P. P. (1998). Facilitating psychotherapy with Asian American clients. In D. R. Atkinson, G. Morten, & D. W. Sue (Eds.), *Counseling American Minorities: A Cross-Cultural Perspective* (pp. 214–234). Boston: McGraw-Hill.

Root, M. P. P. (2001). Negotiating the margins. In J. G. Ponterotto, J. M. Casas, L. A. Suzuki, & C. M. Alexander (Eds.). *Handbook of multicultural counseling.* Thousand Oaks, CA: Sage.

Rosenblatt, P. C., Karis, T. A., & Powell, R. D. (1995). *Multiracial couples.* Thousand Oaks, CA: Sage.

Rosenthal, R., & Jacobson, L. (1968). *Pygmalion in the classroom.* New York: Holt, Rinehart, & Winston.

Rotter, J. (1966). Generalized expectancies for internal versus external control of reinforcement. *Psychological Monographs, 80,* 1–28.

Rotter, J. (1975). Some problems and misconceptions related to the construct of internal versus external control of reinforcement. *Journal of Consulting and Clinical Psychology, 43,* 56–67.

Rouse, B. A., Carter, J. H., & Rodriguez-Andrew, S. (1995). Race/ethnicity and other sociocultural influences on alcoholism treatment for women. *Recent developments in alcoholism, 12,* 343–367.

Rowe, W., Bennett, S., & Atkinson, D. R. (1994). White racial identity models: A critique and alternative proposal. *The Counseling Psychologist, 22,* 120–146.

Rudman, L. A. (1998). Self-promotion as a risk factor for women: The costs and benefits of counter-stereotypical impression management. *Journal of Personality and Social Psychology, 74,* 629–645.

Ruiz, A. (1981). Cultural and historical perspectives in counseling Hispanics. In D. W. Sue (Ed.), *Counseling the culturally different: Theory & practice* (pp. 186–215). New York: Wiley.

Ruiz, A. S. (1990). Ethnic identity: Crisis and resolution. *Journal of Multicultural Counseling and Development, 18,* 29–40.

Ruiz, P. (1995). Assessing, diagnosing and treating culturally diverse individuals: A Hispanic perspective. *Psychiatric Quarterly, 66,* 329–341.

Russell, S. (1988). *At home among strangers.* Washington, DC: Gallaudet University Press.

Russell, S. T., Franz, B. T., & Driscoll, A. K. (2001). Same-sex romantic attraction and experience of violence in adolescence. *American Journal of Public Health, 91,* 903–906.

Russell, S. T., & Joyner, K. (2001). Suicide attempts more likely among adolescents with same-sex sexual orientation. *American Journal of Public Health, 91,* 1276–1281.

Russo, N. F., & Denious, J. E. (2001). Violence in the lives of women having abortions: Implications for practice and public policy. *Professional Psychology: Research and Practice, 32,* 142–150.

Rutter, M. (1991). Nature, nurture, and psychopathology: A new look at an old topic. *Developmental Psychopathology, 3,* 125–136.

Ryan, A. (1995). Apocalypse now? In R. Jacoby & N. Glauberman (Eds.), *The bell curve debate* (pp. 14–29). New York: Times Book.

Ryan, C., & Futterman, D. (2001a). Experience, vulnerabilities and risks of lesbian and gay students. *The Prevention Researcher, 8,* 6–8.

Ryan, C., & Futterman, D. (2001b). Lesbian and gay adolescents: Identity development. *The Prevention Researcher, 8,* 1–5.

Ryan, W. (1971). *Blaming the victim.* New York: Pantheon.

Sabnani, H. B., Ponterotto, J. G., & Borodovsky, L. G. (1991). White racial identity development and cross-cultural counselor training. *The Counselor Psychologist, 19,* 76–102.

Sage, G. P. (1997). Counseling American Indian adults. In C. C. Lee (Ed.), *Multicultural issues in counseling* (2nd ed., pp. 35–52). Alexandria, VA: American Counseling Association.

Samovar, L. A., & Porter, R. E. (1982). *Intercultural*

communication: A reader. Belmont, CA: Wadsworth.

Samuda, R. J. (1975). From ethnocentrism to a multicultural perspective in educational testing. *Journal of Afro-American Issues, 3,* 4–18.

Samuda, R. J. (1998). *Psychological testing of American minorities.* Thousand Oaks, CA: Sage.

Sandhu, D. S. (1997). Psychocultural profiles of Asian and Pacific Islander Americans: Implications for counseling and psychotherapy. *Journal of Multicultural Counseling and Development, 25,* 7–22.

Sands, T. (1998). Feminist counseling and female adolescents: Treatment strategies for depression. *Journal of Mental Health Counseling, 20,* 42–54.

San Francisco Chronicle. (2001, March 12). *San Francisco Chronicle,* pp. A1, A 17.

Sanger, S. P., & Alker, H. A. (1972). Dimensions of internal-external locus of control and the women's liberation movement. *Journal of Social Issues, 28,* 15–129.

Satir, V. (1967). *Conjoint family therapy.* Palo Alto, CA: Science & Behavior Books.

Satir, V. (1983). *Conjoint family therapy* (3rd ed.). Palo Alto, CA: Science and Behavior Books.

Saunders, P. A. (1998). "My brain's on strike." The construction of identity through memory accounts by dementia patients. *Research on Aging, 20,* 65–90.

Saxton, L. (1968). *The individual, marriage, and the family.* Belmont, CA: Wadsworth.

Schein, E. H. (1990). Organizational Culture. *American Psychologist, 45(2),* 109–119.

Schindler-Rainman, E. (1967). The poor and the PTA. *PTA Magazine, 61(8),* 4–5.

Schinke, S. P., Schilling, R. F., II, Gilchrist, L. D., Barth, R. P., Bobo, J. K., Trimble, J. E., & Cvetkovich, G. T. (1985). Preventing substance abuse with American Indian youth. *Social Casework, 66,* 213–217.

Schmidt, L. D., & Strong, S. R. (1971). Attractiveness and influence in counseling. *Journal of Counseling Psychology, 18,* 348–351.

Schneider, K. T., Swan, S., & Fitzgerald, L. F. (1997). Job-related and psychological effects of sexual harassment in the workplace: Empirical evidence from two organizations. *Journal of Applied Psychology, 82,* 401–415.

Schofield, W. (1964). *Psychotherapy: The purchase of friendship.* Englewood Cliffs, NJ: Prentice Hall.

Schwartzman, J. B., & Glaus, K. D. (2000). Depression and coronary heart disease in women: Implications for clinical practice and research. *Professional Psychology: Research and Practice, 31,* 48–57.

Seattle Public Schools. (1986). *Disproportionality task force preliminary report.* Seattle: Seattle Public Schools.

Seem, S. R., & Johnson, B. (1998). Gender bias among counseling trainees: A study of case conceptualization. *Counselor Education and Supervision, 37,* 257–268.

Seligman, M. E. P. (1982). *Helplessness: On depression, development and death.* San Francisco: Freeman.

Seligman, M. E. P., & Csikszentmihalyi, M. (2000). Positive psychology: An introduction. *American Psychologist, 55,* 5–14.

Seligman, M. E. P., & Csikszentmihalyi, M. (2001). Reply to comments. *American Psychologist, 56,* 89–90.

Serrano, R. A. (1998, March 4). Study counts record number of hate groups, 20% jump in year. *San Francisco Chronicle,* p. A5.

Shade, B. J., & New, C. A. (1993). Cultural influences on learning: Teaching implications. In J. A. Banks & C. A. McGee Banks (Eds.), *Multicultural Education* (pp. 317–331). Boston: Allyn Bacon.

Shannon, J. W., & Woods, W. J. (1998). Affirmative psychotherapy for gay men. In D. R. Atkinson & G. Hackett (Eds.), *Counseling diverse populations* (2nd ed., pp. 335–351). Boston: McGraw-Hill.

Shapiro, D. H. (1982). Overview: Clinical and physiological comparison of meditation with other self control strategies. *American Journal of Psychiatry, 139,* 267–274.

Shine, K. I. (1984). Anxiety in patients with heart disease. *Psychosomatics, 25,* 27–31.

Shockley, W. (1972). Determination of human intelligence. *Journal of Criminal Law and Criminology, 7,* 530–543.

Shook, V. E. (1985). *Ho'oponopono.* Honolulu, HI: University of Hawaii Press.

Shorter-Gooden, K., & Washington, N. C. (1996). Young, Black, and female: The challenge of weaving an identity. *Journal of Adolescence, 19,* 465–475.

Shostrom, E. L. (Producer). (1966). *Three approaches to psychotherapy: II* [Film]. Santa Ana, CA: Psychological Films.

Shuey, A. (1966). *The testing of Negro intelligence.* New York: Social Science Press.

Shukovsky, P. (1998, April 8). Indians, neighbors square off: Drums, singing enliven hearing on Gorton bill. *Seattle Post-Intelligencer,* p. B1.

Shukovsky, P. (2001, March 29). "Urban Indians" are going home. *Seattle Post-Intelligencer,* pp. A1, A13.

Silverman, J. G., Raj, A., Mucci, L. A., & Hathaway, J. E. (2001). Dating violence against adolescent girls and associated substance use, unhealthy weight control, sexual risk behavior, pregnancy, and suicidality. *Journal of the American Medical Association, 286,* 572–579.

Singelis, T. (1994). Nonverbal communication in intercultural interactions. In R. W. Brislin & T. Yoshida (Eds.), *Improving intercultural interactions* (pp. 268–294). Thousand Oaks, CA: Sage.

Skolnik, S. (2001, November 2). Same-sex estate rights backed. *The Seattle Post-Intelligencer,* p. B1.

Sleek, S. (1998, July). Mental disabilities no barrier to smooth and efficient work. *Monitor,* p. 15.

Smalley, W. A. (1984). Adoptive language strategies of the Hmong: From Asian mountains to American ghettos. *Language Science, 1,* 241–269.

Smith, E. J. (1981). Cultural and historical perspectives in counseling Blacks. In D. W. Sue (Ed.), *Counseling the culturally different: Theory and practice* (pp. 141–185). New York: Wiley.

Smith, E. J. (1991). Ethnic identity development: Toward the development of a theory within the context of majority/minority status. *Journal of Counseling and Development, 70,* 181–188.

Smith, M. E. (1957). Progress in the use of English after twenty-two years by children of Chinese ancestry in Honolulu. *Journal of Genetic Psychology, 90,* 255–258.

Smith, M. E., & Kasdon, L. M. (1961). Progress in the use of English after twenty years by children of Filipino and Japanese ancestry in Hawaii. *Journal of Genetic Psychology, 99,* 129–138.

Smothers, R. (1998, June 22). Church blesses union of 2 men in adoption case. *New York Times,* p. 5.

Snowden, L. R., & Cheung, F. H. (1990). Use of inpatient mental health services by members of ethnic minority groups. *American Psychologist, 45,* 347–355.

Sodowsky, G. R., Kwan, K. K., & Pannu, R. (1995). Ethnic identity of Asians in the United States. In J. G. Ponterotto, J. M. Casas, L. A. Suzuki, & C. M. Alexander (Eds.), *Handbook of multicultural counseling* (pp. 123–154). Thousand Oaks, CA: Sage.

Spiegel, J., & Papajohn, J. (1983). *Final report: Training program on ethnicity and mental health.* Waltham, MA: The Florence Heller School, Branders University.

Spiegel, S. B. (1976). Expertness, similarity, and perceived counselor competence. *Journal of Counseling Psychology, 23,* 436–441.

Sprafkin, R. P. (1970). Communicator expertness and changes in word meaning in psychological treatment. *Journal of Counseling Psychology, 17,* 191–196.

Stanback, M. H., & Pearce, W. B. (1985). Talking to "the man": Some communication strategies used by members of "subordinate" social groups. In L. A. Samovar & R. E. Porter (Eds.), *Intercultural communication: A reader* (pp. 236–253). Belmont, CA: Wadsworth.

Steele, C. M. (1997). A threat in the air: How stereotypes shape intellectual identity and performance. *American Psychologist, 52,* 613–629.

Steele, C. M., & Aronson, J. (1995). Stereotype threat and the intellectual test performance of African Americans. *Journal of Personality and Social Psychology, 69,* 797–811.

Steinberg, L. (1998, July 18). A summer of promise: YMCA camp helps adolescent girls gain confidence in themselves and their abilities. *Seattle Post-Intelligencer*, p. Cl.

Stewart, A. J., & Ostrove, J. M. (1998). Women's personality in middle age: Gender, history, and midcourse corrections. *American Psychologist, 53,* 1185–1194.

Stewart, E. C. (1971). *American cultural patterns: A cross-cultural perspective.* Pittsburgh, PA: Regional Council for International Understanding.

Stice, E., & Bearman, S. K. (2001). Body-image and eating disturbances prospectively predict increases in depressive symptoms in adolescent girls: A growth curve analysis. *Developmental Psychology, 37,* 597–607.

Stice, E., Shaw, H., & Nemeroff, C. (1998). Dual pathway model of bulimia nervosa: Longitudinal support for dietary restraint and affect-regulation mechanisms. *Journal of Social and Clinical Psychology, 17,* 129–149.

Stoltenberg, C. C., McNeill, B. W., & Elliot, T. R. (1995). Selected translations of social psychology to counseling psychology. *The Counseling Psychologist, 23,* 603–610.

Stonequist, E. V. (1937). *The marginal man.* New York: Charles Scribner's Sons.

Strawbridge, W. J., Cohen, R. D., Shema, S. J., & Kaplan, G. A. (1997). Frequent attendance at religious services and mortality over 28 years. *American Journal of Public Health, 87,* 957–961.

Strickland, B. (1971). Aspiration responses among Negro and White adolescents. *Journal of Personality and Social Psychology, 19,* 315–320.

Strickland, B. (1973). Delay of gratification and internal locus of control in children. *Journal of Counseling and Clinical Psychology, 40,* 338.

Strickland, B. R. (1995). Research on sexual orientation and human development: A commentary. *Developmental Psychology, 31,* 137–140.

Strickland, B. R. (2000). Misassumptions, misadventures, and the misuse of psychology. *American Psychologist, 55,* 331–338.

Strock, C. (1998, May 18). A painful discovery. *Newsweek*, p. 16.

Strong, S. R. (1969). Counseling: An interpersonal influence process. *Journal of Counseling Psychology, 15,* 215–224.

Strong, S. R., & Schmidt, L. D. (1970). Expertness and influence in counseling. *Journal of Counseling Psychology, 15,* 31–35.

Sudarkasa, N. (1988). Interpreting the African heritage in Afro-American family organization. In H. P. McAdoo (Ed.), *Black families* (pp. 27–43). Newbury Park, CA: Sage.

Sue, D. (1990). Culture in transition: Counseling Asian-American men. In D. Moore and F. Leafgren (Eds.), *Men in conflict* (pp. 53–165). Alexandria, VA: American Association for Counseling and Development.

Sue, D. (1994). Incorporating cultural diversity in family therapy. *The Family Psychologist, 10,* 19–21.

Sue, D. (1997). Counseling strategies for Chinese Americans. In C. C . Lee (Ed.), *Multicultural issues in counseling* (2nd ed., pp. 173–187). Alexandria, VA: American Counseling Association.

Sue, D. (1997). Multicultural training. *International Journal of Intercultural Relations, 21,* 175–193.

Sue, D., Ino, S., & Sue, D. W. (1983). Nonassertiveness of Asian Americans: An inaccurate assumption? *Journal of Counseling Psychology, 30,* 581–588.

Sue, D., Sue, D. W., & Ino, S. (1990). Assertiveness and social anxiety in Chinese-American women. *Journal of Psychology, 124,* 155–164.

Sue, D., Sue, D. W., & Sue, S. (1994). *Understanding abnormal behavior* (4th ed.). Boston: Houghton Mifflin.

Sue, D., Sue, D. W., & Sue, S. (1997). *Understanding abnormal behavior* (5th ed.). Boston: Houghton Mifflin.

Sue, D., Sue, D. W., & Sue, S. (2000). *Understanding abnormal behavior* (6th ed.). Boston: Houghton Mifflin.

Sue, D. W. (1977a). Barriers to effective cross-cultural counseling. *Journal of Counseling Psychology, 24,* 420–429.

Sue, D. W. (1977b). Counseling the culturally different: A conceptual analysis. *Personnel and Guidance Journal, 55,* 422–424.

Sue, D. W. (1978). Eliminating cultural oppression in counseling: Toward a general theory. *Journal of Counseling Psychology, 25,* 419–428.

Sue, D. W. (1981). Evaluating process variables in cross-cultural counseling and psychotherapy. In A. J. Marsell & P. B. Pedersen (Eds.), *Cross-cultural counseling and psychotherapy.* New York: Pergamon.

Sue, D. W. (1990). Culture specific techniques in counseling: A conceptual framework. *Professional Psychology, 21,* 424–433.

Sue, D. W. (1991a). A conceptual model for cultural diversity training. *Journal of Counseling and Development, 70,* 99–105.

Sue, D. W. (1991b). A diversity perspective on contextualism. *Journal of Counseling and Development, 70,* 300–301.

Sue, D. W. (1992). The challenge of multiculturalism: The road less traveled. *American Counselor, 1,* 7–14.

Sue, D. W. (1993). Confronting ourselves: The White and racial/ethnic minority researcher. *The Counseling Psychologist, 21,* 244–249.

Sue, D. W. (1994). Asian-American mental health and help-seeking behavior: Comment on Solberg et al. (1994), Tata and Leong (1994), and Lin (1994). *Journal of Counseling Psychology, 41,* 292–295.

Sue, D. W. (1994). U.S. business and the challenge of cultural diversity. *The Diversity Factor,* pp.24–28.

Sue, D. W. (1995a). Multicultural organizational development: Implications for the counseling profession. In J. G. Ponterotto, J. M. Casas, L. A. Suzuki, & C. M. Alexander (Eds.), (pp. 474–492). Thousand Oaks, CA: Sage.

Sue, D. W. (1995b). Toward a theory of multicultural counseling and therapy. In J. A. Banks & C. A. M. Banks (Eds.), *Handbook of research on multicultural education* (pp. 647–659). New York: Macmillan.

Sue, D. W. (1997). Multiculturalism and discomfort, *Spectrum, 57*(3), 7–9.

Sue, D. W. (2001). Multidimensional facets of cultural competence. *The Counseling Psychologist, 29,* 790–821.

Sue, D. W. (2002). *You are a racist: The painful journey to understanding and combating racism.* Manuscript in preparation.

Sue, D. W. (in press). Racial-cultural competence: Awareness, knowledge, and skills. In R. T. Carter (Ed.), *Handbook of multicultural psychology and education.* New York: Wiley.

Sue, D. W., Arredondo, P., & McDavis, R. J. (1992). Multicultural competencies/standards: A call to the profession. *Journal of Counseling and Development, 70*(4), 477–486.

Sue, D. W., Bingham, R., Porche-Burke, L., & Vasquez, M. (1999). The diversification of psychology: A multicultural revolution. *American Psychologist, 54,* 1061–1069.

Sue, D. W., Bernier, J. B., Durran, M., Feinberg, L., Pedersen, P., Smith, E., & Vasquez-Nuttall, E. (1982). Position paper: Cross-cultural counseling competencies. *The Counseling Psychologist, 10,* 45–52.

Sue, D. W., Carter, R. T., Casas, J. M., Fouad, N. A., Ivey, A. E., Jensen, M., LaFromboise, T., Manese, J. E., Ponterotto, J. G., & Vasquez-Nuttall, E. (1998). *Multicultural counseling competencies: Individual and organizational development.* Thousand Oaks, CA: Sage.

Sue, D. W., & Constantine, M. (in press). Optimal human functioning among racial-ethnic minorities. In B. Walsh (Ed.), *Counseling psychology and optimal human functioning.* Mahwah, NJ: Erlbaum.

Sue, D. W., & Frank, A. C. (1973). A topological approach to the study of Chinese- and Japanese-American college males. *Journal of Social Issues, 29,* 129–148.

Sue, D. W., Ivey, A. E., & Pedersen, P. B. (1996). *A theory of multicultural counseling and therapy.* Pacific Grove, CA: Brooks Cole.

Sue, D. W., & Kirk, B. A. (1973). Differential characteristics of Japanese-American and Chinese-American college students. *Journal of Counseling Psychology, 20,* 142–148.

Sue, D. W., & Kirk, B. A. (1975). Asian Americans: Use of counseling and psychiatric services on a college campus. *Journal of Counseling Psychology, 22,* 84–86.

Sue, D. W., & Sue, D. (1972). Ethnic minorities: Resistance to being researched. *Professional Psychology, 2,* 11–17.

Sue, D. W., & Sue, D. (1973). Understanding Asian Americans: The neglected minority. *Personnel and Guidance Journal, 51,* 386–389.

Sue, D. W., & Sue, D. (1977). Barriers to effective cross-cultural counseling. *Journal of Counseling Psychology, 24,* 420–429.

Sue, D. W., & Sue, D. (1977b). Ethnic minorities: Failures and responsibilities of the social sciences. *Journal of Non-White Concerns in Personnel and Guidance, 5,* 99–106.

Sue, D. W., & Sue, D. (1990): *Counseling the culturally different: Theory and practice.* New York: Wiley.

Sue, D. W., & Sue, D. (1999). Counseling the culturally different: Theory and practice (3rd ed.). New York: Wiley.

Sue, D. W., & Sue, S. (1972). Counseling Chinese-Americans. *Personnel & Guidance Journal, 50,* 637–644.

Sue, S. (1977). Community mental health services to minority groups: Some optimism, some pessimism. *American Psychologist, 32,* 616–624.

Sue, S. (1999). Science, ethnicity and bias: Where have we gone wrong? *American Psychologist, 54,* 1070–1077.

Sue, S., Allen, D., & Conaway, L. (1975). The responsiveness and equality of mental health care to Chicanos and Native Americans. *American Journal of Community Psychology, 45,* 111–118.

Sue, S., Fujino, D. C., Hu, L., Takeuchi, D. T., & Zane, N. W. S. (1991). Community mental health services for ethnic minority groups: A test of the cultural responsiveness hypothesis. *Journal of Consulting and Clinical Psychology, 59,* 533–540.

Sue, S., & Kitano, H. H. L. (1973). Stereotypes as a measure of success. *Journal of Social Issues, 29,* 83–98.

Sue, S., & McKinney, H. (1974). Delivery of community health services to black and white clients. *Journal of Consulting and Clinical Psychology, 42,* 794–801.

Sue, S., & McKinney, H. (1975). Asian Americans in the community mental health care system. *American Journal of Orthopsychiatry, 45,* 111–118.

Sue, S., McKinney, H., Allen, D., & Hall, J. (1974). Delivery of community health services to Black & White clients. *Journal of Consulting Psychology, 42,* 794–801.

Sue, S., & Sue, D. W. (1971 a). Chinese-American personality and mental health. *Amerasian Journal, 1,* 36–49.

Sue, S., & Sue, D. W. (1971 b). *The reflection of culture conflicts in the psychological problems of Chinese and Japanese students.* Paper presented at the American Psychological Association Convention, Honolulu, HI.

Sue, S. & Sue, D. W. (1972). Chinese American personality and mental health: A reply to Tong's criticisms. *Amerasian Journal, 1,* 60–65.

Sue, S., Sue, D. W., & Sue, D. (1975). Asian Americans as a minority group. *American Psychologist, 31,* 906–910.

Sue, S., Sue, D. W., Sue, L. & Takeuchi, D. T. (1995). Psychopathology among Asian Americans: A model minority? *Cultural diversity and mental health, 1,* 39–51.

Sue, S., & Zane, N. W. S. (1985). Academic achievement and socioemotional adjustment among Chinese university students. *Journal of Counseling Psychology, 32,* 913–920.

Sue, S., & Zane, N. (1987). The role of culture and cultural techniques in psychotherapy: A reformation. *American Psychologist, 42,* 37–45.

Sullivan, K. R., & Mahalik, J. R. (2000). Increasing career self-efficacy for women: Evaluating a group intervention. *Journal of Counseling and Development, 78,* 54–62.

Sun, L. H. (1997, September 11). Asian names scrutinized at White House; guards stopped citizens who looked "foreign." *The Washington Post,* p. A1.

Sundberg, N. D. (1981). Cross-cultural counseling and psychotherapy: A research overview. In A. J. Mansella & P. B. Pedersen (Eds.), *Cross-cultural counseling and psychotherapy* (pp. 29–38). New York: Pergamon.

Surgeon General. (2000). Supplement to *Mental health: A report of the Surgeon General—Disparities in mental health care for racial and ethnic minorities.* Washington, DC: U.S. Public Health Service.

Susman, N. M., & Rosenfeld, H. M. (1982). Influence of culture, language and sex on conversation distance. *Journal of Personality and Social Psychology, 42,* 66–74.

Sutton, C. T., & Broken Nose, M. (1996). American Indian families: An overview In M. McGoldrick, J. Giordano, & J. K. Pearce (Eds.), *Ethnicity and family therapy* (pp. 31–54). New York: Guilford Press.

Swinomish Tribal Mental Health Project. (1991). *A gathering of wisdoms.* LaConner, WA: Sinomish Tribal Community.

Szapocznik, J., & Kurtines, W. M. (1993). Family psychology and cultural diversity: Opportunities for theory, research, and application. *American Psychologist, 48,* 400–407.

Szapocznik, J., Santisteban, D., Kurtines, W. M., Hervis, O. E., & Spencer, F. (1982). Life enhancements counseling: A psychosocial model of services for Cuban elders. In E. E. Jones & S. J. Korchin (Eds.), *Minority mental health* (pp. 296–329). New York: Praeger.

Szapocznik, J., Scopetta, M. A., Kurtines, W., & Aranalde, M. A. (1978). Theory and measurement of acculturation. *International Journal of Psychology, 12,* 113–130.

Szasz, T. S. (1970). The crime of commitment. In *Readings in clinical psychology today* (pp. 167–169). Del Mar, CA: CRM Books.

Szasz, T. S. (1971). *The myth of mental illness.* New York: Hoeber.

Szasz, T. S. (1987). The case against suicide prevention. *American Psychologist, 41,* 806–812.

Szasz, T. S. (1999). *Fatal freedom: The ethics and politics of suicide.* Westport, CT: Praeger.

Taggart, C. (2001, October 14). Disability for a day is enlightening. *Spokesman Review,* p. B1.

Talvi, S. J. A. (1997). The silent epidemic: The challenge of HIV prevention within communities of color. *The Humanist, 57,* 6–10.

Tart, C. (1986). *Waking up: Overcoming the obstacles to human potential.* Boston: New Science Library.

Taylor, M. J. (2000). The influence of self-efficacy on alcohol use among American Indians. *Cultural Diversity and Ethnic Minority Psychology, 6,* 152–167.

Tepper, M. S. (2001). *Sexual healing with a disability.* Sexual Health Network. Available at www.sexualhealth.com.

Terman, L. M. (1916). *The measurement of intelligence.* Boston: Houghton Mifflin.

Thigpen, C. H., & Cleckley, H. M. (1954). A case of multiple personality. *Journal of Abnormal Social Psychology, 49,* 135–151.

Thomas, A. (2001). The multidimensional character of bias perceptions of individuals with disabilities. *Journal of Rehabilitation, 67,* 3–9.

Thomas, A., & Sillen, S. (1972). *Racism and psychiatry.* New York: Brunner/Mazel.

Thomas, A. J. (2000). Impact of racial identity on African American child-rearing beliefs. *Journal of Black Psychology, 26,* 317–329.

Thomas, C. W. (1970). Different strokes for different folks. *Psychology Today, 4,* 49–53, 80.

Thomas, C. W. (1971). *Boys no more.* Beverly Hills, CA: Glencoe Press.

Thomas, M. B., & Dansby, P. G. (1985). Black clients: Family structures, therapeutic issues, and strengths. *Psychotherapy, 22,* 398–407.

Thomason, T. C. (2000). Issues in the treatment of Native Americans with alcohol problems. *Journal of Multicultural Counseling and Development, 28,* 243–252.

Thompson, C. E. (1995). Helms' White racial identity development (WRID) theory: Another look. *The Counseling Psychologist, 22,* 645–649.

Thoresen, C. E. (1998). Spirituality, health and science: The coming revival? In S. R. Roemer, S. R. Kurpius, & C. Carmin (Eds.), *The emerging role of counseling psychology in health care.* New York: Norton.

Thurow, L. (1995, November 19). Why their world might crumble. *New York Times Magazine.*

Tilove, J. (2001, July 11). Gap in Black-White views growing, poll finds. *Seattle Post-Intelligencer,* p. A1.

Toarmino, D., & Chun, C.-A. (1997). Issues and strategies in counseling Korean Americans. In C. C. Lee (Ed.), *Multicultural issues in counseling* (2nd ed., pp. 233–254).

Tobin, J. J., & Friedman, J. (1983). Spirits, shamans, and nightmare death: Survivor stress in a Hmong refugee. *American Journal of Orthopsychiatry, 53,* 439–448.

Tofoya, N., & Del Vecchio, A. (1996). Back to the future: An examination of the Native American Holocaust. In M. McGoldrick, J. Giordano, & J. K. Pearce (Eds), *Ethnicity and family therapy* (pp. 45–54). New York: Guilford.

Toomer, J. E. (1982). Counseling psychologists in business and industry. *The Counseling Psychologist, 10,* 9–18.

Torres, M. M. (1998). *Understanding the multiracial*

experience through children's literature: A protocol. Unpublished doctoral dissertation, California School of Professional Psychology, Alameda.

Tortolero, S. R., & Roberts, R. E. (2001). Differences in nonfatal suicide behaviors among Mexican and European American middle school children. *Suicide and Life Threatening Behavior, 31,* 214–223.

Trevino, J. G. (1996). Worldview and change in cross-cultural counseling. *The Counseling Psychologist, 24,* 198–215.

Triandis, H. C. (2000). Cultural syndromes and subjective well-being. In E. Diener & E. M. Suh (Eds.), *Culture and subjective well-being.* London: MIT Press.

Trimble, J. E. (1990). Application of psychological knowledge for American Indians and Alaska Natives. *The Journal of Training and Practice in Professional Psychology, 4,* 45–63.

Trimble, J. E., Fleming, C. M., Beauvais, F., & Jumper-Thurman, P. (1996). Essential cultural and social strategies for counseling Native American Indians. In P. B. Pedersen, J. G. Draguns, W. J. Lonner, & J. E. Trimble (Eds.), *Counseling across cultures* (4th ed., pp. 177–209). Thousand Oaks, CA: Sage Publications.

Tsui, P., & Schultz, G. L. (1985). Failure of rapport: When psychotherapeutic engagement fails in the treatment of Asian clients. *American Journal of Orthopsychiatry, 55,* 561–569.

Tulkin, S. (1968). Race, class, family and school achievement. *Journal of Personality and Social Psychology, 9,* 31–37.

Tune, L. (2001). Assessing psychiatric illness in geriatric patients. *Clinical Cornerstone, 3,* 23–36.

Turner, C. B., & Wilson, W. J. (1976). Dimensions of racial ideology: A study of urban Black attitudes. *Journal of Social Issues 32,* 193–252.

Uba, L. (1994). *Asian Americans.* New York: Guilford Press.

United Cerebral Palsy. (2001). *Etiquette tips for people with physical disabilities.* Portland, OR: Author.

U.S. Bureau of the Census. (1992). *Statistical abstract of the United States: The national data book* (112th ed.). Washington, DC: Bureau of the Census.

U.S. Bureau of the Census. (1995). *Population profile of the United States.* Washington, DC: U.S. Government Printing Office.

U.S. Bureau of the Census. (2000). *Data highlights.* Available at www.census.gov.

U.S. Bureau of the Census. (2001). *Population profile of the United States.* Washington, DC: U.S. Government Printing Office.

U.S. Department of Commerce. (1997). *Census Bureau current population reports,* Series P-60. Washington, DC: U.S. Government Printing Office.

U.S. Department of Commerce. (2001). *Profiles of general demographic characteristics 2000.* Washington, DC: U.S. Government Printing Office.

U.S. Department of Commerce. (1998). *Census Bureau current population reports,* Series P-60, Selected Issues. Washington, DC: U.S. Government Printing Office.

U.S. Department of Education. (1987). *Percent of minority enrollment in U.S. colleges and universities, Fall 1968–1984.* State Task Force on Minority Student Achievement. Washington, DC: U.S. Government Printing Office.

U.S. Department of Health and Human Services. (1998). *The national elder abuse incidence study.* Washington, DC: U.S. Government Printing Office.

U.S. Department of Labor. (1998). *Bureau of Labor Statistics.* Washington, DC: U.S. Government Printing Office.

U.S. Public Health Service. (1999). *Mental health: A report of the surgeon general.* Rockville, MD: U.S. Department of Health and Human Services.

U.S. Public Health Service. (2001). *A report of the surgeon general on minority mental health.* Rockville, MD: U.S. Department of Health and Human Services.

Urdaneta, M. L., Saldana, D. H., & Winkler, A. (1995). Mexican-American perceptions of severe mental illness. *Human Organization, 54,* 70–77.

Vacc, N. A., & Clifford, K. (1995). Individuals with a physical disability. In N. A. Vacc, S. B. DeVaney, & J. Wittmer (Eds.), *Experiencing and counseling multicultural and diverse populations* (3rd ed., pp. 251–272). Bristol, PA: Accelerated Development.

Vandiver, B. J. (2001). Psychological nigrescence revisited: Introduction and overview. *Journal of Multicultural Counseling and Development, 29,* 165–173.

Vandiver, B. J., Fhagen-Smith, P. E., Cokley, K. O., Cross, W. E., & Worrell, F. C. (2001). Cross's nigrescence model: From theory to scale to theory. *Journal of Multicultural Counseling and Development, 29,* 174–200.

Vasquez, J. A. (1998). Distinctive traits of Hispanic students. *The Prevention Researcher, 5,* 1–4.

Vazquez, J. M. (1997). Puerto Ricans in the counseling process: The dynamics of ethnicity & its societal context. In C. C. Lee (Ed.), *Multicultural issue in counseling* (2nd ed., pp. 315–330). Alexandria, VA: American Counseling Association.

Velasquez, R. J., Gonzales, M., Butcher, J. N., Castillo-Canez, I., Apodaca, J. X., & Chavira, D. (1997). Use of the MMPI-2 with Chicanos: Strategies for counselors. *Journal of Multicultural Counseling and Development, 25,* 107–120.

Vontress, C. E. (1971). Racial differences: Impediments to rapport. *Journal of Counseling Psychology, 18,* 7–13.

Vontress, C. E. (1981). Racial and ethnic barriers in counseling. In P. Pedersen, J. G. Draguns, W. J. Lonner, & J. E. Trimble (Eds.), *Counseling across cultures.* Honolulu, HI: University of Hawaii Press.

Vontress, C. E., & Epp, L. R. (1997). Historical hostility in the African American client: Implications for counseling. *Journal of Multicultural Counseling and Development, 25,* 170–184.

Wagner, M. M., & Blackorby, J. (1996). Transition from high school to work or college: How special education students fare. *The Future of Students, 6,* 103–120.

Walsh, R. (1995). Asian psychotherapies. In R. J. Corsini & D. Wedding (Eds.), *Current psychotherapies.* Itasca, IL: F. E. Peacock.

Walsh, R., & Vaughan, F. (Eds.). (1993). *Paths beyond ego. The transpersonal vision* (pp. 387–398). Los Angeles: J. P. Tarcher.

Warner, C. M. & Morris, J. R. (1997). African-Americans and consultation. *Journal of Multicultural Counseling and Development, 25,* 244–255.

Watson, T. (1998, June 9). Justices to hear "environmental racism" case. *USA Today,* 3A.

Weber, S. N. (1985). The need to be: The sociocultural significance of Black language. In L. A. Samovar & R. E. Porter (Eds.), *Intercultural communication: A reader* (pp. 244–253). Belmont, CA: Wadsworth.

Wehrly, B. (1995). *Pathways to multicultural counseling competence.* Pacific Grove, CA: Brooks Cole.

Wehrly, B., Kenney, K. R., & Kenney, M. E. (1999). *Counseling multiracial families.* Thousand Oaks, CA: Sage.

Weinrach, S. G. (1987). Ellis and Gloria: Positive or negative model? *Psychotherapy, 23,* 642–647.

Weller, S., Martin, J. A., & Ledeerach, J. P. (2001). Fostering culturally responsive courts: The case of family dispute resolution for Latinos. *Family Court Review, 39,* 185–202.

Wellner, A. S. (2001). Americans with disabilities. *Forecast, 21,* 1–2.

Werner-Wilson, R. J., Price, S. J., Zimmerman, T. S., & Murphy, M. J. (1997). Client gender as a process variable in marriage and family therapy: Are women clients interrupted more than men clients? *Journal of Family Psychology, 11,* 373–377.

West, M. (1987). *The psychology of meditation.* Oxford: Clarendon Press.

Whaley, A. L. (2001). Cultural mistrust and mental health services for African Americans: A review and meta-analysis. *Counseling Psychologist, 29,* 513–521.

White, J. L., & Parham, T. A. (1990). *The psychology of Blacks.* Englewood Cliffs, NJ: Prentice Hall.

White, M. (1993). Deconstruction and therapy. In S. Gilligan & R. Price (Eds.), *Therapeutic conversations* (pp. 22–61). New York: Norton.

White, R. W. (1963). Ego and reality in psychoanalytic theory: A proposal regarding independent ego energies. *Psychological Issues, 3,* 1–210.

Wilkinson, D. (1993). Family ethnicity in American. In H. P McAdoo (Ed.), *Family ethnicity: Strength in diversity.* Newbury Park, CA: Sage.

Williams, J. H., Ayers, C. D., Abbott, R. D., Hawkins,

J. D., & Catalano, R. F. (1999). Racial differences in risk factors for delinquency and substance use among adolescents. *Social Work Research, 23,* 241–256.

Williams, R. L. (1974). The death of White research in the Black community. *Journal of Non-White Concerns in Personnel and Guidance, 2,* 116–132.

Willie, C. V. (1981). *A new look at Black families.* Bayside, NY: General Hall.

Willie, C. V. (1995). The relativity of genotypes and phenotypes. *Journal of Negro Education, 64,* 267–276.

Willie, C. V., Kramer, B. M., & Brown, B. S. (1973). *Racism and mental health.* Pittsburgh, PA: University of Pittsburgh Press.

Wilson, L. L., & Stith, S. M. (1991). Culturally sensitive therapy with Black clients. *Journal of Multicultural Counseling and Development, 19,* 32–43.

Wingert, P., & Kantrowitz, B. (2000, March 20). Two kids and two moms. *Newsweek,* 50–53.

Winn, N. N., & Priest, R. (1993). Counseling biracial children: A forgotten component of multicultural counseling. *Family Therapy, 20,* 29–36.

Winter, S. (1977). Rooting out racism. *Issues in Radical Therapy, 17,* 24–30.

Wolfgang, A. (1973). Cross-cultural comparison of locus of control, optimism towards the future, and time horizon among Italian, Italo-Canadian, and new Canadian youth. *Proceedings of the 81st Annual Convention of the American Psychological Association, 8,* 229–330.

Wolfgang, A. (1985). The function and importance of nonverbal behavior in intercultural counseling. In P. B. Pedersen (Ed.), *Handbook of cross-cultural counseling and therapy* (pp. 99–105). Westport, CT: Greenwood Press.

Women's Program Office. (1998). *Mental health and substance abuse problems among women on welfare.* Washington, DC: American Psychological Association.

Wood, P. S., & Mallinckrodt, B. (1990). Culturally sensitive assertiveness training for ethnic minority clients. *Professional Psychology: Research & Practice, 21,* 5–11.

Wren, C. S. (1998, June 5). Many women 60 and older abuse alcohol and prescribed drugs, study says. *New York Times,* p. 12.

Wrenn, C. G. (1962). The culturally-encapsulated counselor. *Harvard Educational Review, 32,* 444–449.

Wrenn, C. G. (1985). Afterward: The culturally-encapsulated counselor revisited. In P. B. Pedersen (Ed.), *Handbook of cross-cultural counseling and therapy* (pp. 323–329). Westport, CT: Greenwood Press.

Wright, J. M. (1998). *Lesbian step families.* Binghamton, NY: Harrington Park Press.

Wright, K. (2001). To be poor and transgender. *The Progressive, 65,* 21–24.

Yamamoto, J., & Acosta, F. X. (1982). Treatment of Asian-Americans and Hispanic-Americans: Similarities and differences. *Journal of the Academy of Psychoanalysis, 10,* 585–607.

Yee, B. W. K., Castro, F. G., Hammond, W. R., John, Wyatt, G. E., & Yung, B. R. (1995). Risk-taking and abusive behavior among ethnic minorities. *Health Psychology, 14,* 622–631.

Yin, X.-H. (2000, May 7). Asian Americans: The two sides of America's "model minority." *The Los Angeles Times,* p. M1.

Ying, Y.-W., Coombs, M., & Lee, P. A. (1999). Family intergenerational relationship of Asian American adolescents. *Cultural Diversity and Ethnic Minority Psychology, 5,* 350–363.

Zeiss, A. M. (2001). *Aging and human sexuality resource guide.* Washington, DC: American Psychological Association.

Zhang, W. (1994). American counseling in the mind of a Chinese counselor. *Journal of Multicultural Counseling and Development, 22,* 79–85.

Zuniga, M. E. (1997). Counseling Mexican American seniors: An overview. *Journal of Multicultural Counseling and Development, 25,* 142–155.

Author Index

Subject Index

503